MANUEL II PALAIOLOGOS (1350–1425)

Few Byzantine emperors had a life as rich and as turbulent as Manuel II Palaiologos. A fascinating figure at the crossroads of Byzantine, Western European and Ottoman history, he endured political turmoil, witnessed no less than three sieges by the Ottomans and travelled as far as France and England. He was a prolific writer, producing a vast corpus of literary, theological and philosophical works. Yet despite his talent, Manuel has largely been ignored as an author. This biography constructs an in-depth picture of him of as a ruler, author and personality, as well as providing insight into his world and times. It offers the first analysis of the emperor's complete oeuvre, focusing on his literary style, self-representation and philosophical/theological thought. By focusing not only on political events, but also on the personality, personal life and literary output of Manuel, this biography paints a new portrait of a multifaceted emperor.

SIREN ÇELIK obtained her PhD at the University of Birmingham. Her main research interests are Late Byzantine history, Byzantine literature, history-writing and daily life. She has been a Junior Fellow at Dumbarton Oaks and has received postdoctoral fellowships from Koç University-ANAMED, Boğaziçi University and Harvard University.

MANUEL II PALAIOLOGOS
(1350–1425)

A Byzantine Emperor in a Time of Tumult

SIREN ÇELIK

Shaftesbury Road, Cambridge CB2 8EA, United Kingdom

One Liberty Plaza, 20th Floor, New York, NY 10006, USA

477 Williamstown Road, Port Melbourne, VIC 3207, Australia

314–321, 3rd Floor, Plot 3, Splendor Forum, Jasola District Centre, New Delhi – 110025, India

103 Penang Road, #05–06/07, Visioncrest Commercial, Singapore 238467

Cambridge University Press is part of Cambridge University Press & Assessment, a department of the University of Cambridge.

We share the University's mission to contribute to society through the pursuit of education, learning and research at the highest international levels of excellence.

www.cambridge.org
Information on this title: www.cambridge.org/9781108812627

DOI: 10.1017/9781108874038

First published 2021
First paperback edition 2022

A catalogue record for this publication is available from the British Library

Library of Congress Cataloging-in-Publication data
NAMES: Çelik, Siren, 1989– author.
TITLE: Manuel II Palaiologos (1350–1425) : a Byzantine emperor in a time of tumult / Siren Çelik.
DESCRIPTION: New York : Cambridge University Press, 2021. | Includes bibliographical references and index.
IDENTIFIERS: LCCN 2020042885 (print) | LCCN 2020042886 (ebook) | ISBN 9781108836593 (hardback) | ISBN 9781108874038 (ebook)
SUBJECTS: LCSH: Manuel II Palaiologus, Emperor of the East, 1350–1425. | Byzantine Empire – History – Manuel II Palaeologus, 1391–1425.
CLASSIFICATION: LCC DF639 .C45 2021 (print) | LCC DF639 (ebook) | DDC 949.5/04092 [B]– dc23
LC record available at https://lccn.loc.gov/2020042885
LC ebook record available at https://lccn.loc.gov/2020042886

ISBN   978-1-108-83659-3   Hardback
ISBN   978-1-108-81262-7   Paperback

In loving memory of Ruth Macrides (1949–2019)

*Here is the work . . . pluck then the sweet fruit for yourself, you who are the cause of it, for it was you who provided us with the seed, and it was by you that the plant was abundantly watered. . .
(Manuel II Palaiologos, upon sending his recent composition to his teacher Demetrios Kydones, Letter 11)*

Contents

Figures and Maps

Figures

Maps

Acknowledgments

This book began its journey as a PhD thesis at the University of Birmingham (2012–16), and my doctoral work there was made possible by a generous scholarship from the College of Arts and Law at the University of Birmingham. While working on Manuel II Palaiologos, I held various fellowships at Dumbarton Oaks, the Research Center for Anatolian Studies, Koç University, the Byzantine Studies Center of Boğaziçi University and finally, at the Center for Middle Eastern Studies, Harvard University. I am grateful to these institutions and their staff for facilitating this project.

My deepest gratitude goes to my supervisors, Dr Ruth Macrides and Professor Dimiter Angelov. For years, Professor Angelov has generously supported my work on Manuel II, and I am grateful to him for his feedback, patience, kindness, encouragement and for many stimulating discussions. Dr Macrides was not only a model mentor, but also a beloved friend; she provided valuable feedback and support, and she shared my enthusiasm for all things Manuel. Her love for Byzantium, her friendship and affection, her joy of life and humour occupied a very special place in my life, and her loss means more to me than words can express – it is to her that this book is dedicated.

Over the years, I have accumulated debts of gratitude to many people. Foremost among them are my parents for their unconditional love and support. This book would not have been possible without them. I would also like to thank Professor Nevra Necipoğlu for her unwavering support since my undergraduate days; on several occasions, the late Dr Niall Livingstone helped me to unravel Manuel's Greek; and at Harvard, as I put the last touches to the book, I had many fruitful discussions with Professor Cemal Kafadar. I am also grateful to Professor Anthony Kaldellis for his support during the last stages of this book. I am indebted to Dr Charalambos Dendrinos for his generous help over years, especially for sharing his own transcriptions of Manuel's then unpublished works with me. Likewise, the

x

late Professor John Barker, whose masterly book on Manuel guided my own research, was always warm and generous in his encouragement. His kindness, and the enthusiasm he showed for my book, meant a lot to me. He will be greatly missed.

I am also indebted to my collegues Alessia Rossi, Aslıhan Akışık, George Makris and Suna Çağaptay, for their support and friendship. Finally, I would like to acknowledge the two anonymous readers of this book for their time and for their insightful feedback. My editor, Dr Michael Sharp has been extremely supportive and patient through all stages of bringing the project to publication, and I am grateful to him and to the team at Cambridge University Press for their professionalism and meticulous work.

Chronology of Manuel II Palaiologos' Life

1350: Manuel II is born

1354: John V becomes the sole emperor; John VI Kantakouzenos abdicates

1366: Manuel accompanies his father John V to Buda and is left behind as a hostage

1369: John V travels to Rome and officially converts to Catholicism; Manuel is made despot of Thessalonike before the emperor's departure

1371: Manuel travels to Venice to bring funds to John V and is left behind as a hostage; the Ottomans defeat the Serbians at the Battle of Maritsa (26 September)

1373: The failed rebellion of Andronikos IV in May, Andronikos is imprisoned; Manuel is made co-emperor and the heir to the throne (25 September)

1376: Andronikos IV escapes from confinement and captures Constantinople; John V, Manuel and Theodore are imprisoned at the Tower of Anemas

1379: John V and his sons escape from Anemas and flee to the Ottoman sultan; aided by the Ottomans, they re-enter Constantinople; Andronikos flees to Pera with members of the imperial family as hostages; more fighting ensues between the factions of John V and Andronikos

1381/2: A truce is signed between John V and Andronikos IV in which the latter is recognized as the heir to throne; Manuel loses his position as heir

1382: Manuel's younger brother Theodore I departs to Morea to assume his position as despot; Manuel establishes a separatist rule in Thessalonike and pursues a policy of aggression towards the Ottomans

1383: The start of the Ottoman siege of Thessalonike

1385: John V and Andronikos IV engage in battle in Melitas near Constantinople; the latter is defeated; Andronikos IV dies of disease (28 June)

1387: Manuel abandons Thessalonike due to the ongoing Ottoman siege and sails to Lesbos; the city surrenders to the Ottomans; Manuel stays for a few months in Lesbos and then moves to Tenedos; afterwards he travels to Bursa to submit to the sultan; John V exiles Manuel to Lemnos

1389: Manuel returns to Constantinople from Lemnos; the Battle of Kosova (15 June), the assassination of the Ottoman Sultan Murad I and the accession of Bayezid I

1390: The rebellion of John VII; he captures Constantinople in April; John V and Manuel lock themselves in the citadel of the Golden Gate; Manuel sails to Rhodes to obtain help from the Hospitallers, accompanied by Rhodian galleys. Manuel re-enters Constantinople in September; John VII flees.

1391: While Manuel accompanies the Ottoman sultan on a campaign, John V dies (15 February); Manuel enters Constantinople as the sole emperor (8 March); in June, Manuel leaves Constantinople again to participate in an Ottoman campaign

1392: Manuel returns from the Ottoman campaign in January; in February, Manuel marries Helena Dragaš and is crowned emperor; Manuel's eldest son, the future John VIII, is born in December.

1393: Bayezid I conquers large territories in Bulgaria, Wallachia and Greece; in 1393/4, Bayezid I gathers his Christian vassals in Serres, including Manuel, Theodore and John VII; the sultan supposedly contemplates murdering them

1394: Manuel disobeys Bayezid's summons and as a result the eight-year long Ottoman blockade of Constantinople commences

1396: The Crusade of Nikopolis (25 September), the Ottomans annihilate the crusading army; in the fall, the Church takes severe action against anti-Palamites and sympathizers of Catholicism, many opt to go into exile; the death of Manuel's mother, Empress Helena (November)

1397/8: Manuel's teacher and friend Demetrios Kydones dies; Manuel starts intense communications with Western European polities for help; Despot Theodore of Morea sells Corinth to the Hospitallers

1399: The French knight Mareschal Boucicaut arrives in Constantinople with a small army; in December, Manuel appoints John VII as regent and leaves Constantinople with Boucicaut for Europe

1400: In spring, Manuel sails away from the Morea, he then tours various Italian cities; in June he arrives in Paris

1401: In December, Manuel arrives in London and returns to Paris before the end of February

1402: Battle of Ankara takes place in July; Bayezid I is defeated and captured by Tamerlane, and the Ottoman Empire starts to disintegrate. Manuel leaves Paris in June

1403: After visiting Genoa and experiencing travel delays in the Morea, Manuel returns to Constantinople (June); Manuel ratifies John VII's peace treaty with Süleyman, the eldest son of Bayezid; John VII is banished to Lemnos and later given the city of Thessalonike to rule

1405: The birth of Manuel's fourth surviving son, the future Constantine XI (8 February)

1407: The death of Manuel's brother Theodore I, despot of Morea; Manuel installs his son Theodore II as the new despot

1408: Manuel travels to the Morea; the death of John VII; Manuel travels to Thessalonike in person and installs his son Andronikos as despot of Thessalonike

1409: The ecclesiastical controversy about the investiture of Patriarch Matthew reaches its peak; Manuel gets significantly involved in the affair; Makarios of Ankyra is tried and condemned

1409–10: Manuel attempts to play one Ottoman prince against the other in order to prevent the unification of the Ottoman Empire

1411: The Ottoman prince Musa lays a brief siege to Constantinople

1413: Battle of Çamurlu (July), supported by the Byzantines, and Mehmed I defeats Musa and unifies the Ottoman lands

1414: John VIII marries Anna of Moscow; Manuel leads an expedition against George Gattilusio for invading Thasos; Manuel Chrysoloras attends the opening of the Council of Constance

1415: Manuel travels to the Morea and renovates the Hexamilion; the Moreans rebel against the emperor on the account of the taxes imposed due to the renovation

1421: The widowed John VIII marries Sophia of Monferrat, Theodore II marries Cleope Malatesta; John VIII is crowned as co-emperor; the death of Mehmed I; the Byzantines support Mustafa, a pretender to the Ottoman throne, against Murad II

1422: Murad II captures Mustafa; Murad II lays siege to Constantinople in July; the Byzantines succeed in lifting the siege in August; the papal legate arrives in Constantinople in September; Manuel has a stroke in October

1423: The Byzantines again support another pretender to the Ottoman throne against Murad II, this scheme, too, fails; the Ottomans attack the Morea and Thessalonike; Despot Andronikos cedes Thessalonike to the Venetians; John VIII travels to Hungary and Italy to seek aid

1424: John VIII continues his travels in Europe; a treaty with the Ottomans is signed to the great disadvantage of Byzantium

1425: Manuel dies in July and is buried at the Pantokrator Monastery in Constantinople

Abbreviations

Anonymous Tevârîh	*Tevârîh-i Âl-i Osman*, ed. F. Giese, re-ed. N. Azamat (Istanbul, 1992)
Argyriou, *Makres*	*Μακαρίου τοῦ Μακρῆ Συγγράμματα*, ed. A. Argyriou (Thessalonike, 1996)
Argyriou, *Makres-Islam*	*Macaire Makres et la Polémique contre l'Islam*, ed. A. Argyriou (Vatican City, 1986)
Aşıkpaşazade	*Âşıkpaşazâde Tarihi (1285–1502)*, ed. N. Öztürk (Istanbul, 2013)
Barker, Manuel II	J. W. Barker. Manuel II Palaeologus *(1391– 1425):A Study in Late Byzantine Statesmanship* (New Brunswick, 1969)
BF	*Byzantinische Forschungen*
BMGS	*Byzantine and Modern Greek Studies*
BSl	*Byzantinoslavica*
BZ	*Byzantinische Zeitschrift*
Chalkokondyles	Laonikos Chalkokondyles. *The Histories*, ed. and trans. A. Kaldellis (Cambridge MA and London, 2014)
Chrysostomides, *Monumenta Peloponnesiaca*	J. Chrysostomides. *Monumenta Peloponnesiaca: Documents for the Study of the Peloponnese in the 14th and 15th Centuries* (Camberley, 1995)
Clavijo	Ruy González de Clavijo. *Embassy to Tamerlane*, trans. Guy Le Strange (London, 1928)
Dennis, *Letters*	*The Letters of Manuel II Palaeologus*, ed. and trans. G. T. Dennis (Washington DC, 1977)
Dennis, *Thessalonica*	G. T. Dennis. *The Reign of Manuel II Palaeologus in Thessalonica (1382–1387)* (Rome, 1960)

Dialogue on Marriage	*Dialogue with the Empress Mother on Marriage*, ed. and trans. A. Angelou (Vienna, 1991)
Dialogue with a Persian	*Dialoge mit einem Perser*, ed. E. Trapp (Vienna, 1966)
Discourse to Iagoup	Ch. Dendrinos. *An Annotated Critical Edition* (editio princeps) *of Emperor Manuel II Palaeologus' treatise On the Procession of the Holy Spirit* (PhD thesis, Royal Holloway and New Bedford College, University of London, 1996), 326–73.
Doukas	Doukas. *Historia Byzantina*, ed. V. Grecu (Bucharest, 1958)
DOP	*Dumbarton Oaks Papers*
Dölger, *Regesten*	F. Dölger. *Regesten der Kaiserurkunden des oströmischen Reiches von 565–1453*, 5: Regesten von 1341–1453 (Munich, 1965)
DVL	Thomas, G. M and Predelli, R. *Deputazione di storei patria per le Venezie. Diplomatarium Veneto-levantinum 1351–1454* (Venice, 1880–99; repr. Cambridge, 2012)
ΕΕΒΣ	Ἑταιρείας Βυζαντινῶν Σπουδῶν
EHB	A. Laiou (ed.) *The Economic History of Byzantium: From the Seventh through the Fifteenth Century*, 3 vols (Washington DC, 2002)
Ethico-Political Orations	C. Kakkoura. 'An Annotated Critical Edition of Emperor Manuel II Palaeologus' "Seven Ethico-political Orations"' (PhD thesis, Royal Holloway, The University of London, 2013)
The Foundations of Imperial Conduct	*PG* 156, cols. 313–84.
Funeral Oration	*Manuel II Palaiologos. Funeral Oration to His Brother Theodore*, ed. and trans. J. Chrysostomides (Thessalonike, 1985)
GRBS	*Greek, Roman and Byzantine Studies*
Gregoras	Nikephoros Gregoras. *Byzantina Historia*, ed. L. Schopen, 3 vols (Bonn, 1853)
Ignatius of Smolensk	G. P. Majeska, *Russian Travelers to Constantinople in the Fourteenth and Fifteenth Centuries* (Washington DC, 1984), 76–113.

Iorga, *Notes et Extraits*   N. Iorga. *Notes et extraits pour servir à l'histoire des Croisades au XVe siècle*, vol. I (Paris, 1899).

Iorga, 'Marea Neagra'   N. Iorga, 'Venetia in Marea Neagra', *Analele Academiei Romane, Memoriile Sectiunii Istorice*, II, 36 (1913–14), Pt. 1, 1043–70; Pt. 2, 1071–88: documents, 1058–70, 1093–118.

JÖB   *Jahrbuch der Österreichischen Byzantinistik*

Kantakouzenos   John Kantakouzenos. *Historiarum Libri IV*, ed. L. Schopen, 3 vols (Bonn, 1828–32)

Loenertz, *La Correspondance de Démétrius Cydonès*   *Démétrius Cydonès Correspondance*, 2 vols, ed. R. J. Loenertz (Rome, Vatican City, 1951–60)

Majeska, *Russian Travellers*   G. P. Majeska, *Russian Travelers to Constantinople in the Fourteenth and Fifteenth Centuries* (Washington DC, 1984)

Mazaris   *Mazaris. Journey to Hades: Or Interviews with Dead Men About Certain Officials of the Imperial Court*, ed. and trans. J. N. Barry et al. (Buffalo, NY, 1975)

Mioni, 'Cronaca'   E. Mioni, 'Una inedita cronaca bizantina dal Mar. gr. 595', *Rivista di Studi Bizantini e Slavici* 3 (1981), 71–88.

MM   F. Miklosich, and W. Müller. *Acta et diplomata graeca medii aevii sacra et profana*, 6 vols. (Vienna, 1860–90)

Necipoğlu, *Byzantium between the Latins and the Ottomans*   N. Necipoğlu. *Byzantium between the Latins and the Ottomans Politics and Society in the Late Empire* (Cambridge, 2009)

Neşri   Neşri. *Kitâb-ı Cihan-nümâ*, 2 vols, eds. F. R. Unat and M. A. Köymen (Ankara, 1949–57)

OCP   *Orientalia Christiana Periodica*

ODB   *The Oxford Dictionary of Byzantium*, 3 vols, ed. A. Kazhdan (Oxford, 1991)

On the Procession of the Holy Spirit   Ch. Dendrinos. 'An Annotated Critical Edition (editio princeps) of Emperor Manuel II Palaeologus' treatise On the Procession of the Holy Spirit' (PhD thesis, Royal Holloway and New Bedford College, University of London, 1996, 1–317.

Panegyric to John V	*Anecdota Graeca*, II, ed. J. Boissonade (Paris, 1844; repr. Hildesheim, 1962), 223–45.
PG	J. P. Migne. *Patrologiae cursus completus*, Series Graeca, 161 vols (Paris, 1857–66)
PLP	E. Trapp. *Prosopographisches Lexikon der Palaiologenzeit*, 14 vols (Vienna, 1976–96)
PRO	Public Record Office
Pseduo-Kodinos	*Pseudo-Kodinos and the Constantinopolitan Court: Offices and Ceremonies*, ed. and trans. R. J. Macrides, J. A. Munitiz and D. G. Angelov (Ashgate, 2013)
Raynaldus, *Annales Annales Ecclesiastici*	C. Baronius and O. Raynaldus. *Ecclesiastici*, vols. 25–27 (Bar-le-Duc, 1872–1880)
REB	*Revue des études byzantines*
RESEE	*Revue des études sud-est européennes*
SBN	*Studi bizantini e neoellenici*
Schreiner, *Kleinchroniken*	P. Schreiner. *Die byzantinischen Kleinchroniken*, 3 vols (Vienna, 1975)
Sphrantzes	*Sphrantzes. Cronaca*, ed. and trans. R. Maisano (Rome, 1990)
TM	*Travaux et Mémoires*
Thiriet, *Régestes*	F. Thiriet. *Régestes des délibérations du Sénat de Venise concernant la Romanie*, 3 vols (Paris, 1958)
Voulgaris, *Bryennios*	Ἰωσὴφ Μοναχοῦ τοῦ Βρυεννίου τὰ Εὑρεθέντα, 2 vols, ed. E. Voulgares (Leipzig 1768, Thessalonike, 1991)

The Family Tree of Manuel II Palaiologos

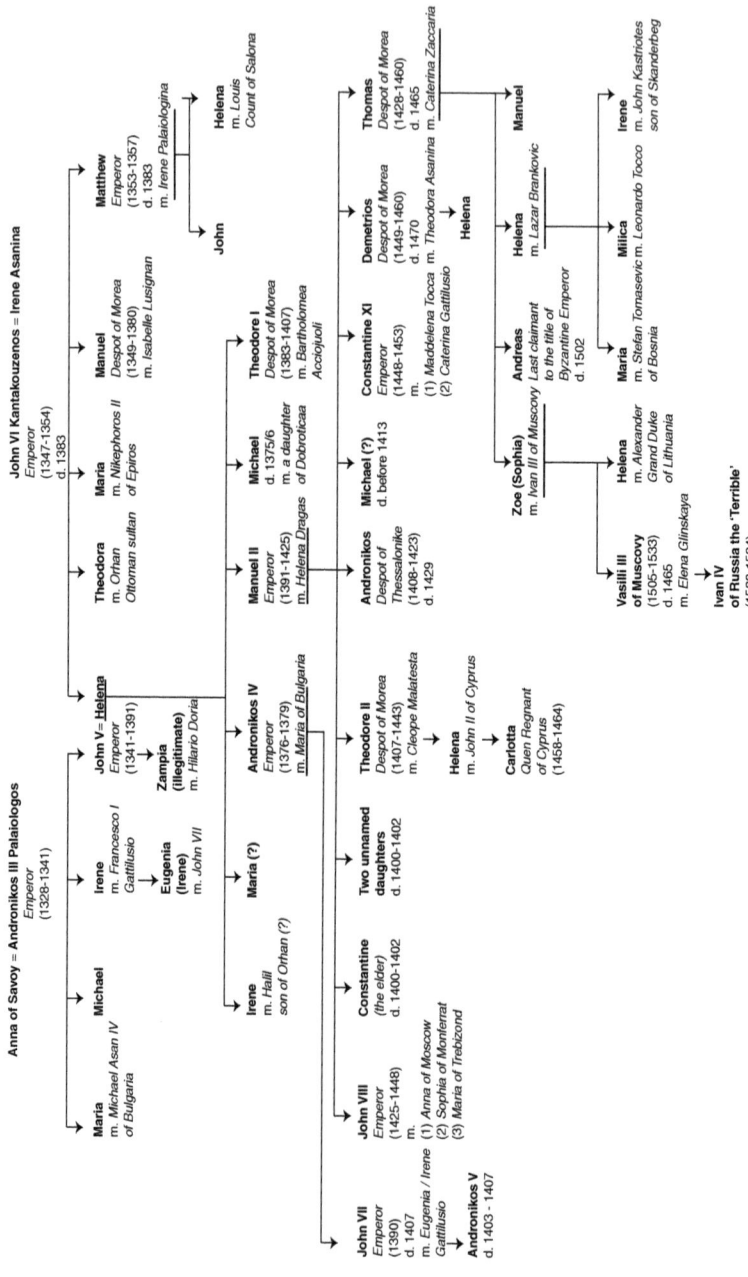

Historical Figures

Byzantine Rulers

John V Palaiologos (1341–91)
John VI Kantakouzenos (1347–54)
Matthew Kantakouzenos (1353–7), Despot of Morea (1380–1)
Andronikos IV Palaiologos (1376–9)
John VII Palaiologos (1390)
Andronikos V Palaiologos, nominally co-emperor, (1400–07?)
John VIII Palaiologos (declared co-emperor before 1408, 1425–48)
Manuel Kantakouzenos, Despot of Morea (1349–80)
Theodore I, Despot of Morea (1381–1407)
Theodore II, Despot of Morea (1407–43)

Ottoman Rulers

Murad I (1382–9)
Bayezid I (1389–1402)
Süleyman, prince and contender for the throne, (1402–11)
Musa, prince and contender to the throne, (1411–13)
Mehmed I (1413–21)
Murad II (1421–51)

Balkan and European Rulers

Charles IV, King of France (1380–1422)
Constantine Dejanović, Serbian ruler in eastern Macedonia (1379–95)
Francesco II Gattilusio, ruler of Lesbos (1384–1403/4)
Gian Galeazzo Visconti, first Lord, then duke of Milan (1385–95, 1395–1402)
Richard II, king of England (1377–99)
Henry IV, king of England (1399–1413)
Martin I, king of Aragon (1396–1410)
Mircae I, ruler of Wallachia (1386–94, 1397–1418)
Nerio I Acciajuoli, duke of Athens (1385–94)

Sigismund of Hungary, king of Hungary and Croatia (1387–1437), among other titles, also Holy Roman Emperor (1433–7)

Stefan Lazarević, ruler of Moravian Serbia (1389–1417)

Popes

Urban V (1362–70)

Boniface IX (1389–1404)

Benedict XIII, pope in Avignon (1394–1415)

Martin V (1417–31)

Family, Literary Circle, Officials

Andronikos Palaiologos: the third surviving son of Manuel; despot of Thessalonike

Antiochos: *parakoimomenos* of Manuel and a member of his entourage during the European journey

Constantine Asanes: a correspondent and *theios* of Manuel

David and Damian: Manuel's spiritual fathers

Demetrios Chrysoloras: Manuel's correspondent and literary collaborator; the *mesazon* of John VII in Thessalonike

Demetrios Kydones: Manuel's teacher and friend, eminent statesman, translator and literary figure

Demetrios Palaiologos: Manuel's fifth surviving son

Helena Dragaš: Manuel's empress consort

Helena Kantakouzene: the youngest daughter of John VI Kantakouzenos; Manuel's mother

Hilario Doria: *mesazon* and Manuel's envoy; also his brother-in-law

George Gemistos Plethon: literatus and philosopher; author of several addresses to Manuel

Isidore Glabas: archbishop of Thessalonike during Manuel's rule in the city in the 1380

Isidore of Kiev: monk and theologian, later the metropolitan of Kiev; Manuel's literary collaborator

Jean de Berry: duke of Berry, French King Charles IV's uncle

Jehan II Le Maingre, Boucicaut: marshal of France, knight

John Chortasmenos: literatus and author of works addressed to Manuel

Joseph Bryennios: theologian; Manuel's literary and theological collaborator

Makarios of Ankyra: metropolitan of Ankyra; Manuel's opponent in an ecclesiastical controversy concerning Patriarch Matthew

Makarios Makres: monk and theologian; Manuel's literary collaborator

Manuel Chrysoloras: literatus, diplomat and teacher; Manuel's correspondent and literary collaborator

Manuel Kalekas: literatus and theologian who engages in a polemic with the emperor

Nicholas Kabasilas: literatus and theologian; Manuel's correspondent

Patriarch Matthew: patriarch during the blockade of Constantinople; his investiture becomes the cause of long-lasting ecclesiastical controversy

Patriarch Euthymios: Manuel's correspondent and literary collaborator

Rhadenos: former student of Demetrios Kydones; Manuel's companion in Thessalonike

Symeon of Thessalonike: archbishop of Thessalonike; Manuel's correspondent

Thomas Palaiologos: the sixth surviving son of Manuel

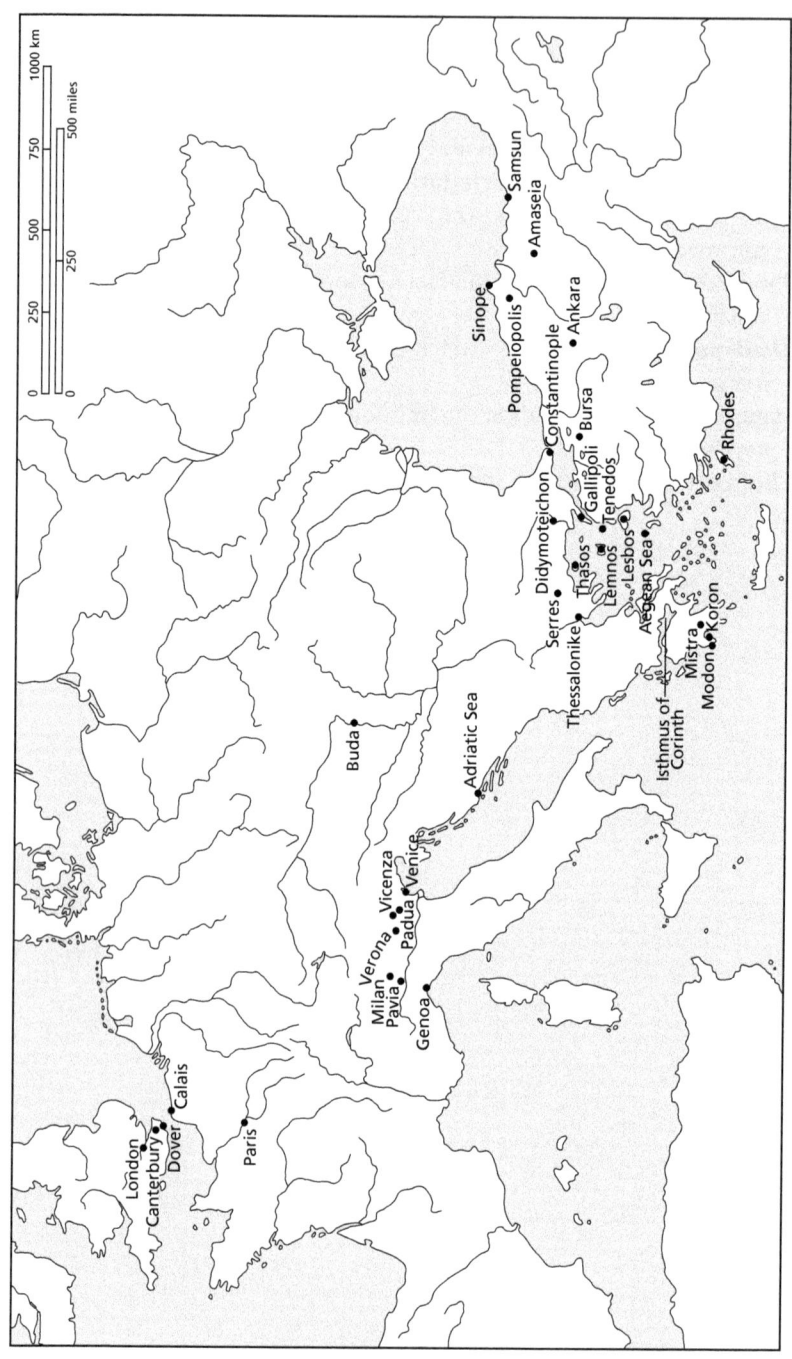

1 The travels of Manuel II Palaiologos (1350–1425)

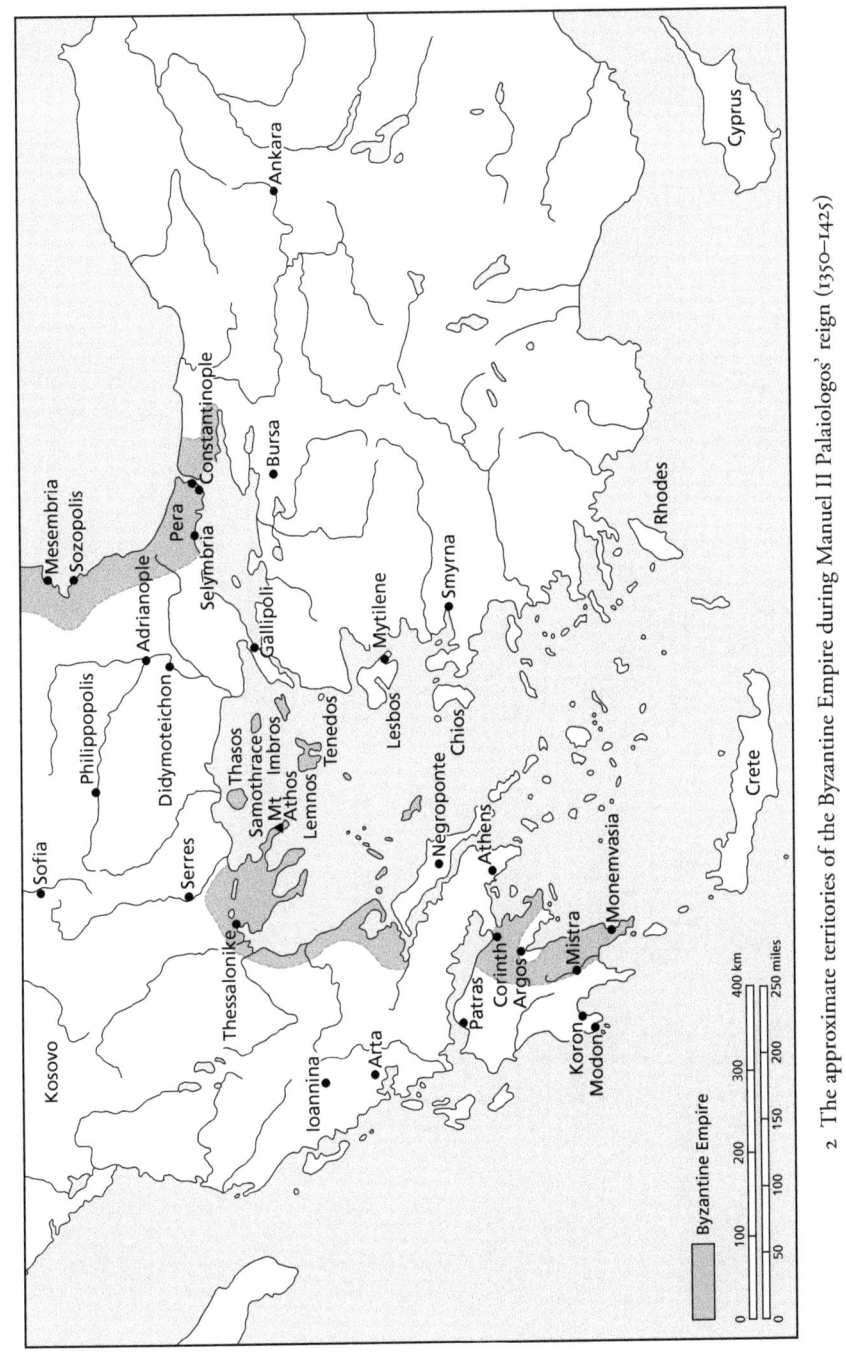

2 The approximate territories of the Byzantine Empire during Manuel II Palaiologos' reign (1350–1425)

Introduction

Few Byzantine emperors had a life as eventful and as rich as Manuel II Palaiologos (1350–1425). Living and ruling during the last decades of the empire, Manuel witnessed rapid territorial loss, dire socio-economic problems and civil wars between his own family members. Both his father, paternal grandfather and maternal grandfathers were emperors – not to mention his brother and nephew. The last two Byzantine emperors were Manuel's sons. His own reign saw the Ottomans lay no less than three sieges on Constantinople and intense communications with Rome for a Church union. Even as a prince, he faced rebellions and was left behind as a hostage in foreign territories by his father. As a young man, Manuel ruled Thessalonike, one of the major cities of the empire, in his own right and withstood a siege of the city for five years. As emperor, he was compelled to accompany the Ottoman sultan on his campaigns, fighting to ensure the success of the rival empire. He had to strive against the centrifugal tendencies of the Byzantine elite and the increasing gap between the rich and the poor. Theological disputes further engulfed his society. In 1399–1402, when he travelled to Western Europe to seek help against the Ottomans, Manuel also became famous as the only Byzantine emperor to visit London and Paris. This celebrated voyage was recorded in Europe both in textual and visual sources.

In short, Manuel sat at the crossroads of Byzantine, Western and Ottoman history. He was part of a fascinating era that witnessed the rise of the Ottoman Empire and the beginnings of the Italian Renaissance. He crossed paths with many influential figures. In Europe he was hosted by Charles VI, the mad king of France, and Henry IV of England, and he visited their courts at a time when authors such as Christine de Pizan and Chaucer flourished. Manuel feasted and exchanged gifts with the uncle of the French king, the renowned art collector Jean de Berry. He campaigned, hunted and clashed with Sultan Bayezid, the Ottoman ruler nicknamed 'the Thunderbolt'. The emperor was also in contact with early Renaissance scholars such as Guarino of Verona, as well as with French and Ottoman theologians. Manuel's own Byzantine literary circle boasted famous figures such as Demetrios Kydones, Manuel Chrysoloras, Joseph Bryennios and Isidore of Kiev; all famed literati, authors and teachers of the period. Even more exceptionally, Manuel himself was a notable author. He penned thirty-three surviving works across an impressive array of genres. These works amount to more than 1000 pages in modern editions: letters, orations, sermons, poems, prayers, dialogues, ethico-philosophical and theological treatises. His oeuvre is remarkable for its erudition, its literary style and the insights it provides into the emperor's own life. The life of the author-emperor, Manuel II Palaiologos offers a fascinating window into the last decades of the Byzantine Empire.

Naturally, this intriguing Byzantine historical figure has attracted a fair amount of scholarly interest. Many works have been devoted to aspects of Manuel's life, especially those concerning his reign and political career.[1] In the last decades, editions of the emperor's works have also significantly progressed, while studies have also started to emerge on selected works of his oeuvre, and of his philosophical and theological thought.[2] Undoubtedly, the monumental monograph by John Barker, written in 1969, remains the

---

[1] J. Berger de Xivrey, 'Mémoire sur la vie et les ouvrages de l'empereur Manuel Paléologue', *Mémoires de l'Institut de France, Académie des Inscriptions et des Belles Lettres XIX, 2* (Paris, 1853). See also, Th. Khoury, 'L'empereur Manuel II Paléologue (1350–1425), esquisse biographique', *Proche-Orient Chrétien* 15 (1965), 127–44; A. A. Vasiliev, 'Putešestvie vizantijskago imperatore Manuila Palaeologa po zapadnoi Evrope (1399–1403)', *Žurnal Ministerstva Naradnago Prosveščeniia*, N. S. 39 (1912), 41–78, 260–304; and G. Schlumberger. *Un empereur de Byzance à Paris et Londres* (Paris, 1916). R. J. Loenertz, 'Manuel Paléologue et Démétrius Cydonès: remarques sur leurs correspondances', *Echos d'Orient* (1937/38), 271–87; 474–87 (1938), 107–24; 'La première insurrection d'Andronic IV Paléologue (1373)', *Echos d'Orient* 38 (1939), 334–45; 'Manuel Paléologue, épitre à Cabasilas', *Μακεδονικά* 4 (1956), 38–46; 'Notes sur le règne de Manuel II à Thessalonique, 1381–1387', *BZ* 50 (1957), 390–6; and 'L'éxil de Manuel II Paléologue à Lemnos 1387–89', *OCP* 38 (1972), 116–40; G. T. Dennis. *The Reign of Manuel II Palaeologus in Thessalonica (1382–1387)* (Rome, 1960). See also the studies in G. T. Dennis, *Byzantium and the Franks, 1350–1420* (London, 1982). Bibliographic references will be abbreviated from Chapter 1 onwards, for reasons of convenience.

[2] *The Letters of Manuel II Palaeologus*, ed. and trans. G. T. Dennis (Washington DC, 1977); *Funeral Oration to his Brother Theodore*, ed. and trans. J. Chrysostomides (Thessalonike, 1985); *Dialogue with the Empress Mother on Marriage*, ed. and trans. A. Angelou (Vienna, 1991); and *Dialoge mit einem Perser*, ed. E. Trapp (Vienna, 1966); Ch. Dendrinos, *An Annotated Critical Edition* (editio princeps) *of Emperor Manuel II Palaeologus' Treatise On the Procession of the Holy Spirit* (PhD thesis, Royal Holloway and New Bedford College, University of London, 1996); C. Kakkoura, *An Annotated Critical Edition of Emperor Manuel II Palaeologus' 'Seven Ethico-political Orations'* (PhD thesis, Royal Holloway, The University of London, 2013), F. Leonte, *Rhetoric in Purple: The Renewal of Imperial Ideology in the Texts of Emperor Manuel II Palaiologos* (PhD thesis, Central European University, 2012). This thesis has now been published as a monograph, but it appeared too late to be included in this biography, see F. Leonte. *Imperial Visions of Late Byzantium. Manuel II Palaiologos and Rhetoric in Purple* (Edinburgh, 2020).

authoritative work on Manuel.[3] It is a comprehensive and masterly study of the political aspects Manuel's reign and is of immense value as a narrative history of the emperor's statesmanship. Since its priorities and aims were different, however, it largely leaves out the voluminous literary output and the personal life of Manuel.

Aims and Methodologies of this Study

This book is not a narration of Manuel's reign, nor is political history at its core. Rather, it is a biography that seeks to construct an in-depth portrait of Manuel as a writer, ruler and a personality. Despite his fame as a scholar-emperor, Manuel's works are generally used to extract information about the political and socio-economic circumstances of the period. The literary features of these works are seldom discussed and Manuel's authorship is mostly valued mainly because he was an emperor. However, he also deserves recognition as an author, and not solely for providing scholars with 'historical data' and ideological insights through his politically charged works. I will focus on Manuel as an author, and on discussing his literary, theological and philosophical works. This biography offers, for the first time, a comprehensive study of his complete oeuvre. Several of the emperor's works are analysed for the first time, while his more well-known works are given new interpretations. The biography focuses especially on Manuel's self-representation in his works and examines some features of his literary style. Related to his study as an author, the book also traces several aspects of Manuel's philosophical and theological views.

Another major theme of this biography is a more 'personalized' study of Manuel's life, including his relationships with family, friends and foes; his everyday life; his thoughts and feelings on people and on events and the world around him. Although a portrayal of the emperor as a personality may not alter the Palaiologan historical narrative, it can enrich our understanding of Manuel as a person; a real human being who once lived, loved, hated and hoped. After all, history is not only about political, socioeconomic, religious or cultural phenomena, but also people themselves. Although the book will offer some new insight into his rulership, an exploration of Manuel's rulership is a subsidiary subject here and thus will not become a central discussion. As a whole, I envision this present

---

[3] J. W. Barker. *Manuel II Palaeologus (1391–1425): A Study in Late Byzantine Statesmanship* (New Brunswick, 1969).

study as an amalgam of literary and personal biography, supplemented by discussion of Manuel's rulership.

The developments in the study of Byzantine literature over the last two decades are especially relevant and merit some discussion for any treatment of Manuel and his oeuvre. It is against this scholarly backdrop that I look at Manuel's works and authorship. Scholarship on Byzantine authors and texts has not only flourished, but also drastically changed its approach. Previously, Byzantine texts were considered a poor imitation of antiquity; their lofty language, veneration of ancient authors and adherence to the classical literary tradition were frowned upon. Their high register Attic Greek, complex and difficult language, metaphors, puns, quotations and allusions were discarded as being mere artifice and unnecessary ornamentation. The abundance of these elements, the reliance on established rhetorical forms, the references to classical and biblical works were all seen as manifestations of a lack of sincerity, creativity and as a sign of the 'unoriginality' of Byzantine texts and those who composed them. Scholars generally conceded that Byzantine texts could very rarely – that is, almost never – be read for pleasure and enjoyment. One could only use these works, be they letters, orations or histories, to extract the historical data that was hidden under 'the veneer of rhetoric'. Similarly, Byzantine authors were deemed as lacking in creativity and thus literary merit. Manuel II Palaiologos, also suffered his fair share of such critiques.

This unfortunate understanding has now been largely discarded. The study of Byzantine literature has been transformed thanks to the pioneering works of scholars such as Alexander Kazhdan, Margaret Mullett, Panagiotis Agapitos, Paolo Odorico and Stratis Papaioannou. Now, Byzantinists emphasize the need to study Byzantine literature in context and on its own terms. These works were composed as 'literary' artefacts, and not as receptacles of historical information for future historians to plunder; they deserve serious study of their literary features.[4] It is also argued that what a Byzantine author

---

[4] Although the bibliography is vast, see especially P. Odorico and P. A. Agapitos (eds.) *Pour une nouvelle histoire de la littérature byzantine: problèmes, méthodes, approches, propositions. Actes du colloque international philologique 25–28 Mai 2000*, (Paris, 2002); M. Mullett, 'The Classical Tradition in the Byzantine Letter', in *Byzantium and the Classical Tradition: University of Birmingham Thirteenth Spring Symposium of Byzantine Studies 1979*, eds. M. Mullett and R. Scott (Birmingham, 1981), 75–93; M. Mullett, 'Originality in the Byzantine Letter: The Case of Exile', in *Originality in Byzantine Art, Literature and Music: a Collection of Essays*, ed. A. Littlewood (Oxford, 1995), 39–53; M. Mullett, *Theophylact of Ochrid: Reading the Letters of a Byzantine Archbishop* (Aldershot, 1997); S. Papaioannou, 'Letter Writing', in *The Byzantine World*, ed. P. Stephenson (Routledge, 2010), 188–99; A. Kazhdan. and S. Franklin (eds.) *Studies on Byzantine Literature of the 11th and the 12th Centuries* (Cambridge, 1984); and I. Ševčenko, 'Levels of Style in Byzantine Prose', *JÖB* 31/1 (1981), 307–12; S. Papaioannou, *Michael Psellos. Rhetoric and Authorship in Byzantium* (Cambridge, 2013), Henceforth, Papaioannou, *Psellos*. N. Gaul, *Thomas Magistros und die spätbyzantinische Sophistik. Studien zum Humanismus urbaner Eliten der frühen*

and reader might have enjoyed in these texts was drastically different from the modern scholar's preferences. Atticizing Greek, complex sentence structures, classical and biblical allusions and rhetorical devices were not considered by the Byzantines to be signs of literary artifice or insincerity. They were an indispensable part of their literary tradition, essential elements that they desired and appreciated in compositions.[5] Quotations, allusions, puns, similes, metaphors and other such devices were the features that imbued these works with their aesthetic quality, lending them beauty and affording pleasure to the reader. More often than not, these also presented the reader and the audience with additional layers of meaning that could be peeled away through slow and careful thought.

Adherence to literary tradition, or established rhetorical forms and devices, was likewise a much-desired feature for the Byzantine audience. Imitation (*mimesis*) of authors such as Plato, Demosthenes or Gregory of Nazianzos was an integral part of the Byzantine literary tradition. Contrary to modern values, *mimesis* was imbued with positive qualities; imitation was seen as a praiseworthy emulation of models of virtue.[6] The preoccupation with 'originality' and 'creative genius' is a far more recent phenomena which chiefly emerged in the eighteenth century. Hence, Byzantine authors and audience did not share this concern with modern readers. Moreover, as recent studies have amply demonstrated, staying within the confines of tradition does not render one author indistinguishable from another. While operating within the established forms and practices, many Byzantine authors developed their own style and introduced 'innovative', personalized touches to the established textual practices. One can thus speak of 'originality' and 'individual style' within tradition – that is, innovation and change did not take place against the tradition, but rather within it. Recent research has also demonstrated that many Byzantine texts were intended for circulation and for oral performance. This also changes our perception of the intended audience and the composition.[7]

Palaiologenzeit (Wiesbaden, 2013) and A. Pizzone (ed.) *The Author in Middle Byzantine Literature. Modes, Functions and Identities* (Berlin, 2014). The following discussion on Byzantine literature is based upon these studies.

[5] See M. Lauxtermann, 'Byzantine didactic poetry', in *Doux Remede, Poésie et poétique à Byzance, Actes du IVe colloque international philologique, Paris 23–24–25 février 2006*, eds. P. Odorico and P. Agapitos (Paris, 2009), 37–46, and the introduction in M. Lauxtermann. *Byzantine Poetry from Pisides to Geometres* (Vienna, 2003) for some observations on this issue.

[6] Papaioannou, *Psellos*, 90.

[7] One such study is I. Toth, 'Rhetorical theatron in Late Byzantium: The Example of Palaiologan Imperial Orations', in *Theatron: Rhetorische Kultur in Spätantike und Mittelalter*, ed. M. Grünbart (Berlin and New York, 2007), 429–48. For scholarship in Western literary history and literary theory, see S. Burke. *The Death and the Return of the Author: Criticism and Subjectivity in Barthes, Foucault*

One example illustrating this change in scholarly approach is the case of Byzantine epistolography. Earlier scholarship considered Byzantine letters to be artificial and empty displays of rhetorical flourish: the language was unduly complex, and they were adorned with puns, metaphors and allusions. Moreover, they were seen to contain little 'concrete' information, as the author seldom referred to his or her life, nor to the socio-political or economic situation of the empire. Letters read as if they had been composed in a timeless vacuum, and were laced with constant themes of separation, friendship and the desire for aesthetic pleasure. What, then, scholars asked, was the purpose of writing a letter at all?

Margaret Mullett's work on the letters of Theophylact of Ochrid, however, demonstrated that Byzantine authors did not compose these works in the same spirit as 'modern' letters, that is, to convey concrete information to their recipient, but rather as beautifully ornate, polished compositions filled with literary features. The chief goal of a Byzantine letter, unlike a 'modern' one, was not to convey information about one's mundane life. Further, if necessary, such messages could be orally delivered by a letter-bearer. Thus in sending a letter the author signalled several things to his/her recipient: that he or she wished for contact, that he/she deemed the recipient worthy of receiving a letter and that he/she valued the recipient's friendship. The mere act of sending of a letter was a message in itself; it expressed a desire for communication and regard for the recipient.

Instead of offering concrete information, a letter thus aimed at providing literary delight to the recipient; sophisticated language, metaphors, allusions and quotations were highly desired and appreciated features in this context. For instance, Manuel's allusions to Aristophanes in his letters from Asia Minor in 1391 were not mere embellishments, they imbued layers of meanings to the text and lent it a sense of humour. A Byzantine letter was meant to be read aloud and re-read many times, discovering new layers of meanings in its metaphors or allusions with each reading. In this context, it now also understood that letters were not private communications between two people. Letters were meant to be circulated among a literary circle, and sometimes performed aloud in literary gatherings called *theatra*. A letter was to be made known to many people, each of

and Derrida (Edinburgh, 1998); M. Biriotti, 'Introduction: Authorship, Authority, Authorization', in *What is an Author?*, eds. M. Biriotti and N. Miller (Manchester and New York, 1993); T. J. Miller. *Poetic License: Authority and Authorship in Medieval and Renaissance Contexts* (New York and Oxford, 1986; J. Pucci. *The Full Knowing Reader: Allusion and the Power of the Reader in the Western Literary Tradition* (New Haven, 1998); and R. Corradini (ed.) *Ego Troubles: Authors and their Identities in the Early Middle Ages* (Vienna, 2010).

whom evaluated its literary features and gave an ear to its political or personal messages. In this manner, one advertised his or her views and formed a network. Through this network, letter writers sought patrons, political and literary support, as well as asked for favours or help. When these letters are analysed in this way, scholars gain invaluable insights into the Byzantines' own aesthetic criteria, as well as into the social and cultural functions of the letter.

Another current research topic in Byzantine literature which has significance for Manuel's biography, is the issue of self-representation. The primary example of this is Stratis Papaioannou's insightful study of Michael Psellos and his self-representation.[8] It produces a detailed examination of Psellos' self-representation and omnipresence in his texts: how did Psellos fashion his self-image in his writings? What were the factors that influenced his opting for a particular persona, and under which circumstances? How did he contextualize his self-representation in the Byzantine literary tradition, and on which models did he build? Psellos' 'I' voice in the texts is not an organic and direct reflection of Psellos himself, but rather a constructed literary persona; an act of self-portraiture. This holds true not only for Psellos, but also for all Byzantine authors. Hence, it is not Psellos' psyche that is examined through his texts, but rather his self-representation. This self-representation bears traces of his predilections, fears and desires, as well as being conditioned by audience, occasion, style and genre. It reflects how the author wished to perceived by the audience and for posterity. Through such analysis of self-representation, one gains invaluable insight into Psellos' authorship and also for other Byzantine authors.

Another crucial debate in the scholarship surrounds the the questions: what is Byzantine literature? How does one decide which Byzantine texts are literature and which are not? And how did the Byzantines conceive their own texts? These are questions that naturally pertain greatly to Manuel's case as an author. Did he produce literature, and how can one classify his texts? It has been amply demonstrated that the Late Antique and Byzantine concept of literature was distinct from our modern sense, if such a concept existed at all. Many of these texts were produced with aesthetic pleasure as a secondary goal. They had political, social and educational goals that have nothing to do with our modern perception of literature. Rhetoric supplied all of the tools for any textual production, be it a letter, poem or theological treatise. All texts sprang from patterns, practices and

---

[8] See footnote 4 above; Papaioannou, *Psellos*, especially 3–4.

devices found in rhetorical manuals and earlier models. The Byzantines did
not even have a word that directly and exclusively corresponded to literature. The term *logos* (pl: *logoi*) was used for literary, rhetorical, philosophical and theological works. *Logos* was also used to signify learning, belles-
lettrès and even literate education in broad subjects. Thus, the modern
term literature and *logoi* do not overlap strictly. The Byzantines also
employed the word *techne*, skill or art, to refer to the act of writing. They
could use the term *logos* to denote any work and refer to an author's *techne*
when speaking about writing. In this regard, a prominent scholar has
pointed out that it is no coincidence that the modern Greek word for
literature is a combination of the two: *logotechnia*.[9]

There is thus no proper definition of literature in a Byzantine context.
Nor is there scholarly consensus on what constitutes Byzantine literature or
on the requirements for a text to be considered 'literary'. As one scholar
succinctly illustrates: '. . . these texts have an undeniable literary dimension –
though it remains to be discovered what it is.'[10] A marked preoccupation
with textual aesthetics can lead to a text being considered literary. A surplus
of rhetorical/literary devices, such as the employment of features like characterization, allusions, sound harmony, metaphors and imagery, can also
result in a particular text being recognized as 'literary', though not always. To
complicate matters further, the boundaries between Byzantine literary,
rhetorical, philosophical and theological were blurred; philosophical works
could be composed as elegant poems, and literary letters could have theological digressions. Further, official documents might include elegantly
composed preambles replete with rhetorical elements. Ultimately, defining
a Byzantine work as 'literary' or 'literature' is a difficult and complicated
issue. Is an imperial oration 'literature' because it makes use of beautiful
imagery? Likewise, when the preamble of an imperial document is laden
with rhetorical/literary elements, does it become literature? What about the
Acts of the church synods? Is a rhetorical school exercise of character
portrayal literary or not? These questions have been met with a wide range
of answers from scholars: some believe that the majority of Byzantine written
artefacts should be considered literary, while others propose that these texts
should be considered non-literary works, albeit with a pronounced rhetorical
flavour. The boundaries for defining the literary are as flexible as opinions are
diverse.

---

[9] See P. Magdalino, 'A History of Byzantine Literature for Historians', in *Pour une nouvelle histoire*, 167–84. See footnote 4 above.
[10] Mullett, *Theophylact of Ochrid*, 3. See footnote 4 above.

Thus, we return to an important question for this book: did Manuel produce literature? None of Manuel's works can be called literature in the modern sense, since they were all composed with political, social and educational goals that have very little to with the function of modern works of literature. As the definition of Byzantine literature is so elusive, in this biography none of Manuel's writings are referred to specifically as works of literature. Nor does this study attempt to strictly categorize his oeuvre as literary, rhetorical or philosophical. Instead, I will speak of 'literary features' or 'literariness'. Although classifying Manuel's orations as rhetorical compositions is easy, in the case of a work like the *Dialogue with a Persian*, a theological dialogue displaying remarkable literary features, it is much more difficult. The *Dialogue* is a theological work, but on occasion, it has almost novel-like qualities. Manuel's entire oeuvre, be it a theological treatise, a letter or a prayer, reveals his remarkable interest in and penchant for literary aspects of writing: characterization, complex strategies of self-representation, imagery and metaphors. And it is in these elements that one can observe Manuel's style as an author as well as his personal touches to the textual traditions. Thus, when attempting to discuss the emperor as an author one needs to study his complete body of work.

How did the Byzantines themselves evaluate their texts? What would have made Manuel's works 'good' in the eyes of his audience? Byzantine rhetorical manuals give us some insight into the Byzantines' own criteria for their *logoi*. These handbooks assign a more secondary role to aesthetics, and instead focus on the ethical and educational dimensions of a text. However, this does not mean that textual aesthetics did not matter; quite the contrary. This is also suggested by the common Byzantine association of painting or sculpture, with writing. Several significant criteria can be gleaned through rhetorical handbooks and the texts of several Byzantine authors, including Michael Psellos, Theodore Metochites and Demetrios Kydones.[11] Notions such as gracefulness and charm (*charis*), clarity (*saphenia*), dignity (*semnotes*) and force (*deinotes*) dominate their criteria. These could be achieved by employing the appropriate style and form for the occasion, by harmonizing the sound, and by combining various rhetorical/literary elements in a seamless, organic fashion.

---

[11] G. Kennedy, *Greek Rhetoric under Christian Emperors* (Princeton, 1983), 4–5, 97–100; *Michael Psellos on Literature and Art: A Byzantine Perspective on Aesthetics*, eds. and trans. C. Barber and S. Papaioannou (Indiana, 2017); *Theodore Metochites on Ancient Authors and Philosophers. Semeioseis gnomikai 1–16 & 71*, ed., trans. and notes K. Hult (Gothenborg, 2002), 156–7, 164–75; *Démétrius Cydonès Correspondance*, 2 vols., ed. R. J. Loenertz (Rome, Vatican City, 1951–60).

An advisory oration, for instance, should have a persuasive and forceful style, and powerful and ear-catching sounds. Similarly, a work of history could charm by incorporating myths or allusions appropriate to the occasion. Along with the flow and rhythm of language, the sound harmony and the well-blended presentation of rhetorical/literary elements, the ideas presented and the emotional expression were of equal importance. Other important criteria included the ability to communicate many things with a few words and to choose the most appropriate style and form for each occasion. Thus, imagery, metaphors, allusions, puns, jokes or quotations were not meant to be piled upon each other indiscriminately, in the best cases they were chosen with care to fit the text; not merely adorning it but enriching its meaning.

All textual composition relied on the earlier models, devices and strategies found in rhetorical handbooks. However, many Byzantine authors introduced their own touches by deviating from set practices, altering and cancelling patterns, and by experimenting with and mixing various elements.[12] An author could thus alternate forms, styles and produce variations on established devices such as commonplace imagery. In this way, if two Byzantine authors relying on the same pre-existing model were to compose, say, imperial orations on the same topic, they never produced identical works. The adherence to established forms and practices, moreover, did not mean that the Byzantines did not appreciate 'personal' touches and departures from tradition. Any variation, whether it pertained to textual structures or elements such as metaphors, was noted and appreciated. This appreciation of variation can be seen in the comments made by many Byzantine authors who evaluated the ancient or contemporary authors.

It has been proposed that looking at verse or prose rhythm, archaic or elated language, fiction, story-telling and the intent to charm, educate or entertain, is beneficial when studying Byzantine texts and their 'literariness'. After all, such features clearly and consciously reveal a preoccupation with the literary. However, this leads to another debate that asks: what is the exact difference between a rhetorical device and a literary feature? And is there a strict division between the two? Characterization, sound patterns, imagery, metaphors and all other such devices were discussed in Byzantine rhetorical handbooks. Similarly, conveying ideas and feelings appropriate to a given text and occasion, setting the mood, or how to evoke the desired emotion, were explained in rhetorical manuals. Rhetoric was indeed the

---

[12] E. Bourbouhakis, 'Rhetoric and Performance', in *The Byzantine World*, ed. P. Stephenson (Oxford and New York, 2010), 175–87.

foundation of the written Byzantine culture and it formed the basis for composing any text, be it an oration, a letter or a philosophical treatise. There was no Byzantine distinction between two; works were not sorted into different categories of 'rhetorical' and 'literary', indeed all texts were *logoi*. When the Byzantines spoke of rhetorical skill or art (*rhetorike techne*) and called each other rhetoricians, they referred to all aspects of textual composition and aesthetics.

Some scholars may prefer to speak of 'rhetorical skill' or 'rhetoricality' when discussing any Byzantine text. Still, there are many scholars who seem to acknowledge implicitly these above-mentioned elements as literary features – that is, as indicators of the 'literariness' of a given text. When looking at the scholarship on Byzantine literature, one can see textual features such as genre combination, imagery, puns, allusions, character portrayal, sound patterns or the evoking of specific feelings as discussed in relation to the literary aspects of texts. It is on the basis of these elements that scholars discuss 'history-writing as literature' or analyse the 'literary' style of letter writers.[13] These features are discussed in Byzantine rhetorical handbooks, but modern scholars refer to them as 'literary'. Furthermore, as previously pointed out, there was no strict distinction between a rhetorical device and a literary feature in a Byzantine context, or even between a rhetorical text and a literary one. For instance, *ethopoiia*, characterization, is seen as a form of rhetorical exercise and is listed as such in Byzantine handbooks. Yet it constitutes the basis of character portrayal not only in texts such as orations, but also in histories and romances – texts that are considered to be 'literary' by some scholars. Thus, one might indeed refer to literary features when discussing Byzantine texts.

Moreover, as previously mentioned, though all Byzantine authors based their text on earlier models and relied on rhetorical manuals, they did not merely reproduce an earlier exemplar or pile on various stylistic devices that they copied from such texts. When employing devices such as amplification, imagery or attempted to lend force or persuasiveness to their text, many Byzantine authors developed their own style and added their personal touches to the suggestions made in the rhetorical manuals. Although they share common sources, models and techniques, no two Byzantine

---

[13] For instance, see A. Pizzone (ed.) *The Author in Middle Byzantine Literature. Modes, Functions and Identities* (Berlin, 2014), A. Littlewood, 'Imagery in the *Chronographia* of Michael Psellos', in *Reading Michael Psellos*, eds. C. Barber and D. Jenkins (Leiden, 2006), 13–56; R. J. Macrides (ed.) *History as Literature in Byzantium. Papers from the 40th Spring Symposium of Byzantine Studies, University of Birmingham, April 2007* (Aldershot, 2010) and R. Beaton, *The Medieval Greek Romance* (Cambridge, 1989).

histories, letters, dialogues or orations are identical. The highly selective process of evaluation means that modern scholars have many subjective reasons for preferring one text or author over another, or finding one text to be more pleasing, moving, graceful, interesting or entertaining than another. The reasons for such preferences (for any text and author from any era) are elusive and subjective. But what becomes apparent is that by modifying, embellishing and combining various models, genres and the devices found in rhetorical manuals, Byzantine authors displayed literary merit and talent.

For these reasons, while discussing Manuel's works in this biography, I have opted to refer to devices such as imagery, metaphors, allusions, sound harmony or character portrayal as literary features.[14] By employing these devices, Manuel displays his own style, personalizing the existing models and commonplaces. His works are not mere pastiches of forms, ideas, emotions and images found it manuals or earlier texts; he exhibits creativity and a penchant for textual aesthetics. In my opinion, all these features help us to discern Manuel's literary merit. Naturally, any such study of Manuel and his oeuvre is a subjective one. I am aware that there may be scholars who arrive at different assessments. Similarly, when evaluating an author and his/her compositions, Byzantine literati did not have a strict and universal definition of what made an author or a text a 'good' one. While their criteria relied on rhetorical handbooks, it was still a matter of personal taste.[15]

Ultimately, this biography seeks to present a portrait of Manuel as an author. This requires that we look at his complete oeuvre rather than a few select texts. Furthermore, when discussing themes such as Manuel's ideas on the imperial office, his political use of his works or his attitude to the Church, all of his texts must come into the discussion. For instance, although the emperor's well-known *Funeral Oration* is politically very charged, two works that deal chiefly with theological matters, the *Dialogue with a Persian* and the *Epistolary Discourse to Iagoup*, are equally laced with political statements. If these works are omitted in a discussion of such themes, such as Manuel's self-representation, his advertisement of his rule, or his views on the Church, the emerging picture will be limited and incomplete.

In this attempt to explore Manuel as an author, this book focuses on select aspects. As many of his works have been now published and the aims

---

[14] When discussing Manuel's orations, I also use the designation rhetorical/literary.

[15] For instance, although Theodore Metochites' (1270–1332) complex style is usually criticized by modern scholars, an editor of his poems disagrees with this assessment; See I. Polemis (ed.), *Theodorus Metochita Carmina* (Turnhout, 2015), especially XLVII.

of this study do not necessitate it, there are no in-depth analyses of his manuscripts and their production process.[16] The emperor's self-representation strategies and their political goals will be a key and recurrent thread throughout this biography. How did Manuel fashion his self-portrait in his works, and what did he strive to achieve through self-representation? Did he ever rely on previous models or adopt a specific persona under varying circumstances? What does his self-representation suggest about Manuel as an author and emperor? Some insights into Manuel's literary style, including his imagery and metaphors, will also be provided. How did the emperor manifest his own literary style while also operating within the Byzantine tradition? How does he converge or diverge from established models and practices, such as text structures or common-place imagery? In this regard, attention is paid to how he shaped his own self-portrait, as well as his imagery and metaphors, as I believe that these best reveal Manuel's creativity and his literary merit.

Further analysis will focus on the allusions Manuel makes to classical authors in order to exhibit his wit and to suggest the presence of different layers of meaning. It has now been demonstrated that allusions or quotations were not mere ornamentation, but that they opened up new layers of meaning that are often lost on the modern reader, including jokes and subtle political statements. Such an analysis of Manuel's works allows for a deeper understanding of the content and the intended meaning of the text. Manuel's portrayal of others, including his family members and the Ottomans, will also be investigated, especially in the case of his dialogues. How did he represent the people in his life and why? Can one gain an insight into Manuel's relationships with his family, friends and foes through his portrayal of others? Finally, where appropriate, some compari-sons are drawn between the emperor and his contemporaries, as well as between Byzantine authors from earlier periods. Ultimately, this biography seeks to make the case that Manuel deserves study not only because he was an emperor-author, but also because he was a gifted one.

The discussion of some aspects of Manuel's ethico-political and theo-logical thought is another recurrent theme in this book. More recently, his

---

[16] I am grateful to Dr Charalambos Dendrinos for sharing with me his transcriptions of Manuel's remaining unpublished works; the *Prayer for those in Peril or Simply at Sea* and the *Sermon on St Mary of Egypt*. He also generously shared his editions of the *Confession to his Spiritual Fathers* and *the Sermon on the Oikonomia and Providence of the Lord*; these works have since been published by S. D. Lamprou. I have consulted the digitized versions of several of the manuscripts containing the emperor's works; Vat. gr. 1619; Vat. Barb. gr. 219; Vat. Barb. gr. 74; and Par. gr. 3041. Another unpublished short work, *Admonitions Leading to Brevity and Peace in Councils*, is transcribed in Appendix 6 of this book.

Seven Ethico-Political Orations and the *On the Procession of the Holy Spirit*
have been the subject of extensive commentaries by their respective editors,
while several articles have explored his theological notions. The works of
Charalambos Dendrinos, John Demetracopoulos and Ioannis Polemis
have greatly advanced our understanding of the emperor's theological
thought, and this work relies heavily on their studies. This biography traces
Manuel's ethico-political thought across his lifetime and in his complete
oeuvre, including in his 'non-philosophical' works. Similarly, some key
themes in his theological thought are highlighted. The main goal here is to
trace some themes and patterns across his life, not to produce an in-depth
analysis of each of his philosophical and theological works. An exploration
of the emperor's thought system is worthwhile, as his period witnessed
significant philosophical and theological phenomena such as Palamism,
increasing fluidity between Orthodox and Catholic theology and the rise of
humanism. In this regard, his friendship with pro-Latin figures such as
Demetrios Kydones, his contacts with Gemistos Plethon, and various
Italian scholars, have raised speculation as to whether Manuel shared
similar views with them. These issues will be touched upon in this
biography.

Various other points of focus include Manuel's blending of ancient philosophy and Christian thought, his stance towards Orthodoxy and Catholicism, his
opinions on the relationship between theology and philosophy and finally, his
interest in Aristotelian ethics. As in the case of the study of Byzantine literature,
scholarship on Byzantine philosophy and theology has also transformed over
the last decades. Recent studies have demonstrated that instead of merely
preserving and transmitting classical philosophy, Byzantine authors actively
engaged with these works. While tension between philosophy and Christianity
did exist in Byzantium, this also resulted in distinctive blends of Christian,
Platonic and Aristotelian thought.[17] The recent scholarly work on Late
Byzantine theology and fifteenth-century Palamism, is especially relevant for

---

[17] See especially these collected volumes and their introductions, K. Ierodiakonou and B. Byden (eds.)
Many Faces of Byzantine Philosophy (Athens, 2012); K. Ierodiakonou (ed.) *Byzantine Philosophy and
its Ancient Sources* (Oxford, 2002); M. Knežević (ed.) *The Ways of Byzantine Philosophy* (Alhambra,
California, 2015) and A. Rigo, P. Ermilov and M. Trizio (eds.) *Byzantine Theology and its
Philosophical Background* (Brepols, 2011). For debates on the study of Byzantine philosophy, see
M. Trizio, 'Byzantine Philosophy as a Contemporary Historiographical Project', *Recherches de
Théologie et Philosophie Médievales* 74 (2007), 247–94; G. Kapriev, 'Modern Study of Byzantine
Philosophy', *Bulletin de Philosophie Médiévale* 48 (2006), 3–13 and F. Ivanović, 'Byzantine
Philosophy and its Historiography', *BSl* 68 (2010), 369–80, J. Meyendorff, *Byzantine Theology:
Historical Trends and Doctrinal Themes* (New York, 1974); A. Louth, *St John Damascene. Tradition
and Originality in Byzantine Theology* (Oxford, 2004); A. Papadakis, *The Christian East and the Rise
of the Papacy: The Church 1071–1453 A.D* (New York, 1994), and K. P. Todt, *Kaiser Johannes VI*

Manuel's biography.[18] It is within this scholarly framework that the emperor's thought will be discussed.

As this study is a biography and not a political narrative, the focus is on Manuel himself rather than on his reign. This book therefore offers a more personal portrait of Manuel as opposed to representing him as a distant figure who merely undertook political decisions and signed imperial documents. Through an in-depth analysis of his writings and other primary sources, I will try to gain an insight into the emperor's personality, as well as his thoughts, feelings and reactions to events. At first glance, perhaps, such an endeavour might seem trivial. After all, Manuel's childhood, family relationships, favourite pastimes or daily life can be seen as insignificant in the grander scheme of things, and these insights do not necessarily alter our understanding of his reign or of the corresponding period of Late Byzantine history. However, history is also about people, and not solely a string of political, socio-economic or cultural narratives. This study of Manuel's life will seek to breathe life into his biography and to flesh out his experiences and world.

It goes without saying that the emperor's works are of immense help in this undertaking; indeed, it is only their very existence that can enable this kind of study of Manuel. Although he has not left a stand-alone autobiography, many of his works have strong autobiographical elements.[19] When analysing his writings, however, one must keep in mind that Manuel had his own literary goals, and that his oeuvre represents the emperor as he wished to be perceived by others. For instance, while an autobiography like Augustine's famed *Confessions* provides ample material and facilitates a scholar's task in writing a biography, it also poses challenges. It is, of course, not a faithful reflection of the individual, but a self-representation – that is, it is a reflection of how Augustine wished readers and posterity to perceive him.

Kantakouzenos und der Islam. Politische Realität und theologische Polemik im palaiologenzeitlichen Byzans (Würzburg, 1991).

[18] N. Russell, 'Palamism in the circle of Demetrius Cydones', in *Porphyrogenita: Essays on Byzantine History and Culture and Latin East Presented to Julian Chrysostomides*, eds. Ch. Dendrinos, et al. (Aldershot, 2003), 7–25; I. Polemis, *Theologica varia inedita saeculi XIV* (Turnhout, 2012); J. A. Demetracopoulos, 'Palamas Transformed, Palamite Interpretation of the Distinction between God's 'Essence' and 'Energies' in Late Byzantium', in *Greeks, Latins, and Intellectual History 1204–1500*, eds. M. Hinterberger and C. Schabel (Leuven, 2011), 263–372; and Demetracopoulos, 'Thomas Aquinas' Impact on Late Byzantine Theology and Philosophy: The Issues of Method or 'Modus Sciendi' and 'Dignitas Hominis', in *Knotenpunkt Byzanz. Wissenformen und Kulturelle Wechselbeziehungen*, eds. A. Speer and P. Steinkrüger (Berlin, 2012), 333–410.

[19] For autobiography in Byzantium, see M. Hinterberger, *Autobiographische Traditionen im Byzanz* (Vienna, 1999); M. Angold, 'The Autobiographical Impulse in Byzantium', *DOP* 52 (1998), 225–57 and Angold, 'Autobiography and Identity: The Case of the Later Byzantine Empire', *BSl* 60 (1999), 18–32.

Similarly, when analysing Manuel's autobiographical narratives in works such as the *Funeral Oration* or the *Discourse to Iagoup*, one should bear in mind that we are looking at a carefully constructed presentation of his self and life. The emperor, too, like Augustine, portrayed his life as he wished his audience to perceive it. Consequently, in analysing autobiographical texts, both a 'naïve' acceptance of the account and total suspicion of the author, are limiting extremes. Rather, scholars should focus on how autobiography reveals the author and what this self-representation suggests about the individual. For a careful analysis of self-representation, how the author wished to be seen can also offer insight into his/her motives, ideas and desires.

As in Augustine's case, the voice of Manuel that can be heard across his oeuvre is a constructed literary persona. One thus has to speak of self-representation and not of self-revelation when analysing his writings. These works are not secret diaries into which Manuel poured out his soul or confided his secrets and private thoughts. The persona he presents to the audience is a carefully, deliberately fashioned, and very often, an idealized image of himself. His autobiographical incursions are likewise minutely moulded narratives with political messages. However, in an ironic twist, even analysing this constructed literary persona reveals something about Manuel: we see how he wished to be perceived by the others and why. This in itself, offers us insights into the emperor.

Through a careful analysis of his writings and self-representation, one gains invaluable glimpses into Manuel's world, such as his relationships with family members, friends and rivals, his piety and his pastimes. Manuel's writings do reflect his reactions to events and the world around him; sieges, civil wars, his travels and his experiences among the Ottomans. By relying on primary sources like letters and travellers' accounts, as well as secondary bibliography, this book also seeks to flesh out Manuel's world. We will envisage the surroundings and the everyday life of the emperor, trying to imagine his environment in Constantinople and other cities, his travels in Asia Minor and Europe, the conditions in the campaigns in which he participated, and his daily life in the palace, fashions and food.

The final goal of this study is to offer some novel discussion of Manuel as a ruler. However, this is a subsidiary theme of the book. His statesmanship has been discussed in-depth by John Barker. Yet as almost fifty years have passed since the publication of Barker's monograph, many scholarly works on the socio-economic and political aspects of Manuel's era have modified our understanding of the fourteenth and the fifteenth centuries.[20] The story of Manuel's reign may thus benefit from an update through a look at these works. His rulership does not form a continuous thread of discussion in this biography, though it is thematically discussed in several instances. Despite its autobiographical aspects, Manuel's rich oeuvre offers little help when studying his governance. He seldom refers to governmental affairs or to concrete political problems. There are no surviving letters from him addressed to his imperial secretaries, and only a very few that are addressed to the members of his government or his envoys. This book therefore does not fuse Manuel's authorship and governance into a single thread of discussion, but rather discusses their points of intersection. The historians narrating Manuel's reign are likewise of little help in this endeavour, and the surviving official documents are meagre. However, by relying on the insights that can be gleaned from Manuel's works, the Venetian senate deliberations and the emperor's official documents, new dimensions may be added to the study of his rulership.

Biography: Uses and Approaches

By focusing on Manuel as an author and a personality through a depiction of his environment and experiences, this book will offer a different kind of biographical writing to the field of Byzantine studies: a more 'personal' biography as opposed to a political narrative.[21] Indeed, monographs on Byzantine emperors are usually studies of their reigns and various aspects of their times.[22] As a writer-emperor, not only does Manuel present a rare case, he also offers ample sources for biography. He is one of the few

---

[20] See K. P. Matschke, *Die Schlacht bei Ankara und das Schicksal von Byzanz* (Weimar, 1981); K. P. Matschke and F. Tinnefeld, *Die Gesellschaft im späten Byzanz. Gruppen, Strukturen und Lebensformen* (Cologne, Weimar and Vienna, 2001) and N. Necipoğlu, *Byzantium between the Ottomans and the Latins: Politics and the Society in the Late Empire* (Cambridge, 2009). Hereafter Necipoğlu, *Byzantium between the Ottomans and the Latins*.

[21] A recent and notable exception is D. G. Angelov, *The Byzantine Hellene. The Life of Emperor Theodore Laskaris and Byzantium in the Thirteenth Century* (Cambridge, 2019).

[22] Of course, the bibliography is vast, but for concerns of space, I have limited my examples. P. Magdalino, *The Empire of Manuel I Komnenos 1143–1180* (Cambridge, 1993); D. Nicol, *The Reluctant Emperor* (Cambridge, 1996) and C. Holmes, *Basil II and Governance of the Empire (976–1025)* (Oxford, 2006); W. Kaegi, *Heraclius: Emperor of Byzantium* (Cambridge, 2003). Manuel's sons, John VIII and Constantine XI have also benefitted from such studies, I. Djuric, *Le Crépuscule de Byzance* (Paris, 1996); D. Nicol, *The Immortal Emperor: The Life and Legend of Constantine Palaeologus, The Last Emperor of the Romans* (Cambridge, 1992); and M. Philippides, *Constantine XI Dragaš Palaeologus (1404–1453): The Last Emperor of Byzantium* (London, 2018). Finally, one should also mention D. Obolensky, *Six Byzantine Portraits* (Oxford, 1988), offering short biographical sketches of six individuals.

emperors, and Byzantines in general, for whom a more 'personal' biography is even possible. The vast number and diverse nature of other primary sources also facilitates this task.

Although not a wide-spread genre in Byzantine studies, biography has been widely used by scholars of antiquity and the medieval West as a genre of modern history writing. Recent decades have seen a further rise in the number of articles and edited volumes devoted to biography as an academic form; its uses, handicaps and challenges.[23] Several influential examples of historical biography include those of Peter Abelard by Michael Clanchy, Augustine by Peter Brown and Frederick II by Ernst Kantorowicz.[24] Special mention should also be made of *The Merchant of Prato* by Iris Origo, an influential and widely read biography of the fourteenth-century Italian merchant, Francesco Datini.[25] Scholars of Western medieval history have produced countless other biographies of royalty, aristocracy and intellectuals. Indeed, its popularity as a genre can be connected to its versatility, which allows scholars to pursue a wide range of research interests in relation to one individual. Moreover, academic biographies are more likely to be accessible to a general audience, and this, too, contributes to their appeal for scholars.

Although biography does possess a certain novelistic style and is arguably more accessible, it must be emphasized that it still is a way of reconstructing the past. The biographer does not merely put sources together, but also analyses these and proposes original arguments. A biography is not a mere narration of a life-story, but a scholarly work that offers new interpretations and ideas pertaining to that individual and their times. By authoring a biography, historians not only narrate an individual's life, but are also compelled to study the socio-political, economic and cultural history of the period. As the subject of the biography does not exist in a vacuum, but interacts with his or her historical context,

---

[23] The following discussion will be drawn from these works, see R. Fleming, 'Writing Biography at the Edge of History', *American Historical Review*, 114 (2009), 606–14; W. Warren, "Biography and the Medieval Historian," in *Medieval Historical Writing in the Christian and Islamic World*, ed. D. Morgan (London, 1982), 5–18; R. Porter (ed.) *Re-writing the Self: Histories from the Renaissance to the Present* (London, 1997); P. France and W. St Clair (eds.) *Mapping Lives: The Uses of Biography* (New York, 2002); J. Le Goff, 'The Whys and Ways of Writing a Biography: The Case of Saint Louis', *Exemplaria* 1, (1989), 207–25; A. Momigliano, *The Development of Greek Biography* (Cambridge, 1991) and D. Bates, et al. (eds.) *Writing Medieval Biography* (Woodbridge, 2006).

[24] M. Clanchy, *Abelard. A Medieval Life* (Oxford, 1997); P. Brown, *Augustine of Hippo: A Biography* (London, 1967);and E. Kantorowicz, *Frederick the Second 1194–1250* (New York, 1967). A well-known biography in Ottoman studies is F. Babinger, *Mehmed II Conqueror and his Times*, trans. R. Manheim (New Jersey, 1994).

[25] I. Origo, *The Merchant of Prato. Francesco di Marco Datini, 1335–1410* (London, 1957).

and although they seem to focus on a single topic – that is, the individual life of the subject – biographies are in fact wider in scope than they might initially seem. Ultimately, the biographer must deal with a broad array of topics and disciplines, such as socio-political history, economics, cultural history, everyday life, art history or the history of a given geography, including the country or the city of the biography's subject. While on the surface, biographies may seem to be narrow and specific, the reality is far more complex.

Consequently, biography not only allows scholars to investigate the life of an individual, but also to pursue their own interests. Naturally, the elements that are emphasized in a biography are not only decided by the scholar alone but are also determined by the nature of the sources to an extent. In this regard, the indispensability of written sources must be emphasized. Although archaeology and material culture offer many insights that cannot be gleaned from other sources, this book relies on written sources to sketch a biography. As for choosing the focus of one's study, the following examples may be illuminating. For instance, Peter Brown focused on Augustine's representation of the self, his relationship with his homeland in Hippo Regius and religion in society. In Abelard's biography, Michel Clanchy emphasizes the love story between Abelard and Heloise, investigating their letters and Abelard's self- representation. Writing the biography of the saint king of France, Louis IX, Jacques le Goff lacks such autobiographical material, and instead relies on the medieval biographies of the king.[26] He focuses on the representation of Louis as a king and a saint. The biography also allows Le Goff to pursue his other interests influenced by the Annales school, such as the long-durée, space and *histoire des méntalities*.

In contrast, thanks to the diaries and letters of Francesco Datini, Iris Origo focuses on the everyday life and the consumption of the merchant; namely, his household items, business interests and his relationship with his wife. It is also possible to write a biography that challenges the scholarly perception – positive or negative – of an individual. One example of this can be seen in David Abulafia's work on Frederick II, who was already the subject of several biographies. In his work, Abulafia seeks to demonstrate that Frederick was not the 'great' emperor that often appears in scholarship, but rather that he had built on his father's legacy.[27] In this regard, biography is also a selective study since the scholar chooses which aspects

---

[26] J. Le Goff, *Saint Louis* (Paris, 1999).
[27] D. Abulafia, *Frederick II: A Medieval Emperor* (Oxford, 1999).

he or she wants to emphasize. Again, although this is a highly subjective decision, it is also influenced by the available sources. Similarly, one may choose to focus on Manuel as author or as a statesman, or even to write an intellectual biography of the emperor as a philosopher and theologian. This biographical selectiveness is moreover determined by the concerns of available space. After all, it is not possible to touch on all aspects or to narrate everything in any individual's life.

Structuring Manuel's Biography

This biography poses several challenges relating to its structuring and content. As the study of a complex and rich life-story, it does not focus on a single topic or thesis, but weaves together several strands of different themes. After examining various models, I have decided to opt for a chronological narrative, embedding my analysis of Manuel's works and the discussion of other issues into this narrative. With regards to the chapter organization, each section will deal with different chronological parts of Manuel's life, tracing him from his birth until his death. I did not adopt separate treatments of Manuel's different faces as a ruler, a writer and a personality, as I felt that it would artificially split his multi-faceted persona and disrupt the narrative of his eventful life. Moreover, in my view what makes Manuel such an intriguing figure is the interlinking of many simultaneous events and his works, his ruling and his personal life, and thus a chronological approach fits his life-story best.

This chosen structure calls for a careful blending of analysis and discussion in order to form a narrative history. While chiefly chronological, I have also inserted thematic topics, such as Constantinople or Manuel's rulership, into appropriate places in the narrative. Although this is a scholarly study, the biography also needs to read as a life story and thus I do not employ an overly argumentative style, such as openly refuting or confirming scholarly theories. My discussions and arguments are instead embedded in the narrative. Similarly, in order to avoid disrupting the flow of the narrative, I did not include methodological discussions in the main text – such as various approaches to Byzantine literature. References are given as footnotes in order to facilitate the reader's consultation of the sources and the quotations of foreign languages. This format is also necessitated by the fact that the notes incorporate supplementary arguments and discussions that could not be incorporated into the main text.

A balance between the discussions of Manuel's writings and personality, and that of his reign and other issues, also has to be maintained. Since a biography is a study of the individual, it is important that the focus remains on Manuel and that the discussions of his reign, surroundings and time are balanced to enrich the background. The biography cannot offer in-depth insights of every aspect of Manuel's reign or era; that would require a Palaiologan encyclopaedia. On the other hand, it is important to place Manuel in his socio-political and historical context, especially because as an emperor and a writer, his biography is an important part of larger Byzantine political and literary history. Despite the fact that this book has an emperor at its core, as a biography it focuses on Manuel and his oeuvre – in other words, it is not intended as a Late Palaiologan political, socio-economic or cultural narrative.

Sources and Notes on Style

For Manuel's biography, the primary source material is extremely rich and diverse: histories and chronicles, Byzantine literary, philosophical and theological works, official documents, traveller accounts, Western European histories and document collections, and Ottoman chronicles. The languages used in these materials range from Greek and Latin to Ottoman Turkish, medieval English, French, Italian and Catalan. The analysis of these primary sources poses many challenges both on account of their vast number and nature. In Manuel's case, unlike the Western medieval kings or saints, no contemporary biography exists, and the available material gives little information as to his personality or private life. For similar reasons, it is often difficult to gain an insight into the other people in Manuel's life. The biographer thus has to be careful when deciding if and how these 'gaps' should be filled. It is important to select the most relevant sources from the vast material that exists, as well as to carefully analyse the influence of the text's agenda and bias on the portraiture of Manuel and the events.

This book relies mostly on textual sources, supported by scholarly studies on material culture and archaeology. Art history and numismatics will seldom be touched upon, as I am not a material culture specialist. Further, as the textual sources are voluminous and Manuel's life-story is densely packed, considerations of space also contributed to this decision. As discussed previously, the emperor's own oeuvre forms the core of his biography. These compositions require a careful and nuanced analysis of Manuel's constructed literary persona and his own idealized accounts of his life. Yet this multi-layered analysis allows him to emerge further as a complex and engaging individual.

The works of the Byzantine literati in the period, form another significant category of sources. Among this vast corpus, one can include the letters and orations of Demetrios Kydones, works of Manuel and Demetrios Chrysoloras, sermons of Isidore Glabas, letters of Manuel Kalekas, sermons and liturgical works of Symeon of Thessalonike, theological works by Makarios Makres and Joseph Bryennios, as well as the treatise on the Procession of the Holy Spirit by Makarios of Ankyra. As in the case of Manuel's writings, these sources, too, need to be analysed carefully. Like the emperor, all these authors had their literary, political and social goals in composing these works. The context of composition thus has to be taken into account in their interpretation. Where appropriate, their work is occasionally compared to that of Manuel in order to reach a more detailed assessment of Manuel as an author. However, in this biography, these sources are secondary to Manuel's own oeuvre and are not discussed in equal depth or length. Many of these works require separate articles, even books, in order to be explored fully and is it not possible to do justice to this here. In short, they are consulted here in order to supplement the emperor's own works and other sources.

Byzantine histories and chronicles are indispensable for the study of the period to the study of Manuel as an emperor. Although two historians who dealt with Manuel's reign, Michael Doukas and Laonikos Chalkokondyles, were not exact contemporaries, their work is nevertheless informative. Both authors wrote in mid- to late fifteenth centuries, after the fall of the empire. While they are our chief historical accounts for the reign of Manuel, both accounts have chronological confusion, mistakes and omissions of several episodes.[28] The account of George Sphrantzes, a member of the courts of Manuel, John VIII and Constantine IX, also contains valuable information. Yet it deals only with the years after Manuel's return from Europe in 1403, and Manuel's reign constitutes a minor part of Sphrantzes' work. Moreover, Sphranztes is clearly biased in favour of Manuel and against his son John VIII. The short chronicles published by Peter Schreiner are equally crucial for Manuel's reign. They supplement the information given by the above-mentioned fifteenth-century historians, as well as in some cases, they are the only source to mention certain events. In order to construct a narrative of Manuel's life, the historian needs to combine and reconcile all these accounts. The histories of Kantakouzenos and Gregoras are also briefly relied upon while investigating Manuel's childhood and early youth. As in the case of the works of the

---

[28] For studies on Chalkokondyles, see A. Akışık, *Self and Other in the Renaissance: Laonikos Chalkokondyles and Late Byzantine intellectuals* (PhD thesis, Harvard University, 2013); and A. Kaldellis, *A New Herodotos: Laonikos Chalkokondyles on the Ottoman Empire, the Fall of Byzantium and the Emergence of the West* (Washington DC, 2014).

literati, who had their own agendas, the histories and chronicles, too, require careful analysis. Finally, Byzantine monastic documents are used while discussing some aspects of Manuel's rulership.

Since Manuel had extensive dealings with Europe, both on account of the political situation and his travels in Europe, Western sources also provide ample material for Manuel's biography. For instance, the anonymous biography of Mareschal Boucicaut, French nobleman and commander, is an informative source for the discussion of the blockade of Constantinople in 1396–1402. Italian chroniclers such as Marino Sanudo the Younger, Rafaino Caresini and Giorgio Stella also offer valuable information both about Byzantine politics and Manuel's voyage to Europe. Manuel's journey is recorded by both English and French sources, most notably by Adam of Usk and Thomas Walsingham for the English side; and by the *Chronicle of Saint Denis* and Jean Juvenal Ursins for the French. These sources not only provide information on chronology and events, they also offer their own representation of Manuel. The deliberations of the Venetian senate, summarized by Freddy Thiriet, Nicholae Iorga and Julian Chrysostomides, form the basis of the discussions of the politics during Manuel's reign. They offer far more concrete information than the Byzantine historians. Papal bulls provide further insight into the political situation of the period. Once more, Manuel's biography requires the synthesis of all these sources written in Latin, medieval French, English, Italian and Catalan.

In relation to Western histories and documentary sources, special mention must be made of travellers' accounts. Thanks to the increasing contact between Byzantium and foreign polities, Manuel's reign was touched upon in many travellers' accounts. One of the most important of these writers is Ruy Gonzalez de Clavijo, a diplomat who visited Constantinople in 1402 on his way to the court of Tamerlane. The account of Johannes Schiltberger, a German knight who was captured at Nikopolis in 1396 by the Ottomans, also provides very valuable material. The Russian pilgrim Ignatius of Smolensk is yet another significant source. Having visited Constantinople in 1390–2, he is an eyewitness to the revolt of John VII and to Manuel's coronation. These travellers' accounts also help the biographer to flesh out Manuel's world through the details they give about Constantinople and the life in the city, as well as providing glimpses into the emperor's daily life.

Albeit to a lesser extent, Ottoman chronicles are also relied upon in this biography. The earliest Ottoman chronicles survive from the later fifteenth century, one notable exception being the *Ahvâl-ı Sultan Mehemmed Han,* completed in the 1410s. The later chronicles of Aşıkpaşazade, Neşri and various anonymous chronicles (Tevârîh-I Âl-i Osman) still provide some information for Manuel's reign. However, they can only be used as sources 'supplementary' to the Byzantine and Western ones. The study of these chronicles are complicated with regards to their sources and their textual relationship with each other. For instance, both Aşıkpaşazade and Neşri contain material attributed to the lost work of Yahşi Fakih and the anonymous chronicles as well as other earlier sources. The early Ottoman chronicles also exist in different versions. Their creation was thus a process of copying, compiling and altering the texts to serve the chronicler's own purposes. Furthermore, since they were written in the fifteenth century, the chronicles reflect the so-called *ghazi* ideology of the period, portraying the early Ottomans as the ideal warriors of Islam who relentlessly fought against the 'infidel' Christians. In most cases, the Byzantine involvement in Ottoman politics and the collaboration between the two, are completely marginalized.[29] The role played by the Ottoman chronicles in Manuel's biography is therefore helpful, but not extensive.

[29] See H. İnalcık, 'How to Read Ashık Pasha-Zade's History', in *Studies in Ottoman History in Honour of Professor V. L. Ménage*, eds. C. Heywood and C. Imber (Istanbul, 1994), 117–38 and the introductions in C. Kafadar, *Between Two Worlds* (Berkeley and Los Angeles, 1995) and D. J. Kastritsis, *The Sons of Bayezid: Empire Building and Representation in the Ottoman Civil War of 1402–1413* (Leiden and Boston, 2007).

CHAPTER I

The Young Manuel

The emperor also allowed his wife Empress Helena to follow him
(John V), accompanied by Manuel, the younger of their sons.[1]

On 21 May 1347, the Feast of Saints Constantine and Helena, an unusual
ceremony was staged in Constantinople. The coronation of John VI
Kantankouzenos, who had emerged victorious from the six-year-long
civil war with the Palaiologos dynasty, took place on that day. Several
factors contributed to the peculiarity of this ceremony. Although he was
certainly not the first usurper-emperor in the long history of the
Byzantine Empire, Kantakouzenos was in a rare position, as the coronation was his second.[2] Perhaps the most striking aspect of all, was the
amicable agreement Kantakouzenos had struck with his opponents, the
boy-emperor John V Palaiologos and his mother Empress Anna of
Savoy.[3]

The civil war of 1341–7 is a long and complicated story; a full account
of it requires its own study. However, it is worth touching upon the main
events, since they provide the backdrop for the life of Manuel
Palaiologos. In 1341, upon the death of Andronikos III Palaiologos
(1328–41), his son John V Palaiologos ascended to the throne. He was

---

[1] Kantakouzenos, III, 328. ʿ Ἐλένην τε βασιλίδα τὴν γαμετὴν ἐπέτρεπεν αὐτῷ συνέπεσθαι, Μανουὴλ
τὸν νεώτερον ἔχουσαν τῶν υἱῶν.ʾ

[2] He had been previously crowned in Adrianople by the Patriarch of Jerusalem. Kantakouzenos, II,
564–5; Gregoras, II, 762–3. Herakleios, another usurper-emperor was also crowned twice; first by the
metropolitan of Kyzikos, and later by the patriarch of Constantinople. Majeska, *Russian
Travellers*, 419.

[3] For a detailed analysis of the civil war of 1341–7, see D. Nicol, *The Last Centuries of Byzantium,
1261–1453* (Cambridge, 1993), 185–209. Henceforth, Nicol, *Last Centuries*; D. Nicol, *The Reluctant
Emperor: A Biography of John Cantacuzene, Byzantine Emperor and Monk, c. 1295–1383* (Cambridge,
1996), 45–83; and P. Charanis, ʿInternal Strife in Byzantium during the Fourteenth Centuryʾ,
Byzantion 15 (1940–1), 208–30. Henceforth, Nicol, *Reluctant Emperor*, and Charanis, ʿStrifeʾ. For
Kantakouzenos and the social dimensions of the civil war, see G. Weiss, *Joannes Kantakuzenos.
Aristokrat, Staatsmann, Kaiser und Mönch, in der Gesellschaftsentwicklung von Byzanz im 14.
Jahrhundert* (Wiesbaden, 1969).

a minor, and John Kantakouzenos, a much esteemed official and personal friend of the late emperor, was appointed as regent. However, Empress Mother Anna of Savoy and her supporters mistrusted Kantakouzenos. They suspected him of having designs on the imperial throne, and soon, fighting broke out between the two factions. In response, Kantakouzenos declared himself emperor in Adrianople and more fighting ensued. This six-year civil war proved perilous for the empire in every way. The already troubled Palaiologan Byzantium was ravaged by social strife, unrest and political and economic instability.

At the end of the war, although it was Kantakouzenos who emerged victorious, he decided to share the throne with the young John. They became co-emperors, with Kantakouzenos serving as the senior emperor and John as his junior colleague for a period of ten years, after which power was equally shared.[4] Accordingly, the coronation ceremony featured not only the victorious emperor, but also the defeated emperor and the empress mother. As a final peculiarity of the coronation, Kantakouzenos became the only emperor to write the history of his own reign. He was hence in the unique position of narrating his own coronation, referring to himself in the third person.[5]

Another unusual feature of the ceremony was the venue for the coronation. It took place in the Church of the Virgin at Blachernai and not in Hagia Sophia as was the ancient custom. Hagia Sophia had been badly damaged in a recent earthquake and parts of its dome and arches were in ruin. The situation prompted Gregoras and Kantakouzenos to reflect with sadness on the condition of the church in their narratives of the event.[6] Still, as Kantakouzenos took special care to emphasize, other aspects of the customary ceremonial were meticulously observed in Blachernai. Five thrones were set on the platform instead of two. Sitting upon them were the two emperors and the three empresses, including Helena, the youngest daughter of Kantakouzenos who was betrothed to the young John Palaiologos. Both of the emperors were called John, an amusing coincidence that did not go unnoticed by the

---

[4] Kantakouzenos, II, 604–15; Gregoras, II, 773–9.

[5] Kantakouzenos, III, 29–30. However, he is mistaken in dating his own coronation, he gives it as the 30th May. T. S. Miller, *The History of John Cantacuzenus (Book IV): Text, Translation, and Commentary* (PhD thesis, The Catholic University of America, 1975), 269. Henceforth, Miller, *History*. For Kantakouzenos' work see also B. McLaughlin, *An Annotated Translation of Emperor John VI Kantakouzenos, History, Book III* (PhD thesis, Royal Holloway, University of London, 2018).

[6] Gregoras, II, 787; Kantakouzenos, III, 29.

historian Gregoras who referred to them in his narrative as 'the two synonymous emperors'.[7]

After the ceremony, mounting their horses and clad in imperial robes, this group of emperors and empresses embarked on a procession to the palace where they appeared to the public from a balcony and afterwards, once more seated upon their five thrones, enjoyed a coronation banquet. Despite the solemnity and grandeur of the occasion, the tableware was of clay and pewter instead of gold and silver. The crowns were made of gilded leather and were adorned with paste gems, not real ones because Anna of Savoy had pawned the crown jewels to Venice in order to finance her troops during the civil war. These treasures would never be recovered.[8]

A week after the coronation, on 28 May, Constantinople witnessed yet another imperial ceremony. The nuptials of John Palaiologos and Helena Kantakouzene were solemnized in the same church.[9] All seemed to be resolved between the houses of Kantakouzenos and Palaiologos.

Manuel Palaiologos was born as the third child of this marriage on 27 June 1350.[10] By that time, the marriage had produced one daughter, Irene, and the future Andronikos IV Palaiologos, who was proclaimed emperor soon after his birth.[11] Manuel's first months would bear witness to more strife among his family members. His father John V left Constantinople shortly after Manuel was born.[12] He and Kantakouzenos sailed to Thessalonike in the fall of 1350 after the city was recovered from the Zealots, a rebellious faction that had established a separatist rule in the city against Kantakouzenos.[13] Soon after, Kantakouzenos returned to

---

[7] Kantakouzenos, III, 29. On Kantakouzenos' emphasis on the ceremonial, see N. Gaul, 'The Partridge's Purple Stockings: Observations on the Historical, Literary and Manuscript Context of Pseudo-Kodinos' Handbook on Court Ceremonies', in *Theatron: Rhetorische Kultur in Spätantike und Mittelalter*, ed. M. Grünbart (Berlin and New York, 2007), 69–103, 72. Gregoras, II, 787, ' . . . δυοῖν τε βασιλέων ὁμωνύμων . . . '.

[8] Gregoras, II, 788–9. On the pawning of the jewels, see P. Hetherington, 'The Jewels from the Crown: Symbol and Substance in the Later Byzantine Imperial Regalia', *BZ* 96 (2003), 157–68.

[9] Both Gregoras and Kantakouzenos agree that the wedding was a week after the coronation, Gregoras, II, 791; Kantakouzenos, III, 30. Another short chronicle, like Gregoras, gives the wedding date as 24 May, Schreiner, *Kleinchroniken*, Chronik 8/48c.

[10] Manuel's birth date has been convincingly calculated by R. J. Loenertz, 'Une erreur singulière de Laonic Chalcocondyle', *REB* 15 (1957), 182–3.

[11] His grandfather Kantakouzenos explicitly names Andronikos as *basileus*, Kantakouzenos, III, 238.

[12] Barker claims that John V was absent at Manuel's birth. Barker, *Manuel II*, 4. So, he slightly predates the entry of the emperors to Thessalonike by a few months. However, Kantakouzenos himself puts the event in the late fall of 1350, after Manuel's birth in the summer, Kantakouzenos, III, 112–14; Nicol, *Last Centuries*, 228–30; Nicol, *Reluctant Emperor*, 110. While in Thessalonike, Kantakouzenos also signed a treaty with Dušan, dated December 1350. Dölger, *Regesten*, no. 2967. See Miller, *History*, 395.

[13] Nicol, *Reluctant Emperor*, 110. For some select literature on the Zealot regime, see Nicol, *Last Centuries*, 194–5; Charanis, 'Strife', 208–30; J. W. Barker, 'Late Byzantine Thessalonike:

Constantinople, leaving his young co-emperor to rule in Thessalonike. John V would not see his infant son again until 1352.

Shortly after Kantakouzenos' departure, nineteen-year-old John sought to establish himself as the sole emperor. He was also found to be corresponding with Stephan Dušan of Serbia; Dušan even suggested that John should send Helena to Serbia as a hostage and instead take a wife from his family. Empress Anna went to Thessalonike with her son to negotiate and ended the crisis and John was transferred to Didymoteichon. Instead, Kantakouzenos' elder son Matthew, who was ruling the city, was sent to Adrianople.[14] John took his wife Helena and two-year old Manuel with him on his travels to his new territories. The presence of Manuel in his father's entourage is recorded in Kantakouzenos' history as 'Manuel, the younger son'.[15] The infant Manuel thus made his first appearance in history in a work written by his own grandfather. His elder siblings Andronikos and Irene were left in Constantinople under the care of their maternal grandmother Irene Kantakouzene.[16]

John Palaiologos and Matthew Kantakouzenos still had a score to settle. Matthew, ranking above a despot, yet below an emperor, resented being overshadowed by John.[17] Fighting started anew in Thrace as John attacked Adrianople and drove Matthew out of the city. Kantakouzenos came to his son's aid with his Turkish and Catalan troops, while John Palaiologos relied on Serbian, Bulgarian and Venetian help. The Kantakouzenos faction emerged victorious in the hostilities, while John was forced to leave Didymoteichon and instead go to Tenedos.[18] In his history, Kantakouzenos points out that once more that John's wife, Helena, followed the young emperor, again accompanied by 'the younger son' Manuel.[19]

Embittered by his exile, John Palaiologos sailed away from Tenedos and made an unsuccessful attempt at entering Constantinople. His attack was

---

A Second City's Challenges and Responses', *DOP* 57 (2003), 5–30; I. Ševčenko, 'Nicolas Cabasilas' "Anti-Zealot" Discourse: A Re-Interpretation', *DOP* 11 (1957), 79–171, and K. P. Matschke, 'Thessalonike und die Zeloten. Bemerkungen zu einem Schlüsselereignis der spätbyzantinischen Stadt und Reichsgeschichte', *BSl* 55 (1994), 19–43. Henceforth, Ševčenko, 'Anti-Zealot'.

[14] Kantakouzenos, III, 200–8; Gregoras, III, 147–50. For a narrative of the events, see Nicol, *Last Centuries*, 228–30 and Nicol, *Reluctant Emperor*, 116.

[15] Kantakouzenos, III, 238, '... Μανουὴλ τὸν νεώτερον'. Manuel is called 'τὸν νεώτερον' with reference to his older brother Andronikos.

[16] Kantakouzenos, III, 238.

[17] Nicol, *Last Centuries*, 238, and Nicol, *Reluctant Emperor*, 119, and D. Nicol. *The Family of Kantakouzenos, 1100–1460* (Washington DC, 1968), 88. Henceforth, Nicol, *The Family of Kantakouzenos*.

[18] For a more detailed narrative of the events, see Nicol, *Last Centuries*, 238 and Nicol, *Reluctant Emperor*, 121.

[19] Kantakouzenos, III, 253. '... Ἑλένη ἡ γυνή, Μανουὴλ τὸν νεώτερον τῶν παιδῶν ἔχουσα ...'.

repelled by his mother-in-law Irene Kantakouzene.[20] John then sailed back to Tenedos, from whence he set off for Thessalonike, to his mother Anna of Savoy. He was accompanied by Helena and once more, with her came Manuel, this time referred to as 'their child, Manuel' by Kantakouzenos.[21] As the constant companion of his mother, the three-year-old Manuel had already travelled to three different locations: Didymoteichon, Tenedos and Thessalonike. In an interesting twist, during his reign he travelled frequently not only in his empire, and became famous as the only Byzantine emperor to visit France and England.

Meanwhile, Kantakouzenos proclaimed his son Matthew as co-emperor, and Manuel's father John V was stripped of his rank of emperor. Nonetheless, the names of John's mother Anna and his son Andronikos were still commemorated in the growing list of emperors and empresses.[22] Now although there were three emperors and four empresses, thanks to the new addition of Matthew's wife Irene Palaiologina, the situation would soon be altered. On 29 November 1354, John entered Constantinople with the help of the Genoese.[23] For a few days, there the city was filled with tension and uncertainty, but on 9 December, John Kantakouzenos announced his decision to abdicate. The next day, he donned the habit of a monk and embraced the monastic life. After a few more years and a little more resistance, in 1357 his son Matthew also relinquished his claim to the crown.[24] Finally, it seemed that the Palaiologan dynasty had firmly re-established itself on the throne.

Byzantium Post-Civil War

These were the events of Manuel's infancy, and the outcomes of this civil war between his family members would determine many aspects of Manuel's future rule and greatly shape his imperial inheritance. The struggle between the Kantakouzenoi and the Palaiologoi was the cause of devastation for the empire until its definite termination in 1357. By 1357, the once vast Byzantine Empire was confined to Constantinople, parts of Thrace, Thessalonike, some Aegean islands, roughly half of the Peloponnesian peninsula and the

---

[20] Kantakouzenos, III, 255; Nicol, *Last Centuries*, 239.

[21] Kantakouzenos, III, 256. '... βασιλίδα Ἑλένην τὴν γυναῖκα ἔχων καὶ Μανουὴλ τὸν παῖδα ...'.

[22] Kantakouzenos, III, 276; Gregoras, III, 204; Schreiner, *Kleinchroniken*, Chronik 22 /10–12; Nicol, *Last Centuries*, 239 and *Reluctant Emperor*, 124.

[23] Kantakouzenos, III, 276, but this time only Helena Kantakouzene is mentioned. Schreiner, *Kleinchroniken*, Chronik 22/12.

[24] Nicol, *Last Centuries*, 239–43 and *Reluctant Emperor*, 124–8.

western part of the Chaldean peninsula.[25] Constantinople, Thessalonike and Mistras were the three major political centres of this drastically diminished territory, the latter two administrated by governors who were appointed by the emperor. Increasingly, they would be ruled by the members of the imperial family. Furthermore, the dramatic loss of territory and constant fighting had led to the decline of agricultural production, causing Byzantium to become increasingly dependent on Genoa for grain. The fisc also suffered as the revenues from taxes plummeted. By now, imperial revenues almost entirely came from Constantinople alone. Commercial privileges given to the Italian maritime cities of Venice and Genoa further exacerbated these dire economic straits. Although the Byzantine political elite continued to enjoy a relative economic power, the majority of the population was growing increasingly poor.

The Byzantine army fared no better; the navy no longer existed. Moreover, the militarily weakened empire faced a serious Turkish threat in Anatolia and recently in Thrace. Although there were several Turkish emirates, Byzantium's chief contender for the region were the Ottomans. Originally founded as one of the many Turkish emirates that had sprung forth in Anatolia after the dissolution of the Seljuk Empire in the thirteenth century, the Ottoman Emirate soon became a major threat for the Byzantines. The civil wars of the fourteenth century allowed for further Ottoman expansion into Byzantine territory. And by seeking them as allies, both Kantakouzenos and Anna of Savoy allowed the Ottomans to meddle in Byzantine political affairs. This Ottoman infiltration into Byzantine affairs would prove to be a great handicap to Manuel as emperor. Some of the lesser Turkish emirates, such as the Karesioğulları or the Aydınoğulları, posed minor challenges to Byzantium as well.[26] Other nearby political entities consisted of the following: on the Black Sea shore, the Byzantine Empire of Trebizond persevered, yet its relations with Constantinople were not always cordial. In the Balkans, by 1357, Dušan's Serbian Empire had crumbled to make way for several principalities – Manuel's empress would come from one of them in 1392. Bulgaria and Wallachia were Byzantium's other contacts in the Balkans. All of these entities, like Byzantium, had to cope with the growing Ottoman expansion. In the south, Morea was home to various Latin principalities. Cyprus, too, was ruled by the Latin Lusignan family.

[25] J. V. A. Fine, Jr., *The Late Medieval Balkans: A Critical Survey from the Late Twelfth Century to the Ottoman Conquest* (Ann Arbor, 1987), 321. Henceforth, Fine, *Balkans*. See also Nicol, *Last Centuries*, 265–315.

[26] *The Cambridge History of Turkey*, ed. K. Fleet (Cambridge, 2009), vol. 1, 102–17.

Byzantium's chief support against the Ottomans came from Venice and Genoa, the two great Italian maritime city states. These cities exercised great influence over Byzantine politics and economy. Like the Ottomans, they too had been instrumental in the civil war. Throughout the fourteenth century, the Byzantine Empire frequently relied on Venice and Genoa for military and economic support. However, it must be emphasized that help was lent only when it suited their own interests. These Italian cities rivalled – sometimes even exceeded – the authority of the emperor in Constantinople. The Venetians had a neighbourhood in Constantinople and a *bailos*, a resident representative in charge of the Venetians in the city. While the Genoese even had their own colony in Pera, which was governed by a *podesta*. Various attempts made by Byzantine emperors to curb their influence or impose even minor taxes, were always thwarted, and Byzantine economy and trade were almost entirely under Italian control. Under Kantakouzenos' rule, the Genoese even burnt the recently built Byzantine naval ships. which they perceived as a threat.[27] The story of Manuel's Byzantium, would also be closely intertwined with these Italian cities.

Alongside Venice and Genoa, the papacy was another option in searching for allies against the Ottomans. However, negotiations with the papacy presented some challenges: they frequently brought up the thorny question of a union between Orthodox Byzantium and the Catholic papacy. Any agreement on a union might potentially require the Byzantines to renounce their Orthodox faith and accept the Latin doctrines. Such an outcome could expect opposition from fervent supporters of the Orthodox Church, after all, this was exactly what happened after similar demands were made at the Council of Lyons in 1274. Any union concluded between the two churches had the potential to intensify Byzantine social strife. Moreover, during Manuel's own reign, the issue would be further complicated by the Papal Schism (1378–1417), which resulted in rival popes in Rome and in Avignon; the Byzantines usually negotiated with the former. The political sphere of Byzantium in the aftermath of the civil war also included those European polities further removed from the Byzantine political sphere, including several other Italian cities, as well as Hungary, France and England. Some forty years later, Manuel would also have to operate within this political map.[28]

---

[27] Nicol, *Last Centuries*, 222.
[28] See Nicol, *Last Centuries*, 265–315 and Necipoğlu, *Byzantium between the Ottomans and the Latins*, 18–27.

A brief outline of the social problems of Byzantium is also in order. On this front, too, circumstances were rather bleak, since on many levels the civil war between the houses of Palaiologoi and Kantakouzenoi had greatly intensified pre-existing social tensions. The socio-political elite was divided between the two warring factions, and the incessant fighting had caused havoc for the populace. Their economic prosperity steadily plummeted during those six turbulent years. In addition, a serious theological dispute had further engulfed society. The fourteenth century had already been marked by many theological debates, both on account of increased contact with the Latins and the translations of important Latin theological works into Greek. During this time, hesychasm, the practice of silent prayer, also become a major point of contention. Soon afterwards, it erupted into a full-fledged theological dispute.

In 1330s, the monk and theologian Gregory Palamas developed this practice into a doctrine known as Palamism. Among other things, Palamas further developed the Orthodox teaching on the distinction between the essence (*ousia*) of God and his energies (*energeia*). While God's essence was entirely unknowable and imparticipable for human, it was possible for one to participate in the divine through God's energies. The major tenet of Palamism proposed that through prayer and spiritual contemplation, it was possible for humans to reach a mystical union with divinity. The teachings of Palamas ultimately led to a great religious controversy that divided not only scholars of theology, but the entire society.[29]

Because theological debates and politics were often intertwined in Byzantine society, Palamism become a significant component of the civil war. John Kantakouzenos championed Palamism, while Anna of Savoy and her supporters opposed it. The supporters of Palamism mostly came from the more conservative Orthodox, such as the monks of Mt. Athos, whereas its opponents were mostly pro-Latins. However, one must keep in mind that these lines were not rigidly drawn – not all Palamites embraced Kantakouzenos' cause and not and anti-Palamites supported the empress. The theological stance regarding Palamism was also fluid. Eventually, the conflict resulted in the victory of Palamites in 1351, and a synod convoked by Kantakouzenos declared Palamism as the official doctrine of the church.[30] Still, the matter was not yet resolved. Its political dimensions

---

[29] On Palamism, see for instance J. Meyendorff, *A Study of Gregory Palamas*, trans. G. Lawrance (London, 1964); and J. Meyendorff, *Byzantine Hesychasm: Historical, Theological and Social Problems* (London, 1974). Palamism will be discussed in more detail in Chapter 6.
[30] Nicol, *Last Centuries*, 210–15.

had further elevated the importance of the question of Palamism. Even many decades later, and throughout Manuel's reign, the tension between the Palamites and the anti-Palamites continued to pose a serious challenge to social stability. All things considered Manuel's imperial inheritance was already in a precarious state, and this background must be taken into account when discussing his reign.

An Imperial Family: Palaiologoi and Kantakouzenoi

No attempts have yet been made to gain an insight into Manuel's perception of these early years. However, they are an important part of his life story and merit some discussion. Manuel never makes mention of the events of the civil war in his writings. Though it is true that he was yet not born during the peak of the civil war and was too young to remember the struggle between his father and grandfather between 1350–4, it is nonetheless possible that he had vague memories of the clash between his maternal uncle Matthew Kantakouzenos and his own father. He may have also heard the stories that were told within the family.[31] It would have been interesting to know something about Manuel's perspective on events, especially since in addition to being a disastrous time for the empire, the civil war was also a family feud. This familial aspect of the struggle is perhaps best reflected in Kantakouzenos' history: the text is full of the kinship terms, such as son, father, mother, son-in-law and wife, that defined the relationships between the emperors and the empresses.[32]

The family members involved in the civil strife lived until the early years of Manuel's youth, and his writings do help us to explore his relationships with some of these figures. The most obscure are Manuel's female relatives, whom he scarcely ever mentions. His maternal grandmother, Irene Kantakouzene, was alive in April 1363, but seems to have died before 1379.[33] She played an active role during the civil war, even defending Didymoteichon and Constantinople in her husband's absence, and both her husband Kantakouzenos, and Gregoras have nothing but the highest praise for her.[34] Still, she can only be seen through the eyes of the men who portrayed her according to their literary goals. Irene's own voice is

---

[31] In 1357, Manuel was seven years old.

[32] Several terms used by Kantakouzenos are υἱός, πατήρ, μήτηρ, γαμβρός and γυναῖκα.

[33] See D. Nicol, *The Byzantine Lady: Ten Portraits, 1250–1500* (Cambridge, 1994), 71–81 for Irene's life. Henceforth, Nicol, *Byzantine Lady*. She must have been dead by 1379, as she is not mentioned among the hostages Andronikos IV took, which included Kantakouzenos and his three daughters.

[34] For some examples, see Kantakouzenos, II, 336; III, 49; Gregoras, II, 625, 692, 805.

missing.[35] Upon her husband's abdication, Irene retired to the monastery of Kyra Martha in 1354.[36] Since she was in Constantinople and it was possible for nuns to see their male relatives, it is almost certain that Manuel knew her in person.[37]

The same possibility exists also for his aunts, the sisters of the Empress Helena, who later retired to the same monastery. They, too, were alive in 1379.[38] As an emperor who was to have especially close contacts with the Ottomans, it is an intriguing question whether Manuel ever conversed with Theodora Kantakouzene (who married the Ottoman ruler Orhan) about her life among the Ottomans.[39] The only passing reference Manuel makes to his maternal aunts can be found in his *Funeral Oration to His Brother Theodore* (c. 1409), in a passage where he mentions them as the hostages of Andronikos IV.[40]

On the other hand, Manuel never mentions his paternal grandmother Anna of Savoy. She established herself as empress in Thessalonike in 1351 and died there in 1366, never returning to Constantinople.[41] It seems that the two did not have much physical contact apart from Manuel's brief stay in Thessalonike with his parents as an infant. Indeed both Kantakouzenos and Gregoras portray the empress as a jealous, bitter and ill-tempered woman.[42]

[35] On the study of women in Byzantium and its challenges, especially through texts, see A. Kaldellis, 'The Study of Women and Children: Methodological Challenges and New Directions', in *The Byzantine World*, ed. P. Stephenson (London, 2010), 61–71.

[36] Irene is the only empress during the Late Byzantine period to retire to a convent because of political pressure, A. M. Talbot, 'Late Byzantine Nuns: By Choice or Necessity?', *BF* 9 (1985), 103–17, 112.

[37] A. M. Talbot, 'Women's Space in Monasteries', *DOP* 52 (1998), 113–27, see 122–3.

[38] Kantakouzenos claims to have inherited Kyra Martha from his family, Nicol, *Byzantine Family of Kantakouzenos*, 30. So his wife and daughters retired there, and Irene Kantakouzene even raised Matthew's daughter in the same monastery, Nicol, *Family of Kantakouzenos*, 27 and 50. Their example was later to be followed by Helena Kantakouzene and Manuel's wife Helena Dragaš, who also retired to Kyra Martha as nuns. For Maria and Theodora Kantakouzene, Nicol, no. 27 and no. 29.

[39] On the marriage of Theodora Kantakouzene, see A. A. M. Bryer, 'Greek Historians on the Turks: The Case of the first Byzantine-Ottoman Marriage', in *Writing of History in the Middle Ages: Essays Presented to R. W. Southern*, eds. R. H. C. Davis and J. M. Wallace-Hadrill, (1981), 471–93. Albeit less detailed, also see J. Gill, 'Matrons and Brides of 14th-Century Byzantium', *BF* 10 (1985), 39–56.

[40] *Funeral Oration*, 110–11.

[41] For Anna of Savoy, see Nicol, *Byzantine Lady*, 82–3 and C. Diehl, *Byzantine Empresses*, trans. H. Bell and T. De Kerpely (London,1963), 288–308. Focusing specifically on her reign in Thessalonike; D. Nicol and S. Bendall, 'Anna of Savoy in Thessalonica: The Numismatic Evidence', *Revue Numismatique, 6th Ser, XIX* (1977), 87–102. Henceforth, Nicol-Bendall, 'Anna of Savoy'. The oldest work on Anna of Savoy is D. Muratore, *Una principessa sabauda sul trono di Bisanzio* (Chambéey, 1909), which narrates the political events.

[42] Kantakouzenos, II, 47–8; 105; Gregoras, II, 748–51, 760–1, 767. For negative views of Anna, see above for the works of Diehl and Nicol. They both reach their negative verdict through their sources Kantakouzenos and Gregoras – enemies of Anna of Savoy.

For more recent work, see S. Origone, *Giovanna di Savoia: Alias Anna Paleologina, Latina e Bisanzio (c. 1306–1365)* (Milan, 1998). See also E. Malamut, 'Jeanne-Anne princesse de Savoie et

Her reign in Thessalonike, however, was a period of peace and prosperity. Years later, when Manuel came to rule the city, there was an inscription on the gate of the Acropolis commemorating her.[43] Manuel certainly knew his maternal uncles. He describes Manuel Kantakouzenos, the despot of Morea, with whom he probably had limited contact, as a man of noble character who knew how to govern well.[44] Although he must have had less admiration for his elder uncle Matthew Kantakouzenos, whose struggle with his own father he knew of, Manuel was tactful in the *Funeral Oration*. In this oration, he merely remarks that Matthew was an exceedingly kind man, of higher rank and older than his brother. It should however be noted that unlike in the case of Manuel Kantakouzenos, he bestows no praise upon him or his rule in Morea. It is a telling omission. Instead, he points out the rebellious conduct of Matthew's son John as a hindrance to peace in Morea.[45] Whatever his personal feelings, later in his life Manuel was cautious and reserved in his criticism. Nonetheless, a close reading reveals that however subtle his remarks might have been, Manuel was indeed critical of his elder uncle.

Unlike the other Kantakouzenoi, John VI was to remain an influential figure in Manuel's early life. Despite his donning of the monastic garb, Kantakouzenos was very much a public figure until his death in 1383. He was involved actively in theological debates, was present at audiences and counselled his son-in-law John Palaiologos.[46] Notably, in the *Funeral Oration*, Manuel represents his grandfather as a direct participant in the family decision of appointing his brother Theodore as the despot of Morea.[47] The young Manuel also personally witnessed his grandfather's speech against the papal legate at the council of 1367, where Kantakouzenos is reported to have advocated the union of the churches only on equal terms.[48] This stance is reminiscent of the ideas that Manuel would advocate later in his life.

---

impératrice de Byzance', in *Impératrices, princesses, aristocrates et saintes souveraines. De l'Orient Chrétien et Musulman au Moyen Age et au début des temps modernes*, ed. E. Malamut and A. Nicolaides (Aix-en-Provence, 2014), 85–117.

[43] Nicol-Bendall, 'Anna of Savoy', 92–3 for the inscription. M. Jugie, 'Nicolas Cabasilas, Panegyriques inédits de Matthieu Cantacuzène et d'Anne Paléologine', *Izvetija Russkago Archeologiceskago Instituta v Konstantinopole, xv*, (1911), 112–21, see especially 119–20. Henceforth, Jugie, 'Nicholas Cabasilas'.

[44] See no. 25 in Nicol, *The Family of Kantakouzenos*. Manuel Kantakouzenos was made the despot of Morea in 1349 and lived there until his death.

[45] *Funeral Oration*, 114–15.   [46] Nicol, *Reluctant Emperor*, 134–9.   [47] *Funeral Oration*, 113–14.

[48] J. Meyendorff, 'Jean-Joasaph Cantacuzène et le projet de concile oecuménique en 1367', in *Akten des XI. Internationalen Byzantinisten-Kongresses, München 1958* (Munich, 1960), 363–9. An account of the council proceedings is also included. Henceforth, Meyendorff, 'Le projet'.

Similarly, Manuel composed an anti-Islamic dialogue in which he partially relied on Kantakouzenos' work on the same topic. In the foreword of the *Dialogue with a Persian* (c. 1392–6), he refers to Kantakouzenos as 'our most blessed grandfather, the excellent and admirable emperor' and pays tribute to his work on Islam.[49] Moreover, in 1384, the year after Kantakouzenos' death, Manuel made a donation to the monastery of Nea Mone in Thessalonike in his memory. This act can be interpreted as indicative of his affection for his grandfather.[50]

Indeed, Manuel bears a striking resemblance to his grandfather Kantakouzenos. Both emperors shared a profound interest in theology and both were avid literati which, to some extent, seems to be a trait of the Kantakouzenos family – Empress Helena and Matthew Kantakouzenos were authors as well. Empress Helena is known to have composed several laudatory speeches in honour of her father, as well as being a correspondent of Demetrios Kydones and Gregoras.[51] These similarities in the interests of Manuel and John Kantakouzenos are often pointed out by modern scholars, and even their marked facial resemblance has been noted.[52] Still, despite all the parallels between them, Manuel's signature never included his mother's Kantakouzenos name.[53]

It is fascinating, however, to ponder whether Manuel read his grandfather's history, in which he makes three appearances as an infant. The last event Kantakouzenos recorded in his work is dated to 1364.[54] Thus, it is highly plausible that the work was in circulation at least among Kantakouzenos' own circle and that Manuel might have read it. Although he produced works in diverse genres and his *Funeral Oration* is a blend of panegyric and historical narrative, as far as we know, Manuel never authored a work of history. Perhaps this was because, unlike his deposed grandfather, he did not feel the need to do so.

---

[49] *Dialogue with a Persian*, 6. '... ὁ θειότατος πάππος ἡμῖν ὁ πάντ᾽ ἄριστος καὶ θαυμάσιος βασιλεύς ...'. Kantakouzenos' son Matthew Kantakouzenos also composed theological works, see Nicol, *Byzantine Family of Kantakouzenos*, 120. In his *enkomion* of Matthew, Kabasilas alludes to Matthew's use of his father's works. Jugie. 'Nicolas Cabasilas', 117.

[50] *Actes de Lavra*, III, *De 1329 à 1500*, eds. A. Guillou, P. Lemerle, D. Papachryssanthou, and N. Svoronos. (Paris, 1979), 163–6. Henceforth, *Actes de Lavra*.

[51] See F. Kianka, 'The Letters of Demetrios Kydones to Empress Helena Kantakouzene Palaiologina', *DOP 46* (1992), 155–64. Henceforth, Kianka, 'Letters'. For Matthew Kantakouzenos, see footnote 43.

[52] Barker, *Manuel II*, 393; Nicol, *Reluctant Emperor*, 181 and Charanis, 'Strife', 286.

[53] Nicol, *Byzantine Family of Kantakouzenos*, 138.

[54] Nicol, *Reluctant Emperor*, 138. Kydones, Letters 9, 15 and 23. The earliest dated manuscript is from 1369 and no manuscripts survive from the 1370s or 1380s. There is nothing to indicate that Kantakouzenos revised his text in the 1370s. See Nicol, *Reluctant Emperor*, 141–2. See also R. H. Trone, *The History of John Kantakouzenos, Book 1. Edition, Translation and Commentary* (PhD thesis, The Catholic University of America, 1979), xii.

No less intriguing is the question why Kantakouzenos chose to emphasize the presence of his grandson in his narrative. As the second son of John V, it was not likely that Manuel would one day succeed his father, and the issue of the succession was not resolved until 1390–1. A possible reading is that this emphasis on infant Manuel's presence among John V's entourage served to highlight the devotion of Kantakouzenos' daughter Helena to her husband. Helena Kantakouzene is represented as an ideal wife who dutifully follows her Palaiologos husband with her *infant* son in tow. The presence of the young Manuel in the narrative can thus be interpreted as an indication of family unity despite Helena's torn loyalties. Or perhaps, it is a more personal indication that Kantakouzenos had a special fondness for his younger grandson. This question, of course, cannot be answered with certainty.

Manuel soon made appearances in other historic writings. Pressed by the dire need for help against the growing Turkish power, John V offered his son as a hostage to Pope Innocent IV in 1355. In exchange for military help, John V promised to secure the conversion of his subjects to the Catholic faith. He also agreed to a permanent papal legate in Constantinople and that his eldest son Andronikos would receive instruction in Latin. It was proposed that his second son Manuel would be sent to Avignon as a hostage and educated there. Should his father fail to honour his pledge, Manuel was to be married according to the wishes of the pope.[55] These lavish and deferential promises from the emperor can only be a reflection of his desperation. However, this plans came to nothing; the pope merely ignored the proposals. John V watched helplessly as his territories shrank: in 1360, the Ottomans captured Didymoteichon, followed by Adrianople in 1362 and Philippopolis in 1363.[56]

Despite the challenges faced by the emperor, young Manuel remained in Constantinople with his family. Meanwhile, two new brothers were born: Michael (after 1351) and Theodore (c. 1355), the future despot of Morea.[57] On the other hand, the number and the identities of John V's daughters are

---

[55] The offer would be renewed in 1357 without success. Dölger, *Regesten*, no. 3052, 42–3; Greek and Latin text in A. Theiner and F. Miklosich, *Monumenta spectantia ad unionem ecclesiarum graeca et romana* (Vienna, 1872), 29–37. Nicol, *Last Centuries*, 258; Barker, *Manuel II*, 4; O. Halecki. *Un empereur de Byzance à Rome* (Warsaw, 1930; reprint. London, 1972), 24–31. Henceforth, Halecki, *Un empereur.*

[56] Barker, *Manuel II*, ix; Nicol, *Last Centuries*, 262–3.

[57] PLP, no. 21352 for Michael Palaiologos and no. 21460 for Theodore I Palaiologos. Respectively no. 85 and no. 87 in A. T. Papadopoulos. *Versuch einer Genealogie der Palaiologen 1259–1453* (Amsterdam, 1962). However, Papadopoulos mistakenly makes Theodore the third brother, although Manuel himself states that he was the fourth brother, *Funeral Oration*, 86–7.

still uncertain. It seems that he had at least two daughters, possibly more.[58] The only one whose name is known for certain, is Manuel's older sister Irene, whom his grandfather also names in his history.[59] Irene was betrothed to Halil, the youngest son of Emir Orhan.[60] Whether the marriage actually took place or not is unclear. Probably another sister named Maria also existed, whom, according to an Italian chronicle, Andronikos IV offered as a bride to the Ottoman sultan Murad I in 1376–7, though she died before the marriage could take place.[61] A Byzantine short chronicle remarks that two of John V's daughters took the veil in August 1373, shortly after Andronikos' rebellion. It is quite possible that these were Irene and Maria. Furthermore, between 1376–9, Kydones indicated that a daughter shared Empress Helena's confinement in the Tower of Anemas.[62] Finally, the Ottoman chronicler Neşri makes the dubious claim that Murad I married two of his sons to daughters of the emperor, as well as marrying one himself.[63]

One vague clue about Manuel's sisters can be found in the *Funeral Oration* where he uses a rather enigmatic metaphor to describe his feelings on Theodore's attainment of the eternal life, likening his situation to

---

[58] A. Lutrell, 'John V's daughters: a Palaiologan Puzzle', *DOP 36* (1986), 103–12, 103. Henceforth, Luttrell, 'Daughters'. Now see Th. Ganchou, 'Les chroniques vénitiennes et les unions ottomanes des filles de l'empereur byzantine Jean V Palaiologos, Eirènè et Maria (1358 et 1376)', in *La transizione bizantino-ottomana nelle cronache veneziane*, eds. S. Kolditz and M. Koller (Rome and Venice, 2018), 163–96. Based on the surviving sources, Ganchou seeks to prove the existence of Maria, as well as proposing that the marriage of Irene and Halil actually took place. He proposes that Irene then returned to Constantinople and took the veil, together with Maria, around 1373.

[59] Kantakouzenos, III, 238; for Irene Palaiologina, see PLP, no. 21352 and Papadopoulos no. 88.

[60] Gregoras, III, 509–10.

[61] In 1373, the possible marriage of one of John V's daughters to the King of Cyprus – probably mistakenly reported as his only daughter – was perhaps negotiated. *Leontios Makhairas. Recital Concerning the Sweet Land of Cyprus entitled 'Chronicle'*, ed. R. M. Dawkins, (Oxford, 1932), vol. 1, 326–31. Ganchou proposes that as Irene had probably been married and widowed, the reference to the emperor's only (*unicam*) virgin daughter should not be interpreted as referring to an only daughter, but the only remaining virgin daughter of John V. Ganchou believes the princess in question to be Maria, see Ganchou, Les chroniques vénitiennes, 184.
Based on the Ottoman chronicler Neşri, three of John V's daughters marry the sultan and his two sons, see A. D. Alderson, *The Structure of the Ottoman Dynasty* (Oxford, 1956), 165–6. These marriages are justifiably dismissed by Luttrell. Maria and her proposed marriage to Murad is mentioned in an Italian chronicle, Raffaino Caresini, *Chronica A. A 1343–1388*, ed. E. Pastorello, (Bologna, 1923), 32. Henceforth, Caresini. Schreiner, *Kleinchroniken*, Chronik 7/35, records the death of (probably the same Maria around 1376.

[62] Kydones, Letter 222, lines 97–102.

[63] Schreiner, *Kleinchroniken*, Chronik 9/27, Neşri, 237–9. One other possibility is that if these marriages had indeed taken place, these may have been illegitimate daughters. However, after Theodora Kantakouzene, both John V and Andronikos IV seem to have offered legitimate princesses to the Ottomans. It is much more likely that Neşri's statement is a mistaken one, see also footnote 61 above.

a mother who was sending off her daughter in marriage to a foreign land.[64] It's an unusual metaphor to express lament about the permanent departure of a loved one to eternity. Moreover, it reveals an understanding of maternal psychology, especially that of an empress, and it may have been inspired by Empress Helena's distress over the prospect of sending her daughters to foreign territories as brides. Among his brothers, Manuel was certainly closest with the youngest Theodore, with whom he retained a strong and cherished bond. Manuel wrote his famous *Funeral Oration* on Theodore's death, and dedicated the *Dialogue with the Persian* to him. In contrast, the nature of his relationship with Andronikos and Michael during their childhood is not known at all. There is no question, however, that any fraternal affection that may have existed between him and Andronikos must have been destroyed during the latter's rebellions.

Imperial Upbringing

Like his family relationships, other aspects of Manuel's childhood have not received much attention. Naturally, as a child or an adolescent, Manuel did not engage in political decisions. None of his compositions dated to this period survive and it is therefore not surprising that his earlier life is hardly studied. Since this biography will discuss Manuel as a *person*, and not merely an emperor, his childhood deserves further study as a crucial part of his fascinating life story.

Along with his siblings, Manuel was raised in a manner befitting the child of an emperor. The ideal of the well-educated prince was a common notion in Byzantine court panegyric; a solid education was seen as an integral part of imperial childhood.[65] Manuel, too, was to stress the importance of the upbringing of an imperial child, proudly stating that his brother Theodore was 'brought up in a royal way'.[66] Byzantine children usually started their elementary education around age six or eight. After a few years, they would start their secondary education around the ages of twelve or fourteen years old. They would then move on to higher education, which could last beyond

---

[64] *Funeral Oration*, 252–3.
[65] On imperial childhood and its representation in court rhetoric, see D. G. Angelov, 'Emperors and Patriarchs as Ideal Children and Adolescents: Literary Conventions and Cultural Expectations' in *Becoming Byzantine: Children and Childhood in Byzantium*, eds. A. Papaconstantinou and A. M. Talbot, (Washington, 2009), 85–125. Henceforth, Angelov, 'Ideal Children'. On Byzantine education during childhood and its stages, see N. Kalogeras, *Byzantine Childhood Education and its Social Role from the Sixth Century until the End of Iconoclasm* (PhD thesis, University of Chicago, 2000), especially 134–5.
[66] *Funeral Oration*, 84–5.

the age of eighteen. At the court, after receiving training in reading and writing, the princes would be instructed in the practicalities of rulership by tutors, often by several different ones.[67] Manuel's narration of his education conforms to this pattern:

> So, then, when I was a child, it was not possible for me to frequent only the haunts of the Muses and to make this my sole employment, so that I could surpass every wise man and those who are exalted with regard to words. But, as I came out of the council chamber, toils followed one upon another. And it was necessary each day to alternate among my many teachers, who taught many other things- how to handle both bow and spear, how to ride horseback . . .[68]

Manuel's account indicates the presence of numerous tutors, and in the *Funeral Oration*, he also refers to Theodore's many instructors.[69] Interestingly, Manuel claims that he also attended some council meetings. This is not inconceivable, as we know that he was present at the restoration of Patriarch Philotheos in 1363 and that in 1367 he attended a council on the church union.[70] In short, this claim should not be dismissed.

Just as Manuel mentions above, the physical education of the princes would have also included some military training as well as archery, horsemanship, sports and games.[71] In the *Funeral Oration*, Manuel tells how he consoled himself in the Tower of Anemas in 1379 during his imprisonment, by imagining Theodore engaging in activities suited to his youth – military exercises, hunting and contests. These activities, Manuel points out, would strengthen men in training, bring health and a life of fame. Although Theodore was no longer a child or an adolescent at the time, the emperor's thoughts on these past times conform to the ideals of princely instruction.[72] Manuel again emphasizes the importance of physical training in his *Foundations of Imperial*

---

[67] Angelov, 'Ideal Children', 105.

[68] This passage from the *Discourse to Iagoup* (*Epistolary Discourse to Alexios Iagoup*) is also translated by Barker in his monograph. Barker, *Manuel II*, 411–12. However, I disagree with Barker's rendering of 'ἀλλ' ἐκ τοῦ βουλευτηρίου ἐξερχόμενον' as 'out of my earliest instruction'. I believe that Manuel is referring to his attending of the council meetings in the palace and thus I have modified Barker's translation accordingly. *Bouleuterion* is given as council, council meeting, deliberation and advice giving in LSJ. In one of his letters Manuel again uses *bouleuterion* to refer to a council, see Letter 45, line 20. *Discourse to Iagoup*, 328, ' Ἐμοὶ τοίνυν παιδὶ μὲν ὄντι οὐχ ὑπῆρξεν ἐς μουσεῖα μόνον φοιτᾶν, καὶ τοῦτ' αὐτὸ μόνον ἔργον ποιεῖσθαι, ὅπως πάντα παρελάσαιμι σοφὸν καὶ τοὺς ἐπὶ λόγοις σεμνυνομένους. ἀλλ' ἐκ βουλευτηρίου ἐξερχόμενον, ἄλλοι ἐπ' ἄλλοις διεδέχοντο πόνοι, καὶ πολλοὺς ἦν ἀνάγκη καθ' ἑκάστην ἡμέραν ἀμεῖψαι τοὺς διδασκάλους, οἳ πολλά τε ἄλλα τόξα τε μεταχειρίζειν καὶ δόρυ καὶ ἱππεύειν ἐδίδασκον . . .'.

[69] *Funeral Oration*, 84–5.   [70] Barker, *Manuel II*, 6; Meyendorff, 'Le projet', 363–9.

[71] Angelov, 'Ideal Children', 107–10.

[72] *Funeral Oration*, 104–5. Theodore would have been around 21–3 at the time of the events. They were imprisoned 1376–9, and it is unclear when exactly Theodore was able to leave, but it should be closer to 1379.

Conduct (c. 1410), an advisory work addressed to his eldest son and heir, John VIII. In the introductory letter to the work, he points out that his adolescent son had already received some instruction in archery and hunting.[73] Strikingly, in the same text Manuel employs metaphors related to hunting while also discussing the importance of wisdom. These include how an eagle is caught by a bird-line, how larks habitually fly over the rocks and how gazelles cannot be easily caught by ropes; all examples that reflect Manuel's own love for hunting. John also could relate to these hunting references.[74] In another chapter, Manuel gives the commonplace advice that hunting was conducive to relaxation and a relief for the mind. He also adds that hunting is good training for warfare and boosts health. The emperor tells his son that in this manner, he will not miss out on pleasure even if he does occasionally miss his prey; 'for', he remarks, 'you are not likely to hit it always'.[75] Hence, his writings bear the marks of his imperial upbringing, and indeed in his adulthood, Manuel retained a notable love of hunting and riding.

In addition to physical training, Manuel was instructed in literature and rhetoric. Rhetorical and literary education was of paramount importance for a ruler, as speaking and writing well were indispensable skills at court. A mastery of these skills could pave the way for political advancement. Moreover, possessing such an education was a shared trait of the Byzantine political and cultural elite. *Paideia* (παιδεία), a solid education in Greek literature, philosophy and rhetoric, functioned as a social marker and indicated belonging to elite circles. However, it was not an end in itself. By delivering orations, exchanging letters, forming literary networks and dedicating works to influential patrons, the elite advanced their political and bureaucratic careers.[76] One notable example is Theodore Metochites in the fourteenth century, whose bureaucratic career prospered thanks to an oration he delivered at the Byzantine court. Similarly, the historian Nikephoros Gregoras was offered a post in the patriarchate after delivering a panegyric for the emperor.

---

[73] *The Foundations of Imperial Conduct*, col. 313.

[74] *The Foundations of Imperial* Conduct, col. 377.

[75] *The Foundations of Imperial Conduct*, col. 372, '... ὁ φίλος σοι ἵππος, ὁ κύων, ὁ ἱέραξ, ἡ πρὸς τὰ θηρία τῶν βελῶν ἄφεσις ... Ταύτῃ καὶ τῆς θήρας ἀποτυχὼν (οὐδὲ γὰρ ἀεὶ τυγχάνειν οἷόν τε), τῆς εὐφροσύνης οὐκ ἂν ἁμάρτοις ...'.

[76] For the relationship of politics and *paideia*, see C. Holmes, 'Political Literacy', in *The Byzantine World*, ed. P. Stephenson (London, 2012), 135–47; N. Gaul, *Thomas Magistros und die spätbyzantinische Sophistik. Studien zum Humanismus urbanen Eliten in der frühen Palaiologenzeit* (Wiesbaden, 2011), especially 1–5. Henceforth, Gaul, *Thomas Magistros*. D. G. Angelov, *Imperial Ideology and Political Thought in Byzantium, 1204–1330* (Cambridge, 2007), 18–20, 73. Henceforth, Angelov, *Imperial Ideology*.

Moreover, practices of imperial government were closely associated with rhetorical skill, such as the composition of state documents. The literati would also subtly – but sometimes rather openly – incorporate political statements into their writings. Consequently, rhetoric provided the main platform for political thought. For the political elite, *logoi* and politics were interlinked. As the son of the emperor, education did not give Manuel exactly the same opportunities for advancement as officials at the court, who could earn promotions and curry imperial favour through their compositions. However, in the future, Manuel, too, would make use of literary networks, and disseminate political messages through his writings.

Manuel would become an avid writer as an adult. One can safely surmise that his rhetorical and literary instruction must have left a deep impression on him as a young man. It is also probable that Empress Helena Kantakouzene played a role in Manuel's education. After all, she had wielded a pen herself and corresponded with the famed literati of the day.[77] Until her death in 1396, Manuel enjoyed a close relationship with his mother, immortalizing the erudite empress in his *Dialogue on Marriage*. In contrast, nothing concrete can be gleaned about the role John V played in his upbringing. Once more, we must turn to his oeuvre to trace their relationship. Manuel's silence on his father in these works, combined with their future clashes, indicate that there was no particularly close bond.

There was another man who dominated Manuel's education and early life: Demetrios Kydones, the eminent statesman, diplomat and writer from whom Manuel seems to have received his instruction.[78] One of the foremost literati of the fourteenth century, Demetrios Kydones hailed from a Thessalonian family and enjoyed the patronage of John VI Kantakouzenos. A stellar bureaucrat and diplomat, Kydones acted as *mesazon*, chief minister, to both John V and John VI. He was involved in many significant political decisions in the period, including John V's conversion and trip to Rome in 1370. His rise in the bureaucracy was also closely connected to his scholarly abilities. In addition to dedicating orations to both emperors, Kydones established a wide literary network

---

[77] *Funeral Oration*, 11–12 and Dennis, *Letters*, xlv; *Dialogue on Marriage*, 39–44, 48–57; Kianka, 'Letters', 155. For the role of the empress in imperial upbringing, see J. Herrin, 'L'enseignement maternel à Byzance', in *Femmes et pouvoirs des femmes à Byzance et en Occident (VIe–XIe siècles)* eds. S. Lebecq et al. (Lille, 1999), 91–102.

[78] Barker, *Manuel II*, 416. Kianka, 'Letters', 155–6. On Kydones, see F. Kianka, *Demetrius Cydones (c. 1324 – c. 1397): Intellectual and Diplomatic Relations between Byzantium and the West in the Fourteenth Century* (PhD thesis, Fordham University, 1981) and J. R. Ryder, *The Career and Writings of Demetrios Kydones: A Study of Fourteenth Century Politics, Religion and Society* (Leiden, 2010).

through his letters and sought political support. His bulky letter collection encompasses almost all of the literati of the period, including Manuel's mother Helena Kantakouzene.

Kydones had the distinction of possessing a fine knowledge of Latin. He employed this skill not only in diplomacy, but also translated many important Latin theological works into Greek, mostly those of Saint Augustine and Thomas Aquinas. These translations were supported by John VI. Despite being a firm Orthodox, Kantakouzenos approved of Kydones' endeavours, partially in order to make use of the translations in his dealings with the Latins. Kydones himself famously converted to Latin Catholicism and remained a major advocate for a Byzantine-Latin rapprochement, in both political and religious spheres. His translations and teaching, especially of Aquinas, helped to disseminate Latin theology among the Byzantine literati. The dissemination of Thomas Aquinas was especially significant on the account of the fact that his theological methodology was based on philosophical inquiry and Aristotelian logic. Aquinas' translated works allowed the Byzantines to familiarize themselves with the methods of Scholastic theology. Some of Kydones' disciples, including Manuel Kalekas, Maximos Chrysoberges and Manuel Chrysoloras, also shared his profound admiration for Latin theology and converted to Latin Catholicism. However, as will be discussed later, it must be pointed out Manuel did not adopt his teacher's enthusiasm for the Latins and their theologians. Nor did he ever learn Latin.

Kydones' letters offer us a glimpse of a learned, eloquent and at times, humorous man. However, nothing more can really be gleaned about his role as Manuel's teacher; the duration and the content of his teaching is unknown. Likewise, it is not possible to trace their relationship before the 1370s, when their earliest surviving correspondence appears. Later in his life, Manuel often acknowledged his debt to Kydones, and sent works to his teacher for assessment. In these letters, Manuel addresses Kydones as 'the father of the writing', saying that he had 'provided us with the seed and watered it'.[79] These remarks clearly indicate a teacher-student relationship between the two.

Contemporary scholars have often relied on this correspondence in their studies of the period and have remarked upon the friendship between the two. However, the literary aspect and the tone of these letters have not received any serious attention. Nonetheless, an analysis of these features

---

[79] Letter 11, lines 24–9, '... καὶ δρέπου καρπὸν ἡδὺν ὡς τούτου αἴτιος ὤν, τά τε γὰρ σπέρματ' αὐτὸς παρέσχες ἡμῖν, ἥ τε ἀρδεία ἀφθόνως ἐκκέχυται παρὰ σοῦ.' and Letter 62, lines 11–13, 'ὁ γὰρ τὸ σπέρμα παρασχὼν οὗτος τῶν φύντων αἴτιος ...'. Here, Manuel is quoting Demosthenes, *De Corona*, 159.

has the potential to offer us a far deeper insight into this relationship. For instance, a close reading of their letters reveals a degree of reverence on Manuel's side and a familiarity on Kydones', despite the imperial rank of his pupil. Yet contrary to the widespread scholarly assessment, it is important not to overestimate Kydones' influence on Manuel. Despite his admiration for Kydones, Manuel never shared his pro-Latin views and as an author his interests differed.

What subjects might Manuel have been taught? Although there can be no definitive answer to this question, it is probable that he received instruction in grammar, rhetoric and philosophy, as well as studying at least some classical literature.[80] Imperial students were also expected to study advisory texts on moral issues. While Manuel composed ethico-political works for his son and heir, we do not know if such texts had been written for him. History, especially the study of good and bad kings of the past, was also seen as an integral part of the imperial education.[81] In his writings, Manuel referenced Herodotos, Thucydides and Xenophon, showing a familiarity with Greek histories. It is unclear whether he studied them as a student or read them later in life. However, Manuel later employed many historical exempla in his ethico-political works such as Cyrus, Xerxes, Caesar and Alexander the Great.

While Manuel almost certainly received instruction at the palace, it is unclear whether his studies were one-to-one or involved any joint classes with his brothers and sisters.[82] His relations with his various tutors and the methods they may have used to instruct their imperial pupil are relegated to the shadows. For younger students, it was not unusual for a teacher to inflict physical punishment on those of their charges who misbehaved. Many years later, while praising a correspondent, Manuel made the following comment: ' … only you alone of the youngsters escaped the

---

[80] On Byzantine education and the subjects taught in general, see P. Lemerle, *Le prémier humanisme byzantin* (Paris, 1971), 101–3; G. Buckler, 'Byzantine Education', in *Byzantium: An Introduction to East Roman Civilization*, ed. N. H. Baynes and H. St. L. B. Moss (Oxford, 1948), 204–7; G. Cavallo, *Lire à Byzance* (Paris, 2006), 23–34; S. Mergiali- Sahas, *L'enseignement pendant l'epoque des Paléologues* (Athens, 1996) and C. N. Constantinides, *Higher Education in Byzantium in the Thirteenth and Early Fourteenth centuries, 1204 – ca. 1310* (Nicosia, 1982) and C. N. Constantinides, 'Teachers and Students of Rhetoric in the Late Byzantine Period', in *Rhetoric in Byzantium: Papers from the 35th Spring Symposium of Byzantine Studies, Exeter College, the University of Oxford, March 2001*, ed. E. Jeffreys (Ashgate, 2003), 39–53. Henceforth, Mergiali-Sahas, *L'enseignement*; Constantinides, *Higher Education*; and Constantinides, 'Teachers and Students'.

[81] Angelov, 'Ideal Children', 105.

[82] It was also possible for girls to receive similar education with their brothers at least as far as some topics, such as literature, were concerned. For instance, Theodore Metochites' sister Irene received the same instruction under Gregoras, see Mergiali-Sahas, *L'enseignement*, 13.

mocking, the rod, the whip and the piercing glance of the schoolmaster'.[83]
After learning to read, write and recite the Psalms, Manuel would have
been instructed in Attic Greek and rhetoric. After all, speaking and writing
well was highly desirable for any courtly career, including an imperial one.

Manuel's writings provide the basis for envisioning the curriculum he
might have been taught. The emperor displayed a good knowledge of
Homer, Theognis, Pindar, Hesiod, Libanios, Demosthenes, Aristophanes
and Plato – authors who were all common choices in *enkyklios paideia*.[84] It
is probable that Manuel studied these authors at some point in his education, as most of his references and allusions to these works demonstrate
a deep acquaintance with them. This may indicate that he had engaged in
more serious study of the authors, as opposed to simply gathering quotations from compendia. An in-depth analysis of his works similarly reveals
the emperor's knowledge of Platonic philosophy. Indeed, Manuel would
later compose dialogues following the Platonic model, often casting himself into the role of Socrates. Among the Platonic dialogues, the emperor
shows a familiarity with the *Phaedrus* and the *Phaedo*, and his abundant
and witty allusions to the latter indicate a fondness for this dialogue in
particular.

Another work that seems to have been favoured by Manuel is Aristophanes'
play *Wealth*. Many humorous allusions in Manuel's works seem to betray the
emperor's partiality. Aristotle's *Nicomachean Ethics* also figures prominently in
the emperor's oeuvre, and he shows a close acquaintance with the text in his
Ethico-Political Orations, the *Foundations of Imperial Conduct* and partially,
the *Dialogue with a Persian*, all of which are influenced by Aristotle's
Nicomachean Ethics. It has also been demonstrated that Manuel's ethico-
political works reveal a knowledge of the well-known rhetorical handbooks
of Menander Rhetor (third century), Hermogenes (second century) and
Pseudo-Menander.[85] The analysis of the two orations dating from his youth
supports this conclusion.[86] Finally, the emperor also composed *progymnasmata*, rhetorical exercises: two *ethopoiia* and an *ekphrasis*, that is, two character
portrayals and a description. All of which indicate a solid instruction in these
rhetorical genres. In his letters, Manuel moreover quotes some *chreiai*, pithy

---

[83] Letter 45, lines 9–11, 'μόνος δὴ νέων διέφυγες σκῶμμα καὶ ῥάβδον καὶ μάστιγα καὶ ὄμμα πλήττειν
δυνάμενον παιδοτριβεῖν πεῖραν ἔχοντος.' I have modified Dennis' translation for νέων from 'young
men' into 'youngsters' as it seems to reflect better the fact that here Manuel is referring to an earlier
stage of education, as evident in his usage of the verb παιδοτριβεῖν.

[84] For the authors whose works were studied in Byzantine education, especially in late Byzantium, see
Constantinides, *Higher Education*, 151; N. G. Wilson, *Scholars of Byzantium* (London, 1996), 8–19
and C. Constantinides, 'Teachers and Students'. Henceforth, Wilson, *Scholars*.

[85] *Ethico-Political Orations*, 38.   [86] They will be analysed in Chapters 3 and 4.

sayings, that are found in the *Progymnasmata* of Aphthonios. Hence, it is probable that Manuel also studied this extremely popular handbook.[87]

Manuel shows a strong affinity with Libanios as well. The emperor makes numerous references to his letters. An analysis of *Reply of Antenor to Odysseus* and the *Declamation regarding a Drunken Man* – little known pieces by Manuel – suggests that he modelled them on Libanios' declamations. It has been already demonstrated that his famous *ekphrasis* on a tapestry in the Louvre betrays the influence of the same author. Similarly, it has been proposed that the *Dialogue on Marriage* was influenced by the *thesis* sample of Libanios, which also dealt with marriage.[88] To these, one should add the fact that Manuel's mentor Kydones seems also to have been interested in this author and even owned one of the oldest extant manuscripts of Libanios' letters. In a letter to Kydones, Manuel refers to Libanios' Letter 75, adding that he had heard Kydones praise the sayings of this man. This particular reference to Libanios has not been noted in the textual apparatus of the edition.[89] Therefore, although it is not possible to verify, it is plausible that Manuel may have studied Libanios with Kydones.

Unsurprisingly, the emperor's oeuvre also manifests an in-depth knowledge of the Bible, the Psalms and Church Fathers such as Gregory of Nazianzos, Basil of Caesarea and John Chrysostom. Manuel reveals a further affinity with Maximos the Confessor, John Klimakos and Pseudo-Dionysios, at the time, mistakenly believed to be Dionysios the Aeropagite. It is not possible, however, to conclude with any certainty which of these authors Manuel studied as a student versus which he explored later. Finally,

---

[87] For instance, Letter 44, lines 58–9; 'οὐδὲ ἔστιν εὑρεῖν βίον ἄλυπον ἐν οὐδενί' and Letter 68, lines 40–1, 'δεῖ δὲ χρημάτων, καὶ ἄνευ τουτῶν οὐδὲν ἔστι γενέσθαι τῶν δεόντων.' H. Rabe, *Progymnasmata*, (Leipzig, 1926), 7.

[88] *Dialogue on Marriage*, 54–5.

[89] Letter 12, lines 29–30. See J. Boissonade, *Anecdota Graeca*, 11 (Paris, 1844; repr. Hildesheim, 1962), 308–9, for the declamation. Henceforth, *Declamation Regarding a Drunken Man*. Libanios' *melete* on Odysseus, after which Manuel composed the *Reply of Antenor to Odysseus*, is in Libanius, *Declamotiones i– xii*, vol. v, ed. R. Foerster (Leipzig, 1909), 228–86.

On Kydones' manuscript of Libanios, see E. Fryde, *The Early Palaeologan Renaissance (1261– c. 1360)* (Leiden, 2000), 388; G. Mercati, *Notizie di Procoro e Demetrio Cidone, Manuele Caleca e Teodoro Meliteniota, ed altri appunti per la storia della teologia e della letteratura bizantina del secolo XIV* (Vatican, 1931), 127; and Th. Ganchou, 'Démetrios Kydones, les fréres Chrysoberges et la Crete (1397–1401)', in *Bisanzio, Venezia e il Mondo Franco-Greco (XIIe–XVe s.)*, eds. C. Maltezou, P. Schreiner (Venice, 2002), 435–98, 498. Henceforth, Fryde, *Renaissance;* Mercati, *Notizie* and Ganchou, 'Kydones'.

In his *Synkrisis of Old and the New Rome*, Manuel Chrysoloras also points out that the emperor had a liking for Libanios, see C. Billò, 'Τοῦ Χρυσωλορᾶ Σύγκρισις Παλαιᾶς καὶ Νέας Ῥώμης', *Medioevo greco* 0 (2000), 1–26, 6.

Manuel's *Epistolary Discourse on Dreams to Andreas Asan* (c. 1392–6?) was found to indicate at least some knowledge of Hippocrates and Galen.[90] All in all, his familiarity with a wide range of authors, rhetorical techniques and genres demonstrates that he must have received a sound education. Combined with his talents, this instruction later enabled Manuel to emerge as a prolific and engaging author.

Manuel as a Child?

As is to be expected, other aspects of Manuel's childhood are obscure. Since reliable sources are meagre, the lives of medieval children are difficult to study. The few sources that do exist usually concern figures such as rulers, ecclesiastic leaders and saints, which represent childhood in a highly idealized manner: the authors employ the *topos* of *puer senex*, where children are depicted as having an adult's mind and manners in a youngster's body. In other words, the idealized child figure behaves like an adult, and a rather stoic one at that.[91] This *topos* was established firmly in Byzantine as well as Western European texts and consequently, these works offer little to no insight into what the actual childhood of the subject.[92]

In Manuel's case, with one exception, the panegyrics written for him make no mention of his childhood. This can be interpreted as an attempt by the orators to purposefully avoid the topic, perhaps in an attempt to gloss over that, as a second son, Manuel was not originally destined for the throne. The only oration which refers to the emperor as a child, unsurprisingly, casts him in the role of *puer senex*. In the work, the orator claims that as a child Manuel sought to toil for his *patris* and *genos,* and surpassed all in knowledge.[93] Even Manuel applied this *topos* to his beloved brother Theodore, narrating how he always acted with wisdom and sense beyond his years .[94]

---

[90] I. R. Alfagame, 'La epístola περὶ ὀνειράτων de Manuel Paleólogo', *Cuadernos de filolología clásica* 2 (1971), 227–55, 236. Henceforth, Alfagame, 'La epístola'.

[91] For childhood in Byzantine Studies, see A. Moffatt, 'The Byzantine Child', *Social Research* 53 (1986), 705–23 and A. Papaconstantinou and A. M. Talbot (eds.), *Becoming Byzantine: Children and Childhood in Byzantium* (Washington, 2009).

[92] On the *topos* of *puer senex,* see Angelov, 'Ideal Children', 87–8; S. Shahar. *Children in the Middle Ages* (London, 1990), 15. Henceforth, Shahar, *Children.*

[93] Ch. Dendrinos, 'An Unpublished Funeral Oration on Manuel II Palaeologus († 1425)', in *Porphyrogenita: Essays on the History and Literature of Byzantium and the Latin East in Honour of Julian Chrysostomides,* eds. Ch. Dendrinos et al. (Aldershot, 2003), 423–57, 442. Henceforth, Dendrinos, *Anonymous Oration.*

[94] *Funeral Oration,* 86–7.

Although not a frequent occurrence, Byzantine emperors could also appear more naturally as smiling, playing or misbehaving children.[95] One such instance is the monody on Andronikos V, the infant son of Manuel's nephew John VII. The orator ponders whether the dead infant-emperor, as a childish trick, might be hiding away somewhere. He exclaims: 'Does my emperor, so young, still play somewhere on earth?', answering the question by sadly remarking that he was now covered by a small tomb.[96] There are no such representations of Manuel's childhood, however, nor does the emperor speak about his own childhood memories.

On the rare occasions that Manuel refers to childhood, it is usually in a metaphorical sense. Conventionally, he uses the metaphor of childhood to denote physical or intellectual inferiority. This silence and conventional usage should not be interpreted as Manuel being hostile to children or not cherishing his childhood memories. Simply, the prescriptions of medieval autobiographical writing did not accord childhood an important role.[97] Authors did not compose these works as earnest and complete accounts of their lives but sought rather to fulfil narrative goals in their self-representation. That is, they narrated their life story as they wished their readers and posterity to perceive it.

It has been argued extensively that medieval autobiographical texts were shaped by the author's perception of him or herself and of the world at the time of writing. For instance, Saint Augustine perceived his whole life, including his childhood, through the prism of his ideological commitment to the Church, and he fashioned his self-representation accordingly. In the narration of his childhood, the young Augustine behaves like a precocious little bishop.[98] The same tendency can be observed in autobiographical passages penned by Manuel. An analysis of his oeuvre, moreover, manifests a very strong awareness of his imperial rank (σχῆμα), which he seeks to emphasize at every chance. Thus, in his works Manuel is always present as *the emperor*, not as an ordinary person. Since in most

---

[95] Angelov, 'Ideal Children', 111–14. See also N. Kalogeras, 'What do they think about Children? Perceptions of Childhood in Early Byzantine Literature', *BMGS 25* (2001), 2–19.

[96] G. T. Dennis, 'An Unknown Byzantine Emperor, Andronicus V Palaeologus (1400–1407?)', *JÖB 16* (1967), 175–87, reprinted in G. T. Dennis, *Byzantium and the Franks, 1350–1420* (London, 1982), Study II, see page 181. 'ὁ χρυσοῦς μου βασιλικώτατος νεοττὸς ἆρα ποῦ γῆς ἐκρύβη; ... μὴ ὁ ἀνθολευκοχρυσοπυρσοιειδέστατος μου βασιλεὺς ἐν νεᾳ τῇ ἡλικίᾳ ὢν καὶ διὰ τοῦτο παιδιᾳ χρώμενος ποῦ ποτε γῆς ἀθύρει; ... οὔ, ἀλλὰ βραχὺς τύμβος τοῦτον καλύψας ἔχει ...'. The author of the monody is Gabriel of Thessalonike. Henceforth, Dennis, 'Andronicus V'.

[97] N. Orme, *Medieval Children* (New Haven, 2001), 340–1. Also see A. Gurevich, *The Origins of European Individualism* (Blackwell, 1995), 204, who discusses medieval autobiography as an account that moves towards a narrative goal.

[98] Shahar, *Children*, 4.

instances, the intimate details of his childhood or adolescence were not directly relevant to his literary goals, he does not provide them for his audience.

One poignant case in which Manuel speaks about his childhood, the aforementioned account in the *Discourse to Iagoup* on his education, is not a random narration. Rather, it underscores Manuel's self-representation as an ideal emperor who is continuously sacrificing his happiness for his imperial duties. When speaking about his education, Manuel noticeably adopts a wistful tone, lamenting that, despite his eagerness, his studies were interrupted by political tumult. However, these educational details are shared with the audience in order to reinforce his self-representation as an all-sacrificing ruler, not from a wish to narrate his childhood. The entire passage serves to emphasize how Manuel's entire life was controlled and hindered by his imperial rank. The intended message is that even as a child, his imperial rank was a burden for this 'ideal' emperor.[99]

Due to lack of sources, it is difficult to imagine Manuel's pastimes as a child. There are no hints as to which games Manuel might have enjoyed playing, although his own account suggests that he devoted ample time to outdoor exercise. Probably he played ball games with other children, and perhaps he played with knucklebones. The young Manuel also may have blown on clay whistles in the shape of birds and various animals, toys whose popularity seems to have endured even into the Ottoman period.[100] Likewise, he must have played outdoors, climbing trees and playing with animals, as these were general children's activities to which both written and visual sources testify.[101]

Some of the curious metaphors Manuel employs may also suggest some vague memories of childhood and an insight into a child's psychology. One such case can be found in the *Funeral Oration*, where Manuel speaks of the irrational and ever-changing stance of Sultan Bayezid I towards himself. The emperor says: ' . . . he (Bayezid) then very naively tried to win me over by greeting me with gifts and sending me home, just as people soothe children by giving them sweets when they cry after they

---

[99] The narrative function of this passage in the *Discourse to Iagoup* will be discussed in more detail in Chapter 6.

[100] B. Pitarakis, 'Material culture of childhood in Byzantium', in *Becoming Byzantine: Children and Childhood in Byzantium*, eds. A. Papaconstantinou and A. M. Talbot (Washington, 2009), 167–251, 228–36. Henceforth, Pitarakis, 'Material culture', C. Hennessy, *Images of Children in Byzantium* (Farnham, 2007). For discussions of Byzantine adolescence, see *Coming of Age in Byzantium: Adolescence and Society*, ed. D. Ariantzi (Leiden and Berlin, 2017).

[101] Pitarakis, 'Material culture', 238–9.

have been punished.'[102] This unusual metaphor is intended to underscore the absurdity and the irrationality of the sultan's behaviour. On the other hand, it is also a strikingly accurate description of a situation which was undoubtedly experienced by many children, perhaps even including Manuel himself.[103]

Another similar instance can be discerned in the *Ethico-Political Orations*. When discussing the inevitability of pleasure, Manuel likens the struggle to resist pleasure with children fighting over toys. Children, Manuel points out, get up and continue fighting even if they are knocked down by one of their playmates.[104] Once more, the metaphor serves to underscore the irrationality and frivolity side of pleasure. It also comes across as a rather peculiar metaphor for a philosophical discussion and again shows some interest in and attention to child behaviour. Finally, Manuel's *Ekphrasis on a Tapestry in the Louvre* describes children playing outdoors. The emperor depicts the games of the children with affection, emphasizing their innocence. Manuel then goes on to narrate in minute detail, how one child tries to catch an insect by using his cap as a net, while another, who has tied two insects by a thread, laughs and dances.[105] Although the *ekphrasis* relates to an imaginary depiction in a tapestry, it nevertheless implies that envisioning such a scene appealed to Manuel.

The Voyage to Buda

Manuel's childhood came to an abrupt end in the winter of 1366. At the age of sixteen he was personally confronted by political turmoil for the first time. Still desperately in need of help against the Ottomans, John V visited King Louis of Hungary to persuade him to raise a crusader army. The emperor took with him two of his sons, Manuel and Michael, while the

---

[102] *Funeral Oration*, 140–1. '... ὥσπερ οἱ τὰ παιδία τρωγαλίοις ἡμερούντες μετὰ τὰς πληγὰς κλάοντα ...'.

[103] Theodore Metochites uses similar imagery in one of his poems; 'I say that I do not appear frightened, nor do I resemble infants who cry when their honey cakes, given by their loving mothers, are taken away ...', Poem XVIII, 334–6 in *Theodore Metochites' Poems to 'Himself': Introduction, Text and Translation*, ed. and trans. M. Featherstone (Vienna, 2000). Brigitte Pitarakis has pointed out that Metochites' imagery seems to be reflective of childhood experiences, see Pitarakis, 'Material culture', 195.

[104] *Ethico-Political Orations*, 376, 'Καὶ καθάπερ ἐπὶ τῶν ἀθρυμάτων οἱ παῖδες, εἰ ὠθισμῷ τῶν συναθυρόντων καταβληθεῖεν, πρὸς πάλην αὖθις ἀνίστανται, καὶ ἑτοίμως ἔχουσι συμπλακῆναι τοῖς κατενεγκοῦσι πολλάκις ...'.

[105] J. Davis, 'Manuel II Palaeologus' A Depiction of Spring in a Dyed, Woven Hanging', in *Porphyrogenita: Essays on the History and Literature of Byzantium and the Latin East in Honour of Julian Chrysostomides*, eds. Ch. Dendrinos et al. (Aldershot, 2003), 411–21; 412. Henceforth, Davis, 'Ekphrasis'.

eldest son, Andronikos, was left behind as regent. Apart from an entry in a short chronicle, none of the Byzantine historians speak about this voyage. What little information can be gleaned about the events, comes from the writings of Kydones.[106] He narrates the journey in his *Oration for Getting Aid from the Latins*, yet his account is far from biased. As the title suggests, Kydones sought to depict the Hungarians negatively in order to press his point that the Byzantines should ally with the Latins. As a result, Kydones does his best to emphasize the poor conditions met by the emperor's retinue.

Kydones recounts that the emperor began his journey in the midst of winter. Sailing to the Danube via the Black Sea, he continued on to Buda, to the court of King Louis. In addition to the two young despots and his ambassador George Manikaites, John V was accompanied by a small entourage. Demetrios Kydones bitterly remarks that there were hardly enough men to serve the emperor at the table.[107] Sailing in the winter undoubtedly had been unpleasant, and in the *prooimion* of the *chrysobull* issued by John V for Manuel's success against the Ottomans in 1371, Kydones again praises the young despot for facing dangers with his father by land and sea. He claims that Manuel braved the fast flow and the rocks of Danube, as well as the trials of sailing in the wintry Black Sea.[108] While such references to the dangers of sea voyages were commonplace in Byzantine texts, there can be no doubt that Kydones had actually heard about these events at the court. Although Kydones undoubtedly emphasized these unpleasant factors in order to highlight Manuel's sacrifices, his account should not be dismissed as 'mere rhetoric'. Furthermore, letters that John V received from the pope while in Buda clearly indicate that the journey had indeed been undertaken in winter.[109] This was the first of many eventful sea voyages Manuel would undertake in his life.

Although the political and diplomatic aspects of this voyage have been researched extensively, nothing can be discerned about the personal experiences of John V and his sons at the Hungarian court. It appears that at first, the relationship between the emperor and King Louis was cordial.[110] Many

---

[106] Schreiner, *Kleinchroniken*, Chronik 9/26.   [107] *PG* 154, col. 1000.

[108] F. Tinnefeld, 'Vier Prooimien zu Kaiserurkunden, verfaßt von Demetrios Kydones,' *BSI* 44 (1982), 13–30, 178–95, 180, lines 104–8. Henceforth, Tinnefeld, 'Vier Prooimien'. The *prooimion* for Manuel's grant is on pages 178–83.

[109] Halecki, *Un empereur*, 112–3.

[110] For the visit to Buda, see Halecki, *Un empereur*, 111–37; Barker, *Manuel II*, 6–9 and J. Gill, *Byzantium and the Papacy, 1198–1400* (New Jersey, 1979), 212–5. Henceforth, Gill, *Papacy*. Also P. Wirth, 'Die Haltung Kaiser Johannes V. bei den Verhandlungen mit König Ludwig I. von Ungarn zu Buda im Jahre 1366', *BZ* 56 (1963), 271–2.

letters were exchanged with the pope; again John V promised his personal conversion to Catholicism, as well as that of Manuel and Michael.[111] The Hungarian and Byzantine rulers also sent a joint embassy to Avignon,[112] but despite the encouragement these proposals received from the pope, they never materialized. A document pertaining to a council in 1367 reports an intriguing incident: according to the text, King Louis demanded the re-baptism of the Byzantine emperor before a crusade could be formed.[113] Regardless of the veracity of this source, it appears that the relationship between the rulers had indeed become strained.[114] An empty-handed John Palaiologos left for Constantinople at the latest by February 1366.[115] His already small retinue had shrunk even more on his return journey, and for reasons unknown, the emperor was compelled to leave Manuel as a hostage in the Hungarian court.[116]

That the emperor's son could be held as a hostage in a foreign court, should be taken as a striking testimony to the weakness of Byzantine political power. Thanks to this feebleness, Manuel was plunged deep into political turbulence at the age of sixteen, despite being merely a second son. Moreover, it soon became clear that leaving Manuel as a hostage was no guarantee of a safe return journey. The Bulgarians blocked the emperor's way, and for several months John Palaiologos had to wait helplessly for the arrival of his cousin Amadeo of Savoy in the fall of 1366 when he succeeded in lifting the blockade, even getting some minor territorial concessions for the Byzantines. John V finally returned to Constantinople in December 1366. Unfortunately, all the difficulties the emperor and his entourage had faced on their journey were in vain. The next year, the Hungarian king abandoned the idea of a crusade against the Ottomans altogether.[117]

---

[111] Dölger, *Regesten*, no. 3107 and no. 3108, 55–6.

[112] The embassy consisted of Archbishop Etienne of Nyitra and George Manikaites. For George Manikaites, see S. Mergiali-Sahas, 'A Byzantine Ambassador to the West and his Office during the Fourteenth and Fifteenth Centuries', *BZ 94* (2001), 588–604, 595–6. Henceforth, Mergiali-Sahas, 'Ambassador'.

[113] Meyendorff, 'Le projet', 173, see lines 139–52.

[114] Joseph Gill believes the council text to be mistaken on this issue, Gill, *Papacy*, 216. For greater detail on the re-baptism issue, see J. Gill, 'John V Palaeologus at the Court of Louis I of Hungary', *BSI* 38 (1977), 31–8. The author claims that re-baptism of the Orthodox Christians became commonplace only after the visit had already taken place.

[115] The papal letter dated 10 March indicates that the emperor had already left, Halecki, *Un empereur*, 112.

[116] This is clearly stated in the *prooimion* of the 1371 document; '. . . καὶ δεῆσαν ἐμὲ μὲν ἐκεῖθεν ἐξελθεῖν, τοῦτον δὲ μένειν, ὡς ἂν οὐκ ἄνευ ὁμήρων τοῦ ῥηγὸς τὴν ἔξοδον συγχωροῦντος . . .', see Tinnefeld, 'Vier Prooimien', 180, lines 113–15. See also F. Pall, 'Encore une fois sur le voyage diplomatique de Jean V Paléologue en 1365/66', *RESEE* 9 (1971), 535–40 for the return journey of John V.

[117] Halecki, *Un empereur*, 136; Gill, *Papacy*, 215.

It is unclear exactly when Manuel was allowed to return to his family. At any rate, he was present in the council proceedings of 1367.[118] In his writings, Manuel makes no explicit mention of his eventful journey to Buda, but an attentive reading of the autobiographical passages in the *Discourse to Iagoup*, reveals one curious instance. While narrating how his education came to an abrupt end, Manuel complains:

> And then, once I had passed the age of children, before reaching manhood, a different fortune ensued with my advancing age, filled with storm and tumults . . .[119]

This narrative implies that this stormy chapter in his life began in his 'adolescence'. He describes this moment as being between childhood (τὴν παίδων ἡλικίαν) and manhood (πρὶν εἰς ἄνδρας ἐλθεῖν). This time frame fits with Manuel's journey to Buda when he was sixteen years old. As such, it can be proposed that in this passage, Manuel was representing the Buda voyage almost as the beginning of his imperial political career.

A similar reference to these events can be traced in the *Panegyric to John V* (1390). In this oration to his father, when narrating how John V had to travel into the midst of savage and rough peoples, Manuel remarks that *those* people who had travelled with him know his sufferings very accurately.[120] John V travelled abroad twice, to Buda in 1366 and to Rome in 1369, but since the account seems to be narrating diplomatic travel, Manuel cannot be speaking about John V's participation in Ottoman campaigns. On the other hand, his references to the boorishness and the roughness of their hosts echo the comments made by Kydones. In this case, it is much more likely that Manuel refers to the Hungarians, and not to the Latins.

Furthermore, an analysis of his orations reveals that Manuel often sought to insert his authorial presence into the picture. His above-mentioned remark about the emperor's entourage can be interpreted as

---

[118] For the discussions, see Meyendorff, 'Le projet'. Manuel also received a letter from the Pope dated 6 November 1367, encouraging him to work for the union of the churches. As the heir to throne, Andronikos received his own letter, yet as the younger sons, Manuel and Michael received a joint one, addressed to 'nobilibus viris Manueli despoto et Michaeli'. The letters are available in Halecki, *Un empereur*, 367.

[119] *Discourse to Iagoup*, 328. 'Τὴν δὲ τῶν παίδων παραλάσαντα ἡλικίαν, πρὶν εἰς ἄνδρας ἐλθεῖν, ἑτέρα τύχη μετὰ τῆς ἡλικίας ἐδέχετο, τρικυμίας οὖσα θορύβων ἀνάπλεως . . .'. See also Barker, *Manuel II*, 412.

[120] *Panegyric to John V*, 224. 'Τὴν γὰρ ἀγροικίαν καὶ τὸ τραχὺ καὶ ἀνήμερον καὶ ἀσύμβατον ἐνίων ἐθνῶν, εἰς οὓς ὁ βασιλεύς ἀνάγκην εἶχε πορεύεσθαι, σιωπῶ . . . ὁπόσων ἀπέλαυε τῶν λυπηρῶν ἴσασι μὲν ἀκριβῶς οἳ τότε τούτῳ συναπεδήμουν. Οὐ χαλεπὸν δὲ ἡγοῦμαι καὶ τοὺς οἴκοι μένοντας τούτων στοχάσασθαι.'

a reference to his own presence in the Buda voyage of 1366; this strategy contributed to the aim of underscoring Manuel's devoted service to his father amidst difficulties. It also suited the circumstances and the aim of the *Panegyric to John V*. Written shortly after his reconciliation with his father in 1390, the oration's chief textual goal was to establish Manuel's loyalty to his father as his rightful heir.[121] Ultimately, the above-mentioned textual instances suggest that this unpleasant journey left its traces on Manuel.

Despite the fiasco in Buda, John V did not give up his hope of obtaining Western aid. In the summer of 1369, having been encouraged by his cousin Amadeo of Savoy and the papal legate Paul, the emperor sailed to Rome in order to make a profession of his Catholic faith. Before he set sail, John V also established Manuel as the governor of Thessalonike.[122] It seemed that for all he had suffered, Manuel finally got his reward. Yet this abrupt end to his adolescence was merely a prelude to the greater tumult to come.

> For many calamities then came upon me as if by signal, difficulties, the struggle with manifold troubles and dangers one upon another, which blowing upon me violently, did not allow me to breath.[123]

---

[121] For the discussion of this oration, see Chapter 4.

[122] Barker, *Manuel II*, 9 points out that it was from Thessalonike that Manuel later came to his father's aid in Venice, which shows that he was already established there.

[123] *Discourse to Iagoup*, 328, 'πολλὰ γὰρ ἄττα ἀθρόα ὥσπερ ἐκ συνθήματος τόθ' ἡμῖν ἐπέθετο, δυσκολίαι τε καὶ διαφόρων πάλη συμφορῶν καὶ ἀλλεπάλληλοι κίνδυνοι, ἃ σφοδρᾷ τινι ῥύμῃ πνεύσαντα καθ' ἡμῶν, οὐδ' ἀναπνεῖν συνεχώρουν.'

CHAPTER 2

Family Affairs

They fought against one another for many days, father against son and son against father; such was the consequence of the inhumanity of the Romans and their hatred of God . . .[1]

Manuel's father John V arrived in Rome in September 1369, accompanied by his *mesazon* Demetrios Kydones. On 18 October, the Byzantine emperor officially converted to Roman Catholicism in a private ceremony. While his purpose, as usual, was to secure aid from the papacy against the Ottomans, this conversion did not bind any of John's subjects. After a few days, a public ceremony was held at the steps of Saint Peter's. The Byzantine emperor genuflected three times, kissing the pope's feet, hands and mouth. Having recited the *Te Deum*, the pope and John V then retired inside to celebrate mass.[2]

How did Manuel react to his father's conversion? The question is an intriguing one, as the issue of a church union and Byzantine conversions to Catholicism constituted a critical problem during Manuel's reign. In the *Discourse to Iagoup*, Manuel does briefly touch upon John V's sojourn in Rome.[3] While narrating how John V travelled to Rome to secure an

---

[1] Doukas, 72–3, 'καὶ πολεμήσαντες ἡμέρας ἱκανὰς πατὴρ πρὸς υἱὸν καὶ υἱὸς πρὸς πατέρα (τοῦτο τῆς Ῥωμαίων ἀπανθρωπίας καὶ τῆς πρὸς θεὸν ἔχθρας) . . .'.
   The translation is from Doukas, *Decline and Fall of Byzantium to the Ottoman Turks. An Annotated Translation of 'Historia Turca-Byzantina'*, trans. H. J. Magulias (Detroit, 1975), 80.

[2] The most detailed study is A. A. Vasiliev, 'Il viaggio di Giovanni V Palaeologo in Italia e l'unione di Roma', *SBN* 3 (1931), 153–92. Vasiliev also gives the Latin text of John V's confession of faith, 180–3. For a general account, Halecki, *Un empereur*, 188–234; Gill, *The Papacy*, 218–21 and F. Kianka, 'Demetrios Kydones and Italy', *DOP* 49 (1995), 99–110. Phillipe de Mézières also narrates the conversion, but not John's journey to Rome. Philippe de Mézières, *The Life of Saint Peter Thomas*, ed. J. Smet (Rome, 1954), 74–5. The English chronicler Walshingam notes John V's conversion, but mistakenly dates it to Christmas, see Walshingam, *Vita Ricardi Secundi*, ed. G. B. Stow (Philadelphia, 1977), 58. He refers to the event in relation to Manuel's visit to London in 1401. Henceforth, Walshingam, *Vita Ricardi*.

[3] *Discourse to Iagoup*, 371. '. . . ὁ θεῖος βασιλεὺς καὶ πατὴρ πρὸς αὐτὸν παρεγένετο ἐπικουρίαν τοῖς ἐνταῦθα πραγματευσόμενος, ἥτις ἄνωθεν ἐθρυλλεῖτό τε καὶ ἠλπίζετο, χαλινὸν τοῖς στόμασιν ἔθετο

alliance against the Ottomans, he emphasizes his father's eagerness for
a reconciliation between the two churches. At every opportunity, Manuel
claims, John V prevented the members of his Byzantine entourage from
arguing with the Latins. At the first glance, Manuel's tone comes across as
rather approving of John V's stance. But in a significant omission, he fails
to mention his father's conversion to Catholicism.

In this regard, as we will later discuss, a close reading of Manuel's
autobiographical works demonstrates that he often employed the rhetorical strategy of omitting unpleasant details. In other words, he tends to
skip over the events that he found shameful or that he felt would undermine his authority. Hence, his silence about John V's conversion speaks
volumes; Manuel probably did not approve, especially later in his life.
Although in his quest for help against the Ottomans, Manuel, too, would
strive to end the quarrel with the papacy, he never accepted Latin supremacy. He also remained sceptical about the possible outcomes of a union,
perhaps, influenced by the ineffective outcome of John V's conversion in
1369.

John V stayed in Rome for about five months. At the end of spring in
1370, he went to Venice and started negotiating the sale of the island of
Tenedos to the city state, a transaction through which he hoped to rid
himself of a number of financial problems.[4] He moreover hoped to retrieve
the Byzantine crown jewels – his mother, Anna of Savoy, had pawned the
jewels to Venice to raise money during the civil war – which had been
conspicuously missing from his joint coronation with Kantakouzenos in
1347. For years, the Venetians had been pressuring the emperor to obtain
Tenedos, an island of great strategic importance. While in Italy, severely in
debt and in desperate need of money, John V was finally compelled to
accede, but as the negotiations dragged on the emperor's financial straits
deteriorated further until he was unable to return to Constantinople.[5]
Once more, the frailty of the Byzantine power became manifest.

Desperate for help, the trapped emperor wrote to Andronikos in
Constantinople, who completely ignored his father's pleas. The exact motives
for Andronikos' refusal remain unclear. The historian Chalkokondyles claims

---

τῶν αὐτοῦ τι λέγειν περὶ τουτωνὶ τῶν ζητημάτων ἐπιχειρούντων. Μηδὲ γὰρ ἀνοῖξαι τὸ στόμα, μηδὲ
φθέγξασθαι τι τοιοῦτον τοῖσδε προσέταξε.'

[4] Barker, *Manuel II*, 11. See also R. J. Loenertz, 'Jean V à Venise (1370–1371)', *REB* 16 (1958), 217–32.
Henceforth, Loenertz, 'Jean V'.
[5] Chalkokondyles claims that John V was actually detained by his debtors. See Chalkokondyles, 80–3.
However, Loenertz points out John V could not return home without the means to finance his
journey. Thus, he claims that insufficient funds were enough to keep John V in Venice. See Loenertz,
'Jean V', 225.

that as regent Andronikos feared that his influence in Constantinople would diminish upon his father's return. All in all, it was a clear act of disobedience, and his refusal should be interpreted as foreshadowing the fierce power struggle that would soon take place between father and son.[6] In the end, it was Manuel who took the burden upon himself and set sail from Thessalonike to assist his father.

Manuel arrived in Venice sometime in the winter of 1371.[7] In the *prooimion* of the *chrysobull* bestowed on Manuel shortly after these events, as in the case of the voyage to Buda, the travels are dramatized. Manuel's journey to Venice presented Demetrios Kydones, the composer of the document, with yet another opportunity to fashion his image as a dutiful son.[8] He also narrates Manuel's route in detail: he crossed the Aegean Sea and stopped at the Peloponnese, then sailed across the Adriatic Sea.[9] A *prostagma* dated to 1415 also mentions that in 1371 he stopped in the Peloponnese on his way to Venice.[10] Even his official documents reflect Manuel's mobility and frequent journeys. Kydones' account in the *prooimion* ends when Manuel reaches his father in Venice. The emperor, Kydones laments, was oppressed by the winter, yet even more so by his financial affairs. His son's arrival 'filled the paternal eyes with joy'.[11]

What exactly Manuel brought with him to Venice to help his father is unclear. He probably brought cash.[12] Chalkokondyles' claim that Manuel brought funds that he had collected in Thessalonike, lends further support to this theory.[13] Whatever the nature of his assistance, it was clearly efficient, since John V was able to return to Constantinople in October 1371. Upon his return, on 5 December, the emperor arrested five high officials. It has been suggested that these officials might have

---

[6] Chalkokondyles remarks that Andronikos refused his father by pointing out that he could not use the Church treasures. Chalkokondyles, 80–3. There was indeed a recent act forbidding such use of church treasures: see, MM, I, 513. In reference to Chalkokondyles and this act, Charanis suggests that it was not impossible for the Church to have had a hand in Andronikos' disobedience: Charanis, 'Strife', 291–2. See also J. Chrysostomides, 'John V Palaeologus in Venice (1370–1371) and the Chronicle of Caroldo: A Re-interpretation, *OCP* 31 (1965), 46–84, re-printed in J. Chrysostomides, *Byzantium and Venice 1204–1453*, eds. M. Heslop and Ch. Dendrinos (Farnham, 2011), Study I. Henceforth, Chrysostomides, 'Venice'.

[7] See Kydones, Letter 21.   [8] Tinnefeld, 'Vier Prooimion', 181, lines 150–1.

[9] Tinnefeld, 'Vier Prooimion', 181, lines 152–3.   [10] *Actes de Lavra*, III, 163–6, lines 11–12.

[11] Tinnefeld, 'Vier Prooimion', 181, lines 155–8. The description of Manuel's arrival in Venice in Kydones' document is strikingly similar to Kydones, Letter 21. In the *prooimion*, Kydones says: '... ἐν τοῖς ἐκείνου μυχοῖς ἡμᾶς εὗρεν ἐν Βενετίᾳ ...', in Letter 21, '... πρὸς τοῖς ἐκείνου μυχοῖς τὸν πατέρα ζητεῖν ...', lines 12–13. It seems that Kydones borrowed from his own letter when drafting the document. The letter is dated to spring–summer 1371, while the *chrysobull* is dated to December 1371 by Tinnefeld, see 'Vier Prooimion', 186.

[12] Chrysostomides, 'Venice', 77.   [13] Chalkokondyles, 80–3.

been conspiring with Andronikos against his father. Still, the emperor seems to have taken no action against his disobedient son.[14]

As in Buda a few years previously, Manuel was compelled to remain behind as a 'guarantee' for his father's good intentions.[15] His activities during his stay in Venice are obscure. He probably had to remain as a guarantor until the debts of his father were settled, as well as taking part in the settlement as his father's representative. During his stay, Manuel received several letters from Kydones in Venice; however, his own replies do not survive.[16] Unsurprisingly, the pro-Latin Kydones does not refer to any mistreatment by the Venetians, merely lamenting Manuel's separation from his beloved ones.[17] It is tempting to wonder about Manuel's first sojourn in Venice. For instance, he must have noticed the Byzantine horses displayed proudly on top of the basilica of San Marco. Like Syropoulos and the Byzantine delegation many years later, perhaps he was even granted permission to see the treasury of the cathedral, which was likewise replete with Byzantine booty from the sack of 1204.[18]

First Taste of Ruling

Manuel was back in Thessalonike at the latest in November 1371.[19] Unfortunately, nothing can be gleaned from the sources about his rule as the despot of Thessalonike in the 1370s. None of his writings survive from these years either. For similar reasons, it is equally difficult to analyse John V's rule during these times. The little information that exists provides only a simple outline of the events that took place. While both Manuel and his father were still away in Italy, the Ottomans inflicted a devastating defeat on the Serbs at the Battle of Maritsa on 26 September 1371. The Ottomans

---

[14] Schreiner, *Kleinchroniken*, Chronik 9/23. The arrested officials were named as Glabas, Manuel Bryennios, John Asanes, the *pansebastos* Tzamplakon and Agalos. Their possible connection to Andronikos' disobedience has been suggested by Charanis, 'Strife', 291.

[15] Tinnefeld, 'Vier Prooimion', 181, lines 161–74.   [16] Kydones, Letters 21 and 24.

[17] For Kydones and Venice, see G. T. Dennis, 'Demetrios Kydones and Venice', *in Bisanzio, Venezia e il mondo Franco-Greco (XIIe–XVe s.)*, eds. C. Maltezou, P. Schreiner (Venice, 2002), 495–502.

[18] Syropoulos notes that enamel icons from the Pantokrator were among the booty which the Venetians believed to be from Hagia Sophia. See H. Klein, 'Refashioning Byzantium in Venice, 1200–1400', in *San Marco, Byzantium and Myths of Venice*, eds. H. Maguire and R. Nelson (Washington, 2010), 193–226, 194–7.

[19] The exact date of his return is unknown; it must have been in summer or autumn, as he recovered some Byzantine cities after the defeat of the Serbians at the Battle of Maritza. Loenertz, 'Jean V', 217. Dennis, *Thessalonica*, 13–14.

then started freely raiding Macedonia as the remnants of Dušan's Serbia crumbled away. The Balkans now lay exposed to the Ottomans.[20]

Several monastic documents reveal that, prompted by these threatening developments, Manuel resorted to confiscating monastic lands in order to provide for the defence of Thessalonike and its vicinity. He converted them to *pronoia*, which was a fiscal establishment that denoted lands or taxes from lands granted to individuals in exchange for military manpower and help. A *prostagma* dated to 1408 specifies that in the 1370s, when the Ottoman raids were especially burdensome, half of the *metochia* of the monasteries of Mount Athos and of Thessalonike were confiscated by Manuel. 'Simply everything', the document states, had been 'pronoiarized'.[21]

Seizing monastic lands and converting them into *pronoia* was not a policy unique to Manuel. Since the beginning of the fourteenth century many emperors, including his fathe,r John V, resorted to this practice in order to strengthen the feeble military power of the empire.[22] Hence, Manuel's decision to confiscate lands for *pronoia* is not a novel tactic. Although clearly compelled by dire necessity, undoubtedly these deeds must have been quite unpopular with the Thessalonian ecclesiastics. For instance, it has been proposed – though remains unproven – that Nicholas Kabasilas, a prominent Thessalonian literati of the period and one of Manuel's future correspondents, possibly composed his famous discourse against land confiscations in response to this policy.[23] Many years later, as emperor, Manuel would return these lands.

All things considered, this policy is a significant and revealing moment in the early career of Manuel Palaiologos. First, it demonstrates that even as a young despot, Manuel did not refrain from confronting the Church. Furthermore, his decisions indicate that he also did not shrink from introducing drastic financial policies. Already by the 1370s, Manuel was slowly establishing his style of government; these above-mentioned tendencies would become even more pronounced during his later life as emperor.

---

[20] Barker, *Manuel II*, 16; Dennis, *Thessalonica*, 32. With reference to the area of Macedonia, the *prooimion* drafted by Kydones claims that 'those cities were now in greater danger than before', see Tinnefeld, 'Vier Prooimion', 183, lines 226–7.

[21] P. Charanis, 'The Monastic Properties and the State in the Byzantine Empire', *DOP* 4 (1948), 53–118. A more up-to-date study is now available, see M. Bartusis, *Land and Privilege in Byzantium: the Institution of Pronoia* (Cambridge, 2012), see, 551–70, for Manuel's policy of seizing monastic properties and converting them into *pronoia* as a response to the Battle of Maritza. προνοιασθῶσαι is translated as 'to pronoiarize' by Bartusis. Henceforth, Bartusis, *Pronoia*. See also K. Smyrlis, 'The State, the Land and Private Property: Confiscating Monastic and Church Properties in the Palaiologan Period', in *Church and Society in Late Byzantium*, ed. D. Angelov (Kalamazoo, 2009), 58–87, especially 66–72.

[22] See ODB, III, 1733–4 for a definition.   [23] I. Ševčenko, 'Anti-Zealot', 79–171.

Despite further unleashing the Ottoman threat against Byzantium, the Battle of Maritza presented the Byzantines with some opportunity. Taking advantage of their current weakness, Manuel recaptured Serres from the Serbians and restored it to the empire. However, this small moment of victory was short lived. Without any support from the papacy and even more desperate after the defeat of the Serbians, it was around this time that John V accepted Ottoman suzerainty. turning Byzantium into a tributary state to the Ottomans, both in economic and military spheres.[24] Although the details pertaining to this agreement are obscure, his father's agreement would be instrumental in shaping Manuel's future relations with the Ottomans.

It was as a reward for the capture of Serres that John V issued the *chrysobull* of 1371 for Manuel, confirming his status as the despot of Thessalonike and granting him any lands that he might yet recover from the Ottomans.[25] The *prooimion* of the *chrysobull* strives to represent Manuel as an ideal imperial son. It dramatizes events, such as the Buda and Venice journeys, in order to showcase Manuel's devotion to the emperor. In addition, the entire document is laced with rhetorical references to the relationship between the imperial father and son, as well as to Manuel's exceptional virtue. Even in the beginning of the *prooimion*, Kydones argues that while emperors love all their sons in accordance with nature, they reward the best of them.[26] It is possible that the intended implication was that, despite being a second son, Manuel's great virtue and devotion made him John V's 'best' son, eclipsing all others. Or perhaps Kydones was merely emphasizing Manuel's filial virtues.

Because of the praise lavished on Manuel in the text, scholars have interpreted the document as an indication that John V was planning to alter the succession in Manuel's favour.[27] This assumption has also been reinforced by several references to crowning in the *prooimion* and a letter from Kydones addressed to Manuel. In this letter, Kydones claims that it

---

[24] Dennis, *Thessalonica*, 32.   [25] Dölger, *Regesten*, no. 3130, 60.

[26] Tinnefeld, 'Vier Prooimion', 178, lines 18–19, '... φιλήσουσι μὲν τοὺς υἱεῖς, τῆς φύσεως αὐτοὺς ἐπὶ τοῦτ' ἀναγκαίως ἀγούσης, ἀμείψονται δὲ τοὺς ἀρίστους ...'.

[27] Dennis, *Thessalonica*, 27, is neutral, but on the basis of this document, he claims that Manuel was the emperor's 'favourite' son. Barker interprets the *prooimion* as evidence that John V had indeed begun to favour Manuel over Andronikos. See Barker, *Manuel II*, xxi and 19. Recently, Raúl Estangüi-Gómez has interpreted the document in the same manner, interpreting the generic 'φίλτατον' as an indication that Manuel was John's favourite son. See R. Estangüi-Gómez, *Byzance face aux Ottomans. Exercice du pouvoir contrôle du territoire sous les derniers Paléologues (milieu XIVe– milieu XVve siècle)* (Paris, 2014), 228–9. Henceforth, Estangüi- Gómez, *Byzance Face aux Ottomans*.

was not himself, but his father who had 'woven' that crown for Manuel. And so, he goes on, the young prince did not need to thank Kydones for the document.[28] This has been interpreted as a reference to the imperial crown and hence as evidence that his father was already intending to make Manuel his heir. These expressions are, however, not necessarily references to the imperial crown. They are mere *topoi* connected to the metaphor of ancient contests and the crowning of their winner with laurels. Such metaphors were frequently employed by Byzantine authors in the sense of bestowing honour on the recipient. Kydones' choice of the verb 'to weave' (πλεκεῖν) reinforces the metaphorical nature of the expression.

Like the letter, the *prooimion* also contained *topoi* pertaining to crowns. Once again, these are metaphorical expressions and should not be taken as references to the imperial crown. The language of the text is quite elaborate and is replete with rhetorical devices, which is not unexpected, since important official documents could have *prooimia* with a pronounced rhetorical colouring, strongly resembling court oratory. The lines between an official state document and a literary/rhetorical work could be blurred.[29] This rhetorical/literary nature of the text is further supported by the fact that Kydones preserved it in manuscripts containing his own works, including letters and sermons.[30] Additionally, the lavish praise came from Kydones, a friend and former teacher of Manuel, and not directly from John V.

Finally, Manuel was already the despot of Thessalonike before this document was issued. The bull merely grants him any land that he might possibly recover from the Ottomans in the future – a hope which Manuel was never able to fulfil. In other words, the document did not alter his position significantly.[31] Moreover, the emperor's third son Michael was the recipient of a similar grant. The *chrysobull* granting Michael, Zagora in

---

[28] Tinnefeld, 'Vier Prooimion', 179, line 61, '… ἀλλ' οὕτω τοὺς πολεμίους στεφανώσομεν πρὸ τῶν ὑπηκόων …', 180, lines 85–6, 'παρὰ τῶν ἐχθρῶν τῆς ἀνδραγαθίας ἐστεφανοῦτο' and 182, line 181, 'στεφάνων φῶ μεγάλων ἀξίαν'. Kydones, Letter 19, lines 9–10, 'γὰρ ὁ πάντα ἄριστος βασιλεὺς καὶ πατὴρ ἔπλεξέ σοι τὸν στέφανον.'

Barker, *Manuel II*, 19, suggests that the reference to a crown might reflect John's intention to bestow the crown on Manuel. Tinnefeld, 'Vier Prooimion', 187, disagrees with Barker and Dennis, but he still interprets the document literally, and proposes that the crowning vocabulary might be related to a despot's crown. Kydones, Letter 19.

[29] Angelov, *Imperial Ideology*, 21.

[30] Tinnefeld, 'Vier Prooimion', 15–17. The literary character of the *prooimion* is also evident when the similarities between the text and Kydones' Letter 21 are considered. It seems that Kydones borrowed some expressions from his own letter in the *prooimion*, see footnote 11 above.

[31] Tinnefeld, 'Vier Prooimion', 191–2, for the *prooimion* of Michael's grant. Tinnefeld dates it to 1369–76, 193.

northern Thrace, again drafted by Kydones, is more moderate in its praise; however, it is very similar to Manuel's *chrysobull*, especially in its emphasis on the father-son relationship. Kydones' *prooimion* and letter to Manuel therefore do not provide any evidence that the emperor was contemplating an alteration to the succession. In short, however grateful the emperor may have been to his son for all his services, there is no indication that at this stage, that John V actually was intending to make Manuel his heir.

The Rebellion of Andronikos

Manuel would not enjoy his new lands in tranquillity. Just a year later, trouble struck the imperial family once again. In May 1373, his older brother Andronikos, who had already shown signs of opposition to John V, rose in rebellion against their father, in co-operation with the Ottoman prince Savcı Çelebi, the eldest son of Sultan Murad. The confused narratives of the Byzantine historians and chronicles give us an outline of the events.[32] While John V and Sultan Murad were away on a campaign in Asia Minor, they left their sons behind as regents. Although it is not possible to securely date the obligation of the Byzantine emperor to serve the sultan in his campaigns, it was most probably imposed some time in 1372–3. The young princes, both seeking to overthrow their fathers, united their forces: Andronikos joined Savcı in Thrace and the two sons openly rebelled against their fathers. Upon hearing the news, John V and Sultan Murad hastened to Thrace. The Byzantine emperor was the first father to capture his rebellious son, as Andronikos surrendered on 30 May.

---

[32] For a narration of the events, see Chalkokondyles, 64–73, who gives the events in the wrong order; Doukas, 70–1, who names Savcı as Kunduz; Schreiner, *Kleinchroniken*, Chronik 22/14; 9/24 and *Ecthesis Chronica and Chronicon Athenarum*, ed. S. P. Lampros (London, 1902), 1, which confuses Savcı with Musa Çelebi, another Ottoman prince contending for the throne in 1402–13.

   For non-Byzantine sources, see the Spanish traveller Clavijo, although his account is full of errors, *Clavijo*, 47, and Chrysostomides, 'Caroldo', 134–42. A Bulgarian chronicle also refers to the joint rebellion, see J. Bogdan, 'Ein Beitrag zur bulgarischen und serbischen Geschichteschreibung', *Archiv für slavische Philologie* 13 (1891), 481–543, 528. Henceforth, Bogdan, 'Bulgarian Chronicle'. Finally, several Italian chronicles record the rebellion, probably prompted by the Venetian and Genoese involvement in the affair in the later stages. See Caresini, 32; Giorgio Stella, *Annales Genuenses*, ed. G. Petti Balbi (Bologna, 1975), 169 and Zeno, Iacobo, *Vita Caroli Zeni*, ed. N. Zanichelli (Bologna, 1940), 12–13. Henceforth, Stella. The Ottoman sources do not mention the events.

   For modern scholarly work, see Barker, *Manuel II*, 19–24; Charanis, 'Strife', 293–6 and 'Internal Strife'; F. Dölger, 'Zum Aufstand des Andronikos IV gegen seinen Vater Johannes V im Mai 1373', *REB* 19 (1961), 328–33; F. Dölger, 'Johannes VII, Kaiser der Rhomaer 1390–1408', *BZ* 31 (1931), 21–36, especially 22–6. Henceforth, Dölger, 'Johannes VII'. See also R. J. Loenertz, 'La première insurrection d'Andronic IV Paléologue (1373)', *Échos d'Orient* 38 (1939), 334–45.

Nothing is known of Andronikos' immediate punishment. At any rate, he lost his place in the succession. On 25 September, Manuel was proclaimed co-emperor and became the new heir designate.[33] Murad captured his own son in Didymoteichon in September. After blinding Savcı, the sultan asked the emperor to carry out the same punishment on Andronikos. Fearing the sultan's anger, John V had his son blinded and confined to the Tower of Anemas. Doukas and Chalkokondyles claim that Andronikos' infant son, the future John VII, was also blinded. Supposedly, he would be left with squinting eyes for the rest of his life.[34]

This was not the first instance in Byzantium of a ruler blinding a son. However, the narratives of Doukas and Chalkokondyles, as well as a few Western sources, stress that John V only complied because of the pressure exerted by the sultan, assigning the severity of the punishment entirely to Murad. Doukas' uneasiness with the idea of a father blinding his own son, as well as at the blinding of the infant John VII, is reflected in his account where he attempts to soften and justify the emperor's actions.[35] The Spanish traveller Clavijo similarly reports that the emperor took pity on his son and only partially blinded him, moreover allowing his eyes to be treated to recover his sight. Clavijo also relates another tale, according to which John again took pity on his son and ordered Andronikos released after he saw a huge snake the latter had killed with his bare hands while in the prison.[36]

The Italian chronicler Caresini also claims that while Murad had his son completely blinded, John refrained from such a punishment.[37] All these authors attempt to soften the harsh punishment and cast John V as more compassionate than the sultan. At first, this narrative bias may appear rather trivial and easy to dismiss, after all, it does not alter the chronology or the gist of the events. Yet these accounts are significant since they clearly indicate that these authors found the blinding of Andronikos disturbing and gruesome – that is, unworthy of a 'civilized' Byzantine emperor. This adds another layer to our understanding of this episode, thereby opening a small window into the perception of the events by near contemporaries.

Since Andronikos would continue in his quest for power – quite aggressively at times – he probably did indeed recover his eyesight to

---

[33] Schreiner, *Kleinchroniken*, Chronik 9/29 and Mioni, 'Cronaca', no. 19'.

[34] Doukas, 70–1. See also Dölger, 'Johannes VII', 24.

[35] Chalkokondyles, 70–3, 96–7; Doukas, 70–1. Schreiner, *Kleinchroniken*, Chronik 12/1; 22/14. In the eighth century, Empress Irene also had her son Constantine VI blinded in order to become ruler herself. In the ninth century, Basil I had his son Leo confined for three years, as he suspected that Leo was plotting against him. It is possible that Basil also contemplated blinding Leo. See S. Tougher, *The Reign of Leo IV: Politics and People (886–912).* (Leiden, 1997), 35.

[36] Clavijo, 47.   [37] Caresini, 32.

a degree. Manuel's own reaction to his sudden elevation or to the blinding of Andronikos is, however, unknown. Nor can we gain any insight into what might have motivated Andronikos to rebel against his father instead of safely assuming the throne upon his death. In his writings, Manuel mentions his eldest brother only once, in the *Funeral Oration,* where he refers to Andronikos as Theodore's 'brother, the emperor' and glosses over his rebellion against their father.[38] As with Matthew Kantakouzenos, Manuel was careful to observe decorum and refrain from speaking ill of his brother after his death.

John V and Manuel: A Joint Rule?

Whatever Manuel and others may have thought about Andronikos' blinding, the pope, for one, was quick to condemn the act, as well as John V's co-operation with the Ottomans. The news actually reached the pope almost a year later, in 1374, when he was endeavouring to form a league against the Ottomans and to fulfil his promise to the emperor. After receiving the news that the Byzantines were now co-operating with Ottomans, the Pope changed his mind and sent the emperor a reproachful letter. John V then dispatched his ambassador, Philip Tzykandyles, to Rome to explain the circumstances, but no help was forthcoming either from the pope or from the Venetians. It became clear that the emperor's conversion had been in vain.

Demetrios Kydones, who had been influential in convincing the emperor to convert, terminated his duties as *mesazon* soon after the trip to Rome.[39] And it seems that it was around this time that Manuel began to have some influence in the governing of the empire as the heir to the throne. For instance, Caroldo's chronicle reports that in 1375, the Venetian ambassador was advised to negotiate with Manuel should his father be too ill to receive him.[40] Though John V might have delegated some tasks to Manuel, nothing indicates that as co-emperor, he was free to exercise power on his own. Nonetheless, being the heir meant that besides being delegated certain government tasks, the young emperor also had the opportunity to observe his father's governance more closely than he might otherwise have done.

---

[38] *Funeral Oration,* 104–5. [39] Barker, *Manuel II,* 34–7; Dennis, *Thessalonica,* 35.

[40] J. Chrysostomides, 'Studies on the Chronicle of Caroldo, with Special Reference to the History of Byzantium from 1370 to 1377', *OCP* 35 (1969), 123–82, re-printed in J. Chrysostomides, *Byzantium and Venice 1204–1453,* eds. M. Heslop and Ch. Dendrinos (Farnham, 2011), Study II. Henceforth, Chrysostomides, 'Caroldo'.

The pre-existing political and socio-economic problems did not present John V with an ideal setting to operate within. The empire was exhausted after years of civil war, and his reign was to witness even more. John V would eventually bequeath Manuel a rather troublesome heritage. For instance, the Italian influence on Byzantine politics and economy were further solidified during his rule. John V granted Lesbos to Franceso I Gattilusio and leased Chios to the Genoese for a very low rent, and he incurred further debts to the Venetians and promised them the island of Tenedos. Although he later changed his mind and sought to retrieve the island from Venice, it would remain a source of strife for the Byzantines, Venetians and the Genoese. John V also strove to limit the Venetian influence on Byzantine trade, even refusing to renew the treaty with Venice after 1376.[41] Ultimately, he was not successful in his efforts to undermine their economic influence and John V was also compelled to accept the suzerainty of the Ottomans.[42] On several occasions, Manuel would later attempt to rid the empire of Italian and Ottoman influence, also to no avail.

The chief characteristic of John V's reign appears to have been an increasing dependence on Western powers for ensuring the survival of the empire. While many emperors before him had turned to the Italians, and especially to the papacy, he made a special effort to obtain military and economic aid from these powers.[43] After all, the further diminishment of the empire's resources made his need for Western help even greater than that of his predecessors. Moreover, John V also had family connections to Italy through his mother Anna of Savoy. In this regard, it must be remembered that Amadeo of Savoy, who had come to John V's aid when the latter's way blocked by the Bulgarians in 1366, was his cousin. And it was probably this family bond that prompted to Amadeo of Savoy to help the Byzantine emperor; he had very little, if anything, to gain from the enterprise.

Despite his conversion and lavish promises, John V failed to obtain help from Europe: he had nothing concrete to offer to them in return. Without any real incentive, Western powers were understandably not keen to offer Byzantium substantial help in the name of charity. Likewise, although the emperor's personal conversion was a grand gesture, it did not benefit the

---

[41] The Veneto-Byzantine treaty was subject to renewal every five years. For John V's dealings with Venice, see D. Nicol, *Byzantium and Venice: A Study in Diplomatic and Cultural Relations* (Cambridge, 1992), 292–322. Henceforth, Nicol, *Byzantium and Venice*.

[42] Nicol, *Last Centuries*, 256–73 for an outline of John V's reign.

[43] See the acts listed in Dölger, *Regesten*, 49–61, for John V's diplomatic missions to the papacy.

papacy in the slightest. His acceptance of the Ottoman suzerainty was furthermore extremely problematic. Not only did the papacy and the Italians perceive this as a treasonous act to Christianity, it also weakened their trust in the emperor's proposals against the Ottomans. Still, given the internal problems of the empire and the increasing power of the Ottomans, the emperor was at least astute in recognizing that Western aid was crucial to the empire's survival. Since Manuel would adopt an almost identical outlook when he became emperor, it is possible to interpret this as a continuation of John V's policies.

Rebellion Rekindled

Only three years after Manuel's proclamation as co-emperor, everything was turned upside down. Civil war was sparked once more. Before mid-July of 1376, with the help of the Genoese, Andronikos escaped from the Monastery of Kauleas, to which he had been moved from Anemas. He then took refuge in Pera with his wife and son. Having also received support from the Ottoman sultan, Murad, Andronikos entered Constantinople on 12 August. His father and his brothers Manuel and Theodore fought him and were defeated in October. Andronikos had them confined in the Anemas.[44]

The Tower of Anemas, located in the suburbs of Blachernai, had served as a prison for high-ranking individuals since the twelfth century.[45] The imprisonment of John V and his sons in Anemas was recorded extensively by contemporary and later authors, indicating that the tale of a usurper emperor confining his father and brothers to a prison was perceived as a note-worthy and particularly dramatic episode. Their narratives generally manifest the authors' sympathy for the emperor and his sons. Doukas dramatizes his account by narrating that the tower shut in the father and the brothers like Tartaros, and likened Andronikos to Zeus who had imprisoned his father Kronos and brothers Ploutos and Poseidon.[46] In his confused narrative, Chalkokondyles makes the bizarre claim that the

---

[44] Schreiner, *Kleinchroniken*, Chronik 22/14. Andronikos was first imprisoned in the Tower of Anemas, but he seems to have been moved to the Monastery of Kauleas, while his sight was also partially restored. The sources agree that he was in this monastery when he escaped. The move has been suggested by Barker, *Manuel II*, 24. Stella, 169 and Danielo di Chinazzo, *Cronoca della guerra di Chioggia*, ed. L. A. Mutatori (Milan, 1864), 22–4, note the alliance between the Genoese and Andronikos. Henceforth, Chinazzo.

[45] A. Van Millingen. *Byzantine Constantinople: The Walls of the City and Adjoining Historical Sites* (London, 1899), 146–7 and 154–63.

[46] Doukas, 72–3. The addition of Pluto and Poseidon are erroneous, but it is probable that Doukas incorporated them to create a parallel for Manuel and Theodore.

emperor and his sons were imprisoned in a wooden cage constructed in a room.[47] Similarly, Demetrios Kydones, a staunch supporter of John and Manuel, uses similar imagery comparing the tower to a labyrinth and bewailing that it was easier for a soul to escape from Tartaros than from Anemas.[48] John V and his sons were to remain in Anemas for three years.[49] Years later, in the *Funeral Oration* and the *Discourse to Iagoup*, Manuel would describe his sufferings in Anemas. Likening his prison to a tomb, he laments the darkness that prevailed within.[50]

Manuel's days of imprisonment were shared by his father and his youngest brother Theodore. The third brother, Michael, about whom we know almost nothing, was absent. After being granted an appanage in Mesembria in 1371, Michael married a daughter of Dobrotica, a prominent Bulgarian nobleman, in 1373. In 1376, either before or shortly after Andronikos' ascent to power, he was murdered in Silistria by his brother-in-law.[51] Thus it can be argued with certainty that Michael was not in Constantinople during the events. While a short chronicle claims that Andronikos also imprisoned the Empress Helena, Manuel's own writings and a letter by Kydones makes it clear that she was not at the Tower of Anemas. Instead, she was attempting to mediate between the two parties, although her attempts met with scorn from both Andronikos and his imprisoned family members.[52] In the *Funeral Oration*, Manuel represents Empress Helena as having contact with her imprisoned family members, establishing her as a direct participant in a secret plan to smuggle Theodore out.[53]

In contrast to his silence on Andronikos and Michael, Manuel's account in the *Funeral Oration* of his days at Anemas is marked in its warm descriptions of his brother Theodore. As the *Funeral Oration* has strong autobiographical digressions, it discloses Manuel's perceptions of his

---

[47] Chalkokondyles, 98–9.   [48] Kydones, Letter 222, lines 86–91 and Letter 167, lines 36–8,

[49] The length of time is confirmed not only by Manuel's own writings, but also by Doukas, Chalkokondyles and a number of short chronicles. See the *Discourse to Iagoup*, 329; Doukas, 72–73; Chalkokondyles, 98–9; Schreiner, *Kleinchroniken*, Chronik 7/19; Chronik 12/1–2; Chronik 22/17–20.

[50] *Funeral Oration*, 106–7; *Discourse to Iagoup*, 329.

[51] In November 1373, Michael made an unsuccessful attack on Trebizond. Schreiner, *Kleinchroniken*, Chronik 22/18–19; Michael Panaretos. *Μιχαὴλ τοῦ Παναρέτου Περὶ τῶν Μεγάλων Κομνηνῶν*, ed. O. Lampsides (Athens, 1958), 78. A Venetian deliberation dated 12 March 1376 also discusses Michael's desire to gain the Trapezuntine throne. Michael's father-in-law, Dobrotica, wanted the throne for Michael, Thiriet, *Régestes*, I, no. 576, 143. He was thus alive in March 1376 but was dead by around July 1376.

[52] Kydones, Letter 222, lines 69–73. *Discourse to Iagoup*, 329, ' Ἔπειτ' εἶχε με φρουρὰ ἅμα τῷ πατρί τε καὶ βασιλεῖ, καὶ δὴ καὶ τῷ ἀδελφῷ.'

[53] *Funeral Oration*, 100–1.

experiences, including the civil war ignited by his elder brother. However, as in the case of every autobiographical narrative, Manuel's account is a carefully crafted version of people and events as he wished his readers to perceive them. In this regard, an analysis of his narrative strategies in the oration will shed light on his relationship not only with Theodore, but also with his father.

In the *Funeral Oration*, Manuel employs the Anemas episode in order to fashion Theodore's image as the epitome of brotherly love and obedience. For instance, in one emotional passage, Manuel narrates that when he was wounded in the head, Theodore rested him on his knees and did not move at all so as to not cause him further pain.[54] He emphasizes that at all times, Theodore obeyed him unconditionally, except for on one occasion. Although there had been a secret plan to smuggle Theodore out of prison, Manuel claims that his brother did not wish to leave him and kept delaying. The detailed narration of their suffering serves to further evoke the audience's sympathy. As befits the protagonist of the *Funeral Oration*, Theodore is represented as being a selfless, devoted son and brother. Further, by highlighting his absolute devotion and obedience as a brother, the episode of Anemas also foreshadows his future political loyalty to Manuel as the despot of Morea.

While the *Funeral Oration* was an *apologia* for Theodore's future political career, this study will later propose that it also functioned as an idealized narrative of Manuel's reign.[55] In this respect, it is significant to note that when narrating the plan to free Theodore, Manuel openly represents himself as a decision maker, along with his father and mother. In other words, he portrays himself as an agent, not as a passive actor. Although Manuel's elaborate account of their imprisonment is a narrative strategy to reinforce the idealized portrayal of Theodore – and of himself – it should not be dismissed as a mere pretext for political statements. The Anemas story also reflects the genuine affection and close bond between the two brothers.

Another key figure in Manuel's account is his father John V, whose portrayal in Manuel's Anemas episode stands in stark contrast to that of Theodore. In a telling passage, Manuel claims that their father changed his mind about letting Theodore escape since he feared for his own life. Manuel then points out that Theodore willingly chose to die because of his father's apprehensions and, as an obedient son, uttered no protest. There were some people who disagreed with the emperor, Manuel says

---

[54] *Funeral Oration*, 100–1.   [55] See Chapter 8.

with emphasis, and he himself was among them.[56] Ultimately, Manuel portrays John V as an indecisive and rather cowardly man, denying his son freedom out of fear for his own life. Moreover, not only does Manuel explicitly point out that he disagreed with the emperor, he also attempts to further tarnish his father's image. By minutely narrating the anguish Theodore felt in prison afterwards, he indirectly puts the blame for his sufferings squarely on John V's shoulders.

While lingering on his own sufferings and those of his brother, Manuel is completely silent about the misery his father must have gone through. Although, as the protagonist, it is to be expected that Theodore dominates the *Funeral Oration*, it is notable that John V has almost no presence in the Anemas episode, in this work or in the *Discourse to Iagoup*. Instead of portraying John V as a capable father who comforted his sons, Manuel opted to represent him as a weak man, and limited himself to merely narrating the bleak outcome of his apprehensions. This negative portrayal was surely influenced by their future confrontation in the 1380s.[57]

Both in the *Funeral Oration* and the *Discourse to Iagoup*, Manuel gives a highly dramatized account of their three-year imprisonment.[58] A passage in the *Discourse to Iagoup*, where Manuel narrates how he coped during this time, has attracted special attention from scholars:

> As for everyone under such circumstances, it was necessary to turn to many activities, so that I could scatter a little the cloud of despair with some leisure and not surrender completely to the present and future evils; no one can do that. So, at this time, it seemed good to me to continuously occupy myself with this activity, spending time with books day and night, along with performing my duty to God … It was necessary to use a lantern whenever I turned to such an occupation. Since I was bereft of an instructor, I could not advance in many respects in proportion to my great labours. Yet, in the continuity of my activity, an utterly tyrannical love for *logoi* was imprinted into my soul and it prevailed over all things as to make me not simply a lover, but a raving one, too.[59]

---

[56] *Funeral Oration*, 100–3. '… ἧκέ τις ἀγγέλων πρός ἐμέ, ὡς ὁ πατήρ μεταμέλοιτο δεδιὼς περὶ τῷ ζῆν, ἂν ὁ δρασμός ὑποπτευθῇ γεγενῆσθαι τῇ ἐκείνου γνώμῃ … ὥστε γνώμῃ τέθνηκε διὰ τὴν τοῦ πατρός ὑποψίαν, πρὸς ἣν ἂν εἶχε μυρία λέγειν, εἴ γε ἐβούλετο παραιτεῖσθαι, ἐπεὶ καὶ ἦσαν οἱ τ'ἀναντία τῷ βασιλεῖ λέγοντες, οἷς γε καὶ αὐτός συνεστοίχουν.'

[57] F. Leonte, 'A Brief "History of the Morea" as seen through the Eyes of an Emperor-Rhetorician: Manuel II Palaiologos' Funeral Oration for Theodore, Despot of the Morea', in *Viewing the Morea Land and People in the Late Medieval Peloponnese*, ed. S. Gerstel, (Washington DC, 2013), 397–417, 400, 414, also notes the minimal role of John V in the *Funeral Oration* and assigns this to the clash between them in the 1380s. However, he does analyse Manuel's portrayal of John V. Henceforth, Leonte, 'Morea'.

[58] *Funeral Oration*, 104–5.

[59] *Discourse to Iagoup*, 329. 'Πᾶσι μὲν οὖν τοῖς οὕτως ἔχουσιν, ἀνάγκη πρὸς ἔργα τρέπεσθαι παντοδαπά, ὥστε μικρὸν γοῦν τῇ περὶ ταῦτα σχολῇ διασκεδάζειν τὸ νέφος τῆς ἀθυμίας, καὶ μὴ

The complete text of the *Discourse to Iagoup* has only been recently edited. Yet the passage on Manuel's childhood and this one immediately following it were first noticed and translated by Berger de Xivrey in the nineteenth century. In 1969, prompted by the extracts made by Berger de Xivrey, John Barker edited and translated the first three folia of the *Discourse*. He did so, and in isolation from the rest of the text, only because he was aware that those passages contained an autobiographical account by Manuel.[60] Since then, several scholars have relied on these passages for an autobiographical account of Manuel's scholarly pursuits, but again, in isolation from the rest of the work. Although these passages do indeed provide an autobiographical account, Manuel's narrative goals in inserting them into the discourse must be taken into account. Scholars have interpreted this excerpt on Anemas as referring to the study of literature or to broader scholarly activities. However, a complete reading of the discourse and an analysis of its narrative goals alters this conclusion. It emerges that in all probability Manuel was referring to chiefly theological pursuits and was fashioning this episode almost as a 'stepping-stone' for his future interest in theology.

The *Discourse to Iagoup* was composed in 1396 as a defensive reply against the theologian Manuel Kalekas. He criticized Manuel for his theological interests, urging the emperor to leave these matters aside and to occupy himself solely with state affairs. On the whole, the goal of the *Discourse to Iagoup* is to combat these criticisms and to present Manuel as an ideal 'scholar-emperor'. In other words, Manuel composed the entire work as a defence of his theological interests and his competence in these matters. Throughout the text, he seizes every chance to represent himself as an dedicated scholar, clinging to his studies even in adversity. Consequently, the autobiographical passages on his tumultuous childhood and imprisonment in Anemas serve the narrative goal of eliciting the audience's sympathy for the emperor and

---

ἀπειπεῖν πρὸς τὰ ὄντα τε καὶ ὑφορώμενα κακά, ὅπερ οὐκ ἀνδρός. Ἐδόκει τοίνυν τηνικαῦτα ἐμοὶ τοῦτ' ἔργον ἔχειν διηνεκές, τὸ βιβλίοις ἐνδιατρίβειν νύκτωρ καὶ μεθημέραν, μετὰ τὸ ἀφοσιοῦσθαι τὸ πρὸς τὸ θεῖον χρέος ... ὅθεν ἔδει λύχνῳ χρῆσθαι τὸν πρὸς οἱανοῦν ἐργασίαν τρεπόμενον ... Ὧν δὲ ἔρημος σοφιστοῦ, πλεῖστα μὲν ἐπιδοῦναι καὶ τῶν πολλῶν ἰσόρροπα πόνων οὐκ ἐδυνήθην. Τῇ δ' οὖν συνεχείᾳ τοῦ ἔργου, ἔρως μοι τῶν λόγων ἄκρως τυραννικὸς ἐντέτηκε τῇ ψυχῇ, καὶ οὕτω γε τοῖς ὅλοις οὗτος κεκράτηκεν, ὥστε με τούτων οὐχ ἁπλῶς ἐραστήν, ἀλλὰ μανικώτατον ἀπεργάσασθαι.' Barker, *Manuel II*, 412, has a translation of this passage. C. Bevegni, 'La lettera ad Alessio Iagoup di Manuele II Paleologo: una rilettura del Par. gr. 3041', *La Parola del Passato 233* (1987), 103–8, has made some corrections to Barker's reading of the text and his translation.

60 Barker, *Manuel II*, 410. See also J. Berger de Xivrey, 'Mémoire sur la vie et les ouvrages de l'empereur Manuel Paléologue', *Mémoires de l'Institut de France, Académie des Inscriptions et des Belles Lettres* XIX, 2 (Paris, 1853), 25–6. Dennis, *Thessalonica*, 14, also translates Berger de Xivrey's French version of the former passage where Manuel narrates his childhood studies, into English.

of underscoring his dedication to theology. As a result, these autobiographical passages help set the tone for Manuel's defence against Kalekas.

While the studies narrated in the passage on Manuel's childhood certainly refer to broader literary and scholarly pursuits, those that take place in Anemas seem to be concerned specifically with theology. The discourse offers ample evidence for this. Significantly, Manuel claims that apart from his books, his other occupation in Anemas was prayer and worship. Immediately after this passage, Manuel remarks that in these pursuits, he has chanced upon men who had not only been granted divine help and strength but were *also* educated in Greek literature. This sentence has been interpreted by scholars to be about very well-educated men who were favoured by God in their endeavours. However, his wording in Greek indicates that these men were theologians, who also had a solid 'outer' education.[61] So, unlike previous assumptions, these men were not just scholars in a general sense; they were scholars of *theology*. Moreover, later in the same passage, Manuel also refers to his study of Scripture. All of these strongly indicate that in the passage on Anemas, the studies that are being referred to, are chiefly theological.

The conclusion of this autobiographical account lends further support to this interpretation. With a touch of false modesty, Manuel protests that he considers himself far from a theologian, but he then proceeds to discuss theology and defend his interests for the remainder of the discourse.[62] The other passage in the discourse where Manuel refers to his preoccupation with books is, once again, specifically about theology.[63] Since the goal of the work was to refute Kalekas' critique of the emperor's interest in theology, it is natural that the text would put a special emphasis on Manuel's theological pursuits. Ultimately, the whole account of his childhood and youth serves to gradually set the tone for Manuel's defence of his interest in theology. A complete reading of the discourse allows for a more precise interpretation of this passage, and also serves to clarify the narrative function of the Anemas episode in the work.

---

[61] *Discourse to Iagoup*, 330, 'ἀνδράσι γὰρ ἐνέτυχον θείας ἐπικουρίας τε καὶ ῥοπῆς μετέχουσιν ἀτεχνῶς, καὶ τὴν ἔξω σοφίαν πεπαιδευμένοις ἐπεικῶς ...'. G. Podskalsky, *Theologie und Philosophie in Byzanz. Der Streit um die theologische Methodik in der spätbyzantinischen Geistesgeschichte (14/15 Jhr. Seine systematischen Grundlagen und seine historische Entwicklung)* (Munich, 1977), 48–64, points out that in addition to the existence of the 'Patriarchal School', it was possible for students to study theology privately, with a mentor. Henceforth, Podskalsky, *Theologie und Philosophie in Byzanz*.

[62] *Discourse to Iagoup*, 331.   [63] *Discourse to Iagoup*, 358.

Re-writing History

During the three years that his father and two brothers were held as captives in Anemas, Andronikos reigned as the sole emperor. Although he had emerged victorious in October 1376, Andronikos was not officially crowned emperor until the following year.[64] However, he does not appear to have received much support from the populace. Having gained the throne with the support of the Genoese and the Ottomans, he was now expected to pay his debts, and Andronikos agreed to give Tenedos, the island that John V had been persuaded to sell to Venice, to the Genoese. When the Genoese arrived in Tenedos to claim the island, the inhabitants refused to surrender, instead, choosing to submit to Venetian rule. This sparked the famous War of Chioggia between Genoa and Venice. Unsurprisingly, Byzantium also was entangled in the struggle, and on 31 July 1376, the Venetians even mounted an attack on Constantinople.[65] Moreover, Andronikos ceded Gallipoli to the Ottomans.[66] Thus his rule succeeded mostly in a further increase of Italian and Ottoman involvement in Byzantine affairs and left Byzantium in a far more precarious state than before.

However, Andronikos IV was not to remain emperor for much longer. In June 1379, John V and his two sons finally managed to escape from the Tower of Anemas. How exactly they did so is unclear. Chalkokondyles reports that a servant brought them an iron saw; while Doukas claims that a certain Angelos, nicknamed the devil, lowered them from the tower to the sea. The satire by Mazaris also refers to a certain Angelos in Manuel's court who enjoyed imperial favour because his grandfather had spent a fortune getting Manuel out of Anemas;[67] and a short chronicle simply states that their escape was miraculous.[68]

Manuel himself mentions an arrangement concerning Theodore in the *Funeral Oration*, according to which Andronikos had agreed to release Theodore on an oath that he would not try to help the remaining captives. Manuel enigmatically remarks that God provided something better, enabling all three of them to come out of Anemas. He then omits the details, claiming that the audience was already familiar with them. While this omission may have eased the narrative flow, it is also a textual strategy

[64] Barker, *Manuel II*, 29; Doukas, 72–3.

[65] Barker *Manuel II*, 29–30; Dennis, *Thessalonica*, 40; L. T. Belgrano, 'Studi e documenti su la Colonia Genovese di Pera (Prima serie),' *Atti della Società Ligure di Storia Patria* 13, 2 (1877), 97–317, 131, no. 24. Henceforth, Belgrano.

[66] Kydones, Letter 154, lines 25–40.   [67] Chalkokondyles, 100–1; Doukas, 72–3; Mazaris, 26–7.

[68] Schreiner, *Kleinchroniken*, Chronik 7/19.

which indicates that for some reason, Manuel did not wish to elaborate further on their escape.[69] Concerning their break out of Anemas, a letter from Kydones hints that the Empress Helena may have helped the captives.[70] John V and his sons then took refuge at the court of Sultan Murad. There, the emperor persuaded the sultan to support them instead of Andronikos, probably by offering him even greater concessions. Having thus secured the crucial Ottoman support, the father and his younger sons entered Constantinople on 1 July 1379.

The fight was not yet over, however. Andronikos fled to Pera and took hostages with him: his mother Empress Helena, his grandfather John Kantakouzenos, and Maria and Theodora Kantakouzene, his maternal aunts.[71] Andronikos also left behind a garrison of 300 Genoese to defend the city against his father and brothers. Venice, John V's ally against his rebellious son and the Genoese, sent ships to help the emperor. Venetian ships blockaded Pera, while the Ottomans attacked from the land. The fight between the father and the son lasted for almost two years, and it was the Venetians, the Genoese and the Ottomans who were the decisive partners, not the Byzantines. The cost of this civil strife for civilians was profound: prolonged siege caused famine and an outbreak of plague in Pera; and the residents of Constantinople also suffered because of the rekindling of the civil war.[72]

Around April 1381, the dispute finally ceased as John V, with Ottoman consent, finally made peace with Andronikos and his Genoese allies.[73] The contents of the treaty that was agreed can be inferred from a synodal document.[74] Andronikos consented to refrain from attacking his father, while John V accepted him and his young son, John VII, as the legitimate successors to the throne. He also received territories in Thrace, including Selymbria,[75] and it is probable that his imperial hostages were released around the same time, since John Kantakouzenos left for Morea, where he would die two years later in 1383, soon after. The truce between father and

---

[69] *Funeral Oration*, 108–9. Manuel usually uses such interjections, not to let the narrative slacken, but when he wishes to omit an episode for reasons of decorum or when he considered the events unpleasant.

[70] Kydones, Letter 22, lines 92–125.

[71] *Funeral Oration*, 110–11. Schreiner, *Kleinchroniken*, Chronik 22/20.

[72] See Dennis, *Thessalonica*, 40–2 for an account of the hostilities. Since the Greek historians ignore the fight in 1379–81, Dennis bases his account on Italian sources. See Stella, 176; Chinazzo, 90–3 and Caresini, 36. For the sufferings of the captives, see Kydones, Letter 222, lines 111–16.

[73] Dennis, *Thessalonica*, 44. Dennis believes that John V could not have come to terms with the Genoese without the consent of the Ottomans.

[74] MM, II, 25–7. Dölger, *Regesten*, no. 3171, 67.

[75] Doukas, 72–3, who mistakenly dates the battle before Andronikos' imprisonment in 1373.

son was confirmed on 2 November 1382 in a Byzantine-Genoese treaty, and
tranquillity was at long last restored – at least temporarily – to
Constantinople and to the little that was left of the Byzantine Empire.[76]
Civil strife, however, had undermined the empire's situation yet again, and
its political, economic and military fragility could no longer be contained.
The struggle between Andronikos IV and John V had effectively turned
Byzantium into a pawn in the hands of the Genoese, the Venetians and the
Ottomans.

The degree of Manuel's involvement in the fight between his father and
brother has not yet been adequately considered. Understandably, this is
partially due the lack of sources. All things considered, it is safe to conclude
that he seems to have mainly followed his father's decisions, fulfilling
a rather secondary role in governing. Although Manuel represents himself
as an active political agent in the *Funeral Oration* during these events, his
role was most likely a passive one. Indeed, all the evidence indicates that his
father was the chief decision maker among his faction: he negotiated with
the Ottomans, the Genoese and the Venetians, and there is nothing to hint
at an active, prominent political role for Manuel. Although Manuel was co-
emperor, it was John V who had been Andronikos' primary opponent.
Manuel and Theodore had been merely caught up in this family struggle as
supporters of their father, and not as significant political actors in their own
right. Even the fact that John V was able to alter the succession in
Andronikos' favour, signals a more passive role on Manuel's part.

Manuel was campaigning with the Ottoman sultan in Anatolia at the
time of the reconciliation. He was probably accompanying the Ottoman
army on behalf of John V.[77] It is not known whether Manuel knew of the
contents of the treaty beforehand, nor when and how he learned of it.
Certainly he cannot be expected to be among those 'who rejoiced and
leaped with joy upon witnessing the peace', as the synodal document put
it.[78] The treaty had removed him from the succession, despite all the
loyalty he had shown and all that he had endured in the service of his
father. In order to gain more insight into his perception of events, we will
now turn to the *Funeral Oration* and the *Discourse to Iagoup*.

---

[76] Dennis, *Thessalonica*, 47. A copy of the treaty is preserved in the Genoese archives, to which Dennis
had access.

[77] Both Barker and Dennis agree with this on the basis of Kydones' letters from the time written to
Manuel in Anatolia. Barker, *Manuel II*, 44; Dennis, *Thessalonica*, 50–1. Kydones, Letters 218, 219
and 220.

[78] MM, II, 25–7. '… οὐδεὶς ὃς οὐ χαίρει καὶ ἀγάλλεται καὶ σκριτᾷ παρρησιαζομένην ὁρῶν τὴν
εἰρήνην.'

In the autobiographical passages of these works, Manuel completely omits the treaty of 1381 and its consequences. Again, this omission can be interpreted as a rhetorical strategy used in order to pass over events which Manuel did not wish to mention. Manuel's account of the civil war in the *Funeral Oration* ends abruptly with his escape from the Tower of Anemas, and more strikingly frames the entire struggle as a war with the Latins, and not a civil strife fuelled by his elder brother. Even the imprisonment of his mother's family is represented as an act of the Latins alone. Manuel omits Andronikos' role altogether, declaring simply that he would say no more of it for various reasons. Once more, this is clearly a convenient rhetorical strategy that allowed him to pass over what he may have considered a shameful civil strife and his own consequent removal from the succession. He may have also been motivated by a wish to refrain from speaking ill of the then dead Andronikos.[79]

After pointing out that the war with the 'Latins' had ended, Manuel narrates the events of Theodore's early rule as the despot of the Morea and does not return to events in Constantinople until 1391, by which time he was emperor; before mentioning that the two brothers are summoned by the Ottoman sultan in 1394. He thus skips the ten years between 1381–91, and thus passes neatly over the alteration in the succession. Since the narrative is shaped by Theodore's central role in the oration, it is not necessarily a surprise that the focus shifts away from Constantinople once he leaves. Nonetheless it is clear that Manuel did not wish to narrate details which undermined his own authority, both political and authorial. He was reluctant to admit in the *Funeral Oration*, which was, of course, designed to eulogize his rule, that there had ever been an occasion, when he had lost his place in the succession.[80]

The narrative of the *Discourse to Iagoup* follows a similar pattern where everything abruptly ends with Manuel's escape from the Tower of Anemas, and once more, he omits any mention of the civil strife between 1380–2. This is an interesting choice, as including the episode would have provided him with an excellent opportunity to lament the hindering of his studies and to underscore the suffering he endured. To put it differently, it would have contributed to his self-representation as an ideal 'scholar-emperor'.[81]

---

[79] *Funeral Oration*, 110–11.

[80] Leonte, 'Morea', 401, also notes that several episodes receive much more attention than others. He attributes this to Manuel's desire to construct a narrative of the history of the Morea. While this is certainly true, I would further add that Manuel also seems to have wished to omit 'unpleasant' episodes in order to represent a much more idealized version of his rule.

[81] *Discourse to Iagoup*, 329.

However, in order to avoid any mention of the succession issues, Manuel chose to let this opportunity pass. Even more significantly, after abruptly finishing his account of his imprisonment in Anemas, the emperor emphasizes that he had returned to his former rank (σχῆμα).[82] Here, his words should be interpreted as a reference to his imperial rank as the heir to the throne. In fact, he uses the word *schema*, a term which he continuously employs in the sense of imperial rank in all of his other works.[83]

As in the case of the *Funeral Oration*, Manuel shapes the narrative so as to avoid mentioning the reversion in the succession. Both the *Funeral Oration* and the *Discourse to Iagoup* therefore read as if these events had never happened. After all, mentioning the reversion in the succession would have undermined his imperial dignity and weakened his authority, both imperial and authorial. By glossing over the alteration of the succession in these two autobiographical works, he sought to distort the political realities and present his audience with an idealized version of his life and reign. Instead he 're-wrote' these historical events. Throughout his life, this gap between real life and Manuel's representation of his reign constitutes an important aspect of his oeuvre.

Aside from his later representation of events, Manuel's immediate actions speak volumes about the disappointment he seems to have suffered. Upon his return to Constantinople around the autumn of 1382, he bid farewell to Theodore who left to assume his duties as the despot of Morea.[84] It is unclear whether or not Manuel was meant to return to Thessalonike once more as its despot, but soon after Theodore's departure, he took the risky step of sailing to Thessalonike in secret. He established himself there not as its despot, but as a rival emperor. For the next five years, he would openly defy his father and his policies by waging war upon the Ottomans.[85] It was now Manuel's turn to be the rebellious son.

---

[82] *Discourse to Iagoup*, 329. "Ὡς δὲ δὴ τρία παρελήλυθεν ἔτη, καὶ φροῦδα πάντα γέγονε χειρὶ Θεοῦ τὰ κατέχοντα, καὶ αὖθις ἐπανήκομεν εἰς τὸ πρότερον σχῆμα . . .'

[83] It is not possible to cite all instances of Manuel's use of σχῆμα. The other instance in the *Discourse to Iagoup* is illustrative of Manuel's use of the word, 'οὐδ' αὖ ἔτι μοι καὶ νῦν τὸ σχῆμα προτρέπει, καὶ πρὸς τούτῳ γε ὁ καιρὸς τἆλλα δεύτερα πάντα θέμενον, τοῦ θεολογεῖν ἀπρὶξ ἔχεσθαι . . .', 332.

[84] Barker, *Manuel II*, 44; Dennis, *Thessalonica*, 50, *Funeral Oration*, 112–15.

[85] Barker, *Manuel II*, 44; Dennis, *Thessalonica*, 50.

CHAPTER 3

Fighting for Freedom

O men! Let us do everything, let us endure all for the sake of freedom.[1]

Sailing away in secret from Constantinople, Manuel arrived in Thessalonike in the autumn of 1382.[2] He was never to mention in his writings the reasons that pushed him to establishing a separatist rule in this city. However, it is beyond doubt that it was an outcome of the bitter frustration he must have felt about the alteration in the succession. Still a relatively young man at age thirty-two, Manuel established an independent rule in Thessalonike and styled himself *emperor* rather than despot of Thessalonike.

Although the city enjoyed a semi-autonomous status since the early the fourteenth century, the governors of Thessalonike did not act independently but answered to the emperor in Constantinople. It must be emphasized that Manuel's rule in 1382–7, unlike that of his despotate in 1369–73, does not fit this pattern at all. He was to wage war against the Ottomans for five years and thereby directly contradict his father's policy of reconciliation.[3] The principal events of Manuel's five-year reign in Thessalonike can be traced mainly through his letters and those of Demetrios Kydones. Several homilies by Isidore Glabas, the metropolitan of Thessalonike, also contribute to the picture.[4] The only Byzantine historian to mention this phase in Manuel's

---

[1] *Discourse to the Thessalonians*, 302, lines 20–1. 'Δρῶμεν τοίνυν, ὧ ἄνδρες, πάντα, ἀνεχώμεθα πάντων ὑπὲρ τῆς ἐλευθερίας.'

[2] Dennis, *Thessalonica*, 57–9 and *Funeral Oration*, 36–7.

[3] Manuel was proclaimed emperor in 1373, but when succession was changed in 1382, he might have lost the title of emperor. For despots of Thessalonike, see R. Rochette, 'Les despotes à Thessalonique', in *Impératrices, princesses, aristocrates et saintes souveraines. de l'Orient Chrétien et Musulman au Moyen Age et au début des temps modernes*, ed. E. Malamut and A. Nicolaides (Aix-en-Provence, 2014), 89–96.

[4] See G. T. Dennis, 'The Late Byzantine Metropolitans of Thessalonike', *DOP* 57 (2003), 255–64 for Isidore Glabas. His homilies are an important source for Manuel's reign in Thessalonike, especially for the discord among the citizens. The editions of his works are B. Laourdas, ed., Ἰσιδώρου Ἀρχιεπισκόπου Θεσσαλονίκης Ὁμίλιαι εἰς τὰς Ἑορτὰς τοῦ Ἁγίου Δημητρίου (Thessalonike, 1954); S. Lampros, ed. Ἰσιδώρου μητροπολίτου Θεσσαλονίκης, ὀκτὼ ἐπιστολαὶ ἀνέκδοτοι', Νέος Ἑλληνομνήμων 9 (1912), 343–414; N. Tsirpanlis ed., 'Συμβολὴ εἰς τὴν ἱστορίαν τῆς Θεσσαλονίκης.

life is Chalkokondyles, but his confused chronology makes it almost impossible to use him as a source.[5] That Manuel was not expected in Thessalonike is evident both in a letter by Kydones and a homily by Isidore Glabas.[6] However, the populace's reaction to his unexpected arrival and his new independent regime cannot be discerned. The Thessalonians were already familiar with Manuel from his rule of the city as despot from 1369 to 1373. But this independent rule was a new phase in the relationship between the Thessalonians and Manuel and it was to have a drastic effect – on both sides.

Manuel's rule in Thessalonike is notable for being a 'separatist' rule, opposing the emperor in Constantinople. Although Manuel had been declared co-emperor in 1373, it is unclear whether his title as emperor was also revoked when he lost his place in the succession. Regardless, his insistence on using this title in Thessalonike emphasizes Manuel's defiance of John V and his break with Constantinople. Overall, his five-year rule should not be viewed as a 'more independent despotate', but rather as a separatist and rival rule to Constantinople.

The city was already accustomed to having relative autonomy from Constantinople. Additionally, it was the seat of another such 'separatist' rule: just a few years before Manuel's birth, Thessalonike had witnessed the disastrous regime of the Zealots (1342–50). Aside from this episode, it had a long tradition of being ruled by the members of the imperial family who were subordinate to the emperor in Constantinople: In the thirteenth century, Yolanda of Montferrat established herself as an independent ruler alongside her husband in Constantinople, Andronikos II; John Kantakouzenos appointed Manuel's father John V as a governor of the city between 1350–2; and Anna of Savoy, Manuel's paternal grandmother, had ruled the city in her own right in 1351–66.[7] The recent history of the

Δύο ἀνέκδοτοι ὁμιλίαι Ἰσιδώρου ἀρχιεπισκόπου Θεσσαλονίκης', Θεολογία 42 (1971), 548–81; B. Ch. Christophorides, Ἰσιδώρου Γλαβᾶ Ἀρχιεπισκόπου Θεσσαλονίκης Ὁμιλίες, 2 vols. (Thessalonike, 1992–6). Henceforth, Laourdas, *Isidore*; Lampros, 'Isidore' and Tsirpanlis, 'Isidore'.

[5] See the three articles by R. J. Loenertz, 'Manuel Paléologue et Démétrius Cydonès: remarques sur leurs correspondances', *Échos d'Orient* (1937), 271–87; 474–87 (1938), 107–14. However, Loenertz modified some of his dating in his edition of the letters of Kydones. It is the dating of the edition that shall be relied upon in this chapter. The main study on Manuel's reign in Thessalonike between 1382–7 is G. T. Dennis, *The Reign of Manuel II Palaeologus in Thessalonica (1382–1387)* (Rome, 1960), cited as Dennis, *Thessalonica*. J. W. Barker mainly follows Dennis' narrative; see Barker, *Manuel II*, 43–65.

[6] Laourdas, *Isidore*, 31 and Kydones, Letter 203, lines 5–6.

[7] See A. Vakalopoulos, *A History of Thessalonike*, trans. T. F. Carney (Thessalonike, 1963), 62–70 and though now dated, see also O. Tafrali, *Thessalonique au quatorzième siècle* (Paris, 1913). Henceforth, Tafrali, *Thessalonique*. See also L. Maksimović, *The Byzantine Provincial Administration under the Palaiologoi* (Amsterdam, 1988), 88–97. Henceforth, Maksimović, *Byzantine Administration*; J. Barker, 'The Problem of Appanages in Byzantium during the Palaiologan Period', *Byzantina 3*

city was thus closely connected to that of Manuel's own family, and during his stay in the city, he would have seen the inscription commemorating the memory of Anna of Savoy at a gate in the acropolis.[8] Certainly, Thessalonike's relative autonomy provided Manuel with a unique and ideal place to establish his separatist rule.

Thessalonike in the Late Fourteenth Century

What was Manuel's Thessalonike like? Founded in the fourth century, Thessalonike occupied a strategic and advantageous location. It lay between the sea and the foothills of Mount Chortaites, in the west and the north, it was neighboured by the plain of Thessalonike and the Mygdonia basin. In the east and southwest, it neighboured the region called Kalamaria. Thanks to its advantageous location, which provided it with trade routes, thriving ports and fertile land, the city enjoyed prosperity. For all these reasons, in 1345, the Thessalonian Demetrios Kydones lavished rhetorical praise on his native city.[9]

In 1380s, however, very different conditions prevailed in the city. The new reality formed a stark contrast to the rhetorical image created by Kydones. Constant warfare and the Zealot regime had taken its toll, and after this point, Byzantine Thessalonike was never to thrive again.[10] Its once famous harbour was less active; the governor's palace was in ruins; and the once orderly urban landscape was now overgrown with vegetation.[11] In 1372, the plain of Thessalonike and the Mygdonian basin were seized by the Ottomans, blocking access to the countryside, and as a result, agricultural production and the economic prosperity of the city rapidly declined.

Tellingly, even the textual accounts of Thessalonike from the period – including inscriptions – tend to focus on themes of disintegration and

---

(1971), 103–22; J. W., Barker, 'Late Byzantine Thessalonike: A Second City's Challenges and Responses', *DOP* 57 (2003), 6–35.

[8] For the inscription, see Nicol-Bendall. 'Anna of Savoy', 93.

[9] A translation is found in J. W. Barker, trans. 'The Monody of Demetrios Kydones on the Zealot Rising of 1345 in Thessaloniki', in *Μελετήματα στὴ Μνήμη Βασιλείου Λαούρδα* (Thessalonike, 1975), 285–90, 292. For the Greek text, see *PG* 109, cols. 640–52.

[10] For a detailed discussion of Late Byzantine Thessalonike, see Ch. Bakirtzis. 'The Urban Continuity and the size of Late Byzantine Thessalonike', *DOP* 57 (2003), 35–64; for land walls, see N. Bakirtzis, 'The Practice, Perception and Experience of Byzantine Fortification', in *The Byzantine World*, ed. P. Stephenson (New York, 2010), 352–71, especially 364–7, discussing Manuel's reference in the *Discourse to the Thessalonians* to fortifications around Thessalonike. See also, M. L. Rautman, 'Observations on the Byzantine Palaces of Thessaloniki', *Byzantion* 60 (1990), 300–6. Henceforth, Bakirtzis, 'Thessalonike'; Bakirtzis, 'Fortification', and Rautman, 'Palaces'.

[11] Bakirtzis, 'Thessalonike', 43.

destruction.[12] No artwork or buildings can be securely dated after 1380s, an indication that building activity in the city had declined considerably.[13] With the possible exception of a tower attributed to him in the village of Hagios Basileos near the Lake Langadas, we do not know if Manuel had any buildings erected while he ruled the city.[14] During his earlier residence in the city as its despot (1369–73), Manuel may also have made an addition to the northwest fortifications of the acropolis. A brick inscription, consisting of four lines, refers to the repair of a tower by the *doux* of Thessalonike, George Apokaukos, on Manuel's orders. Although the repair was poorly executed, the claims made in the inscription are flamboyant.[15] This contrast between words and deeds remained a salient theme throughout Manuel's imperial career.

Although he does not speak about the city in his letters from this period, Manuel refers to the walls of Thessalonike in a letter from the 1410s. He also remarks that it was possible to walk in the city without the need for a horse as everything was within the walls.[16] The palace of the governor was destroyed during the uprising of the Zealots, and the citadel at the acropolis had been used as the imperial residence since the governorship of John V. Located in the north corner of the upper city, it offered security to its residents.[17] Presumably, Manuel lived in this citadel. (Fig 3.1)

The socio-economic circumstances Manuel faced in Thessalonike were not promising, to say the least. Around the 1380s, pre-existing problems had become especially troublesome. Thessalonike's relative autonomy from Constantinople and its special economic privileges, meant that the

---

[12] Rautman, 'Palaces', 306, makes this observation.   [13] Bakirtzis, 'Thessalonike', 39.

[14] The tower served the purpose of being able to watch for enemies. Bakirtzis, 'Thessalonike', 37.

[15] 'Σθένει Μανουὴλ δεσπότου. ''Ηγειρε τόνδε πύργον αὐτῷ τειχίῳ/ Γεώργιος δοὺξ Ἀπόκαυκος ἐκ βάθρων/ Σθένει Μανουὴλ τοῦ κρατίστου', published in J. M. Spieser, 'Inventaires en vue d'un recueil des inscriptions historiques de Byzance, 1 : les inscriptions de Thessalonique', *TM* 5 (1972), 145–80, 176–7. See also Bakirtzis, 'Thessalonike', 37. Bakirtzis, 'Fortification', 361, remarks on the contrast between the poor restoration work and the exaggerated claims of the inscription. In addenda to his first article, Spieser later pointed out that it was impossible to completely rule out the possibility that the inscription dates from 1382–7; D. Feissel and J. M. Spieser, 'Inventaires en vue d'un recueil des inscriptions historiques de Byzance, 11: les inscriptions de Thessalonique. supplément', *TM* 7 (1979), 303–46, 339–40. However, during 1382–7, Manuel referred to himself as *basileus*, as did Isidore Glabas and Kydones.

[16] See Letter 43, dated 1403–8, when Demetrios Chrysoloras was in the service of John VII in Thessalonike.

[17] Rautman, 'Palaces', 302; Bakirtzis, 'Thessalonike', 46–7. The citadel had also become a symbol of civic identity in the late period and was represented on Thessalonian coins; see A. Akışık, 'Praising a City: Nicea, Trebizond and Thessalonike', in *Journal of Turkish Studies, in Memoriam Angeliki E. Laiou*, eds. N. Necipoğlu and C. Kafadar (Leiden, 2011), 1–25, 5.

Figure 3.1 Walls of Thessalonike. Photo by DeAgostini / Getty Images.

aristocratic presence in the city was strong. The exact nature of these privileges are as yet unclear; however, they seemed to present the aristocracy with the means to extend their power further, both through land possessions and trade. Members of prominent families, such as Angeloi, Deblitzenoi, Kasandrenoi and Rhadenoi, resided in Thessalonike, and made up a very crucial part of the *archontes* – the political elite of the city. Thus, Thessalonike was not merely a prosperous city, it was also an important and relatively independent source of local power.

In the second half of the fourteenth century, however, the economic life of the city went into drastic decline. Wars and raids in the region had diminished Thessalonike's importance as a trade centre, and agricultural production was in such a state that by 1350s the city was already heavily dependent on grain imports. The society was increasingly divided into the extremely wealthy and the excruciatingly poor. The *mesoi*, or middle class, had long since disappeared, but the rich avoided taxes and the *archontes* oppressed the poor mercilessly. This bleak atmosphere of social inequality and corruption would prove a great challenge to Manuel.

It must also be taken into account that under the Palaiologoi, the power of the government outside Constantinople had weakened considerably. As central authority declined, cities emerged as independent sources of local power and during the process, Thessalonike's autonomy was further enhanced. In lieu of the state, the aristocracy became responsible for the defence and the administration of the city, and ecclesiastics likewise overtook judiciary posts. Due to the weakening of the state authority, the city was governed to a large extent, by its local elite, and as a result, the poor found themselves completely at their mercy.[18] It can be even argued that, in some aspects, the Thessalonike of 1380s resembled an ancient Greek *polis* – albeit one in a precarious state. This comparison should be kept in mind when discussing Manuel's rule in the city, because despite all his aspirations of absolute ruler over Thessalonike, he actually held a position that was more of *primus inter pares*.

Manuel's Thessalonian Network

Manuel's rule as the despot of Thessalonike between 1369–73 cannot be fully sketched out save for fleeting references. However, his new reign in the 1380s provides only a few sources that allow us to discern his activities. The first letters in his collection date from this period, and these years consequently offer the first concrete glimpses of Manuel as a ruler. Shortly after his arrival, in autumn 1382, he relieved Serres from the siege laid by the Turks.[19] This victory, quickly achieved, made an impact on the region. The despot of Epiros, Thomas Preljubović, submitted to Manuel and accepted him as his overlord.[20]

Kydones lavishes praise on Manuel, enthusing that Constantinople was filled with the news of the victory.[21] In a highly amusing letter, he speaks of Manuel's booty capture, elaborating on its impact the tales of the booty's abundance had on the inhabitants of Constantinople. Apparently, even a beggar sleeping in the marketplace thought of rushing to Manuel in Thessalonike, who suddenly transformed the Iros into Kallias.[22] This entertaining letter by Kydones bears testimony to the optimistic atmosphere

---

[18] See also Necipoğlu, 'The Aristocracy in Late Byzantine Thessalonike: A Case Study of the city's Archontes (late 14th and early 15th centuries)', *DOP* 57 (2003), 133–51; Necipoğlu, *Byzantium between the Ottomans and the Latins*, 78–9; and D. Jacoby, 'Foreigners and the Urban Economy in Thessalonike ca. 1150–ca. 1450), *DOP* 57 (2003), 86–113. Hereafter Necipoğlu, 'Archontes' and Jacoby, 'Thessalonike'.

[19] Dennis, *Thessalonica*, 65. On the basis of two of Kydones' letters and a patriarchal act, Dennis convincingly argues that this was a mere relief and not a recapture, since Serres was still in Byzantine hands in 1382. For the patriarchal act, see MM, II, 77–9 and Kydones, Letters 244 and 249.

[20] Dennis, *Thessalonica*, 106. See *Chronicle of Epirus*, ed. S. Cirac Estopañan. *Bizancio y España. El Legato de la Basilissa Maria y de los Déspotas Thomas y Esaú de Joannina* (Barcelona, 1943), 48.

[21] Kydones, Letter 244, lines 4–9 and Letter 247, lines 1–11.

[22] Kydones, Letter 247, lines 24–35. Iros is the beggar in Homer's *Odyssey*, and Kallias is the spendthrift in Aristophanes' *The Birds*. Both figures were used by the Byzantine authors to allude to poverty and wealth.

created by Manuel's early success. It also clearly indicates just how much the promise of prosperity appealed to the impoverished Constantinopolitans. This early promise of financial gain was now starting to attract followers to Manuel, but he would soon learn just how quickly financial troubles could alienate people.

Manuel was not entirely alone in his enterprises against the Ottomans. Through Kydones' letters it is possible to gain an understanding of who formed Manuel's entourage in Thessalonike; for instance, he refers to Theodore Mouzalon's daily attendance on Manuel and his involvement in Turkish affairs.[23] Mouzalon, it seems, occupied a key place in Manuel's entourage. Another person in his service was Demetrios Kabasilas. He probably was the imperial secretary, since Kydones refers to him as reading the emperor's letters before Manuel did.[24] Several letters by Kydones make it clear that Manuel's victory in Serres prompted people to come to Thessalonike to enter into his service.

Another such person was Rhadenos, one of Kydones' most esteemed students. The son of a wealthy Thessalonian merchant, Rhadenos was close to Manuel in age and possessed a great love for literature and philosophy. His first name is not known, however the many letters that Kydones wrote to Rhadenos in Thessalonike indicate that he was close to Manuel, possibly acting as an advisor to him.[25] Another such follower was Theodore Kantakouzenos: Kydones wrote a letter of recommendation to Manuel on his behalf.[26] Two of Manuel's followers thus came to him directly through Kydones. This demonstrates the robust support Kydones gave to his imperial pupil, which must have risked incurring the displeasure of John V in Constantinople.

Significantly, all of these followers had connections with Thessalonike and came from families who possessed land in the environs of the city. It has been already pointed out that this connection might have given them an additional motive for joining Manuel.[27] They must have greatly valued their properties in the city, as joining him in this city meant opposing his father. Breaking relations with John V's government in Constantinople,

---

[23] Kydones, Letter 323, lines 13–14. For Theodore Mouzalon, see PLP 19432.
[24] Kydones, Letter 329, lines 5–6. For Demetrios Kabasilas, see PLP 23986.
[25] See G. T. Dennis, 'Rhadenos of Thessalonica, correspondent of Demetrius Cydones', *Byzantina* 13 (1985), 261–72 and F. Tinnefeld, 'Freundschaft und Παιδεία. Die Korrespondenz des Demetrios Kydones mit Rhadenos (1375–1387/8)', *Byzantion* 55 (1985), 210–44. Tinnefeld focuses especially on the 'triangular' relationship of the three and on Kydones' approach to Rhadenos as a teacher. For Rhadenos, PLP 23986.
[26] Kydones, Letter 250, lines 11–15; PLP 10965.
[27] Necipoğlu, *Byzantium between the Ottomans and the Latins*, 60–1.

these followers of mostly aristocratic background effectively formed an opposing political faction with Manuel in Thessalonike. Indeed, Kydones' letters reveal that these defections to Thessalonike were greatly disapproved of by John V. In one illustrative case, he writes to John Asan that his prolonged stay in Euboea had caused the slanderers at court to accuse him of intending to join Manuel in Thessalonike, which was dubbed 'the new empire'.[28]

Thessalonike not only offered Manuel a base for his offensive against the Ottomans, but also a literary milieu. After Constantinople, Thessalonike was an important intellectual centre in Late Byzantium. Many famed literati, such as John Pothos Pediasimos, Thomas Magistros and Demetrios Triklinos, hailed from there.[29] Manuel's own teacher Demetrios Kydones and another of his esteemed correspondents, Nicholas Kabasilas, were also natives of this city; however, they continued to reside in Constantinople during Manuel's reign in the city. Thessalonike was a spiritual centre as well. In the fourteenth century, more than fifty ecclesiastical structures, including the Thessalonian Hagia Sophia and the famous church of St Demetrios functioned in the city, and many *metochia* adorned the cityscape. A future correspondent of Manuel, Gabriel of Thessalonike, was a novice in the monastery of Nea Mone at the time. Later in life, Manuel would make further Thessalonian friends, including his spiritual fathers, the monks David and Damian, as well as Makarios Makres.[30]

Manuel seems to have appreciated the literary milieu of the city. Many years later, he would reminisce about Thessalonike in these words:

> ... the city, which could be justly termed the Mother of Rhetoricians, or rather, the font of literature. Made fruitful by the sagacity and seriousness of her inhabitants, she has always had numerous offspring of this sort.[31]

---

[28] Kydones, Letter 264, lines 79–81.

[29] For Late Byzantine Thessalonike as an intellectual centre, see F. Tinnefeld, 'Intellectuals in Late Byzantine Thessalonike', *DOP* 57 (2003), 153–72. Henceforth, Tinnefeld, 'Intellectuals'; K. Konstantinides. 'Οἱ ἀπαρχὲς πνευματικῆς ἀκμῆς στὴ Θεσσαλονίκη κατὰ τὸν 14° αἰῶνα', Δωδώνη (1992), 133–50 and D. Nicol, 'Thessalonica as a Cultural Centre in the 14th Century', Ἡ Θεσσαλονίκη μεταξὺ Ἀνατολῆς καὶ Δύσεως. Πρακτικὰ Συμποσίου Τεσσαρακονταετηρίδος, Ἑταιρείας Μακεδονικῶν Σπουδῶν (1980), 121–31, re-printed in D. Nicol, *Studies in Late Byzantine History and Prosopography* (London, 1986), Study X. Henceforth, Nicol, 'Thessalonica'. Also, Constantinides. *Higher Education*, 127–8.

[30] See Tinnefeld, 'Intellectuals', 154; Nicol, 'Thessalonica', 123 and S. Gerstel, 'Civic and Monastic Influences on Church Decoration in Thessalonike: In Loving Memory of Thalia Gouma-Peterson', *DOP* 57 (2003), 225–339; 301. Henceforth, Gerstel, 'Thessalonike Church'. J. Meyendorff, 'Mount Athos in the 14th Century: Spiritual and Intellectual Legacy', *DOP* 42 (1988), 157–65. For Gabriel and Nea Mone, see V. Laurent, 'Une nouvelle fondation monastique des Chumnos: la Néa Moni de Thessalonique', *REB* 13 (1955), 109–32 and Dennis, *Letters*, xi.

[31] Letter 45, lines 83–5.

It must nevertheless be emphasized that many Thessalonian literati of the period, including Kydones and Nicholas Kabasilas, went to Constantinople for their education and the advancement of their careers. Although Thessalonike was a prominent political centre, Constantinople had the advantage of being home to the imperial court. In the capital, rhetorical and literary talent could earn the favour and support of powerful members of the socio-political elite, possibly even that of the emperor himself. Evidence for the presence of libraries in Thessalonike is scarce for the period, and so it seems clear that for the literati, Thessalonike could not offer the same opportunities as Constantinople.[32]

While in the city, either as a despot in 1369–72 or as emperor in the 1380s, Manuel seems to have received significant instruction and guidance from Ivankos, a rhetorician who ran a school in the city.[33] In his *Epistolary Discourse to Ivankos* (1404–8), Manuel reminisced about their past, and twice explicitly refers to Ivankos as his teacher and as the one who 'had provided him with the seed of *logoi*'.[34] This expression closely mirrors those used by Manuel for Kydones. In the epistolary discourse, the emperor vividly describes how Ivankos used to guess his thoughts from his expressions, and reminiscences about how his teacher would recite his favourite authors, who, sadly, are not named.[35] Manuel moreover remarks that he provided him counsel and comfort during his troubles as the ruler of the city.[36] This is significant since it indicates that Ivankos may have influenced Manuel's actions as ruler. Unfortunately, save for these fleeting references, no more can be discerned about their relationship. Nonetheless, more than twenty years after their time together in Thessalonike, Manuel addressed this lengthy and carefully composed discourse to him. Since not many people received such compositions, one can conclude that he must have particularly cherished Ivankos' friendship.

Manuel's first datable letters and his famed *Discourse to the Thessalonians* are from his reign in Thessalonike. This period can be characterized as almost an 'early phase' in Manuel's authorship. In this regard, a discussion of his letters also invites a discussion of literary networks, the *theatron* and the circulation of his works. Most Byzantine texts, be it an oration, dialogue, poem or a philosophical treatise, would have been circulated

---

[32] Tinnefeld, 'Intellectuals', 161–5.

[33] For Ivankos, see Dennis, *Letters*, xivi and PLP 7973. His school is discussed in Mergiali, *L'enseignement*, 150. He is also mentioned by John Argyropoulos as a judge in Thessalonike; see J. Argyropoulos, 'La comédie de Katablattas', eds. P. Canivet and N. Oikonomides, Δίπτυχα 3 (1982–83), 5–92, 46–7. Henceforth, 'La comédie de Katablattas'.

[34] Letter 45, lines 66–71, 209–10.   [35] Letter 45, lines 32–4.   [36] Letter 45, lines 70–1.

amongst the literati and even performed to an audience in a *theatron* – a literary gathering. This tendency was especially marked as far as letters were concerned. *Theatra* could by organized by a patron who offered his/ her support for the authors belonging to this literary circle. In *theatra*, the literati would evaluate the performed pieces, and it was a place to receive acclaim and feedback – or critique. Furthermore, having their works circulated and performed could help the authors to spread their political views and messages through their writings. Ultimately, *theatra* could effectively fuse *logoi* and politics.[37] Thanks to *theatra* and the circulation of works among the literati, pieces usually reached a far wider audience than the direct addressee of the work. Byzantine authors were thus writing not only for their direct addressees but were also targeting a much broader network of interconnected literati. Throughout his lifetime, Manuel would make ample use of his network to advertise his political stance and strengthen his position as emperor.

It is difficult to gain detailed insight into Manuel's literary network and his *theatron* while in Thessalonike. For this period of five years, only nine letters by Manuel survive.[38] Five of Manuel's surviving letters were written to Kydones, two to Nicholas Kabasilas and one to Triboles, the secretary of Despot Theodore in the Morea. Although the replies of Kydones survive, those of Kabasilas and Triboles do not. Although there are no hints regarding the existence of other *theatra* under other Thessalonian literati, Manuel's letters do refer to the existence of a *theatron* under him in Thessalonike.[39] This is not surprising at all, since as an emperor-author, Manuel was in an ideal position to reside over a *theatron* in Thessalonike.

Similarly, it is not possible to discern precisely the identities of people in Manuel's *theatron*. It is safe to assume that the officials and literati close to him would have been present. In fact, Kydones' letters indicate that Rhadenos was present during the performances of the letters Manuel received, as well as that of the *Discourse to Thessalonians*.[40] Further, Kydones' letters to Manuel often hint at an audience who listened to the letters sent by him and others.[41] One can therefore conclude that letters from and to Manuel clearly circulated beyond their intended recipient.

---

[37] Gaul, *Magistros*, 17–33; I. Toth, 'Rhetorical Theatron in Late Byzantium: The Example of Palaiologan Imperial Orations', in *Theatron: Rhetorische Kultur in Spätantike und Mittelalter*, ed. M. Grünbart (Berlin and New York, 2008), 429–49, and P. Marciniak, 'Byzantine Theatron: A Place of Performance?', in *Theatron: Rhetorische Kultur in Spätantike und Mittelalter*, ed. M. Grünbart (Berlin and New York, 2007), 277–85.
[38] Letters 3 to 11.   [39] See especially Letter 9.   [40] Kydones, Letter 262, 270.
[41] For instance, Kydones, Letter 254 and 294.

During the years 1382–7, Kydones corresponded with Tarchaneiotes, Manikiates, Calopheros, John Asan, Neilos and Nicolas Kabasilas, and with Manuel's brother Theodore, the despot of Morea. His letters to the Despot Theodore indicate that Kydones was also in touch with Triboles, another of Manuel's correspondents from this period.[42] Moreover, Kydones was in frequent contact with Rhadenos in Thessalonike. He also wrote to Theodore Kantakouzenos, yet another member of Manuel's entourage.[43] Finally, Kydones addressed several other Thessalonians of unknown names. In one instance, he tells his recipient that Manuel had already informed him via letters of the new political affairs that the latter had reported.[44] Kydones' frequent and dense correspondence with Thessalonike further demonstrates his support for Manuel's regime. On the whole, these letters indicate the existence of a tightly knit literary network around Manuel in Thessalonike. At least through Kydones, his letters were certainly circulated among the Constantinopolitan literati, and this is a crucial factor in analysing the political messages that Manuel embedded in his Thessalonian letters.

This networking around Manuel was also significant for the dissemination of political messages in the letters concerning his separatist regime in Thessalonike. A Byzantine letter was not just a 'private' message addressed to one single individual, it could also serve as a medium of self-promotion for the authors. In his Thessalonian letters, Manuel seeks to promote and legitimize his rule and always refers to himself as *basileus*, or emperor. He also carefully moulds his image as an idealized, selfless ruler facing turmoil and casts himself in the role of a victim of circumstances. Through his self-representation, Manuel attempted to rouse sympathy for his rule in Thessalonike, and perhaps, also aimed at gaining more supporters.

During his reign in the city, Manuel appears to have written to many literati in Constantinople. Twice Kydones refers to Philalites, Manuel's letter bearer, as 'filling' the city with his letters.[45] He boasted of his victories and represented his regime as a heroic stance against the Ottomans. The politicized nature of these networks is also evident from the difficulties the letter bearers faced in Constantinople under pressure from John V. In one instance, the letters had their seals broken, read by the officials of the emperor and only then delivered to their recipients.[46] Similarly, on another

---

[42] See for instance Kydones, Letter 293.
[43] There are numerous letters addressed to Rhadenos; Letter 254 for Theodore Palaiologos.
[44] Kydones, Letter 314, referring to the negotiations with the papacy in 1385.
[45] Kydones, Letter 247 and 250. [46] Kydones, Letter 303.

occasion, for reasons of safety, Rhadenos refrained from keeping Kydones informed via letters.[47]

Manuel's letters allow us invaluable insights into his life over a period of many years. His first datable letters are from his time in Thessalonike. In the earlier scholarship, the emperor's letters were criticized for their high style prose, literary features and their lack of 'concrete' information about events. However, Manuel composed these letters in the tradition of Byzantine epistolography and thus his understanding of a letter was very different from that of modern scholars.[48] The primary purpose of a letter was not to convey information; this could be delivered by the letter bearer as an oral message. Instead, the letter was supposed to betoken a friendship and to be used as a literary artefact. The mere composition of a letter signalled a desire to communicate, while abundant allusions, quotations and other such literary features flaunted not only the author's talent, but also the great esteem felt for his correspondent. These layers of meaning were to be peeled away slowly and savoured. A letter was, in some ways, a written conversation between correspondents. Its careful, elaborate language allowed the correspondents to transcend daily life and to immerse themselves in literary pleasures. The high style and the literary features of a Byzantine letter were thus essential components meant to be appreciated and desired, both by the author and the audience.

Manuel's letters are adorned with the traditional themes of Byzantine epistolography: friendship, silence, absence and separation. Most of the time, the letters lack what modern scholars call 'concrete', factual information. Instead his letter collection consists of elegantly written compositions, adorned with literary features that are notable for their vivid imagery. As an emperor, Manuel did not write letters to seek patronage or help, though he clearly sought to idealize his rule, subtly promoting, legitimizing and defending his deeds, through careful self-representation. A meticulous reading of his letters and an analysis of their literary features, such as allusions, metaphors and self-representation, allow us to discern Manuel's aspirations, thoughts and emotions.

---

[47] Kydones, Letter 316.

[48] For Byzantine letters, see M. Mullett, 'The Classical Tradition in the Byzantine Letter', in *Byzantium and the Classical Tradition: University of Birmingham Thirteenth Spring Symposium of Byzantine Studies 1979*, eds. M. Mullett and R. Scott (Birmingham, 1981), 75–93; M. Mullett, 'Originality in the Byzantine Letter: the Case of Exile', in *Originality in Byzantine Art, Literature and Music: A Collection of Essays*, ed. A. Littlewood (Oxford, 1995), 39–53. Henceforth, Mullett, 'Originality'; S. Papaioannou, 'Letter Writing', in *The Byzantine World*, ed. P. Stephenson (Routledge, 2010), 188–99. See P. Hatlie, 'Life and Artistry in the Publication of Demetrios Kydones' Letter Collection', *GRBS* 37/1 (Spring 1996), 75–102; F. Tinnefeld, 'Kriterien und Varianten des Stils im Briefcorpus des Demetrios Kydones', *JÖB* 32/2 (1982), 257–64; F. Tinnefeld, *Briefe des Demetrios Kydones: Themen und literarische Form* (Wiesbaden, 2010).

Literary Exchanges, Dire Realities

Manuel's reign in Thessalonike witnessed the emergence of new literary themes in his correspondence. These themes underscore Manuel and Kydones' desire to promote the new regime in Thessalonike. For instance, both Manuel and Kydones make frequent references to freedom, using it in the sense of liberty from the Ottomans. Kydones is especially fond of this theme of freedom. In one letter he even addresses Manuel as the 'free one', expressing hope that one day they would make public sacrifices to God on behalf of freedom.[49] Freedom was a prominent discourse in Ancient Greek political culture. It furthermore had Christian connotations, since alongside that of free-will and free choice, freedom was seen as an important Christian ideal. Arguably, Manuel and Kydones' references to freedom were influenced by both traditions. Kydones' above-quoted expression also hints at the imagined atmosphere of a Greek city state, which would have provided a fitting model for Manuel's Thessalonike. It resembled a resilient 'Hellenic' city state facing 'barbarian' conquest; only the role of the Persians in this case, was filled by the Ottomans.[50] In another letter, Kydones writes to Manuel that he will honour the *patris* by making it rule over freedom.[51] As a native of Thessalonike, the city was indeed Kydones' *patris*, but in this context, it equally becomes Manuel's *patris*. In a third letter, Kydones proudly tells Manuel that nothing shall prevent him from being called the founder of a free commonwealth.[52] While Kydones employed the theme of freedom in his orations and other writings, this emphasis in his correspondence with Manuel is unique to the latter's reign in this city. During this period, freedom almost becomes a 'Thessalonian' theme in the correspondence of Manuel and Kydones.

Other such 'Thessalonian' themes that emerge in Manuel and Kydones' letters are *patris*, fatherland, and St Demetrios. Unsurprisingly, Kydones always underlines that the city was his *patris*, and Manuel emphasizes this notion of fatherland to his two Thessalonian correspondents, Kydones and Nicholas Kabasilas. When Manuel rebukes the two for not paying enough attention to how precarious Thessalonian affairs had become, he does this by pointing out that Thessalonike is their *patris*. Likewise, on one occasion,

---

[49] Kydones, Letter 244, lines 21–2.

[50] It is worth noting that the juxtaposition of freedom and servitude in the political sphere had its origins in fifth-century BC, the aftermath of the Persian wars. D. G. Angelov, 'Three Kinds of Liberty as Political Ideals in Byzantium, Twelfth to Fifteenth Century', in *Proceedings of the 22nd International Congress of Byzantine Studies*, I: *Plenary Sessions* (Sofia, 2011), 312.

[51] Kydones, Letter 247, lines 41–2.

[52] Kydones, Letter 249, lines 60–1. '. . . οὐδέν σε κωλύσει τῆς κοινῆς ἐλευθερίας ἀρχηγέτην κληθῆναι.'

he reminds Kydones that the Thessalonians are his own citizens.[53] Both Manuel and Kydones invoke, moreover, the cult of St Demetrios, the patron saint of Thessalonike and a potent symbol of the city. Manuel expresses to Nicholas Kabasilas his firm belief in the help provided by the saint in the struggles against the Ottomans.[54] By highlighting the notion of *patris* and evoking the city's native saint, Manuel seems to have attempted to escalate the urgency of his plight for his Thessalonian correspondents. Through the Thessalonian motifs he used in his letters, Manuel strove to stress his new and strengthened ties with the city as its emperor. All these themes vanish from his letters after the end of his reign in Thessalonike.

Despite the optimistic tone of Manuel's early Thessalonian letters, circumstances soon turned sour on the political front. The jubilant atmosphere of the Serres victory did not last long. Less than a year later, at the beginning of September 1383, the Ottomans conquered large sections of Macedonia.[55] A more devastating blow came on 19 September when the Ottomans finally captured Serres. The city passed under Turkish rule for good.[56] The tone Kydones' letters alter significantly after these events; plunging into deep despair.[57] But much worse was to come for Thessalonike and Manuel: by November 1383, at the latest, the Ottomans had laid siege to the city.[58]

The siege hit Thessalonike hard. Manuel was soon writing to Kydones about the unwillingness of the populace to defend their city, and their correspondence suggests that the populace preferred to surrender to the Ottomans. These letters offer insight not only on Manuel's troubles, but also on his witty and playful side. He laments his pressing need for money and playfully complains that although Kydones' gift of *Souda*, a popular Byzantine lexicon, made him rich in words, he needed coins. Still able to retain a sense of humour under the circumstances, Manuel goes on to argue that all Thessalonians could be called 'Soudases' since they were able to come up with so many excuses for their lack of co-operation. The Thessalonians, he argues more seriously, had to be persuaded that to suffer willingly for the sake of freedom was far nobler than to submit to the Ottomans for safety. This letter demonstrates that the Thessalonians

---

[53] Letter 4, lines 10–11; Letter 3, line 19; Letter 6, line 22.
[54] Letter 6, lines 46–50 and Kydones, Letter 299, line 72.   [55] Dennis, *Thessalonica*, 74.
[56] Dennis, *Thessalonica*, 75–6. Schreiner, *Kleinchroniken*, Chronik 55/6; 60/ 9; 72/555; 74/1; 107/13. Neşri, 210–11, notes the capture of Serres. The chronology of the narrative also places the event in 1382.
[57] Kydones, Letter 289, lines 4–5.
[58] Dennis, *Thessalonica*, 76, who calculates the date of Thessalonike's fall as April 1387 and claims that the siege lasted for four years.

favoured surrender as soon as the siege started, rather than to follow Manuel to freedom.

Despite his disillusionment with the Thessalonians, Manuel acknowledged that poverty was choking the city; his letter hints that the population's desire to surrender to the Ottomans was chiefly to attain financial privileges.[59] This inclination was practical and should not be viewed as cowardice: according to Islamic law, cities that had willingly surrendered could not be sacked, nor could their citizens be enslaved. Those most inclined to surrender were likely the poor, whose situation had already deteriorated because of the siege. This, coupled with the very real threat of enslavement, naturally led many to favour submitting to the Ottomans from whom they would receive some minor financial protection. True, they would be taxed by the Ottomans, but Manuel's administration was already imposing taxes.

Ultimately, the Ottoman pressure greatly accelerated the pre-existing socio-economic tensions between the population and the *archontes*. Despite the danger, the latter continued to amass wealth and neglected the plight of the suffering citizens. The *archontes* neither contributed to the defence costs, nor shared their wealth in order to ease the hunger of the citizens.[60] Though he was the ruler of Thessalonike, it is clear that Manuel's authority over the *archontes* was not strong enough to bend them to his will. And without the necessary economic resources he could not ease the suffering of the poor. This increasing poverty and polarization was Manuel's main obstacle in persuading the Thessalonians to fight, and for the remainder of his reign in Thessalonike, he struggled against his own subjects.

Demetrios Kydones was the one correspondent to whom the young emperor could confide. Despite the public and politicized nature of most Byzantine letters, a close reading of these texts offer us a glimpse into the 'public intimacy' that existed between the two men. Manuel's letters are illustrative of his deep affection for his former teacher. Although their relationship is much celebrated among scholars, its more personal aspects have not received much attention. Instead their correspondence has been used as a means to obtain data on the events of the period; however, a careful analysis of these letters reveals many layers of intimacy between the two, particularly in the relaxed, informal tone of the writing and the

---

[59] Letter 4, lines 8–22.
[60] Necipoğlu, *Byzantium between the Ottomans and the Latins*, 42–3 and 71–2. See also Necipoğlu, 'Archontes', especially 138.

inclusion of several personal jokes. One such joke concerns a manuscript of Plato.

Amidst all the trouble in Thessalonike, at Kydones' request Manuel obtained a copy of Plato from the monks of Mount Athos and sent it to his friend. This is a remarkable gift, as manuscripts, which were expensive, and were usually lent, rather than sent through letter exchange in this manner.[61] The exact contents of the manuscript are unknown, but it had an eventful journey before it finally reached Kydones, falling into the hands of Turkish pirates almost immediately after it was sent. In a letter, Kydones playfully personified the book as Plato:

> He suffered the fate of prisoners, after having been freed (μετὰ τὴν ἐλευθερίαν), the pirates captured him. Moreover, he suffered this in front of the gates of his fatherland … he also became enslaved to the Turks, so that none of the Hellenes, even if they died a long time ago, would escape feeling the humiliation of the success of the Turks … Since you have delivered such a man from slavery, we pray that you may do the same in the case of our enemies and that freedom returns to all of the genos …[62]

As in his previous letters, Kydones places an emphasis on freedom, elegantly weaving this ideal and other political statements into his narration of the eventful journey of the book. Thessalonike here symbolically becomes Plato's *patris*, yet another 'Thessalonian' theme that Kydones employed in his letters. Consequently, Manuel's city is represented as the last bastion of the Hellenes, either ancient or contemporary.

For his part, Manuel jokes that 'Plato' had reason to be grateful to him for being delivered from the monks. Since the monks had not used the manuscript at all, Manuel claims, it was not alive at the time. He alludes here to a passage in Plato's *Phaedrus* which discusses the immortality of the soul, claiming that something that does not move is a not alive. Kydones, Manuel continues, not only brought Plato to life, he also allowed him to

[61] See I. Ševčenko, 'Society and Intellectual Life in the 14th Century', in *Actes du XIVe Congres International des Études Byzantins, Bucarest 1971*, vol. 1, (Bucharest, 1974), 69–92, re-printed in I. Ševčenko, *Society and Intellectual Life in Byzantium*, (London, 1981), Study I, 91. Henceforth, Ševčenko, 'Intellectual life'. For manuscript lending, see A. Karpozilos, 'Realia in Byzantine Epistolography X–XII c.', *BZ* 77 (1984), 20–37, 31.

[62] Kydones, Letter 259, lines 10–13, 20–1, '… μετὰ τὴν ἐλευθερίαν πειρατῶν ἐπειράθη, καὶ ἡ τῶν αἰχμαλώτων αὐτὸν διεδέξατο τύχη, καὶ ταῦτ' ἐν προθύροις τῆς αὐτοῦ πατρίδος, ἵνα καὶ τοῦτο τῷ προτέρῳ Πλάτωνι παραπλήσιον ἔχῃ. καὶ ὡς ἔοικεν εἵμαρτο καὶ τοῦτον νῦν Τούρκοις δουλεῦσαι, ἵνα μηδεὶς Ἑλλήνων κᾶν πάλαι τεθνηκὼς ᾖ τὴν τῶν καθαρμάτων τούτων ὕβριν ἐκφύγῃ … ᾖ τὸν ἄνδρα τοῦτον τῆς δουλείας ἀπήλλαξας, εὐχόμενοι δὲ ταύτην κἀπὶ τῶν κοινῶν πολεμίων ἐνδείξασθαι, καὶ διὰ σοῦ τῷ κοινῷ γένει τὴν ἐλευθερίαν ἐπανελθεῖν …'.

live as a philosopher.[63] Such jokes are not found in the letters addressed to other correspondents of both Manuel and Kydones. This further indicates their intimacy and mutual affection. The tale of the Plato manuscript offered the two correspondents an opportunity to demonstrate their literary wit, accentuating it with political and philosophical digressions. These letters can be considered fine specimens of Byzantine epistolography, which seamlessly blend the literary, with the political and the philosophical.

Another such letter exchange concerns the production of a manuscript. Manuel appears to have ordered that Kydones' letters and other works be compiled into a book in Thessalonike, and that blank pages should be left for future letters.[64] With feigned modesty, Kydones seems to have requested his writings back. Manuel fiercely protested in his reply, suggesting that even if Kydones' feelings towards him had changed, he would preserve his love for his teacher.[65] Kydones, in his turn, teases Manuel for wishing to make him a figure of ridicule for future generations by compiling his works.

This amusing letter exchange contains a rather enigmatic joke between them: Kydones declares that he consents to the compliment, only because he fears that he might otherwise be forced to consume the lentil soup or dish of 'Chalazas.' The editor of the letter, Raymond Joseph Loenertz, offers no explanation for these lines; however, Mazaris' satire mentions a Chalazas, as a doctor in Thessalonike. As no other Chalazas can be identified for the period, the reference was probably to the same person. One can surmise that Manuel and Kydones were enjoying a joke at Chalazas' expense. Perhaps, Chalazas prescribed a foul-tasting lentil soup or dish to his patients, as a dietary requirement,[66] or he may have once served such a meal to his guests. Whatever the actual meaning of this joke, it serves to reflect the intimacy between Manuel and Kydones.

The letter exchange between the two men in this period offers further such insights. In his letters, Manuel repeatedly summons his teacher to his side and pleads for help in persuading the Thessalonians to endure the

---

[63] Letter 3, lines 4–17. Plato, *Phaedrus*, 24D.

[64] Letter 5 and Kydones, Letter 263 to Akakios, lines 10–11, 17–19. The contents of this manuscript are not known, except that they clearly contained some of Kydones' letters. Kakkoura has identified textual parallels between Manuel's *Ethico-Political Orations* and Kydones' *On Despising Death*. See *Ethico-Political Orations*, 95. Thus, this work, too, was perhaps included in the manuscript.

[65] Letter 5, lines 16–17.

[66] Kydones, Letter 326, lines 24–5, 'ἡμεῖς δὲ σιγήσομεν ἵνα μὴ καὶ ἡμῶν τις τὴν τοῦ Χαλαζᾶ φακῆν κατεχέῃ.' Mazaris, 66–7. Concerning this surname, a certain Andronikos Chalazas is also attested in a monastic act from the thirteenth century, see PLP 30359. Φακῆ, *phake*, could refer both to a lentil itself and to a lentil soup, A. Dalby. *Tastes of Byzantium* (New York, 2003), 222.

siege. He complains that even the 'manuscript Plato' had braved the seas in the middle of winter, but Kydones pays no heed to his *patris* or to his friend. Plato was lucky, Manuel continues, he *alone* could enjoy Kydones' company, but if affairs were to go smoothly, Manuel's desire to see Kydones would make one hour seem like a lifetime.[67] Like the personalized jokes, such fervent declarations of affection are not found in the letters he addressed to others.

On another occasion, he again asks Kydones to help him persuade his fellow Thessalonians, strongly emphasizing that of all people, it was Kydones that he needed. This demonstrates Manuel's exceptionally high regard for him both as a politician and orator. 'Do not employ your rhetoric on us', Manuel writes, 'that rhetoric we require you to employ with others on our behalf'.[68] In contrast to his insistent pleading with Kydones, Manuel never summons Nicholas Kabasilas, another Thessalonian and his other correspondent from the period, to his side.[69] This difference in tone is an indication of Manuel's special affection and regard for his former teacher. For his part, his letters reveal that Kydones felt enough at ease with his imperial student to share jokes with him, to advise and sometimes to even mildly rebuke him.

The Discourse to the Thessalonians

Aside from his letters, circumstances soon prompted Manuel to compose one of his first works. Early on during the siege, as mentioned by Isidore Glabas, the Ottomans sent an ultimatum to the Thessalonians offering a choice between paying a heavy tribute or having their city captured.[70] Manuel delivered an advisory speech (*Advisory Discourse to the Thessalonians when They Were Besieged*) to an assembly in response to this ultimatum.[71] Convoking an assembly in times of crisis to was by no means unprecedented in Byzantium, and the practice was also common in Thessalonike. For instance, Manuel's grandfather John VI Kantakouzenos had convoked another such assembly in 1347. *Archontes*, ecclesiastics and other leading figures in the city would be present, and sometimes ordinary people would also be allowed to attend.[72]

---

[67] Letter 3, lines 17–28.

[68] Letter 4, lines 30–1, '… ὅρα δὲ μὴ χρήσῃ τῇ ῥητορείᾳ πρὸς ἡμᾶς παραιτούμενος ἢ σε πρὸς ἄλλους ὑπὲρ ἡμῶν χρήσασθαι ἀξιοῦμεν.'

[69] See Letters 6 and 7.   [70] Laourdas, *Isidore*, 31, lines 9–11.

[71] B. Laourdas, 'Ὁ συμβουλευτικὸς πρὸς τοὺς Θεσσαλονικεῖς τοῦ Μανουὴλ Παλαιολόγου', *Μακεδονικά* 3 (1955), 290–307. Henceforth, the *Discourse to the Thessalonians*.

[72] See Tafrali, *Thessalonique*, 71–5; Maksimović, *Byzantine Administration*, 225; C. N. Tsirpanlis, 'Byzantine parliaments and representative assemblies from 1081 to 1351', *Byzantion* 43 (1973), 432–83. Henceforth, Tsirpanlis, 'Parliament'. D. Kyritses, 'The Imperial Council in Byzantium

That Manuel's advisory oration was delivered is clear from the letters that were exchanged between Manuel and Kydones; thus, it is clear the oration was not composed as a rhetorical exercise. Furthermore, in one of his homilies, Isidore Glabas refers to Manuel as advisor (βουλευτής). This epithet was usually not applied to emperors.[73] He seems to have taken note of the oration, and perhaps sought to acknowledge Manuel's wish to present himself as an advisor to the city. However, it is not possible to define Manuel's audience. Whether Manuel was only addressing the *archontes* or also ordinary citizens is unclear. The only tantalizing reference to the intended audience can found in a letter by Kydones, who mentions the presence of Rhadenos.[74]

Alongside the 1380s letters, *The Discourse to the Thessalonians* is one of Manuel's earliest surviving works. More crucially, it is one of his two orations and his only advisory speech (*symbouleutikos*). The oration often comes up in scholarly literature because of what it reveals about the political circumstances; yet, despite being frequently referred to, it has never been studied in its entirety or on its own merits, and its themes and literary/rhetorical features remain unexplored.[75] The discussion below will address these issues. On the whole, the *Discourse to the Thessalonians* occupies a special place among Manuel's oeuvre not just as an early work, but also for its rhetorical/literary features.

From the very beginning, the oration mentions that some people considered paying the tribute demanded, or even surrendering the city to the Ottomans. The main goal of the oration, therefore, was to persuade the Thessalonians to fight, and this 'persuasive' aspect of the oration is very dominant. On the whole, the oration emphasizes its 'forcefulness' (δεινότης), a rhetorical element described by Hermogenes. Following the rules set by Hermogenes, Manuel lists every thesis and expands upon them in order to persuade his audience. Remarks such as 'the majority (οἱ πλείους) is disposed carelessly when the dangers are not immediate' and 'many people push me to do these things (accepting the terms of the

---

73 and the Tradition of Consultative Decision-Making in Byzantium', in *Power and Subversion in Byzantium, Papers from the 43rd Spring Symposium of Byzantine Studies, Birmingham, March 2010*, eds. D. Angelov and M. Saxby (Farnham, 2013), 57–67, 63; Kantakouzenos, III, 33–41.

73 Letter 8; Kydones, Letter 262, line 4. Laourdas, *Isidore*, 31, line 17. Tsirpanlis, 'Parliament', 444–5, remarks that *ekklesia* was used to denote a gathering.

74 For Manuel's own references to the assembly, *Discourse to Thessalonians*, 295, line 2; 298, line 35. 'La comédie de Katablattas', 50–1, also mentions a senate (συγκλήτος) of the Despot Andronikos, son of Manuel, in 1408–23.

75 Even Dennis' book on Manuel's rule in Thessalonike merely summarizes its main points, see Dennis, *Thessalonica*, 81–5.

Ottomans) ... ' strongly indicate the presence of a non-cooperating faction.[76] The emperor points out to his audience that it is not their material goods (τὴν ἔξω οὐσίαν) that the Ottomans desire, but rather to master the citizens themselves (ὑμᾶς αὐτοὺς χειρώσασθαι).[77] Consequently, Manuel signifies that what is at stake is not a matter of mere tribute, but of independence, and this forms one the chief themes of the oration.

Another theme that Manuel expands upon are the perilous finances of the city. As previously discussed, the *archontes* refused to contribute to defence expenses. Likewise, the poor protested the newly imposed taxes. In the *Discourse*, Manuel often targets the *archontes* in his constant emphasis on the need to contribute financially to the defence of the city.[78] He argues that the problems can be solved by 'spending *a little* money' (μικρὰ χρήματα ἀναλίσκοντες); it is crucial that none of the citizens spare his property. In another part of the oration, he urges citizens to contribute generously (μεγαλοψυχίᾳ) and to spend ungrudgingly (ἀφθονῶς) for the defence of the city.[79] Manuel seems to have viewed finances as the greatest obstacle for victory, probably correctly. The great emphasis he places on this suggests that the citizens not only disagreed with the emperor's policy of resistance, but also did not want to give financial help. All in all, these themes in the oration make manifest the clear dissent between Manuel and his subjects.

Manuel's advisory speech stands apart from his other works for the following reason: it places an exceptional emphasis on the opposition of freedom and servitude (δουλεία); references to freedom and its derivatives occur no less than twenty times.[80] As in Kydones' letters, Manuel uses freedom in the sense of liberty from political servitude. This is a widespread political concept that can easily be found in the works of any Byzantine author, but here Manuel innovatively categorizes three types of servitude.[81] The *Discourse* represents an occasion where Manuel comes up with a minor political theory. One type of servitude, he claims, is the lawful kind that is

---

[76] *Discourse to the Thessalonians*, 296, lines 6–7; 300, lines 34–6; 298, lines 34–5.

[77] *Discourse to the Thessalonians*, 298, lines 21–3.

[78] Some of the *archontes* even resorted to burying their money. Necipoğlu, *Byzantium between the Ottomans and the Latins*, 71–2.

[79] *Discourse to the Thessalonians*, 295, lines 6–7; 302, line 5.

[80] Manuel also refers to *douleia* in the *Dialogue with a Persian*, but in the sense of being enslaved to impiety and his discussion is very brief. He does not use the word *eleutheria* in that work.

[81] It is worth noting that in his oration Περί Καλλιπόλεως, Kydones also refers to the choice of the Byzantines as one between freedom and servitude. *PG* 154, cols. 1009–36. For Manuel's use of these concepts, Angelov, 'Liberty', 321–6.

owed to the rulers. The second is enslavement to tyrants, for whom ruling means only the daily oppression of those under them. The third and the worst form is enslavement to 'barbarians', whose chief goal is to trample upon Christians.[82] Naturally, the first form of 'lawful' servitude coincides with that expected of the Thessalonians towards Manuel, and the last and worst form, corresponds with submission to the Ottomans. By offering this original categorization of servitude, Manuel subtly pushes his audience towards the first option: obeying him as their ruler.

In addition to these categories, Manuel characterizes the economic privileges of Thessalonike as a type of freedom: 'You, for whom freedom is significant and well-known, never had masters . . . . you did not owe the taxes that Romans and all other free people owe to the emperors. Instead of these, you had benevolence . . . .'[83] He argues that, for the Thessalonians, it would be unbearable if other cities should have more claim to freedom. The emperor targets here a very specific 'Thessalonian' concept in order to persuade his audience to fight for their freedom, both in a political and an economic sense. Like any good orator, Manuel customized his speech for his intended audience in an attempt to increase its persuasiveness.

In his oration, Manuel similarly highlighted other components of the Thessalonian civic identity. In the first lines of his speech, he addressed the assembly as 'those who dwell in the city of Philip'. In another passage, he urged the Thessalonians to remember that they share the same *patris* with Alexander and Philip, and that they descend from their *genos*.[84] By emphasizing the Hellenistic past of the city he was able to draw comparisons between the Ancient Greek conflict with the Persians and his own with the Ottomans. Furthermore, Manuel refers to the patron saint of the city, St Demetrios, calling him 'our guardian' and reminding his audience of the saint's past assistance to the city.[85] He also presents himself as a devotee to

---

[82] *Discourse to the Thessalonians*, 296–7, lines 34–9; 1–2.

[83] *Discourse to Thessalonians*, 297, lines 3–9. The exact nature of these privileges is not clear. See Maksimović, *Byzantine Administration*, 249–58; E. Patlagean, 'L'immunité des Thessaloniciens', in Εὐψυχία. *Mélanges Offerts à Hélène Ahrweiler*, 2 vols. (Paris, 1998), 591–601 and A. E. Laiou, 'Economic Concerns and Attitudes of the Intellectuals of Thessalonike', *DOP* 57 (2003), 205–23. In his 'Anti-Zealot' Discourse, Nicholas Kabasilas also refers to it in this sense. See Ševčenko, 'Anti-Zealot', 26.

[84] *Discourse to Thessalonians*, 295, line 1. For Thessalonike as the city of Phillip, see E. Russell, *Literature and Culture in Late Byzantine Thessalonica* (London, 2013), xviii; for the usage of Alexander in late Byzantine literature, see A. Karathanassis, 'Philip and Alexander of Macedon in the literature of the Palaiologan era', in *Byzantine Macedonia, Identity, Image and History*, eds. J. Burke and R. Scott (Melbourne, 2000), 111–15, 112.

[85] For the special status St Demetrios enjoyed in the city, see Tafrali, *Thessalonique*, 130–48; E. Russell, *St. Demetrius of Thessalonica: Cult and Devotion in the Middle Ages* (Oxford, 2010); S. Gerstel,

St Demetrios, and a citizen of Thessalonike, by using the possessive 'our' for the saint as opposed to his usual usage of 'your' when addressing the Thessalonians. In order to appeal to his Thessalonian subjects, Manuel stresses the most important elements of their civic identity. Tellingly, one of his major focuses in the entire work is the topic of finances. In introducing this subject he was probably trying to address the issue that had driven a wedge between him and the citizens.

An analysis of the oration reveals several intriguing Aristotelian influences. In fact, the first instances of Manuel's lifelong use of Aristotle as an ethical framework can be traced in this oration. Aristotelian ethics had been widely copied and commented upon among the Byzantine literati for many centuries, and especially enjoyed an upsurge in the twelfth century. Its ability to blend with Christian ethical thought contributed to its popularity, and as a result many Byzantine literati relied on Aristotelian ethics in their philosophical work.[86] While Manuel's acquaintance with the work is nothing out of the ordinary, throughout his lifetime he showed an especially and unusually intense preoccupation with Aristotelian ethics. In the future Aristotelian ethics coloured his dialogues, and he composed ethico-political works under the same influence, including the *Foundations of Imperial Conduct* and the *Seven Ethico-Political Orations*.

In the *Discourse to Thessalonians*, Manuel presents his audience with four alternatives; slavery, death, to live and to 'live well' (εὖ ζῆν).[87] *Eu zen*, which can be roughly translated as 'to live well', is used in Aristotle in the sense of leading a rational, virtuous life through choice (προαίρεσις).[88] Following Aristotle, Manuel differentiates in the oration between merely living and 'living well', claiming the superiority of the latter and equating 'living well' with leading a virtuous life as a free Christian.

He further laces his oration with the concepts of voluntary (τὸ ἑκούσιον) and involuntary action (τὸ ἀκούσιον). These are key categories in

---

'Thessalonike Church', 229; C. Morrison, 'The Emperor, the Saint and the City: Coinage and Money in Thessalonike from the Thirteenth to Fifteenth Centuries', *DOP* 57 (2003), 173–203, 189 and especially R. J. Macrides, 'Subversion and Loyalty in the Cult of Saint Demetrios', *BSl* 51 (1990), 189–97, which highlights the 'separatist' nature of the saint's cult and its uniqueness to Thessalonike. *Discourse to the Thessalonians*, 295, line 10. '... λαμπροτέρου καὶ ἡμετέρου πολιούχου ...'.

[86] For Aristotelian ethics in Byzantium, see the essays in C. Barber and D. Jenkins (eds.) *Medieval Greek Commentaries on the Nicomachean Ethics*, (Leiden, 2009).

[87] *Discourse to the Thessalonians*, 299, lines 36–9.

[88] Aristotle, *Nicomachean Ethics*, I, iv, 4–5. In her commentary to the *Ethico-Political Orations*, noting the difficulty of translating the term, Kakkoura defines *proairesis* as 'committed, deliberative disposition' and chooses to leave the term untranslated. See *Ethico-Political Orations*, 79. For reasons of convenience, I have translated the term as 'choice', but gave the Greek term in brackets whenever the term was referred to for the first time in a chapter.

Aristotelian ethics where choice (προαίρεσις), which leads to virtue, can only come into being through voluntary action.[89] Manuel emphasizes the voluntary nature of the actions of the Thessalonians; for instance, he urges them to become friends with death willingly (ἑκόντες) for the sake of freedom. Likewise, he speaks of the shame of becoming enslaved with a willing conscience (ἐθελουσίῳ γνώμη). Their voluntary actions will lead them to virtue, Manuel argues, which in turn, will lead to 'living well'. The underlying argument here is that the Thessalonians should 'voluntarily' join him in resisting the Ottomans and that it is the correct action in order to obtain virtue and the good life.

Similarly, the emperor criticizes people who see no difference between a life of slavery and that of free will (αὐτεξούσιον).[90] This last example does not stem from Aristotle, but from Christian thought. The notion of a free will (αὐτεξουσία) was a frequent topic of discussion in Byzantine theology, especially in the Fathers. It was accepted that free will, the capability to will things and to choose the virtuous action as opposed to a sinful one, was what differentiated humans from animals.[91] By using this term, Manuel implies that those Thessalonians who fail to distinguish between a life of slavery and that of free will, are also unable to distinguish between a life directed by Christian morality and a life under the oppression of the 'infidel' Ottomans. In a final twist, the Ottomans are represented as the voluntary (ἑκούσιοι) slaves of demons. Manuel subtly implies that their impiety is voluntary and a result of choice, further vilifying their portrayal in the oration.[92] Thus, it can be argued that the whole oration is oriented within an ethical framework influenced by Aristotle.

The oration is Manuel's only *symbouleutikos*, as a result it stands out from the rest of his oeuvre for being very politically charged. Here, fittingly, Manuel adopts the persona of a Greek orator advising the senate of a city state.[93] It has been noted that the assemblies convoked in Byzantium still bore some resemblance to those of antiquity; a parallel that Manuel also seems to have been aware of.[94] Moreover, the circumstances strengthened

---

[89] Aristotle, *Nicomachean Ethics*, III, ii, 13.

[90] *Discourse to the Thessalonians*, 299, lines 9, 28; 300, line 7.

[91] *Autexousia* is absent in Aristotelian ethics and is instead found in the Fathers, especially John of Damascus. See W. Telfer, 'Autexousia', *Journal of Theological Studies* 8.1 (1957), 123–9. Henceforth, Telfer, 'Autexousia'.

[92] *Discourse to the Thessalonians*, 299, line 14.

[93] See P. Brown, *Power and Persuasion in the Late Antiquity* (Madison, 1992), 35–70 for the relationship of *paideia*, rhetoric and politics among the elite in Late Antiquity.

[94] Tsirpanlis, 'Parliament', 449.

this parallel. Manuel was acting as advisor in an environment which essentially functioned now as a city state, albeit one ruled by an emperor, and Thessalonike, like the Greek cities threated by the Persians, faced enslavement by outsiders. In the oration, Manuel also creates a 'Hellenistic' atmosphere. He refers to the citizens as the descendants of Philip and draws explicit links between them and the past Greeks, as well as between the Persians and the Ottomans.[95] Still, he does not neglect Christianity, but instead incorporates it as an identity marker against the Ottomans: the Thessalonians are not only fighting to preserve the political autonomy of their city, but they are also defending the Christian faith against the 'infidels'.

Manuel emphasizes his role as an advisory orator, explaining and weighing each political option available to the city. He engages with the audience and creates the setting of a Greek city's senate, as if the decision with regard to the Ottomans is to be taken collectively. While it is possible that in such assemblies, decisions were sometimes made by voting, there is no such indication of this in Manuel's oration.[96] Although his oration might have encouraged the otherwise uncooperative citizens, it was taken for granted that the final decision lay with Manuel. And indeed, he would continue resisting the Ottomans despite the unwillingness of the Thessalonians. Nonetheless, in the oration the ultimate decision is represented as being a democratic one.

It possible that for the *Discourse* Manuel had the example of a specific orator in mind: that of Demosthenes, who was very widely studied and emulated by the Byzantine literati.[97] Not only does Manuel borrow directly from the *First Olynthiac*, but his depiction of the Ottomans also has some vague parallels with that of Philip in the *Philippics* and *the*

---

[95] *Discourse to the Thessalonians*, 296, line 1; 297, lines 26–32. ' . . . ἐκηβόλοις τόξοισιν ἐξηρτημένα, ποιητὴς ἂν εἴποι τις, δόρασι καὶ ἱππικῇ σεμνυνόμενα. . . .'

    The expression 'ἐκηβόλοις τόξοισιν ἐξηρτημένα' seems to be a direct borrowing from Aeschylus, *Prometheus Bound*, where Prometheus uses the exact same expression to describe the Scythians, just like Manuel. Aeschylus, *Prometheus Bound*, line 711. This play was edited by Demetrios Triklinos in Thessalonike in the fourteenth century (c. 1320–30). Moreover, after the new edition was made, it was sometimes studied in schools. In the fifteenth century, scholars such as Andronikos Kallistos were familiar with the editions of Triklinos, Fryde, *Renaissance*, 278–9, 289. Thus, combined with Manuel's precise use of Aeschylus' expression, it is possible that Manuel was familiar with the play.

[96] This possibility is raised by Tsirpanlis, 'Parliament', 444–5.

[97] Hermogenes also gives *Philippics* as an example for *symbouleutikos* and claims that Demosthenes has the best combination of force, beauty and other elements, Περί Ἰδεῶν, *Hermogenis Opera*, ed. H. Rabe (Leipzig, 1913; reprinted 1969), 380–5. See also the example of Thomas Magistros, who wrote a declamation based on Demosthenes' *Against Leptines* to subtly criticize the tax policies of his time, G. Martin, 'Rhetorical Exercise or Political Pamphlet? Thomas Magistros' exploitation of Demosthenes' Against Leptines', *GRBS* 46 (2006), 207–26.

Olynthiacs.[98] Like Philip, the Ottomans are haughty, militarily superior and trick the cities into surrendering with false promises, but treat them badly regardless of promises made.[99] Manuel's circumstances and those of Demosthenes in these orations are also very similar. Both are trying to persuade an unwilling audience, which does not perceive how critical the situation is, to resist the enemy. Both point out that the citizens are fighting for their freedom; it is not their material goods, but their liberty that the enemy desires. When Manuel proudly sent his work to his beloved Kydones, the latter was not remiss in noting the echos of Demosthenes in the oration.[100]

Manuel underlines these parallels with Demosthenes also from a stylistic point of view. In contrast with his other oration, the *Panegyric to John V* (1390), he frequently employs the vocative, such as 'O Men' and 'O those present'.[101] His Greek is very elevated and the sentence structures are extremely complex, much more so than in his other works.[102] The reasons for Manuel's decision to opt for such difficult language in this early work is not known, but one can make several guesses. It is possible that while trying to emulate Demosthenes' style, in this early work, Manuel also attempted to show off his own sophistication by employing complex sentence structures and ambiguity. There is nothing to suggest that the existing oration is a revised version of a much simpler text. Although he may have revised the oration, he does not seem to have altered it significantly. In his later works, however, the emperor never again opted for such difficult language.

This oration moreover stands out from Manuel's other works on account of its masculinity; manliness and a vigilant fighting spirit are emphasized at every opportunity. In one instance, Manuel directly accuses

---

[98] *Discourse to the Thessalonians*, 296, line 28–9: 'ὁ νῦν καιρὸς μονονουχὶ φωνὴν ἀφιεὶς προσδιαναγκάζων ...' and 'Ὁ μὲν οὖν παρὼν καιρός ὦ ἄνδρες Ἀθηναῖοι, μόνον οὐχὶ λέγει φωνὴν ἀφιεὶς ...'; Demosthenes, *First Olynthiac*, 2.

    Even the first lines of the *Discourse* seem to bear a resemblance to Demosthenes: for instance, compare ' Ἔδει μέν, ὦ παρόντες...' and the opening lines of the *First Olynthiac*, 1, ' Ἀντὶ πολλῶν ἄν, ὦ ἄνδρες Ἀθηναῖοι....'

[99] Even some of Manuel's wording resembles the description of Philip by Demosthenes. Compare the Ottomans in the *Discourse to the Thessalonians*; '... ἐν ᾗ τοῖς πεπραγμένοις μεθύοντες ...', 300, lines 28–9 and the *First Philippic*, '... μεθύειν τῷ μεγέθει τῶν πεπραγμένων...', 47. However, this is a vague connection as the metaphor of being drunk with arrogance/haughtiness, especially for the 'barbarians', was commonplace in Byzantium.

[100] Manuel's Letter 11; Kydones, Letter 262, lines 24–5, '... ὥσπερ τινὰ Δημοσθένους ἠχὼ τοῖς ἀκούουσιν ἐπιπέμπεις.'

[101] *Discourse to the Thessalonians*, 245, line 1; 296; line 4–6; 296, line 19; 300, line 67.

[102] While clarity was an important feature in Byzantine rhetoric, obscurity could still be appreciated, G. Kennedy, *Greek Rhetoric under Christian Emperors* (Princeton, 1983), 95–100.

the dissidents of unmanliness, claiming that no one would listen to such a man in the council: as a blemish to manhood, his place is at home with the women and the Romans should not allow him even to enter the council.[103] As in antiquity, rhetoric employed in the political sphere was closely connected with masculinity, the 'masculine' tone in the oration is therefore worth noting.[104] Manuel's advisory oration also builds on this heritage.

The Last Struggles

The Thessalonians did not heed Manuel's counsel in the slightest, and discord continued among the citizens. Isidore Glabas still emphasized the importance of unity and co-operation, on one occasion, even condemning the miserliness of the *archontes*.[105] Moreover, around this time, notably Isidore defended Manuel against the Thessalonians in his homilies. Furthermore, the emperor seems to have imposed a new tax upon the citizens, no doubt to finance the defence of the city.[106] Nothing else can be gleaned about this tax; however, it is clear that the on-going blockade of Thessalonike greatly impacted the economic circumstances. The poor suffered the most, barely able to keep starvation at bay, but the *archontes* also endured hardship in the loss of further lands through the Ottoman raids in the countryside.[107] In this regard, Isidore's homilies are full of hints of Manuel's growing unpopularity with his subjects, both on account of the city's sufferings and the financial measures he introduced. While imposing a new tax was a logical decision for a ruler to raise money for defence, it can also be considered an ill-advised move. The new taxation only served to further alienate the oppressed populace from Manuel and his cause.

As in the aftermath of the battle of Maritsa in 1371, Manuel resorted to confiscating ecclesiastical property. It was yet another risky decision. In one

---

[103] *Discourse to Thessalonians*, 299, lines 26–34.

[104] M. W. Gleason, *Making Men: Sophists and Self-Presentation in Ancient Rome* (Princeton, 1995), especially xx–xii, 62–3, 160. In his discussion of Late Antiquity, the author emphasizes the orators' displays of masculinity in their sheer exertion, addressing a large audience in an unamplified voice. Although the effect is now lost on the modern reader, Gleason argues that delivering a speech was a rhetorical test of masculinity.

[105] Lampros, 'Isidore', 350; Tsirpanlis, 'Isidore', 567. For Isidore's references to *philargyria*; Tsipanlis, 'Isidore', 560, 565.

[106] Laourdas, *Isidore*, 31–2: 'εἰ δ ἡ τῶν πραγμάτων νῦν ἂν to refer to taxes or tribute payment, and not to burden in a more general sense. dzenstance of 'ὡμαλος φορὰ πρὸς συστολὴν ἀναγκάζει...' Isidore consistently uses φόρα to refer to taxes or tribute payment, and not to burden in a more general sense.

[107] Necipoğlu, *Byzantium between the Ottomans and the Latins*, 39–70.

of his homilies, Isidore Glabas condemns the confiscation of the properties of the monastery of St Sozon. Isidore does not blame Manuel directly, but rather those men who 'push the emperor into this'. Yet he makes the rather curious remark that he would never cease to speak against these acts, even if 'one threatened to cut his tongue off'.[108] This stands in clear contrast to his other homilies where Isidore lavishes praise upon Manuel. Ultimately, Manuel's necessary but harsh fiscal policies even alienated Isidore, one of the few who supported his stance against the Ottomans.

Whether Manuel himself was present during this particular homily, cannot be discerned.[109] A few months after this homily was delivered, in spring 1384, Isidore Glabas sailed to Constantinople and abandoned his see. He was not to return until the city passed into Ottoman hands. Although the reasons for his abrupt departure are unknown, it is not impossible that the archbishop left his see because of a clash with Manuel over the issue of confiscations. At any rate, Isidore was later accused of abandoning his see, which suggests that his departure was not authorized by Manuel.[110]

The 'tongue cutting' threat referred to by Isidore is especially intriguing. In this regard, Manuel's oeuvre reveals a notable tendency to employ 'tongue' related imagery concerning disputes and confrontation. Could Isidore's remark that he would continue to protest, 'even if one were to threaten to cut off his tongue', be a reference to Manuel? Or was it simply a rhetorical expression? In one prominent instance, Manuel addresses a 'certain foolish person' in his Anacreontic verses (composition date unknown). This person, he claims, would cause a nuisance even if 'one were to tear off his tongue from its root'.[111] There is nothing to suggest that this poem was addressed to Isidore,

---

[108] Lampros, 'Isidore', 350–1: 'Ἐγὼ δὲ οὔτ' ἐλέγχειν ἀποστήσομαι τὰ θεομισῆ, εἰ καὶ τὴν γλῶτταν τὴν ἐμὴν ἐκτεμεῖν τις ἠπείλησεν . . . .' Dennis also makes the suggestion that the 'Anti-Zealot' Discourse of Kabasilas might have been addressed to Manuel on account of his confiscations in 1383; see Dennis, *Thessalonica*, 91. Kabasilas indeed refers to the fact that monastic properties were seized for the purposes of defence and to fund repair of the walls; Ševčenko, 'Anti-Zealot', 100–101. But, as argued by Ševčenko in a later article, this theory cannot be supported further, see I. Ševčenko, 'A Postscript on Nicholas Cabasilas' "Anti-Zealot" Discourse', *DOP* 16 (1962), 403–8; 405–6.

[109] As the archbishop, Isidore could be expected to preach in Hagia Sophia, which probably was the episcopal seat of the city, see Bakirtzis, 'Thessalonike', 52. In another homily, Isidore explicitly refers to Manuel's presence among the congregation, see Tsirpanlis, 'Isidore', 565.

[110] See Dennis, *Thessalonica*, 93–4 for various theories, including the clash with Manuel and the possibility that he may have been on a mission for Manuel. However, there is no evidence to support the latter theory and Isidore does not mention such a reason when defending himself against the accusation for deserting his see. In his letter to Dositheos Karantenos, Isidore glosses over the reasons for his departure, Lampros, 'Isidore', 379.

[111] This poem is found in *PG* 156, cols. 575–6, '. . . τίς σου τὴν γλῶσσαν πρόρριζον ἐξανασπάσῃ . . .'. See Appendix 2 for the poem and its translation.

and yet the similarity between the expressions is striking.[112] Ultimately, Isidore's 'tongue' remark might reflect a real threat made by Manuel, who frequently employed such imagery.

If this were indeed the case, it would not be a unique instance in Manuel's life. He was to clash many times with ecclesiastical figures, such as Makarios of Ankyra and Patriarch Euthymios, as well as engaging in heated disputes with theologians such as Manuel Kalekas. Significantly, all cases resulted in the disgrace of Manuel's opponent. The one exception was Euthymios, who died before the dispute became more heated. An examination of Manuel's relations with ecclesiastics does reveal a pattern of fall outs. On the whole, it is not improbable that Isidore Glabas left Thessalonike on account of a dispute with Manuel. Though in autumn 1384 he sent a letter to Thessalonians urging them to obey their ruler, it is nevertheless telling that Isidore chose not to return until Manuel abandoned the city.[113]

Thessalonike's situation did not improve in the slightest and Manuel's unpopularity further increased.[114] By 1384, he was in dire need of military help. He was to receive no help from Epiros, as its despot Thomas Preljubović died, effectively ending the submission of the despotate to Thessalonike.[115] The caesar of Thessaly, Alexios Angelos, was another ally to whom Manuel turned for help. Alexios Angelos is an obscure figure who is chiefly known from a synodal act of 1382, in which the emperors recognize him as caesar of Thessaly. He was also the recipient of grants by Manuel and Despot Theodore of Morea during the 1380s.[116] Yet it is unclear whether Angelos was able to provide Manuel with any military support. After Angelos' death, Manuel instead formed a triple alliance with his brother Despot Theodore of Morea and Nerio Acciajuoli, the lord of Corinth. He helped his brother and Nerio against the Navarrese, while the latter supported him against the Ottomans.[117] In the winter of 1384/85

---

[112] This will be discussed in Chapter 9.   [113] Lampros, 'Isidore', 385.

[114] Kydones, Letter 299 and 324. Both Kydones and Isidore Glabas complained of the citizens' hostility towards Manuel, see Lampros, 'Isidore', 385. Kydones, Letter 273, lines 19–23.

[115] Dennis, *Thessalonica*, 108. Thomas Preljubović's successor chose to pledge his loyalty to Constantinople.

[116] Dennis, *Thessalonica*, 104–5. For a discussion of Alexis Angelos and these grants, see R. J. Loenertz, 'Notes sur le règne de Manuel II à Thessalonique, 1381–1387', *BZ* 50 (1957), 390–6, 392; and R. J. Loenertz, 'Un prostagma perdu de Théodore I Paléologue regardant Thessalonique (1380/ 82?)', *EEBΣ* 25 (1955), 170–2; G. Theocharides, 'Δύο νέα ἔγγραφα ἀφορῶντα εἰς τὴν Νέαν Μονὴν Θεσσαλονίκης', *Μακεδονίκα* 4 (1957), 315–51; Laurent, 'Thessalonique', 109–32; Dölger, *Regesten*, nos. 3173a, 3175a, 3175b, 3180a, 3181c, 68–70.

[117] Dennis, *Thessalonica*, 114–24. The main source for this alliance is a letter from James, the bishop of Argos. Dennis cites his letter in *Thessalonica*, 119–21. Despite his confused chronology, Chalkokondyles, 82–3, is also aware of this alliance between Manuel and Theodore.

Manuel sent Theodore 100 cavalrymen though he does not seem to have received any military support in return.[118]

Theodore also married Nerio's daughter, Bartolomea, in order to cement this alliance. It is intriguing – and remarkable – that Manuel himself did not marry in order to obtain an advantageous alliance. Clearly, as he was acting independently, he was in no need of his father's approval. But in the end, although Theodore's marriage allowed Nerio Acciajuoli to achieve his dream of becoming the duke of Athens, it brought Manuel no help against the Ottomans. Manuel instead turned to Venice, requesting military assistance and a loan of 6,000 ducats. In turn, both Manuel and Theodore agreed to cede some territory to Venice. Their proposals, however, were met with refusal in the senate.[119] It is likely that Venice believed that Manuel was doomed for failure and that Thessalonike would eventually fall to the Ottomans, whose displeasure they did not wish to incur.

Manuel's alliance with Theodore not only demonstrates his desperate need for military aid, it also reflects his esteem for his younger brother. Theodore, who had been such a comfort to Manuel during their imprisonment in Anemas, was now a key figure in the Peloponnese. From the moment of his accession as the despot in 1382 until his death in 1407, Theodore, like his elder brother, would face many adverse political and socio-economic conditions. As the despot of Morea, Theodore had to contend with the Navarrese Company in Achaia and the Venetian presence in Modon and Koron. In this volatile political geography where the alliances were continually shifting, Theodore also struggled against his rebellious Morean subjects.[120] While Theodore's political career can be thus sketched, his personality eludes us: there are no texts that shed light on his person. In Manuel's writings Theodore is always seen though the lense of the emperor; an ideal younger brother who readily follows him in all things. While in Thessalonike, Manuel addressed a letter to Triboles, Theodore's secretary, voicing his ardent desire to see his brother:

> For that land holds my dearest brother and friend and son. Can you imagine how much I desire to see it? You know how passionately I yearn to be able to see him, whom I regard as myself, whenever I wish to do so. If it were not possible with gold, I would readily choose to purchase at the price of my

[118] Dennis, *Thessalonica*, 119–21.
[119] Dennis believes that Manuel may have offered Lemnos, Thasos or Kitros to Venice, as the republic was mostly interested in acquiring naval bases, see Dennis, *Thessalonica*, 124. For Manuel's proposal to the Senate, see Loenertz, *Démétrius Cydonès Correspondance*, I, Appendix A and Thiriet, *Régestes*, I, no. 693, 168; Chrysostomides, *Monumenta*, no. 28, 60–1.
[120] See the introduction by Julian Chrysostomides, *Funeral Oration*, 16–25.

own limbs either the harp of Orpheus or the arrow of Abaris. More than anything else I would choose never to be separated in body from him to whom I am united in spirit night and day.[121]

His language conveys Manuel's great affection for Theodore. Tellingly, he claims that their separation has nothing to do with their own desires and wishes but rather because both have put the common good of the Romans first. Again, he fuses his declaration of affection with politics in order to promote his self-image as a ruler.[122] As in the *Funeral Oration*, Manuel's his relationship with Theodore is portrayed as a means of highlighting his sacrifices as a dutiful ruler.

During this period, Manuel also wrote a letter of recommendation to Theodore on behalf of a certain Kanonas, who seems to have come to Thessalonike in order to assist Manuel.[123] Through Kanonas, Manuel lavishes praise on his brother, but he also inserts yet another political statement: that 'he and I are one and the same person' – in other words, to serve Theodore was the same as serving Manuel. Though his statement certainly reflects the close bond and mutual love between the brothers, which equated loyalty to one as loyalty to both, Manuel also generally sought to highlight this 'unity' when he wanted to make a political statement. This tendency is apparent both in his letters and in the *Funeral Oration*, where Theodore's policies are actually that of Manuel and his successes are in part appropriated by his brother. While this letter is a token

---

[121] Letter 9, lines 29–36. 'ὡς δὲ καὶ αὐτὴν τὴν τοῦ Πέλοπος ἣν οἰκεῖς νῦν, ἔχουσαν γάρ μοι τὸν γλυκύτατον ἀδελφὸν καὶ φίλον καὶ υἱόν. Πῶς οἴει με ταύτην ποθεῖν ἰδεῖν; ἴσθι με ἔφεσιν κεκτημένον τοσαύτην τοῦ δεδυνῆσθαι βλέπειν ὁπόταν ἐθέλοιμι ὃν ἔγωγε ἴσον ἄγω τῇ ἐμῇ κεφαλῇ, ὡς καὶ μέλους ἐμοῦ πρίασθαι ἑλέσθαι ἑτοίμως εἴπερ οὐκ ἐνῆν χρυσίου ἢ τὴν τοῦ Ὀρφέως κιθάραν ἤγουν τὸν Ἀβάριδος ὀϊστόν. ἑλοίμην γὰρ ἂν ἀντὶ πάντων ᾧ γε σύνειμι τῇ ψυχῇ νύκτωρ καὶ μεθ' ἡμέραν μηδὲ τῷ σώματι κεχωρίσθαι.'
　　Manuel also calls Theodore his 'son' in the *Funeral Oration*, in order to stress his dominance over Theodore as his elder brother, *Funeral Oration*, 218–19.
[122] Letter 9, lines 37–8.
[123] Letter 13. Dennis dates this letter to 1390 on the assumption that Theodore must have sent Kanonas to help Manuel suppress the rebellion of John VII. However, he cites no evidence for this dating. For a number of reasons, I believe that this letter was written around 1384–5, when the two brothers were allied. First, of all, there is nothing in the manuscript arrangements which indicate that this letter did not belong to the group of the Thessalonian letters. As Dennis himself notes, the letters were arranged in chronological 'packets', but the letters were not chronologically ordered within that 'packet'. Thus, this letter could be the 'last' letter of the Thessalonike 'packet', and there is no evidence to show that it was written after Letter 12 (1390). Letter 13 could chronologically precede Letter 12. Moreover, it would have been very difficult for Theodore to send Kanonas to Constantinople during the siege of 1390, as the sea entrance to the city was blocked. Thessalonike on the other hand was open to the sea during 1383–7, as well as being accessible via land to a degree that John V was able to send envoys who were able to come in front of the city walls. Furthermore, for the greater part of the 1390 siege, Manuel was not in Constantinople, but was trying to secure help in Rhodes.

of genuine affection for his brother, Manuel still seizes the opportunity to make subtle political propositions to his audience.[124]

Without imminent help, Thessalonike continued to suffer. Even as early as 1384, Kydones was advising Rhadenos to leave Thessalonike, claiming that Manuel would not object.[125] Significantly, even Kydones seems to have lost his faith in the enterprise, though Manuel was still entertaining hopes for a truce with the Ottomans as a plausibility. He asked the Venetian Senate to mediate between the two parties, and John V also sent envoys to the Ottoman commander Hayreddin Pasha.[126] These attempts failed, and Manuel avowed to Kydones that he would do anything to avoid poverty. His dire need for money is also demonstrated by his confiscation of the cargo of two Catalan ships in 1385.[127] Around the same time, in a letter to Kydones, Manuel quotes from the New Testament: 'Ask, and you shall be given', followed by the announcement that he has placed his hopes in Rome and sent the pope an embassy.[128]

The only information regarding Manuel's negotiations with the papacy comes once more from the letters of Demetrios Kydones. A papal legate was received in Thessalonike, who by mistake had first gone to Constantinople and was met with a frosty reception. Once more, it is worth noting that Manuel did not attempt to create a marriage alliance for himself through the papacy. On the whole, it seems that a union was not concluded, and that these negotiations brought no benefit to Manuel.[129] Demetrios Kydones, as might be expected, comes across as rather enthusiastic about the project.[130] He offered to contact his connections in Rome on Manuel's behalf; however, his letter also makes plain that Manuel had not informed him initially of his intentions. Therefore, the decision to negotiate with the papacy cannot be assigned to Kydones' influence or advice.[131]

In the spring of 1385, while Manuel was struggling against the Ottomans in Thessalonike, his father and Andronikos clashed once more.[132] A battle was fought near Melitas, between Constantinople and Selymbria, and,

---

[124] Letter 13, lines 21–2. [125] Kydones, Letter 324. [126] Kydones, Letter 318, lines 5–7, 21–2.
[127] Dennis, *Thessalonica*, 130–1. [128] Letter 8, especially lines 1–7 and 8–19.
[129] Dennis argues that a union was concluded. However, he himself notes that no source, Byzantine or Western, mentions such a union, which would have certainly been mentioned had it been concluded. His claim is based on Kydones' letter 327, where Kydones states that Thessalonike was persuaded to render the same honours to the Son as to the Father, Letter 327, lines 14–15. Yet, this seems to be a rhetorical remark which conveys Kydones' belief that the project was soon to materialize.
[130] See Dennis, *Thessalonica*, 132–50 for a detailed discussion of the contacts between Manuel and Pope Urban VI. As the evidence is scarce, Dennis himself is not able to do more than summarize Kydones' letters and offer some hypotheses.
[131] Kydones, Letters 302, 314 and 327. [132] Kydones, Letter 308, narrates the events to Manuel.

after great bloodshed, Andronikos was defeated. He retreated to Selymbria, and this time it would not be the Venetians or the Genoese who intervened, but death. After a brief illness, Andronikos died on 28 June. His claim to the Byzantine throne would be taken up by his son John VII, and like his father before him, John would stir up civil strife in his attempts to gain the crown.[133] Manuel's thoughts on the battle and on his estranged brother's death are unknown. The only reference he would ever make to Andronikos was to mention him as Theodore's brother, the emperor, in a brief remark in the *Funeral Oration*.[134]

During the remaining two years of the siege, the situation in the city did not improve. Kydones, who once called Thessalonike the 'New Empire', now urged his student Rhadenos to flee the city.[135] Moreover, John V's displeasure with Manuel became even more bitter, and he was angered further by the imminent loss of the city. Already by 1385, Kydones was commenting upon how the letters from Thessalonike had their seals broken and their contents read before they reached their addressees.[136] More alarmingly, John V convoked an assembly to make a decision about Manuel's future and to draw up a formal document of reprimand against his son. Kydones was not allowed to the meeting on the account of his intimacy with Manuel.[137]

At this point, it is clear from Kydones' letters that Manuel was intending to leave the city. Guided by his great esteem for his teacher, Manuel once more turned to Kydones for advice about to what to do.[138] This explicit request for advice represents a unique moment in Manuel's life; he would never make such a request again, and the fact that he does so must be a reflection of his great despondency. In reply, Kydones advised Manuel against going to a foreign land. Though Manuel also considered joining his brother Theodore in the Morea, Kydones cautioned him against this idea, too, claiming that the two brothers were likely to end up engaging in power struggles in the Peloponnese.[139] Instead, he urged Manuel to submit to his father in Constantinople, as he believed that John V would forgive his son.[140]

[133] Dennis, *Thessalonica*, 109–11. Schreiner, *Kleinchroniken*, Chronik 7/ 20; 10/4.
[134] *Funeral Oration*, 104–5.   [135] Kydones, Letter 332, lines 16–26.
[136] Kydones, Letter 305, lines 18–22.
[137] Kydones, Letter 342, lines 16–22 and Letter 346, lines 1–12. Kydones also alludes to the *prooimion* he had drafted in 1371 for Manuel and expresses his fear that now he might be ordered to write a document of reprimand.
[138] The letter suggests the request for advice came from Manuel. Kydones, Letter 342, lines 1–13.
[139] Kydones' advice was far-sighted; after Manuel's death, his own sons would strive against each other over the empire's Morean territories.
[140] Kydones, Letter 342.

Manuel's thoughts on the subject can only be traced in Kydones' letters. It is evident that he had finally decided that his cause in Thessalonike was lost. Despite his initial success against the Ottomans, Manuel had failed in his enterprise. Moreover, what lay at the root of his failure was his unpopularity with the Thessalonians. It must have been a bitter experience for him. Both Kydones and Isidore Glabas commented upon the hostility of the Thessalonians toward Manuel. Even Chalkokondyles, despite his confusion about the events, was to note the harsh attitude of the citizens towardsthe future emperor.[141]

Manuel's brief rule in Thessalonike is notable for its radical break from Constantinople. It is also a rather significant turning point in his political career. Despite his best efforts, Manuel did not manage to assert authority over the *archonte*s. Similarly, his taxation policies alienated the population. It is also during this period that Manuel began to make use of his network to advocate his political stance, as well as employing his rhetorical skills to the same end. All these aspects of his rule would be later repeated in his career. While Manuel did his best not to let Thessalonike fall, it must also be pointed out that he had personal motives for his stubborn perseverance. After all, he had established himself in Thessalonike out of wounded pride, to defy his father. While his efforts to keep the city in Byzantine hands and the harsh fiscal measures he took were in the best interest of his territories, they were also to further his own aims. He must have been aware that should the city fall he would be disgraced. Ultimately, despite his bravery against the Ottomans, Manuel's reign in Thessalonike was not an disinterested or inherently heroic enterprise.

For the remainder of his life, apart from a brief passage in the *Discourse to Kabasilas* (c. 1387), Manuel would never speak about his brief rule in the city. Yet his remark in the *Funeral Oration* on the relationship between Theodore and the Moreans is suggestive: ' . . . he retained their love for him, which is something rare, for people's love usually diminishes with time . . . '[142] Might this be a reflection of his own bitter experiences in Thessalonike? Similarly, in his *Ethico-Political Orations*, Manuel pointed out that when a city was divided, it would inevitably be lost, and that citizens should follow a 'good' ruler.[143] Clearly, this episode in his life had

---

[141] Chalkokondyles, 74–5.

[142] *Funeral Oration*, 114–15, '. . .οὐ προϊὼν ἡμαύρωσε τὸν εἰς αὐτὸν ἔρωτα (τοῦτο δὴ τὸ σύνηθες οἶμαι ὡς τὰ πολλὰ πανταχοῦ γίνεσθαι). . . .' In reality, Theodore was not very popular among the Moreans, but what is interesting here is Manuel's side remark that people's love for their rulers usually diminishes, which seems to be based on personal experience.

[143] *Ethico-Political Orations*, 334, also noted by the editor, Kakkoura.

taught Manuel a lesson: he was never again to pursue a policy of military offensive against the Ottomans.

Manuel sailed away from Thessalonike in April 1387 as secretly as he had arrived five years earlier, and a few days later, the city willingly surrendered to the Ottomans. Like everything else, *The Discourse to Thessalonians* had utterly failed to fulfil its purpose. Manuel himself did not heed Kydones' advice. Instead, with a small group of followers, he sailed to the island of Lesbos. For the next three years, he languished in exile, uncertain about his imperial title and future.

CHAPTER 4

In Limbo

It seems that I have been destined to live with continuous war, with every kind of war.[1]

Manuel's ship laid anchor at Lesbos probably a few days after he sailed away from Thessalonike.[2] Why he decided to take refuge in Lesbos, an Aegean island under Genoese rule, is unclear, as are the events that took place during his stay there. The years 1387–9 are probably the most obscure period in Manuel's life. His whereabouts and activities can scarcely be discerned. Possibly, Kydones, who had rather friendly relations with Francesco Gattilusio, the Genoese ruler of Lesbos, influenced his decision to seek refuge in Lesbos. In a letter to Rhadenos, Kydones mentions having written to Gattilusio on Manuel's behalf, yet despite his intercession, the ruler refused to allow Manuel entry into the island's capital, Mytilene. His refusal was based either on the account of Manuel's large entourage, or because he feared the anger of Sultan Murad.[3] Exiled and humiliated, Manuel camped on a barren spot on the island under the burning sun.[4]

---

[1] *Discourse to Kabasilas*, (Letter 67), lines 18–19. 'Εἵμαρτο γάρ μοι, ὡς ἔοικε, πολέμῳ συζῆν ἀεί, καὶ τούτῳ παντοδαπῷ.'
[2] See Barker, *Manuel II*, 59–82, which relies on Kydones' letters to construct a narrative. Also, S. W. Reinert, 'The Palaiologoi, Yildririm Bayezid and Constantinople: June 1389–March 1391', in *Tὸ Ἑλληνικόν: Studies in Honor of Speros Vryonis Jr.*, ed. J. S. Langdon, et al., 2 vols. (New Rochelle, NY, 1993), i, 289–365, reprinted in S. W. Reinert ed. *Studies in Late Byzantine and Early Ottoman History* (Farnham, 2014), Study IV, for events leading to the uprising of John VII in 1390. Henceforth, Reinert, 'The Palaiologoi and Yildirim Bayezid'. Although now outdated, Charanis, 'Strife', 286–314 also deals with the years in question.
[3] Kydones, Letter 350. Despite his confused narrative of Manuel's rule in Thessalonike and its aftermath, Chalkokondyles takes note of Manuel's refuge in Lesbos, as well as the refusal of Francesco Gattilusio to allow him into town; see Chalkokondyles, 84–5.
[4] *Discourse to Kabasilas*, lines 1–18. For the family of Gattilusio and Lesbos under their rule, see W. Miller, 'The Gattilusj of Lesbos (1355–1462)', in W. Miller, *Essays on the Latin Orient* (Amsterdam, 1964), 313–54.

The Discourse to Kabasilas

During the two months he spent on Lesbos, Manuel wrote his *Epistolary Discourse to Kabasilas* (c. 1387). It is a relatively short, but engaging work. Although often dismissed by scholars for its lack of 'historical data', Manuel's self-representation, ideas on authorship and the subtle political messages he weaves into the text, render the discourse a notable work.[5] After all, Manuel's goal in penning the composition was not simply to bequeath 'historical data' for future scholars, he had other literary and political goals.

The Discourse to Kabasilas opens with a vivid elaboration on Manuel's surroundings. The scene is established as unbearably hot, rocky and barren. Manuel adds that he is not only fighting with the stifling heat outside his tent, but also with his own stifling thoughts.[6] Though this depiction of the summer in Lesbos corresponds to the climate of the island, it is also a literary strategy that introduces a pessimistic atmosphere for the work and appeals to the sympathy of the audience. The oppressive tone is reinforced only a few lines later when Manuel voices his bitterness over the Thessalonian affair. Slowly, it is revealed that the discourse functions as his *apologia* for events in Thessalonike.

> It seems that I have been destined to live with continuous war, with every kind of war. When I had to dwell in the Great City I warred, as everyone knows, against those attempting to take it by war, and never neglected a single one of my duties. Then, in your native city I kept on fighting against the enemies of the faith. But, those on whose behalf I chose to face death each day and night ought to have responded in like manner … these same people were fighting along with the enemy … they gave themselves to weaving subtle intrigues against us who were tyrannizing over them – indeed this was their constant

---

[5] This epistolary discourse was first edited by Loenertz, who points out that Manuel did not include the discourse among his letters. R. J. Loenertz, 'Manuel Paléologue, épitre à Cabasilas', Μακεδονικά 4 (1956), 38–46. Yet Dennis included this work in his edition of Manuel's letters since he believed that it also seemed to be a personal letter, see Dennis, *Letters*, 204. The only article that deals with it is S. W. Reinert, 'Coping with Political Catastrophe in 1387: Representations of Nature in Manuel II Palaiologos' *Epistolary Discourse to Kabasilas*', in S. W. Reinert, *Studies on Late Byzantine and Early Ottoman History* (Farnham, 2014), 1–21, Study V. Henceforth, Reinert, 'Kabasilas'. He notes some of the political messages in the text and focuses on the data provided by the discourse on Lesbos.

[6] *Discourse to Kabasilas*, lines 4–9, 15–17. 'τὸ δ' ἐφ' ᾧ χωρίον ἤδη παροικοῦμεν, μηδὲ τέγους γοῦν εὐποροῦντες ἀλλ' ἐν σκηναῖς, πρῶτον μὲν λιθώδους οὔσης τῆς νήσου λιθῶδές ἐστι καὶ αὐτό, ἔπειτ' οὐδὲ ὕλῃ κομᾷ. Γυμνὸν δὲ ὂν καὶ ἡλίῳ προσομιλοῦν ἀνίσχοντί τε ἅμα καὶ περὶ μεσημβρίαν καὶ δὴ καὶ μέχρι δυσμῶν, βαρύ τι καὶ οὐ φορητόν, πῶς οἴει, τοῦτο ποιεῖ …. καὶ τοίνυν πολεμοῦμεν μὲν τῷ πνίγει τῷ αἰσθητῷ προσβάλλοντι θύραζε σφοδρῶς, ἔνδοθεν δὲ πρὸς τούτῳ συμπλέκεσθαι ἀνάγκη καὶ τῷ τῶν λογισμῶν …'.

accusation – and were not allowing them to betray their freedom in a vile manner.⁷

Manuel strives to portray himself as an ideal ruler, one whose sacrifices were disregarded by ungrateful subjects. Through this literary strategy, he shifts the blame for the fall of the city onto the shoulders of the Thessalonians. His goal, arguably, was to redeem himself not only in the eyes of his Thessalonian addressee, Kabasilas, but anyone who might read or listen to the work. The whole discourse is thus permeated with strong political undertones.

It is worth reflecting upon the fact that Manuel seems to have been accused of tyranny by the Thessalonians. One interpretation of this is that the Thessalonians may have indirectly accused him of oppressing the population for his own interests. As one might expect, Manuel treats this accusation as an outrageous slander. Yet it was not without basis. He had, after all, imposed himself upon the citizens as a ruler without the permission of the reigning emperor, and his rule was therefore unlawful. This was perhaps overlooked by the citizens in the early days of his victories against the Ottomans, though not towards the end. While preserving Thessalonike was in the best interests of the empire and was a noble goal, Manuel's persistence was also promoted by his own self-interest: should the city fall, he would be left with nothing. By fashioning an idealized self-image in the *Discourse to Kabasilas*, Manuel seeks to deflect these accusations. He again employs his writings as a means of political legitimization. These brief lines were the first and only time that Manuel would reminiscence about his Thessalonian rule.

Alongside its subtle political messages, the discourse contains other engaging aspects. One is Manuel's musings on authorship; should an author combine pleasantry (παιδιά) and gravity (σπουδή)? What is the proper occasion to do so? The discussion on how to combine pleasantry and gravity in one's works is not unique to Manuel; it was frequently

---

⁷ *Discourse to Kabasilas*, lines 18–26. 'εἵμαρτο γάρ μοι, ὡς ἔοικε, πολέμῳ συζῆν ἀεί, καὶ τούτῳ παντοδαπῷ. ὅθεν καὶ ἐν τῇ μεγάλῃ Πόλει δεῆσαν με διατρίβειν τοῖς ταύτην πολέμῳ πειρωμένοις ἑλεῖν ὡς πάντες ἴσασιν ἐπολέμουν, μηδὲ ἕν τι τῶν εἰς ἡμᾶς ἡκόντων μηδεπώποτε παρειείς, ἐν δὲ τῇ πατρίδι τῇ σῇ τοῖς τῆς πίστεως ἐχθροῖς μαχόμενος διετέλουν. Οἵ δ' ὑπὲρ ὧν νύκτωρ καὶ μεθημέραν ἠρούμην ἀποθανεῖν, ὀφείλοντες τοῖς ἴσοις ἀμείβεσθαι ἢ γοῦν χάριν ἡμῖν τῶν ὑπὲρ αὐτῶν κινδύνων εἰδέναι ... οἱ δὲ καὶ στρατηγοῦντες ἦσαν τοῖς ἐχθροῖς ... ἀλλὰ καὶ τῷ δόλους ποικίλους συντόνως πλέκειν ἡμῖν τοῖς τυραννοῦσιν αὐτοῖς -τοῦτο δὴ παρ' ἐκείνων ἀεὶ λεγόμενον καθ' ἡμῶν- καὶ οὐκ ἐπιτρέπουσιν αἰσχρῶς τὴν σφῶν ἐλευθερίαν προδοῦναι.' I have slightly modified Dennis' translation. He translates 'μηδὲ ἕν τι τῶν εἰς ἡμᾶς ἡκόντων μηδεπώποτε παρειείς' as 'I have never failed in a single one of my duties'. I believe that the participle *pareieis* is used in the sense of neglecting, or a slackening of one's efforts.

touched upon by Byzantine authors. The two may appear discordant to many people, Manuel explains, but he believes that they can be successfully blended. An attentive reading of the *Discourse to Kabasilas* reveals the text itself to be an amalgamation of pleasantry and gravity. Manuel not only argues for this approach to authorship, his discourse is the embodiment of the literary technique that he advocates. This can be seen for instance, in a joke on the breezes of Constantinople which Manuel incorporates into the introduction, and which allows him to give an explanation for including the pleasantry into the text.[8] It was incorporated, he claims, in order to introduce some 'lightness' into his writing, but also to let Kabasilas know:

> ... I have not been drowned, as might be expected of one whom adversity has tossed into the midst of the tempestuous sea. Even though I never learned to swim, I am floating on the surface, and am writing this so that you may not become frantic or be dragged under yourself.[9]

Throughout the text, Manuel argues that the best time to engage in literary pleasantries is not in times of prosperity but during hard times, in order to gain the strength to persevere. He continually highlights the close relationship between writing and amusement.[10] Indeed, he would maintain this outlook throughout his life and sought solace in his writing. This passage reflects his view of writing as an outlet and as a possible channel of pleasure. Moreover, this literary discussion also has political overtones, since Manuel, engages in literary pleasantries to alleviate his distress over the events in Thessalonike. The 'light' tone and the jokes in *Discourse to Kabasilas* are meant to embody his own steadfastness amidst adversity. In other words, Manuel signals to Kabasilas and the wider audience that he has not 'drowned'.

Another key discussion is again interwoven with political implications: the question of what increases a man's troubles so greatly that all consolation is in vain? At this point in the discourse, Manuel switches from epistolary style to a Platonic dialogue, hence combining two literary forms in a single work. Dialogue was a popular form in Byzantium

---

[8] *Discourse to Kabasilas*, lines 45–7. 'εὖ γὰρ οἶδ' ὅτι ἐπέλθοι σοι θαυμάσαι τὸ σὺν παιδιᾷ ἡμᾶς τὰ τῆς τραγῳδίας εὐθὺς ἄρξασθαι, τὸ περὶ τῶν πνευμάτων φημί, καί σοι δόξομεν ἴσως τὰ ἄμεικτα μειγνύναι.'

[9] *Discourse to Kabasilas*, lines 56–61. 'κοινωνεῖ γὰρ πῶς ταύτης ὁ λόγος ... ἔπειθ' ἵν' ἀκούσας ὡς οὐ καταβεβάπτισμαι ἢ εἰκὸς ἐν μέσῳ πελάγει καὶ σάλῳ τοῖς δυσχερέσι ῥιφείς ... ἀλλ' ἐπιπολάζω νήχεσθαι μὴ μεμαθηκώς, μὴ ἁλύῃς μηδὲ καταβαπτισθῇς καὶ αὐτός.' Although here Manuel is using his favoured and conventional tempestuous sea metaphor, his extension of the metaphor to drowning and to floating on the sea surface goes beyond the *topoi*.

[10] *Discourse to Kabasilas*, lines 106–7. 'εἰ γοῦν ἡδύ τι καὶ ἡ παιδιά, ἡδύ τι καὶ λόγοι. Οὐ πάνυ τοι ἄν τις ἁμάρτοι εἰ παίζοντα τὸν λέγοντα γε προσερεῖ.'

throughout the centuries; several prominent examples are the works of John of Damascus (eighth century), Soterichos Panteugenos, Eustratios of Nicaea, Theodore Prodromos (all twelfth century), George Scholarios (fifteenth century) and two well-known satire: the *Timarion* (twelfth century) the *Journey of Mazaris to Hades* (fifteenth century).[11] Byzantine dialogues built on the heritage of Ancient Greek and Hellenistic dialogues, the most two prominent models being Lucian and Plato. The latter was the preferred model for theological and philosophical discussions.

The second half of the *Discourse to Kabasilas* is clearly modelled on a Platonic dialogue. It shares several prominent literary features with the dialogues, such as the work opening with a gathering of friends, Platonic modes of address, a quick flow 'question and answer' section, and at times, the *elenctic* method of Socrates. As in the case of many Platonic dialogues, the *Discourse* is in reported speech, where Manuel is both a speaker and the narrator. Finally, to some extent, Manuel's decision to combine an epistolary style with Platonic dialogue adheres to the tradition of 'embedded' dialogues in Byzantium. Indeed, many Byzantine authors inserted dialogues into panegyrics, funeral orations and other genres.[12] However, in the *Discourse to Kabasilas*, Manuel does not insert the dialogue into the letter. Instead, he completely switches from the epistolary style to the Platonic dialogue. Such experimenting with genres was popular among many Late Byzantine authors, and Manuel also attempted to combine these two forms in a literary experiment. His success in this blending bears witness to his talent as an author.

The *Discourse* takes place as Manuel and his companions sit under an oak tree near a spring. This vivid imagery strongly resembles that of the *Phaedrus*, one of Manuel's favourite Platonic dialogues, where Socrates and Phaedrus converse under a tree, also near a spring, and this obvious allusion to the *Phaedrus* is duly picked up by Kydones.[13] Significantly, Manuel emphasizes his imperial rank by mentioning that the companions who sat with him had been granted the privilege to do so. Kydones seems to have

---

[11] A recent volume, A. Cameron and N. Gaul (eds.) *Dialogues and Debates from Late Antiquity to Late Byzantium* (London and New York, 2017), deals extensively with various types of dialogue in Byzantium and offers case studies of many significant specimens. Henceforth, *Dialogues and Debates*.

[12] See N. Gaul, 'Embedded Dialogues and Dialogical Voices in Palaiologan Rhetoric', in *Dialogues and Debates*, 184–202.

[13] *Discourse to Kabasilas*, lines 140–9; Plato, *Phaedrus* 5C; Kydones, Letter 380, lines 34–7, 'ἐγὼ δὲ ἐμακάρισα καὶ τὴν δρῦν καὶ τὴ ὑπὸ ταύτην σκιὰν καὶ τὴν πηγὴν ἥ τοὺς πολλοὺς καὶ καλοὺς . . ., ὑφ' ἣν τοῖς καλοῖς περὶ τοῦ καλοῦ λόγοις τὸν Φαῖδρον ὁ Σωκράτης ἑστία.' Finally, although the scenery was clearly intended to mirror that of the *Phaedrus*, Clavijo also reports that a plain with water springs indeed existed just outside Mytilene. Clavijo, 26.

taken note of this instance as well, since in his letter on the work, he, too, highlights Manuel's special status as emperor.[14] Manuel's assertion of his superiority over his collocutors as an emperor can be interpreted as a defence of his imperial rank. This was especially important after the Thessalonike fiasco, and now that he was a fugitive in Lesbos and in deep disgrace with John V. As in many of his writings, Manuel aims at offering an authoritative, idealized self-representation, both in a literal and a political sense.

While pursuing this strategy of self-representation, Manuel seems to have cast himself in the role of Socrates. Indeed, the parallels between the two figures are striking. As with Socrates in the Platonic dialogues, the discussion begins when a companion asks to hear Manuel's opinions on what might cause a man such distress as to make consolation impossible; the others are unable to come up with a satisfactory answer to the question. Like Socrates, Manuel's companions are very deferential, and his views dominate the entire dialogue. Manuel employs Socrates' famed *elenctic* method, dealing with one person at a time and refuting the collocutor's view through questions that allowing the person to discover the fault in his reasoning.[15] Manuel presents himself, like Socrates, as dominating the dialogue and thus establishes himself as the 'superior' collocutor, both as the emperor and as a discussant.

His companions present various arguments and answers to the question. One claims that consolation may be impossible when one is blamed despite being innocent. Yet another argues that having no precedent for his own misfortunes, may lead a man to despair. Manuel promptly dismisses both arguments; nevertheless, both cases are appropriate to Manuel's adopted position: he was betrayed by the Thessalonians and unjustly punished by his father, and there was no exact precedent for his current, somewhat bizarre, situation. Ultimately, this discussion was not written simply for the

---

[14] *Discourse to Kabasilas*, lines, 190–1. "'Ἐκαθήμην ὡς εἰώθειν πρὸς τῇ πηγῇ καὶ παρεκάθηντο μοι τῶν σὺν ἐμοὶ πολλοὶ οἷς τοῦτο δέδοται ποιεῖν . . .'.

Kydones, Letter 380, lines 49–52, 'Ἀλλά σοι μὲν ὑπὲρ δόξης ἐξέστω καὶ παράδοξα λέγειν. Πάντως ὥσπερ ἄλλο τι γέρας βασιλέων καὶ τοῦτο. ἡμῶν ἰδιωτῶν οὐδεὶς ἂν ᾐσχύνθη αὐτόν τε καὶ τὴν αὐτοῦ δόξαν πάντων εἰπὼν προτιμᾶν, ὃ τήν τε φύσιν ἴσασι πάντες ψηφιζομένην καὶ τὸν Θεὸν ἐπιτάττοντα.'

[15] See R. Blondell, *The Play of Character in Plato's Dialogues* (Cambridge, 2002), especially 42–3, 185 for these characteristics of Socrates in Platonic dialogues. See also T. C. Brickhouse and N. D. Smith, *Plato's Socrates* (New York, 1994), 3–16, for the *elenctic* method employed by Socrates.

sake of writing a Platonic dialogue, the whole dialogue serves to flesh out the resemblance between Manuel and the abstract man in the question; he is actually speaking of his own predicament.

His self-representation as an ideal ruler and an innocent victim charge the text with strong political undertones. Tellingly, Manuel equates his misfortunes to those of Christ. The sufferings of Christ, he laments, were unprecedented – like his own.[16] Similarly, he compares himself to another lofty Christian figure, Jonas, who was also left to suffer underneath a burning sun. Manuel strikingly points out that while Jonas was merely given a plane tree by God as a consolation, he was given an oak tree; moreover, Jonas was old and frail, while he was healthy and 'just halfway through life' – the implication here is that Manuel has actually fared better than Jonas.[17] These comparisons with Christ and Jonas elevate were undoubtedly intended to elevate Manuel to their level and disclose his dignity in the face of disgrace. Despite everything, Manuel implies, he could not be crushed by his misfortunes.

His own verdict on the question of what drives a man to despair further augments these political implications. Manuel argues that being treated unjustly by someone that you love greatly, is the greatest suffering.[18] This should be interpreted as a clear political statement against his father, John V, who had 'unjustly' exiled Manuel and perhaps would even deprive him of the throne. His reference to his services in the civil war of 1370s further reinforces his father's 'ingratitude'.[19] All things considered, *The Discourse to Kabasilas* skilfully blends philosophical dialogue and political messages.

The political messages in the discourse begs the question of circulation for the text. Although the addressee was Nicholas Kabasilas, there are many hints that the discourse was in fact intended for a wider circulation. First of all, as an *apologia* for Manuel's actions in Thessalonike, the discourse had significant literary and political goals. Thus, it is almost certain that Manuel's intended audience did not consist of merely Nicholas Kabasilas. Indeed, a letter of Demetrios Kydones indicates that Kabasilas passed the work to him.[20] However, the circulation of the text beyond that is unknown, and Kabasilas' letters concerning these exchanges do not survive. However, several of Kydones' later letters to Manuel indicate that he, at least, arranged performances of Manuel's works in a *theatron*.

---

[16] *Discourse to Kabasilas*, lines 120–90.
[17] *Discourse to Kabasilas*, lines 150–60, 'ἐρρωμένως μὲν τοῦ σώματος ἔχοντες σὺν Θεῷ τὴν δ' ἡλικίαν οὐ τὴν αὐτὴν κεκτημένοι τῷ γέροντι -εἰς γὰρ τὴν μέσην ἤδη τελοῦμεν . . . .'
[18] *Discourse to Kabasilas*, lines 335–43. [19] See the translated passage above.
[20] Kydones, Letter 380.

It is quite possible, therefore, that other literati in Constantinople were acquainted with the discourse through Kabasilas and Kydones' large literary networks. Another intriguing question is whether the text was merely circulated among the supporters of Manuel, or if it was also known to the people in his father's circle, perhaps even by John V himself? Sadly, this question cannot be properly investigated.

The *Discourse to Kabasilas* is a notable early work in Manuel's oeuvre due to the subtle political messages he weaves into seemingly irrelevant discussions, as well as his ideas regarding the act of writing. As a blending of an epistolary discourse and a Platonic dialogue, it is also interesting form-wise and represents an early stage in Manuel's dialogues.[21] The fusion of solemn political messages and jokes, a lucid Platonic atmosphere and Manuel's rich self-representation, all enhance the literary merit of the work.

Uncertain Years: 1387–9

The *Discourse to Kabasilas* is the only source that provides hints about Manuel's stay in Lesbos. Around the end of July or the beginning of August, Manuel moved to Tenedos. The move was probably undertaken in order to facilitate the contacts between him and Sultan Murad, who seems to have approached Manuel via his ambassadors.[22] Manuel then went to Bursa and submitted to the sultan in person. He had finally been forced to adopt his father's policy of appeasement.[23] There is scarcely any information on early Ottoman Bursa. Johannes Schiltberger, a crusader captured by the Ottomans in 1396, describes Bursa as a large, vibrant city possessing around 200, 000 houses and eight hospitals that offered free care to people of all faiths. Nothing is known about Manuel's stay in this city except that his loyal companion Rhadenos from Thessalonike died here.[24]

After his reconciliation with the Ottoman sultan, Manuel finally returned to Constantinople. His submission to the sultan must have been instrumental in John V 's decision to finally allow his son into the

---

[21] Platonic dialogues in Byzantium and Manuel's use of this form will be further discussed in Chapter 5.

[22] Kydones, Letter 352 and Chalkokondyles, 84–5.

[23] Chalkokondyles, 76–7 and 84–5, speaks of Manuel's submission to Murad, although he narrates the same event twice due to his confused narrative. Kydones, Letter 354, also speaks of Manuel's submission to the Ottomans.

[24] Johannes Schiltberger, *The Bondage and Travels of Johann Schiltberger, 1396–1427* ed. and trans. J. B. Telfer (London, 1879), 190. Henceforth, Schiltberger. Kydones, Letter 362, lines 28–38, offers his condolences to Manuel. The cause of Rhadenos' death is unknown.

city.[25] How the father and the son first met after so many years, and how exactly the emperor treated Manuel, is not known. It is probable that John V was still suspicious of his son, since Demetrios Kydones was not allowed to speak with or visit Manuel.[26] In the end, John V decided to exile his son to Lemnos, one of the few Aegean islands that still remained under Byzantine control.[27]

Manuel's two-year-long exile in Lemnos can only be traced through Kydones' letters. Although it is clear that Manuel wrote back to him, his own letters do not survive.[28] As in Thessalonike, their voluminous letter exchange illustrates the close bond between the two correspondents. On one occasion, Kydones also refers to reading a letter that Manuel sent to Empress Helena, thus, Manuel seems to have had contact with her as well.[29] He was not alone in Lemnos either. Theodore Palaiologos, one of his companions in Thessalonike, appears to have followed him into exile, and Kydones refers to Maximos Chrysoberges, an eminent theologian, residing with Manuel in Lemnos as well.[30] Like Kydones, Chrysoberges, too, was a convert to Catholicism. This demonstrates that despite the firm Orthodoxy he would display later in his life, Manuel's tolerance for converts was not limited to Kydones; however, in later life he does not seem to have preserved his contact with Chrysoberges. Furthermore, a certain Angelos is mentioned frequently by Kydones as having acted as a letter-bearer and messenger between Lemnos and Constantinople.[31]

Manuel's everyday life in Lemnos is shrouded in obscurity. In a rare glimpse, Kydones' letters reveal that Manuel focused his energies on hunting, and he jocularly chastises him for neglecting his literary pursuits:

---

[25] Chalkokondlyles claims, albeit erroneously, that Manuel tried to sail to Constantinople without being reconciled with the sultan and had been rejected by his father who only allowed Manuel to enter the city after Sultan Murad had given his approval. Chalkokondyles, 76–7.

[26] Kydones, Letters 370 and 372, addressed to Manuel when the latter was in Constantinople.

[27] Kydones, Letters 372 and 374. The circumstances of this decision are not known. Schreiner, *Kleinchroniken*, Chronik 12/28 also refers to John V exiling his son to Lemnos. The only study on this period in Manuel's life is R. J. Loenertz, 'L'éxil de Manuel II Paléologue à Lemnos 1387–89', *OCP* 38 (1972), 116–40. The article summarizes Kydones' letters from the period and attempts to construct a chronology for the events.

[28] Barker, *Manuel II*, 66, suggests that Manuel might have deliberately chosen not to preserve any letters from the period.

[29] Kydones, Letter 353, lines 20–1.

[30] Kydones, Letter 382. Kydones, Letters 385, 387 and 402 for Maximos Chrysoberges.

[31] Kydones, Letters 383, 390, 391 and 402. The identity of this Angelos is unclear, yet it is tempting to ask whether he could be the same Angelos from the history of Doukas and the satire of Mazaris, who had smuggled Manuel and John V out of Anemas in 1379. Since this Angelos was acting as a messenger between Lemnos and Constantinople, even visiting the palace to deliver letters from Manuel (Kydones, Letter 391), he must have been esteemed both by Manuel and John V.

How could one not use such licence of speech to a person who has utterly given himself up to trifles and to hunting, forsaking the care for letters? . . . Is the dog now more precious to you than Plato, the hare more pleasant than Demosthenes, the wild boar, which is led to the ambush by howls, more exalted than Aristotle? Have you suddenly exchanged orderly speech for ignorant cries?[32]

Manuel was indeed fond of hunting and would retain that love into his old age. But following the conventional juxtaposition of physical and literary pursuits, Kydones expresses his concern for Manuel's excessive zeal.[33]

As in Thessalonike, the tone of these letters reveals the personal side of their relationship. The reprimand is especially illuminating. It indicates that Kydones felt sufficiently at ease with Manuel to criticise him, albeit in a playful manner. In this regard, Kydones' friendly, and at times, fatherly tone contrasts sharply with the formality of his letters addressed to John VI Kantakouzenos and John V. In those letters, Kydones strictly addresses them as 'emperor'. As letters written to literary patrons, any hint of intimacy is absent.[34] Moreover, in the surviving letters, none of Manuel's other correspondents employ a similarly 'intimate' tone when addressing him. This intimacy can be seen in Kydones' request of a sheepskin coat from Manuel. Lemnos, at the time, was famous for its flocks.[35]

Despite having boasted in the *Discourse to Kabasilas* of being in good health, Manuel fell ill on Lemnos. The illness was so grave that even John V was alarmed. He duly dispatched Angelos to the island to obtain news about his son's health. Kydones' account that Manuel suffered from pains on one side of his body, headache, fever and sleeplessness, offers a rare glimpse into his health.[36] He recovered however, albeit slowly, and in the meantime, misfortune struck the empire.

On 15 June 1389, the Ottomans crushed the Serbian army at Kosovo, effectively subjugating the Serbians to their rule. Another significant

---

[32] Kydones, Letter 388, lines 23–8. 'πῶς γὰρ οὐ καὶ τοιαύτη τις ἂν χρήσαιτο παρρησίᾳ πρὸς τὸν ἀνέδην οὕτωσὶ ἐπὶ παίγνια καὶ θήραν εἰπόντα μεταθεῖναι τὴν τῶν λόγων φροντίδα; τί ταῦτ' ὢ βασιλέων ἀγαθώτατε καὶ μετὰ νοῦ πάντα φθεγγόμενε σύ; γέγονε γὰρ σοὶ νῦν κύων Πλάτωνος τιμιώτερος καὶ λαγὼς Δημοσθένους ἡδίων καὶ σῦς ἐπὶ λόγχην ταῖς ὑλακαῖς ἐπειγόμενος Ἀριστοτέλους σεμνότερος, καὶ τοῦ σὺν κόσμῳ λέγειν ἐξαίφνης τὰς τῶν ἀπαιδεύτων βοὰς ἀντηλλάξω . . .'.

[33] While hunting was a traditional imperial pastime and was moreover seen as military training, an excessive love of hunt could evoke criticism of the emperor. See E. Patlagean, 'De la chasse et du souverain', *DOP* 46 (1992), 257–63.

[34] For some of these letters addressed to John V and VI, see Letters 6–16, 70, 83 and 118.

[35] Kydones, Letters 397 and 404 for the coat request. See H. W. Lowry, *Fifteenth Century Ottoman Realities: Christian Peasant Life on the Aegean Island of Limnos* (Istanbul, 2002), 6, for the flock economy on Lemnos.

[36] Kydones, Letter 395.

outcome of the battle was the death of Sultan Murad and the subsequent accession of Bayezid I. Manuel couldn't know it then, but Bayezid would prove himself to be his great nemesis. He was to have a very personal enmity with Bayezid, whom he would portray in demonic guise in his works.[37]

After two years in exile in Lemnos and almost seven years after having secretly set sail for Thessalonike, Manuel finally made a permanent return to Constantinople sometime around the mid-autumn of 1389.[38] It is highly probable that he returned to the capital on account of John V's failing health. He appears to have been seriously ill. Another motive may have been to prevent John VII, the son of the deceased Andronikos IV, from entering the capital should the old emperor die. John VII had taken up his father's mantle, setting himself against Manuel as a rival for the throne. As with Andronikos, nothing can be gleaned about the person of the rebellious prince except that John had inherited not only his father's political designs, but also his Genoese connections and support. In fact, during the period of Manuel's return, the young John was in Genoa, seeking support for his bid for the Byzantine throne.[39] Sometime before April 1390, however his grandfather John V unexpectedly recovered from his illness.

The *Panegyric to John V*

This felicitous turn of events prompted Manuel to deliver a panegyric to celebrate the occasion.[40] The audience for the panegyric included

---

[37] Kydones, Letter 396. Schreiner, *Kleinchroniken*, Chronik 53/7–8; 54/7–8; Neşri, 302–7 and Aşıkpaşazade, 85–7. For the political outcomes of Kosovo, Barker, *Manuel II*, 67 and Reinert, 'The Palaiologoi and Yıldırım Bayezid' and, 295. See also S. W. Reinert, 'A Byzantine Source on the Battles of Bileća (?) and Kosova Polje, 'Kydones' letters 396 and 398 reconsidered', in *Studies in Ottoman History in Honour of Professor V. L. Ménage*, eds. C. Heywood and C. Imber (Istanbul, 1994), 249–72, reprinted in S. W. Reinert (ed.) *Studies on Late Byzantine and Early Ottoman History* (Farnham, 2014), Study III.

[38] The exact date of Manuel's return is unclear. On the basis of Kydones, Letter 398, Reinert argues that Manuel did not return to Constantinople until around 21 October. He also bases his argument on a Latin letter addressed to Amadeo of Savoy from the Despot Theodore, dated 21 October 1389, which quite possibly refers to Manuel as residing in Constantinople. Reinert, 'Yıldırım Bayezid and the Palaiologoi', 295, 304–5.

[39] Reinert, 'The Palaiologoi and Yıldırım Bayezid', 298–301, 307–8. Chalkokondyles, 101–2, claims that in 1390, Manuel helped the Ottomans conquer Philadelphia, which is rejected by Reinert. Schreiner also questions the Chalkokondyles account, yet accepts the autumn 1390 date for the capture of the city, P. Schreiner, 'Zur Geschichte Philadelphias in 14 Jahrhundert (1293–1390)', *OCP* 35 (1969), 375–431. Barker, *Manuel II*, 79 also accepts the dating, as well as the assumption that Manuel took part in the campaign. On John VII in Genoa, see J. Barker, 'John VII in Genoa: A Problem in Late Byzantine Source Confusion', *OCP* 28 (1962), 213–8 and E. Lappa-Zizicas, 'Le voyage de Jean Paléologue en Italie', *REB* 34 (1976), 139–42.

[40] The full title of the work is *Panegyric to his Father on the Occasion of his Recovery*. In this book, it is abbreviated as *Panegyric to John V*.

Demetrios Kydones, and John V later rewarded Kydones with money as a nod to his son's former teacher.[41] It is safe to presume that this oration celebrating the emperor's recovery and performed in his presence, was delivered in the palace. Many members of the political elite, including high ranking government officials, bureaucrats and ecclesiastics, were probably in the audience. As with many of Manuel's works, however, this panegyric has mostly escaped scholarly interest.[42]

This only surviving panegyric by Manuel has some interesting ideological and rhetorical aspects. First of all, Manuel wholeheartedly adopts the persona of a court panegyrist. Through the adoption of a panegyrist persona, he seeks to curry his father's favour and advocate his own candidacy for the throne. This work is also notable for being the only instance where Manuel opts an 'inferior' position as opposed to an authoritative one. The focus of the work is the 'miraculous' recovery of John V, which Manuel conventionally presents as a divine favour to the empire. The dramatic contrast between the great moral strength of John V and his ailing body, is a dominant theme.

Yet another dual theme in the work is that of the divine and earthly empires, commonplace designations signifying the kingdom of heaven and Byzantium, between which John V kept alternating. Manuel furthers this theme through literary plays on the link between God the divine emperor and John the earthly emperor. He envisions a literal 'chain' of rulership wherby John rules over his people and is himself ruled by God.[43] Overall, Manuel places great emphasis on the divine nature of the imperial office, a commonplace notion that he would expand upon further in future works.

Manuel's portrayal of John V departs significantly from Byzantine rhetorical tradition. Panegyrics generally dwelt on the virtues, deeds and the policies of the emperor in question. Following the handbook of Menander Rhetor, they would also extol his birth and native city, as well as comparing him to ancient kings. Manuel's panegyric contains none of these salient characteristics. There are no comparisons of John V to any ancient kings or other such figures, and Manuel even omits altogether the four cardinal virtues (justice, wisdom, temperance and courage). By

---

[41] Kydones, Letters 82 and 83 and Manuel's Letter 12 make this clear.

[42] The only scholar who makes any use of this oration is Reinert, who is interested in Manuel's references to John VII. Even he is dismissive of the oration: '... the text conveys little discernible historical data ...'. Reinert, ' The Palaiologoi and Yıldırım Bayezid', 311.

[43] *Panegyric to John V*, 228. Ὁ τοίνυν κρατῶν μὲν ἡμῶν, κρατοῦντα δ᾽ αὐτοῦ κεκτημένος παρ᾽ οὗ τὸ σκῆπτρον εἴληφει ...'. For such other references, see pages 224, 229 and 231.

contrast, he was to make lavish use of these virtues in the portrayal of his brother Theodore in the *Funeral Oration*.

Instead, in order to bestow praise upon his father, Manuel recounts the long and tiresome journeys John V undertook for the sake of his people. He narrates how John braved the sea while travelling to Buda and to Venice, and finally touches upon his campaigns with the Ottoman sultan. As previously suggested, Manuel certainly included himself when he spoke of 'those people' who endured dangers during the emperor's voyages, and so, as an orator, he managed to subtly insert himself into the picture.[44] Furthermore, his limited praise of John V double functions as self-promotion. Having just been reconciled to his father, he seems to be reminding John V and the audience of his former services, and concludes his account by remarking that the emperor had not been able to tame those 'savage' peoples since they were not likely to be subdued. Manuel thus effectively admits the political weakness of his father in a panegyric dedicated to him. This presents an ironic and notable contrast to his depiction of the emperor just a few lines before, which alleged that John V had won many trophies against his enemies.[45] In short, while Manuel does briefly praise his father, he also peppers the oration with mentions of his failures.

As a panegyrist, Manuel unsurprisingly depicts John V as a good ruler. However, his praise is lukewarm and his portrayal of his father strikes the reader as rather impersonal. The portrayal of John V lacks warmth and provides a stark contrast to that of Theodore in the *Funeral Oration*, or Empress Helena in the *Dialogue on Marriage*. Unlike these works, in the panegyric, Manuel never says anything personal about his father or about their relationship. It is telling that he does not even refer to John V as his father, but merely as the emperor.

Manuel embarks on a narration of the sorrow of the people at the news of the emperor's illness, but he abruptly terminates his account, suggesting that it is not necessary to narrate this in detail, as the day (of the panegyric celebrating his recovery) was one of rejoicing and not of grief.[46] While this is certainly used as a rhetorical strategy to keep the pace of the oration flowing, it also passes over a perfect opportunity to depict John V as a beloved

---

[44] *Panegyric to John V*, 224, '... ὁπόσων ἀπέλαυε τῶν λυπηρῶν ἴσασι μὲν ἀκριβῶς οἵ τότε τούτῳ συναπεδήμουν. Οὐ χαλεπὸν δὲ ἡγοῦμαι καὶ τοὺς οἴκοι μένοντας τούτων στοχάσασθαι.'

[45] *Panegyric to John V*, 224. '... οὓς μήτε τιθασσεύειν δυνάμενος (οὐδὲ γὰρ οἷοί τε ἦσαν τοῦτο παθεῖν), μήτε πρὸς τἀκείνων ἤθη μεταβαλεῖν δεῖν ἀξιῶν (οὐδὲ γὰρ προσῆκε τηλικῷδε ἀνδρί, καὶ ἄλλως βασιλεῖ) ...'.

[46] *Panegyric to John V*, 224.

emperor.[47] Moreover, the praise of John V only occupies a very small portion of the panegyric. The oration quickly changes course to become an advisory speech as to how the empire can flourish and the emperor quickly ceases to occupy a central role.[48] This double textual structure consisting of laudatory and advisory parts, was not a blend invented by Manuel. Known as the political panegyric, this form enjoyed a revival in Late Byzantine rhetoric.[49] Orators would first praise the emperor in the *enkomion*, then proceed to the advisory speech. Furthermore, the two parts were tightly linked, since the *enkomion* set the tone for the advice that was to follow. Thus, Manuel's oration can certainly be classified as a political panegyric. By adopting this form, not only did Manuel follow the rhetorical trends of his era, he also restricted the laudatory aspect of his oration. On the whole, while he seems to be celebrating the emperor's recovery as a dutiful subject and son, his impersonal depiction of John V echoes his other lukewarm portrayals in the *Discourse to Kabasilas* and the *Funeral Oration*. One might conclude, therefore, that the breach between the father and the son did not heal without leaving some scars, or at least not on Manuel's side.

The *Panegyric to John V* is politically charged in one further way. Manuel makes the intriguing remark that when a rumour that John V was dead spread, people who seemed to be friends betrayed the emperor.[50] Yet in another part of the oration, he emphasizes that *true* friends were restored to safety upon the emperor's recovery.[51] Although Manuel is not explicit about the identity of these people, it is probable that he is referring to John VII and his faction.[52] The implication that Manuel is one of those *good* friends, is made clear in the fact that he celebrates John V's recovery with a panegyric. Manuel openly accuses John VII, his rival for the throne, of treachery and lobbies for his own political cause.

The implicit indication in the panegyric is that John, who took advantage of his grandfather's illness, is therefore unworthy to succeed him. On

---

[47] See M. Mullett, 'How to Criticize the Laudandus', in *Power and Subversion in Byzantium, Papers from the 43rd Spring Symposium of Byzantine Studies, Birmingham, March 2010*, eds. D. Angelov and M. Saxby (Farnham, 2013), 247–62, for veiled criticism in panegyrics.

[48] This will be discussed below.

[49] See Angelov, *Imperial Ideology*, 49–63. for political panegyric.

[50] *Panegyric to John V*, 225. 'φήμη τις ὡς ὁ βασιλεὺς ἐτεθνήκει, τῶν πτηνῶν ζηλώσασα τὰ κουφότερον τὸ πτερὸν κεκτημένα … διεγείρει μὲν τοὺς δυσμενεῖς καθ' ἡμῶν … τῶν δὲ δοκούντων φίλων οὓς μὲν φρονεῖν τὰ δυσμενῶν … νομιζομένους καὶ κίονας ἀστραβεῖς κατέπεισε καὶ κατέβαλεν.'

[51] *Panegyric to John V*, 226. 'φίλοι δὲ ἀληθεῖς, συνάμα πᾶσι Ῥωμαίοις, εἰς τὴν προτέραν αὖθις καταστάντες ἀσφάλειαν …'.

[52] Reinert also believes that it is to John VII that Manuel refers here. Reinert, 'The Palaiologoi and Yıldırım Bayezid', 309.

the other hand, the 'panegyrist' candidate for the throne, who rejoiced in the recovery of John V – and celebrated the occasion with an oration – is the worthy heir. Manuel is here embracing the persona of a 'princely panegyrist'. While court orators advertised their political and rhetorical skills by delivering orations to promote their careers, Manuel, an emperor's son, advertises himself as his father's legitimate and worthy successor. As in the case of the *Discourse to Thessalonians*, he resorts to oratory to achieve his political aims. Although his oeuvre is replete with hints that Manuel truly enjoyed writing, the absence of other alternatives perhaps prompted him to also embrace *logoi* as a venue of political expression.

Manuel imbues his oration with further political statements. When the panegyric part of the oration gives way to the advisory part, he divests himself of the panegyrist role and adopts once more an advisory role. Despite his adopted stance of a humble, dutiful son and subject, Manuel still represents himself as a political authority. He openly gives advice to the audience and his father on the future of the empire. Like the *Discourse to Thessalonians*, his advice is moreover fused with philosophical meanings.

This time Manuel discusses *eudaimonia* (εὐδαιμονία), probably again in reference to Aristotelian ethics. *Eudaimonia* was a term in Greek philosophy signifying a perfect state of flourishing through virtue and reason.[53] While *eudaimonia* was amply used by Byzantine historians and orators to refer to mere 'good fortune'/'prosperity', the passage hints that Manuel gave the term a more profound philosophical meaning, as he would later in his ethico-philosophical works.[54] His underlying and commonplace advice is that as fortune is reversible, the Byzantine empire will therefore flourish again. Meanwhile the fortune of the Ottomans will wane, especially if the Byzantines persevere in virtue and faith to obtain *eudaimonia*. Manuel also offers much more concrete advice on the matter:

---

[53] Aristotle, *Nicomachean Ethics*, i, vii, 9–16. Although *eudaimonia* is a common theme in many Greek philosophers, I have chosen to refer to Aristotle as Manuel relied on him in his own ethico-political works.

[54] The generic use of *eudaimonia* as mere 'good fortune' or 'happiness' is common. Another author who also gave *eudaimonia* more of a philosophical content was John Chortasmenos, who in an oration, contrasts *eudaimonia* and good fortune (εὐτυχία), claiming that the former stemmed from virtue and blessedness, while the latter from mere luck. J. Chortasmenos, 'Address to Manuel II on his Return from Thessalonike', ed. H. Hunger. *Johannes Chortasmenos, ca. 1370 – ca 1436/37. Briefe, Gedichte und kleine Schriften. Einleitung, Regesten, Prosopographie, Text* (Vienna, 1969), 217–24, 221. Henceforth, Chortasmenos, 'Address to Manuel'.

For those, who have fallen from the heights of this honour to where we are *now*, it is not easy to rise up again. But I believe that it is necessary to hold on to lesser and more humble territory rather than to be utterly shattered.[55]

These words contrast sharply with his aggressive position on the Ottomans only a few years earlier. Now, Manuel seems to be advocating a reconciliatory stance as opposed to an aggressive, expansionist one. Had his failure in Thessalonike caused him to indeed undergo a change of heart? Or is this a political statement to prove to the audience and especially to John V, that Manuel had now embraced his father's policy of submission to the Ottomans? Possibly, it was a combination of both. While the passage subtly renounces Manuel's former and contradictory ideas, it also reflects some aspects of his later stance towards the Ottomans as sole emperor.

Rebellion of John VII

The unexpected recovery of John V did not deter the ambitions of his grandson. Sometime towards the end of March 1390, John VII left Genoa and made his way into Bayezid's court. He obtained military support from the sultan, and then, like his father Andronikos almost fifteen years before, he marched to Constantinople. When the news of John's advance reached the city, it must have provoked panic. Manuel sailed to Lemnos and returned with some galleys on 31 March.[56] Manuel and his father then sought refuge in the citadel of the Golden Gate and resisted John VII for two weeks. But, on the night of 13 April, John VII's followers in the city, possibly people of the lower classes, opened the Charisios Gate to the young pretender and to his Greek troops, though they denied entry to the Ottoman soldiers.[57] The Russian pilgrim Ignatius of Smolensk narrates

---

[55] *Panegyric to John V*, 232–3. 'ἔπειτ' οὐδὲ ῥᾴδιον ἔστι πεσόντας τοῦ τῆς τιμῆς ἐκείνης ὕψους, ἔνθα νῦν γοῦν ἱστάμεθα, αὖθις στῆναι. ἀλλ' ἀνάγκη χείρονος, οἶμαι, χώρας καὶ ταπεινοτέρας μεθέξειν ἢ καὶ παντελῶς συντριβῆναι.'

[56] For a detailed analysis of John VII's uprising, see Reinert, 'Yıldırım Bayezid and the Palaiologoi', 311–27. This episode has previously been analysed by G. T. Kolias, "Η ἀνταρσία Ἰωάννου Ζ΄ Παλαιολόγου ἐναντίον Ἰωάννου Ε΄ Παλαιολόγου (1390)', Ἑλληνικά 12 (1952), 34–64. The approximate time for John VII's move has been calculated by Reinert, 'Yıldırım Bayezid and the Palaiologoi', 311. Manuel's arrival in Constantinople is noted by Ignatius of Smolensk, 100.

[57] Ignatius of Smolensk, 100–1. '... Пасхы и среду о попунощи долнѣишаа люди отвориша врата градаа калоану андрониковичу и пустиша его ...'. The identity of these followers of John VII is unclear. Majeska takes 'долнѣишаа' to refer to the people, hence he translates as 'common people.' Reinert is unsure whether these followers were the lower classes or simply people who resided in 'lower' parts of Constantinople. Reinert, 'Yıldırım Bayezid and the Palaiologoi', 313. Sonja Mešarović points out that the reference is to the lowest gate and not to people, see S. Mesarović. *Jovan VII Paleolog* (Belgrade, 1996), 68 and 141. Indeed, долнѣишаа could also be agreeing with врата, gate. Yet Charisios Gate was not the 'lowest' gate on the city walls. Moreover,

that the fighting continued until the morning. A confused atmosphere of both joy and terror reigned in the city as the inhabitants joined the acclamatory cries of John VII's troops.[58] Some of the elite fled to Hagia Sophia while John V sealed himself inside the citadel. Manuel managed to sail away from the capital.[59]

His destination was Rhodes, where he intended to ask for help from the Knights Hospitaller who resided there. On his way to Rhodes, he briefly stopped in the island of Kos on 22 April.[60] Ignatius of Smolensk casually remarks that Manuel had fled with his possessions. This was indeed the case, for Manuel took with him many precious liturgical objects, including votive crowns decorated with gems and icons made of silver and gold. He deposited these with the Hospitallers as security for a loan.[61] Having thus obtained the military support of the Hospitallers, he probably left Rhodes in May and returned to Lemnos. From this island, he twice tried to penetrate the harbour with the aid of the Hospitallers. He failed on both occasions.[62] It was on 17 September 1390 that he finally succeeded in entering the city, and John VII, having lost the throne that he had occupied for only a few months, fled to Pera.[63]

A comparison of the uprising of John VII and that of Andronikos yields several differences and is significant for Manuel's imperial career. One aspect is the role of the populace. As evidenced by the account of Ignatius of Smolensk, not only did John VII have the support of the Ottomans and the Genoese, he also had followers among the populace. Whereas, there is no indication that Andronikos IV ever had public support.[64] Although Andronikos IV, John V and later, to some extent, Manuel would preserve

Doukas also claims that in 1396–9, John VII was supported by the lower classes, 'χυδαῖος λαός' and 'κοινὸς λαός', Doukas, 80–5. Thus, it is probable that Majeska's translation was correct.

[58] Ignatius of Smolensk, 102–3. E. Zachariadou has demonstrated that Ignatius' report that John VII was acclaimed as Andronikos was not a mistake. Apparently, John VII briefly adopted his father's name, probably in order to avoid confusion with his grandfather John V. See E. A. Zachariadou, 'John VII (alias Andronicus) Palaeologus', *DOP* 91 (1977), 339–42.

[59] Ignatius of Smolensk, 100–1, mistakenly claims that Manuel went to Lemnos.

[60] This information comes from a notice published in P. Wirth, 'Manuel II Palaiologos und der Johanniterorden', *Byzantina* 6 (1974), 387–9.

[61] The full list of the items is found in a letter addressed to Phillip of Naillac from Manuel, dated 1396. For the original text of this letter, see R. J. Loenertz, 'Pour l'histoire du Péloponnese au XIVe siècle', in *Byzantina et Franco-Graeca*, eds. R. J. Loenertz and P. Schreiner (Rome, 1970), 227–65, 264–5. The list has been translated by S. Reinert, 'Yıldırım Bayezid and the Palaiologoi', 316–17. See also J. W. Barker, 'Byzantium and the Hospitallers, 1306–1421', in *Bisanzio, Venezia e il mondo Franco-Greco (XIIe–XVe s.)*, eds. C. Maltezou and P. Schreiner (Venice, 2002), 41–64.

[62] Reinert, 'Yıldırım Bayezid and the Palaiologoi', 319; Schreiner, *Kleinchroniken*, Chronik 7/ 21.

[63] Ignatius of Smolensk, 102–3.

[64] See A. Kaldellis, *The Byzantine Republic* (Leiden, 2015), especially chapter 5 for the importance of public opinion during uprisings in Byzantium.

their throne with help from foreign powers, John VII seems to have commanded the loyalty of the masses, or at least a portion of them. While the populace mostly supported John V against Andronikos, in the case of John VII, some of them seem to have shifted their loyalty. Although his nephew's popularity would also prove to be a great challenge to Manuel later, the rebellion is significant in Manuel's career for other reasons as well. Like in previous civil wars, John VII's rebellion further weakened and destabilized the empire that Manuel would inherit. Moreover, in contrast to his more passive role during the rebellion of Andronikos, Manuel also appears to have played a more active one. Not only did he sail to Rhodes and obtain the Hospitallers' aid, but he also personally commanded attacks on Constantinople on two occasions.

This was the second time that Manuel had fought against a family member for the throne. Just as in the uprising of 1376, he and John V had lost their authority only to regain it by 're-conquering' their own capital. Now, Manuel had witnessed no fewer than three civil wars among his family. He had been imprisoned for years at Anemas and had lost the throne not only once, but twice. Arguably, as a prince, he had experienced more tumult and strife than most Byzantine emperors. A remark that he was to make years later in his *Foundations of Imperial Conduct* may reflect these experiences:

> It is clear that for men, there is nothing as fearsome as the loss of time. For it is possible to regain money, glory, *the throne* and other such things when they are lost, and to recover them with additions, even if it is not very easy.[65]

The rebellion had been quelled, but Manuel's toils and troubles were not yet over. Instead, he was obliged by Sultan Bayezid to accompany the Ottoman army during their campaign. Manuel joined the Ottoman army, probably in Konya, and returned with Bayezid to Bursa, spending the winter at the Ottoman court.[66] No details are known of Manuel's first sojourn with Bayezid, but all of his writings indicate his profound personal enmity against the sultan. Perhaps the seeds of hostility were sown on this occasion, for it seems that the sultan considered him to be a quasi-hostage, ordering John V to dismantle the Golden Gate citadel by threatening to

---

[65] *Foundations of Imperial Conduct*, col. 360. 'Χρήματα μὲν γάρ, καὶ δόξαν, καὶ θρόνον, καὶ τὰ τοιαῦτα, ἔνεστιν ἀποβαλόντα ἀνακαλέσασθαι, καὶ μετὰ προσθήκης ἐπανακτήσασθαι εἰ καὶ μὴ πάνυ ῥάδιον ... .' Although the idea that wealth is perishable and that all material things are temporary is a *topos* found in advisory texts, such as that of Agapetos the Deacon, the notion that a throne can be lost and recovered is unique to Manuel. This will be further discussed in Chapter 9.

[66] This is noted both by Ignatius of Smolensk, 102–4 and Doukas, 76–7. Reinert, 'Yıldırım Bayezid and the Palaiologoi', 331.

blind Manuel should he not oblige. Having no other alternative, John V obeyed.

Shortly afterwards, the old emperor died on 15 February. Manuel was still in Bursa when he received the news of his father's death.[67] Indicated by his rather critical portrayals of his father, Manuel would exhibit a number of differences from John V as a ruler: on occasion, he would attempt to resist and curb the power of the Ottomans; he would refrain from concluding a Church Union; and his interest in scholarship and patronage of the literati would be in stark contrast to his father's reign. Yet Manuel would also continue some aspects of John V's legacy: for instance, like his father, he would look towards the West for the empire's salvation.

Returning from the Ottoman court and arriving at the Byzantine capital in a Genoese galley, Manuel entered Constantinople around 8 March 1391.[68] Finally, after many years of struggle, uncertainty and anguish, Manuel was the sole emperor of Byzantium.

> I have received the news that by good fortune, you have received the sceptre from God ... I shall come and address him who has been anticipated in ancient times, *the philosopher emperor* ...[69] (Letter 430 of Kydones)

---

[67] The story of Bayezid's ultimatum is narrated both by Ignatius of Smolensk, 102–4 and Doukas, 76–7, who claim that John V died out of shock and grief. Schreiner, *Kleinchroniken*, Chronik 10/7; 12/4.

[68] Although Doukas narrates that Manuel escaped from the Ottoman camp unknown to Bayezid, this is not likely. This is further strengthened by his claim that the blockade of Constantinople was immediately brought about by Manuel's supposed escape in 1391, whereas the blockade actually started in 1394. Moreover, the Genoese provided Manuel with his travel needs, and it is quite plausible that they would not have helped him without Bayezid's consent. See also Reinert, 'Yıldırım Bayezid and the Palaiologoi', 332. Barker, *Manuel II*, 82 for the Genoese expenditure entries. Doukas, 48–9 for Manuel's 'flight'.

[69] Kydones, Letter 430, lines 6–11, written upon receiving the news of Manuel's accession. 'τοῦτον ... λαβόμενον, ὅτε καὶ αὐτὸς παρὰ Θεοῦ τύχῃ ἀγαθῇ τὸ σκῆπτρον ἐδέξω ... ἥξω, προσερῶν μέν, τὸ πάλαι θρυλλούμενον, τὸν φιλόσοφον βασιλέα ...'.

CHAPTER 5

The Vassal Emperor[1]

I have marched with the Romans from our own land to wage war with
the Scythians in the land of the Scythians and to command troops for
our enemies.[2]

Only a few months after his accession, Manuel was compelled to accompany Sultan Bayezid on a campaign that took place between June and
January 1391/2. Unlike his predecessors, Bayezid was bent on uniting
Anatolia under his rule and to subjugate all other rulers. The campaign
was directed against the Turkish emirates in the Black Sea region,
especially the Emirate of Isfendiyar. The sultan also intended to force
Kadı Burhan-al-din, the ruler of the Eretna Emirate, to abandon his
designs on those territories.[3] The new emperor thus left Constantinople
on 8 June 1391.[4] During this campaign, Manuel not only fought for the
enemies of his own empire, he also produced some of his best-known
works: the often-cited eight letters from the campaign, and the famous
Dialogue with a Persian.

Exactly where Manuel joined the Ottoman army is unclear. Bayezid
defeated and killed Süleyman Pasha, the ruler of Kastamonu, sometime

---

[1] I do not use the word 'vassal' in the sense of Western feudal terminology, but to denote Manuel's obligation to the Ottoman sultan to accompany him in campaigns and to appear before him when summoned. See, H. İnalcık, 'Ottoman Methods of Conquest', *Studia Islamica* 2 (1954), 103–29, especially 104, who refers to the Christian rulers with these obligations as 'vassal lords', *beys*, who were overlords in their lands before these territories were finally incorporated into the Ottoman Empire.

[2] Letter 14, lines 10–13. Ὸ γὰρ Ῥωμαίους καὶ αὐτὸν ἄφεντας τὴν αὐτῶν ἐν τῇ Σκυθῶν τοῖς Σκύθαις πολεμεῖν καὶ στρατηγεῖν τοῖς ἐχθροῖς . . . '.

[3] The most detailed study on this campaign is E. A. Zachariadou, 'Manuel II Palaeologus on the strife between Bayezid I and Kadi Burhan al-Din Ahmad', *Bulletin of the School of Oriental and African Studies 43* (1980), 471–81. Henceforth, Zachariadou, 'Strife'.

[4] Schreiner, *Kleinchroniken*, Chronik 10/ 8. A Venetian document in Iorga, 'Venetia in Maera Negra', no. 24, 1106, also refers to Manuel having left Constantinople in July. See also Thiriet, *Régestes*, I, nos. 797 and 798, 191. It is not possible to evaluate this campaign in the light of the Ottoman chronicles as they do not deal with this episode.

before 5 July, but the emperor does not mention the conquest of Kastamonu in his letters.[5] Bayezid's next objective seems to have been subduing Süleyman Pasha's brother Mubariz al-din İsfendiyaroğlu, who ruled over the territories around Sinope and Amisios (Samsun). The sultan then intended to proceed to Amaseia in order to put an end to the aspirations of Kadı Burhan al-Din concerning these territories.[6] Manuel's letters do not indicate a clear route; he only mentions that the army passed through Zenopolis and Pompeiopolis, the latter being in modern Taşköprü. Afterwards it marched to the east, with Sinop on the left and the Halys on the right.[7] Manuel gives a vivid description of the savage slaughter that took place there, in which Bayezid's other Christian vassals seem to have readily participated, much to the emperor's disapproval.[8]

Manuel's letters indicate that he was aware of Bayezid's designs for these territories; he writes that the sultan intended either to conquer Sinope or at least to subdue Mubariz al-din İsfendiyaroğlu in order to intimidate Kadı Burhan al-Din.[9] Although the Ottomans did not succeed in conquering Sinope on that campaign, they conquered Osmancık and Kırk Dilim. These events are not mentioned by the emperor in his letters.[10] He merely comments that Kadı Burhan al-Din kept retreating while the Ottoman army advanced unrestrained.[11] Manuel's subsequent letters indicate that the Ottoman army reached Ankara and then crossed the river Halys, which was blocked by bandits.[12] The emperor pointed out to Kydones that the Ottomans had significantly consolidated their power in Anatolia, and – in an ironic twist – that he had contributed to this Ottoman success.[13]

Under these distressing circumstances, Manuel resorts to literary humour. He jokes that if Aristophanes could see Bayezid, he would compose a play on 'Blind Fortune', just as he did on 'Blind Wealth'.[14] In Aristophanes' play *Wealth*, the blind deity Wealth goes to undeserving people. The emperor's allusion to Aristophanes hints that since fortune, like Wealth, is blind it can also favour the unworthy – namely Bayezid. While his letter is also humorous, this allusion also serves to point out that Bayezid's success is undeserved in Manuel's opinion. Without an understanding of the Aristophanes illusion,

---

[5] Zachariadou, 'Strife', 473.   [6] Zachariadou, 'Strife', 477.
[7] Letter 16, lines 24–53. The city of Zenopolis remains unidentified.   [8] Letter 16, lines 10–20.
[9] Letter 16, lines 54–63.
[10] Kırk Dilim is located near modern Yozgat. Zachariadou, 'Strife', 477 suggests that Manuel might have ignored these conquests if the operations had been quick and easy.
[11] Letter 18, lines 14–20.   [12] Letter 20, lines 8–22.   [13] Letter 19, lines 34–8.
[14] Letter 19, lines 31–4. On humour in Byzantine writers, see J. Haldon, 'Humour and Everyday Life in Byzantium', in *Humour, History and Politics in Late Antiquity and Early Middle Ages*, ed. G. Halsall (Cambridge, 2002), 42–72.

the joke and its subtle political statement are easily missed and can be written off by the modern reader as mere artifice.

Letters from Asia Minor

As in the case of the Aristophanes allusion, Manuel's letters from the campaign deserve study within the context of Byzantine letter theory, and not just as a source of 'historical data'. Although these eight letters are often cited for the important information they provide about the campaign, they have never been studied as letters, as literary compositions. On the contrary, the elevated language and style of the letters has been disparaged by several scholars as a barrier to historical investigation. However, Manuel's aim in writing these letters was not to provide precise details about various aspects of the campaign. Once more, we must remember that in Byzantine letter theory and writing, the priority was not to convey concrete information; eloquent language and literary features were considered essential and desirable elements.

These letters claim a special place in the emperor's letter collection on the account of their sophisticated literary features, and Manuel's self-representation here deserves attention. As might be expected, the letters are full of complaints relating to the difficulties of warfare and his humiliation in serving his enemies.[15] He also describes Anatolian topography: while the Ottoman army was camping in the area of Sinope, the emperor narrates that they were encamped on a tiny plain that could barely contain the army, encircled by mighty mountains. It had only a little wood and some murky water, having been deserted by its inhabitants who had fled to escape slaughter.[16] In another letter, he also complains that the soil in the area was dry and devoid of any greenery, which made finding provisions for the army extremely difficult.[17] Although Manuel's descriptions do correspond to the climate of the region, his complaints about the topography and provisioning also serve the literary purpose of creating an atmosphere of misery. This imagery further accentuates his sufferings in the Ottoman army.

---

[15] See Ch. Messis, 'La memoire de 'Je Souffrant'. Construire et écrire la mémoire personelle dans les récits de voyage', in *L'écriture de la mémoire: la littérarité de 'historiographie, Actes du colloque international sur la littérature Byzantine, Nicosie 6–8 mai,* 2004 eds. P. Odorico and P. Agapitos (Paris, 2006), 107–46 for some examples, such as Gregory Palamas and John Caminiates, for the representation of self and the 'barbaric' other during travel or captivity.

[16] Letter 16, lines 2–10.

[17] Letter 18, lines 21–7. The same complaints about the scarcity of supplies are also found in Letter 16, line 64 and Letter 19, line 5.

His Anatolian letters also give insight into Manuel as a ruler. A seasoned soldier himself, the emperor seems to have taken a genuine interest in the problems of provisioning. For instance, he reports the case of a man who had to sell his horse in order to buy barley. The man learned that he would receive only five coins for each horse but would have to pay forty-five coins for barley only to feed a single horse once. In the end, he was left distraught by the realization that he would have to sell nine horses each day for the fodder of a single horse. Employing a simile that befits his current military atmosphere and adapting his imagery to the circumstances, Manuel compares the soldier's cry of despair to the screams of the wounded.[18]

Manuel says very little about the Ottoman army itself. He indicates the presence of the sultan's other Christian vassals but does not speak about other commanders. Yet it is highly probable that Bayezid was also accompanied by the Janissaries and possibly also by the *akıncıs*, the raiders' troops within the Ottoman army.[19] The sultan's entourage possibly included some of his close associates, including his *vezir* Çandarlı Halil Pasha.[20] It is difficult to sketch a picture of Manuel's military experiences among the Ottomans as there are no contemporary sources that provide insight into the Ottoman military. The only time he makes a reference to his surroundings in the Ottoman encampment is in his narration of how writing letters at night in his tent, but he gives no further details.[21] In the *Funeral Oration,* while describing the Ottoman soldiers' surveillance of Theodore in Serres on Bayezid's orders, Manuel recounts how it was the sultan himself who decided where the tent of the despot should be pitched. He also narrates how the Ottoman guards lit fires and sang at night.[22] One imagines that an atmosphere similar to the Serres camp pervaded that of the Asia Minor campaign of 1391.

A letter to Kydones offers a striking vignette of the itinerant Ottoman court. In it Manuel complains to Kydones about an interesting aspect of

---

[18] Letter 18, lines 32–3.

[19] See Sp. Vryonis, 'Isidore Glabas and the *Devshirme*', *Speculum* 31 (July 1956), 433–43, and C. Imber, *The Ottoman Empire, 1300–1650: Structures of Power* (New York, 2002), 134. The *akıncıs* could also be made up of Christian soldiers, see H. Lowry, *The Nature of the Early Ottoman State* (New York, 2003), 51–2. Henceforth, Lowry, *The Nature of the Early Ottoman State.*

[20] Although narrating the Crusade of Varna during the reign of Murad II, the *Anonymous Gazavâtnâme* dating from the fifteenth century illustrates the close collaboration between the Ottoman sultan and his commanders. Since we have no contemporary sources for the reign of Bayezid I, is possible to use the *Gazavâtnâme* to partially visualize the military environment during the reign of Bayezid some fifty years earlier. See *Gazavât-ı Sultan Murad b. Mehemmed Han: İzladi ve Varna Savaşları (1443–1444) üzerine Anonim Gazavâtnâme*, eds. H. İnalcık and M. Oğuz (Ankara, 1989). I thank Dr Rhoads Murphey for suggesting this source.

[21] Letter 19, lines 19–20.   [22] *Funeral Oration,* 148–50.

his participation in the campaign: he was frequently expected to join the Ottoman sultan in drinking parties. Although Islam forbade the use of alcohol, Bayezid's love of wine was remarked upon by the Ottoman chroniclers Aşıkpaşazade, Neşri and Ahmedi. However, it should also be noted that they emphasized his drinking in order to underscore the sultan's deviation from the accepted norms of a *ghazi* warrior. The message is that this deviation from the *ghazi* ideology brought about Bayezid's defeat at the Battle of Ankara in 1402.[23] The fact that they do mention the drinking, however, in combination with Manuel's testimonies, leaves us in no doubt that the sultan did in fact consume wine.

In the letter, Manuel complains that Bayezid wanted to drink a few toasts before dinner with the Christian lords, forcing them to fill themselves with wine from his varied collection of golden bowls and cups. Manuel also remarks that the sultan believed that drinking together dispelled the sorrows of the campaigns. Yet, Manuel remarks, even if he had been in a good mood, these cups could only fill him with sadness. Manuel laments to Kydones about being forced to spend time in the sultan's circle, and he protests that he was unable to see, hear or do anything for the betterment of his spirit. Neither his nature nor his education predisposed him to enjoy things the Ottomans did; namely, indulge in idle pleasures.[24]

The *topos* of a drunk and pleasure loving 'barbarian' was commonplace in Byzantine literature, but it is noteworthy that Manuel confines these depictions only to the case of Bayezid, a portrait which is also partially confirmed by the Ottoman sources.[25] Moreover, he describes their unpleasant time in each other's company in minute detail. All these factors indicate that Manuel's portrayal of Bayezid was not a mere *topos* but stemmed from strong personal dislike. This instance has further significance with regard to his self-representation. While his words do reflect genuine anguish, they also serve to represent the emperor – the morally 'superior' and educated Byzantine – as a fish out of water among the pleasure-loving and unsophisticated 'barbaric' army. Manuel seeks to portray himself as a sophisticated and scholarly ruler who, through misfortune, is forced to dwell among 'barbarians'. Not only does the emperor flaunt his virtues and learnedness here, but he also strives to elicit sympathy from his audience.

---

[23] See Aşıkpaşazade, 95; Neşri, 333 and Lowry, *The Nature of the Early Ottoman State*, 24–9; 136–7; and Manuel's Letter 16, lines 98–104.
[24] Letter 16, lines 69–75.   [25] See footnote 23.

Manuel's letters are also laced with complaints about lack of time for writing. Nonetheless, he wrote at least eight long, polished letters in a span of a few months. Both the manuscript tradition of the letters and the replies to them do not indicate any serious revisions. This suggests that despite his complaints, he did find enough time to concentrate on his writing during the campaign. Moreover, throughout his life the emperor displayed a tendency to immerse himself in writing during difficult times.[26] Perhaps, this was partially due to his fondness for writing, and partially because he also sought to enhance his political authority through his compositions. Manuel had already attempted to legitimize his political decisions in Thessalonike through his writings, both during and after his rule in the city. The Asia Minor campaign was not only a period of personal distress for him, but also an extremely humiliating episode for him as a ruler. Hence, in these Asia Minor letters, Manuel again endeavours to combat criticism and assert his authority through his self-representation.

The emperor represents himself as an idealized man of letters and also draws attention to his military surroundings in order to demonstrate his devotion to his writing. For instance, Manuel is described as composing replies just as he is about to mount his horse for battle. We are also told that he writes letters in his tent during the night, choosing to 'nourish' himself with *logoi* instead of sleep. In addition, he remarks, rather enigmatically, to Kydones that the people who could not bear to see the emperor devote time to literary pursuits at home, would be even more critical if they could see Manuel doing the same on campaign. These people, he claims, blamed his literary occupations for the problems of the empire, and the emperor felt that he had to 'hide' while writing in his tent.[27] These remarks suggest that he faced blame for his literary pursuits, probably on the grounds that an emperor should devote his time entirely to governing, but through his self-representation, Manuel strove to deflect these anonymous critics and defend his passion for *logoi*.

In the same letters, Manuel highlights the irony of serving the Ottomans in lands that once belonged to his own empire. He complains of marching with the Romans to wage war with the Scythians in the land of the Scythians and commanding troops for his enemies.[28] Significantly, that while Manuel conceives Constantinople as the land of Romans (Ῥωμαίους ... τὴν αὐτῶν), Anatolia is referred to here as the land of the Scythians (ἐν τῇ Σκυθῶν): the emperor now perceives this once Byzantine

---

[26] This tendency has also been noted by Angelou, see *Dialogue on Marriage*, 47–8.
[27] Letter 19, lines 19–23.   [28] Letter 14, lines 10–11.

landscape as being alien and 'barbaric', despite the fact that the ancient
ruins adorning the landscape were his own heritage:

> Most of these cities now lie in ruins, a pitiable spectacle for the people
> whose ancestors once possessed them. But not even the names have
> survived, since they were destroyed so long ago. Actually, when
> I inquired after the names of these cities, and the people I asked would
> reply: 'We destroyed those cities, but time has erased their names', I was
> seized with sorrow . . . . when someone having no idea of the ancient
> name of the city would instead call it by some barbaric and strange-
> sounding name, I lamented loudly . . . . You have heard of the city of
> Pompey, beautiful, marvellous, extensive; rather, that is how it once was,
> for now you can barely make out its ruins. The small plain in which we
> are now staying certainly had some name when it was fortunate enough
> to be inhabited and ruled by the Romans . . .[29]

The emperor emphasizes that it was not only the physical elements of the
cities that had declined, but also the Greco-Roman cultural heritage, as
evidenced in the change of place names. Though he was a descendant of
the people who once possessed these territories, Manuel represents himself
as a stranger in these now 'barbaric' lands. His letters bear testimony to the
humiliation and sorrow experienced by the Byzantine emperor, who was
now functioning almost as an Ottoman mercenary.

Apart from the insights they offer into Manuel's thoughts and feelings,
the letters from the Asia Minor campaign can be considered among his
most notable literary works. As a group of eight letters, they are thematically and stylistically coherent. In this regard, one of the most striking aspect
of these letters is the military atmosphere Manuel seems to have attempted
to create through several allusions to the *Iliad* and Xenophon's *Anabasis*.

---

[29] Letter 16, lines 22–36 and 43–9. 'αἱ δὲ πλείους καὶ κεῖνται θέαμα τούτοις ἐλεεινὸν ὧν πάλαι κτῆμα
τοῖς προγόνοις ὑπῆρχον, ἀλλ' οὐδὲ τοὔνομα γοῦν ταυταισὶ τῷ διεφθάρθαι ἄνωθεν περιλείπεται.
Καὶ μὴν ἐρόμενος πῶς αἱ πόλεις ὀνομάζοιντο, ἐπειδὰν μὲν ἀποκρίνοιντο πρὸς οὓς τὴν πεῦσιν
ποιοῦμαι ὡς "ἡμεῖς μὲν ταύτας, ὁ χρόνος δὲ τὴν προσηγορίαν ἠφάνιεν", ἀνιῶμαι μὲν εὐθύς, σιγῇ δὲ
τέως πενθῶ σωφρονεῖν ἔτι δυνάμενος. Εἰ δέ τις ἀφαιροῖτο μὲν τὴν ἣν προσηγορίαν αἱ πόλεις
ἐκέκτηντο, προσθήσει δέ τινα βάρβαρον καὶ ἀλλόκοτον, σὺν βοῇ λοιπὸν πενθῶν οὐδὲ κρύπτεσθαι
σχεδόν, πῶς οἴει, βουλόμενος πολλῶν εἵνεκα δύναμαι ... Ἀκούεις τὴν Πομπηΐου τὴν καλὴν καὶ
θαυμαστὴν καὶ μεγάλην, μᾶλλον δὲ τὴν ποτε τοιαύτην οὖσαν, νῦν γὰρ μόγις που λείψανα ταύτης
φαίνεται, πρὸς ὄχθῃ κειμένην τοῦ ποταμοῦ ἔχοντος γέφυραν ἐκ λίθων θαυμαστῶν διὰ στοῶν τῷ τε
μεγέθει καὶ τῷ κάλλει καὶ τῇ τέχνῃ κεκοσμημένων. ἥτις δὴ πόλις τὸν δειμάμενον μέγαν παρὰ
Ῥωμαίοις προσαγορευθέντα . . . .'

Several other writers also described the ruins of Byzantine cities while they were contrasting the current
state of the Byzantine Empire and its glorious past. See A. Kaldellis, 'Historicism in Byzantine Thought
and Literature', *DOP* 61 (2007), 1–24 and I. Ševčenko, 'The Decline of Byzantium seen through the Eyes
of the Intellectuals', *DOP* 15 (1961), 167–86. Henceforth, Kaldellis, 'Historicism'.

For instance, in Letter 16, when describing the landscape of northern Asia Minor to Kydones, Manuel calls the formidable mountains *oresi helibatoisin* (ὄρεσι ἡλιβάτοισιν). This usage is not found in any of his other works.[30] The adjective *helibatos* (ἡλίβατος) is found in book fifteen of the *Iliad* and means lofty. The word is employed in the description of the reaction of the Greeks upon seeing Hector, who are compared to game animals dispersing. This Homeric image of animals fleeing to escape death, is reminiscent of Manuel's description of the flight in Asia Minor that immediately follows this description of the mountains.[31] Manuel's word choice of *helibatos*, and the slight resemblance between his narrative and that of the *Iliad*, may suggest the influence of Homer, who also narrated a war and ironically described lands that were very close to those in which the emperor now found himself.

Moreover, when describing the flight of the inhabitants to the clefts of the rocks, Manuel uses the word *cheramos* (χήραμος), from the *Iliad*, book twenty-one. Homer uses the word *cheramos* to describe a cleft while narrating the flight of the goddess Artemis after being defeated by Hera.[32] Manuel's usage of *cheramos* too, occurs in the same context of flight from battle into wilderness.[33] The Homeric vocabulary in the letter is reinforced by Manuel's remark; 'as a poet would say . . . '[34] The recipient of the letter, Kydones, must have recognised these Homeric influences since he replies that Manuel's sea of misfortunes did not need his ship, but rather the Muse of Homer.[35]

The emperor alludes to yet another epic narrative that, in part, took place in Asia Minor. In Letter 19, he writes that the men he took with him experienced hardships on the campaign that were far greater than any in the past, elsewhere adding that all these hardships the army endured called for a historian and not a letter writer. In another letter, Manuel complains that even Xenophon, the general of the 10,000, would scarcely have been able to give an exact account of the campaign.[36] It can thus be proposed that Manuel sought to represent the campaign almost as another *Anabasis*. The latter work narrates the return journey of Greek mercenaries in 401 BC. At

---

[30] Letter 16, lines 1–5. '. . . ἐν πεδίῳ τινὶ πάνυ σμικρῷ. ὄρεσι γὰρ συνεχέσι κυκλούμενον ἡλιβάτοισιν, εἶπεν ἂν ποιητής, σταθμὸς μόγις ἥρκεσε τῇ στρατιᾷ γενέσθαι.'

[31] Homer, *Iliad*, Book 15, 273. Letter 16, lines 7–10. [32] Homer, *Iliad*, Book 21, 494–5.

[33] These two words are also listed as Homeric in the *Souda*, a copy of which Manuel might have owned. See Chapter 3.

[34] Homer was referred to as 'ὁ ποιητής' in Byzantium, Wilson, *Scholars*, 18. Usually, when Manuel refers to 'the poet' or to 'a poet' without using the definite article, he means Homer. See also R. Browning, 'Homer in Byzantium', *Viator* 6 (1975), 15–33.

[35] Kydones, Letter 432, lines 37–8. [36] Letter 15, lines 26–9.

one point, it takes place in northern Asia Minor, very near where the emperor himself was campaigning. The *Anabasis* tells the story of a group of mercenaries who fought for the Persian king, a situation that was ironically similar to Manuel's position in the Ottoman sultan's army. In a way, the campaign was an indeed an *Anabasis* for him, and the emperor took care to convey these parallels to his correspondents.

Manuel's Homeric vocabulary and allusions to Xenophon served to create an atmosphere of epic warfare. This not only lent a 'heroic' flavour to the emperor's humiliating campaign, but also provided literary enjoyment for his recipients. These allusions were meant to display the author's erudition and to delight the recipient with their wittiness. They were not mere 'decorations' in the text but were literary features that the Byzantine audience enjoyed listening to and reading. In this regard, Manuel's decision to preserve these eight letters from this unpleasant episode seems to indicate that he did not view them as unpleasant souvenirs, but as a noteworthy authorial achievement.[37] These eight letters, containing Manuel's insights on Ottoman Anatolia, his self-representation, his use of metaphors and his allusions to epic narratives, were not merely receptacles of 'historical' information, and they deserve recognition as literary pieces in their own right.

The *Dialogue with a Persian*

The campaign soon ended, and around December the Ottoman army retreated to Ankara for the winter.[38] On Ottoman Ankara, Manuel only mentioned that although the city had abounded in piety under Byzantine rule, it now flourished in impiety. Indeed, Ankara would not have looked very familiar to the emperor: most of the antique remains of the city had been severely damaged during the Persian attacks of the seventh century, though he probably would have seen some Byzantine remnants, including several military towers and Emperor Julian's column.[39] In Ankara, Manuel was hosted at the house of a *müderris*, a scholar of Islamic theology. Echoing the experiences of Gregory Palamas in Bithynia earlier in the fourteenth century, the two men seem to have held debates concerning Islam and Christianity, often in front of a curious audience. It was on the

---

[37] For instance, Barker remarks that it is surprising that Manuel chose to preserve so many letters from such an unpleasant episode in his life, Barker, *Manuel II*, 88.

[38] For Byzantine Ankara, see C. Foss, 'Late Antique and Byzantine Ankara', *DOP* 31 (1977), 27–87, which however, deals with earlier centuries.

[39] *Dialogue with a Persian*, 5.

basis of these debates that Manuel would compose one of his most famous works, the *Dialogue with a Persian*.[40] *Dialogue with a Persian* holds a special place in Manuel's oeuvre. Its theological contents are not only engaging, but the literary aspects of the work are also notable. Consequently, it merits lengthy discussion. The *Dialogue with a Persian* acquired global fame in 2006, when Pope Benedict XVI quoted from the seventh dialogue to criticise Islam, and it regularly features in the scholarly literature, especially concerning the identity of the *müderris* and the theological aspects of the work. The following discussion will focus on some of the literary aspects of the work, especially in the portrayal of the characters.[41]

[40] Although the work consists of twenty-six dialogues, since the work is formed of consecutive dialogues and thus forms one coherent, unified work, I will refer to the text as *Dialogue*, and not *Dialogues*. Th. Khoury, *Manuel II Paléologue. Entretiens avec un Musulman, 7e controverse* (Paris, 1966), consists of only the seventh dialogue with a French translation; Manuel Palaeologus, *Dialoge mit einem Perser*, ed. E. Trapp (Vienna, 1966); K. Förstel, *Dialoge mit einem Muslim*, 3 vols. (Würzburg, 1995); *Kaiser Manuel II Palaiologos: Dialog Über den Islam und Erziehungsratschläge*, trans. W. Baum and R. Senoner (Vienna, 2003), also has a German translation of the seventh dialogue. In this book, I will rely on the well-known Trapp version. See also E. Voordecker, 'Les 'Entretiens avec un Perse' de l'empereur Manuel II Paléologue (à propos de deux éditions récentes)', *Byzantion* 36, (1966), 311–17.

[41] The following discussion has been published in a slightly modified version; S. Çelik, 'The Emperor, the Sultan and the Scholar: The Portrayal of the Ottomans in the *Dialogue with a Persian* of Manuel II Palaiologos', *BMGS* 41 2 (2017), 208–28.

Barker points out that he was not able to consult the work at the time of the publication of his monograph, Barker, *Manuel II*, 97. S. Reinert, 'Manuel II Palaeologus and his Müderris', in *The Twilight of Byzantium*, eds. S. Ćurčić and D. Mouriki (Princeton, 1991), 39–51, reprinted in S. Reinert, *Studies on Late Byzantine and Early Ottoman History* (Farnham, 2014), Study IX. Henceforth, Reinert, 'Müderris' and C. J. G. Turner, 'Pages from the Late Byzantine Philosophy of History', *BZ* 57 (1964), 348–57; J. A. Demetracopoulos, 'Pope Benedict XVI's use of the Byzantine Emperor Manuel II Palaiologos' dialogue with a Muslim *muteritzes*', *Archiv für Mittelalterliche Philosophie und Kultur* 14 (2008), 264–304; I. Polemis, 'Manuel II Palaiologos between Gregory Palamas and Thomas Aquinas', in *The Ways of Byzantine Philosophy*, ed. M. Knežević (Alhambra, California, 2015), 353–60. Henceforth, Reinert, 'Müderris', Demetracopoulos, 'Pope' and Polemis, 'Palamas'.

Also see A. Karpozilos, 'Byzantine Apologetic and Polemic Writings of the Palaeologian Epoch against Islam', *Greek Orthodox Theological Review* 15 (1970), 213–48; E. Trapp, 'Quelques textes peu connus illustrant les relations entre le Christianisme et l'Islam', *BF* 29 (2007), 437–50; E. Trapp, 'Der Sprachgebrauch Manuels II in den Dialogen mit einem 'Perser'', *JÖBG* 16 (1967), 189–97; M. Balivet, 'Rhomania Byzantine et Diyar-ı Rum Turc une aire de conciliation religieuse (XIe–XVe siècles)', in *Byzantins et Ottomans: relations, interaction, succesion, in Byzantins et Ottomans*, ed. M. Balivet (Istanbul, 1999), 11–79; S. Vryonis, *The Decline of Medieval Hellenism in Asia Minor and the Process of Islamization from the Eleventh through the Fifteenth Century* (Berkeley, 1972), 428; A. Ducellier, *Chrétiens d'Orient et Islam au Moyen Age, VIIe–XVe siecle* (Paris, 1966), 90–106; Ducellier, 'L'Islam et les musulmanes vus de Byzance au XIVe siecle', *Byzantina* 12 (1983), 95–134; E. A. Zachariadou, 'Religious Dialogue between the Byzantines and Turks during the Ottoman Expansion', in *Religionsgespräche im Mittelalter*, eds. B. Lewis and F. Niewöhner (Wiesbaden, 1992), 289–304, re-printed in E. A. Zachariadou, *Studies in Pre-Ottoman Turkey and the Ottomans* (Aldershot, 2007), Study II; J. Meyendorff, 'Byzantine Views of Islam', *DOP* 18 (1964), 263–86.

The *Dialogue with a Persian* consists of twenty-six dialogues written in the form of a Platonic dialogue. Previously, Manuel had employed the same form in the *Discourse to Kabasilas*. That the emperor was interested in dialogic form, is not surprising. As discussed earlier, dialogue was a popular literary form in Byzantium for centuries, and it was favoured by many Byzantine authors to discuss philosophical and theological issues.[42] Manuel's decision to compose an anti-Islamic treatise as a dialogue was rooted in this well-established Byzantine literary tradition. For Byzantine authors, Plato was the preferred model for theological and philosophical discussions. As in the case of the *Discourse to Kabasilas*, there can be no doubt that the *Dialogue with a Persian* is also modelled on Plato.[43] Despite employing the Socratic *elentic* method – that is to guide and to refute the arguments of the opponent through questions – in the *Dialogue*, the emperor chiefly employs the Platonic model as a literary ploy.[44]

For instance, several Platonic dialogues start with a collocutor asking Socrates' opinion on a philosophical question; usually, the collocutors sit with a group of friends. Manuel's *Dialogue*, too, begins as the two collocutors and several other people are sitting by the fire after the dinner. The *müderris* asks the emperor to satisfy his curiosity about Christianity. Platonic modes of address (ὦ βέλτιστε, ὦ ἀγαθέ) are likewise sprinkled throughout the entire work. Although at times the discussions become long monologues, the many quick 'question and answer' sections found in the text also closely resemble the style of Plato. As in the case of many Platonic dialogues, the *Dialogue with a Persian* is reported speech, thus making the emperor both a speaker and the narrator.

The *Dialogue with a Persian* also belongs to the tradition of Byzantine anti-Islamic treatises. The tradition of writing polemical treatises against Islam emerged in the eighth century as a response to the rise of Islam, and can be traced throughout the centuries.[45] Although the corpus of these works is rather vast, some notable works include those of John of Damascus (eighth century), Niketas Byzantios (ninth century), George Monachos (ninth century),

---

[42] See *Dialogues and Debates*; for dialogue especially in the twelfth century, Cameron, *Arguing it Out: Discussion in Twelfth-Century Byzantium* (Budapest, 2016), 10–52.

[43] For the depiction of Socrates in Platonic dialogues, see R. Blondell, *The Play of Character in Plato's Dialogues* (Cambridge, 2002), 42–3, 185; T.C., Brickhouse and N. D., Smith. *Plato's Socrates*, (New York, 1994) 3–16.

[44] For the uses of the Platonic dialogue by Byzantine authors as a literary ploy, E. Kechagia-Ovseiko, 'Plutarch's Dialogues: beyond the Platonic Example', in *Dialogue and Debates*, 8–19, especially 8–10.

[45] The following discussion is based upon Trapp's introduction, *Dialogue with a Persian*, *13–35; Th. Khoury, *Les théologiens Byzantins et l'Islam: texts et auteurs (VIIIe–XIIIe siècles)*. (Louvain and Paris, 1969); Cameron. *Arguing It Out*, 120–35.

Zigabenos (twelfth century) and Niketas Choniates (twelfth century). Anti-Islamic works had their roots in the *Adversus Iudaeos* literature; works written against Judaism. It must be emphasized that neither the *Adversus Iudaeos* texts, nor the anti-Islamic ones were composed as comparative studies of Christianity and the opposing religion. Their function was to refute the opponent and to vindicate Christianity, and both were ultimately composed with the sole goal of establishing Christianity's superiority.

Despite the breadth of the topics found in Byzantine anti-Islamic works, ranging from the life of the Prophet Mohammed to the origins of Islam, polygamy and the authenticity of the Quran, Islam was never accurately represented. Instead, the authors would insert rather fanciful stories. Byzantine authors did not conduct in-depth studies of Islam and its various aspects, but usually recycled the 'distorted' information found in earlier and contemporary anti-Islamic texts. These texts did not engage objectively with Islam, but attempted instead to refute it, frequently by relying on statements from the previous literature. Thus, although they may contain some interesting factual details, the information offered by the authors of anti-Islamic works cannot be used to reconstruct the realities Islam of the time.

In the fourteenth and fifteenth centuries, the rapid Ottoman conquests, increasing conversions to Islam and face-to-face contacts between the Christians and the Muslims led to a further proliferation of anti-Islamic works. One such notable example is that of Gregory Palamas, who held debates with the Ottoman audience on Islam and Christianity during his captivity and later composed works based on these discussions. Most crucially, Demetrios Kydones translated Ricoldo di Monte Croce's *Contra Saraceneroum,* an important anti-Islamic Latin text, into Greek. Manuel's maternal grandfather John VI Kantakouzenos penned anti-Islamic works relying on this Greek translation of Ricoldo di Monte Croce's *Contra Saraceneroum.*[46] Moreover, many people among Manuel's literary circle, such as Makarios Makres and Joseph Bryennios, also wrote anti-Islamic texts.[47]

---

[46] Kantakouzenos' work, consisting of four apologies and four orations, is found in *PG* 154, cols. 371–692 and Kydones' translation of Ricaldo di Monte Croce's *Contra Legem Sarracenorum* in *PG* 154, cols. 1035–170. On Kantakouzenos' work, see also K. P. Todt, *Kaiser Johannes VI Kantakouzenos und der Islam. Politische Realität und theologische Polemik im palaiologenzeitlichen Byzanz.* (Würzburg, 1991). Also see W. Eichner, 'Accounts of Islam', in *Doctrine and Debate in the East Christian World,* eds. A. Cameron and R. Hoyland (Farnham, 2011), 109–72, 115, points out that Kantakouzenos' knowledge of Islam seems to be solely based on Kydones' translation of Ricoldo.

[47] However, these works are dated later than the *Dialogue with a Persian.* See Argyriou, *Makres-Islam* 239–330 for the treatise of Makres. See A. Argyriou, Ἰωσὴφ τοῦ Βρυεννίου μετὰ τίνος Ἰσμαηλίτου Διάλεξις', *EEBΣ* 35 (1966–1967), 141–95 for the dialogue of Joseph Bryennios.

Manuel's *Dialogue with a Persian* fits well within the broader framework of Byzantine anti-Islamic works. The majority of the topics touched upon by Manuel, such as the life of the Prophet Mohammed, polygamy, violence in religion and the Islamic perception of Trinitarian theology, were quite commonplace in the genre. The emperor also does not represent Islam accurately, but instead weaves many spurious stories into his discussions. As is the case with other anti-Islamic or *Adversus Iudaeos* dialogues, in his work Christianity utterly prevails. The *Dialogue with a Persian* does not reveal strong textual parallels or influences from former anti-Islamic literature, and only two pieces seem to have been essential to Manuel's dialogue; namely, those of Kydones and Kantakouzenos.

Kantakouzenos' heavy reliance on Kydones' translation of Ricoldo has now been demonstrated. In turn, Manuel seems to have relied, to an extent, on Kantakouzenos' work.[48] Not only does Manuel's discussion of the life of the Prophet Mohammed display remarkable similarities with that of Kantakouzenos, but several textual parallels between the works have been attested concerning the discussions of pleasure, the arc of Noah, polygamy and violence in Islam.[49] The emperor openly acknowledges his debt to Kantakouzenos, recalling him as 'our blessed grandfather the emperor'.[50] Apart from Kantakouzenos, Manuel betrays only a very few parallels with other anti-Islamic works.[51] Instead, the emperor chiefly relies on the four gospels, the psalms and the Church Fathers. All in all, despite being part of the much wider anti-Islamic polemical tradition, his dialogue does not reveal a strong reliance on earlier Byzantine polemical writings. Rather, it stems from a new line of Byzantine treatises generated by Kydones' translation of Ricoldo di Monte Croce.[52]

On the other hand, albeit relying partially on Kantakouzenos, Manuel's work differs from that of his grandfather in its breadth of content. The discussions are much more wide-ranging, including, among other subjects, the nature of the angels, paradise, rationality in men and animals, the life of the Prophet Mohammed, Trinity, Christology, icons and the lives of the apostles.[53] For instance, although Manuel relies on Kantakouzenos' and

---

[48] This has been studied in detail and demonstrated by Trapp, see *Dialogue with a Persian*, *66–86. For several textual parallels with Kantakouzenos, identified by Trapp, *Dialogue with a Persian*, 29, 33,34, 51,52,54,79,134.

[49] *Dialogue with a Persian*, *66.

[50] *Dialogue with a Persian*, 6. 'ὁ θειότατος πάππος ἡμῖν, ὁ πάντ' ἄριστος καὶ θαυμάσιος βασιλεύς. . . '.

[51] Once with Niketas Byzantios and a few times with John of Damascus, see *Dialogue with a Persian*, 58 and 195–6.

[52] *Dialogue with a Persian*, *66.

[53] *Dialogue with a Persian*, *62–84, for an extensive summary of these discussions.

Kydones' translations of Ricoldo for the discussion of the life of the
Prophet, his own discussion is much more extensive.[54] Similarly, the topics
of rationality in men and animals, and icons are absent in the works by
Kantakouzenos and Kydones. What is most striking, however, is the fact
that several of Manuel's discussions are not attested in any other work. In
this regard, the most prominent is the discussion of the nature of the
angels, where Manuel represents Islam as viewing the angels as mortal and
corruptible. This is an argument that has no precedent either in Byzantine
or in Islamic sources. Other such topics include a tale of Enoch and Elias
and the so-called Islamic belief of Mohammed as the Paraklete.[55]

Unlike other examples of anti-Islamic polemical texts, discussions in
the *Dialogue with a Persian* are not limited to the defence of Christian
dogma. Manuel moreover touches upon other issues such as choice
(προαίρεσις), free-will, desire and the changeability of fortune; questions
in which he shows a continuous interest throughout his life. In the 1410s,
these topics would form the central questions of his ethico-political
works, namely the *Foundations of Imperial Conduct* and the *Seven Ethico-
Political Orations*. Despite being a chiefly theological work, the *Dialogue
with a Persian* bears witness to Manuel's lifelong interest in ethics and
philosophy.

The theological 'originality' of the work also poses an important question. As mentioned above, Manuel draws upon the Byzantine theological
and patristic literature in the *Dialogue*. The majority of the material and
the arguments he presents, are borrowed from these sources. However, it
would be unfair to label Manuel's reliance on the existing theological
literature as a sign of unoriginality and thus to dismiss his theological
work out of hand. Originality in the modern sense, that is, to produce
distinct, original ideas that depart from a tradition, was not a priority for
Byzantine theologians. The Palaiologan era did indeed see two theologians
who, while adhering to the tradition, came up with 'novel' arguments –
Gregory II of Cyprus (1241–90) and Gregory Palamas (1296–1356) – this
was not the case for Manuel. Rather, it was the norm to reproduce
discussions from the teachings of the Fathers and other established theological authorities. The Byzantines did not perceive this reliance as unori-
ginal or restrictive but rather as operating within the framework of
theological tradition and as an expression of the tradition of the living
theology. Thus, even John of Damascus declared proudly that he would

---

[54] *Dialogue with a Persian*, *66.   [55] *Dialogue with a Persian*, *86.

say nothing on his own, but instead, refer to the Fathers throughout his work.[56]

Indeed, any attempts to add to patristic teachings could easily lead to accusations of 'innovation' (καινοτομία) and impiety. Deviating from the established corpus of theology and proposing new ideas was thus a problematic issue. Moreover, Byzantine theological works were usually composed as responses to perceived heresies, be it Islam, Judaism or a differing view of Christianity, and thus, they were usually exegetical or polemical treatises. They did not seek to find new arguments but to refute claims made by the opposing side. In short, these works and their authors sought to define and defend the Orthodox teachings, not to create a new theological system.[57]

Manuel's aim in composing the *Dialogue* was likewise to produce a detailed apology of Christianity vis-à-vis Islam. He did not need to and did not seek to produce new ideas or arguments. Unlike the modern reader, the emperor's audience did not expect new arguments from his work. Scholars should also refrain from condemning Manuel's reliance on previous theological work as a mark of unoriginality or to dismiss him altogether as a theologian. Throughout the *Dialogue*, it is evident that he had a good command of the topics and the sources he was discussing. Furthermore, as mentioned, the *Dialogue* also discusses a few unattested topics concerning Islam: such as the tale of Enoch and Elias, Mohammed as the Paraklete, the corruptible nature of the angels, the story of Ashoka and the column.[58] In these few instances Manuel does introduce new discussions to the genre whose origin cannot be discerned. However, it must also be pointed out that these discussions do not represent original or distinctive theological arguments by Manuel. They are merely anecdotes and stories pertaining to supposedly Islamic beliefs.

---

[56] Dialectae sive capita philosophica, ed. B. Kotter, *Die Schriften des Iohannes von Damaskos* I (Berlin, 1969), 55, 9–11. Cited by C. Triantafyllopoulos, Makarios of Ankyra. *An Annotated Critical Edition of the Treatise Against the Errors of the Latins by Makarios, Metropolitan of Ankyra (1397–1405)*, 2 vols. (PhD thesis, Royal Holloway, University of London, 2009), 33*. Henceforth, Makarios of Ankyra.

[57] See Makarios of Ankyra, *33–4; Podskalsky, *Theologie und Philosophie*, 80–1; A. Papadakis, 'The Byzantines and the Rise of Papacy: Points for Reflection (1204–1453)', in *Greeks, Latins, and Intellectual History 1204–1500*, eds. M. Hinterberger and C. Schabel (Leuven, 2011), 19–42, 38–9 and in the same volume, T. Kolbaba, 'Repercussions of the Second Council of Lyon (1274): Theological Polemic and the Boundaries of Orthodoxy', (Leuven 2011), 43–68, 66–7. For the case of Gregory of Cyprus, see A. Papadakis, *Crisis in Byzantium: The Filioque Controversy in the Patriarchate of Gregory II of Cyprus (1283–1289)* (New York, 1983; repr. 1997). Henceforth, Papadakis, 'The Byzantines and the Rise of Papacy', Kolbaba, 'Council of Lyon' and Papadakis, *Crisis*.

[58] *Dialogue with a Persian*, *86.

Another key question raised by the dialogue is related to its fictional qualities. While the emperor refers to his collocutor merely as *müderris* (μουτερίτζης), there are many hints in the dialogue which indicate that he was a real person and that actual conversations took place. In the preface to his work, Manuel says that the *müderris* was an old man who was a newcomer, having arrived from Babylon. For this reason, he was greatly honoured: all judges and all teachers of 'their' wisdom hung upon his words. He was called *mouteritzes*, which Manuel explains was an epithet of precedence and honour.[59] Based on this, we can conclude that the emperor's collocutor was an Islamic theologian of high standing. Throughout the dialogues it is clear that he has command of both Persian and Arabic and is sometimes summoned by the dignitaries of the city, a mark of the great esteem he seems to have commanded. The emperor explains that the *müderris* and his circle conversed in Turkish and he, in Greek. Their words were translated by an Ottoman translator whom Manuel refers to as a 'Christian offspring'. He was either a recently converted Greek, or a second-generation Muslim born of Greek parents.[60]

Recently, Michel Balivet has attempted to identify this *müderris*; he suggests two candidates, Hacı Bayram Veli and Şemsettin Fenari. While his arguments are convincing, it is unfortunately not possible to answer this question definitively, since no separate source concerning Manuel's debates besides the *Dialogue* exists.[61] Finally, as mentioned, some of the discussions of the *müderris* are not attested in any Byzantine or Latin source. It is possible therefore that Manuel instead heard these in an actual conversation while he was among the Ottomans.[62]

With further regard to the question of fictionality, one must bear in mind that the emperor did not write the dialogue as a transcription of the conversations nor as documentary evidence of his sojourn in Ankara. This blurred line between 'reality' and fiction is prevalent in most of the other Platonic dialogues in Byzantium.[63] Although some parts of the debates

---

[59] *Dialogue with a Persian*, 5.

[60] I am grateful to the late Prof. John W. Barker for warning me that I had neglected to speak about the languages spoken by Manuel and the *müderris* in these debates. His insight allowed me to clarify this point.

[61] *Dialogue with a Persian*, 8, for the sons. See M. Balivet, 'Le soufi et le *basileus*: Haci Bayram Veli et Manuel II Palaéologue', *Medievo Greco* 4 (2004), 19–31.

[62] This point has been convincingly made by Trapp, *Dialogue with a Persian*, *86; also followed by Demetracopoulos, 'Pope', 295–300, concerning the story of Ashoka.

[63] See P. Andrist, 'Literary Distance and Complexity in Late Antique and Early Byzantine Greek dialogues Adversus Iudaeos', in *Dialogues and Debates*, 43–64, for this observation. For fiction in Byzantium, especially in hagiography, see Ch. Messis, 'Fiction and/or Novelisation in Byzantine Hagiography', in *The Ashgate Companion to Byzantine Hagiography*, vol. 2, ed. S. Efthymiadis (Farnham, 2014), 313–42.

recounted in the *Dialogue with a Persian* may have indeed taken place and some of the everyday life scenes scattered across the work probably did stem from Manuel's actual experiences, most of the work is fiction or a fictionalized, modified and embellished version of actual conversations. This is also made plain in Manuel's representation of himself and of Christianity as the utterly prevailing side: remarkably, the *müderris* never makes a sound argument, nor does he quote the Quran or other Islamic theological texts. The lengthy argumentations on Manuel's part further indicate that the emperor expanded upon and modified actual debates. One should not expect to find a depiction of 'reality' or a faithful report of the debates that took place. Simply put, this was not the purpose of the work. The emperor penned the *Dialogue* as a defence of his Christian faith vis-à-vis Islam, contributing to the bulk of similar treatises that were 'in vogue' amongst his circle.

What renders the *Dialogue* so remarkable is its vividness as a Platonic dialogue, its adornment with amusing anecdotes and the complex, multi-layered representation of the characters. While the *Dialogue* is a theological treatise refuting Islam, those stylistic features set it apart from other such contemporary compositions, posing a sharp contrast to the 'dryness' of the usual offerings. There is no attempt, for instance, at characterization of the collocutors in Joseph Bryennios' theological dialogues. Similarly, a dialogue by Demetrios Chrysoloras has only a single, feeble instance of such characterization, in which one of the collocutors, Demetrios Kydones, is depicted as becoming angry when refuted.[64] Otherwise, the collocutors are cartoon-like, mouthpieces for conventional arguments. However, the *Dialogue* displays strong 'literariness' through its liveliness, witty style and vivid language, suggesting that Manuel endeavoured to fashion a more literary text as opposed to a mere theological treatise.

Manuel's self-representation in the *Dialogue* is directed once more towards enhancing his authority, both in the text and in reality, as the ruling emperor. By positioning himself as the superior discussant in the debates, he was also seeking to assert himself as a theological authority. Not only does the emperor portray himself as being intelligent and learned, he also fashions his own portrayal as an emperor-scholar: one whose ideas are wholeheartedly embraced by the Ottoman audience.

---

[64] Demetrios Chrysoloras authored a dialogue between the then deceased Kydones, Neilos Kabasilas and himself. See V. Pasiourtides, *An Annotated Critical Edition of Demetrios Chrysoloras' Dialogue on Demetrios Kydones' Antirrhetic Against Neilos Kabasilas* (PhD thesis, Royal Holloway and Bedford New College, University of London, 2013), especially 28 for the author's comments on the style of the dialogue.

As in the case of his former works, Manuel adopts varying strategies to offer an idealized, authoritative self-representation to his audience. Unsurprisingly, throughout the *Dialogue* he emerges as the undisputed winner of each debate. While Christianity is expanded upon, the *müderris* speaks very superficially, and the emperor openly represents himself as the intellectually superior party. Moreover, the *müderris* and the Ottoman audience are represented as acknowledging Manuel's intellectual superiority. After all, it is the *müderris* who first approaches the emperor to converse, with the claim that he had never met with a Christian who could completely satisfy his curiosity. This speech functions as a subtle tribute to Manuel. Although, at first, he graciously declines the offer, Manuel represents himself as accomplishing what all the others failed: convincing the *müderris* of Christianity's worth.[65]

In the face of his authoritative persona, the *müderris* is represented as extremely excited and overjoyed by the debates. Each morning, he eagerly arrives in Manuel's chambers at very early hours. He is even unable to sleep at night since he ponders the arguments with such intensity. On one occasion, the *müderris* is so enthusiastic about the emperor's conversation that he threatens to kill the roosters, since they announce the arrival of morning and the end of the debate.[66] The audience is also depicted as showering praise on the emperor. At one point some audience members even cling to Manuel's cloak to prevent him from leaving.[67]

On the other hand, Manuel is full of self-control, engaging in the discussions only in order to enlighten his host. While Palamas and Kantakozuenos also employ the conventional literary trope of reluctance to engage in a debate with Muslims that would 'enlighten' them, Manuel's self-representation as a sought-after teacher of Christianity goes beyond these examples.[68] The emperor shows neither any sign of excitement concerning the debate, nor any curiosity about Islam, and this contrast between him and the *müderris* serves to highlight his own intellectual 'superiority'. It moreover demonstrates his 'cultural' superiority as a calm, restrained Christian – freed from the almost childish curiosity of his Ottoman opponent.

Manuel again adopts the role of Socrates, as he had previously done in the *Discourse to Kabasilas*. Once more, he is the one who is approached to enlighten the collocutors. Throughout the work, he is clearly in control of

---

[65] *Dialogue with a Persian*, 8.   [66] *Dialogue with a Persian*, 250.   [67] *Dialogue with a Persian*, 119.
[68] See A. Philippides-Braat, 'La captivité de Palamas chez les Turcs, dossier et commentaire', *TM* 7 (1979), 109–221, 142–5.

the discussions, and like Socrates, the participants look up to him; sometimes employing the *elenctic* method, he unravels all counter-arguments.
Also significant, is that the emperor represents himself as operating
unaided in the debates, whereas the *müderris* is aided by his two sons and
the audience. Manuel describes the Ottomans as gathering in private to
prepare in advance and switching to Arabic or Persian when they wish to
discuss amongst themselves, so as to avoid being translated.[69]

The *müderris* is the also depicted as the more passive collocutor during the
debates. His part of the dialogue is also far shorter than that of Manuel.
Indeed, in the preface, the emperor refers to him as 'a lover of listening'
(φιλήκοος), thus neatly assigning the *müderris* a passive role from the very
beginning.[70] When compared to the figure of Manuel, he comes across
almost as a young student, despite his white beard. Another contrast between
the two can be seen in the cool demeanour of the emperor, while the *müderris*
is described as continuously blushing and saddened by his defeats. On one
occasion, he almost becomes tearful.[71] Manuel laces his text with accusations
that his opponent was 'fleeing' (φυγεῖν), especially when the latter tries to
avoid answering his questions. This sense of incompetence is further
enhanced by the *müderris*' protests that defending himself against Manuel
was not easy.[72] Ultimately, at the very end of the work, the *müderris* professes
a wish to visit Constantinople to become better acquainted with Christianity.
The closure adds the final touch to the triumph of the emperor over his
opponent, and of Christianity over Islam.[73]

Manuel does not seek to triumph over Islam only through his character
portrayals.[74] A part of the fifth dialogue is entirely devoted to the question of
the durability of the current Ottoman prosperity. At this point, the text
almost completely breaks from the theological debates. Instead, the discussion takes a radically different turn and focuses on the rise and fall of empires.
The *müderris* boasts that the Ottomans' current successes stems from Islam
being the 'true religion.' As in the *Panegyric to John V*, Manuel contextualizes
Islam's success within a framework of volatile fortune but expands the theme
in great detail. He claims that many past empires that flourished achieved

---

[69] *Dialogue with a Persian*, 94, 190 and 212.   [70] *Dialogue with a Persian*, 4.

[71] *Dialogue with a Persian*, 25, 35 and 106.

[72] *Dialogue with a Persian*, 65–6, 92, 198 for a few examples.

[73] *Dialogue with a Persian*, 299. Reinert takes this wish as almost a conversion to Christianity, Reinert,
'Müderris', 45–8. Yet in my view, this should not be interpreted as leading to a conversion since in
his preface Manuel explains to his brother Theodore that on account of his old age, his opponent did
not abandon his 'erroneous' faith. *Dialogue with a Persian*, 5.

[74] Arguably it is this part of the work that has drawn the most attention, see the two articles focusing on
this discussion; Turner, 'Pages' and Reinert, 'Müderris'.

success by means of their virtue and zeal, giving as examples those built by Philip and Alexander. Did they, asks the emperor, differ from their opponents in their mode of worship, displaying a greater reverence for God? He then answers his own question in the negative, pointing out that both the ruling and the ruled peoples sacrificed to demons at that time – that is, they were all pagans. They succeeded because they were virtuous and strove hard for glory, not because of their religion.[75] He thus separates virtue and faith, claiming that the former allowed empires to flourish. Here Manuel does not seem to consider faith a type of virtue.

This passage has a further interesting aspect: Manuel displays 'historical awareness' in his open acknowledgement of the virtue of these empires despite their paganism.[76] He respects those empires for following their own notions of virtue and piety, and refrains from debasing them as pagans. The emperor further expands his arguments and brings forth yet another category of empires, namely those that flourished completely undeservedly and through an inexplicable providence of God. Unsurprisingly, the empires of Nero, Sardanopoulos, Xerxes and Cyrus fall into this second category; these were all, by Byzantine standards, examples of (mostly 'Oriental') tyranny. Manuel then goes on to narrate the struggle between Xerxes and the Greeks, ultimately resulting in Xerxes' unexpected defeat, which he argues was a complete reversal of fortune.

The emperor here seems to be drawing on a very commonplace parallel between the struggle of the Byzantines against the Ottomans and that of the Greeks against Xerxes. His implication is that as an empire in the second category – a tyrannical one – the Ottoman Empire would eventually meet the same fate as the Persians.[77] He concludes his passionate defence by stating that fortune will again be reversed and the Byzantines will be restored to their former glory, and also that as true Christians, they will not attribute this to their own virtue but to their faith.[78] While trying to redeem his own faith, Manuel essentially contradicts his own former claim that empires flourish by virtue and not by faith. He thus refutes the logic of his own argument within the span of a few passages – which goes unnoticed by the *müderris* and the Ottoman audience.

---

[75] *Dialogue with a Persian*, 58.
[76] See Kaldellis, 'Historicism', giving examples of Byzantine literati of a similar outlook to that of Manuel here, notably Attaleiates, who praises the Roman Republic for being virtuous and revering its own religion. See also A. Kaldellis, 'A Byzantine Argument for the Equivalence of all Religions: Michael Attaleiates on Ancient and Modern Romans,' *International Journal of the Classical Tradition* 14 (2007) 1–22.
[77] *Dialogue with a Persian*, 58–9.   [78] *Dialogue with a Persian*, 62.

Manuel's stance against Islam and his glowing self-representation does not, however, lead him to portray the *müderris* as a cartoonish, ignorant 'barbarian' stereotype. A noteworthy feature of the *Dialogue* is Manuel's more nuanced representation of the Ottomans. Although he is depicted as being the intellectual inferior of the Byzantine emperor, the portrayal of the *müderris* does not correspond to the uncivilized barbarian portrait that one might expect to find in such a work. Instead, Manuel portrays him as a learned, witty and amiable person. It is indeed possible to sense throughout the dialogue that, despite their religious differences, the emperor enjoyed the company of his anonymous host.[79] When the *müderris* makes witty jokes, he admits to being taken by these pleasantries. He even endows his collocutor with the quality of urbanity (ἀστειότης) that is often ascribed to Byzantine literati.[80]

Significantly, when informing his brother Theodore that the *müderris* did not abandon Islam, Manuel admits that that was to be expected. The *müderris* was very old and Islam was, after all, the faith of his forefathers.[81] It warrants attention here that the emperor reveals a sensitive approach in the matters of faith. Similarly, the Ottoman audience is depicted as being exceptionally tolerant during the religious debates, more so than Manuel himself. At one point, the emperor insults the Prophet Mohammed. It is only then that the *müderris* becomes angry and asks Manuel to use more considerate words. Notably, this is the only time the verb 'to get angry (ὀργίζεσθαι)' is used in the entire work. Immediately after, in an intimate gesture, the *müderris* touches Manuel's knee and consoles him by saying that friends have great licence of speech.[82] He himself is represented as being very respectful of Christianity. Once, he even claims that Christ belonged more to him than to the emperor, as Manuel believed Christ was crucified, while Islam argued that he directly ascended to heaven. While Manuel uses this exchange to emphasize the *müderris'* high regard for Christianity, it is worth noting that this direct ascension of Christ to heaven is referred to in the Quran.[83]

---

[79] In his *Verses Against an Atheist*, Manuel displays a similarly tolerant stance. This poem consisting of 800 lines is addressed to an atheist (ἄθεος). The emperor uses the term in the sense of a godless person, an unbeliever. Perhaps, Manuel wished to denote that the unbeliever was a Muslim, a Jew or a Christian with 'heretical' beliefs. Based on some textual parallels with the *Dialogue with a Persian*, the editor of the poem, Ioannis Vassis, proposes 1392–6 as the poem's composition date. See I. Vassis, 'Οι ανέκδοτοι στίχοι πρὸς ἄθεον ἄνδρα του Μανουὴλ Β' Παλαιολόγου', *Βυζαντινά* 32 (2012) 37–100.

[80] *Dialogue with a Persian*, 50, 190. [81] *Dialogue with a Persian*, 5.

[82] *Dialogue with a Persian*, 71.

[83] *Dialogue with a Persian*, 146. Islam does indeed recognize Christianity and considers Christ to be a major prophet; a *sura* of the Quran is specifically devoted to the Virgin Mary.

From time to time, Manuel still highlights the 'otherness' of the Ottoman collocutors. This can be observed in the few instances where a member of the audience disagrees with Manuel. Tellingly, Manuel refers to the audience as *theatron*, contextualizing their debates in a Byzantine framework.[84] Whenever there are disagreements from the audience, the emperor characterizes their speech as 'barbaric'.[85] Even in the preface, after praising the character and the learning of the *müderris*, Manuel says that both in character and in speech, he was nevertheless a barbarian, and he often accuses the *müderris* of subverting the *taxis* during the course of debates.[86] The emperor suggests that the Ottoman scholar could not really grasp this significant Byzantine concept.[87] Similarly, in an amusing passage, while Manuel tries to demonstrate the implausibility of Mohammed being the only one to announce his own coming as a prophet, without any mentions in the Old and the New Testament or the former prophets, the following exchange takes place:

> 'Was he the only one to do so, or do any of the
> prophets of the old agree with him?
> And he replied: 'It was he (αὐτός) who said so.'
> I said: 'You could say he himself (αὐτότατος), if you
> wish to allude to the Comedian.'
> 'We', he replied, 'do not know the Comedian ... '[88]

In Aristophanes' *Wealth*, the deity Wealth uses the word *autotatos* in an amusing scene where he desperately tries to convince the others about his identity. By alluding to Aristophanes and within the context of the Prophet's self-acclamation, Manuel not only undermines, but also ridicules the argument of his opponent. It is a display of wit that would have been much appreciated by his Byzantine audience, but is lost on his Ottoman collocutor. The emperor seems to have employed this particular exchange to stress their 'cultural' differences, pointing out the *müderris*' lack of knowledge of Greek literature. For all his good qualities, this lack sets the *müderris* apart from Byzantine literati and lowers his level of erudition in Manuel's eyes.

Manuel allows glimpses into his life among the Ottomans and the warm hospitality of the *müderris*. In one instance, the emperor narrates how he had breakfast with the *müderris* on a cold and stormy winter morning:

---

[84] *Dialogue with a Persian*, 154–5, 188–9 and 241 for some examples.
[85] *Dialogue with a Persian*, 22 and 290 for two such instances.   [86] *Dialogue with a Persian*, 7.
[87] *Dialogue with a Persian*, 76, 89.
[88] *Dialogue with a Persian*, 54. ʽΚαὶ τίς τῶν προφητῶν ταῦτα λέγει; Μωάμεθ ὁ ἡμέτερος. Μόνος ἦ καί τινας ἔχων τῶν πάλαι συμφθεγγομένους; Καὶ ὅς, "αὐτὸς" ἀπεκρίνατο. Πρόσθες δὴ καὶ τὸ "αὐτότατος" ἔφην, εἴ σοι δοκεῖ τῷ Κωμικῷ χαριζόμενος. Οὐκ ἴσμεν, ἔφην, τὸν Κωμικόν. ὄντι δὲ τηλικούτῳ προφήτῃ δεήσει γε μαρτύρων καὶ συνηγόρων', Aristophanes, *Wealth*, 83.

... Someone from among his people came in carrying wood to light a great fire. He also brought a considerable amount of nuts and honey to us – such was the hospitality of the Persians. The old man, who pointed at these with his finger, started joking as on previous occasions: 'I have come to you bringing arms, with which we shall scare away the present storm.' And since I was pleased with those words, I said: 'This is well thought of, we shall not be bothered by the snow while having breakfast.' I sat down and partook in the offering, so that I did not dishonour the hosts and distributed all remainders to those standing nearby ...[89]

The offering of nuts and sweets that the emperor describes above would indeed have been considered a mark of hospitality. For instance, the traveller Ibn Battuta was also served nuts and sweetmeats by almost all his hosts in Turkish Anatolia.[90] Curiously, Manuel takes note of the Ottomans' eating habits. He takes special care to distinguish breakfast from other meals by referring to it as *ariston* (ἄριστον).[91] Throughout the work, Manuel often refers to the Ottomans visiting him after having had breakfast. He does not refer to breakfast merely to indicate that the debates began in the morning, but because he seems to have been especially intrigued by the Ottomans' breakfast habits. In one case, he conveys their eagerness by remarking that they had come even before the sun's rays and *even before* having eaten anything, despite their custom of having breakfast before settling down to their tasks.[92] While such vignettes serve to enrich the atmosphere of the work, they also seems to indicate the emperor's particular notice of these customs.

Yet another such episode is the return of Manuel and his party from the hunt. Their spoils include some wild boars, and when the *müderris* jokingly asks whether they could also feast on the game meat, Manuel replies similarly:

'Of course', I replied to him, 'yet if you wish to taste from all, since we cannot divide the game; this is not the custom for hunters.' I said this in jest, and I will now explain the joke. Someone from our party had hunted a big

[89] *Dialogue with a Persian*, 50. Ταῦτα τούτου μεθ' ἡδονῆς εἰρηκότος εἰσῄει τις τῶν αὐτοῦ ξύλα τε μεγίστην ἀνάψαι πυρὰν ἱκανὰ καὶ κάρυα καὶ μέλι κομίζων ἡμῖν (τοιαῦτα γὰρ τὰ ξένια τῶν Περσῶν). Ταῦτα τοίνυν τῷ δακτύλῳ μοι δείξας ἔφη πάλιν ὁ γέρων τοῖς προτέροις παραπλήσια παίζων. Ἥκω σοι κομίζων ὅπλα, οἷς τὸν ἐπιόντα χειμῶνα ἀποσοβήσομεν. Καὶ ἡσθεὶς τῷ τῶν ῥημάτων ἀστείῳ, τοιγαροῦν καταφρακτέον ἔφην, καλῶς, ὅπως ἐν τῷ ἀριστᾶν μὴ ταῖς νιφάσι διενοχλώμεθα. Καθίσας δὲ καὶ τῶν ξενίων ἁψάμενος, ὅσον ἐκείνους μὴ ἀτιμάσαι, ἔπειτα τοῖς περιεστηκόσι πάντα διένειμα.'

[90] Ibn Battuta, *The Travels of Ibn Battuta: A.D 1325–1354*, 2 vols., eds. C. Defremery and B. R. Sanguinetti (Cambridge, 1962), 411, 428 and 432. Henceforth, Ibn Battuta.

[91] See ODB 1, 170 for *ariston* in Byzantium, which is usually referred to as a morning meal as opposed to the later ones. However, many Byzantine authors used *ariston* to denote a midday meal; its Classical usage as breakfast shifted in Byzantine Greek. Here, the text makes it clear that Manuel used it in the sense of breakfast.

[92] In *Dialogue with a Persian*, see for instance, 120 and 231.

and fat wild boar with his spear and without anyone noticing, he had
concealed it in grass while bringing it, so that he was not subjected to
many curses and abuses, and accidentally also blows, of those who could not
bear even to see pigs . . .[93]

The emperor here is, of course, referring to Islamic dietary regulations that
forbid the consumption of pork. This amusing exchange highlights the
dietary and religious differences between the Byzantine party and their
Ottoman hosts. Manuel likewise narrates their Ottoman dinner in detail:

I got down from my horse and taking me by hand, the old man led me to the
house, being hospitable in accordance with his customs. Torches had been
lit, as well as a fire sufficient to combat the severity of winter. Near the fire,
was a sizable bronze platter, full of winter fruits, adorned with bread loaves,
which you recognize, those ones which are of a paper-like appearance
(χαρτοειδεῖς) and are badly baked . . .[94]

Manuel here is describing the custom of eating around a round bronze
platter called *sini*, which functioned as a dining table.[95] The bread loaves that
the emperor described seem to be the Turkish flatbread. In order to describe
this bread, the emperor coined a new word: *chartoeidos*. Significantly,
Manuel strongly hints that he did not like this bread; it was badly baked.
While it is also possible that he did indeed dislike the flatbread, his negative
description might have also served to debase Ottoman baking, thus implying
a culinary and hence 'cultural' inferiority.[96]

Apart from the *müderris*, the other prominent Ottoman in the *Dialogue
with a Persian* is Bayezid. He and Manuel seem have had a very personal

---

[93] *Dialogue with a Persian*, 190. 'Κἀγὼ ταὐτὸν ἐκείνῳ ποιῶν καί, μάλ᾽ ἔξεστιν, εἶπον, εἰ πάντων
ἐθελήσαιεν ἀπογεύσασθαι, οὐδὲ γὰρ τὰ μὲν μερίζειν, τὰ δὲ μὴ θεμιτὸν θηραταῖς. Τοῦτο δὲ εἶπον
παίζων, τὴν δὲ παιδιὰν ἤδη λέξω. Κάπρον τις τῶν ἡμετέρων μέγαν τε καὶ πίονα σφόδρα δόρατί
που κατενεγκὼν μηδενός τινος συνειδότος συρφετώδει χόρτῳ ἑλίξας, ὡς ἂν μὴ ὑπὸ τῶν μηδὲ
βλέπειν χοίρους ἀνεχομένων συχνὰς ἀρὰς καὶ προπηλακισμούς, τυχὸν δὲ καὶ πληγὰς δέξαιτο,
ἐκόμιζεν ἐφ᾽ ἵππου.'

[94] *Dialogue with a Persian*, 190. '῾Ηδομένων οὖν πάντων τῷ τοῦ γέροντος λόγῳ (ἀστεῖος γάρ τις
ἔδοξεν εἶναι) κατέβην εὐθὺς τοῦ ἵππου καὶ τῆς χειρός με λαβόμενος ὁ πρεσβύτης ἦγεν ἐπὶ τὸν οἶκον
ἐπιχωρίως ξενίσων. Δᾷδες οὖν ἦσαν ἡμμέναι καὶ πῦρ ἱκανὸν χειμῶνος ἐλέγχειν δριμύτητα καὶ πρὸς
αὐτῷ τι σκεῦος χαλκοῦν οὐ σμικρόν, γέμον μὲν ὀπωρῶν τούτων δὴ τῶν χειμερίων, ἔχον δὲ καὶ
ἄρτους, οὓς οἶσθα, τοὺς χαρτοειδεῖς ἐκείνους καὶ κακῶς ὠπτημένους . . . .'

[95] Bertrandon de la Brocquière also describes a *sini*, calling it 'un pié de rondeur'. Bertrandon de la
Broquière, *Le voyage d'outremer de Bertrandon de la Broquière.* ed. Ch. Scafel (Paris, 1892), 89.

[96] It has been noted by several scholars that a negative description of foreign food could serve to
emphasize the cultural inferiority of the consumers vis-à-vis the Byzantines. See P. Tuffin and
M. McEvoy, 'Steak à la Hun: Food, Drink and Dietary Habits in Ammianus Marcellinus', in *Feast,
Fast or Famine: Food and Drink in Byzantium*, eds. W. Mayer and S. Trzcionka (Brisbane, 2005),
69–84; C. Galatarioutou, 'Travel and Perception in Byzantium', *DOP* 47 (1993), 221–41 and
T. Kolbaba. *The Byzantine Lists: Errors of the Latins* (Chicago, 2000), especially, 150. Henceforth,
Galatariotou, 'Travel'.

enmity. Indeed, the emperor's detailed and extremely hostile depictions of Bayezid stand out from those of other sultans and transcend the *topoi* concerning the Ottomans. In the dialogue, he refers to Bayezid's nickname Yıldırım, meaning thunderbolt as *keraunos* (κεραυνός). He claims that the sultan received this epithet because of the swiftness of his evil actions.[97] This is remarkable as no other contemporary source speaks about Bayezid's epithet. Manuel constantly describes the sultan's immoderate love of hunting, and the only full description of Bayezid in the *Dialogue* is an almost demonic portrait:

> As an extraordinary snow fell and it was very cold, the satrap was confined at home. Being bereft of his customary hunt because of the severity of the storm, he was greatly vexed and resembled a madman. Since he could not comfort his soul which thirsted for murdering people, with animal blood, he thence drank at home, pouring out his anger on those who had by ill-fortune, offended him ever so slightly (perhaps not so slightly), sometimes insulting them and uttering blasphemies, sometimes using his sword. It seemed that, he was not able not to say or not to do something evil.[98]

This description of Bayezid stands in stark contrast to the portrayal of the *müderris*, especially since the scene that immediately follows the sultan's depiction is that of the *müderris* bringing in food to Manuel amidst a flurry of jokes. Moreover, the host expresses his delight in the fact that the storm had prevented the emperor from accompanying the sultan to the hunt; he can keep Manuel's company for himself.[99] It warrants attention that throughout the *Dialogue*, the *müderris* and the audience are represented as siding with Manuel against their own sultan. They openly declare their displeasure when the former is summoned to the hunt and are critical of Bayezid's displays of immoderation. The *müderris* even encourages the emperor to find an excuse not to go, effectively suggesting disobedience to his own ruler. While their demeanor emphasizes the Ottomans' high regard for Manuel's company, the Ottoman audience is nevertheless represented as disapproving of their own ruler.[100]

---

[97] *Dialogue with a Persian*, 17. For Bayezid, see H. İnalcık, 'Bayezid I', in *The Encyclopedia of Islam*, vol. 1, eds. H. A. R. Gibb, J. H. Kramer, E. Levi-Provencal and J. Schact (Leiden, 1986), 1117–19.

[98] *Dialogue with a Persian*, 50. 'Νιφετοῦ δὲ ἐξαισίου γεγονότος καὶ ψύχους ὅτι πλείστου εἴρκτο τε ἐν τῷ οἴκῳ ὁ σατράπης καὶ τῆς εἰωθυίας ἐπὶ τὰ θηρία ἐξόδου στερόμενος τῇ τοῦ χειμῶνος δριμύτητι σφόδρα τε ἐδυσφόρει καὶ μαινομένῳ ἑῴκει, καὶ ἐπεὶ μὴ αἵμασι θηρίων παρεμυθεῖτο τὴν ἐπ' ἀνθρώπους αὐτοῦ φονῶσαν ψυχήν, ἐκένου δήπου τὸν θυμὸν οἴκοι πίνων ἐπὶ τοὺς οὐκ ἀγαθῇ τινι τύχῃ σμικρόν τι προσκεκρουκότας αὐτῷ (ἴσως δὲ οὐδὲ σμικρόν) πῇ μὲν ὡς μάλισθ' ὑβρίζων καὶ βλασφημῶν, πῇ δὲ σιδήρῳ διεργαζόμενος (οὐδὲ γάρ, ὡς ἔοικεν, οἷος τ' ἦν μὴ οὐχὶ κακῶς ἢ λέγειν ἢ ποιεῖν).'

[99] *Dialogue with a Persian*, 121.   [100] *Dialogue with a Persian*, 50, 120, 124–5, 250.

Manuel dramatically uses the *müderris* and his circle as a foil to the pleasure loving court of the sultan:

> ... the daily hunt, the enjoyment of the dinner which follows the hunt, the crowd of mimes, choirs of flute players and singers, an entire nation of dancers, the sound of cymbals, the roaring laughter accompanying this *immoderation* (τὸ ἄκρατον) ... All these are sufficient to fill the soul with foolishness ...
>
> I do not see you (the *müderris*) sharing meals with those who are considered to be the happy (τούς εὐδαίμονας) people amongst you. Those people sleep, then eat once more as if in a vicious circle, their life is one of laziness and luxury, which is not suitable to men at all ...[101]

Yet in another point, the emperor again stresses the difference in the lifestyles of these two factions. He remarks that the *müderris* and his circle are seeking the perfect (εὐτελῆ) and the simple (ἀπέριττον) life in order to pursue a life of philosophy.[102] While the representation of these two parties can be seen within the context of a general juxtaposition of a life of philosophy and pleasure, it can also be interpreted as a sign of the influence of the *Nicomachean Ethics*. Manuel's criticism of the sultan and his court is grounded in their immoderation, a crucial vice in Aristotelian ethics since virtue can be achieved by acting moderately with respect to everything. In his own ethico-political works, Manuel would put great emphasis on moderation, especially in reference to *Nicomachean Ethics* the main source of his future ethico-political works.

A member of the audience is also depicted as criticizing Bayezid for his immoderation in hunting. The hunt is good, he argues, only if practiced in moderation.[103] Moreover, as in the *Panegyric to John V*, Manuel seems to be using *eudaimonia* in this passage not in the general sense of happiness; he utilizes it as a philosophical concept of true well-being, of reaching the highest form of contentment and fulfilment in life. According to Aristotle, *eudaimonia* was perceived differently by different individuals who choose

---

[101] *Dialogue with a Persian*, 121. 'Οὔκουν οὐδ' ἐκεῖνα παραδραμεῖν δεῖ τὴν μεθ' ἡμέραν θήραν, τὴν περὶ τὰ δεῖπνα μετὰ ταῦτα διάχυσιν μίμων τε ὄχλους καὶ αὐλητῶν συστήματα καὶ χορούς ᾀδόντων καὶ ἔθνη ὀρχηστῶν καὶ ἠχὼ κυμβάλων καὶ τὸν μετὰ τὸν ἄκρατον προπετῆ γέλωτα, ὧν ὀλίγα ἱκανὰ τὴν ψυχὴν ἀφροσύνης ἐμπλῆσαι. ... Οὐδὲ γὰρ ὁρῶ γε ὑμᾶς ἀρίστῳ μὲν δεῖπνα συνάπτοντας κατά γε τούς ἐν ὑμῖν εὐδαίμονας εἶναι νομιζομένους, ταυτὶ δὲ αὖ ὕπνοις κἀκείνους πάλιν ἀρίστῳ καθάπερ ἐν κύκλῳ βαδίζοντας, ὡς εἶναι σφίσι τὴν ζωὴν ἐν ἀργίᾳ καὶ χλιδῇ ἀνδράσιν οὐδαμῶς προσηκούσῃ.'

[102] *Dialogue with a Persian*, 65.

[103] *Dialogue with a Persian*, 94. In his writings, Manuel seems to refer to 'τὸ μέτρον' and the importance of moderation in the context of Aristotelian Ethics. This will be discussed in Chapter 9.

to follow different lifestyles in order to achieve this goal. Again, these ideas are adopted by Manuel in his own works.

In this regard, two lifestyles stand out in Aristotle: the Life of Pleasure (βίος ἀπολαυστικός) and the Life of Contemplation (βίος θεωρητικός), the basest and loftiest forms respectively, with the latter leading to true *eudaimonia*.[104] Here, Manuel's depiction of those at the Ottoman court who are *supposed* to be *eudaimon*, seems to be correspond to the Life of Pleasure. In contrast, the *müderris* and his circle are represented as attempting to pursue the Life of Contemplation.[105] The emperor may have relied on an Aristotelian framework when contrasting these two factions, and it is clear that he, unsurprisingly, identified with the scholars.

The criticism of Bayezid by the *müderris* and his circle serves to showcase their sympathy for Manuel vis-à-vis the sultan. Although these depictions are clearly literary representations fashioned by the emperor, they should not be dismissed. Manuel may have had a negative bias towards Bayezid, but it is significant to note that the Ottoman chroniclers also depict him as a pleasure-loving man and recount tales of his volatility. Both Neşri and Aşıkpaşazade narrate a curious episode where upon becoming angry at the *kadıs* (the judges) the sultan orders all of them to be burned alive. He is persuaded, with difficulty, to abandon these plans on the grounds that the *kadıs* were scholars.[106]

Furthermore, a *menakıbname*, or Ottoman saints' life, points out that the sultan received criticism from religious sheikhs, especially concerning his drinking. Hacı Bayram Veli – a possible candidate for the identity of the *müderris* in Manuel's *Dialogue*, is reported to have proposed that taverns be built on the four corners of the Grand Mosque in Bursa in order to encourage the sultan's visit.[107] Manuel's literary portrayals of Bayezid and the Ottoman audience therefore corresponds to the Ottoman sources. The *müderris* with whom Manuel conversed might indeed have been one of those critical scholars, possibly contributing to Manuel's obvious sympathy for him. After all, the emperor could have

---

[104] Aristotle, *Nicomachean Ethics*, I, VII, 4–9; I, IV, 5–6; X, VI–VII.

[105] Manuel's *Address as if from a Benevolent Ruler to his Subjects* (date unknown) has a similar depiction of the *Life of Pleasure*, see Appendix 3.

[106] Anonymous Tevarih citation should stay, it tells the same story as with Aşıkpaşazade 95–6 and Neşri, 336–9 and *Anonymous Tevârîh*, 34; Neşri, 336–9; Aşıkpaşazade, 95–6. Schiltberger, 11–12, also narrates that Bayezid wanted to kill him and his comrades but relented when the advisors entreated him to change his mind.

[107] See M. Balivet, 'Rhomania Byzantine et Diyar-ı Rum Turc: une aire de conciliation religieuse (XIe–XVe siècles)', in *Byzantins et Ottomans: relations, interaction, succession*, ed. M. Balivet (Istanbul, 1999), 111–79; 130, who refers to the *menakıbname* of Hacı Bayram Veli.

easily depicted the *müderris* as a stereotypical 'barbarian', which would have fulfilled his aims just as well. Manuel's nuanced and generally positive portrayal, however, hints at genuine regard.[108]

The character portrayal, flow, witty jokes and novel-like style of the *Dialogue with a Persian* render it a significant work among Manuel's oeuvre. Although Manuel shows great care and a penchant for literary features in all of his compositions in his use of language, metaphors, allusions, displays of wit and complex self-representation strategies, the *Dialogue* is especially remarkable. The work displays a concern for elegant, carefully constructed language and the flow of the text, and it attempts at characterization, displays of wit and episodes of story-telling that are highly fictionalized. On account of its pronounced 'literariness', the *Dialogue* cannot be considered solely a theological work, it must also be understood as a 'literary' one. While the boundaries between the theological, philosophical, rhetorical and the literary are indeed already blurred in Byzantine authorship, Manuel further amalgamates these in the *Dialogue with a Persian*. This, in turn, bears further witness to his interest in and talent for writing as an aesthetic venture.

A Wedding and a Coronation

Manuel's sojourn with his 'Persian' did not last long. Sometime in January 1392, the emperor finally returned to Constantinople where he made a decision that would alter not only his personal life, but the future of the dynasty: at the age of forty-two, Manuel finally decided to marry. His bride was Helena Dragaš, the daughter of the Serbian prince Constantine Dejanović (also known as Dragaš), who ruled over a large territorial lordship in northern Macedonia and titled himself a despot.[109] He also served Bayezid in his campaigns as a vassal, and it is almost certain that Manuel knew him in person. The advantages the marriage brought to the Byzantine emperor, if any, are unclear, and both rulers were in the same difficult position of having submitted to the Ottoman sultan.[110] At any

---

[108] Aşıkpaşazade, 113, notes that Manuel was on friendly terms with Fazlullah, the *kadı*, judge, of Gebze. The remark is made within the context of the war between Mehmed and Musa Çelebi in 1410–13. Thus, Manuel seems to have sympathy for several Ottoman scholars.

[109] Belgrano, no. 38, 169; Thiriet, *Régestes*, I, no. 808, 193 and Loenertz, *Lettres de Démetrius Kydones*, II, 445–6. The only article about Helena is D. Anastasjević, 'Jedina vizantijska carica Srpkinja', *Brastvo* 30 (1939), 26–48. A more recent book is now available, but it mostly deals with the political events of the period; L. Petanović, *Elena. L'ultima imperatrice bizantina* (Milan, 2002).

[110] Chalkokondyles, 80–1 claims that the marriage was agreed upon when both Manuel and Constantine were with Bayezid in Serres in 1394. However, all the sources, the Venetian Senate

rate, any alliance that might have resulted from the marriage was not to last long. Three years later Constantine Dejanović was killed at the Battle of Rovine in 1395 fighting in the Ottoman ranks.[111]

The person of Helena Dragaš is as obscure as the reasons for her marriage. She never appears in any of Manuel's writings. Her absence in the *Dialogue on Marriage*, where her husband represents marriage merely as a means to beget children and to secure the dynasty, is especially notable. This stands in great contrast to Manuel's treatment of the other Empress Helena in his life, his mother Helena Kantakouzene. Other Byzantine sources of the period observe a similar silence. For instance, the marriage is only recorded by Chalkokondyles who dates it erroneously, and by an entry in a short chronicle. This entry refers to her as being one-eyed or having sight in one eye (τῆς μονοφθάλμου).[112] It is difficult to determine whether this statement was true. Had Helena been deformed in one eye, or partially blind, is it likely that she would not have been considered a particularly eligible bride. If there was any truth to this statement, perhaps she might have lost eyesight in one eye after her marriage, due to illness or advanced age. Helena appears more often in the sources after Manuel's death, when she retired to the nunnery of Kyra Martha under the monastic name Hypomone. Later, she was to be recognized as a saint by the Orthodox Church.[113] All things considered, it can be suggested that her influence was stronger as a dowager empress than as Manuel's consort. During her husband's reign Helena does not seem to have exercised any influence either on politics, or on the emperor himself.

None of the sources touch upon the question of Helena's intellect or wisdom. When compared with the glowing praise bestowed upon empresses like Eirene Kantakouzene and Helena Kantakouzene, this silence can be interpreted as Helena Dragaš's more passive role during her husband's reign. After Manuel's death, Sphrantzes, himself a loyal supporter of Constantine XI, emphasizes Helena's strong political support for his younger son. Tellingly, Constantine XI was also known by the Greek version his mother's Serbian name, Dragatses.[114]

Like Sphrantzes, the funeral oration for Helena by Gemistos Plethon focuses on her role as a mother. He praises her for bearing many children,

---

deliberations, the Genoese expense books, Ignatius of Smolensk's account, point out that it took place in 1392, two years prior to the Serres meeting. Moreover, John VIII was born in 1393.

[111] See Fine, *The Late Medieval Balkans*, 382, 424 and 429 on Constantine Dejanović and Manuel's marriage.

[112] Chalkokondyles, 80–1; Schreiner, *Kleinchroniken*, Chronik 22/23.

[113] The feast day of St Hypomone is celebrated on 13th March, while her memory is also celebrated on 29th May, the anniversary of Constantinople's conquest and the death of her son Constantine XI.

[114] Sphrantzes, 36–7 and 100–1.

several of whom also became emperors. Helena appears as a mother figure while her role as the consort empress is represented as passive. For instance, Plethon extols her for sharing dangers with her husband during the blockade of Constantinople (1394–1402) and for her patient endurance during Manuel's European journey. Plethon ends his account of Helena's *genos* and *patris*, with astute, but rather unconventional comments. The waters of the river Axios of Helena's native land were clear and beautiful, but she nevertheless hailed from a relatively minor royal dynasty: her father was 'not insignificant'. In marrying the Byzantine emperor, Plethon remarks, she had made a marriage far above her station.[115]

Helena Dragaš seems to have arrived in Constantinople sometime before 7 February, since on this date, the expense book of the Genoese colony in Pera refers to a purchase of small value coins for her arrival ceremony.[116] According to Pseudo-Kodinos, if travelling by land, an imperial bride would usually dismount at Pege, where she would be greeted by the emperor and his entourage. If she arrived by sea, her ships would dock near the Church of Blachernai, outside the city. The emperor, his entourage and the wives of dignitaries would then greet her near the Acropolis at the Eugenios Gate.[117] Neither the route of Helena's journey, nor her reception in Constantinople are recorded. Still, when she entered the city, the coins mentioned in the Genoese expense accounts were scattered over her, and the wedding, a description of which does not survive, was celebrated shortly thereafter.[118]

The joint coronation of Helena and Manuel is narrated by Ignatius of Smolensk in meticulous detail.[119] As perhaps the last demonstration of Byzantium's imperial grandeur, the coronation is a vivid vignette of

---

[115] Plethon, *Monody for Helena Palaiologina*, in ΠΠ, III, 266–80; 267, 270 and especially 271–2. '. . . μήτηρ τῷ τούτων πατρὶ πολλῷ κρείττονι τήν τε ἀξίαν καὶ τύχην ἢ κατὰ τοὺς ἑαυτῆς γονέας . . .'. Also see Gennadios Scholarios, 'Consolatory Oration to the Emperor Constantine on the Death of his Mother', in Georgios Scholarios, *Oeuvres complètes*, eds. L. Petit, A. Siderides and M. Jugie, vol. I, (Paris, 1928), 262–270.

[116] Belgrano, 169. See S. Reinert, 'What the Genoese cast upon Helena Dragash's Head: Coins, not "Confecti"', *BF* 20 (1994), 235–46 in S. Reinert, *Studies on Late Byzantine and Early Ottoman History* (Farnham, 2014), Study VIII, who argues that the items being cast upon Helena's head were coins of small denomination, and not confetti.

[117] *Pseudo Kodinos*, 267–9 for the description of this ceremony. Although Pseudo-Kodinos' text dates to the mid-fourteenth century, it preserves a protocol of the reception of a foreign bride which has many parallels in earlier receptions and also contemporary ones. It is therefore possible that a similar ceremony, took place while welcoming Helena in the capital.

[118] P. Schreiner, 'Hochzeit und Krönung Kaiser Manuels II im Jahre 1392', *BZ* 60 (1967), 70–85, deals with the coronation ceremony in the light of Ignatius' account and the anonymous description found in Verpeaux's edition of Psedo-Kodinos, see the footnote below.

[119] Schreiner, *Kleinchroniken*, Chronik 10/9 agrees on the date. Schreiner argues that Manuel was not crowned twice, but was merely proclaimed emperor in 1373, as opposed to his coronation in 1392, see Schreiner, 'Hochzeit und Krönung', 74–5; and Ignatius of Smolensk, 103–13 for the coronation

ceremony. On the morning of 11 February, Hagia Sophia was already crowded with people. The singers were dressed in wide, belted robes of silk and brocade decorated with gold braids on the shoulder, they also wore pointed hats with braids. Two golden thrones had been set on a platform, covered with red cloth on the right corner under the galleries. The procession was extremely slow; Ignatius claims that it took the emperor three hours to reach the platform. It must have been taxing for all those involved, including Manuel. Twelve men at arms walked at his sides and two black haired standard bearers at the front, dressed in red, carried red standards. At the front of the procession heralds carried silver staffs. When Manuel and Helena were finally seated on their thrones, the liturgy began.

After the procession, Manuel was crowned by Patriarch Anthony in the ambo, then, the emperor crowned Helena himself.[120] As the sound of the Cherubic hymn filled the church, the Russian pilgrim was moved by the whole spectacle; who, he exclaimed, could describe the beauty of that moment? When the emperor left the church, Ignatius reports that the crowds tried to catch *staurata* that were thrown unto them. The account of the pilgrim ends at this point, but according to the anonymous description of Manuel's coronation, the emperor and the empress then proceeded on horseback, accompanied by dignitaries, to a residence (οἶκος) where the emperor and the empress appeared on a balcony. Finally, an imperial banquet was held, and the imperial couple were served by dignitaries.[121]

The Sole Emperor: Some Observations on Manuel's Rule

Despite this picture of splendour painted by Ignatius of Smolensk, Manuel's reign was anything but grand. His reign had commenced with a humiliating campaign as Bayezid's vassal, and even upon his return from his Ottoman campaign, Venetian envoys were instructed to remind Manuel of the Byzantine debt of 17,173 *hyperpyra* that he had inherited

account. Another account of the coronation also survives. This anonymous text is found in Pseudo-Kodinos, *Traité des offices*, ed. and trans. J. Verpeaux (Paris, 1966), 353–61.

[120] While Manuel was almost certainly also anointed by the patriarch, Ignatius omits this detail, perhaps since it was a custom foreign to him, Majeska, *Russian Travellers*, 420. *Pseudo-Kodinos*, 220–1, includes anointment with *chrism*. For anointment in Late Byzantium, see D. Nicol, 'Kaiseralbung. The Unction of the Emperor in Late Byzantine Coronation Ritual', *BMGS* 11 (1976), 37–52, re-printed in D. Nicol, *Studies in Late Byzantine History and Prosopography* (London, 1986), Study 1.

[121] See the anonymous account, 359–60 in footnote 119. Perhaps the residence in question was the Great Palace or the Blachernai, *Pseudo Kodinos*, 426.

while bidding him welcome to his capital.[122] The issue of debt owed to Venice constituted a major theme in the late Palaiologan era. His father, John V, had also received such a congratulatory message on his own accession, having inherited Andronikos III's debt of 19,000 *hyperpyra*. John V had paid 4,000 *hyperpyra*, but he and his mother Anna of Savoy accumulated further debts.[123] Indeed, Manuel made no payment – and would never do so.

From 1391 to his death in 1425, Manuel's rule was characterized by debt and political dissent. Despite having ruled for thirty-six years, it is difficult to study him as an administrator, as none of the Byzantine historians narrating his reign touch upon his administrative or economic policies. The few *chrysobulls* and *prostagmata* that have survived do offer some insight into his policies on landholding. This scarcity of source material stands in stark contrast with the abundance of documentary evidence at the disposal of biographers, for instance, of sixteenth and seventeenth-century European rulers such as Henry VIII of England, Charles V the Holy Roman Emperor and Philip II of Spain. Similarly, very few of Manuel's seals survive and are not particularly illuminating with regards to his rulership. Furthermore, due to his precarious financial straits, the emperor did not commission buildings or decorative programmes. Apart from two surviving manuscript illuminations, there are no surviving contemporary Byzantine depictions of the emperor. The surviving art artefacts that were produced in relation to Manuel consist of an ivory pyxis commissioned by a follower of John VII and an older manuscript enriched by illuminations containing the works of Pseudo-Dionysios.[124]

One might expect that Manuel's sizeable bulk of writings has yielded many insights into his actual governing of the empire; however, his voluminous oeuvre actually offers little help in this venture, since Manuel almost never speaks of his day-to-day ruling. His surviving letters seldom touch upon concrete matters that pertain to the governing of the empire, and no such letters addressed to him survive; any notes or mementos that were exchanged between Manuel and his officials, do not survive. For the same reasons, despite the autobiographic character of Manuel's works, one cannot construct a detailed portrait of him as an administrator

---

[122] Thiriet, *Régestes*, 1, no. 809, 193.

[123] Nicol, *Venice and Byzantium*, 257–60. By 1381, John V's debts stood at 17,163 *hyperpyra*, almost the exact sum Manuel inherited. Thiriet, *Régestes*, 1, no. 609, 149. Thus, although he had been able make at least some payment upon his accession, by 1381, John V, too, was unable to pay any part of the Byzantine debts until the end of his reign in 1391.

[124] These artefacts will be discussed in Chapters 7 and 8.

on the basis of his writings. One can, however, study the emperor's idealized and carefully constructed literary persona, and his strategies to legitimize and defend his political decisions. Indeed, almost all of his writings have embedded political messages. He also frequently complains of the difficulties he faced as the emperor of a weakened empire; and all of this provides insight into his rulership. Nontheless, Manuel's daily running of the government, his bureaucracy, and administrative and economic policies cannot be easily discerned through his oeuvre.

In this regard, the first three to four years of his reign are the most obscure period in Manuel's rule; his only known act as emperor is his decision in 1394/5 to reduce the metal content of the silver and copper coinage. This time period coincides with the early stages of the Ottomans blockade of Constantinople. It is rather telling that Manuel's only known act from these early years is reducing the metal content of coinage. On the whole, the empire of which Manuel was now the sole ruler was even weaker than during his childhood and youth in every sense. The accession of Bayezid I had accelerated the territorial expansion of the Ottoman Empire, and in 1393, he conquered Wallachia, Bulgaria and parts of Greece. Byzantine lands in Thrace also shrunk further. In Anatolia, Bayezid terminated the Aydınoğlu, Saruhan and Menteşe emirates. More crucially, as we may remember, sometime during the later years of John V's rule, Byzantium had become tributary to the Ottomans.[125]

To complicate matters further for the new emperor, Byzantine society was also divided on many levels. The situation strongly resembled Manuel's predicament in Thessalonike. The 'middle class', the *mesoi*, had disappeared to a large extent, and instead, society was polarized between the very wealthy, such as the *archontes* – members of the aristocracy and influential merchants – and the poor populace. The emperor could neither ease the suffering of the poor, nor exercise control over the wealthy, and money was the source of problems for everyone.

But perhaps the greatest problem of all, was the threat posed by John VII. Although Manuel was now officially the sole emperor of Byzantium, he still had a serious rival in his nephew. It can even be argued that Byzantium had two, opposing emperors. The activities of John after his short-lived rule in 1390 remain in the shadows. He resided in and ruled Selymbria, and was undoubtedly still hostile to his uncle Manuel. Despite the fact that several of his followers were exiled after his overthrow in 1390,

---

[125] Nicol, *Last Centuries*, 314–20. See also Chapter 2.

John still commanded a wide base of supporters. Not only had a part of the populace welcomed him to Constantinople during his rebellion, but members of prominent families also openly sided with John. Among these was his aunt by marriage Anna Palaiologina and members of the Goudeles family. As influential merchants, the support of the Goudeles family would prove especially troublesome for Manuel as would the support that John VII also enjoyed from the Ottomans and the Genoese. Through marriage, John VII was allied with the Genoese rulers of Lesbos, the Gattilusio family, and during the first years of Manuel's rule, he would also eventually become allies with Bayezid against his uncle. In short, Manuel had every reason to be apprehensive.

So, what did it really mean for Manuel Palaiologos to be emperor? Although the popular notion of a Byzantine emperor is one of absolute power and authority, Manuel's reality was rather different. In court rhetoric and imperial ceremony, Manuel was an omnipotent figure. However, as the emperor of a drastically weakened empire, his imperial authority was precarious. Politically, he was subsidiary to the Ottoman sultan, and economically, to a large degree, he was dependent on Venice and Genoa.[126] In the domestic sphere, moreover, Manuel's imperial authority was restricted severely by the elite and by the threat of his rival John VII.

Due to the loss of lands, the aristocracy was dependent on Manuel for their income; yet many engaged in trade and thus prospered. Furthermore, through their wealth, merchants also began acquiring governmental, diplomatic and bureaucratic posts. The aristocracy and this new elite always had the option to switch to John VII's side, who could potentially offer them land in Selymbria and economic privileges through his Genoese contacts; thus it can be argued that John VII and his faction became almost an 'alternative' court to that of Manuel. The populace (δῆμος) could be influential in politics as well, as demonstrated by the popular support offered to John VII during his uprising. Although erroneous, a story reported by Chalkokondyles in which Bayezid offers the people a choice between Andronikos IV and Manuel and they choose the latter, is illustrative of the power of the populace. Manuel becomes emperor *only* through the consent of the populace and the Ottoman sultan.[127]

In 1391, at the beginning of his reign, Manuel was aware of the difficulties he and his empire were facing. His letters are filled with complaints

---

[126] T. Kiousopulou, *Emperor or Manager: Power and Political Ideology in Byzantium before 1453*, trans. P. Magdalino (Geneva, 2011), 5–6. Henceforth, Kiousopoulou, *Emperor or Manager*.
[127] Chalkokondyles, 101–2.

concerning the 'present' circumstances and hints relating to his struggles to at least retain the status-quo. Tellingly, Manuel never speaks of territorial or economic expansion, nor does he ever express a certainty that the empire might be returned to its former glory. After all, ever since childhood, he had been witness to almost continual loss and chaos. Even after the civil war between the Palaiologoi and the Kantakouzenoi had ended, the meagre heritage his predecessors had bequeathed him was further debilitated by the uprisings of Andronikos IV and John VII, as well as by the empire's plummeting revenues. During John V's reign, Byzantium had moreover been compelled to accept Ottoman suzerainty; the very reason that the emperor was now at the beck and call of Bayezid. The civil wars, the increasing economic and political power of the Italian maritime cities and his father's submission to the Ottomans, had shaped many aspects of Manuel's reign.

The loss of lands and income left Manuel very little room in his attempts to improve the situation. Throughout his reign, whenever confronted by a major economic problem, he resorted to confiscation and taxation. Arguably, this was a reasonable policy to follow, and yet, as seen in Thessalonike, it continuously backfired and alienated his subjects. Throughout Manuel's reign, it is also possible to trace attempts to curb the economic influence of Venice. Before Manuel, both John VI Kantakouzenos and John V had sought to restrict Venetian economic power in Constantinople. They were especially concerned about the tax-free wine sold by Venetians in the taverns – a significant hindrance for local merchants – and attempted to impose embargoes and taxation on it.[128] John V had also refused to renew the Veneto-Byzantine treaty for fourteen years up to his death.[129] In this respect Manuel followed in his predecessors' footsteps and eventually did succeed in imposing some taxation on the Venetians. Like John V, he did not renew the treaty with the Venetians until 1406. Furthermore, Manuel wholeheartedly adopted another of his father's policies: to perpetually petition the West for help.

How much agency did Manuel manage to retain under these circumstances? Did he manage to control negotiations and remain proactive or

---

[128] The wine sold by the Venetians in taverns had been exempt from taxation since the reign of Michael VIII Palaiologos (1259–82), see J. Chrysostomides, 'Venetian Commercial Privileges under the Paleologi', *Studi Veneziana* 12 (1970), 267–356, re-printed in J. Chrysostomides, *Byzantium and Venice 1204–1453*, eds. M. Heslop and Ch. Dendrinos (Farnham, 2011), Study III, 273–7, 311. Henceforth, Chrysostomides, 'Venetian Privileges'. Nicol, *Byzantium and Venice*, 292–3.

[129] During his reign, which lasted a few months, John VII renewed the treaty and accepted the Venetian ownership of Tenedos, undoubtedly in order to gain Venetian support for his usurpation, MM, III, 135–44; DVL, II, no. 135, 224–9. This treaty became null after his deposition, requiring ratification from John V.

was he forced to respond to adverse circumstances? Analysing the deliberations of the Venetian Senate does shed some light on this matter, but as is to be expected these conditions can at times turn Manuel into a largely passive figure. Likewise, his political moves emerge as having usually been formulated in response to adverse situations. For instance, a study of the Venetian deliberations demonstrates how little power and brokerage he had in his dealings with Venice. In most of cases, Manuel's requests are usually turned down and his proposals dismissed. Even though he faced dire threat from the Ottomans, only some of his more minor petitions are granted.

However, the same documents also show that Manuel often held firm and acted accordingly. As an illustrative case, the matter of the debt owed to Venice comes up regularly in the deliberations, but throughout Manuel's reign, the Venetians did not manage to extract any payment. Indeed, this debt would never be settled.[130] Of course, Manuel lacked the financial means to make any payment, and Venice was aware of this. Although the Venetians had the upper hand in this relationship, they also did not wish to alienate the Byzantine emperor, in whose territories they had significant economic interests. It is also notable that Manuel was not compelled to give significant concessions to Venice in exchange for the debts he owed or the help he received, be it political, economic or territorial.[131] By contrast, his father had been forced to promised them Tenedos. In 1418, Manuel even managed to impose a tax on the wine consumed by the Venetians in taverns and their homes. Moreover, despite the Senate's protests that he violated the treaty, he did not lift the tax, instead increasing it in the following months. In 1419, he made an exemption only for the wine consumed in Venetian homes, and the taxation imposed on wines sold in retail remained in force.[132] Hence, despite his weak position vis-à-vis Venice, in some cases Manuel held firm.

Similarly, the emperor evaded the question of Tenedos. Despite his promise to Venice, John V changed his mind and tried to take it back, but the island never reverted to Byzantine control.[133] Although Venice held ownership of Tenedos by the Treaty of Turin, like the Genoese, they were not allowed to arm the island or to fortify it. Still, they regarded the island as their property and used it as a port. Throughout his reign, despite continuously petitioning Venice for military and economic help,

---

[130] Thiriet, *Régestes*, I, no. 809, 198; II, no. 1165, 48, no. 1463, 108–9.　[131] See Chapter 8.
[132] Chrysostomides, 'Venetian Privileges', 308–10.
[133] For John V and Tenedos, see Nicol, *Byzantium and Venice*, 299–312, 322.

Manuel, like his father before him, refrained from accepting Venetian rights over the island. One Senate deliberation speculates that when the envoy brought up the subject, the emperor actually refused to discuss the issue of Tenedos.[134] Even during the blockade of Constantinople (1394–1402), and despite his dire need for help, Manuel did not offer to accept Venetian ownership of the island as a bargaining tool. It seems that the emperor still hoped to be able re-claim Tenedos for Byzantium. Furthermore, his firm stance on the issue might have stemmed from another reason: Manuel must have been aware that should he accept Venetian ownership of the island, he ran the risk of alienating and inciting the Genoese; perhaps even a re-kindling the war between Genoa and Venice.

Much later, in 1404–5, Manuel still held firm regarding Tenedos, and it was chiefly on account of this issue that he refused to sign the Veneto-Byzantine treaty, which had not been renewed since 1376. In 1395, he tried to change the clause that pertained to Tenedos, asking Venice to completely renounce its claim of ownership. The Senate refused, and in 1406, Manuel finally accepted Venetian rights over the island under the condition that it be refortified at common expense. He also requested transportation to the Byzantine territories and the Venetian colonies in the Morea. He seems to have changed his mind as the senate considered his offer. A year later in 1406, a Senate deliberation complains that the Byzantine ambassadors were still pressuring Venice regarding Tenedos.[135] The Veneto-Byzantine treaty of 1406 left the question of Tenedos open-ended.[136] Despite his perpetual reliance on Venice for help, Manuel thus did not give up the Byzantine claim over the island and compelled the Venetians to adopt a more lukewarm stance in the treaty. Although he never succeeded in re-claiming the island for Byzantine rule, this small concession that Manuel obtained should not be completely dismissed. While by that time, the island functioned as a neutral territory for Venice and Genoa, the Venetian insistence on having their rights acknowledged in the treaty, implies that the issue still had some significance.

Some Senate deliberations are also permeated with anger towards Manuel. One such theme in these documents is that despite petitioning the Senate for money and military help, Manuel did not curb the anti-Venetian activities of his brother Theodore in the Morea, and later, those

---

[134] Thiriet, *Régestes*, II, no. 1165, 48.   [135] Thiriet, *Régestes*, I, no. 871, 206.
[136] Thiriet, *Régestes*, II, nos. 1175 and 1176, 50–1. Nicol, *Venice and Byzantium*, 348. For the treaty of 1406, see MM, III, 144–63; DVL, II, no. 163, 301–2. From that point onwards, despite being renewed every five years, the text of the Veneto-Byzantine treaty never changed.

of his own sons. On the contrary, he perhaps secretly encouraged them to undermine the political and economic influence of Venice in the region. Likewise, in 1410, the Senate points out that the emperor was not respecting Venetian economic privileges.[137] All these cases hint that Manuel was not entirely reduced to a passive political player. Rather, he emerges as a resourceful and shrewd ruler who could find effective routes around unpleasant issues.

As an author-emperor, Manuel sought to enhance his feeble imperial prestige through the power of his words. We have already seen that in his early career, Manuel permeated the *Discourse to the Thessalonians*, the *Discourse to Kabasilas* and *Panegyric to John V* with political messages and self-aggrandizement. During his sojourn in Asia Minor, he sought to combat the critics at home through his letters, as well as attempting to represent his presence in the Ottoman campaign as a part of an 'epic' narrative. In the *Dialogue with a Persian*, he portrayed himself as a supreme theological authority whom both the Byzantines and the Ottomans revered.

Throughout his reign, the emperor persevered in this practice. Manuel always sought to offer his audience an idealized self-representation, sometimes seeking political support, and sometimes defending himself against critics. It should be emphasized that he employed writing as a means of asserting his authority and superiority, and not as a place to discuss his decisions or seek advice. He never represented himself as a *primus inter pares* or as a 'fellow literatus'; he always occupies the superior position vis-à-vis the literati and the members of the *theatron*. In other words, he is always present as the emperor. From 1390s onwards, Manuel would increasingly adopt the persona of an ideal scholar-emperor, one who was potent in literary, philosophical and also, theological matters. The *Dialogue with a Persian* is a testimony to this tendency. Arguably, through such self-representation, Manuel strove to enhance his own authority not only in political, but also in other spheres that he wished to dominate, such as theological matters.

How did Manuel project his carefully constructed image to an elite audience? His works were circulated among the literati and probably also performed, and his letters and other works contain many references to performance in a *theatron*. Undoubtedly, as in Thessalonike in the 1380s, the emperor did preside over a *theatron* in Constantinople, and possibly, gatherings were also held by other literati. Unfortunately, several factors

---

[137] Thiriet, *Régestes*, 11, no. 1247, 66, no. 1260, 69, no. 1364, 89, no. 1948, 219.

hinder a detailed study of Manuel's literary network. For instance, it is not possible to study changes in his network across his lifetime. There are a few reasons for this: first, Manuel's letter collection is rather small. It consists of sixty-four letters in contrast to the 450 of Demetrios Kydones, or the similarly massive one of Nikephoros Gregoras. Furthermore, with the exception of Kydones and Manuel Kalekas, no other major letter collection survives from the period. Figures such as Joseph Bryennios, John Chortasmenos or Nicholas Kabasilas, for instance, also have very few surviving letters, and none of them are addressed to the emperor. Manuel has few letters dating to this period and his manuscripts, with the exception of the first half of Par. gr. 3041, all date to post 1402.

However, unsurprisingly, a close analysis of the available material reveals that the literati with whom Manuel corresponded were all interlinked.[138] The most prominent members of this large literary network compromised the following: Demetrios Kydones, Manuel and Demetrios Chrysoloras, Nicholas Kabasilas, Joseph Bryennios, Isidore of Kiev, Constantine Asanes and Manuel Kalekas. Among others, one can count John Chortasmenos, Theodore Kaukadenos, Michael Balsamon and Manuel Pothos. Yet it is not possible to discern when exactly many of these friendships started. This holds true even for prominent figures such as Manuel Chrysoloras and Joseph Bryennios; for instance, although the emperor was close to the famous author, diplomat and teacher Manuel Chrysoloras, their relationship cannot really be traced before the former's trip to Europe.

It should also be noted that Manuel's literary circle united people with diverse political and theological stances. For instance, anti-Palamites, such as Constantine Asan and Manuel Raoul, were included in Manuel's circle alongside the conservative Orthodox and Palamites Joseph Bryennios and Makarios Makres. Similarly, the future *mesazon* of John VII, Demetrios Chrysoloras, was a cherished member of the emperor's network. Thus, Manuel's literary network was not restricted to only those who shared his theological or political ideals, but also encompassed a much wider and heterogeneous group of people. Although he enjoys a reputation among modern scholars as a devout Orthodox, one must not assume that Manuel had no tolerance for differing beliefs.

Overall, the role of the literati in formulating Manuel's governing policies is unclear. For instance, none of the emperor's surviving letters discuss matters of governance, neither are they addressed to any of the prominent officials, such as the *mesazon*. None of the literati that Manuel

---

[138] This will be further discussed in Chapter 9.

was especially close to held an important office during his reign, not even Kydones. Thus, the two groups – Manuel's literary circle and his officials – appear to have been largely separate entities. There were a few members of his literary circle, however, who were active in the government. Demetrios Chrysoloras, one of Manuel's cherished collaborators, would later become John VII's *mesazon* in Thessalonike. The emperor likewise employed Manuel Chrysoloras as an ambassador for many years, and the future Patriarch Euthymios would also become a correspondent and literary collaborator. In an amusing twist, the Mazaris' satire mocks the emperor's penchant for employing at court those with literary talents. The protagonist of the work, Manuel Holobolos, is a rhetorician, imperial secretary and doctor at the court.[139] Yet, while Manuel's court did indeed fuse *logoi* and politics, whether the emperor actually relied on the literati for government decisions, or actively sought their advice, remains unknown. The silence of the sources on this matter, also given the separation between Manuel's literary circle and officials, seems to suggest that this was not the case.

Manuel, Bayezid and John VII

It was under such circumstances that Manuel's eldest son, the future John VIII, was born on 18 December 1393. This birth fulfilled the emperor's urgent need for an heir against the claims of John VII.[140] After all, his nephew was the chief threat to Manuel's authority. It is even possible to interpret his coronation in 1392 as a political act against John VII, one which advertised Manuel's legitimacy through elaborate ceremony. The anonymous coronation account also notes that the reading of Scripture during the ceremony included John 10: 1–8, the Parable of the Good Shepherd. It has been proposed that this reading possibly functioned as an allusion to Manuel's status as the legitimate emperor, linking him with the figure of the Good Shepherd.[141] Concerning his nephew and the birth of John VIII, in the *Dialogue on Marriage* (c. 1396), Manuel refers to an interesting dynastic arrangement. The emperor claims that he gave his heir

---

[139] Mazaris, 12–3.

[140] Schreiner, *Kleinchroniken*, Chronik 10/10. See also P. Schreiner, 'Chronologische Untersuchungen zur Familie Kaiser Manuels II', *BZ 63* (1970), 258–99; 287–8. Henceforth, Schreiner, 'Untersuchungen'.

[141] Majeska, *Russian Travellers*, 431. See also S. W. Reinert, 'Political Dimensions of Manuel II Palaiologos' 1392 marriage and coronation: some new evidence', in *Novum Millennium: Studies on Byzantine History and Culture Dedicated to Paul Speck*, eds. C. Sode and S. Takács (Aldershot 2001), 291–303, reprinted in S.W. Reinert, *Studies on Late Byzantine and Early Ottoman History* (Farnham, 2014), Study VII.

to John VII as an adoptive son and adopted the latter's son Andronikos as his own. The agreement supposedly entailed John VII succeeding Manuel, who in turn, would be succeeded by John VIII.[142]

Manuel's real intentions cannot be discerned here, since the *Dialogue on Marriage* was written around 1396, three years after the birth of his son. At the time of composition, this arrangement for the succession had already been shattered. A careful reading of the text suggests that the entire *Dialogue* is an attack on John VII. The emperor does not refrain from using strong language to describe his nephew: 'that despicable person – that is what he is, not my nephew – that disastrous threat to the Rhomaic people . . .'.[143] Resorting to his usual strategy and in direct contrast with his nephew, Manuel portrays himself as an ideal emperor, lamenting that he put the common good above his own family in sacrificing his own son. It is not impossible, however, that Manuel envisioned this arrangement as a temporary one, concocted to pacify John VII. We will never be sure whether the emperor really intended to fulfil this pledge or not.

Any existing agreement between Manuel and his nephew vanished in the autumn or winter of 1393/4. The sultan summoned Despot Theodore, Manuel and all his Christian lords to Serres, where a strange episode took place.[144] According to the *Funeral Oration*, Manuel and Theodore did not know that they had been summoned together; they never went together to Bayezid as he had previously plotted to murder them.[145] There was great panic among the Christian lords when Theodore and Manuel both found themselves at Bayezid's side. The shock was amplified when John VII also arrived. Manuel then tell how Bayezid decided to murder both him and his brother and entrusted the deed to a eunuch, who refrained from carrying out the order. The sultan did not get angry however; in fact, having changed his mind during the night and regretted his decision he was actually pleased to have been disobeyed. Bayezid then tried to win over the emperor again, sending him home with gifts but keeping Theodore with him.[146]

It is remarkable that while giving this account of the murderous scheme of Bayezid, Manuel does not mention John VII during the entire episode.

[142] *Dialogue on Marriage*, 112–13.
[143] *Dialogue on Marriage*, 98–9. '. . . ὁ μέντοι γε μᾶλλον ἔχθιστος ἢ ἀδελφιδοὺς ἐμός, κακίστη μὲν μοῖρα Ῥωμαίων . . . .'
[144] *Funeral Oration*, 129–33; Barker, *Manuel II*, 113–14.
[145] Doukas also narrates a similar story, claiming that Bayezid had intended to murder Manuel during the Asia Minor campaign prior to John V's death, Doukas, 76–7.
[146] *Funeral Oration*, 132–40 and Chalkokondyles, 128–33.

The narrative represents the two brothers as the sole targets of Bayezid's wrath, and thus implies that John was collaborating with the sultan and did not meet with any mistreatment. Chalkokondyles lends support to Manuel's narrative in the *Funeral Oration*, claiming that while it was Mamonas, a Morean landlord, who was responsible for Bayezid's wrath against Theodore, it was his nephew that had incited the sultan against Manuel. Indeed, it is quite possible that John was behind this dreadful gathering in Serres.

Manuel's narration of these events in the *Funeral Oration* merits close attention. A careful reading suggests that his account functions as an *apologia* for the turmoil that was to follow. Overall in the *Funeral Oration*, especially during this episode, Manuel represents the sultan as a fickle, irrational and dangerous man. He makes every effort to emphasize that it was impossible to accommodate Bayezid, especially after his murderous scheme in Serres. It should be remembered that although his writings from Asia Minor already displayed a personal enmity against Bayezid, the Serres episode indeed seems to have been a turning point in the relationship between Bayezid and Manuel. Directly after his narration of these events, Chalkokondyles tells us that the emperor disobeyed Bayezid's next summons.[147] After this incident, Manuel probably did not wish to take such a risk again by going to Bayezid's camp. Manuel's disobedience, however, summoned Bayezid and his army to the walls of Constantinople.[148]

After the Serres episode in the *Funeral Oration*, Manuel immediately turns to the narration of Theodore's affairs in the Morea. Significantly, he never mentions how the blockade of Constantinople began. This silence could be interpreted as a deliberate omission of the reason for the blockade – namely his own disobedience. Quite possibly, Manuel's intense personal dislike contributed to his decision to disobey the sultan, but highlighting Bayezid's murderous scheme further strengthened Manuel's *apologia* for his

---

[147] Chalkokondyles, 132–3. Unlike Chalkokondyles, Doukas claims that the attack of the Ottoman army was prompted by a different reason. He narrates that upon Manuel's accession in 1391, Bayezid demanded that Manuel install a *kadı*, a Muslim judge in Constantinople, and that Manuel declined. However, Doukas' account is not credible, both because there was a *kadı* already in residence in Constantinople and because furthermore the historian has erroneously dated the blockade to 1391. See Doukas, 76–7.

[148] Aşıkpaşazade, 93, tells us that Bayezid demanded that the *tekfur* install a judge and establish a Muslim neighbourhood in Constantinople, and that the latter accepted. However, Aşıkpaşazade also places this event in the aftermath of Nikopolis, in 1396, and narrates that the siege had already begun. *Anonymous Tevârîh*, 31, reports the same. See Jacoby, 'Thessalonike', 86–133, 121, ft 255, for the *kadı* issue, who points out that a *kadı* was resident in 1391 and that in 1396, the agreement was probably renewed by John VII.

disobedience. The implication was that the emperor had no other choice. As in other cases, he again modifies the actual events and fashions a glowing self-image, offering an idealized version of his reign and of himself. Ultimately, although the fall-out probably served as a mere pretext for Bayezid, Manuel's disobedience was to have drastic consequences: Constantinople would remain under Ottoman blockade for the next eight years.

CHAPTER 6

Besieged

This most violent time, which already brings forth unspeakable
troubles and also threatens future ones ... Thence, I could not defend
myself at first.[1]

By spring of 1394, Constantinople was completely surrounded by Ottoman
troops. That the blockade is recorded extensively in both Byzantine and
Ottoman sources reveals the impact that it had on both sides.[2] The
Ottomans blockaded Constantinople both by sea and famine soon started
to devastate the city. The early stages of the blockade can mainly be traced
through the deliberations of the Venetian Senate. By December, Manuel
was compelled to ask Venice for provisions, and to petition for military
help. Venice sent two galleys.[3]

A Venetian deliberation reveals the despair Manuel seems to have
felt: in his desperation the emperor appears to have considered selling
Lemnos, one of the last remaining Byzantine possessions, to Venice.[4]
Furthermore, another deliberation reveals that Venice offered the
emperor and his family refuge on Venetian ships should the need
arise. This is a significant clause, as it indicates that even in the early
stages of the blockade, Manuel and the Venetian Senate were already
envisioning the danger of an Ottoman incursion into the city, or

---

[1] *Discourse to Iagoup*, 327. '... καὶ με πρὸς ἔπος ἀποκρίνασθαι, πῶς οἴει, παρακαλεῖ. ὁ δὲ βιαιότατος
οὑτοσὶ καιρὸς οὐ δίδωσιν, οὐδὲ συγχωρεῖ, ἀμυθήτους δυσχερείας τὰς μὲν ἤδη ἐπάγων, τάσδ'
ἀπειλῶν. ὅθεν καὶ μηδ' ὁπωσοῦν τὴν πρώτην χωρῆσαι πρὸς ἀπολογίαν δεῖν ἔγνων'.
[2] For various accounts of the blockade; Doukas, 76–89; Chalkokondyles, 132–3; Schreiner,
Kleinchroniken, Chronik 22/26; 12/ 6; Neşri, 327; Aşıkpaşazade, 91. The biographer of Stefan
Lazarević, Konstantin the Philosopher, also mentions the siege, see Konstantin the Philosopher,
Lebensbeschreibung des Despoten Stefan Lazarevics, ed. and trans. M. Braun (The Hague, 1956), 14.
Henceforth, Konstantin the Philosopher.
   See also P. Gautier, 'Action de graces pour l'anniversaire de la bataille d'Ankara (28 Juillet 1403)',
REB 19 (1961), 340–357 and Gautier, 'Un récit inédit du siege de Constantinople par les Turcs
(1394–1402)', *REB* 23 (1965), 100–17 for other Byzantine narratives. Henceforth, Gautier, 'Action des
graces'.
[3] Thiriet, *Régestes*, I, no. 851, 202.   [4] Thiriet, *Régestes*, I, no. 860, 203–4.

173

military action.[5] Despite dispatching the requested grain and the offer
of refuge, however, the senate gave no clear answer as to whether
Venice would participate in a league against the Ottomans. Manuel
himself is silent during these early years. The only exception is a letter
in which he speaks about leaving the city with a small number of men
and relieving a nearby fortress from an Ottoman attack.[6] All other
sources indicate that at the very beginning of the eight-year blockade,
Constantinople and its inhabitants were struggling with famine and
dire economic problems.

Manuel's Constantinople

The drastic effects that the blockade would have on Constantinople mean
that a short digression to flesh out the surroundings of Manuel's capital is
in order. After all, it was against this backdrop that the majority of his
biography unfolds. During Manuel's lifetime, the Byzantine capital was
the subject of numerous panegyrics. The city still excited the imagination
of the foreigners as the famed capital of a once prosperous empire.
Byzantine literati endlessly extolled the city's buildings and monuments,
proudly elaborating on the city's long history and its Greco-Roman
heritage.[7] Manuel himself exalts his capital. In the *Panegyric to John V*,
Constantinople is called 'the queen, the metropolis and the eye of the
universe, a stream of great goods … ', and in the *Funeral Oration*, he
praises the city in similar terms. He moreover remarks that, as the 'queen'
of cities, Constantinople's great glory made any praise unnecessary.[8]

He makes no other mention of his Constantinopolitan surroundings,
and we cannot discern what he thought or felt about particular spaces,
palaces or monuments. Certainly under Manuel the city was by then

---

[5] Thiriet, *Régestes*, 1, no. 868, 205. In view of the persistence of the famine in the capital and the
complete blockade by both land and sea, a question has been raised by Necipoğlu as to whether the
provisions sent by Venice ever reached Constantinople, see Necipoğlu, *Byzantium between the
Ottomans and the Latins*, 149.

[6] Letter 29, which must be dated before 1396/97 as Kydones, the addressee, is still alive and seems to be
in the capital.

[7] See for some examples, Manuel Chrysoloras, *Comparison of the Old and New Rome*, ed. C. Billò, 'Τοῦ
Χρυσωλορᾶ Σύγκρισις Παλαιᾶς καὶ Νέας 'Ρώμης', *Medioevo Greco* 0 (2000), 1–26; Isidore of Kiev,
'*Panegyric for Manuel and John VIII Palaiologos*', ed. S.P. Lampros, *ΠΠ*, III, 132–99, 152. Henceforth,
Isidore of Kiev, 'Panegyric'. See also G. Dagron, 'Manuel Chrysoloras: Constantinople ou Rome',
BF 12 (1987), 281–8 and A. Kiousopoulou, 'La notion de ville chez Manuel Chrysoloras:
A. Kiousopoulou, 'La notion de ville chez Manuel Chrysoloras: Σύγκρισις Παλαίας καὶ Νέας
Ρώμης', *BSl* 59 (1998), 71–9.

[8] *Panegyric to John V*, 230. *Funeral Oration*, 82–3.

a small space. It is worth noting that for the authors of the period, the city of Constantinople (ἡ πόλις) and fatherland (ἡ πάτρις) become almost synonymous. Significantly, in many of his works Manuel also uses the word *polis*, and not *basileia*, to refer to his territories.[9] This usage can be interpreted as the effect of the shrinking territories upon the literati's perception of their empire, which was now almost entirely confined to Constantinople.

These authors exalted Constantinople partly out of patriotic sentiment and partly according to the rhetorical conventions of the panegyric. However, despite the glowing picture painted by these texts, there can be no doubt that Manuel's Constantinople was a mere shadow of its former self.[10] Its size and population had shrunk significantly; the cityscape was now adorned with gardens and vineyards. As early as the 1330s, despite bestowing praise on the city walls, the traveller Ibn Battuta described Constantinople as consisting of thirteen villages. His account is a striking account of how rural the city looked.[11] The blockade of Bayezid would only contribute further to its decay and to the decrease in the population.

The walls seemed to indicate the borders of Constantinople, but the real boundaries of the city space were by then much more restricted. City life unfolded in the area containing the Blachernai Palace, the Church of the Holy Apostles, Forum Tauri, the Forum of Constantine, Augusteion and Hagia Sophia, terminating at the Golden Horn and the shores of the Marmara Sea.[12] Restorations carried out by Manuel's father on the Golden Gate, as well as the fortifications that he built on the site, had long been demolished on Bayezid's orders.[13] The Hippodrome was covered partially by trees, and only certain parts of the Great Palace were used on special occasions. The Mese – main road – still functioned but retained commercial functions only in the Eastern part, and the imperial market was situated on the Golden Horn near the Imperial Gate. Other markets were scattered through the city. The political centre of Constantinople was Blachernai, where the imperial palace and the residences of the elite were

---

[9] *Discourse to Iagoup*, 361. Letter 38, line 13 and Letter 42, line 8.
[10] A detailed picture of Constantinople in late fourteenth and early fifteenth centuries is given by Kiousopoulou, *Emperor or Manager*, 13–26, who relies on various primary and secondary sources. The following description of Constantinople will follow that of Kiousopoulou.
[11] Ibn Battuta, 508. K. P. Matschke, 'The Late Byzantine Urban Economy, Thirteenth-Fifteenth Centuries', in *EHB* (2002), 463–95, especially 465–6.
[12] *Pseudo-Kodinos*, 194–5, mentions the Forum of Constantine.
[13] See S. Guberti Bassett, 'John V Palaiologos and the Golden Gate in Constantinople', in τό Ἑλληνικόν: *Studies in Honour of Speros Vryonis Jr*, vol. 1, eds. J. S. Langdon, et al. (New Rochelle and New York, 1993), 117–27.

located.[14] Manuel resided in the Blachernai Palace and probably left his palace only to visit a limited number of these venues, such as the Great Palace, Hagia Sophia or the Pantokrator. He also indulged his love of hunting in nearby forests.[15]

Even in its current state of decay, Constantinople attracted many visitors. The Russian pilgrims who visited the city during Manuel's lifetime give long lists of the sights they visited. Their accounts can offer insight into what the emperor himself might have seen had he wandered around in his capital. The pilgrims mention visiting Justinian's Column, Hagia Sophia, Milion, Blachernai, the Great Palace, the Hippodrome, Pantokrator, Hodegetria, Peribleptos and the Monastery of Studios.[16] The Spanish traveller Clavijo, who visited Constantinople in 1403, was also given a tour of many of these sites, and he too noted the orchards and cornfields encroaching on the urban landscape, and how most of the buildings were in ruins.[17]

The churches of Constantinople housed many valuable relics which were dear to Manuel. Indeed, both the French traveller Ghillebert de Lannoy and Clavijo comment upon his love of relics, and the latter even points out that Manuel personally kept the keys to the chests in the Church of Saint John the Baptist in Petra. Though no record of the incident survives, Clavijo claimed that the emperor appropriated the little finger of the hand of Saint Anne for his private devotion and that a lawsuit was being brought against Manuel for this appropriation.[18]

Manuel made much greater use of these relics. In December 1395, he offered the tunic of Christ to Venice as a security for a loan and was promptly refused. Manuel's novel use of relics in diplomacy has already been discussed in previous studies, but such anecdotes offer insight into Manuel as a shrewd and practical statesman.[19] Unable to offer any other

---

[14] Majeska, *Russian Travellers*, 140, for the markets and 242–7 for the decline of the Great Palace.

[15] *Pseudo-Kodinos*, 196–203, lists the churches the emperor would visit on special occasions.

[16] Clavijo, 61–2, gives an extensive list of the monasteries he visited. Stephen of Novgorod (c. 1349) in Majeska, *Russian Travellers*, 28–47 and Ignatius of Smolensk, 90–101. Alexander the Clerk (c. 1394/95), reports seeing similar sights; Majeska, *Russian Travellers*, 160–5. These pilgrims visited many other churches, those mentioned are the more significant ones.

[17] Clavijo, 32–48. See also M. Angold, 'The Decline of Byzantium seen through the Eyes of Western Travellers', in *Travel in the Byzantine World, Papers from the 34th Spring Symposium of Byzantine Studies, Birmingham, April 2000*, ed. R. J. Macrides (Aldershot, 2002), 213–32.

[18] Clavijo, 34 and 50. For Ghillebert de Lannoy's comments, *Oeuvres de Ghillebert de Lannoy, voyageur, diplomate et moraliste*, ed. Ch. Potvin (Louvain, 1878), 11 and 65–6. Henceforth, Ghillebert de Lannoy.

[19] It is not clear exactly which tunic of Christ is being referred to here. Mergiali-Sahas has pointed out that it does not seem to be identical with the so-called Seamless Tunic of Christ, which Manuel was later to cut to pieces for further diplomatic use. See S. Mergiali-Sahas, 'An Ultimate Wealth for

solid or tempting proposals to potential allies, he was forced to resort to the unconventional tactic of using relics as bargaining tools.

During the blockade, Manuel's dealings with such holy objects were not confined to relics. One curious case concerns a special icon of the Virgin, called *Kouboukalaria*. Thought to be a miracle-working icon, the *Kouboukalaria* was in the possession of a brother and a sister from the Gabras family. It was passed down through generations and housed in a Constantinopolitan church. The revenues generated by the icon were shared between this church and the heirs. Compelled by her sufferings during the blockade, however, the sister fled Constantinople – taking the icon with her. She was intercepted by the authorities and was forced to leave it behind to her brother's sole ownership, which he obtained through a 300 *hyperpyra* deposit to Manuel as a guarantee that the icon would not be taken out of the city. Eventually, when Gabras also abandoned Constantinople, the icon went into the hands of the emperor, and he in turn entrusted it to the *archon* Manuel Boullotes, who deposited 200 *hyperpyra* as a guarantee. Boullotes had the icon placed in another church, and this gave rise to further dispute. Finally, in July 1401, the patriarchal tribune decided that the icon should remain in this new church, but that one third of its revenue should go to the former one.[20] This intriguing case reveals Manuel's interest in the precious religious objects of his capital. Moreover, it bears testimony to his penchant for seizing on all opportunities to obtain money. After all, these deposits made him 500 *hyperpyra* richer, a sum that was no doubt appreciated under these dire straits.

The Crusade of Nikopolis

Besides the woes of the siege, another blow struck the imperial family in May. Manuel's father-in-law Constantine Dejanović died at the Battle of Rovine while fighting in the Ottoman ranks.[21] The imperial couple made a donation to the Monastery of Saint John the Baptist in Petra in his memory, a considerate gesture towards his wife on Manuel's part. It should be noted that this monastery was in close proximity to the Blachernai Palace and also boasted a scriptorium that was associated with the imperial

---

Inauspicious Times: Holy Relics in Rescue of Manuel Palaeologus' Reign', *Byzantion 76* (2006), 265–75, 270. Henceforth, Mergiali-Sahas, 'Relics'. Thiriet, *Régestes*, I, nos. 892 and 896, 210–11.
[20] N. Oikonomides, 'The Holy Icon as an Asset', *DOP* 45 (1991), 35–44; 41–2.
[21] Barker, *Manuel II*, 128.

court.[22] Furthermore, as Clavijo mentions that Manuel kept the keys of the reliquaries of the monastery, it is reasonable to assume that the emperor had personal ties with Saint John the Baptist in Petra. It is also plausible that the imperial couple paid yet another tribute to Constantine Dejanović; their second son may have been named after him, though this Constantine would die young.[23]

Desperate for help, Manuel eventually began communicating with Sigismund of Hungary. Why should the emperor have turned to Hungary in particular? After all, some thirty years earlier, his father John V had returned from Buda empty-handed and humiliated. By 1396, however, Hungary was in a position to offer support to the emperor against the Ottomans.[24] The early years of Manuel's reign had witnessed a rapprochement between Byzantium and Hungary. Not only the emperor, but also the Patriarch Anthony had been in correspondence with Sigismund regarding ecclesiastical affairs that pertained to the Balkans, and it seemed that Byzantium and Hungary were already also in discussion regarding the Ottoman threat acerbated by Bayezid's aggressive expansionist policies. Many of the Serbian princes had been compelled to accept Ottoman suzerainity and were not likely to be persuaded to fight the Ottomans. Bayezid had already conquered Trnovo by 1393; the Bulgarian tsar was either executed or died in captivity. Indeed, the Ottoman expansion in the Balkans was a serious problem for both sides, and halting this progress was of extreme importance.

Moreover, the recently crowned Hungarian king, Sigismund, harboured his own expansionist designs on the Balkans. In this regard, the ambitious and energetic personality of Sigismund must be also taken into consideration; another ruler might not have come so wholeheartedly to Manuel's aid. The gradual Ottoman expansion in the Balkans posed a grave threat for Sigismund. Not only did it challenge his designs on the Balkans, it also posed and eventual threat to his own realm. Thus, Sigismund's appeals to the West on the behalf of the Byzantines did not

[22] MM, II, 260–4; Dölger, *Regesten*, no. 3257, 83. See E. D. Kakulide, 'Βιβλιοθήκη τῆς Μονῆς Προδρόμου-Πέτρας στὴν Κωνσταντινούπολη', *Ἑλληνικά* 21 (1968), 3–39.

[23] This son, born c. 1393–8 should not be confused with Constantine XI, see Schreiner, 'Unterschungen', 292. It should be noted that the name Constantine does not seem to have been popular in Manuel's immediate family. Thus, it is not implausible that this name was chosen to honour the memory of Manuel's father-in-law, a hypothesis that only works, of course, if the son was born after May 1395. Or perhaps, he was named after his maternal grandfather while the latter was still alive.

[24] See D. I. Mureşan, 'Une histoire de trois empereurs: aspects des relations de Sigismond de Luxembourg avec Manuel II et Jean Paléologue', in *Emperor Sigismund and the Orthodox World*, ed. E. Mitsou (Vienna, 2010), 41–100, for extensive discussion of the Byzantine-Hungarian relations. Henceforth, Mureşan, 'Trois empereurs'.

stem from a purely altruistic desire to help besieged Constantinople. Using Bayezid's expansionist policies and aggression as a pretext, he sought to encourage the West to rescue fellow Christians from the Muslim threat. Not only would the Balkans and Constantinople be saved from the Ottomans, but Sigismund would also be free to pursue his own ambitions in the region.

The traffic of Venetian Senate documents on this alliance has already been cited in several studies: to summarize, the Venetian Senate had previously offered its help in negotiating a peace between Byzantium and the Ottomans. However, after learning of the new alliance between Byzantium, Hungary and various Balkan rulers, the Senate cancelled its embassy to the Ottoman court and instead sent an envoy to Constantinople to learn more. Venice ultimately refrained from joining the newly formed league.[25]

Manuel's efforts to obtain military help succeeded in this instance, a unique occurrence in his entire reign. Thanks especially to Sigismund's efforts, a great crusading army was formed in 1396 consisting not only of Hungarian, Wallachian and Serbian, but also of French and English troops obtained through the intercessions of Sigismund. Without his endeavours, the army would probably have never been assembled. The goal was to engage the Ottoman army on the Balkan frontier and to force the sultan to raise the blockade. However, Manuel's hopes evaporated on 25 September 1396 when the Ottomans annihilated the crusading army in Nikopolis.[26] This defeat is also profoundly lamented in the English and French sources, echoing the battle's devastating effect even on these remote lands – if for no other reason than that many prominent English and French noblemen had perished on battlefield.

Manuel is one of the few actors in this last crusading movement that left a great impact not only in the Balkans, but also in Europe. After Nikopolis, Varna (1444) would be the last serious (and unsuccessful) attempt to dislodge the Ottomans from the Balkans. Although the prime actor in this was Sigismund, the emperor also contributed to the formation of the Nikopolis Crusade, which ultimately solidified Ottoman presence in the Balkans. Manuel's intentions, of course, had been the exact opposite. About a fortnight after this resounding defeat,

---

[25] Barker, *Manuel II*, 129–30. A. S. Atiya, *The Crusade of Nicopolis* (London,1934), 33–49, albeit now outdated in some respects, gives a more detailed account of the formulation of the alliance. Henceforth, Atiya, *Nicopolis*. Dölger, *Regesten*, nos. 3249–51, 82–3, for the communications with Sigismund. Doukas, 78–9 and Chalkokondyles, 120–3 also refer to the alliance. Thiriet, *Régestes*, I, nos. 900 and 901, 211–12.

[26] Atiya, *Nicopolis*, 33–49. Doukas, 78–9; Aşıkpaşazade, 91–2 and Neşri, 327–9.

the Venetian Senate was giving out instructions concerning the likely fall of Constantinople.[27]

Manuel poured out his despair in the longest letter of his collection, addressed to his beloved Kydones who had just left Constantinople, never to return.[28] A close reading of this letter, paying special attention to its literary features, opens a window into Manuel's mood. It's pessimistic tone stands out from among his entire collection. Filled with dark imagery and devoid of one single witty Classical allusion, it is a reflection of the emperor's anguish. In particular, storm imagery is expanded upon in great detail – a storm, which Manuel claims, destroyed all hope. Instead of his usual elegant and witty language, the letter is adorned with harsh insults levelled against Islam. Likewise, solemn Biblical allusions are scattered throughout the text. The outpouring of anger, the insults and the discussion of the total 'barbarisation' of the Ottomans also stand in stark contrast with the emperor's treatment of them in the *Dialogue with a Persian*. This sombre imagery and negative tone in Manuel's unusually long letter is testimony to his understandable bitterness over events.

The emperor had even more reason to be gloomy. In the fall of 1396, not only was Manuel confronted by this highly precarious political situation, for reasons unknown, the Palamite controversy also flared up. Although in 1351, Palamism had been declared the official doctrine of the Church, there were still many who held anti-Palamite beliefs. During the summer and the autumn of 1396, ecclesiastical authorities began taking action against the anti-Palamites and the Catholic converts in the capital.[29] How and why exactly the Church decided to crush the anti-Palamite faction in 1396 is not clear, nor is Manuel's role in the affair.

Manuel, A Moderate Palamite

Although in Late Byzantium, the Church could challenge imperial intervention into ecclesiastical affairs, Palaiologan emperors still enjoyed great

---

[27] Thiriet, 1, *Régestes*, no. 917, 214–15.   [28] Letter 31.
[29] See *Correspondance de Manuel Calécas*, ed. R. J. Loenertz (Vatican, 1950), 23–4. Henceforth, Loenertz, *Calécas*. For professions of faith by anti-Palamites, see J. Darrouzes, *Les régestes des actes du patriarchat de Constantinople*, 1/6 (Paris, 1979), no. 3017, 282, no. 3019, 284, no. 3021, 284–5, no. 3022, 285, no. 3026, 290. Henceforth, Darrouzes, *Régestes*. See also N. Russell, 'Prochoros Cydones and the Fourteenth- Century Understanding of Orthodoxy', in *Byzantine Orthodoxies. Papers from the 36th Spring Symposium of Byzantine Studies, University of Durham, 23–25 March 2002*, eds. A. Louth and A. Casiday (Farnham, 2006), 75–94 and N. Russell, 'Palamism in the circle of Demetrius Cydones', in *Porphyrogenita: Essays on Byzantine History and Culture and Latin East Presented to Julian Chrysostomides*, eds. Ch. Dendrinos, et al. (Aldershot, 2003), 7–25.

authority over the Church and were directly involved in many significant decisions.[30] Indeed, throughout his reign, Manuel would seek to assert his authority over the Church and intervene in ecclesiastical matters.[31] Although on one hand it is very likely that he was an initiator of these anti-Palamite purges, it is also possible that the Church took action against the anti-Palamites without Manuel's initiation.

Either way, it must still be pointed out that he seems to have done nothing to hold it in check. This was an especially poignant decision considering that these persecutions also affected people in his own circle. The most striking example is that of Demetrios Kydones, who opted to leave Constantinople for good; Maximos Chrysoberges, who had shared Manuel's exile in Lemnos, also left for Pera. Another such intimate of Manuel to be targeted by the authorities was his *theios* and correspondent Constantine Asan, who held anti-Palamite views.[32]

Manuel's stance towards these persecutions has not been considered. Yet, as we will discuss, Manuel was not an emperor who refrained from confrontations with the Church. Several of the patriarchs during his reign were moreover elevated to the throne chiefly thanks to his favour. So his tacit approval or lack of apparent dissent in this instance, suggests that these purges do not seem to have seriously vexed the emperor. Even though the accused were members of his circle, he does not appear to have combatted the actions of the Church. This already suggests that albeit tolerant to a degree, Manuel did not sympathize with anti-Palamism. Furthermore, the offices of patriarchs Anthony IV, Kallistos Xanthapoulos and Matthew I saw a rise in the opposition to anti-Palamites during the same time period of Manuel's accession and rule (1391–1410).[33] Even more significantly, recent scholarship has shown that the emperor's theological works contain Palamite tendencies and contain explicit condemnations of anti-Palamite views.[34]

---

[30] See R. J. Macrides, 'Emperor and Church in the Last Centuries of Byzantium', *Studies in Church History* 54 (2018), 123–43. Henceforth, Macrides, 'Emperor and Church'.

[31] This will be discussed in detail in Chapter 8.

[32] However, Asan duly signed a confirmation of faith and avoided any persecution. For Constantine Asan, see Dennis, *Letters*, xxvii-xxviii and PLP 1503. On his involvement in the affairs of summer/fall 1396, Loenertz, *Calécas*, 23–4.

[33] Loenertz, *Calécas*, 24–6 for these patriarchs and their offices.

[34] Hans Georg Beck characterized Manuel as a 'moderate' Palamite; H. G. Beck. *Kirsche und theologische Literatur im byzantinischen Reich* (Munich, 1959), 748. However, he was not able to consult most of Manuel's theological works. In recent years, Manuel's Palamite references in his works have been increasingly discussed by Dendrinos, Demetracopoulos and Polemis, see below. Their studies focus on the *Dialogue with a Persian* and the *On the Procession of the Holy Spirit*. I follow their discussions on the issue of Palamism in these texts.

What were, then, the main tenets of Palamism?[35] The chief doctrine concerned the distinction between God's essence and energies. According to Orthodox theology, God's essence (*ousia*) is entirely inaccessible, undefinable and imparticipable. God enters into a direct communion with his creation not through his essence, but through his energies (*energeia*). Like essence, God's energies are eternal, uncreated and shared by the three hypostases of the Trinity. His energies are divine activities, outpourings of grace, which permeate all his creation, and it is only through these that God can be known. Thus, God is paradoxically both transcendent and particable. Although the discussion of God's essence and energies was already found in the works of the Cappadocian Fathers, Palamas further developed and accentuated this issue.[36]

While God's essence is all-transcending and imparticipable, Palamas argued that humans could be united with the divine through God's energies; humans could become God through divine grace. It was thus possible to be united with God, and this mystical union was known as *theosis* or deification. Again, this was an idea that could be traced back to the patristic tradition, but Palamas bestowed further significance to this discussion. According to him, through participating in God's energy, man would see the vision of the uncreated divine light, the one that illuminated Christ at his Transfiguration on Mount Thabor. Palamas argued that such a mystical union could be achieved through leading a true Christian life and unceasing prayer.

[35] This discussion of Palamism is based on the following: Dendrinos, *On the Procession of the Holy Spirit*, 95–7; J. A. Demetracopoulos, 'Palamas Transformed, Palamite Interpretation of the Distinction between God's 'Essence' and 'Energies' in Late Byzantium', in *Greeks, Latins, and Intellectual History 1204–1500*, eds. M. Hinterberger and C. Schabel (Leuven, 2011), 263–372, 333–4; J. A. Demetracopoulos, 'Thomas Aquinas' impact on late Byzantine theology and philosophy: The issues of method or 'Modus Sciendi' and 'Dignitas Hominis', in *Knotenpunkt Byzanz. Wissenformen und Kulturelle Wechselbeziehungungen*, eds. A. Speer and P. Steinkrüger (Berlin, 2012), 333–410. Henceforth, Demetracopoulos, 'Dignitas Homini'; I. Polemis, 'Manuel II Palaiologos between Gregory Palamas and Thomas Aquinas', in *The Ways of Byzantine Philosophy*, ed. M. Knežević (Alhambra, 2015), 353–60; I. Polemis, *Theologica varia inedita saeculi XIV* (Turnhout, 2012), CXXXVIII-CXLI; J. Meyendorff, *Introduction a l'étude de Palamas* (Paris, 1956); L. C. Contos, 'The Essence-Energies Structure of Saint Gregory Palamas with a Brief Examination of its Patristic Foundation', *The Greek Orthodox Theological Review* 12 (1967–8), 283–94; A. Torrance, 'Precedents for Palamas' Essence-Energies Theology in the Cappadocian Fathers', *Vigilae Christianae* 63 (2009), 47–70; Ch. Triantafyllopoulos, 'The Thomist Base of Prochoros Kydones' anti-Palamite treatise "De essential et operatione Dei" and the reaction of the Byzantine Church', in *Knotenpunkt Byzanz. Wissensformen und Kulturelle Wechselbeziehungen*, eds. A. Speer and P. Steinkrüger (Berlin, 2012), 411–30. Henceforth, Demetracopoulos, 'Palamas Transformed', Polemis, 'Palamas' and Triantafyllopoulos, 'Thomist Base'. See also Gregory Palamas, *The One Hundred and Fifty Chapters*, ed. and trans. R. E. Sinkewicz (Toronto, 1988) and Gregory Palamas, *The Triads*. ed. with an introduction by J. Meyendorff, trans. N. Gendle (New Jersey, 1983).

[36] The Cappadocian Fathers did not really focus on the distinction between essence and energies, and their interpretations regarding this issue and *theosis* are not identical with that of Palamas, see Torrance, 'Palamas' in footnote 35.

Palamas also intensified the debates as to whether philosophy was compatible with theology, and whether logical reasoning and syllogisms, could be used in theological inquiry.[37] For Palamas, human reason could not grasp any aspect of the divine: the use of philosophy and logic in theological inquiry was to be strongly cautioned against. Any knowledge of the divine could only be attained by mystical revelation; saints and other holy figures accessed this knowledge through divine illumination. Syllogisms could only be used in the manner of the Greek Church Fathers; their premises had to be based on the revelation. Thus, while approving the use of syllogisms in the manner of the Fathers, Palamas expressed doubts about the methods of Scholastic theology.

Some of Palamas' later followers interpreted this stance more radically. They condemned reliance on 'Hellenic' philosophy, namely the teachings of Plato and especially Aristotelian logic, as well as the use of syllogisms in theological inquiry. In some ways, Palamites came to be identified as proponents of 'obscurantism' and an 'anti-logical' or 'anti-rational' outlook. Their stance contrasted with the trends of Latin theology in the fourteenth and fifteenth centuries, which employed syllogisms and Aristotelian logic. Especially under Thomas Aquinas' influence, the Latin theologians and their Byzantine followers, such as Prochoros and Demetrios Kydones, incorporated syllogisms and Aristotelian philosophy into theology. However, these boundaries concerning theological methodology were blurred and fluid.

As a response to Palamas, following Barlaam of Calabria and Gregory Akyndinos, the critics of Palamite theology argued that a sharp distinction between essence and energies was not compatible with the simplicity of God's essence. Such a distinction divided the Godhead and violated this fundamental theological concept. On the contrary, they argued, any distinction between essence and energies was purely mental. Moreover, they disapproved of the Palamites' opposition to the use of syllogisms in theology. For them, while phenomena such as the Incarnation or the Trinity were beyond human reason and were not demonstrable by philosophical methods, the use of syllogisms in theology was legitimate.[38]

However, many Orthodox theologians with Palamite views were also influenced by Latin theologians such as Augustine, and especially Thomas Aquinas. They drew influences from the latter's philosophy-based theology,

---

[37] Syllogism is a deductive scheme of a formal argument consisting of a major and a minor premise and a conclusion. Through these premises that are held to be true, a conclusion is reached; for instance, A) Socrates is a human and B) All humans are mortal, and the conclusion is 'Therefore, Socrates is mortal'.

[38] Demetracopoulos, 'Dignitas Hominis', 344–7.

and to a degree, they also employed syllogisms in their own works. Even Palamas' own works was influenced by Augustine. Similarly, there were anti-Palamites who were opposed to the use of logic in theology, and thus, the differences between the Latins, anti-Palamites and Palamites concerning theological methodology were not rigid.[39] There were no sharply drawn boundaries. Orthodox or Palamite theologians were not closed to Latin theology or the use of logic; on the contrary, they were receptive towards it.

That Manuel himself held Palamite views is not surprising. After all, despite the existence of dissident voices, Palamism was by then the official doctrine of the church. Manuel's stance on Palamism can be traced in his *Discourse to Iagoup*. As we will discuss, this polemical discourse was composed during the persecutions of 1396 and targeted Manuel Kalekas, a Latin convert and an anti-Palamite. In the *Discourse*, the emperor harshly criticizes Kalekas for his anti-Palamism and advises Kalekas to 'purge the heresy of Barlaam and Akyndinos from his soul as if purifying his hands from a putrid smell.'[40] In *On the Procession of the Holy Spirit* a theological treatise composed around 1400–2, the emperor reveals a similar outlook. As in the *Discourse*, in several instances he openly condemns the anti-Palamite teachings of Barlaam and Akyndinos. These passages offer strong evidence that Manuel himself did not hold anti-Palamite beliefs.[41]

Apart from these instances, the *Discourse to Iagoup* and the *On the Procession of the Holy Spirit* have further Palamite colouring. For instance, in both works, Manuel opposes the use of syllogisms and other such philosophical methods in theological inquiry. This reflects not only the traditional Orthodox position, but also the influence of Palamite teachings. Like the Palamites, Manuel, too, is opposed to 'Hellenic' philosophy and the use of logical reasoning in theology. He underscores at every opportunity that divine knowledge is obtained through mystical revelation, and not through human reason. More crucially, the *Procession of the Holy Spirit* has extensive discussions on essence and energies: the central tenet of

---

[39] See the two articles by Demetracopolous cited above for insights into the evolvement of Palamism. For the fluidity of Orthodox and Latin theological methodologies, see *Never the Twain Shall Meet? Latins and Greeks Learning from Each Other in Byzantium.* ed. D. Searby (Berlin and Leiden, 2018), especially M. Plested, 'Reconfiguring East and West in Byzantine and Modern Orthodoxy', 21–46, arguing that the East/West divide in theology is a later scholarly product; that the reality of the fourteenth and fifteenth centuries was one of flexible and blurred lines. Henceforth, Plested, 'Reconfiguring East and West'.

[40] *Discourse to Iagoup*, 370, 'τὴν δὲ Βαρλαάμ τε καὶ Ἀκινδύνου εἴτε μανίαν, εἴτε δόξης ἔμπληκτον ἐπιθυμίαν προσκαίρου, ἢ οὐκ οἶδ'ὅ τι τοιοῦτον χρὴ ἀκριβῶς ταύτῃ συμβαῖνον εἰπεῖν, ἀπορριπτέον -ἐμοὶ πειθόμενον τὸν συνήθη σοι- τῆς ψυχῆς, ὥσπερ ὀσμήν τιν' ἄχαριν τῶν χειρῶν'.

[41] *On the Procession of the Holy Spirit*, 1, 100, 118, 374. Both instances have also been noted by the editor of these works, Dendrinos.

Palamism.[42] Manuel argues that God's essence and energies are distinguished from each other: while the first is completely unknowable and imparticipable, the second is participable, thus denying the distinction between the two, leads to a wholly erroneous theology. Those who do so are called 'the children of Hellenes' – a reference to the anti-Palamites and their philosophical methods of theological inquiry. Again, following the Palamite doctrine, the emperor argues that this distinction between essence and energies does not divide the Godhead, nor does it contradict God's simplicity – one of the main objections of the anti-Palamites. Finally, Manuel associates God's energy with the light on Mount Thabor, which also seems to manifest a Palamite influence.[43]

A recent study proposes that the *Dialogue with a Persian* also contains some Palamite influences.[44] In the fourth dialogue, the *müderris* asks the emperor how mortal men filled with passions can participate in God's energies, who is immortal and beyond passion. Manuel replies to this question by proposing a distinction between God's essence and energies, and he suggests that God's wisdom and goodness are divine energies. Not only does he have the same outlook later in the ninth dialogue, but the influence of Palamite teachings on essence-energies and deification can be traced in the work in many other instances.[45]

However, while agreeing with the doctrines of Palamas, Manuel also seems to have been a 'moderate' Palamite. Unlike his grandfather, John VI Kantakouzenos, he never penned works specifically dedicated to the defence of Palamism. Still, as Palamism was by that time the official doctrine of the church, unlike his grandfather, Manuel did not have a pressing need to defend Palamite arguments. Nonetheless, the emperor never refers to Palamas or his writings by name, and though he is influenced by Palamas' writings, he never directly quotes him. Moreover, it has been pointed out that on one particular occasion, Manuel seems to contradict Palamas. This is concerning an expression of Maximos Confessor; 'infinite times inifinitely', *apeirakis apeiros*. Palamas interpreted this expression as being a reference to the infinite gap between God's essence and his energies. Yet it has been noted that in his *On the Order in the Trinity*, a short theological treatise probably composed soon after the *On the Procession*, Manuel uses Maximos' expression in its original sense: as referring to the gap between God's nature

---

[42] *On the Procession of the Holy Spirit*, 72–119.   [43] *On the Procession of the Holy Spirit*, 119.
[44] See Polemis, 'Palamas'.   [45] *Dialogue with a Persian*, 46, 83, 122, 200.

and energies on one hand, and human nature on the other. This was also the anti-Palamite interpretation of this expression.[46]

Manuel's association with anti-Palamite and pro-Latin figures, combined with his knowledge of Plato and Aristotle, may invite speculation that he actually held similar views; all factors, however, suggest otherwise. The emperor's friendship with several anti-Palamites, such as Demetrios Kydones, Constantine Asan and Maximos Chrysoberges, should not be interpreted as evidence that Manuel shared all their opinions and doctrines. Rather, it hints at a certain tolerance. Neither should these friendships be considered surprising, as many literati bonded with each other despite their theological differences. The same also held true for Manuel and the anti-Palamite members of his circle.

The *Discourse to Iagoup*

During the anti-Palamite persecutions, trouble ensued when another of the accused, Manuel Kalekas, fled to Pera in autumn 1396. Kalekas ran a school in Constantinople and was a disciple of Kydones. He was a convert to Catholicism and associated with Kydones' anti-Palamite circle, which included Asan, Chrysoberges and Manuel Raoul.[47] From his exile in Pera, Kalekas wrote a bitter letter to Constantine Asan. The letter, which does not survive, was apparently filled with insults, and it fell into Manuel's hands. The emperor, in turn, composed a similar letter attacking Kalekas to Asanes.

The language of Manuel's letter is unusually pejorative. Stating from the outset that he will imitate the manner of Kalekas' letter, the emperor likens Kalekas to animals that give birth to large litters. He further complains that comparing some people to drunks and swine, calling them liars and imposters, was a behaviour that did not befit a man seeking to pursue philosophy.[48] Such insults are not found anywhere else in Manuel's oeuvre and indicate the extent of the emperor's rage. Further, the length and the passionate tone of his letter make it evident that he was infuriated. This bizarre letter exchange was not to be the only exhibition of tension between Kalekas and the emperor. Again, during the autumn of 1396, Manuel

---

[46] *On the Order in the Trinity* is edited in *On the Procession of the Holy Spirit*, 318–321. Demetracopoulos, 'Palamas transformed', 333–40. See also Maximos Confessor, Περὶ Θεολογίας καὶ τῆς Ἐνσάρκου Οἰκονομίας Υἱοῦ τοῦ Θεοῦ, PG 90, 1083–176, 1101A and 1085B.

[47] For a detailed biography of Kalekas, see Loenertz, *Calécas*, 16–46.

[48] Letter 30, lines 4–10 and 50–3.

attacked him in an epistolary discourse addressed to another member of his circle and his *oikeios*, Alexios Iagoup.[49]

The *Discourse to Iagoup (Epistolary Discourse to Alexios Iagoup)* is one of Manuel's least known works. A few scholars have referred to the first three pages of the work, made available by Berger de Xivrey, on Manuel's education and his early life, and they have done so in almost complete isolation from the remainder of the text.[50] Since in the text, the emperor attacks Kalekas' Scholastic methods in order to refute him, scholars have also been led to consider the work merely as a discourse on the study of theology. However, the following discussion will argue that the text was composed as an *apologia* in the polemic between the emperor and Kalekas.[51] Since it offers insight into Manuel's personality and contains many digressions on his ideas about Byzantine identity and the study of theology, the *Discourse to Iagoup* merits lengthy discussion.

As in the case of many of Manuel's works, it was probably circulated in his literary circle. The *Discourse to Iagoup* is certainly related to the events of the autumn of 1396, and the emperor makes clear references to the prosecution and flight of Kalekas. Although Manuel does not refer to his opponent by name, the striking parallels between the discourse and his letter to Constantine Asan strongly indicate that the person in question was Kalekas.[52] His letters also testify that Kalekas was in correspondence with several members of Manuel's literary circle, including Kydones, Constantine Asan, Manuel Raoul, Manuel Chrysoloras, Demetrios Skaranos and Joseph Bryennios.[53] It is highly probable that Manuel not only wished to address Iagoup and the members of his immediate literary circle, but also his principal opponent on the matter. The subsequent reply of the opponent and this networking strongly indicate that the discourse reached Kalekas.

Manuel opens the work by addressing Iagoup on the subject of 'an acquaintance' of his. Iagoup's 'friend' was concerned that although the

---

[49] Alexios Iagoup appears as an *apogrepheus* in Lemnos in 1396–7, and is also listed as an *oikeios* of Manuel in 1401, in the synod convoked against Makarios of Ankyra. *On the Procession of the Holy Spirit*, 419–20.

[50] See Chapter 2. The editor of the work, Dendrinos, provides a brief commentary on the work, identifying the events and the persons, *On the Procession of the Holy Spirit*, 419–29. See also Ch. Dendrinos, "Ἡ ἐπιστολὴ τοῦ αὐτοκράτορος Μανουὴλ Β′ Παλαιολόγου πρὸς τὸν Ἀλέξιο Ἰαγούπ καὶ οἱ ἀντιλήψεις του περὶ τῆς σπουδῆς τῆς θεολογίας καὶ τῶν σχέσεων Ἐκκλησίας καὶ Πολιτείας', *Φιλοσοφίας Ἀνάλεκτα*, vol. 1 (2001), 58–74. Henceforth, Dendrinos, "Ἡ ἐπιστολή'.

[51] *Dialogue on Marriage*, 13, Dennis, *Letters*, xvii and xxiii. Barker, *Manuel II*, 410, *Procession of the Holy Spirit*, 419 and "Ἡ ἐπιστολή', 59. Manuel himself refers to his work as ἀπολογία in the text, *Discourse to Iagoup*, 364 and 393.

[52] *On the Procession of the Holy Spirit*, 410–20 and "Ἡ ἐπιστολή', 63–5, also argues that this person was Kalekas.

[53] Loenertz, *Calécas*, 47–105.

cares of ruling scarcely allowed the emperor to breathe, he still wanted to study theology. This person advised Manuel to direct his zeal to matters of state only, and to refrain from pursuing theology; a discipline that did not befit him. The anonymous critic seems to have subtly implied that the emperor lacked the necessary knowledge to deal with theology.[54] This person, of course, was Kalekas. Hence, the introduction of the text immediately sets out Manuel's motivation for penning the discourse, which is revealed to be Kalekas' critique of his theological interests, not Kalekas' own Catholicism or anti-Palamism. An analysis of the discourse demonstrates that Manuel was extremely offended, both personally and also as the emperor, by these criticisms questioning his authority in theology. It manifests a previously unseen side to him and reveals that the emperor was disposed to react rather harshly to criticism, especially when his scholarly abilities were questioned.

The language of the discourse thus stands out from the rest of Manuel's works in its aggressive tone. The text is tightly woven with military metaphors and battle imagery, and although such imagery could well be an influence of the Psalms and was commonplace, Manuel confines their use solely to instances of theological and ecclesiastical dispute.[55] Manuel creates an atmosphere of 'intellectual battle' for his audience, and he and Kalekas are portrayed as the two enemy lines. In one prominent instance, the emperor labels the situation as a 'spiritual war'; this accentuation of the tense textual atmosphere is unique in the emperor's oeuvre.[56] Thus, it is probable that Manuel adapted his imagery to suit the tone of his work.

He also adopts an unusually derogatory tone when referring to Kalekas. The emperor never explicitly names Kalekas, but instead refers to him as 'that person' or 'your friend'. At certain points in the discourse, Manuel even abandons the pretence that his addressee was Iagoup, and directly attacks Kalekas in the second person. In a striking passage, the emperor draws a vivid picture of Kalekas extolling his own theological erudition while downgrading that of Manuel. The emperor implies that Kalekas has treated him as a child or as a student, but he retaliates by pointing out that Kalekas had not received a vote from God that instated him as the teacher of the *genos* and the guide of the faith.[57] These remarks are of crucial significance. They indicate that Manuel was offended not only by the

---

[54] *Discourse to Iagoup*, 326, lines 1–16.
[55] Apart from the *Discourse to Iagoup*, the *kephalia* on the Church in the *Foundations* stand out with regards to battle and weapon metaphors. *On the Procession of the Holy Spirit* also has a few, milder instances.
[56] *Discourse to Iagoup*, 333–5, for a few examples.   [57] *Discourse to Iagoup*, 351.

belittlement of his erudition, but also for being treated as 'intellectually inferior'.

Kalekas' scorning of Manuel's theological competence threatened to undermine his projected image as a scholar-emperor; a figure who was equally well-versed in philosophy and theology as well as in state affairs. We have seen that Manuel's self-representation in the *Dialogue with a Persian* sought to establish him not only as a political, but also as a theological authority. Kalekas' critique was thus seen as an attack on Manuel's authority in theology. As will become clear in the following chapters, the emperor sought to exert influence over theological debates and Church affairs as the teacher of the *genos* and the guide of the faith. The *Discourse to Iagoup* is therefore especially poignant in the fashioning of the persona of a scholar-emperor. Manuel opens the work with the disclaimer – a *topos* of modesty – that he does not consider himself to be a theologian and would never aspire to become one. Yet despite the frequency of such protests, they do not hold up under close scrutiny, and it quickly becomes manifest that many passages actually advertise his theological erudition.

One recurring theme revolves around the disadvantages attendant upon Manuel's imperial rank both as a young prince and later as emperor. Throughout the text, the emperor laments that the troubles brought about by the difficult times left him little opportunity for scholarly pursuits.[58] Even the 'autobiographical' passages of the work, such as those narrating Manuel's tumultuous childhood and youth, serve to arouse the audience's sympathy. The message, of course, is that despite all the obstacles placed in his path, Manuel displayed an incredible aptitude and yearning for scholarship.[59] Similarly, the emperor laments that he could not devote himself to theology as a child, as he was prevented by both the circumstances and by his status.[60] This remark hints that *had* he been free do so, Manuel would have devoted his whole life to theology.

Against Kalekas' criticisms that he ought to leave theology aside and tend to his duties as a ruler, Manuel represents himself as a model scholar-emperor, fusing these two aspects in his person. Finally, once he finishes

---

[58] *Discourse to Iagoup*, 326–7, 365, 373, for a few examples.

[59] *Discourse to Iagoup*, 329–30. For autobiographical narratives in Late Byzantium, see M. Angold, 'Autobiography and Identity: The Case of the Later Byzantine Empire', *BSl* 60 (1999), 18–30. For instance, the Patriarch Matthew also speaks of his love for spiritual life as a child, representing himself as an ideal clergyman. His 'autobiographical' account, too, has apologetic qualities as the testament in part refutes the accusation that he had collaborated with the Ottomans during the blockade. See H. Hunger, 'Das Testament des Patriarchen Matthaios I (1397–1410)', *BZ* 51 (1958), 288–309, 295. Henceforth, Hunger, 'Das Testament des Patriarchen Matthaios'.

[60] *Discourse to Iagoup*, 332.

the account of his early life, he immediately proceeds to *discuss* theology in a highly learned manner and refutes Kalekas' Scholastic methods. Ultimately, Manuel also defines the 'correct' way to study theology by championing the Orthodox position vis-à-vis the Catholic converts and the anti-Palamites. The emperor therefore attempts to establish himself not only as a political, but a theological authority.

A significant discussion in the discourse is the usage of syllogisms in theological inquiry. As previously noted, while this had always been significant point of a contention in Byzantine theology, the debate was further intensified with the rise of Palamism and the conversions to Catholicism. During Manuel's time, generally, it was pro-Latin and anti-Palamite theologians who approved the use of syllogisms in theology. Orthodox and Palamite scholars, on the other hand, chiefly opposed their use unless their premises were based on revelation.[61] While addressing this prominent debate, Manuel firmly defends this Orthodox – and to an extent, Palamite – position and argues that use of syllogisms in theology is improper. He equates the use of syllogisms to sophistry. Hence, as emperor, he sanctions the Orthodox theological methodology vis-à-vis that of the Latins and also, of the anti-Palamites.

Related to the use of syllogisms in theological inquiry, is the question of the role of Greek philosophy, especially the teachings of Plato and Aristotle, in theology. Manuel discusses these two issues together. The reliance on philosophy was a much-debated topic in both Latin and Orthodox theology, with the latter opposing any such use of philosophy. The same contention also existed between the Palamites and anti-Palamites. However, as previously discussed, the lines between these groups were not rigidly drawn concerning these issues. This contested relationship between philosophy and theology had added significance in Byzantium: the boundaries between theology and philosophy were sometimes blurred, and a fusion of the two could easily bring about accusations of heresy. Some prominent examples would be the condemnations of John Italos in the eleventh century and Prochoros Kydones in the mid-fourteenth century.[62] In a poignant passage in the *Discourse to Iagoup*,

---

[61] See Demetracopoulos, 'Dignitas Hominis', 369 and 394–401; Podskalsky, *Philosophie und Theologie*, 124–73; Kapriev, *Philsophie in Byzanz*, 2788–9 and K. Ierodiakonou, 'The Anti-Logical Movement in the Fourteenth Century' in *Byzantine Philosophy and its Ancient Sources*, ed. K. Ierodiakonou (New York, 2002), 219–37. For Makarios Makres and Joseph Bryennios' opposition to syllogisms, see respectively their treatises in, Voulgaris, *Bryennios*, vol. 1, 1–406; 82–97 and Argyrios, *Makres*, 49–63; 49–50.

[62] See R. Browning, 'Enlightenment and Repression in Byzantium in the Eleventh and the Twelfth Centuries', *Past and Present* 69 (1975), 3–29; A. Kaldellis, *Hellenism in Byzantium: The Transformations*

Manuel claims that any use of Greek philosophy in theology was highly improper:

> Is it not clear that these people (true theologians) do not use syllogisms or clever sophistry? They are neither exalted by the help of *enkyklios paideia* nor take courage from Plato and those others who are contentious in accordance with him. But, as we have already said, do they not simply put into our souls, the simple *logos* about the simple Trinity and that the Trinity does not achieve an absolute fusion since it is tripartite? And the simple *logos* about its *oikonomia*, the manner of which is still unknown even to the angels? For if it were possible for men to find God through the outer wisdom, if the intellect could grasp God, then Pythagorases, Socrateses and the remainder of the ancients – from whose wisdom we have fallen so short that it is not easy to find such accomplishments – would have been the first ones to undertake this contest.[63]

Manuel further expresses his contempt for the use of Greek philosophy in many other passages of the work. The Fathers, he says, trampled and 'spit upon' pagan philosophy. The emperor argues that faith (πίστις) and knowledge (γνῶσις) are distinct from each other and are, in fact, opposites. According to him, piety stems from a right will, a good disposition and a gentleness of conscience, not from *paideia*.[64] He criticizes people who praise 'the wisdom of the Hellenes', pointing out that the study of pagan philosophy could confound one's faith. This stance bears witness to Manuel's adherence to traditional Orthodox teachings. As previously discussed, it also hints at his Palamite leanings.

Although he is not referred to by name, the target of these attacks is once again Kalekas. Having 'deviated' from the Orthodox faith through his 'improper' study of philosophy, Kalekas is the embodiment of Manuel's

---

of Greek Identity and the Reception of Classical Tradition (Cambridge, 2007), 120–66; A. Kaldellis, 'Byzantine Philosophy Inside and Out: Orthodoxy and Dissidence in Counterpoint,' in *The Many Faces of Byzantine Philosophy*, eds. K. Ierodiakonou and B. Bydén (Athens, 2012) 129–51; J. Meyendorff, *Byzantine Theology. Historical Trends and Doctrinal Themes* (New York, 1974), 11–12; Kapriev, *Philosophie in Byzanz*, 13–14. Henceforth, Kaldellis, *Hellenism* and Meyendorff, *Byzantine Theology*.

[63] *Discourse to Iagoup*, 337, "Ἡ δῆλον, ὡς οὐ συλλογισμοῖς καὶ σοφίσμαισι χρώμενοι, οὐδὲ τῇ τῆς ἐγκυκλίου παιδεύσεως σεμνυνόμενοι συμμαχίᾳ, οὐδὲ Πλάτωνι θαρροῦντες καὶ τοῖς κατ' αὐτὸν οἶς ἀμέλει μαχόμενοι διετέλουν, ἀλλ' ἁπλῶς, ἧπερ ἔφην, τὸν ἁπλοῦν ταῖς ἡμετέραις ψυχαῖς ἐνέθετο λόγον περί τε τῆς ἁπλῆς Τριάδος καὶ μὴ τὸ παράπαν σύνθεσιν δεχομένης ὅτι τριάς, καὶ αὐτῆς δὴ ταύτης τῆς οἰκονομίας, ἧς καὶ ἀγγέλοις ὁ τρόπος ἔτι καὶ νῦν ἄγνωστος ὢν τυγχάνει; Εἴπερ γάρ, ὦ τὰν ἀνθρώπους ἐνῆν ἀπὸ τῆς ἔξω σοφίας εὑρεῖν τὸν θεόν, καὶ εἰ ἐδύνατο νοῦς περιλαβεῖν τὸν θεόν, Πυθαγόραι καὶ Σωκράτεις καὶ οἱ λοιποὶ τῶν παλαιῶν ἀνδρῶν, ὧν τοσοῦτον τῆς σοφίας ἀφεστηκότες ἐσμέν, ὡς οὐδὲ ῥᾴδιόν ἐστιν εὑρεῖν ὅσον, αὐτοὶ ἂν πρῶτοι τουτονὶ τὸν ἀγῶνα ἠνυκότες ἐφαίνοντο.'

[64] *Discourse to Iagoup*, 336, 338, 340–1, 343–5.

criticisms. Since he is not just any author, but the emperor, Manuel adopts
a defence which seeks to establish Orthodoxy as the 'correct' and legitimate
dogma vis-à-vis Kalekas and other deviants – that is, other pro-Latin and
anti-Palamite theologians. Thus, in both debates, he uses his imperial
authority to lend further sanctity to the Orthodox position, and to an
extent, Palamism. Despite his condemnation of pagan philosophy, however, Manuel still praises ancient philosophers. Although he acknowledges
that his contemporaries lagged behind in terms of 'secular learning', he
does emphasize that this shortcoming was excused as the contemporaries
excelled in matters of faith.[65]

How can one reconcile Manuel's exceedingly negative attitude towards
Greek philosophy in the *Discourse to Iagoup,* and the admiration he
displays elsewhere? After all, the emperor's other works are adorned
with Platonic allusions, his dialogues are modelled on Plato and his
ethico-political works are dominated by Aristotelian ethics. Even the
Discourse to Iagoup contains some Platonic quotations, although they
do not pertain to philosophical ideas. Moreover, in this very same work,
Manuel also openly acknowledges his love of the 'outer wisdom' and
paideia. 'I would never reproach these things', he remarks, 'in which
I rejoice; things without which one could not lead a life that befits
mankind.'[66] He further identifies some of the practical uses of *paideia*:
first, it is useful in protecting oneself against wicked sophistry in matters
of faith; second, it helps divinely inspired people to enlighten others
through their speech.[67] Therefore, Manuel envisions a very traditional
Orthodox role for *paideia*.

The *Discourse* offers insight into Manuel's perception of the relationship
between theology and philosophy. Although his status as a 'philosopher-
emperor' is much celebrated, his actual stance regarding philosophy has
never been discussed. In the *Discourse,* the emperor proposes that philosophy is helpful in those things that pertain to character formation (εἰς τὰ
ἤθη) and in the governance of public affairs (τό πολιτεύεσθαι), as well as in
other matters belonging to *this life*.[68] He makes a clear differentiation
between ethico-political philosophy and the use of philosophy in theological inquiry. In other passages, he again argues that orthodox faith
(εὐσεβεία) and philosophy are completely unrelated to one and the
other; they have different boundaries.[69] When touching on the debate

---

[65] *Discourse to Iagoup,* 341.   [66] *Discourse to Iagoup,* 357–8.   [67] *Discourse to Iagoup,* 342–3.
[68] *Discourse to Iagoup,* 342, 'βοηθεῖ μεν γὰρ εἰς τε τὰ ἤθη καὶ τὸ πολιτύεσθαι τοῖς ἀνθρώποις, καὶ ἄλλ'
ἄττα τῷ βίῳ πρέποντα τούτῳ.'
[69] *Discourse to Iagoup,* 347.

concerning the relationship between faith and philosophy, the emperor is at pains to separate the two.

Manuel's friendship with figures such as Demetrios Kydones, and later, the tolerance he exhibited to Plethon, should not be interpreted as him approving such use of philosophy. Neither should the criticism he pours down upon Greek philosophy in the *Discourse*, be seen as a contradiction of the positive approach he displays elsewhere. Manuel here envisages clear boundaries between philosophy and theology, where the former deals with ethics and politics, and the latter with divine matters. Ultimately, in order to distinguish clearly between the two, the only form of philosophy he accepts is ethico-political philosophy. In this regard, it is also noteworthy that the ethical and political ideas promulgated by Plato and Aristotle are easier to reconcile with Christian thought, as opposed to, for instance, Platonic idealism. Throughout his life, Manuel was to stay within these boundaries in his own works, where he was to deal with Plato and Aristotle only in terms of ethical and political philosophy.

Finally, *Discourse to Iagoup* sheds light on the emperor's views on identity. Although Byzantine identity has become a popular area of study in recent years, Manuel hardly makes an appearance in them. In this regard, a passage on Kalekas is rather illuminating and deserves full quotation:

> He has received all *our* teaching on literature, as well as that of the Latins, and he has also learned their doctrines regarding the divine. Despite that he stayed amongst *us* for a great many years. But, when his head became full of grey hair, when he would be expected to think in the same manner as he had spoken during his youth and prime, those things were dimmed by the passage of time and decay; we see this happening to many people. Now, he is seen manifestly trampling upon what he used to praise before, as if he cannot help it . . . But even now, he rejoices more in living with *us* rather than with *them*. Concerning sacred hymns, customs, literature and other things through which by nature people unite, bind and become of the same mind with their own, he rejoices in *ours* rather than that of those to whom he has deserted. His clothes, mantle, riding equipment, rod and yoke, his fine things, his manner of dressing, sitting, standing and walking, not least his couch, bed, table, food and drink, all other things he uses, these belong to the *Hellenes*, to their lifestyle and order. These are the things he inherited and by which he had been raised. There is nothing in common between him and the Latins.[70]

---

[70] *Discourse to Iagoup*, 368–9. ἐκ γὰρ τῶν πρὶν αὐτομολησάντων ὡς αὐτούς, εἶτ᾽ ἐπανελθόντων ὡς ἡμᾶς, δῆλον ἂν εἴη ὡς οὐδὲ τούτῳ πάνυ πιστεύοντες ἔσονται. Οὐ γὰρ ἐπειδήπερ εἰς ἄνδρας ἀφίκετο, καὶ τὴν ἡμετέραν ὁπόσην ἔχει παιδείαν περὶ τοὺς λόγους, καὶ δὴ καὶ τὴν Λατίνων παιδευθείς, καὶ τὴν ἐκείνων περὶ τὸ θεῖον δόξαν μαθών, καὶ πρός γε ἔτι ὕστερον μετὰ πολλὰς

This passage makes manifest that Manuel did not perceive Kalekas' conversion and subsequent fleeing to Pera as a mere betrayal of his Orthodox faith, he perceived it as a complete rejection of his identity as a Byzantine.[71] Manuel signifies here that the Latins and the Byzantines did not differ from each other only in terms of religion, but also in terms of language, literature, customs and everyday life. In his view, these were inherited from one's ancestors and one became familiar with them from early childhood; they united people with other members of their *genos*. The emperor remarks that it was only natural and to be expected for a person to cherish the things by which he was reared as a child. Hence, it can be argued that Manuel assigns identity largely to one's upbringing rather than one's ethnicity or to biological factors.

It is also worth noting that he displays a similar outlook in the *Dialogue with a Persian*, where he admits that it was understandable that the old *müderris* did not convert from Islam, the faith in which he had been reared. The emperor thus implicitly acknowledges that even the devotion of the *müderris* to his ancestral faith was to be expected. The implication is that Islam constituted a part of his identity as an Ottoman.[72] Manuel's views relating to identity and upbringing were therefore not restricted to his fellow Byzantines, but extended even to the Ottomans, his foes.

In the *Discourse to Iagoup*, Manuel's attempts to construct a Byzantine identity vis-à-vis the Latins prompts him to use the word *Hellene* in reference to the Byzantines. This usage is not present in any of his other

---

ἐτῶν περιόδους διέστηκεν ἡμῶν, ἀλλ᾽ ἡνίκα πολιὸς ἐγεγόνει, καὶ ἦν εἰκὸς νομίζειν ὡς καὶ ἅπερ ἐν νεότητι καὶ ἀκμῇ συνελέξατο, καὶ ταῦτ᾽ ἠμβλύνθη τυχὸν τῷ χρόνῳ τε καὶ τῇ παρακμῇ, ὡς ἐν οὐκ ὀλίγοις τοῦθ᾽ ὁρῶμεν γινόμενον, τότ᾽ ὤφθη διασύρων φανερῶς, ὡς μὴ ὤφελεν, ἃ τὸ πρὶν ὕμνει. Καὶ μήν, μέχρι χθὲς καὶ πρώην καὶ μετὰ τὸ διαβάλλειν ἀξιοῦν τὰ ἡμέτερα, τοὺς ἡμετέρους ἱερέας προπηλακίζων μὲν οὔκουν ἀφίστατο. Τούτοις δ᾽ οὖν ὅμως ἑαυτὸν προσαγγέλλων ἐφαίνετο, εἴ που τι σύνοιδεν ἀνθρώπινον ἑαυτῷ, καὶ παρ᾽ αὐτῶν ἠξίου καθαίρεσθαί τε καὶ ἁγιάζεσθαι. Ἀλλὰ καὶ νῦν ἡμῖν μᾶλλον, ἢ σφίσι χαίρει συνὼν τοῖς τε ἱεροῖς ὕμνοις, καὶ ἔθεσι, καὶ λόγοις, καὶ οἷς ἁπλῶς πεφύκασιν ἄνθρωποι εἰς ταὐτὸ συνέρχεσθαι καὶ συνδεδέσθαι, καὶ ὁμογνωμονεῖν, τοῖς ἡμετέροις ἥδεται μᾶλλον, ἢ τοῖς πρὸς οὓς ηὐτομόλησεν. Ἔτι τοίνυν, καὶ ἐσθής, καὶ ἐφεστρίς, καὶ ἱππασία, καὶ μάστιξ, καὶ κέντρον, τὰ εὐτελέστατα καὶ τὸ ὑποδεδέσθαι, καὶ καθῆσθαι, καὶ ἵστασθαι, καὶ βαδίζειν, καὶ δὴ καὶ σκίμπους, καὶ εὐνή, καὶ τράπεζα, καὶ σιτία, καὶ ποτά, καὶ συνελόντα φάναι τἄλλα πάνθ᾽ οἷς τισι χρῆται, ταῦτα δὲ Ἑλλήνων καὶ τῆς τούτων διαίτης καὶ τάξεως, ἃ δὴ καὶ οὗτος παρ᾽ ὧν ἔφυ πεπαίδευταί τε καὶ διεδέξατο. Καὶ οὐδὲν αὐτῷ καὶ Λατίνοις ἔστι κοινόν.᾽

71 For some prominent discussions, see P. Magdalino, 'Hellenism and Nationalism in Byzantium', in *Tradition and Transformation in Medieval Byzantium*, ed. P. Magdalino (Aldershot, 1991), Study XIV, 1–29; Kaldellis, *Hellenism* and also Kaldellis, *Ethnography*; G. Page. *Being Byzantine. Greek Identity before the Ottomans* (Cambridge, 2008); A. D. Angelou, 'Who am I? Scholarios' Answers and the Hellenic Identity', in *Philhellene: Studies in Honour of Robert Browning*, eds. C. Constantinides, N. Pamagiotakes et al. (Venice, 1996), 1–19. Henceforth, Page, *Being Byzantine*.

72 *Dialogue with a Persian*, 5–6.

works and has not been noted.[73] The emperor normally uses *Hellene* to refer to pagan Greeks, which is also evident in his usage of the word elsewhere in the discourse. Yet while trying to define a Byzantine identity versus the Latins in terms of customs, language and everyday life, it is significant that Manuel chooses to use the term *Hellene*, and not *Roman*, on the basis of the Greek language and inheritance of Byzantium.

The aftermath of the *Discourse to Iagoup* is rather telling in exposing the depth of Manuel's resentment towards Kalekas. Kalekas' letter collection contains seven letters addressed to him after these events, usually dated around 1396/8, in which he asks the emperor's forgiveness in a beseeching and humble tone.[74] However, Kalekas never directly refers to the events or to his previous criticism. No replies to Kalekas survive in Manuel's own letter collection, and a study of Kalekas' letters suggests that he never received a pardon from the emperor despite the fact that in the letters he adopts the persona of a penitent petitioner and continually emphasizes Manuel's rank as the emperor and his own 'unworthiness' as his subject. In addition to portraying himself as a quiet, harmless scholar, his letters are adorned with praises of Manuel's literary skills, his multi-faceted personality as an emperor, rhetor and military commander. He further extolls Manuel's ability to continue his scholarly occupations amidst all his troubles.[75]

All this stands in stark contrast with Kalekas' earlier criticisms of Manuel and instead conforms completely to the emperor's self-representation in the *Discourse to Iagoup*. These strengthen the possibility that Kalekas had either read or heard about the discourse. Ultimately, his opponent seems to have sought forgiveness by reflecting back Manuel's own constructed self-image. Even six years later, during Manuel's sojourn in Paris in 1401, Kalekas was still writing to the emperor, hoping to be restored to his favour.[76] After that point, however, nothing more can be discerned about the affair. At some point, Kalekas migrated to Crete from Pera and ended his days there. The Kalekas of 1396 affair is illustrative of Manuel's sensitivity to criticism, especially when contesting his authority as a scholar-emperor, and it is a trait that he would display throughout his life.

---

[73] For the use of the terms *Hellene* and Greek as referring to the Byzantines, especially after 1204, see Kaldellis, *Hellenism*, 334–79, Angelov, *Imperial Ideology*, 95–8 and in general, Page, *Being Byzantine*. Gill Page, who only analyses Manuel's *Funeral Oration* argues that Manuel exclusively used the term Roman, 25–6.

[74] These are Letters 14, 26, 34, 39, 47 and 71 in Kalekas' letter collection.

[75] Kalekas, Letter 26, lines 4–10 and Letter 34, line 26.   [76] See Kalekas, Letter 71.

A Flurry of Writing: The *Dialogue on Marriage*

During the blockade of Constantinople, Manuel composed many works. This probably stemmed from a combination of Manuel's pleasure in writing and his need to enhance his authority under immense political pressure. In addition to the *Discourse to Iagoup*, the *Epistolary Discourse to Andreas Asan on Dreams* probably dates from this period.[77] This short work deals with the question of whether it is possible for the soul to prophesize in sleep.

Again, Manuel is the dominant figure in the discussion, giving an authoritative verdict on the issue as a scholar-emperor. Combining Platonic and Christian thought, the emperor concludes that the soul, as it is still connected to the body during sleep, may prophesize, but only in a very foggy manner. This is a curious instance, as Manuel does not display an interest in such matters elsewhere. It is possible that Asan initiated this new discussion,

During the blockade, some parts of the *Dialogue with a Persian* were probably still in progress. Around this same time, Manuel also composed his famous *Dialogue on Marriage*, where he and the Empress Mother Helena are the collocutors.[78] Despite its relatively short length and slightly less vivid characters in comparison to those in *Dialogue with a Persian*, it is still a fascinating work with regard to its embedded political messages and representation of the collocutors.

Although the *Dialogue on Marriage* is one of Manuel's most studied works, we will now seek to add few more insights to existing studies.[79] The representation of the Empress Helena in this work is remarkable; she is portrayed as the leading party in the philosophical discussion. Indeed, she was a literary figure in her own right and a correspondent of Demetrios Kydones and Nikephoros Gregoras. Indeed, Kydones' letters to Helena hint that he had been her teacher in her youth, just as he was for her son Manuel. Although none of Helena's compositions survive, Kydones' letters indicate that at least during her youth, Helena wielded the pen, composing

---

[77] Two articles exist on the *Epistolary Discourse to Andreas Asan on Dreams*; I. R. Alfagame, 'La epístola περὶ ὀνειράτων de Manuel Paleólogo', *Cuadernos de filolología clásica* 2 (1971), 227–55.', and G. Calofanos, 'Manuel II Palaiologos: Interpreter of Dreams?' in *Manzikert to Lepanto: The Byzantine World and the Turks (1071–1517). Papers given at the 19th Spring Symposium of Byzantine Studies, Birmingham, March 1985*, eds. A. A. Bryer and M. Ursinus, *BF* 16 (1991), 447–55.

[78] The work exists in two editions; Manuel Palaeologus, *Dialogue with the Empress Mother on Marriage*, ed. and trans. A. Angelou (Vienna, 1991) and *Dialogum de matrimonio*, ed. C. Bevegni (Catania, 1989).

[79] These works will be cited in the following discussion.

a panegyric in honour of her father John Kantakouzenos.[80] Kydones even sent her his sermon on St Laurence and his translations of some works of St Augustine, which indicate that Helena had the intellectual capacity and learning to deal with such complex theological works.[81] In his depiction of the empress in the dialogue as an extremely able discussant, it is clear that Manuel valued his mother's scholarly abilities highly. She also possesses the notable distinction of being the only female in his compositions.

While Helena's strength of character and intelligence in the *Dialogue on Marriage* stem partially from Manuel's admiration for his mother, Kydones' letters also hint at her personal strength. Helena acted as a patron for her former teacher during the reign of her husband, for instance, and on occasion shielded Kydones from John V's displeasure.[82] An analysis of Manuel's *Funeral Oration* reveals a similar stance. Manuel portrays Helena as being politically involved, claiming that Helena exercised 'the strongest influence' on her sons; he also emphasizes her wisdom both in private and public affairs.[83] Even more significantly, Manuel makes Helena a direct participant in politics, underscoring that Theodore ceded Corinth to the Hospitallers not only with his consent, but also that of their mother.[84] The emperor essentially represents his mother as having an equal say in politics and a status and authority equal to him; this is a crucial representation given his careful emphasis in his writings on his unique role as the emperor. A further substantiation of Manuel's regard for Helena is her regency during Manuel's absence from Constantinople in 1391.[85]

In addition to their political bond, the mother and son seem to have enjoyed a close relationship. This is further reflected in Manuel's only surviving letter to his mother. The letter cannot be dated precisely, but it seems to have been written before Manuel's reign in Thessalonike.[86] It is a letter of consolation to the Empress Helena on the death of some children in her care. As suggested by the editor of the letters, these were perhaps Manuel's own illegitimate children.[87] The tone of the letter conveys the great affection the emperor felt for his mother, as well as the concern he felt on account of her excessive grief. He touchingly pleads with his mother to

---

[80] For a discussion of the letters of Kydones to Helena, see, Kianka, 'Letters'; Kydones, Letter 25 and 256.
[81] Kianka, 'Letters', 156.   [82] Kianka, 'Letters', 161.   [83] *Funeral Oration*, 102–3 and 240–1.
[84] *Funeral Oration*, 166–7. For other instances of Helena's representation as a significant political figure, see 112–13, 148–9.
[85] See the appendix in Loenertz, *Les letters de Démétrius Cydonès*, ii, 444–5 for the Venetian document pointing to Helena's regency.
[86] Letter 1. John Kantakouzenos, who died in June 1383, is referred to as still alive.
[87] The editor of the letters, Dennis, also raises this possibility.

take care of her own health, as he needs her more than his own breath; apart from Christ and the Virgin Mary, Helena is the only person with whom Manuel adopts the role of a supplicant.

The emperor's actions after her death in 1396 also reveal the very deep affection he felt for Helena. In November 1397, on the first anniversary of Helena's death, the emperor intervened with a *prostagma* to ensure that the memorial service would still be held during the vacancy of the patriarchal throne. This act would later by criticized by the Patriarch Matthew.[88]

In the *Dialogue on Marriage*, Helena is represented as a very strong, confident and on occasion, almost stern figure. During the conversation it is she who is the superior discussant, incessantly providing her son with answers and challenging Manuel's arguments. On occasion, she even mildly scolds him. As in the cases of the *Discourse to Kabasilas* and the *Dialogue with a Persian*, the *Dialogue on Marriage*, too, is modelled as a Platonic dialogue. In contrast to these works where Manuel adopts the role of Socrates, here it is Helena who is cast into that role.[89] It is significant that Manuel, who always seeks to depict himself as the superior party in the discussions, relinquishes that role to his mother and adopts that of a less polished interlocutor. The imbalance of rhetorical power and confidence between the mother and the son can also be traced in Manuel's use of hunting metaphors. Helena becomes the competent hunter and Manuel her prey, and readily admitting his pleasure at becoming one.[90] This imagery highlights the imbalance of power between the two, and it also creates an atmosphere of excitement and tension: the dialogue ends with the empress catching her 'willing' prey.

As remarked by several scholars, the dialogue opens a window onto Manuel's views on marriage.[91] He complains that he married rather unwillingly, only in order to beget heirs. Moreover, he largely ascribes his marriage to the insistence of his mother. Throughout the dialogue, Manuel approaches marriage with the mind of a ruler, and not of a private individual. His emphasis is on his status as an emperor and his analysis of

---

[88] Helena became a nun around 1394, see Schreiner, *Kleinchroniken*, Chronik 22/22. Mioni, 'Cronaca', no. 24, refers to her death. G. T. Dennis, 'Official documents of Manuel II Palaeologus', *Byzantion* 61 (1971), 45–58, reprinted in G.T. Dennis, *Byzantium and the Franks, 1350–1420* (London, 1982), Study IX, 47 for the issuing of this *prostagma*. Also, Darrouzes, *Les Régestes*, no. 3058, 319, for the discontent of Patriarch Matthew. Henceforth, Dennis, 'Official Documents'.

[89] Helena's resemblance to Socrates in this work has also been noted by P. Hatlie, 'Images of Motherhood and Self in Byzantine Literature', *DOP* 63 (2009), 41–57, 54.

[90] Dialogue on Marriage, 78–9.

[91] M. Dabrowska, 'Ought One to Marry? Manuel II Palaiologos' Point of View', *BMGS* 31 no. 2 (2007), 146–56.

marriage focuses solely on the benefit to the state. The emperor declares that he did not wish to marry, as the circumstances were complicated enough, and he refers to the frictions with John VII and the on-going blockade. He also protests that he did not want to divide his attention between the affairs of the state and the obligations of married life.[92] The empress argues that it is precisely these circumstances that necessitate Manuel's marriage: he needs heirs in order to secure his dynasty, especially against the claims of John VII, and thus the whole discussion of marriage has strong political undertones.

Despite its political content, the *Dialogue* also reveals Manuel's personal stance on marriage. His arguments should not be interpreted as being adopted solely for a philosophical discussion, neither are they purely political. In the work, Manuel envisages marriage only in terms of begetting children, and apart from a very brief mention by the Empress Helena, there is no discussion of the relationship between the husband and wife, either from a Christian point of view, or as portrayed in Aristotelian ethics, which he favoured greatly. Furthermore, although the topic is marriage, his wife, the younger Empress Helena, is never mentioned. Despite the fact that Manuel focuses on the procreation of children in marriage as a dynastic tool, his 'lukewarm' stance in this dialogue should not be dismissed as merely having been adopted for the sake of discussion. He did, after all, remain unmarried into his forties despite there being plenty of occasions when a marriage alliance would have benefitted him politically.

In Manuel's other works he displays a similar stance concerning marriage. In the *Dialogue with a Persian*, he suggests that Adam and Eve were bonded by God for the procreation of children. Although this reflects the Christian view, it is significant that he never mentions other Christian ideals pertaining to matrimony. Notions such as marriage preventing one from falling into fornication, or husband and wife as helpmates, are completely absent. For instance, while his grandfather John Kantakouzenos promulgates the same procreation argument in his own treatise, he does mention these Christian ideals.[93] The same attitude can be discerned in the *Declamation regarding a Drunken Man*, a short work based on Libanios' declamations. In the text, Manuel has the father figure claim that he had married solely for the purpose of begetting children.[94] It can thus be proposed that Manuel's 'lukewarm' attitude to marriage was not a mere adopted stance in the *Dialogue with*

---

[92] Dialogue on Marriage, 96–7.
[93] *Dialogue with a Persian*, 33. For Kantakouzenos, see *PG* 155, 545D-53.
[94] *Declamation regarding a Drunken Man*, 277. Although the father is modelled on the tyrannical father figure found in the declamations of Libanios, these statements stem from Manuel himself.

a Marriage. His exceptionally delayed marriage, combined with these statements, seem to suggest a true hesitancy when it came to matrimony.

There are further hints in the *Dialogue on Marriage* about some of Manuel's reservations concerning marriage. On one occasion, the Empress Helena points out the contradictions between married life and a life of philosophy (βίος φιλόσοφος). She elaborates on how the soul tries to free itself from worldly and bodily cares in the pursuit of philosophy. But, Manuel, she claims, cannot follow this life: he is a ruler.[95] In yet another passage, the empress argues that subjects imitate their rulers, and therefore Manuel's bachelor state may cause them to follow a philosopher's life, though many are unfit for the lifestyle.[96]

In Manuel's other works, this notion of a philosopher's life, influenced by Plato and Aristotle, appears as an ideal, and in these discussions the emperor presents marriage as being contradictory to this ideal life of philosophy. Manuel subtly hints that although his heart's desire was to follow the solitary philosopher's path, he became a reluctant husband because his status as a ruler demanded it. It is also interesting to note that all of the literati with whom the emperor was close, such as Demetrios Kydones, Manuel and Demetrios Chrysoloras and Nicholas Kabasilas, were unmarried. Many friends, such as Makarios Makres and Joseph Bryennios were monks, while others were ecclesiastics. In an interesting twist, Manuel's circle largely consisted of men who were bachelor literati and whose lifestyles did more closely resemble the ideal of a philosopher's life. The emperor's stance on marriage therefore does not seem to be a mere literary ploy, but rather a reflection of his actual opinions of the institution.

The *Dialogue on Marriage* also raises some questions as to whether Manuel had any illegitimate children prior to his marriage. It has been recently argued rather convincingly that Zampia (Isabella) Palaiologina, the wife of Hilario Doria, was not an illegitimate daughter of Manuel, but his half-sister.[97] But the dialogue drops vague hints that perhaps Manuel had illegitimate children who died young. Indeed, when he discusses the troubles brought about by marriage, he refers to the illnesses and the deaths of children, which, he laments, cause great disturbance – as the Empress

---

[95] *Dialogue on Marriage*, 86–7.   [96] *Dialogue on Marriage*, 88–9.
[97] For Zampia, see PLP 21374. Nothing is known about her except that she married Hilario Doria in the early 1390s. See Th. Ganchou, 'Ilario Doria le gambros génois de Manuel II Paléologos: beau-frère ou gendre?', *REB* 66 (2008), 71–94. See also, Th. Ganchou, 'Zampia Palaiologina Doria: épouse du prétendant ottoman Mustafa', in *Impératrices, princesses, aristocrates et saintes souveraines. De l'Orient Chrétien et Musulman au Moyen Age et au début des temps modernes*, eds. E. Malamut and A. Nicolaides (Aix-en-Provence, 2014), 133–69. Henceforth, Ganchou, 'Zampia'.

knew better than himself.[98] A few passages later, the empress complains that Manuel forgets all the joy brought by children, though it was something within his experience.[99] By the time he began composing the work, we know that Manuel had fathered John VIII, fatherhood was therefore indeed within the realm of his experience. Despite the remark that his mother was more knowledgeable about these matters, the emperor's complaints about the early deaths of children may suggest personal events. Although his son Constantine and two daughters were to die during infancy, these deaths probably occurred only after Manuel's departure for Europe and therefore long after the dialogue was composed.[100]

Is it possible that the emperor had illegitimate children whom he lost at a young age? Manuel's only surviving letter to his mother, discussed above, seems to suggest this. He consoles the empress over the deaths of some young children in her care, who also were her relatives, and he describes their relationship lovingly. This letter is the earliest in his correspondence and no other letters from that period survive, nor do other letters addressed to Helena. Manuel's decision to preserve this early letter certainly stems from his great affection for his mother, but he may also have been influenced by its contents – namely, the mention of deceased children.

More significantly, Manuel crossed out two lines while he was later editing the letter that ascribed the deaths of these children to his own sins.[101] The crossed-out words are found in Par. gr. 3041 f. 2, line 8. However, these lines are entirely absent from the later edition of the letter in Vat. Barb. gr. 219, f. 53 v, which was also produced under Manuel's own supervision. This revision suggests that he may have been the father of the children in question: the emperor perhaps deleted these lines in order to preserve his projected image as a virtuous ruler.

The *Dialogue on Marriage* can also be interpreted as propaganda against John VII.[102] This aspect of the work has already been demonstrated, so I will merely add a few more points to the previous studies. For instance, it

---

[98] *Dialogue on Marriage*, 96–7.   [99] *Dialogue on Marriage*, 106–7.

[100] Angelou's edition indicates that these were not later additions. See Appendix 7 for the deaths of Manuel's older son Constantine and two unnamed daughters.

[101] Dennis, *Letters*, 4.

[102] F. Leonte, 'Advice and praise for the ruler: making political strategies in Manuel II Palaiologos' Dialogue on Marriage', in *Papers from the First and Second Postgraduate Forums in Byzantine Studies: Sailing to Byzantium*, ed. S. Neocleous (Newcastle, 2009), 163–83, also argues that the dialogue functioned as political propaganda against John VII. However, he focuses only on the passages directly attacking John. Henceforth, Leonte, 'Dialogue on Marriage'. F. Leonte, *Rhetoric in Purple: the Renewal of Imperial Ideology in the Texts of Emperor Manuel II Palaiologos* (PhD thesis, Central European University, 2012) Henceforth, Leonte, *Rhetoric in Purple*, 129–41, offers an extended version of the author's earlier article. Also see F. Leonte, 'Dramatisation and Narrative in Late Byzantine Dialogues: Manuel II Palaiologos' On Marriage and Mazaris' Journey to Hades', in *Dialogues and Debates*, 220–36.

is not the only the direct passages on John VII which fulfil the function of propaganda, but also the metaphors and character portrayal. Towards the end of the 1390s, the threat posed by John was growing. Not only did he have the support of the Ottoman sultan against his uncle, but John VII was also starting to gain in popularity among the Constantinopolitan populace. The sufferings brought upon by the blockade prompted many people to favour John over Manuel. In the *Dialogue*, the empress argues that as long as Manuel remains childless, John VII would be perceived as his heir, and this, she continues, will cause great instability for the empire.[103]

Manuel furthermore devotes lengthy passages to John VII and Bayezid's schemes. John is represented as a man who breaks his promises, betrays his own family and conspires with the enemies of his empire.[104] Manuel is at pains to emphasize that John is effectively ruining himself and the empire through his scheming with Bayezid. Arguably, this portrayal also serves to illustrate his unfitness to rule. Tellingly, the emperor points out that Constantinople was not John's to offer.

Even the end of the dialogue, where Manuel presents his mother with the winner's crown, can be interpreted as a ridicule of John. The emperor claims that Helena's crown had to be of roses and branches, and not of gold as promised, since golden crowns, he jokes, were in short supply and were in danger of being stolen during the award ceremony.[105] Clearly, 'the thief' in question is John. Another particularly strong statement against John can be found in a passage where Manuel refers to the letters of conspiracy between Bayezid and his nephew. The emperor declares that he had these letters with him and that everyone among the audience was welcome to inspect them.[106]

Manuel also pursued his propaganda campaign against John VII in subtler ways. Even the beginning of the work, which is a playful exchange between the mother and the son concerning the question of deceit, may be interpreted as a vague critique of John VII. Manuel claims to have only pretended to have deceived his mother by feigning ignorance. Although this is a form of deceit, he asks his mother about the verdict she would give for a man who approaches another cunningly, pretending to be his friend, and deceives the person who trusted him. This hypothetical question fits perfectly with the emperor's portrayal of John who, like this hypothetical man, once pretended to be at peace with his uncle.[107] Another strategy

---

[103] *Dialogue on Marriage*, 110–11.   [104] *Dialogue on Marriage*, 98–9.
[105] *Dialogue on Marriage*, 117–18.   [106] *Dialogue on Marriage*, 98–9.
[107] *Dialogue on Marriage*, 65–9.

which Manuel employs in order to downplay John's claims to the throne is to contrast his own rank as emperor and status as a mature man with his nephew's youth.[108]

Manuel is at pains to use his idealized self-image as a foil for the self-seeking representation of John. Ultimately, his marriage comes across as a sacrifice that the he must make for the good of his people. Similarly, he laments that he was forced to offer his own son as a hostage to John VII, referring to the 'adoption' agreement they seem to have reached earlier on, only to be bitterly deceived.[109] Manuel is always the blameless party, and his cause is further advocated through the support of the empress mother, who at every chance, emphasizes his wisdom and condemns the behaviour of her grandson. As the politically experienced empress mother figure, Helena's advocacy of Manuel's cause serves the depiction of him as the undisputed legitimate ruler of the empire.

The *Dialogue on Marriage* is a work where Manuel embeds political statements into philosophical discussion in order to enhance the legitimacy of his rule. However, the *Dialogue* should not be viewed as a mere political pamphlet. Although it is not as intricate as, for instance, the *Dialogue with a Persian*, Manuel still displays his continuous interest in the literary features of the text. Once more, the work is adorned with jokes, metaphors and allusions which enhance its literary aspects, and likewise reveal the emperor's care for the work's sound harmony. As in the case of many Byzantine authors, the emperor blended the political and the literary in his oeuvre.

Teacher and Friend

Manuel sent the *Dialogue on Marriage* to Demetrios Kydones, who by then had left Constantinople for good and was residing in Venice.[110] The emperor acknowledges his debt to him as 'the father of the writing' and attributes any success of the dialogue to him, who 'supplied the seed'. In a rare display of eagerness and excitement, Manuel exclaims that the dialogue might have surpassed everything he had written up to that poiny. This is ironic considering that the emperor would later make many changes to the work, even crossing it out completely in one manuscript.[111]

---

[108] *Dialogue on Marriage*, 63–5, 110–11. Doukas also highlights John's youth while narrating his rivalry with Manuel, calling him μεῖραξ, Doukas, 82–3.

[109] See Chapter 5 for this arrangement, which stipulated that Manuel would adopt John's son Andronikos V and John VII would adopt John VIII.

[110] Letter 62.   [111] Letter 62, lines 8–10. *Dialogue on Marriage*, 19.

His letter makes clear that Manuel genuinely desired Kydones' praise for the *Dialogue*, as in the case of the *Discourse to the Thessalonians*. Such a strong desire to please is not found in letters addressed to others. This yearning for approval is a sign of the deep regard Manuel had for Kydones. Like the earlier periods in Manuel's life, the time of the blockade also was one of intense letter exchange between the two. Again, a close reading of these letters offers a glimpse into their 'public intimacy' and fleshes out the more personal aspect of their relationship. In addition to pouring out his despair to Kydones on the defeat at Nikopolis, Manuel shows genuine concern on the occasions when Kydones seems to have fallen ill, asking to be informed should he need anything.[112] Such concerns can also be traced on Kydones' part. In a letter written perhaps shortly before Manuel's exile to Lemnos, he professes to care greatly for Manuel's health, and Kydones narrates that he had come to Manuel's door, only to be told by a guard that he was still in bed, not having slept the night because of a fever. He begs for news of Manuel's health.[113]

Manuel and Kydones also seem to have continued in their scholarly pursuits together. In one of these letters dating to the time of the blockade, Manuel refers to a copy of John Chrysostom's *To An Unbelieving Father* that Kydones had lent him. He remarks that Kydones' suggestion of the work had deepened his knowledge of this author.[114] Despite their differences concerning the Christian faith, Manuel and Kydones could still share their interest in theology with each other – to an extent. Manuel's affection for his teacher is also evident in an expensive gift that he sent to Kydones during the same period – a horse to replace his dead one.[115] Previously, as we have seen, he sent a sheepskin coat to Kydones from Lemnos during his exile; this horse and the coat are the only gift items that appear in the emperor's correspondence and Kydones, is the only recipient of both. While sending the horse, Manuel adds a new jest to their stock of jokes about Plato, claiming that Kydones' dead horse had generated a new horse, in an allusion to the theory of generation found in his favourite Platonic work, the *Phaedo*.[116] As in Thessalonike in the 1380s, the two again share philosophical jokes.

---

[112] See Letters 22 and 29.   [113] Kydones, Letter 84.
[114] Letter 25. Mercati, *Notizie*, 157–8, for a discussion of Kydones' manuscript of John Chrysostom.
[115] A. Karpozilos, 'Realia in Byzantine epistolography X–XII c.', *BZ 77* (1984), 20–37 and A. Karpozilos, 'Realia in Byzantine epistolography XIII–XV c.', *BZ 88* (1995), 68–84 for various instances of horses being requested or sent as gifts by means of letter exchange.
[116] Letter 26, lines 8–11. Plato, *Phaedo* 70 E-71 B.

Manuel's letter accompanying the *Dialogue on Marriage* reproaches Kydones for abandoning his fatherland during a time of hardship. Yet it should be pointed out that the tone of these criticisms is mild. Manuel even attempts to dispel the loneliness of his teacher in a foreign land by telling Kydones that the dialogue would bring to him the people with whom he loved to converse at home – namely himself and the empress mother.[117] This letter exchange proved to be one of their last. Sometime during the winter of 1397/8, Kydones died.[118] He did not forget his imperial pupil even in death, leaving part of his book collection to Manuel, the four Gospels, a Herodotos and a manuscript containing some works of Plato. This was quite possibly the very same manuscript that Manuel had obtained for Kydones from the monks of Mount Athos many years before.[119]

With Kydones' death Manuel had lost a very close friend and a mentor. Their close friendship has often raised the question of the extent of Kydones' influence on Manuel, especially as far the emperor's Western political policies and attitude to Catholicism were concerned. Although Manuel had very great admiration for Kydones as a mentor and a literary figure, and at times, such as during his earlier rule in Thessalonike, turned to him for political advice, his influence on Manuel should not be over-stated. The emperor never adopted Kydones' theological stance on Catholicism and anti-Palamism, nor his fervent desire for a Church union. Despite the fact that he sought Kydones' advice in Thessalonike, there is no indication that Manuel relied on him after becoming sole emperor in 1392. And significantly, Kydones was never appointed *mesazon* under Manuel, though it is possible, of course, that he no longer desired the position. Moreover, although the friendship of the two is a celebrated one, scholars also should take one important factor into account: Kydones left Constantinople a mere five years after Manuel's accession and died soon afterwards. Manuel's ruled for almost thirty more years after Kydones' death, and thus his direct influence during Manuel's reign was limited.

Similarly, a comparison between the oeuvre of the two men yields more differences than similarities. Although Manuel seems to have been influenced by Kydones' *On Despising Death* in some passages of the *Ethico-Political*

---

[117] For Hellenistic and Byzantine theories of the letter as a 'winged visit' and as a way of uniting separated friends, see Mullett, 'The Classical Tradition', 75–93.

[118] Kalekas, Letter 38, line 40; Loenertz, *Calécas*, 31 and Ganchou, 'Kydones', 443.

[119] Loenertz, *Les lettres de Démétrius Cydonès*, Appendix E for the arrangement of the delivery of these manuscripts through the Venetian authorities. See also Sevčenko, 'Intellectual Life', 91 and Ganchou, 'Kydones', 472–8.

Orations, his textual output is different from that of his teacher.[120] For starters, he displays little interest in Latin theologians and their work. Unlike Kydones, Manuel also wrote poems, rhetorical exercises, dialogues, ethico-political works and liturgical texts, and demonstrated more interest in mixing various genres. This sets Manuel further apart from Kydones as an author. Stylistically, too, there are many differences between the two, and thus, however tempting it may be, one must not attempt to see Kydones' influence on every aspect of Manuel's life and literary output.

In Search of Aid

Manuel's anguish at the deaths of his mother and Kydones would soon be aggravated by the political situation. Although Sultan Bayezid seems to have ceased being actively involved in the siege, by 1397 the situation in the capital was becoming increasingly desperate.[121] In April of the same year, Manuel was so pressured that he offered again to cede Lemnos and Imbros to Venice. He also proposed leaving Constantinople to the Venetian authorities should he be obliged to abandon it, perhaps considering giving Constantinople to the Venetians rather than to let it fall to the Ottomans, in the same manner that he had sanctioned the sale of Corinth to the Hospitallers. Moreover, several sources mention that Bayezid wished Manuel to leave the city to John VII; an idea that seems to have been favoured by some citizens as well.[122] Perhaps, in considering a scenario where he would be forced to hand over Constantinople to John VII, Manuel opted to cede the city to Venice instead.[123] However, Venice refused all offers and appeared to have no desire to form a league against the Ottomans. A contemporary French source also adds a further dimension to our knowledge of this situation, telling us that Rhodes sent two galleys to Constantinople.[124] It thus appears that the emperor was still relying on the Hospitallers of Rhodes. Under these dire circumstances, he now also sought help from other Western powers, reaching beyond his neighbouring political sphere. In 1398, four years into the blockade, he began sending a string of embassies to France, England, the Spanish kingdoms and to various other Italian city states to obtain assistance.

The reasons for this diplomatic manoeuvre require further discussion. It should be emphasized that although seeking Western help was

---

[120] Kakkoura points out this influence, *Ethico-Political Orations*, 95.   [121] Barker, *Manuel II*, 148.
[122] See below.   [123] Thiriet, *Régestes*, I, no. 932, 218.
[124] *Le livre des faits du bon messire Jehan Le Maingre, dit Bociquaut, Mareschal de France et gouverneur de Jennes*, ed. D. Lalande (Geneva, 1985), 113. Henceforth, *Le livre de faits*.

a long-established policy in Late Byzantine politics, such contacts were usually confined to Venice, Genoa and the papacy. However, Manuel is not unique for having contacts with France, England and various Spanish kingdoms. Michael VIII Palaiologos (1259–81), for instance, also had contacts with France. Similarly, the English king Edward II (1307–27) sent a letter to Andronikos II (1282–1328).[125] Futhermore, Manuel's own grandfather John VI Kantakouzenos was allied with Aragon, the Spanish kingdom that also had strong trade interests in the region. However, Manuel's diplomacy is notable for the extent and density of these contacts with England, France and other Italian cities. He thus not only followed but expanded upon the Western policy of John V and his predecessors. It must be pointed that back in 1394, Venice had already suggested that Manuel contact France and England for help. Indeed, through Sigismund's mediations, England and France had participated in the Crusade of Nikopolis in 1396.[126] Around 1398, the increasing precariousness of the situation is probably what compelled Manuel to seek other allies with even more zeal.

It should likewise be remembered that the emperor's father-in-law Constantine Dejanović, died in 1395, and many remaining Serbian rulers, including Stefan Lazarević, were all Ottoman vassals as Dejanović had been. The greatest power in the greater region was Sigismund of Hungary, but thanks to the resounding defeat at Nikopolis, he could no longer offer any significant military help. Manuel's new diplomatic endeavours were thus based on solid reasoning: both France and England had once been, Byzantium's allies and the crusading army in Nikopolis had boasted significant number of English and French troops. France was considered an especially viable source of help, as its recently acquired overlordship of Genoa and its colonies meant that its interest in the affairs of the Mediterrenean and the Aegean had grown.

The Byzantine ambassadors, Nicholas Notaras and Theodore Palaiologos Kantakouzenos, were well received in Paris by Charles VI. The French king gave them a sum of 12,000 gold francs and wrote to the Venetian doge on their behalf.[127] Nicholas Notaras also seems to have

---

[125] For instance, Michael VIII Palaiologos (1259–81) also had contacts with France. Similarly, the English king, Edward II (1307–27) sent a letter to Andronikos II (1282–1328), see J. Harris, 'Edward II, Andronicus II and Giles of Argenteim: A Neglected Episode in Anglo-Byzantine Relations, in *Porphyrogenita: Essays on the History and Literature of Byzantium and the Latin East in Honour of Julian Chrysostomides*, eds. Ch. Dendrinos et al. (Aldershot, 2003), 77–84.

[126] Thiriet, *Régestes*, no. 851, 202.

[127] A letter supposedly written by Manuel to Charles IV has been preserved in *Chronique du Religieux de Saint-Denis concernant le Regne de Charles VI de 1380 à 1422*, ed. and trans. L. Bellaguet, in *Collection de documents inédits sur l'histoire de France*, vol. 2 (Paris, 1840), XVIII, VIII, II, 558–60,

gone to England to garner further support.[128] The patriarch wrote to the duke of Lithuania and the metropolitan of Kiev, while another embassy was dispatched to the duke of Burgundy.[129] Hilario Doria, who was married to Manuel's half- sister, was sent to Rome to collect funds raised for the aid of Constantinople. Prompted by his presence, the pope issued bulls granting indulgences to all those who would contribute.[130] Although the cities of Lucca and Siena contributed 500 ducats each, problems arose in the transfer of the 2,000 pounds raised in England and the money never reached Constantinople.[131] Ultimately, Martin I of Aragon sent Dalmau Damius to fight alongside the Byzantines in Constantinople.[132]

These gestures of help could do very little to ease the situation in the capital, however. The severe famine caused by the blockade continued to oppress the populace and grain prices continued to rise dramatically.[133] Between 1399–1402 wheat prices went up to 20–31 *hyperpyra*, falling to 7–8

---

translated in Barker, *Manuel II*, 155–6, who believes that the source of the letter was an original document, an opinion that I share. Moreover, since then, Bernard Guenée has demonstrated that Michel Pintoin, the author of the chronicle, had access to royal archives. See B. Guenée, 'Documents insérés et documents abrégées dans la Chronique Religieux du Saint Denis', *Bibiliothèque de L'école des Chartes* 152, 2 (1994), 375–428. Henceforth, Guenée, 'Documents'.

See DVL, no. 149, 261, for the letter to the doge concerning the sum given by the French king. For Theodore Palaiologos Kantakouzenos and Nicholas Notaras, PLP 21461 and 20733.

[128] Barker, *Manuel II*, 154 cites Du Cange, who reports some French treasury accounts for provisions made for Notaras' passage to England. See C. Du Cange, *Familiae Augustae Byzantinae (Historia Byzantiae, Pt. 1)* (Paris, 1680), 238. Also, A. Champollion-Figéac, *Louis et Charles, Ducs d'Orléans, leur influence sur les arts, la littérature et l'esprit de leur siècle* (Paris, 1844), vol. 3, 40.

[129] MM, II, 280–2 for the letter to the duke of Lithuania, 282–5 for the letter to the metropolitan of Kiev, Dennis, 'Official Documents', 48, for the embassy to Burgundy.

[130] Barker, *Manuel II*, 158–9; Raynaldus, *Annales Ecclesiastici*, vol. 27, 41–3.

[131] Dölger, *Regesten*, no. 3275, 86 and Sp. Lampros, Ἐπιστολὴ Μανουὴλ Παλαιολόγου πρὸς τοὺς Σιεναίους, *Νέος Ἑλληνομνήστημων* 6 (1909), 102–4. On the English funds, see Barker, *Manuel II*, 159 and especially D. Nicol, 'A Byzantine Emperor in England: Manuel II's visit to London in 1400–1401', *University of Birmingham Historical Journal* 12.2 (1971), 204–25, reprinted in Nicol, *Byzantium: its Ecclesiastical History and Relations with the Western World*, (London, 1972), Study x, who has the most detailed account of the funds raised in England. Henceforth, Nicol, 'A Byzantine emperor'.

[132] A. Rubió I Lluch, *Diplomatari de l'Orient Català (1301–1409)* (Barcelona, 1947), nos. 651 and 679 and C. Marinesco, 'Du nouveau sur les rélations de Manuel Paleologue (1391–1425) avec l'Espagne', *Studi Bizantini e Neoellenici* 7 (1953), 420–36, 410. Henceforth, *Diplomatari de l'Orient Català* and Marinesco, 'Les rélations'.

[133] See Necipoğlu, *Byzantium Between the Ottomans and the Latins*, 149–83 and Necipoğlu, 'Economic conditions in Constantinople during the siege of Bayezid I (1394–1402)', in *Constantinople and its Hinterland*, eds. C. Mango and G. Dagron (Aldershot, 1995), 157–67. Also, D. Bernicolas-Hatzapoulos, 'The First Siege of Constantinople by the Ottomans (1394–1402) and its Repercussions on the Civilian Population of the City', *Byzantine Studies* 10/11 (1983), 39–51. The only instance where some grain supply actually did reach the capital is recorded in a Bulgarian chronicle, which reports that in 1397, grain supplies arrived from Trebizond, Amastris, Kaffa, Venice and Mytilene. See Bogdan, 'Bulgarian Chronicle', 542.

hyperpyra after the blockade.[134] The prices of fields and vineyards, as well as interest rates also shot up, and people resorted to selling their houses, businesses and even cashing in their wives' dowries. These economic problems and the famine in the capital were only made worse by some members of the upper class trying to profit by selling wheat at an inflated price. Some members of the Goudeles family, who were also supporters of John VII, were among those who engaged in these black-market practices. These supporters of John indirectly increased social tensions and further weakened Manuel's authority, especially among the suffering populace.[135] The emperor seems to have been unable to take any action against these tactics.

Due to the blockade, people were also hindered from entering or leaving the city.[136] Because of the harsh conditions, some people fled to the Ottomans and embraced Islam and others were captured by the Ottomans when they tried to escape from the city by lowering themselves with ropes around 1400.[137] During this atmosphere of despair and tension even the Patriarch Matthew was accused of collaborating with the Ottomans.[138] There was a growing desire amongst the populace to surrender the city to avoid more suffering. This is reflected in a story preserved in a short chronicle: in 1402, a group of citizens were on their way to present the keys of the city to the sultan when the news of Bayezid's defeat in Ankara reached Constantinople.[139]

Although Manuel is not blamed in the scholarship for triggering the blockade, the textual evidence suggests that a section of Constantinopolitans seem to have held him responsible for their misery. As in Thessalonike in the 1380s, the economic troubles caused by the Ottoman siege, negatively affected Manuel's popularity, and there was at least one section of the population who wished to surrender Constantinople as a means of ending the suffering. This desire to surrender the city can also be traced in Doukas' account of the blockade. The historian moreover hints that the sufferings endured by the

---

[134] Necipoğlu, *Byzantium between the Ottomans and the Latins*, 152. She uses Doukas, 78–9, referring to the dramatic increase in the prices and C. Morrison and J. C. Cheynet, 'Prices and Wages in the Byzantine World', *EHB*, 815–78, Table 8 on pages 833–5.

[135] Necipoğlu, *Byzantium between the Ottomans and the Latins*, 159–66. Necipoğlu uses cases from the patriarchal register to illustrate the economic problems faced by the citizens. See MM, II, nos. 609, 617 and 631 for a few cases of property sale and debts, cited in the above-mentioned study.

[136] Necipoğlu, *Byzantium between the Ottomans and the Latins*, 173–4. Demetrios Chrysoloras also seems to be implying that the gates remained shut, Gautier, 'Action de grâces', 354–5.

[137] Necipoğlu, *Byzantium between the Ottomans and the Latins*, 146–9.

[138] Hunger, 'Das Testament des Patriarchen Matthaios', 300–1.

[139] Necipoğlu, *Byzantium between the Ottomans and the Latins*, 151; Schreiner, *Kleinchroniken*, Chronik 22/ 28.

population had caused some of them to lend their support to John VII against Manuel.

John already had support from among the upper classes, as well as that of the Genoese.[140] Doukas underlines that these new supporters were from the lower classes –he uses the expressions 'lowly people' (χυδαῖος λαός) and 'common people' (κοινὸς λαός). His reference to the low socio-economic standing of these citizens, bring to mind the remarks made by Ignatius of Smolensk in the 1390 revolt in which he also claims that the lower classes supported John VII.[141] Later, in 1403, the Spanish traveller Clavijo would also remark that some people in the capital supported John VII's claim to rule. While John VII was already an 'alternative emperor' to his uncle prior to the blockade, the woes of the populace seem to have further alienated them from Manuel.

Although the exact details cannot be discerned, John VII also had the support of Bayezid. It should be remembered that he had been at least partially responsible for Bayezid's murderous intentions in Serres, and it even appears that John held his appanage in Selymbria through Ottoman consent. Undoubtedly, Bayezid employed John as a threat against Manuel, to establish a 'divide and rule' policy. Doukas claims that Bayezid went as far as to order the emperor to leave the city to John VII with the promise that he would grant peace to the people. In his account, Manuel's reconciliation with his nephew was only on account of the suffering of the people, as he did not wish to rule 'tyrannically' (τυραννικῶς)but for the common good. In an interesting twist, this discontent greatly resembles the Thessalonians' accusations of tyranny. They, too, appear to have accused the emperor of tyranny in his refusal to surrender the city. Doukas' narrative suggests that there was growing support towards John VII in the capital, as well as a dissatisfaction with Manuel. After all, in the eyes of the populace, his unyielding stance towards Bayezid had caused the continuation of the blockade and the famine.

A passage in the *Dialogue on Marriage* can be interpreted as reflecting a similar dissatisfaction with Manuel's resistance to the sultan's demands. The emperor protests that he had never offended Bayezid, he merely did not give in to his demands which were offensive to Christians. Thus, the emperor strives to clear himself from any blame of triggering the blockade,

[140] Doukas, 80–5; Clavijo, 47–8. For the upper-class supporters of John VII, see Th. Ganchou, 'Autour de Jean VII: Luttes dynastiques, interventions étrangères et résistance Orthodoxe à Byzance (1373–1409)', in *Coloniser au Moyen Age*, ed. M. Balard, A. Ducellier (Paris, 1995), 367–85 and Necipoğlu, *Byzantium between the Ottomans and the Latins*, 132–3. Henceforth, Ganchou, 'Autour de Jean VII'.
[141] See Chapter 4.

instead arguing that an individual's duty is to choose to die, if the need arises, together with his people of the same race and faith. Moreover, he adds, an emperor's duty is to accept any risk in order to save his people when freedom and faith are at stake.[142] As in Thessalonike in the 1380s, Manuel is outlining here the ideal behaviour expected from his citizens and seems to be referring to the possibility of surrendering the city, as indicated by his emphasis on freedom and the Christian faith. When one takes into account the political messages in the dialogue, it is possible to interpret this passage almost as an *apologia* for his unyielding stance towards the Ottomans.

In the *Funeral Oration*, Manuel takes pains to stress the 'irrational' behaviour of Bayezid in Serres in 1394, and he emphasizes that after that event, it was impossible to accommodate the sultan.[143] As in the *Dialogue*, he attempts to clear himself of blame for giving Bayezid the pretext to start the blockade, and this apologetic aspect of both works suggest that Manuel had in fact been accused and resented for the blockade of Constantinople. It also seems that not just Bayezid, but also some of the population wanted Manuel to leave Constantinople. Doukas' narrative points to this scenario, as do the emperor's remarks to the Venetian Senate in which he offered Constantinople to Venice should he be obliged to leave it for some reason.[144] Just as he had been compelled to leave Thessalonike, Manuel would also eventually leave Constantinople. But he would do so in a very different manner.

The embassies sent to Charles VI of France did not only result in financial aid, but they did prompt the king to send one of his most famous generals to Constantinople. In spring of 1399, Mareschal Boucicaut arrived in the city with a small army. He had taken part in the Crusade of Nikopolis when French troops did manage to win some minor victories over the Ottomans.[145] But it soon became clear that aid was needed on a far grander scale. Mareschal Boucicaut also proved himself a skilled mediator, and his biography claims that he was instrumental in reconciling Manuel with his nephew when, on 4 December, he brought John VII from Selymbria to Constantinople.[146] Boucicaut also seems to have been influential in a decision that would make

---

[142] *Dialogue on Marriage*, 98–9.   [143] *Funeral Oration*, 129–33.
[144] Thiriet, *Régestes*, I, no. 932, 218.
[145] *Chronique de Saint Denis*, xx, iii, 690 and *Le livre de faits*, 189. Henceforth, Chronique de Saint Denis.
[146] *Le livre des faits*, 149. Of course, this great credit given to Boucicaut here may partially stem from the bias of his biographer. Clavijo, 51–2, also reports the same, but remarks that John had been unwilling. John VII previously offered to sell his succession rights to the French king for cash and a castle in France. Dölger, *Regesten*, no. 3194, 74 and Sp. Lampros, Ἰωάννου Ζ Παλαιολόγος, ἐκχωρήσης τῶν ἐπὶ τῆς βυζαντίακης αὐτοκράτοριας δικαίωματων εἰς τον βασίλεα τῆς Γαλλιάς

Manuel famous for many centuries. In his desperate search for help, the emperor decided to entrust the governance of the empire to his nephew and to visit Western Europe in person.

On 10 December 1399, the emperor boarded a Venetian galley for the Morea, from whence he proceeded to Italy.[147] One wonders what Manuel thoughts were as he watched the towers of his capital gradually fade before into the distance. All things considered, the situation of his empire was so precarious and the journey by sea so perilous that it was unclear whether he would ever return home.

Καρόλου ς', Νέος Ἑλληνομνήμων 10 (1913), 248–52. See also P. Wirth, 'Zum Geschichtsbild Kaiser Johannes VII Palaiologos', Byzantion 35 (1965–67), 592–4.

[147] Chalkokondyles, 134–7; Doukas, 84–5; Schreiner, Kleinchroniken, Chronik 22/27; Chronik 35/5 and Mioni, 'Cronaca', no. 25.

CHAPTER 7

The New Odysseus

He left his homeland, he left his friends, he left behind everything; he went to the Western lands as the sole 'self-appointed' ambassador . . .[1]

After leaving Constantinople on 10 December, Manuel sailed to the Morea. From here the emperor negotiated with the Venetians for his journey. On 27 February, the Senate allotted him galleys and funds. The families of the Despot Theodore and the Emperor Manuel were promised refuge in Modon and Coron in the likely event of an Ottoman invasion, as well as further and permanent transport to Venice.[2] The mood was so bleak that even before Manuel set off, the possibility that he and the rest of the imperial family might have to leave the Byzantine dominions for good was openly contemplated.[3]

Manuel's decision to visit Europe in person was a novel diplomatic tactic. True, his father John V had visited Buda and Rome, but these had been short visits and were closer to Byzantine territory. No Byzantine emperor had undertaken a European 'tour' before. By embarking upon this tour of several Italian cities, France and England, Manuel was essentially presenting himself as a diplomat-emperor. This was duly noted by a Byzantine panegyrist who calls Manuel the 'self-appointed ambassador'.

As in the case of other Western sources, the biography of Mareschal Boucicaut, who accompanied the emperor on this voyage, is adorned with

---

[1] Dendrinos, *Anonymous Oration*, 444; 'ἀπολιπὼν τὴν πατρίδα, ἀπολιπὼν φίλους, ἀπολιπὼν ἅπαντα, μόνος αὐτοχειροτόνητος ἧκε πρεσβευτὴς εἰς τὰ ἑσπέρια . . . .'
[2] Thiriet, *Régestes*, II, no. 978, 10; Dölger, *Regesten*, no. 3279, 86; Iorga, *Notes et Extraits*, 96–7.
[3] Manuel's journey to Europe has been extensively discussed as far as its political aspects are concerned. The most important and detailed study is A. A. Vasiliev, 'Puteševstvie vizantijskago imperator Manuila Palaeologa po zapadnoi Evrope (1399–1403)', *Žurnal Ministerstva Naradnago Prosveščeniia*, N. S. 39 (1912), 41–78, 260–304. Other studies, which are more superficial, are G. Schlumberger, *Un empereur de Byzance à Paris et Londres* (Paris, 1916), A. Mompherratos, *Διπλωματικαὶ Ἐνέργειαι Μανουὴλ Β´ τοῦ Παλαιολόγου ἐν Εὐρώπῃ καὶ Ἀσίᾳ* (Athens, 1913) and M. Jugie, 'Le voyage de l'empereur Manuel Paléologue en Occident (1399–1403)', *Echos d'Orient* 15 (1912), 322–32.

remarks on Manuel's wisdom and regal bearing.[4] This sentiment of admiration was apparently reciprocated by Manuel, as the emperor's references
to Boucicaut are rather favourable. Did Boucicaut believe that Manuel's
presence in Europe would persuade the Western rulers to aid
Constantinople? Perhaps, he counted upon the emperor's presence and
bearing to elicit favourable responses. Many Western sources that touch
upon this journey indeed portray Manuel as an impressive figure, and all
things considered, it is reasonable to assume that the decision to visit
Europe was influenced by Boucicaut. After all, not only did he accompany
the emperor on his journey, the chief destination was Boucicaut's homeland – France.

Furthermore, Boucicaut seems to have been instrumental in reconciling
Manuel and John VII; it was John VII's acceptance of the role of regent
that enabled his uncle to leave Constantinople. His departure from
Constantinople at such a critical time has led several scholars to speculate
whether Manuel was in fact 'escaping' the city. In this regard, Manuel's
voyage may have also served a double purpose: not only did he leave to seek
help, he also effectively left the city to John VII, and in a way, John's desire
to be emperor was fulfilled via his uncle's departure. Furthermore, Doukas'
narrative also implies that Bayezid wanted Manuel to leave Constantinople
to John.[5]

The deliberations of the Venetian Senate bear witness to the Venetian
distrust of John VII during his regency at Constantinople. They suspected
him of being ready to surrender the city to the Ottomans. Indeed, John's
inclination towards surrendering Constantinople was also previously hinted
by Manuel in his writings. Considering the uncertainty of Manuel's eventual
return, his embarking on the journey effectively made John the master of
Constantinople. The blockade had already turned a part of the population
against Manuel; the widespread suffering had caused his popularity to
decline. Thus, the European journey not only functioned as a means to
secure aid, Manuel's departure was probably also intended to pacify John
VII and his supporter Bayezid, as well as the Constantinopolitan populace.

In the *Funeral Oration*, Manuel makes passing reference to the reasons
that compelled him to undertake such a journey, pointing out that he went
to Europe to persuade the rulers in person to provide assistance.[6] The
emperor further attempts to justify his appointment of John VII as regent.
It was, after all, a very risky decision considering the two were not on good
terms, and there was no guarantee that John would not usurp the throne

---

[4] *Le livre de faits*, 155.   [5] Doukas, 80–5.   [6] *Funeral Oration*, 162–3.

for himself and refuse to allow Manuel back into the city. Manuel argues, however, that he could not have made any man regent: the ship of state was not a merchant vessel that could be trusted to anyone. He needed to select a worthy candidate – that is, someone from the immediate imperial family – and John, also a proclaimed emperor, was the only reasonable choice while his own son was still underage.

Thus began Manuel's celebrated journey to Europe. Having taken leave of his wife, children and brother, Manuel sailed away from Modon on a Venetian galley.[7] It would be years before the emperor saw his family again. A new son, Andronikos, would welcome him, but there would also be absences. His second son Constantine and two unnamed daughters died probably during their father's long voyage.[8]

The Outward Journey

On his way to Venice, Manuel was accompanied by Mareschal Boucicaut and a small entourage consisting of his *oikeioi*. The Venetian documents are silent about their identities, but some names can be gleaned from various other sources: Aspietes, Staphidakis, Antiochos, Alexios Branas, Demetrios Palaiologos, Constantine Rhalles and his son Theodore. A major character in Mazaris' satire, Manuel 'Holobolos' was present as Manuel's secretary.[9] And an ecclesiastic, Makarios of Ankyra, served as the emperor's personal chaplain. Makarios would also accompany the emperor on his visits to various churches in Europe, preserving the memories of the visits in his treatise against the Latins. It should be considered significant that most of the people in the emperor's entourage were diplomats with experience of Western Europe, and in most cases, also with knowledge of Latin. The emperor seems to have aimed at selecting the best suited candidates for his journey.

However, not everyone who possessed these skills was chosen for this mission. A letter by Manuel Kalekas informs us of a curious case: an addressee of Kalekas, the *hegoumenos* of a monastery and an *oikeios* of Manuel, who possessed knowledge of both the Latin language and faith but was left behind. Kalekas points out that the emperor trusted this

---

[7] Doukas, 84–5; Schreiner, *Kleinchroniken*, Chronicle 35/ 5; 22/ 24; Chalkokondyles, 136–7; Isidore of Kiev, 'Panegyric', 161–2 and *Le livre des faits*, 15.

[8] See Appendix 7 on the deaths of these children.

[9] Mergiali-Sahas, 'Ambassador', 600; Mazaris, 12–13 and 40–3. See also E. Trapp, 'Zur Identifizierung der Personen in der Hadesfahrt des Mazaris', *JÖB* 18 (1969), 95–9 and L. Garland, 'Mazaris' Journey to Hades: further reflections and reappraisal', *DOP* 61 (2007), 183–214.

person, employing him in many of his other affairs but argues that this person was left behind because of the jealousy among the emperor's inner circle.[10] While Manuel seems to have selected his entourage carefully and with the aim of making the most of their skills and experience, his the decisions were possibly also influenced by people from his inner circle who might have advised the emperor according to their own agenda. The other possibility is Manuel had other criteria for his selection, in addition to the knowledge of Latin, that Kalekas' correspondent simply did not meet.

No records are left of Manuel's experiences aboard the galley.[11] A Venetian galley like the one he boarded would have had a deck around 22 feet wide and 106 feet long, with 25 to 30 benches for the oarsmen. As an honoured passenger, Manuel would have had his own small, enclosed space on the ship. Life on the deck was difficult; hygiene and comfort standards were low. An average galley required around 200 people on board, and the deck, cramped for space, was a place where oarsmen from various ethnicities ate, worked and slept on their benches. The duration of a journey could vary greatly depending on the weather, the type of ship, its crew and the number of stops at various harbours. On this occasion, it would take Manuel and his entourage around a month to reach Venice.[12]

In Venice, although we know the Byzantine emperor held extensive discussions with the Senate, no further details can be gathered about these meetings. Manuel then set out for France and proceeded through various Italian cities, including Padua, Pavia, Vicenza and Verona, before finally stopping at Milan.[13] In Milan, the emperor enjoyed a reunion with his friend Manuel Chrysoloras, a famous diplomat, teacher and author of the

---

[10] Kalekas, Letter 67.

[11] The following account of galleys is drawn from various sources; G. Makris, 'Ships' *EHB*, 91–100, 97; A. Avramea, 'Land and Sea Communications, Fourth to Fifteenth Centuries', *EHB* (2002), 57–90, 78–82; S. Andriopoulou, *Diplomatic communications between Byzantium and the West under the Palaiologoi (1354–1453)* (PhD thesis, The University of Birmingham, 2010), 40–1; B. Doumerc, 'Cosmopolitanism on board Venetian Ships (Fourteenth-Fifteenth Centuries)', *Medieval Encounters* 13 (2007), 78–95, 81–8; F. Chapin Lane, *Venetian Ships and Shipbuilders of the Renaissance* (Baltimore, 1934), 9–24.

[12] A typical diplomatic journey to Venice could follow the course of the Adriatic and the Ionian Seas, Corfu, Patras, Koron and Negroponte, see footnote 11. On 4 April, the Senate allocated 200 ducats for Manuel's expenses; he seems to have been expected very soon, Iorga, *Notes et Extraits*, I, 97.

[13] *Le livre des faits*, 154. A. Gataro, *Historia Padovana 1311–1506*, ed. Muratori, *RIS* 17 (Milan, 1730), col. 837 D; *Annales Mediolanenses*, ed. L. A. Muratori, *RIS* 16 (Milan, 1730), col. 833. Henceforth, Gataro and *Annales Mediolanenses*. Makarios of Ankyra, 336, is the only source to mention Verona among these cities. G. Kohl, *Padua under the Carrara, 1318–1405* (Baltimore and London, 1998), 317, claims that the ruler of Padua, Francesco Carrara had taken residence in Ca' Corner and had been granted duty free provisions by Venice on the occasion of Manuel's visit. The documents referred to are Senato, Misti, reg. 45 fol 38r, 9 Nov. 1400; fol 67r, 5 April 1401. Henceforth, Kohl, *Padua*.

period, and was welcomed into the city by the Duke Gian Galeazzo Visconti.[14]

The emperor presented the duke with a thorn from the crown of Christ, as well as an icon of the Virgin that he had probably obtained in Thessalonike many years earlier. The icon has recently been the subject of several studies. Now known as the Freising icon, this work was originally commissioned in the thirteenth century by Manuel Dishypatos in Thessalonike. Thus, Manuel's gift to the duke was not a specifically commissioned, new one, but rather a second-hand item. This was a reasonable manoeuvre on the emperor's behalf, given how limited his resources were. Furthermore, various aspects of the icon allowed him to imbue his gift with deeper meaning. On the icon, the Virgin was named the 'hope of the hopeless'. This, in some ways, also reflected the position of Manuel and Constantinople vis-à-vis Western Europe. They were the 'hopeless' waiting for 'hope' – that is, for Western help. Moreover, the emperor had the same name as the original owner, Dishypatos, which was engraved on the icon. This coincidence must have lent a more personal touch to the icon as a diplomatic gift.[15]

The significance of Gian Galeazzo Visconti as the emperor's host has not been really considered. Around 1400, Gian Visconti had emerged as a key figure in Italy and had united many cities under his rule. His ambitious policies strove to make the duke and his family the masters of Italy.[16] It is noteworthy that most of the cities Manuel passed through in Italy, were under the direct or indirect domination of Gian Visconti. Although the discussions between the rulers remain in shadows, one can surmise that the emperor recognized the duke as a powerful statesman and a highly promising candidate to supply the required help. After all, at this point, the duke not only exercised great political influence in Italy, he also possessed

---

[14] Barker, *Manuel II*, 172; G. Cammelli, *I dotti Bizantini e le origini dell'Umanesimo, I, Manuele Crisolora* (Florence, 1941), 36. Henceforth, Cammelli, *Crisolora*. For Manuel Chrysoloras, see also S. Mergiali-Sahas, 'Manuel Chrysoloras (ca. 1350–1415), an Ideal Model of a Scholar-Ambassador', *Byzantine Studies* 3 (1998), 1–12. On Manuel Chrysoloras' scholarly activities, see L. Thorn-Wickert, *Manuel Chrysoloras (ca. 1350–1415): eine Biographie des byzantinischen Intellektuellen vor dem Hintergrund der hellenistichen Studien in der italienischen Renaissance* (Frankfurt, 2006) and I. Thomson, 'Manuel Chrysoloras and the early Italian Renaissance', *GRBS* 7 (1966), 63–82; 76–7.

[15] F. De Mély, *Exuviae Sacrae Constantinopolitanae*, III, (Paris, 1904), 268; 342; M. Vassilaki, 'Praying for the Salvation of the Empire?', in *Images of the Mother of God: Perceptions of the Theotokos of Byzantium*, ed. M. Vassilaki (Aldershot, 2004), 263–74; 266. Henceforth, Vassilaki, 'Salvation' for the interpretation of the icon. See also C. Hilsdale, *Byzantine Art and Diplomacy in an Age of Decline* (Cambridge, 2014), 232–4. Henceforth, Hilsdale, *Decline*.

[16] For Visconti's power in the region, see J. Black, *Absolutism in Renaissance Milan* (Oxford, 2009), 72 and Kohl. *Padua*, 317.

military might. The emperor gave Visconti not one, but two gifts, one of which was a relic from the crown of thorns that Manuel reserved only for highly influential figures. The other recipients of this relic reads like a who's who of medieval Europe: the kings of France, England, Aragon and the powerful Jean de Berry, the uncle of the French ruler. Although, the ambitious duke must have considered hosting the Byzantine emperor a demonstration of his prestige and power, enhancing his image across Europe, in the end, Manuel would receive no help from Visconti.

A grand banquet was given in Manuel's honour in Padua, and the emperor stayed there for eight days.[17] At this time, splendid buildings were being built all over Lombardy. Manuel would have seen construction and many new churches built in the past fifty years; a very different sight from Constantinople during his reign. He would have also witnessed the displays of power in Gian Galeazzo Visconti's numerous projects, including the famous Castello Visconteo in Pavia and the Cathedral of Milan. In addition, new universities were also being founded, and libraries were amassing huge collections. During Manuel's visit in 1400, even the public library of Verona, a relatively small city, boasted more than 1000 manuscripts.[18]

The First Stay in Paris: Banquets, Letters and Relics

After receiving gifts and horses from Visconti, Manuel proceeded to France.[19] On 3 June, Manuel reached Charanton near Paris where he was welcomed by nearly 2000 of the city's citizens who had gathered to see the Byzantine emperor. Michel Pintoin, the author of the *Chronicle of Saint Denis*, recorded Manuel's reception in meticulous detail.[20] After the

---

[17] Gataro, col. 837.

[18] J. Larner, *Culture and Society in Italy, 1220–1420* (London, 1971), especially 134–5, 138, 169 and 182–3.

[19] It is unclear whether Manuel passed through Rome to meet with the pope, who issued a bull for the emperor on 27 May 1400, Raynaldus, *Annales Ecclesiastici*, vol. 27, 68–9. Halecki, *Un Empereur*, 514, believes that this bull indicates that such a visit indeed had taken place. However, there is no hint in the bull itself that this was the case. The often erroneous and confused *Ekthesis Chronica* narrates that Manuel visited the pope in Rome, angering him by refusing to pay him obeisance, *Ekthesis Chronica*, 20.

[20] *Chronique de Saint Denis*, XXI, i, 754–8 for the reception. Jean Juvenal Ursins is another French historian to mention Manuel's visit, albeit very briefly, see Jean Juvenal des Ursins, *Histoire de Charles VI*, ed. J. F. Michaud and J. J. F. Poujoulat, in *Nouvelle collection des mémoires pour servir à l'histoire de France*, vol. 2 (Paris, 1836), 418–19. Henceforth, Ursins.

For Michel Pintoin and the various aspects of his chronicle, see B. Guenée, 'Le vœu de Charles VI. Essai sur la dévotion des rois de France aux XIIIe et XIVe siècles', *Journal des Savants*, n° 1, (1996), 67–135; B. Guenée, 'Le portrait de Charles VI dans la *Chronique du religieux de Saint-Denis*', *Journal des Savants*, n° 1, (1997), 125–65; B. Guenée, 'Documents'. Henceforth, Guenée, 'Le voeu' and Guenée, 'Le portrait'.

Chancellor of France and the members of the Parliament greeted the emperor, with music and colourful banners, the king himself arrived. The two rulers exchanged a peace kiss and Charles IV presented Manuel with a white horse; the emperor delighted the crowd by mounting it with his foot scarcely touching the stirrup.

The chronicler also meticulously records Manuel's appearance. Dressed in white silk, he was of a medium height with a strong, shapely chest and limbs. He had flowing white hair and a beard. Michel Pintoin noted the appearance of kings and other royal personages only if he found them remarkable and 'majestic' looking. If he found them otherwise, he simply refrained from commenting on their looks. This held true even in the case of his own king, Charles VI – who was not a particularly prepossessing figure.[21] Manuel's assessment by Pintoin has not been included in such scholarly discussions, but the chronicler's detailed and admiring description of the emperor's appearance can be interpreted as genuine approval. Other Western sources also provided a similar verdict on the emperor's person, emphasizing his bravery, wisdom and gallantry and lamenting the state to which he had been reduced. Nevertheless, chroniclers never fail to mention that all his expenses were covered by his hosts.[22]

Manuel and Charles VI entered Paris together, where the Princes of Blood, the king's uncles and brother, were waiting for them. Although a banquet was given in the palace, no records survive to describe it; however, the reception of Wladislav IV of Bohemia in 1397 may serve as a parallel. On this occasion, the kings were seated on thrones at the table of honour and were served by high-ranking courtiers carrying golden vessels. After dinner, they retreated to a chamber laden with golden tapestries to enjoy wine and confectionery. Michel Pintoin depicts the king of Bohemia as displaying excessive admiration, though such remarks are absent for Manuel.[23] After the banquet, the emperor was conducted to his lodgings in the Louvre.

During his first days in Paris, Manuel met with the Royal Council, which consisted of the chancellors Arnault Corbier and Pierre de Giac, Mareschal Bouciaut and other laymen, as well as some churchmen.[24]

---

[21] Guenée, 'Le portrait', 134–6.

[22] These are independent sources. Walsingham, 403–8; Stella, 419; Ursins, 421; *Le livre des faits*, 155.

[23] For the reception of Wladislav, see *Chronique de Saint Denis*, xviii, viii, 568–9.

[24] A. Tuetey, *Journal de Nicolas de Baye, greffier du parlement de Paris, 1400–1417*, vol. 1 (Paris, 1885), 7–8. This diary of the notary of the parliament has been used by Dendrinos to illustrate the makeup of the royal council at the time of Manuel's visit, see Ch. Dendrinos, 'Manuel II Palaeologus in Paris (1400–1402): Theology, Diplomacy and Politics', in *Greeks, Latins, and Intellectual History 1204–1500*, eds. M. Hinterberger and C. Schabel (Leuven, 2011), 397–422, 416. Henceforth, Dendrinos, 'Paris'.

Without knowledge of French or Latin, he must have relied on an inter-preter during the discussions.[25] Early in the summer, the emperor also wrote to Peter Holt, the prior of the Hospital of St John of Jerusalem in Ireland, to arrange a visit to England. Throughout Manuel's stay in Europe, Peter Holt would act as an intermediary between the emperor and England.[26] During that time, the emperor made contact with the Spanish kingdoms of Aragon and Castile, as well as with Navarre. These communications would last throughout his stay in Europe.[27]

One device used by Manuel to attract the attention of Western rulers was to give them various relics as gifts. Indeed, his use of relics as a diplomatic tool is the most studied aspect of his European journey, and perhaps even of his entire rule.[28] These items served both as precious presents and as reminders of the significance of Constantinople for Christian Europe. Unable to offer economic or political benefits, Manuel gifted to the rulers objects that were imbued with Christian prestige. Such a use of relics should be considered a shrewd diplomatic move on his behalf. After all, should any of these powers offer help to Constantinople, they would do so only out of 'Christian charity' or to enhance their prestige. Another objective for any potential allies, would also have been to prevent Constantinople falling into the hands of the Muslim Ottomans. Not only would such a loss represent ideological devastation for Christian polities, it might further facilitate Ottoman expansion into Europe. Ultimately, Western powers knew that any help they could provide was not likely to be politically or economically rewarded by the feeble Byzantine Empire.

---

[25] *Chronique de Saint Denis*, XXI, i, 759–60.

[26] F. C. Hingeston, *Royal and Historical Letters During the Reign of Henry the Fourth, King of England, and of France, and of Lord of Ireland*, vol. I, AD 1399–1404 (London, 1860), no. 17, 39–40. Henceforth, Hingeston, Letters.

[27] See *Diplomatari de l'Orient Català*, no. 656, 683–4, no. 658, 68; no. 659, 685–6; no. 660, 688–9, no 664, 689, no. 665, 690, no. 666, 691.

[28] The most extensive study of Manuel's use of relics is Mergiali-Sahas, 'Relics'. More generally see Mergiali-Sahas, 'Byzantine Emperors and Holy Relics. Use and Misuse of Sanctity and Authority, *JÖB* 51 (2001), 41–60; G. T. Dennis, 'Two Unknown Documents of Manuel II Palaeologus, *TM 3* (1968), 397–404; reprinted in G. T. Dennis, *Byzantium and the Franks, 1350–1420* (London, 1982), Study VIII, for the two *chrysobulls* Manuel sent to Pope Benedict and Queen Margrethe of Denmark; C. Estopañán, 'Ein Chrysobulles des Kaisers Manuel II Palaiologos (1391–1425) für den Gegenpapst Bennedikt XIII (1394–1417/23) vom 20. Juni 1402', *BZ* 44 (1951), 89–93, for the relic sent to Pope Benedict; C. Marinesco, 'Manuel II Paléologue et les rois d'Aragon, commentaire sur quatre lettres inéedites en Latin, expédiées par la chancellerie byzantine', *Académie Roumanie, Bulletin de la Section Historique*, 11 (1924), 192–206; C. Marinesco, 'Les rélations'; S. Cirac Estopañán, *La Unión, Manuel II Paléologo y sus Recuerdos en España* (Barcelona, 1952) for the relics sent to Spain. Also see H. Klein, 'Eastern Objects and Western Desires: Relics and Reliquaries between Byzantium and the West', *DOP* 58 (2004), 283–313. Henceforth, Marinesco, 'Les rois'; Dennis, 'Two unknown documents' and Estopáñan, 'Chrysobull'.

Recipients of the relics, either in person or through envoys: Boniface IX, Benedict XIII, Margrethe of Denmark and Martin of Aragon all received pieces from Christ's tunic which had healed a woman; Charles III of Navarre and Jean, the duke of Berry, received pieces of wood from the Holy Cross; the duke of Milan, Gian Visconti received a thorn from the crown of Christ; and Henry IV of England received a piece from the Seamless Tunic of Christ.[29] Finally, Martin of Aragon, who was eager to obtain relics for his new cathedral, also received a piece of the Holy Sponge.[30] By 1400, however, Byzantine relics were not as prestigious as they had once been, and many European rulers had by that time acquired relics that were far more precious and prestigious than those offered by the emperor. Still, Manuel's extensive use of relics as a means of diplomacy during his European sojourn had no precedent and is a noteworthy aspect of his reign. His decision to cut the tunic of Christ into pieces for distribution is particularly notable; ultimately, his piety did not restrain him from mutilating the relic for reasons of convenience.

These precious objects came with an official document guaranteeing authenticity, which was drafted in Manuel's lodging in the Louvre.[31] These Byzantine documents composed in Paris are stylistically a conflation of a *chrysobull* and a *prostagma*. They betray strong influences of Latin *patentes litterae*, and some of them seem to have even been composed first in Latin instead of Greek.[32] In drafting these unusual documents, Manuel's mobile Byzantine chancery seemed able to adapt to unique circumstances. Echoes of the emperor's considerable distress and desperation can also be heard in the documents: 'Because of the attacks of the despicable Turks, we came to these Western territories and to other Christian lands . . . '[33] Thus, it can be argued that the documents drafted in the Louvre not only confirmed the authenticity of the relics they also served to convey Manuel's plight to the recipient through emotive language.

---

[29] Identifying the Tunic of Christ is not entirely easy, however, it does not seem to be identical to the famous Seamless Tunic, pieces of which Manuel would present to the king of England. On the tunic, see Mergiali-Sahas, 'Relics', 600.

[30] The contacts between Manuel and Aragon concerning relics would continue until 1407, see Marinesco, 'Les rois', 3; Mergali-Sahas, 'Relics', 274.

[31] The location was often noted as the Louvre. For one such instance, see the text in Marinesco, 'Les rélations', 425, '. . . ἐδόθη εἰς τὴν πόλιν Παρισίου ἐν τῷ τοῦ ῥηγὸς παλατίῳ τῷ λουπαρᾶ, ἐν ᾧ ἤδη καταμένομεν. . . .'

[32] Dennis, 'Two unknown documents', 398–404; Estopañán, 'Chrysobull', 91.

[33] Estopañán, 'Chrysobull', 91.

The palace of the Louvre would host Manuel for the greater part of his stay in Europe.[34] So, what was the French residence of the emperor like? In 1400, the Louvre was a recently restored royal residence to which Charles VI retreated only occasionally, since his court was usually installed at the Hôtel de Saint Paul. The Louvre had many towers with blue turrets, and gates that overlooked the Seine and Saint Germain- l'Auxerrois. If Manuel had strolled in the gardens located in the north, he would have easily reached the *hôtels* of the royal family. Inside the palace, the meals took place in the Salle de Saint Louis, which was decorated with frescoes depicting birds and hunting scenes. Louvre also housed the famous library of Charles V that contained around 1000 books.[35] The royal apartments overlooked the Seine, and when in residence the king stayed on the first floor. Where exactly Manuel was staying is not known, but according to royal custom he may have been given the royal chambers as a mark of respect.

The *Chronicle of Saint Denis* notes that Manuel was present at court occasions such as celebrations and royal hunts. At those gatherings, the emperor would mingle with some of the most famous figures in medieval French history. He certainly must have witnessed displays of splendour now absent from his impoverished Byzantine court. At the French court, the king's brother and uncles stood out. These uncles – Louis d'Anjou, Philippe de Bourgogne and Jean de Berry – all had residences near the Louvre, and their homes were often frequented by the king.[36] They had large retinues, splendid clothes and exchanged many precious gifts. The king's brother, the duke of Orléans, for instance, had a magnificent robe ornately embellished with musical notes and a love ballad sewn in pearls.[37] Likewise, Jean de Berry was famed for his collection of rare and precious items, artworks and illuminated manuscripts.

In the new year of 1401, Jean de Berry was to give 231 luxury gifts and receive 331 in return.[38] This exchange of gifts for the new year at the French

---

[34] The following account of the Louvre at the time of Manuel's visit is based upon L. Gosset, *Le palais du Louvre* (Paris, 1933), 5–10.

[35] F. Autrand, *Charles VI. La folie au pouvoir* (Paris, 1986), 66–7. Henceforth, Autrand, *Charles VI*.

[36] S. Roux, *Paris in the Middle Ages*. trans. J. A. McNamara (Philadelphia, 2009), 84–5. Henceforth, Roux, *Paris in the Middle Ages*. On the king's uncles and their influence, see R. C. Famiglietti, *Royal Intrigue. Crisis at the Court of Charles VI 1392–1420* (New York, 1986) and Autrand, *Charles VI*, 16–17. Henceforth, Famiglietti, *Intrigue*.

[37] Roux, *Paris in the Middle Ages*, 183.

[38] See M. Meiss, *French Art in the Time of Jean de Berry. The Limbourgs and their Contemporaries*, 2 vols (London and New York, 1974), 48 and Famiglietti, *Intrigue*, 111. Henceforth, Meiss, *French Art*. See B. Buettner, 'Past Presents: New Year's Gifts at the Valois Courts, ca. 1400', *The Art Bulletin*, 83, no. 4 (December 2001), 598–625, for *étrennes*.

court was called *étrennes*. It was not merely a matter of exchanging luxury gifts for pleasure, it also served to reinforce familial and social bonds; essentially, it was a ceremonial display of prestige and wealth. The inventories of Jean de Berry indicate that Manuel was also a participant in these exchanges, and that he presented Jean de Berry, an avid relic collector, with a piece of the True Cross.

The inventory of 1416 also contains gift from Manuel that is overlooked: a luxury textile – probably a banner or a wall tapestry – adorned with a crowned double-headed eagle decorated with animals, birds and floral designs, bordered with a white-red fabric.[39] The crowned double-headed eagle was depicted on the border; the textile had the dimensions of 3.5 *aulnes* in length, and 2.5 *aulnes* in width.[40] It was lined with red-yellow taffeta and had tassels of red, green and yellow taffeta. Furthermore, the cost is noted as thirty *livres tournois*. Although not the most expensive of Manuel's gifts it was nevertheless a costly item in the duke's 1416 inventory.

Being lightweight, easy to transport, but also luxurious, this kind of item was a convenient present. Unlike in the cases of the Freising icon and the 'recycled' manuscript that Manuel would later send to Paris; it is difficult to determine whether this textile was another second-hand item. It has been noted, however, that luxury textiles sent as diplomatic gifts in the Palaiologan era were usually imported.[41] In this regard, it is interesting that de Berry's inventory characterizes the piece as a 'work of Greece' (ouvreage de Grèce). This could either indicate that the textile was of Byzantine origin, or perhaps that it had been produced in a region of Greece.

Manuel received a royal invitation to the wedding of Jean de Berry's daughter as well. At the wedding reception, the emperor was seated on a dais decorated with golden ornaments of fleur de lys. He was accompanied by the cardinal of Thury, Charles VI, the bride, Queen Isabeau, the king of Sicily and his brother, the prince of Tarente. Jean de Berry also hosted a feast in Hôtel Nesle where a wooden chamber was specifically constructed for this occasion and laden with golden silk tapestries.[42] The *Chronicle of Saint Denis* gives no more details about the occasion.

---

[39] See *Inventoires de Jean duc de Berry (1401–1416)*, 2 vols., ed. and annotated J. Guiffrey (Paris, 1894), vol. II, 35, no 214 for the crucifix and 262, no 791 for the textile. Jean de Berry had the relic enclosed in a golden crucifix. Henceforth, *Inventoires de Jean de Berry*.

[40] *Aulne* or *aune* is the French equivalent of ell, a measurement usually used in the tailoring businesses. Originally, it was the combined length of the forearm and extended hand. However, the measurement varied across centuries and geographies.

[41] Hilsdale, *Decline*, 228, on the issue of these imported textiles. See also F. E. Schlosser, 'Wearing a Precious Web: The Use of Textiles in Diplomacy', *BSI* 63 (2005), 42–52.

[42] *Chronique de Saint Denis*, XXI, i, 759–60.

Certainly, the feast must have included an impressive set of dishes accompanied by music, dancing and perhaps acrobatic displays. The dishes would have followed a fixed order of foods such as salads and fruits, then broths, followed by roast meats. The final course would have been the entréments, which consisted of cheese, candied fruits, light cakes and a wine called *hypocras*. The most prized dishes, in addition to the saltcellar, would have been within the reach of the most honoured guest – possibly Manuel in this case. Each guest would have a trencher before him, a thick plate fashioned out of bread to soak the meat juices and sometimes even coloured with herbs. At the end of the meal, the company would retire to another chamber to enjoy delicacies, dragées, candied coriander seeds and ginger root.[43]

Thanks to these details provided by the Western sources, the emperor's European journey opens up a fascinating window onto his experiences for the modern reader. However, Manuel himself is silent about all these moments. In his letters he does not mention the people or the sights encountered. This silence would have been entirely expected for Manuel and for his Byzantine audience. After all, the function of Byzantine letters was not to convey concrete information about the circumstances of the sender, rather they were intended to elevate the sender and recipient above such daily concerns in pursuit of literary enjoyment. The emperor composed his letters following these traditions of Byzantine letter writing by creating beautifully polished, small, rich literary creations for his friends, eschewing detailed descriptions of his experiences in Paris or on his travels. Still, his letters do mirror Manuel's emotions abroad: his loneliness, his anxiety at the uncertainty of things and the pain of separation from his *patris* and friends.

It was an established *topos* in Byzantine epistolography for travelling writers to complain about the separation from their *patris*. Furthermore, themes of yearning and separation were also essential features of Byzantine epistolography, since letters were considered tokens of friendship and were supposed to bridge the physical gap between correspondents, functioning as a written conversation. Thus, Byzantine letter writers often lament separation from friends and display a strong sense of yearning. Both prompted by this *topos* and possibly by his actual plight as an emperor forced to seek aid abroad, Manuel's letters are similarly filled with suggestions of homesickness for his city and friends.[44]

---

[43] For feasts and food in fourteenth- and fifteenth-century France, see O. Redon, F. Sabban and S. Servent (eds.) *The Medieval Kitchen: Recipes from France and Italy*, trans. E. Scheider (Chicago, London, 1998), especially 10–11 and M. P. Cosman, *Fabulous Feasts: Medieval Cookery and Ceremony* (New York, 1992), especially 15–30. Henceforth, Cosman, *Fabulous Feasts*.

[44] For this *topos*, see M. Mullett, 'Originality', 39–53.

In his very first letter to Manuel Chrysoloras written from Paris, he mentions that the journey had been difficult and complains that the difference in language did not allow him to converse. He then narrates the details of the promised military aid and concludes his brief letter with his wish for a swift return.[45] It is significant that the emperor immediately highlights the difference in language and expresses a desire to return. In these very first lines penned in Paris we see Manuel as a stranger in an alien environment. Indeed, all of his letters from Europe include mention of a desire to return to his *patris*. The vivid imagery in his letter paints of picture of Chrysoloras leaping with excitement as he received one letter after the other and culminates in the return of the author himself.[46] Manuel's yearning for his *patris* and for his loved ones stems partially from the *topoi* of letter writing, but under the circumstances it was surely also a genuine reflection of the emperor's state of mind.

Although he warrants a brief mention in Manuel's very first letter, Charles VI is otherwise notably absent from the emperor's communications. This is possibly due to the fact that soon after the emperor arrived, around August, Charles had one of his episodes of insanity. In these moments of crisis, Charles was completely secluded, refusing to eat, sleep or see anyone. He tore and broke all objects in his grasp, even throwing them into the fire, even believing at times that he was a lion. The king may have been suffering from some form of schizophrenia; at any rate, he clearly had a serious psychiatric illness.[47] Arguably, the absence of Charles from Manuel's letters may have stemmed from the emperor's gradual realization of the king's state of mind. When and how exactly the emperor came to fully grasp the situation cannot be determined, but a comparison of his letters and the French sources indicate that the intensifying of his plans to visit England coincided with the early phases of the king's illness, and by October, Manuel was already in Calais.[48]

Crossing the Channel: Manuel's Sea Imagery

The emperor waited in Calais for two months before crossing the English Channel in December. This was due to uncertainty along the Anglo-

[45] Letter 37, lines 2–6.
[46] See Letters 37, 38, 40 and 42, all of which elaborate on this theme of return.
[47] *Chronique de Saint Denis*, XXI, i, 763, records the king's uncles receiving ambassadors on his behalf at this time because he was ill. On the madness of Charles IV, which surfaced periodically, see Autrand, *Charles VI*, 289–318; Guenée, 'La voeu'. Famigletti, *Intrigue*, 1–21, argues that the king could have had some form of schizophrenia, based on modern medical theories. Chalkokondyles is the only Byzantine source to note Charles' insanity, see Chalkokondyles, 136–7 and 156–7.
[48] Ursins, 419, claims Manuel left in September.

Scottish borders.[49] As might be expected, the wintry journey was tumultuous. Manuel himself labelled the situation a 'twofold tempest', referring both to the circumstances and to the disagreeable weather.[50] While this was to be his first crossing of the Channel, it certainly was not the first time the emperor had found himself storm tossed.

Although it is tempting to trace a link between Manuel's frequent sea journeys and the ample use of sea imagery in his writing, sea imagery and metaphors, such as that of a stormy sea or the state as ship, were in fact commonplace in Byzantine literature and were employed by almost every author.[51] For instance, in homilies, life could be represented with the metaphor of sea, and faith with that of an anchor. Similarly, in histories and chronicles, time could become a flowing river that washed away all unrecorded memories. Thus, while he does display a special interest in water and sea imagery, Manuel is not unique in this regard.

While such sea imagery was indeed commonplace, a close reading of Manuel's works reveals that his own usage does transcend the *topoi*, and suggests some personal insight. Whatever the reason for his particular fondness, the emperor's sea imagery and metaphors also have distinctive, personal touches. He introduces variations to existing *topoi* and employs new ideas, and his water imagery is noticeably vivid and varied. 'They (sea storms) penetrate men's souls and make their hearts tremble, as those who have experienced those things know very well', he remarks in 1416. Elsewhere he dramatically depicts the apprehension of people looking at what lies below the surface of the sea.[52] Furthermore, Manuel composed a prayer for those in peril at sea by collating sentences from the Psalms.[53] It is interesting that he chose this topic out of all the other possibilities.

Regardless of whether his experiences formed the impetus for this imagery, Manuel seems to have had a particular fascination with the sea:

[49] Nicol, 'A Byzantine Emperor', 212; *Proceedings and Ordinances of the Privy Council of England*, I, ed. H. Nicolas, (London, 1834), 82. Manuel's stay in Calais cost £ 400, *Issues of the Exchequer; Being a Collection of Payments Made Out of His Majesty's Revenue, from King Henry III to King Henry VI Inclusive*, ed. F. Devon (London, 1837), 283–4. Henceforth, *Issues of the Exchequer*.
[50] Letter 38, lines 29–30.
[51] See A. Kazhdan, 'Ships in Storms: On Imagery and Historical Interpretations', in *Studies on Byzantine Literature of the 11th and the 12th Centuries*, eds. A. Kazhdan and S. Franklin (Cambridge, 1984), 264–78. For another case of personal variations on commonplace imagery, see A. R. Littlewood, 'Imagery in the *Chronographia* of Michael Psellos', in *Reading Michael Psellos*, eds. C. Barber and D. Jenkins (Leiden, 2006), 13–56.
[52] Letter 68, lines 23–5, '. . . ἃ δὴ πάνθ᾽ ὁμοῦ συνελθόντα ἐς βάθος ἐφικνεῖσθαι τῶν ψυχῶν καὶ τρόμον ταῖς καρδίαις ἐμποιεῖν καὶ ὅλως γε δεδίττεσθαι πέφυκε καὶ συγχεῖν, ὅσον περ᾽ ἴσασιν ἀκριβῶς οἱ τούτων πεπειραμένοι'. *Dialogue on Marriage*, 96–97, see below for the Greek text.
[53] This composition survives in two manuscripts; Par. gr 3041, f. 127v; Vat. Barb. gr. 219, ff. 91v –92.

a ship may be a metaphor for the state, for the act of writing or for Manuel's feelings; the sea can reflect tranquillity, but it is mostly full of waves and disturbance; or the sea may be a symbol for political circumstances, writing or human life.[54] In the *Funeral Oration*, Theodore is meticulously portrayed as trying to steer the ship of state while it lets out terrible cracking sounds and refuses to be piloted. Another similarly striking passage is a lively description of the damage time has caused the ship of state in the *Dialogue on Marriage*.[55] In accordance with the *topos*, the Church is a harbour for the pious. To bestow great honour on them, the Virgin and the Despot Theodore are also personified as harbours.[56] Even theological disputes are likened to sea storms: Manuel's opponent in vain seeks refuge in the harbour of syllogisms but sinks and is drowned as an outcome of the dispute.

Moreover, Manuel's sea imagery is sometimes highly unusual and at times, outright bizarre. In the *Funeral Oration* Bayezid is described as using his oars to move his boat without realizing that he is also being moved with the boat. In the *Discourse to Kabasilas*, the emperor claims that he has not drowned in his calamities and is instead merely floating on the sea surface. But the most striking instance is in the *Discourse to the Thessalonians* where, in a complicated passage, Manuel likens lengthening his speech to someone who tries to drag a ship that sails in a good wind with a rope by attaching one end to its bow while holding the other end and sitting at the stern of the ship. The attempt is not only futile, but ridiculous.[57]

Manuel's sea imagery is not only vivid, but also very appropriate to the texts which they adorn. For instance, his 'floating' on the sea surface in the

---

[54] *Funeral Oration*, 162–6; *Discourse to Iagoup*, 336; *Kanon*, Ode γ, in E. Legrand, *Lettres de l'empereur Manuel Paleologue*, ed. E. Legrand (Amsterdam, 1962), 94–102; Letters 16 and 33.

[55] *Funeral Oration*, 198–9, '. . . εἶτα τῶν ἀνέμων ὥσπερ λυσσώντων καὶ μαινομένης ἀγριώτερον τῆς θαλάσσης καὶ τῶν μὲν σκευῶν αὐτῷ ποιησάντων, τινῶν δὲ καὶ συντριβέντων ἤδη, τῆς τε νεὼς, ὡς ἔπος εἰπεῖν, ἀφηνιαζούσης καὶ μονονοὺ φωνὴν ἀφιείσης ὡς αὐτίκα καταδύσεται, μὴ μεταβαλούσης αὐτῇ τῆς τύχης . . .' *Dialogue on Marriage*, 96–7, '. . . νεὼς σεσαθρωμένης τῷ χρόνῳ, ᾗ δὴ καὶ τὰ σκεύη πεπόνηκεν, ὑπ' ἀτακτούντων πνευμάτων, κύμασι χειμῶνος μαχομένοις ἅμα καὶ πειραταῖς, ὑφάλυς τε ὑποπτεύουσι, καὶ μὴ δὲ λιμένα ἐγγύς που γοῦν ἔχουσι, καὶ ταῦτα πάντ' ἐν ἀσελήνῳ νυκτί, πυκνότητι νεφῶν κατεζοφωμένῃ, ῥαγδαῖον τε ὑόντων, καὶ βροντὰς ἀλλεπαλλήλους ἀφιέντων, αἳ δὴ καὶ σκηπτὸν ἀπειλοῦσιν ὀλέθριον'.

[56] In Byzantine texts, the person likened to a harbour would usually have been the writer's patron. Thus, as emperor, Manuel is extremely selective in his use of this metaphor. See some cases in *Funeral Oration*, 94–95; Letter 13; *Kanon*, Ode γ; *Foundations of Imperial Conduct*, col. 325.

[57] *Funeral Oration*, 132–3, '. . . ὥσπερ τις χρώμενος ἐν ἀκατίῳ κώπαις ἄγει μὲν τῇ εἰρεσίᾳ τὸ σκάφος, φέρεται δ' αὖθις ὑπὸ τοῦ σκάφους. . .'; *Discourse to Kabasilas*, lines 57–61 '. . . ἀλλ' ἐπιπολάζω νήχεσθαι μὴ μεμαθηκώς, μὴ ἀλύῃς μηδὲ καταβαπτισθῇς καὶ αὐτός'; *Discourse to the Thessalonians*, 296, '. . . τῆς ἐξ οὐρίας πλεούσης νεὼς ἀπὸ τῆς πρῴρας καθήμενος ἕλκων μετὰ κάλῳ τὴν πρύμναν, ὅπως δῆθεν τάχιον διανύσῃ τὸν πλοῦν.'

Discourse to Kabasilas conveys to the audience the precariousness of his situation, as well as a sense of loneliness and despair. Similarly, Bayezid's struggle with the oars emphasizes his irrationality. The emperor uses these metaphors not merely to 'adorn' his texts, through them he also enriches his character portrayals, sets the atmosphere, and conveys his feelings and thoughts to his audience. These above-mentioned metaphors are thus unique to Manuel and hint at his creativity in breathing new life to the *topoi*. While he adheres to the traditions of Byzantine literary texts, he nevertheless introduces his own personal touches. As in the case of many other Byzantine authors, while operating within the Byzantine tradition the emperor shows originality by modifying established literary practices. On the whole, his carefully crafted, eloquent and at times, rather original sea imagery again bears witness to Manuel's interest in and care for the literary features in his works.

Visiting London

Despite the physical and literary storms on the Channel, Manuel finally disembarked at Dover on 11 December, and on the 13 December, he was welcomed at Canterbury.[58] On 21 December, the emperor met with Henry IV in Blackheath. The two rulers then proceeded to London.[59] There, twelve of the aldermen of the city and their sons performed a masquerade for Manuel, and a few days later, at Christmas, Henry IV gave a splendid feast at Eltham Palace. A tournament was also held in the emperor's honour.[60]

---

[58] Nicol, 'A Byzantine Emperor', 213. This article is the most extensive study of Manuel's stay in London, especially of its financial aspects. For other brief remarks, see D. Nicol, 'Byzantium and England', *Balkan Studies* XV (1974), 179–203; reprinted D. Nicol, *Studies in Late Byzantine History and Prosopography* (London, 1986), Study XVII.

[59] Thomas Walsingham, *Historia Anglicana*, ed. H. T. Riley (London, 1864), II, 247; Adam of Usk, *The Chronicle of Adam Usk, 1377–1421*, ed. C. Given-Wilson (Oxford, 1997), 118–19; the short chronicles Bradford MS 32D86/42, Guildhall 3313 and Harley 565, transcribed in M. R. McLaren, *The London Chronicles of the Fifteenth Century: A Revolution in English Writing* (Cambridge, 2002), 181 and *Eulogium (Historiarum sive Temporis): Chronicon ab orbe condito usque ad annum Domini M. CCC.LXVI, a monacho quondam Malmesburiensi exaratum*, ed. F. S. Haydon, (London, 1863), III, 388 and *Vita Ricardi Secundi*, 169–70. Henceforth, Adam of Usk; Walsingham and *Eulogium*. I have not added the English chronicles from later centuries as they merely replicate the sources above.

[60] Harley 565; Adam of Usk, 120–1; J. H. Wylie, *History of England under Henry the Fourth*, (1399–1404), 4 vols. (London, 1884), IV, Appendix IV, 200, cites an entry from the Wardrobe Accounts; PRO, Enrolled Wardrobe Accounts, L.T.R Roll XI. M 12, concerning various purchases for this tournament. Henceforth, Wylie, *Henry the Fourth*. A. Sussman, *Anglo-Byzantine Relations during the Middle Ages*. (PhD thesis, University of Pennsylvania, 1966), 248–9, cites a chancery document, PRO E20/12/40. It reports that in December, Henry IV ordered a gilded bed to be brought to Eltham. Sussman suggests that the bed was for the use of Manuel. Henceforth, Sussman, *Anglo-Byzantine Relations*.

Sadly, no details of this occasion have survived, but since feasts were also political occasions to impress, it must have been quite a sight. 'Subtleties', which were models of castles, ships and animals made of food, would have been paraded and live birds may have been hidden in pies. The menu from Henry IV's coronation banquet two years earlier may give an idea of the dishes that may have been served: three courses consisting of dishes such as meat in pepper sauce, a boar's head and tusks, pheasants, cygnets, sturgeon, jelly, peacocks, roast venison, tarts, quails, glazed eggs and an eagle.[61]

In stark contrast to his silence on Charles VI, Manuel writes a laudatory portrait of Henry IV in his sole surviving letter from London. He extolls the king for abounding in good qualities and virtues. Significantly, the emperor calls the king 'the ruler of Great Britain, or one might say, the second *oikoumene*'. He thus associates Henry and his realm with the Byzantine political and religious sphere, *oikoumene*. The emperor contextualizes his praise within a Byzantine ideological framework, stressing the importance he gave to the English king. He even uses the harbour metaphor for the English king, describing Henry as a haven for Manuel amidst the 'twofold tempest' and providing a refuge for the emperor in his person and character.[62] Since the harbour metaphor also could have implications of patronage, and Manuel previously only used it in relation to his brother and the Virgin, it is clear that the he felt genuine admiration for the king.

Henry IV made extensive inquiries into the matter of the lost funds raised by Richard II and succeeded in recovering some of the money.[63] While Manuel's praise of the king was certainly based on the lavish promises Henry made to him, the emperor also notes his pleasant manners and engaging conversation. Although Henry is not a very impressive figure in English sources, some of his contemporaries also seem to have noted his pleasant disposition.[64] As a token of gratitude, the emperor gave Henry a piece from the Seamless Tunic of Christ, which was further diminished when Henry cut it in two to give one piece to the archbishop of Canterbury, who in turn split his portion further into three.[65] Despite

---

[61] Cosman, *Fabulous Feasts*, 20, 24–6 and 311.   [62] Letter 38, lines 20–21 and 29–30.

[63] Nicol, 'A Byzantine Emperor', convincingly demonstrates that only a fraction of the money could be recovered and given to Manuel, around £3,000. See Manuel's letter of thanks to Henry IV, Hingeston, *Letters*, no. 25, 56–7.

[64] Wylie, *Henry the Fourth*, III, 128–9, 135–6, citing Froissart concerning the period of Henry's exile in France.

[65] Mergiali-Sahas, 'Relics', 272. I thank Prof. Chris Given-Wilson for generously sharing with me a transcription of the manuscript folium containing these details, Lambeth Palace Library MS 78, f. 25.

these gestures, the internal problems faced by Henry IV would eventually prevent him from assisting Constantinople.

After Eltham, Manuel seems to have stayed in the house of St John at Smithfield and perhaps also in the Priory of the Hospital in Clerkenwell.[66] The English historians of the day were particularly interested in the Orthodox rites that the Byzantine party observed, as well as their long, uniform clothes and flowing beards; Adam of Usk makes the intriguing claim that the Byzantines disliked English fashions.[67] Apart from these remarks, the emperor's visit is not elaborated upon, though many years later in 1525, the bishop of London, Cuthbert Tunstal referred to Manuel's presence in the city. While discussing the English translations of the New Testament, the bishop quotes a curious report from a book that he had come across: the emperor and his entourage had been asked whether the populace at home could understand when Scripture was read or recited from. The answer was negative: the language of the Scriptures and the one spoken by people were completely different.[68]

Around 1400, London, like Paris, was a big and bustling medieval city. Manuel would have seen many churches and convents that had been built or renovated in the last century.[69] Undoubtedly, he would have seen the Tower and London Bridge. Westminster Hall, whose roof had been recently rebuilt by Richard II, was the largest hall in Europe at the time.[70] In this respect, like the Italian and French cities, London, too, provided a stark contrast to declining Constantinople in the 1400s.

Back in Paris: Prayers and Gifts

Manuel's stay in London lasted only two months. By the end of February, he was back in Paris with the recently recovered Charles VI.[71] The

---

[66] Nicol, 'A Byzantine emperor', 215 citing *Chronicles of London*, ed. C. L. Kingsford (Oxford, 1905), Appendix 1, 267: 'And this yere the emperour of Constantyne the noble come unto England, and he was lodged atte the gous of Saynt John in Smythfeld.' For Clarkenwell, see E. J. King, *The Grand Priory of the Order of the Hospital of St John of Jerusalem in England. A Short History* (London, 1924), 46–7.

[67] Adam of Usk, 118–21; *Eulogium*, 388. On the English court attire of the time, see D. W. Robertson, Jr., *Chaucers' London* (New York, 1968), 19 and M. G. Houston, *Medieval Costume in England and France* (London, 1939; reprinted 1996), 72–3; 181–3. Henceforth, Robertson, *Chaucer's London.*

[68] J. Harris, 'Manuel II Palaiologos (1391–1425) and the Lollards', *Greek Orthodox Theological Review* 57 (2012), 213–34; 214–15. Henceforth, Harris, 'Lollards.'

[69] Robertson, *Chaucer's London*, 12–32, 53.   [70] Roberston, *Chaucer's London*, 36–7, 57, 65–6.

[71] *Chronique de Saint Denis*, XXI, i, 771. Some members of Manuel's entourage stayed in England for some time; they were given tours of various cities. See the entry from the Queen's Wardrobe as cited in Wylie, *Henry IV*, IV, Appendix B, 198; PRO, Wardrobe Accounts (Q. R. Wardrobe, 68/3), 7 May 1401.

Chronicle of Saint Denis records the Catholic king and the Orthodox emperor attending a Latin mass in the Abbey of Saint Denis. In an interesting twist, it was also the custom of Charles VI to attend mass in Saint Denis after his recoveries. The chronicler notes the shock of the French people at the Orthodox emperor's presence in the Latin mass. In his theological treatise composed around the same time, Makarios of Ankyra – a member of Manuel's entourage – was to fiercely oppose Latins and the Orthodox attending liturgy together. One wonders what his reaction was to the emperor's presence in Saint Denis.[72] Although his writings testify to Manuel's strong Orthodoxy, his attendance of a Latin mass also demonstrates his political tact.

At the time of Manuel's visit, Saint Denis was the royal abbey of Paris, home to the tombs of many French kings. Rumour also had it that the head of St Denis was buried under the basilica, though the Byzantines knew him as Dionysios the Aeropagite. Yet the theological writings they attributed to him actually belonged to another author, now known as Pseudo-Dionysios.[73] In his theological treatise that he was to compose in Paris, Manuel would refer to Dionysios as being 'martyred and lying here, in Paris'.[74] Inside the abbey, Manuel may have also seen a ninth-century manuscript of Dionysios, which had been donated by the Byzantine emperor Michael II.

Around 1407, via Manuel Chrysoloras, Manuel would present to the abbey another manuscript of Dionysios, illuminated with the famous portrait of the imperial family.[75] It has been suggested that Manuel's gift might have also functioned as a 'sequel' to the ninth-century manuscript.[76] As in the case of the Freising icon, the manuscript, too, was an older item.

---

[72] *Chronique de Saint Denis*, xxi, i, 775. Guenée, 'Le voeu', especially 67. In his treatise against the Latins, Makarios of Ankyra, 399–400.

[73] For Saint Denis at the time of Manuel's visit, see S. M. Crosby, *L'abbaye de S. Denis* (Paris, 1953), 66–7 and Guenée, 'Le voeu', 70.

[74] *Procession of the Holy Spirit*, 147.

[75] This illumination has been extensively studied; it was probably completed sometime between 1403–5. See K. Wessel, 'Manuel II Palaiologos und seine Familie. Zur Miniature des Cod. Ivoires A 53 des Louvre', in *Beiträge zur Kunst des Mittelalters. Fetschrift für Hans Wenzel*, ed. R. Becksmann (Berlin, 1975), 219–29; E. Lamberz, 'Das Geschenk des Kaisers Manuel II an das Kloster Saint-Denis und der 'Metochitesschreiber' Michael Klostomates', in Λιθόστρωτον: *Studien zur byzantinischen Kunst und Geschicte. Festschrift für Marcel Restle*, eds. B. Barkopp and T. Steppan (Stuttgart, 2000), 156–9; I. Spatharakis, *The Portait in Byzantine Illuminated Manuscripts* (Leiden, 1976), 140–1; for more general remarks, see J. Lowden, 'The Luxury Book as Diplomatic Gift', in *Byzantine Diplomacy, Papers from the Twenty- fourth Spring Symposium of Byzantine Studies, Cambridge March 1990*, eds. J. Shepard and S. Franklin (Aldershot, 1992), 249–60. Hilsdale, *Decline*, 246–62.

[76] This has been noted by Hilsdale, *Decline*, 238, who suggests that Manuel's own gift might have been a 'sequel' to this previous Byzantine manuscript.

It had been written and bound in the first third of the fourteenth century. Once more, refashioning an already existing item as a diplomatic gift was a convenient solution to both financial and time constraints; however, the decision to opt for this older manuscript may have had another motive, as it consisted of higher quality, more valuable parchment than that of contemporary manuscripts.

Furthermore, two high–quality illuminations were added to the manuscript, thus increasing its value and prestige. The first depicted Dionysios, the author of the text, and the second is a group portrait of the imperial family.[77] It depicts the emperor, his wife Helena and their three sons, John, Theodore and Andronikos. (**Fig 7.1**) Manuel's facial features correspond to his own portrait in the Parisinus manuscript of his *Funeral Oration*, as well as those found in European artefacts. Dressed in full imperial regalia, he and Helena are blessed by the Virgin and child depicted above their heads, an indication that the source of their imperial power is divine, and that Manuel derives his power from God and enjoys divine protection. The younger sons, Theodore and Andronikos wear the diadems of despots and their clothing is similar to that of their mother. John's costume, on the other hand, is identical to that of Manuel, and like his parents he is represented with a halo. It is thus made clear visually that the son had already been declared co-emperor and was his father's legitimate successor, not the emperor's nephew John VII. This is further reinforced by the positioning of John's figure. While his brothers –distinguished from each other only by their height – are standing between the imperial couple, John is on his father's right. The figures of Manuel and John also overlap, visually strengthening their bond as co-emperors. The illumination thus conveys a subtle political message of authority and legitimacy, as well as lending the manuscript gift a more personal touch.

During his second and longer stay in Paris, Manuel worked to get help for his besieged capital. Although Charles VI had recovered temporarily, the governance of the kingdom was practically in the hands of his uncles. Manuel contacted the pope in Avignon, and various Italian cities, also negotiating with Aragon. Although he sought the support of Rome with more fervour, the emperor also curried Avignon's favour and gifted relics to the Avignonese pope. Unfortunately, all his plans came to naught.[78] In one of his letters, Manuel enthusiastically spoke of plans to assemble a joint army of the French and the English which would be commanded by

---

[77] Hilsdale, *Decline*, 246–62, makes the following arguments.
[78] See *ΠΠ*, III, 124–5. For Aragon, *Diplomatari de l'Orient Català*, no. 664, 689; no. 665, 690. Marinesceo, 'Les rois', 427–30; Dölger, *Regesten*, no. 3290, 88–9 for Avignon.

Figure 7.1 Portrait of Manuel II and his family. Paris, Louvre, MR 416 fol. 2r (RMN-Grand Palais). Photo: Louvre, Paris, France / Bridgeman Images.

Mareschal Boucicaut. The emperor's joy in the choice of Boucicaut is a reflection of his genuine liking for the mareschal. 'All that is left' Manuel writes, 'is to set our return date.'[79] He was to be sorely disappointed:

[79] Letter 39, lines 26–7.

Boucicaut was instead appointed the governor of Genoa, and as for the army, it was never assembled.

On the Procession of the Holy Spirit

Manuel's stay in Paris may not have resulted in the military help he had hoped for, but it did provide time for the creation of one of his most extensive theological works. At some point in Paris, the emperor received a Latin tract concerning the procession of the Holy Spirit, probably presented to him by a Benedictine monk of Saint Denis. Although the original Latin tract is now lost, it was in response to this tract that Manuel was to compose his own treatise on the procession of the Holy Spirit.[80]

The filioque controversy that concerned the procession of the Holy Spirit, was a crucial point of doctrinal difference in the Schism.[81] The Latins proposed a double procession of the Spirit, arguing that it emanated both from the Father and the Son, and they claimed that the Greek prepositions *ek* and *dia* could be used interchangeably within this context, incorporating supporting statements from the Fathers. Thus, they argued, the Scripture could be interpreted as stating that the Spirit also proceeded from the Son, which could be expressed as *filioque* in Latin. The Orthodox, on the other hand, opposed this double procession and argued that it was a misinterpretation of the Scripture. They found it further problematic as the double procession elevated the Son to the same rank as the Father. The Orthodox argued that it confounded the order of the Trinity and destroyed the monarchy of the Father, as well as degrading the Spirit. While this debate had been ongoing, it was accelerated in the eleventh century upon the introduction of the *filioque* clause into the Nicene creed by the Latins. The Orthodox Church further rejected this addition as contradicting the decrees of ecumenical councils, which prohibited any additions to the creed. The *filioque* consequently became one of the major reasons for the Schism of 1054.

In the fifteenth century, this debate gained further importance through the increasing theological contact between Byzantium and the West. Church councils and translations of authors such as Thomas Aquinas

---

[80] Based on internal textual evidence, the editor, Dendrinos argues that although it might have been revised at a later point, the majority of the treatise was composed in Paris, *On the Procession of the Holy Spirit*, xvii-iii.

[81] For debates on the procession, see *On the Procession of the Holy Spirit*, xxx-xi, Papadakis, *Crisis*, 1–27, 86–99, 117–20; Meyendorff, *Byzantine Theology*, 91–5. For the Procession in the Fathers, see, J. Meyendorff, 'La procession du Saint-esprit chez les Pères orientaux', *Russie et Chrétiennité* 3/4 (1950), 158–78.

into Greek contributed to these contacts.[82] As a significant point of debate between the Orthodox and Latin Christianity, many Byzantine literati of the time devoted treatises to the procession of the Holy Spirit. As was the case with authoring anti-Islamic works, writing treatises on the procession was also very popular; both the Orthodox and convert Catholics wrote such works, among them Makarios of Ankyra, Joseph Bryennios, Manuel Kalekas and Demetrios Chrysoloras. Thus, like the *Dialogue with a Persian*, this treatise by Manuel should again be considered within the dominant 'trends' of his times and circle. The discussions here will focus on some trends in Manuel's philosophical/theological thought and again, on the literary features of the work.

It has been demonstrated that in the lengthy treatise, Manuel demonstrates knowledge of both Byzantine and Latin theological traditions.[83] As previously discussed, the emperor also reveals the influence of Palamas. Indeed, the treatise includes extensive discussions on the distinction between essence and energies that agree with the doctrines of Palamas. Moreover, Manuel makes a brief reference to the light on Mount Thabor within the context of energies.[84] The emperor also demonstrates a knowledge of Thomas Aquinas through the latter's Greek translations.[85] At first glance, this may be surprising given the emperor's Orthodox and Palamite theological stance; however, as previously pointed out, Orthodox theologians and even those with Palamite views consulted Aquinas as well as other Latin theologians. If nothing else, they could draw support from these Latin works in their own arguments. For instance, Manuel's grandfather John Kantakouzenos not only supported the translations of Aquinas, but was also influenced by his arguments that man could not know God directly but only what was reflected from Him.[86] Moreover, he cited this theologian while combatting the arguments of Prochoros Kydones, an anti-Palamite and adherent of Aquinas.[87] Kantakouzenos thus sought to use Prochoros' his own 'weapon' against him.

In *On the Procession*, Manuel adopts the same stance as his grandfather: to use Aquinas while seeking to refute the views of the theologian's adherents. Namely, he refers to Aquinas not because he wishes to engage

[82] See Meyendorff, *Byzantine Theology*, 91–100; Kolbaba, 'Council of Lyon', 43–68; A. Papadakis, *The Christian East and the Rise of the Papacy: The Church 1071–1453 A.D* (New York, 1994) and A. Papadakis, 'The Byzantines and the Rise of Papacy'.
[83] *On the Procession of the Holy Spirit*, xi-xxxix.   [84] See Chapter 6.
[85] Demetracopoulos, 'Palamas', 334–9 and 'Dignitas Hominis' 393 and 400.
[86] Demetracopoulos, 'Palamas', 292–305. The author proposes that Kantakouzenos introduced a 'Thomistic Palamism'.
[87] Triantafyllopoulos, 'The Thomist base', 419; *Ioahannis Cantacouzeni refutationes duae Prochori Cydonii et Disputatio cum Paulo Patriarcha Latino epistulis septem tradita*. eds. E. Voordeckers and F. Tinnefeld. (Brepols, 1987)

deeply with the Latin arguments, but as a means to refute his opponent and
further solidify his own position. While refuting the argument that essence
and energy may be interpreted as synonyms, the emperor refers to a passage
from Aquinas where the multiplicity of divine names is treated through the
use of Aristotelian logic. In this instance, it has been demonstrated that
Manuel combines Kydones' translation of Aquinas with the arguments of
Joseph Calotheos, a fourteenth-century Orthodox theologian.[88] Although
he uses Aquinas to defend his Orthodox and Palamite views, his consultation of Kydones' translation still shows that Manuel, like many of his
contemporaries, was receptive to Latin theology, at least to a degree.

   With regard to the procession, Manuel wholeheartedly defends the
Orthodox doctrine of a single procession in which the Spirit proceedes
from the Father alone. To summarize, he argued that procession (*ekpor-
eusis*) of the Spirit has to be distinguished from its hypostatic emanation
(*hypostatike proodos*). The latter is caused only by the Father and the
temporal energetic emanation (*energetike proodos, ekfanasis*) of the Spirit.
This emanates from all three hypostases in their common energy. This is
not to be confused with the procession, he argued. All the Scriptural
passages speaking of the Son as giving, sending or distributing the
Spirit – cited by the Latins to support their cause – should be understood
as referring to this energetic emanation, and not procession.[89]

   It has been convincingly argued that in the sense that he strictly follows
the traditional arguments, Manuel does not add any distinctive, novel
theological arguments to the debates.[90] However, this point also needs to
be treated cautiously by scholars. While Manuel is certainly not, for
instance, a Gregory of Cyprus, it should be remembered that strict adherence to Scripture and the Fathers was the norm in Byzantine theological
texts. Furthermore, coming up with new arguments could be equated to
'innovating' (καινοτομία), that is, distorting and adding personal beliefs to
the doctrines. On occasion, this could elicit accusations of heresy. Thus, as
in the case of the *Dialogue with a Persian*, Manuel operated carefully within
this framework of Byzantine theological traditions. He did not need to, or
wish to, offer new discussions and ideas, and his treatise was therefore not
expected to create new arguments. Its intended function was rather to
refute Latin claims by upholding traditional Orthodox doctrines.[91]

---

[88] Demetracopoulos, 'Palamas', 292–305, identified Manuel's sources and makes these arguments.
Procession of the Holy Spirit, 157.
[89] Dendrinos, *On the Procession of the Holy Spirit*, xxxvii–iii, for an extensive summary of Manuel's
arguments.
[90] Dendrinos, *On the Procession of the Holy Spirit*, xxxviii.   [91] See Chapter 5 on this issue.

As in the *Dialogue with a Persian*, Manuel's range of discussion in *On the Procession* is broad: the refutation of specific Latin arguments concerning the Trinity and the procession, essence and energies, *theosis,* the pursuit of knowledge of God, the relationship between God and his creation, man's salvation and papal supremacy. The present discussion will focus on only some select aspects, such as Manuel's views of syllogisms, his insight into Latin theology and the relationship between theology and philosophy. These key themes offer insight into Manuel's philosophical and theological thought, as well as forming links with his other works.

While many other literati indeed wrote such treatises following the traditional arguments, it is worth noting that no treatise is identical with any other. Even when the authors share the same theological stance, one can observe differences among them, and each author has his own particular interests.[92] For instance, while Manuel's *Dialogue with a Persian* is an extensive explanation of the Christian dogma and a detailed refutation of Islam, Makarios Makres' treatise on Islam focuses on virginity in both religions, indicating his own interests as a monk. Similarly, in his own treatise on the procession, Makarios of Ankyra especially focuses on canons, ecumenical councils and the emperor's rights over the Church. By contrast, these topics are absent in the emperor's work. He instead has extensive discussions on the use of syllogisms, the boundaries between theology and philosophy and the limits of human reason in divine matters.

Previously, these issues had been discussed in the *Discourse to Iagoup*; they are themes in which Manuel seems to have had a lifelong interest. The first chapters of the treatise are entirely devoted the issue of the use of syllogisms and philosophy in theology. The emperor discusses these topics as deeply as he discusses the specific points regarding the procession. Indeed, many Orthodox theologians objected to these methods of theological inquiry. For instance, Makarios of Ankyra refers to this issue in his own treatise and exhibits the same stance as Manuel. Although, like the emperor, he also opposes both, when the treatises of Manuel and Makarios are compared, the emperor comes across as being far more interested in these matters. At times, the discussion of syllogisms and the use of philosophy dominates the text, and it appears throughout the entire treatise. In contrast, Makarios' treatment of this issue is brief. He is much more interested in canon law and Church councils, in which he seems to have found a strong base for rejecting papal primacy. Although it may adhere to

---

[92] See Argyriou, *Makres-Islam*, 238–330 for the text; 57–9 and 176–7 for the editor's comments concerning the role of virginity in the treatise.

traditional arguments, *On the Procession of the Holy Spirit* should be still considered as a reflection of Manuel's own particular interests.

As in the *Discourse to Iagoup*, Manuel argues that theological inquiry cannot be subjected to *techne* (τέχνη) – that is, to syllogisms or any other such philosophical method. Once more, he is manifesting his adherence to Orthodox doctrines. The emperor targets the proponents of Scholastic theology, the Latins, the pro-Latin Byzantines and the anti-Palamites. According to him, the divine transcends the human mind and understanding. Thus, the divine cannot be reached through syllogisms, dialectic or philosophical speculation. Not only are these methods futile in theological inquiry, it is also wrong to employ them since the divine cannot be subjected to human reason. Theologians are divinely inspired, and it is God's voice that speaks within them.

As has been pointed out by the editor of the treatise, in order to refute the syllogistic Latin arguments, Manuel also had to resort to the same method, at least to a degree.[93] The refutations of syllogistic arguments also required syllogisms, and thus, to an extent, employing them was inevitable for both their supporters and opponents. Moreover, the Fathers also employed logical reasoning in their works. Both in this treatise and the *Discourse to Iagoup*, Manuel points out that this is precisely the only legitimate use of syllogisms and philosophy: to defend the doctrines and combat their opponents using their own methods.

Manuel further accuses his Latin opponent of *techne*, lifting sentences from Scripture and weaving them together to suit his own arguments. This is not God's voice, Manuel argues, but the Latin's own, human creation, and it is plainly wrong.[94] He also argues that those who treat theology as a branch of philosophy exceed the limits of the latter. 'The subject of philosophy', Manuel writes, 'is existing things, that of theology is He who is above existence'.[95] Again, as in the *Discourse to Iagoup*, the emperor is clearly setting out boundaries between these two disciplines. For him, theology should deal with divine matters and philosophy only with worldly existence. In his later ethico-political works, the emperor would adhere to the division he envisions.

This above-mentioned passage is of the utmost importance for manifesting Manuel's stance in these matters. Both the *Discourse to Iagoup* and *On the Procession* indicate that Manuel saw the perceived relationship

---

[93] *On the Procession of the Holy Spirit*, 19, xxii. See also Demetracopoulos, 'Dignitas Hominis', 393–4.
[94] *On the Procession of the Holy Spirit*, 5–12.
[95] *On the Procession of the Holy Spirit*, 16–17 '. . . τῷ γὰρ μὴ κεράσαι τούτους θελῆσαι τὴν φιλοσοφίαν τῇ μετριότητι . . . .'; 'ὕλη γὰρ φιλοσοφίᾳ τὰ ὄντα, θεολογίᾳ δὲ ὁ ὑπὲρ τὰ ὄντα.', 18.

between philosophy and theology as a problematic one that required clarification. Clearly, he did not agree to the use of philosophy as in Latin theology.
The emperor merely points out that it is useful to know philosophy as it helps
to refute syllogisms. This was an established Orthodox position that was also
promulgated by late Palaiologan theologians such as Makarios of Ankyra,
John Kantakouzenos and John Bryennios. Thus, despite their friendship,
Manuel's views on the use of philosophy differed from Demetrios Kydones,
also coming nowhere near the Neo-platonism of Plethon: the emperor
envisioned philosophy as pertaining only to worldly matters.

It has been demonstrated that in *On the Procession* Manuel displays
knowledge of the current problems of the Catholic Church. The emperor
fiercely condemns the Avignon schism, which, he significantly claims,
came into being through the excessive use of philosophy in the study of
theology. Even on this occasion, he lays the blame on syllogisms and
philosophical reasoning. Manuel also criticizes threats to excommunicate
the Avignonese pope. He moreover refers to the existence of a 'moderate'
party that was against such measures, a group led by the chancellor of the
University of Paris, Jean Gerson. The emperor even briefly mentions the
differences between the Franciscans and the Dominicans concerning
the Immaculate Conception.[96] In keeping with his era – a time of intense
contact between the Orthodox and Latin Christianity – Manuel is well
informed about the current problems and trends of the latter.

He furthermore makes an interesting reference to 'the threat of fire' in
relation to the divergent thoughts within the Catholic Church. Perhaps, he
was referring to the practice of death by fire.[97] Manuel's tone is noticeably
critical as he himself was firmly against the use of violence in matters of faith.
Like Makarios of Ankyra, who has left a detailed description of a fresco icon
of the Throne of Grace, Manuel also briefly discusses Latin iconography. He
was no doubt inspired by his extensive tours of European churches, but his
own discussion is brief and less detailed than that of Makarios of Ankyra.[98]

---

[96] The Immaculate Conception refers to the conception of the Virgin by St Anne as being free from
sin. This is a Catholic doctrine; in Orthodox theology, it was Mary who was holy and pure, and not
her conception. See F. Dvornik, 'The Byzantine Church and the Immaculate Conception', in *The
Dogma of Immaculate Conception: Its History and Significance*, ed. E. D. O' Conor (Indiana, 1958),
87–112. Henceforth, Dvornik, 'Immaculate Conception'.

[97] *On the Procession of the Holy Spirit*, 20–1. '... ὡς πυρὸς ἀπειλὴ καλύπτει....' Dendrinos has
identified this 'moderate party' as the group led by Jean Gerson, xvii. He has also associated this
'threat of fire' with the death penalty imposed by the Church, pointing out that such trials took
place during Manuel's stay in London, 384.

[98] Makarios of Ankyra, 336–7; *On the Procession of the Holy Spirit*, 30–3. Manuel criticizes the divergent
depictions found in the Latin icons and how they portray the Spirit as emanating from both the Father
and the Son.

On the Procession of the Holy Spirit also touches upon the question of identity. As in the *Discourse to Iagoup,* Manuel comments on Byzantine and Latin identities, but this time, he only touches upon the religious aspect of these identities. This selectiveness was probably influenced by the context; the treatise was not an attack on a convert who had left his *patris,* but a refutation of Latin theology. In the treatise, contrasts between 'us' and 'you' are sprinkled throughout.[99] Similarly, religious conversion is imagined as a change between these two opposing groups. Latinophrones leave 'us' to join 'you', and whoever leaves 'you' at once becomes 'our' brother. Yet, Manuel admits that there is still some common ground between these two opposing groups, such as the excessive use of philosophy. The emperor likewise points out that Gregory of Nazianzos is admired by both Byzantines and Latins.[100]

Ultimately, the Byzantines and the Latins are envisioned as separate, opposing blocks with some similarities. The Latinophrone Byzantines emerge as the 'guilty' party in the disagreements between the two groups: 'Some of our people', Manuel writes on the Latinophones, 'that differ from us regarding their thoughts on divinity . . . '. The emperor argues that it is the Latinophone Byzantines who cause clashes between the two groups, since they have abandoned their own *patris* and try to be of like mind with the Latins. He points out that they flock to foreign lands like fugitives though no one chases them.[101] This final claim has a defensive ring to it, especially when one considers the measures taken against the anti-Palamites and the Catholic converts in 1396, which caused some of them to leave Constantinople, including Kydones.

One final, important insight provided by *On the Procession,* is that of Manuel's views on a Church union. Although the treatise refutes the Latin arguments on papal supremacy, the emperor is clearly not averse to the idea of a Church union.[102] His treatise is also not polemical; for instance, it contains no insults or harsh words. Even the introduction hints that Manuel did not intend for his treatise to be polemical; indeed the title explicitly states that the text was not composed *against* the Latins. This stands in stark contrast to Makarios of Ankyra, who, unlike the emperor,

---

[99] For some such instances, see *On the Procession of the Holy Spirit,* 22, 55, 59, 62, 194, 221, 223–5, 230.
[100] *On the Procession of the Holy Spirit,* 22, 194.
[101] *On the Procession of the Holy Spirit,* 58–9. '. . . Ὅτι τινὲς τῶν ἡμετέρων ἡμῶν διαστάντες τῇ περὶ τὸ θεῖον δόξῃ . . .', and 'ἐπίδηδες συγκρούειν ὑμᾶς ἡμῖν καὶ διϊστᾶν ὅση δύναμις . . . πρὸς τὴν ἀλλοτρίαν καθάπερ φυγάδες ᾤχοντο παρὰ μηδενὸς διωκόμενοι.'
[102] Manuel devotes three chapters to papal supremacy, rejecting it, *On the Procession of the Holy Spirit,* 273–82. On papal supremacy, see F. Dvornik, *Byzantium and the Roman Primacy,* trans. E. A. Quain (New York, 1966).

continuously blamed the Schism entirely on the Latins, and referred to their faith as being evil (κακοδοξία).[103] Manuel, on the other hand, laments the Schism as 'the breaking of the limbs of Christ'.[104] This same stance towards the Latins, either in terms of religion or politics, can be traced in the emperor's other works. Manuel does not make disparaging comments about them, either in reference to the Catholic Christians, Italians or to other Western Europeans. Thus, his Orthodoxy should not be equated with an 'anti-Latin' perspective.[105]

Still, while not averse to the idea of a union, Manuel does envisage a union on Orthodox terms and concludes his treatise by expressing his wish that the two parties come together. Significantly, he points out that this will be possible only if the Latins accept that the Spirit proceeded from the Father alone: namely, the Orthodox position.[106] Although the papacy did wish to impose its own views for the union, but, in some ways, so too did Manuel. In interpreting his stance, it is of importance to remember, however, that both the Council of Lyons and the Council of Florence were concluded on Latin terms. None of these unions, agreed with a great concessions on the Orthodox side, brought any significant political benefit; likewise, the conversion of John V was in vain. Perhaps, the emperor feared that the Church union would only further divide Byzantine society without bringing any benefit. It is in this context that the Byzantine courtier and historian Sphrantzes famously portrayed Manuel as warning his son John VIII on the possible social strife a union might bring about.[107]

Furthermore, one should keep in mind that in the eyes of Manuel and those of his contemporaries, a Church union was not a mere political event. The theological issues discussed were not inconsequential or trivial points, they formed the very core of faith. This was not something that Manuel and like-minded Byzantines could sacrifice for political or military help. Their Orthodox faith, in turn, regulated a great part of lives, and it was an

---

[103] *On the Procession of the Holy Spirit*, 1. See Makarios of Ankyra, 33, 50, 362, 366, for a few such references.

[104] *On the Procession of the Holy Spirit*, 30, '... δεῖ γὰρ καὶ θρηνῆσαι πικρὸν ἐνταῦθα ... ὥστε διαρρῆξαι τὰ τοῦ Χριστοῦ μέλη.' See also pages 271–85. Makarios of Ankyra, 362, claims that a group from the French *parlement* visited Manuel during his stay in Paris to discuss the Church union.

[105] For the fluidity of the relations between the Orthodox 'East' and the Catholic 'West', see M. Plested, 'Reconfiguring East and West', 21–46.

[106] *On the Procession of the Holy Spirit*, 316–17. 'συνελθῶμεν ἀλλήλοις, ὦ φίλοι, τὸ τοῦ Χριστοῦ ποίμνιον ... τὸ δὲ συνελθεῖν ἔσται πῶς; Ἂν Θεὸν ἕνα μὲν τὴν παναιτίαν Τριάδα εἶναι φρονῶμεν ... ταῦτα δὴ φρονοῦντες καὶ λέγοντες, ἀναίτιον μὲν τὸν Πατέρα νοῶμεν, αἰτιατὸν δὲ οὐδαμῶς, γεννητὸν δὲ τὸν Υἱὸν μόνον ἐκ μόνου τοῦ φύσαντος καὶ τὸ Πνεῦμα ἐκπορευτὸν ἐκ τοῦ ἀναιτίου καὶ οὐχ ἑτέρωθεν.'

[107] Sphrantzes, 83.

indispensable component of their identity. While treatise does not have a harsh polemical tone, it also embodies the firmness of Manuel's ideas regarding the Church union.

On the Procession: Some Literary Observations

The literary aspects of this work also deserve discussion. As opposed to a 'dry' theological treatise that merely examines one argument after the other, Manuel's *Procession* is an elegant composition with flashes of humour and a strong literary quality. With regard to its literary style, *On the Procession* stands out from other such contemporary theological treatises. For instance, Manuel's quotations of sources are well-blended into his text; the treatise does not come across as a web of quoted sentences. By contrast, Makarios of Ankyra's treatise on the procession or Kantakouzenos' refutations of Prochoros Kydones and the papal legate Paul, can at times read as a pastiche of quotations.[108]

Manuel alternates between long and short sentences in order to ease the flow of this complicated treatise. The emperor's distinct language, including his preferred vocabulary and imagery, is still reflected in the treatise, and Manuel adorns the work with well-crafted imagery and allusions. By contrast, Makarios of Ankyra's work does not contain one single Classical allusion, nor does his treatise on the procession contain any imagery or metaphors. Even though Manuel fiercely criticizes the use of philosophy in theology, his treatise is peppered with literary allusions to Plato and Aristotle.[109]

At times, Manuel also employs Homeric allusions in order to ridicule his opponent. He wittily envisions a 'Siren of the Holy Spirit' and likens the Latins to the sailors who block their ears with wax. Even while discussing a serious theological topic such as the procession, the emperor preserves his sense of humour and a penchant for literary features. Moreover, Manuel's vivid language colours his polemics against the Latin monk and his own self-representation. On many occasions, he mocks his opponent through the use of his customary sea imagery, for instance he describes the Latin as being continuously tossed by waves of blasphemy, seeking refuge in the harbours of syllogism, yet buffeted by his own arguments and eventually sinking.[110]

---

[108] Ioahannis Cantacouzeni Refutationes.
[109] *On the Procession of the Holy Spirit*, 202; Plato, *Phaedo*, 71b, *Procession of the Holy Spirit*, 109.
[110] *On the Procession of the Holy Spirit*, 32, 139, 199, 229 for a few such instances.

As in the *Discourse to Iagoup*, battle imagery is also employed, albeit less frequently. The Latin is described as shooting an argument at the emperor, but his missile turns against him and his bow is back to its unbent position. Elsewhere, the Latin's argument is described as fleeing from him to join Manuel's ranks: it fights its own advocate, having now become the emperor's weapon.[111] Once more, Manuel seems to have attempted to create a more literary text as opposed to a 'dry, academic' theological treatise. The emperor's unusual interest in incorporating allusions, metaphors, imagery and humour into a theological treatise demonstrates his desire to imbue his works with literary qualities.

While the treatise is not a dialogue and hence lacks visible characters, the presence of both Manuel and his opponent are very much felt within the text. Although the work may lack a harsh polemical tone, the Latin monk is still depicted as being arrogant and easily overpowered in arguments. Like the *müderris* in the *Dialogue with a Persian*, he is continuously compared to a child. 'You cannot leap from one spot to another', Manuel exclaims to his opponent concerning his use of syllogisms, 'like sparrows playing on tree branches'.[112] In contrast, the emperor's own voice in the text is calm and confident. He undermines all arguments with utmost conviction and never misses an occasion to point out how easily he does so. He continuously patronizes his opponent with phrases like: 'you have now learnt this' 'heed these words' 'I would advise you' or 'I would pay a lot to see you set right . . . '.[113] Manuel thus openly represents himself as the superior discussant and scholar.

Through his self-representation, as in the *Dialogue with a Persian* and the *Discourse to Iagoup*, the emperor strives to put himself forth as a theological authority. The text of the treatise contains many indications that, like his other works, Manuel intended for it to be circulated. An anonymous oration dated to post-1402 indeed makes a reference to *On the Procession*.[114] It is important to stress that although composed as a reply to a Latin tract, the treatise's intended audience was a Byzantine one. Not only is it in Greek, there is also no indication that Manuel ever attempted to have it translated into Latin. Thus, his defence of the Orthodox doctrines, and to a degree of Palamite views, were aimed at a Byzantine audience. Regarding issues such as the procession, the distinction between essence and energies, the use syllogisms and the boundaries between

---

[111] *On the Procession of the Holy Spirit*, 115, 170 and 306.
[112] *On the Procession of the Holy Spirit*, 109.
[113] *On the Procession of the Holy Spirit*, 173, 178, 202, 254, 256 for a few such examples.
[114] See *On the Procession of the Holy Spirit*, 10, 378 for direct references to an audience, 'ὦ παρόντες'. Dendrinos, *Anonymous Oration*, 449.

philosophy and theology, Manuel seeks to advertise and legitimize his own views. More than the European Latin theologians, it is the pro-Latin and anti-Palamite Byzantines upon whom Manuel was trying to impose his views. Since Manuel was no ordinary author, but the emperor, his defence of the Orthodox dogma and Palamism lends them political sanction. Once more, the emperor attempts to become not only a political, but also a theological authority.

Alongside the persona of a model scholar of theology, Manuel also represents himself as a dutiful emperor through subtle references to his long journey. Both in the title and the preface, he appears as 'the *autokrator* of the Romans, who is abroad in France'.[115] On one occasion Manuel even concludes a chapter by claiming that circumstances do not allow him to reply further. He is engaged in affairs in which, should he be successful, the whole *genos* will be saved. If he fails, however, it will be shipwrecked.[116] Manuel thus ensures that his audience is reminded of the burdens he has undertaken on his journey by incorporating subtle political messages in his theological treatise. As always, he is present in the text not as any author, but as the emperor.

The *ekphrasis* and the Final Months

Manuel's stay in Paris also witnessed the creation of his famous *ekphrasis* of a tapestry in the Louvre depicting spring and children playing outdoors.[117] It has been argued that the fact that Manuel chose to describe this tapestry rather than any other thing he had seen in Paris, is a manifestation of his respect for tradition, since the topic fits well with the theme of spring found in Byzantine textual tradition.[118] While the emperor draws on the works of Libanios and Gregory of Nazianzos, his own voice still dominates the *ekphrasis*. The scene opens with the description of the riverbanks; our gaze is then directed to a boy catching fish with his hands. This vivid imagery is followed by a description of the birds and various insects, and the scene ends with a loving description of young children playing in the garden. The whole work is adorned with alliteration and the imagery is

[115] *On the Procession of the Holy Spirit*, 1*, 2.   [116] *On the Procession of the Holy Spirit*, 125.
[117] The most extensive study is Davis, 'Ekphrasis'. See also G. Peers, 'Manuel II Palaeologos' Ekphrasis on a Tapestry in the Louvre: Word Over Image', *REB 61* (2003), 201–14 and P. Agapitos, E. Metse and M. Hinterberger, Εἰκών καὶ Λόγος: Ἑξι Βυζαντινές Περιγραφές Ἔργων τέχνης (Athens, 2006), 121–2. Henceforth, Peers, 'Ekphrasis'.
[118] Davis, 'Ekphrasis', 146–7.

lively; it is as if we are taking a walk in the surroundings Manuel describes.[119]

Even the scholars who view the *ekphrasis* positively, have regarded this work as merely a pleasant rhetorical exercise, perhaps indicating an optimistic and sunny mood on Manuel's part.[120] However, there is no evidence that Manuel himself or a member of his Byzantine audience would have regarded this work as such, or as in any way less 'serious' a work. Though it is true that students might have composed such texts in school, it does not mean that an *ekphrasis* was not perceived as a piece worthy of attention. While a modern scholar may be tempted to view a Byzantine letter as a more literary text and an *ekphrasis* simply as a rhetorical exercise, the Byzantine authors and audience had no such distinction for *logoi*. The care that Manuel devoted to imagery, alliteration and sound harmony in the *ekphrasis* again reveals his quest for textual aesthetics. The *ekphrasis* may not have deep theological, philosophical or political undertones, but we should not dismiss it out of hand. For Manuel and his audience, the work was not simply a frivolous, meaningless schoolbook exercise. On the contrary, the emperor composed the text in order to allow the audience to experience what he had seen, delighting in the harmony of the sounds and imagery.

Apart from his writings, Manuel's other activities during his second stay in Paris are unknown. It was clear by then, however, that no help from any Western ruler was forthcoming. Manuel's European mission is often considered a failure by scholars, and though it was clearly not a success, the political situation in Europe needs to be taken into consideration in any analysis. First, none of the rulers, be it in England, France, Denmark or the Italian cities, had any real motive for sending help to Constantinople. Any military or economic support would, in essence, have been an act of charity, since the Byzantine Empire had nothing to offer in exchange for help. Rescuing Constantinople from the 'infidel' was indeed a strong ideological motive, but there was little practicality in the notion. Likewise, although preventing the fall of Constantinople would have slowed the Ottoman expansion into the Balkans, and into Europe in general, this incursion into the European continent did not pose an immediate threat to these European polities – they were simply

---

[119] See R. Webb, *Ekphrasis, Imagination and Persuasion in Ancient Rhetorical Theory and Practice* (Farnham, 2009), especially 10–27 and 71, who argues that the goal of an *ekphrasis* was to give the audience a verbal experience of what was being described; it was a verbal work of art.

[120] Davis, 'Ekphrasis', 421; Peers, 'Ekphrasis', 203–5. Barker, *Manuel II*, 192 and J. Harris, *End of Byzantium* (New Haven and London, 2010), 19. Henceforth, Harris, *End of Byzantium*.

too far away. While it is true that hosting Manuel would have boosted their prestige among their own people and abroad, going any further than duties as a host had little concrete benefit for the European rulers.

Moreover, the years 1399–1402 were a particularly problematic period for many Western rulers: the papacy was still divided between Rome and Avignon; the Italian cities were struggling with the attacks of Gian Galeazzo Visconti; and in turn, Visconti was too preoccupied with his own battles to offer Manuel any assistance, and died shortly thereafter, in September 1402. Likewise, France – Manuel's intended destination when he first set out – was ruled by a mentally unstable king. Charles' illness returned soon after Manuel's arrival in Paris and his mental health would only decline further in coming years. The temporary regency created by the king's three uncles focused its energies on preserving the government from being shattered by his illness. Despite the promise of sending Boucicaut to Constantinople with an army, France was too engrossed by its own internal struggles.

In England, Henry IV had just ascended the throne after having deposed Richard II in an uprising. He was essentially a usurper and was also grappling with many troubles of his own: heretical controversies, economic problems, rebellions and hostility from Scotland. Furthermore, his rule was contested by many members of the English nobility.[121] Under such circumstances, it is perhaps natural that none of these polities offered sufficient help to Constantinople. The situation in Western Europe was thus a significant obstacle in Manuel's quest for help abroad. Despite the promises and assurances that had given Manuel so much hope, the negative outcome of his mission was not a surprise.

By spring 1402, arrangements were being made for the emperor's return journey. Although several scholars have proposed that Manuel actually did not intend to return to his besieged capital, possibly considering lingering on in Europe for good, the Venetian Senate records refute this claim. They indicate that in spring 1402, Manuel's return journey was being discussed in earnest. The journey was delayed only because of an outbreak of plague in Modon, where the emperor would disembark. Moreover, in the case of an Ottoman invasion, the Venetian Senate had already promised Despot Theodore and Manuel's family refuge in Venice. Therefore is reasonable to believe that a similar arrangement would have been made for Manuel to reside in Venice with his family as opposed to him living in Paris, a dependent of the

---

[121] See *The New Cambridge Medieval History*, vol. 6, ed. M. Jones (Cambridge, 2008).

French king.[122] In short, there was no need for the emperor to stay in France should Constantinople fall.

Bayezid's Fall, Manuel's Return

In July 1402, something happened that can only described as nothing short of a miracle. Manuel's long-standing nemesis Bayezid was defeated and captured by the Mongol ruler Tamerlane at the Battle of Ankara. The blockade of Constantinople suddenly evaporated and the Ottoman empire disintegrated: the subjugated Turkish emirates declared their independence and Bayezid's sons started fighting each other for the Ottoman throne. In one stroke, events took a whole different turn. The exact moment when Manuel heard the news is not known, but by August the French court had received a full report of events.

The importance of this can be traced in both Byzantine and Western texts. The *Chronicle of Saint Denis* notes the joy of the French nobles, and Ursins recounts in detail how Bayezid was promenaded in chains by Tamerlane. The author of *Vita Ricardi* gives us a fanciful account of the battle, describing how Manuel returned in time to see the dead Christian soldiers on the ground, miraculously facing right.[123] The Byzantine texts are even more excited. The authors relish the fate of Bayezid, narrating how he was imprisoned by Tamerlane, his wealth confiscated, and his wife forced to serve as a wine bearer.[124] They also note with satisfaction how both the victor and the vanquished shared the same faith, a point that was meant to make Bayezid's defeat even more shameful.[125]

---

[122] Thiriet, *Régestes*, II, no. 1039, 23, no. 1055, 27; Iorga, *Notes et Extraits*, II, 118–19. For these claims, see G. Ostrogorsky, *History of the Byzantine State* (New Brunswick, 1957), 494 and Harris, *End of Byzantium*, 19.

[123] *Chronique de Saint Denis*, XXII, iii, 50–1; Ursins, 423; *Vita Ricardi*, 169–70. On Tamerlane's campaign in Anatolia, see M. M. Alexandrescu-Dersca, *La campagne de Timur en Anatolie (1402)* (Athens, 1956). For the Western reactions on the Battle of Ankara as reflected in diplomatic correspondence, see A. Knobler, 'The Rise of Timur and Western Diplomatic Response, 1390–1405', *Journal of the Royal Asiatic Society of Great Britain and Ireland* 3, 5 (1995), 314–49.

[124] Schreiner, *Kleinchroniken*, Chronik 7/25; 12/ 7, 11/ 22, 29;/49, 10. Ottoman chroniclers Aşıkpaşazade and Neşri narrate the battle. They also speak of a possibility that Bayezid may have committed suicide on account of his deep grief. Aşıkpaşazade, 105–8; Neşri, 349–63. Moreover, Neşri narrates that Bayezid was exhibited in a cage by Tamerlane. *Anonymous Tevârîh*, 46–9, reports the same. Interestingly, these stories about a cage have parallels in the accounts of Ursins, 423 and Doukas, 109.

[125] See Doukas, 87–91 and 99–103; Chortasmenos, 'Address to Manuel', 218–19; Isidore of Kiev, 'Panegyric', 162–3. On Tamerlane's conquest policies and his use of force, see B. Forbes Manz, *The Rise and the Rule of Tamerlane* (Cambridge, 1989), especially 15.

Manuel celebrated the occasion with two short works, a hymn of thanksgiving and an *ethopoiia* of Tamerlane addressing Bayezid.[126] Both pieces reflect Manuel's great joy at the fall of his nemesis. As in his letters and in the *Dialogue with a Persian*, the emperor's very personal and particular hatred for this sultan is evident. In many of his works, Manuel expands on Bayezid's portrait in detail, and his allusions and imagery have the most degrading connotations. Such portrayals are not found for the other sultans, whose depictions generally do not go beyond the commonplace. We must not forget that the relationship between the two had also been one of frequent personal contact: in 1390, Bayezid had used Manuel as a hostage to force John V to dismantle fortifications; later, they had spent a long time together fighting in a campaign that had been so humiliating for Manuel; the Serres episode in 1394 had been yet another turning point, prompting Manuel to disobey Bayezid and initiating the siege of Constantinople. In short, Manuel and Bayezid's deeper personal conflicts went beyond their political enmity as Byzantine and Ottoman rulers.

In these pieces, too, Bayezid is depicted as an epitome of arrogance, hostility and irrational behaviour. In the hymn he tries to rival God, even dreaming of subjecting the heavens to his rule; he boasts of his wealth and allies in a portrayal that of course, calls Xerxes to mind. Even the title of the *ethopoiia* is derogatory towards Bayezid. Whereas Tamerlane is the 'leader' (ὁ ἐξηγούμενος) of the Persians and the Scythians, Bayezid is called the 'tyrant' of the Turks, and his rule is thus effectively 'delegitimized'. Many sources reports stories that Bayezid and Tamerlane exchanged insulting letters in which they supposedly told each other that the vanquished should be divorced of all his wives, a very harsh insult in Islamic cultures.[127] It is tempting therefore to ponder whether the emperor knew of these personal exchanges while composing the *ethopoiia*.

The characterization of Tamerlane in the text is especially worth noting. He speaks entirely with Manuel's voice, for instance, pointing out the volatility of human affairs to Bayezid. This is a philosophical concept that was greatly favoured by the emperor in his own ethico-political works. Tamerlane complains that Bayezid is not a man of great virtue as he had

---

[126] These works are found in *Lettres de l'empereur Manuel Paleologue*, ed. E. Legrand (Amsterdam, 1962), 103–4. Barker, *Manuel II*, 516–17, has English translations. See Appendix 5 for my own translation of the *ethopoiia*.

[127] See Clavijo, 71; Ibn Arabshah, *Timur the Great Amir*, trans. J. H. Sanders (London, 1936), 188–9; *Anonymous Tevârîh*, 38–9. Aşıkpaşazde, 103, does not mention the insults concerning the wives, but notes that Bayezid's reply to Tamerlane's ambassador was harsh; 'darblû.' Henceforth, Ibn Arabshah.

previously believed him to be, for he does not bear up under misfortune in a manly manner. This notion also comes across as an important mark of the virtuous man in Manuel's ethico-political works.[128] As in the case of Manuel's arguments concerning the success of the Ottomans, Tamerlane assigns Bayezid's former victories to fortune, not to virtue. 'Let all the gold, all the spoils, all your great wealth be gone', he sighs, 'the glory I desired is absent. I now see that my toil was in vain'.[129] Manuel takes his ultimate revenge by using Tamerlane as a mouthpiece, and the work concludes that Bayezid's base character has made even Tamerlane's victory utterly worthless.

European and Byzantine Reflections

Manuel left Paris on 21 November 1402.[130] His voyage in Europe had lasted almost three and a half years and did not bring about any material assistance. Instead, Byzantium was momentarily saved by the 'miracle' of Tamerlane. Manuel's long stay in Paris might not have brought him any political benefits, but for its part the French court would preserve memories of the Byzantine emperor, and his figure would grace numerous artefacts.[131]

Around 1402–3, the king's uncle Jean de Berry purchased medallions depicting Constantine and Herakleios.[132] These medallions are not of Byzantine origin and were bought from Antonio Mancini, a Florentine merchant living in Paris.[133] Jean de Berry's inventories dating to 1413–14

---

[128] For a few such instances, see *Foundations of Imperial Conduct*, cols. 353 and 356.

[129] "Ἐρρέτω τοίνυν χρυσός, ἐρρέτω λάφυρον ἅπαν καὶ ὁ πολύς σοι πλοῦτος πολλαχόθεν συνειλεγμένος, ἀπούσης δόξης ἧς ἥρων', see footnote 125.

[130] *Chronique de Saint Denis*, XXIII, iii, 450–1.

[131] The pioneering works on the impact of Manuel's visit on French art are C. Marinesco, 'Deux empereurs byzantins en Occident: Manuel II et Jean VIII Paléologue, vus par des artistes parisiens et italiens', *Bulletin de la Société Nationale des Antiquaires de France* (1958), 38–40 and P. H. Spaak, 'Deux empereurs byzantins, Manuel II et Jean VIII Paléologue, vus par des artistes occidentaux', *Le Flambeau*, nov.–déc. (1957),758–62.

[132] These medals are recorded in the duke's inventories, Guiffrey, *Inventoires de Jean de Berry*, I, 72, no. 199 and 200. The appearance of the medals is described in detail, including the formulae on them. See also Meiss, *French Art*, 54–5; R. Weiss, 'The Medieval Medallions of Constantine and Heraklios', *Numismatic Chronicle* VII, 3 (1963), 129–44 and H. Th. Colenbrander, 'The Limburg Brothers, the 'Joyaux' of Constantine and Heraclius, the Très Riches Heures and the Visit of the Byzantine Emperor Manuel II Palaeologus', in *Flanders in a European Perspective. Manuscript Illumination Around 1400 in Flanders and Abroad. Proceedings of the International Colloquium of Illuminated Manuscripts, Leuven 7–10 September*, eds. M. Smeyers and B. Cardon (Leuven, 1995), 171–84. Henceforth, Colenbrander, 'Limbourg Brothers'.

[133] Along with the medallions, Antonio Mancini sold the duke two *tables d'or* depicting John the Baptist and the legend of St Eugenia, decorated with precious stones and Greek inscriptions. Colenbranders suggests that Mancini might have bought those (but not the medallions) from Manuel himself, who needed money as he was about to set onto his return journey. Colenbrander, 'Limbourg Brothers', 179.

show that he possessed other such medallions, those of Phillip the Arab, Tiberios and Augustus. The latter two were also bought around 1402. The three Roman emperors and the two 'Eastern' Roman-Byzantine emperors, Constantine and Herakleios, were linked through a Christian theme, as the earlier emperors' reigns all had connections to the life of Christ, while Constantine and Herakleios were connected with the True Cross. This was already a popular theme in European art at the time, and thus Jean de Berry's acquisition of Constantine and Herakleios medallions was related to a 'themed' collection. These purchases coincide with Manuel's visit, which may suggest that Jean de Berry's desire to collect these items could have been partially influenced by the emperor's presence in Paris.

The two medallions depicting Constantine and Herakleios also have inscriptions that betray influences of Byzantine chancery formulas. In this regard, it should be noted that Jean de Berry's residence Hôtel de Nesle was opposite the Louvre, where Manuel and his entourage were lodged. Indeed, a Byzantine official travelling with the emperor might have even supplied the artist with the necessary information. Herakleios' portrait bears a striking resemblance to the emperor, and it seems that Manuel was used as the model for the image. **(Fig 7.2)**

Figure 7.2 Manuel II as Herakleios? Medal depicting Emperor Herakleios commissioned by Jean duc de Berry, later cast. Word History Archive / Alamy Stock Photo.

Although the originals of these medals are now lost, they were copied numerous times. The Limbourg brothers also used Constantine and Herakleios as models for figures in two famous manuscripts they illuminated for Jean de Berry: *Les Très Riches Heures* and *Les Belles Heures*. In several scenes in *Les Très Riches Heures*, a Manuel-like figure is depicted as one of the magi, Melchior, and as the Roman Emperor Augustus. (**Fig 7.3**) The emperor seems to have graced other French manuscripts as well. In *Les Grandes Chroniques de France*, he may have also been the model for Charles of Luxembourg.[134] Quite possibly, he was also the inspiration for an illumination in the *Chevalier Errant* of Thomas of Saluzzo by the Cité des Dames Master, depicting the convocation of the princes of East.[135] Finally, Manuel's visit is also reflected in one English illumination. His meeting with Henry IV is depicted in a late fifteenth-century manuscript of St Alban's Chronicle in which the two rulers are shown greeting each other. Although Manuel's costume contains English influences, he is wearing a Byzantine hat that is similar to those depicted in French illuminations. The emperor's facial features and long beard are nevertheless quite recognizable.[136] (**Fig 7.4**)

Manuel's frequent appearances in French artefacts from the period are a testament to the excitement elicited by his visit. The French interest in Byzantium and the 'east' in general, had already been roused by travellers who had visited the empire. The defeat at Nikopolis further intensified this interest, and indeed, many French illuminations from the early fifteenth century betray both Byzantine, Ottoman, Hungarian and Mamluk influences regarding the clothing and headgear depicted.[137] These fashions may have also had an 'exotic' or 'oriental' appeal for the artists and patrons. The portraits thought to be that of Manuel generally figure in such contexts: depictions of the Magi, Eastern princes and the Roman emperor Augustus. He is thus usually used as a model for more 'exotic' or eastern figures.

---

[134] Melchior is found in *Les Très Riches Heures*, f. 51v and 52r, Augustus in f. 22. Charles of Luxembourg is depicted in *Grandes Chroniques de France*, Bibliothèque nationale, MS fr. 6465 ff. 444v–r and 446r. The folia depicting Augustus and Charles of Luxembourg could not be reproduced in this book. Barker, *Manuel II*, 173 has small sized reproductions of the illuminations depicting Charles of Luxembourg.

[135] This illumination is found in Bibliothèque nationale MS fr. 12559, f. 162, which is reproduced in an article by Kubiski. The author proposes that one of the figures in this illumination could have been based on Manuel. The figure's facial features and beard display similarities to those of the emperor. He is also wearing a wide-brimmed hat identical to the ones depicted in the European portraits of Manuel's son John VIII. See J. Kubiski, 'Orientalizing Costume in early Fifteenth-Century French Manuscript Painting (Cité des Dames Master, Limbourg Brothers, Boucicaut Master, and Bedford Master)', *Gesta* 40 (2001), 161–80, 162–3.

[136] Lambeth Palace Library, MS 6, f 240r.   [137] See Kubiski above in footnote 135.

Figure 7.3 Manuel II as Melchior? The meeting of the Magi. Chantilly, Musée Condé, *Les très riches heures du duc de Berry*, f 51 v. Photo by Archiv Gerstenberg/ullstein bild via Getty Images.

Figure 7.4 The meeting of Manuel II and Henry IV. MS6f240, *St. Alban's Chronicle*, fifteenth century. Image courtesy of Lambeth Palace Library & The Courtauld Institute of Art.

Indeed, with his long, flowing white beard and Byzantine garb, Manuel must have looked the part in the eyes of the French.

Overall, the emperor's presence in Paris served to further increase the French interest in Byzantium. This interest had already been roused through after the battle of Nikopolis and the travels of prominent court figures such as Philippe de Meziérès and Boucicaut to the Byzantine realm. These people also acted as patrons of literature, and one notable example of their patronage can be seen in a work by Christine de Pizan. During the period, she composed a work that shows Byzantine influences. Her *Long Road of Learning* mentions Constantinople and the realm of Bayezid, and it is entirely possible that she was influenced by her patrons de Meziérès and Boucicaut, and that her interest was further intensified by Manuel's presence in Paris. She may have even seen or met the emperor in person at court.[138]

For the time, Manuel's long voyage in Europe was quite a rare and unprecedented experience for a Byzantine ruler. The obvious question that springs to mind when considering it, is what sort of impact this unusual episode had on him. Neither his writings from this voyage, nor those from the later periods, hint at any significant impact, though in *On the Procession of the Holy Spirit*, he does demonstrate a working knowledge of the Western European theological controversies of the time. Nontheless, in this work the emperor still opts for a refutation based on established Byzantine tradition. Similarly, it has been pointed out that although the subject of his *ekphrasis* is a tapestry in the Louvre, it was still an object depicting spring – a conventional theme for Byzantine *ekphraseis*. While in Paris, among all the new and unusual things he must have seen, Manuel chose to write about an object that could easily fit into established Byzantine literary traditions and conventions.

Likewise, the later life of the emperor does not reveal any significant or lasting influence from his European journey. It does not appear that he bonded with the French or English literati, or that he was influenced by their philosophical or literary culture. Also significant is that although he resided in Europe for three and a half years, Manuel does not seem to have learned Latin. Given his literary talent, it is reasonable to assume that he had a flair for languages. But perhaps, the emperor deliberately avoided learning Latin in order to not compromise his Orthodox stance in the eyes of his contemporaries.

Manuel's long journey, especially the time he spent in Italy, raises the question of his role in the early Renaissance. It should be pointed out that the peak of the Byzantine interest in the Renaissance, dates to the period after Manuel's reign, to the 1430s. It is after this date that figures such as Plethon, Isidore of Kiev, Bessarion and George of Trebizond came into close contact with Italy. However, Manuel's reign witnessed the earliest phases of this cultural relationship, especially thanks to the efforts of Manuel Chrysoloras. Had the emperor also been influenced by the Italian scholars and the advent of humanism during his travels? After all,

---

[138] On Christine de Pizan and her patrons, see, C. C. Willard, *Christine de Pizan: Her Life and Works* (New York, 1984), especially 16, and N. Margolis. *An Introduction to Christine de Pizan* (Florida, 2011), 103–4, who argues for a possible influence of Manuel on the *Long Road of Learning*.

not only was he associated with figures such as Kydones and Manuel Chrysoloras, he also spent time in Italy. It is inconceivable that Manuel Chrysoloras did not introduce him to several Italian scholars while in Europe.

The emperor was certainly astute in choosing Manuel Chrysoloras for his diplomatic missions. Chrysoloras was not only a skilled diplomat, but also shared interests with Western scholars. He astutely sought to advertise the Greek language, literature and philosophy in order to prompt Western Europe to help Byzantium. Manuel seems to have recognized the value of Chrysoloras, and yet it seems that he did not really share the same views. Despite his extensive travels and contacts with Italian scholars, there is no hint that these experiences brought him any closer to the scholars of the Early Renaissance, or that he was inspired by their scholarly interests. He was to send his *Funeral Oration* to Guarino of Verona in 1417, but Guarino had lived in Constantinople between 1403–8.[139] Although his travels in the West were a unique experience for a Byzantine emperor at the time, the episode does not seem to have impacted his scholarly outlook at all. Furthermore, Manuel's scholarly and literary interests make this apparent lack of influence even more intriguing.

To understand Manuel's lack of interest in such contacts, one needs to further consider his scholarly and religious inclinations. Many of the pro-Italian Byzantine scholars of Manuel's time were Catholic converts. Examples that spring to mind include Kydones, Manuel Kalekas, Manuel Chrysoloras and later, Bessarion. Most of these men were drawn to Italy not only by their interest in Greek language, but also by their theological interests. Manuel, on the other hand, was a firm Orthodox who cherished traditional methods of theological inquiry. Likewise, his interests in Plato and Aristotle were very different from those of the Italian scholars. Manuel relied on Aristotle's ethics and emulated Plato exclusively as literary models. Ultimately, his interest in Greek philosophy was limited, nor was he interested in Greek grammar or philological issues. He did not know Latin and hence he was not interested in translations. All in all, his outlook was far removed from Manuel Chrysoloras and the Italian scholars. Despite witnessing the dawn of the Renaissance, Manuel had only limited interactions with its culture.

After Paris, Manuel's first stop on his way home was Genoa, which was now governed by his longtime ally Mareschal Boucicaut. He arrived on 23 January 1403, and Boucicaut duly hosted a feast in Manuel's honour.

---

[139] This will be discussed in Chapter 9.

The emperor seems to have been lodged in a friary during his stay.[140] Manuel also continued to correspond with Venice concerning his return journey and the new political situation in Asia Minor. On 10 February he departed for Venice and stayed there until April to wait out problems concerning the arrangements for the journey. Manuel finally sailed away at the beginning of April. On the 13th and the 14th, he sailed past Ragusa and shortly afterwards, he finally arrived in Modon, where he was reunited with his family. He had been away for almost four years.[141]

While Manuel's long journey ended at this point, echoes of it would endure for much longer in Byzantine texts. No other episode in his reign has received as much attention as his journey to Europe.[142] It also appears that his visit to Europe intensified the Byzantine interest in Western Europe. For instance, the emperor's travels seem to have prompted Byzantine authors to refer to Western geography: Doukas takes care to list all the cities Manuel visited, including some imaginary routes; and Chalkokondyles seizes the opportunity to make lengthy digressions into English and French customs, and even into the flow of the Thames River.[143]

In panegyrics, his voyage to Europe is represented as the ultimate sacrifice made for his people. Authors emphasized the great distance the emperor travelled and labelled Manuel as a new Odysseus; one anonymous

---

[140] See Stella, 262–3, who also points out that Manuel came to Genoa as the other Western rulers were busy. Iorga, *Notes et extraits*, 1, 30–1.

[141] Doukas, 84–5. After leaving Genoa on 10 February, Manuel's whereabouts for the next thirty-two days are not known, raising the question of whether he may have visited the Roman pope in Florence, Ferrara or in Rome, see Barker, *Manuel II*, 121 and G. T. Dennis, 'The Byzantine-Turkish Treaty of 1403', *OCP* 33 (1967), 72–88; 73–7, re-printed in G. T. Dennis, *Byzantium and the Franks 1350–1420*, (London, 1983), Study XII. Henceforth, Dennis, 'The Turkish Treaty'. On this matter of a presumed visit to the pope, nothing can be concluded with certainty unless new evidence emerges.

For the negotiations concerning the arrangements for Manuel's return journey and the new political situation on the Turkish front, see Thiriet, *Régestes*, 11, nos. 1088, 1092, 1097, 1098, 1104, 1107, 34–48 and Iorga, *Notes et extraits*, 1, 126, 131–4. Finally, although Manuel was expected to stop in Ragusa, he did not, presumably because of the long delays he had already suffered, see M. A. Andreeva, 'Zur Reise Manuels II. Palaiologos nach West-europa', *BZ* 34 (1934), 37–47.

[142] Doukas, Chalkokondyles, Mazaris, Schreiner, *Kleinchroniken*, Chronik 12, 22, 35 all refer to the journey. For orations, see footnotes 143 and 44.

[143] Doukas, 85–6; Chalkokondyles, 134–44. See also A. Ducellier, 'La France et les îles Britanniques vue par un byzantin du XVe siècle: Laonikos Chalkokondylis', in *Economies et sociétés au Moyen âge; mélanges offerts à Edouard Perroy* (Paris, 1973), 439–45. See Makarios of Ankyra, 336; Mazaris, 12–13; Demetrios Chrysoloras, 'Comparison between the Emperor of Today and Ancient Emperors', ed. S. Lampros, *ΠΠ*, 111, 222–45, 239; Isidore of Kiev, 'Pangeyric', 161–2; Dendrinos, *Anonymous Oration*, 443; ' I. Polemis, 'Two Praises of the Emperor Manuel II Palaiologos: Problems of Authorship', *BZ* 103 (2010), 699–714, 707–8 for other references to geography. Henceforth, Demetrios Chrysoloras, 'Synkrisis' and Polemis, 'Anonymous Panegyric'.

author even names Manuel 'the self-appointed' ambassador.[144] The novelty of Manuel's status as a diplomat-emperor was thus noted by this orator. The emperor's journey was seized by the panegyrists as an opportunity to laud an otherwise feeble reign, and to go beyond the usual categories of imperial deeds extolled in Byzantine orations.

Although his voyage was depicted as a great quest undertaken for the sake of his people, the authors fail to mention the fact that it brought no concrete results. Instead, the miraculous outcome of the Battle of Ankara is indirectly credited to the emperor. Isidore of Kiev, for instance, claims that Manuel saved the city with his prayers despite being abroad.[145] The tone in some of these texts, however, is somewhat defensive. One short chronicle emphasizes that the emperor went abroad *only* in order to get help. Similarly, a panegyric stresses that Manuel did *not* leave the city and its valuables to the barbarians.[146] Such remarks might be an indication that perhaps some people accused the emperor of using the journey as a pretext to flee from the besieged capital.

The authors furthermore strive to conceal Manuel's plight as the ruler of an impoverished and drastically declining empire. They highlight instead the honours he received and depict Manuel as being showered with admiration for his virtue. In this context, wealth, armies and vast territories are not the true signs of imperial dignity.[147] This provides a stark contrast with the tone of the Western authors. Despite depicting Manuel as an impressive and admirable figure, they unsurprisingly emphasize the generosity of their own rulers to the Byzantine emperor in distress. All of them underscore that his expenses were paid by their rulers; further, they refer to him as the 'Emperor of the Greeks' or 'Emperor of Constantinople'.[148] Byzantine authors fashioned an idealized picture of Manuel's voyage, while

---

[144] Symeon of Thessalonike, 'Oration on Saint Demetrios', ed. D. Balfour, *Politico-Historical Works of Symeon Archbishop of Thessalonica (1416/17 to 1429)*. (Vienna, 1979), 39–69, 43–5; Bessarion, 'Monody on Manuel Palaiologos', ed. S. P. Lampros, *ΠΠ*, III, 284–90, 287; Polemis, 'Anonymous Panegyric', 708; Dendrinos, *Anonymous Oration*, 443–4, 'μόνος αὐτοχειροτόνητος ἧκε πρεσβευτὴς εἰς τὰ ἑσπέρια ... ' Henceforth, Symeon of Thessalonike, 'Oration on St Demetrios' and Bessarion, 'Monody'. Hunger, 'Das Testament des Patriarchen Matthaios', 300, also mentions Manuel's journey.

[145] Chortasmenos, 'Address to Manuel II', 218–19; Polemis, 'Anonymous Panegyric', 707–8.

[146] Schreiner, *Kleinchroniken*, Chronik 22/ 27; Dendrinos, *Anonymous Oration*, 447.

[147] Doukas, 85–6; Isidore of Kiev, 'Panegyric', 161–2; Chortasmenos, 'Address to Manuel II', 218–19; Bessarion, 'Monody', 287.

[148] *Chronique de Saint Denis,* XXI, i, 754–58; Ursins, 418; Walsingham, *Historia*, 247; *Eulogium*, 388; Adam of Usk, 118–21; *Vita Ricardi*, 169–70; *Le livre des faits*, II, 215–16.

In official documents, too, Manuel is always referred to as the Emperor of Constantinople or of the Greeks, see *(Memorials of the Reign of King Henry IV). Official Correspondence of Thomas Bekynton, Secretary to King Henry IV, Bishop of Bath and Wells*, ed. G. Williams (London, 1872), I, no. CCIII, 285–6; *Issues of the Exchequer*, 272; *Proceedings and Ordinances of the Privy Council of*

the European texts peddled a drastically different version. Undoubtedly, the latter came closer to reality.

Manuel stayed in the Morea for about two months. The Venetians kept delaying the assignment of a galley for his return to Constantinople, and Manuel contacted Bouciacut and met with him at the mouth of Vassilipotamo. Alarmed by the emperor's renewed association with the governor of Genoa, the Venetians moved with more alacrity and preparations were completed. At last, Manuel and his family finally boarded a Venetian galley and were welcomed in Gallipoli by his nephew John VII. On 9 June 1403, they entered Constantinople.[149] The emperor was home at last.

England, 1, ed. H. Nicolas, (London, 1834), 82. See also *Diplomatari Català*, no. 658, 685; no. 666, 691 for some examples.

  Manuel is Emperor of Constantinople even in the inventories of Jean de Berry, in contrast to Charles of Luxembourg, who is merely referred to as 'l'empereur'. Guiffrey, *Inventoires de Jean de Berry*, I, no. 791, 262; no. 1249, 335; II, no. 214, 35.

[149] For these negotiations concerning Manuel's return journey, see, *Le livre des faits*, II, xii, 622–3; Thiriet, *Régestes*, II, no. 1122, 40–1; Barker, *Manuel II*, 236–7. For his return, see Schreiner, *Kleinchroniken*, Chronik 12/13; 22/ 30; Mioni, 'Cronaca', no. 27 and Konstantin the Philosopher, 21.

CHAPTER 8

A Clamorous Tranquillity

It is absurd to think of luxury, absurd to think of repose . . . [1]

After his return from Europe, Manuel was to enjoy relative stability for a few years. This was an unprecedented phase in his tumultuous life. The death of Bayezid had not only scattered the Ottoman army besieging Constantinople, it had also shattered his newly formed empire. It was not possible for Tamerlane to rule Anatolia directly from Samarkand, and instead he dismembered Bayezid's Ottoman lands and re-established the former Turkish emirates. The unitary Ottoman Anatolia was no more. Strife also broke out for the succession right to Bayezid's throne, and the remaining Ottoman lands fell into a chaos. For the next ten years, Bayezid's sons Süleyman, Musa, Isa and Mehmed were to fight among themselves for the coveted Ottoman throne. Manuel would do his best to play the brothers against each other in order to preserve his own empire. [2] The Battle of Ankara had changed the whole outlook for the Byzantines.

Months before the return of his uncle, John VII had already signed a treaty with Bayezid's eldest son Süleyman, the most likely candidate for Bayezid's throne. Whether Manuel knew of this treaty at the time is uncertain, but he did ratify it in September 1403. [3] Through this treaty, Süleyman acknowledged him as 'his father', promising not to attack Byzantium, as well as giving the emperor large territorial concessions including Thessalonike. As Süleyman needed the good will of the Byzantines to establish his rule in the now shattered Anatolia, the terms

---

[1] Letter 44, lines 25–6. 'ὅθεν δὴ λῆρος τρυφή, λῆρος ἄνεσις.'

[2] See D. J. Kastritsis, *The Sons of Bayezid: Empire Building and Representation in the Ottoman Civil War of 1402–1413* (Leiden and Boston, 2007) Henceforth, Kastritsis, *Sons of Bayezid* for a detailed analysis of the Ottoman civil wars between 1402–13; Barker, *Manuel II*, 233–45. For the aftermath of the Battle of Ankara and its socio-economic and political implications, see K. P. Matchske, *Die Schlacht bei Ankara und das Schicksal von Byzanz* (Weimar, 1981).

[3] See Chapter 7 and Dennis, 'The Turkish Treaty' for a detailed discussion; Konstatin the Philosopher, 23 also mentions the treaty.

were exceptionally advantageous for the empire. Thanks to the unexpected 'miracle' of the Battle of Ankara, Byzantium seemed be safe from any serious Turkish threat, for the time being at least.

This tranquillity did not stop Manuel from continuing to seek help from Europe, however. Even on his return journey from Italy to the Morea, he asked Venice to correspond with Genoa and France in order to form a league against the Ottomans.[4] Later on, the emperor persevered in dispatching his ambassadors to the Roman pope and various European kings. In 1405, the pope even issued a new bull.[5] In May 1406, Manuel also finally renewed treaty with the Venetians.[6] Meanwhile, Manuel Chrysoloras made two more diplomatic trips to Italy, also visiting London and Paris in 1408.[7] As late as 1410, Manuel was still corresponding with Aragon for military aid. Between, 1411–14, the emperor exchanged letters with Sigismund of Hungary, also discussing a possible church union.[8] All those missions came to naught, and yet they bear witness to his awareness of how fragile the current peace was. The emperor never stopped looking for allies against the Ottomans.

The Turkish front had calmed down, but the immediate aftermath of Manuel's return from Europe saw yet another clash with his nephew John VII. John had been regent in his uncle's stead for almost four years. Despite Manuel's suspicions, John didn't give into the Ottoman demands to surrender the city and honoured his pledge to safeguarded Constantinople. Yet for reasons that are not entirely clear, instead of giving him Thessalonike in reward as had been promised, Manuel banished John to Lemnos.

It is quite possible that the emperor's displeasure with his nephew had to do with the latter's proclamation of his son as emperor and his signing of the treaty of 1403 without Manuel's explicit consent.[9] Or perhaps, despite John's successful regency, the emperor still held a grudge against his nephew and simply wanted him out of the way. After all, John was still popular among his supporters and very much remained a contender for the throne. John did not obey Manuel, and instead of going to Lemnos he joined his father-in-law Francesco Gattilusio on Lesbos. There, the two contemplated a naval attack on the recently recovered Thessalonike in

---

[4] Thiriet, *Régestes*, II, no. 1092, 35.

[5] Raynaldus, *Annales Ecclesiastici*, vol. 27, 126–8; Barker, *Manuel II*, 248–72.

[6] Iorga, *Notes et Extraits*, 131–2; MM, III, 144–53; DVL, 301–2; Dölger, *Regesten*, nos. 3310–11, 92–3. From that point onwards, the treaty would be renewed in 1411, 1418 and 1423, without modifications to the text. See also Chapter 5.

[7] Cammelli, *Crisolora*, 139–42.   [8] Mureşan, 'Trois empereurs', 70–5.

[9] See Dennis, 'Andronicus V', 180. This son of John VII, Andronikos, was to die young. Although the exact date is unknown, he predeceased his father, see Dennis, 'The Turkish Treaty', 76. Clavijo, 27, notes the initial stages of this clash and John's banishment to Lesbos.

mid-September. Although the attack never took place, Manuel conceded quickly to his nephew. In November 1403, John was given Thessalonike and Thessaly to rule.[10] That he conceded such a large territory to John, including the prized city of Thessalonike, is a testimony to Manuel's political weakness in this affair. He was probably aware that he could not decisively put an end to John's claims. All in all, giving into his nephew's demands and refraining from rekindling the civil war was also a wise decision, especially at a moment when relative stability had been restored to the empire.

This political act also prompted the creation of a rather famous Palaiologan artwork. (**Fig 8.1**) A small ivory pyxis was commissioned to commemorate the reconciliation of the imperial family. It depicts the two emperors and their families in union – a visual testimony to the dynastic power sharing between John and Manuel. In it the imperial family is flanked by a celebratory frieze depicting musicians and dancers and the figures are divided into two units. One unit consists of Manuel, Empress Helena and his sons and the other of John VII, his wife and son. The subtle differences between the figures seems to suggest a dynastic agreement: Manuel has a longer beard than John VII, while John VIII is taller than the latter's son Andronikos (V). Perhaps, these visual cues hint that John VII would be next in the line of sucession after Manuel, followed by John VIII and Andronikos V. This would conform to the succession scheme of the 1390s, that was narrated by Manuel in the *Dialogue on Marriage*.

Yet even this token of peace reflected some tension. The commissioner of the ivory pyxis, probably one of John's followers, seems to betray a bias towards his patron.[11] The figures of Manuel and his family are unnamed and portrayed in less detail than those of John and his family members. Furthermore, even though the model of Thessalonike is presented to John, it is not Manuel who is depicted as giving it. As the senior emperor and the bestower of the city, he should have been the one presenting it. That he does not, effectively portrays him as of equal rank with John rather than as the senior emperor. Despite the visual tension depicted in the ivory pyxis, this agreement between the uncle and the nephew was to be a lasting one.

---

[10] Doukas, 110–11; Schreiner, *Kleinchroniken*, Chronik 7/27 and 22/30. Konstantine the Philosopher, 22, remarks that when John VII was in Thessalonike, he had designs on Constantinople.

[11] For a detailed discussion of this miniature object, see N. Oikonomides, 'John VII Palaeologus and the Ivory Pyxis at Dumbarton Oaks', *DOP* 31 (1977), 329–38. Oikonomides draws attention to the fact that the figures of Manuel and his family are less detailed and unnamed. He interprets this as a bias in favour of John VII, strengthening the argument that the commissioner was one of his followers.

Figure 8.1 a and b Ivory pyxis depicting Manuel II, John VII and their families.
© Dumbarton Oaks, Byzantine Collection, Washington DC.

With the Ottoman threat pacified, it finally seemed to usher in a period of political calm.

Public Privacy: Manuel's Daily Life

Manuel was greeted on his return from Europe by his two elder sons, John and Theodore. Another son, Andronikos was born during his father's absence, and thus Manuel saw his young son for the first time when the latter was approximately three years old. Several more sons soon followed: Constantine, Demetrios and Thomas, and possibly also another one named Michael, who seems to have died of plague as an infant.[12] Manuel's relationship with his wife cannot be traced at all. However, there is no source hinting at problems between the imperial couple, and their marriage was a very fruitful one, so one can assume that it was at the very least a cordial union. These first years after the emperor's return were to be a time of reunion with his family and his court at Blachernai, and therefore it is only fitting that at this point in his biography that we take a glimpse into Manuel's daily routines.

It is difficult to reconstruct the Palace of Blachernai from the sources. (**Fig 8.2**) Although the Great Palace was also sometimes used, Blachernai was the main imperial residence. Today the only remaining building from the Blachernai Palace is the Palace of the Porphyrogennitos, today known as Tekfur Sarayı. Decorated with brickwork, this three-storeyed building

---

[12] Sphrantzes, 6–7.

Figure 8.2 Palace of the Porphyrogennitos, Tekfur Saray (pre-restoration). Photo by
DeAgostini / Getty Images.

lay adjacent to the land walls and is thought to have been an annex to the
palace. As opposed to the complex web of buildings of the Great Palace, the
main building of Blachernai was a single block, multi-storeyed palace with
a balcony facing the city.[13] The emperor's apartments faced the inner
courtyard. They were flanked by the palace church and a *triklinos* – main
hall. At present, no further details can be gleaned about this palace either
through the textual sources or through archaeological investigation, but we
do know that within the palace, the furniture was mostly movable and that
curtains hung in many places. In the *triklinos*, Manuel's throne was on
a raised platform.[14] Rare representations of thrones in Late Byzantine art
illustrate box-like thrones with a backrest and no arms, adorned with

---

[13] *Pseudo-Kodinos*, 365; K. P. Matschke, 'Die Stadt Konstantinopel und die Dynastie der Palaiologen',
in K. P. Matschke, *Das spätbyzantinische Konstantinopel. Alte und neue Beiträge zur Stadtgeschichte
zwischen 1261 und 1453* (Hamburg, 2008), 8–87; 36–8, and A. Berger, 'The Byzantine Court as
Physical Space', in *The Byzantine Court. Source of Power and Culture. Papers from the Second Sevgi
Gönül Symposium, Istanbul 21–23 June 2010*, eds. A. Ödekan, N. Necipoğlu and E. Akyürek
(Istanbul, 2013), 3–12, especially 10–12. Henceforth, Berger, 'Court'. Schiltberger, 79–80, reports
that the emperor had two palaces, the bigger one was decorated with gold and lazuli. It had a plain
for tilting and a statue of Justinian in front. He is probably referring to the Great Palace.

[14] *Pseudo-Kodinos*, 375.

cushions, but a manuscript illumination of Manuel's grandfather John Kantakouzenos depicts a golden throne with a curved back.[15] Perhaps, Manuel sat on something similar.

What sort of a life then did Manuel lead in the Blachernai Palace? At first, this may seem a trivial question in the grander scheme of things. Yet an exploration of Manuel's daily life serves to breathe life into his experiences and surroundings, thereby enriching his biography. Reconstructing the daily life of any medieval ruler presents a challenge, as usually very little information survives concerning daily activities in the period. This is especially true for Byzantine emperors' daily lives, such as their toilette, their meals, or their solitary moments in private chambers. By contrast, it is easier to construct the daily life of figures such as Charlemagne or Charles V of France.[16] After all, their contemporary biographers did take the trouble to record many of these mundane details. The sixteenth-century Tudor monarch Henry VIII's life is brought to life by his accounts, expense books and even wardrobe inventories. But no such texts exist for Manuel. His case is aided slightly by the fact that he was also an author and some of his writings do have an autobiographic character. However, it is also important to bear in mind that the emperor did not pen these instances in order to share his daily life with his audience. Instead, these narrations have everything to do with self-representation. Although this does not mean that these were not his 'real' experiences, Manuel nevertheless chose to share those intimate details with his audience that best served to represent himself as a dutiful, self-sacrificing emperor.

A tantalizing glimpse into the emperor's day can be found in one of his letters, in which Manuel complains about his busy schedule:

> . . . . I have chased sleep away from my eyes, and often my bed receives me at dawn, just when those sweeping the whole house and all the domestic servants have to get up out of the bed and dutifully go about their appointed tasks. These people are the most annoying as they buzz about the doors; then there is the shouting of the judges, plaintiffs, and defendants . . . Moreover, the clamour of the attendants resounding throughout the house, where I would like to sleep, would even easily awaken Dardanus himself . . . And then, there is our own Antiochos, the old man who loves to sleep so much . . . When the tumult at the door prevents him from snoring

---

[15] M. Parani, *Reconstructing the Reality of Images* (Leiden, 2003), 160–97 on furniture. Henceforth, Parani, *Reconstructing the Reality*.

[16] See especially G. Duby and P. Ariès (eds.) *A History of Private Life, II, Revelations of the Medieval World*, trans. A. Goldhammer (Cambridge MA, 1988), 5–7 and M. Brauer, 'Politics or Leisure? A Day in the Life of King Charles V of France' (1364–80)', *The Medieval History Journal* 18,1 (2015), 46–63.

away in his usual fashion, he curses the noise makers, puts on some kind of shepherd's cap, stuffs his fingers to his ears, and fits his head into the deepest corner . . . Everything, is filled with turmoil . . .'[17]

Manuel peppers this account with his humorous portrayal of Antiochos, who seems to have been the emperor's *paroikoimomenos tou koitonos*.[18] The *paroikoimomenoi* would sleep at the door of the imperial bedchamber and cater to the emperor's personal needs.[19] The clamour and the noise outside his chamber, preventing him from sleeping, serve to emphasize how preoccupied the 'dutiful' emperor was with governmental affairs. Although Manuel does not describe the interior of his chamber, we can imagine that it probably contained a large, valuable bed, laden with mattresses, blankets, quilts and pillows. These items may have been covered in silk. Only the wealthy had beds; Manuel's poorer subjects would have slept on benches or on the floor.[20]

Upon waking, the emperor was dressed by servants. The typical Palaiologan garment for the wealthy consisted of an ankle length, tight-fitting caftan, either worn on its own or under a mantle, and decorated with geometric or floral motifs.[21] Depictions of such garments can be found in abundance in manuscript images, mosaics and frescoes from the Palaiologan era. The historian Sphrantzes, one of Manuel's courtiers, narrates how the emperor gave him one of his own garments; a grey damask cloak lined with heavy wool. This grey cloak came from an old chest where

---

[17] Letter 44, lines 1–19. Ἐμοὶ δὲ πλῆθος πραγμάτων ἀναγκαζόντων τῷ κατεπείγειν πρὸς ἕτερα μικροῦ με καὶ ἐκείνων ἀπέχεσθαι ὧν χωρὶς οὐ δυνατὸν περιεῖναι. ἐπιλέλησμαι τραπέζης καιροῦ καὶ τῶν σιτίων μικρὰ φροντὶς ὁποῖ᾽ ἄττ᾽ ἂν εἴη. Ἀπεσεισάμην ὕπνον ἐξ ὀφθαλμῶν, καὶ ἔχει με ἡ κλίνη πολλάκις ὄρθρου, ὅτε δεῖ καὶ τοὺς κορόωντας τὸν ὅλον οἶκον καὶ ἁπλῶς τὴν ἔνδον πᾶσαν διακονίαν ἐξανίστασθαι τῆς κλίνης ὅπως ἔργων ἅψαιντο δεομένης ἐπισκέψεως, οἳ περὶ τὰς θύρας βομβοῦντες διενοχλοῦσιν. ἔπειτα βοὴ δικαζόντων, δικαζομένων, ἀμυνομένων, τἄλλα ὅσα περίεργον λέγειν, εἰδότι γὰρ ἂν λέγοιτο. Πλὴν κἂν Δάρδανον, κἂν τὸν ἐκίνου πολὺ ὑπηηλότερον, ῥᾳδίως ἀφύπνισεν ἡ τῆς ὑπηρεσίας βοὴ περιηχοῦσα τὸν οἶκον οὗ καθεύδοιμι. Ἐπεὶ καὶ ὁ Ἀντίοχος ὁ παρ᾽ ἡμῖν, ὕπνοις δὲ τοσοῦτον φίλος ὁ γέρων, ὡς καθεύδειν ἱππεύων καὶ πάντα ἂν ἡλλάξατο ὕπνου, ῥέγχειν μὴ δυνάμενος εἰωθότως διὰ τὴν θύραζε ταραχήν, τοῖς μὴ ἡσυχάζουσι καταρώμενος κυνῆν τινα ποιμαντικὴν ὑποδύς, βύσας τοῖς δακτύλοις τὰ ὦτα γωνίᾳ προσαρμόσας βαθυτάτῃ τὴν κεφαλὴν μόλις ἀναπαύλης τυγχάνει. Οὕτω θορύβου πάντα μεστὰ καὶ τὸ τῆς χρείας ἀπαραίτητον εἴργει κωλύσαι τὸ θορυβοῦν.᾽

[18] *Mazaris*, 40–5, also mentions an Antiochos who had accompanied Manuel to Europe. The Antiochos in the letter and in Mazaris are quite possibly the same person.

[19] *Pseudo-Kodinos*, 86–9. See also F. Schrijver, 'Daily life at the Blachernai Palace: The Servants of the Imperial Bedchamber (1261–1354)', in *The Byzantine Court. Source of Power and Culture. Papers from the Second Sevgi Gönül Symposium, Istanbul 21–23 June 2010*, eds. A. Ödekan, N. Necipoğlu and E. Akyürek (Istanbul, 2013), 83–7.

[20] N. Oikonomides, 'The Contents of the Byzantine House from the Eleventh to the Fifteenth Centuries', *DOP* 44 (1990), 205–14; 209.

[21] Parani, *Reconstructing the Reality*, 58–60.

Manuel kept many other similar clothing items that he had inherited from his father. In turn, as an old man, Manuel distributed these clothes to his eldest son and to some of his own courtiers.[22] Although Sphrantzes conveys these details in order to depict himself as an especially favoured courtier of the emperor, the historian unintentionally offers us a rare and fascinating glimpse into the imperial wardrobe.

According to the stipulations of the Late Byzantine ceremonial book, the Pseudo-Kodinos, Manuel's day would typically have been spent receiving petitioners. The emperor would have also had a daily reception to receive ambassadors, state officials and other types of people. He might also sometimes ride out to receive petitions.[23] Indeed various people would bring a multitude of matters before Manuel, requests that could sometimes be overwhelming:

> ... It is impossible to excuse oneself from seeing the people outside, the people within, and whoever is oppressed with some serious problem. But here stands a Latin, a Persian, a citizen, a foreigner, not least of all, a monk, each one demanding something different and shouting that he would be unjustly treated if his request is not granted immediately ...[24]

When the emperor was ill, especially in his later years, ambassadors and other visitors would be received by other officials. One such insight into his audiences comes from Clavijo. The Spanish traveller reports having a private audience with the emperor just after the latter had returned from Mass. Accompanied by his attendants, the empress and his three eldest sons, Manuel conversed with the Spanish party. He was seated on a dais covered with carpets and a lion skin, and at his back, there was a gold embroidered black cushion.[25]

Matins and vespers would be attended at the palace church. In the *Discourse to Iagoup*, Manuel refers to his regular attendance at church service.[26] Demetrios Chrysoloras notes his fondness for singing hymns and how he ordered absolute silence at those moments. Chrysoloras' description fits in well with the panegyrical image of the pious emperor in Byzantine court ideology. However, his statement should not be dismissed

---

[22] Sphrantzes, 28–9.
[23] *Pseudo-Kodinos*, 90–1. On emperors receiving petitions, see R. J. Macrides, 'The Ritual of Petition', in *Greek Ritual Poetics*, eds. P. Roilos and D. Yatromanolakis (Cambridge MA, 2004), 356–70.
[24] Letter 44, lines 21–5, 'οὐ γὰρ ἐνὸν παραιτήσασθαι πρὸς τοὺς ἐκτός, πρὸς τοὺς ἔνδον, πρὸς ὀντινοῦν πιεζόμενον ὑπό του δεινοῦ πράγματος, ἀλλ' ἔστηκε Λατῖνος, Πέρσης, πολίτης, ξένος, οὐχ ἥκιστα γε καὶ μοναχός, ἕκαστος ἕτερον ἀπαιτῶν καὶ βοῶν ὡς ἀδικοῖτο ἢν μὴ λάβῃ τὸ ζητούμενον εὐθύς.'
[25] Clavijo, 37, Sphrantzes, 26–7. [26] *Pseudo-Kodinos*, 90–1; *Discourse to Iagoup*, 327.

as being mere *topos*. Many foreign sources, such as Clavijo, Ghillebert de Lannoy, Jean Juvenal Ursins and Adam of Usk, do note Manuel's piety. Furthermore, the emperor's composition of a *kanon* in 1411 supports the claim that he was indeed devoted to religious chant.[27] His writings, especially the theological ones, bear further witness to his genuine piety.

Palace life also had more light-hearted aspects. For instance, there would be feasts on special days. In his letters, Manuel's teacher and friend Demetrios Kydones makes a few references to food, such as cheese and fruits, as well as to the infamous lentil dish of the Thessalonian Chalazas. Unlike him, Manuel makes no mention of specific food items in any of his writings. Yet in his *Foundations of Imperial Conduct*, the emperor does make a passing reference to lavish court food. In this text, Manuel refers to the palace food only to make a comparison between luxurious feasts and the stoic pleasure derived from simple food, but it is telling that the emperor opts to give as an example, a banquet in the palace instead of any other sumptuous meal. No details of banquets in the imperial palace in Manuel's reign survive. When one considers the dire economic straits of the emperor, one cannot expect these occasions to have been spectacularly magnificent. In the 1390s, when the Genoese *podesta* gave a banquet in Pera, melons, bread, mutton, milk, vegetables, sugar, confectionary and large quantities of wine were purchased. It is probable that similar purchases would have been made for the imperial palace. These generic items do not allow us any special insight to the dishes that were consumed, however.[28]

Music and other performances were also a part of Manuel's life. The emperor himself touches upon the joy of listening to a singer. Demetrios Chrysoloras remarks that he frequently requested lyre playing. Likewise, the well-known satire, *Mazaris' Journey to Hades*, has a comic story to tell. It mocks a son of a certain Lampadarios. This young man, although a cantor at a monastery, pleaded ill whenever Manuel requested him to sing or to play the lyre.[29] The fact that Manuel's writings are adorned with motifs of music and dancing may also suggest such a fondness on the emperor's behalf. Members of the court also played games such as *tzykanion*, and some-times, tournaments were held.[30] Finally, imperial ceremonies occupied

---

[27] Demetrios Chrysoloras, 'Synkrisis', 226.

[28] *Foundations of Imperial Conduct*, cols. 369–72; Belgrano, 170.

[29] *Foundations of Imperial Conduct*, cols. 369–72; *Mazaris*, 54–5; Demetrios Chrysoloras, 'Synkrisis', 226.

[30] Clavijo, 37, notes that tournaments were held in the Hippodrome. Although Clavijo may have been mistaken on this point, other sources do refer to tournaments among the courtly circles, but not specifically in Manuel's reign. See S. Kyriakidis, *Warfare in Late Byzantium (1204–1453)* (Leiden, 2011), 55–6. Henceforth, Kyriakidis, *Warfare*.

an important part of the emperor's life. Feast days were marked with elaborate ceremonies. The Palaiologan book of ceremonies, Pseudo-Kodinos, dates earlier than Manuel's reign, and it is thus risky to assume that all of the ceremonies in this text were still observed exactly in the same manner during his lifetime. However, major celebrations, such as Christmas and Epiphany, were probably held in a similar manner.[31]

Court and Government

The imperial court was also where the lives of the socio-economic elite, such as the courtiers, officials, ambassadors, the literati, influential merchants, intersected. These groups overlapped significantly: imperial relatives served as ambassadors, merchants held courtly titles and many of the elite had strong business interests. Although they were dependent on the emperor for land and tax-farming, there was no longer much land at the disposal of the imperial authority. Instead, trade became the major source of income, even for old aristocratic families. These aristocratic families now existed side by side with new merchant families. Overall, the Palaiologoi, Kantakouzenoi, Asanes, Laskarides, Philanthropenoi, Goudeles and Notarades dominated court life, with the latter two constituting examples of the new merchant families taking up positions in the Byzantine administration.[32]

At court, officials and title holders wore specified colours and fabrics, carried distinctive staffs and had their names embroidered with gold thread on their clothes.[33] Behind a veil of civility, the court seethed with rivalry. The satire of Mazaris gives us an exaggerated account of court life which nevertheless rings true. The narrative is populated with individuals who serve as imperial secretaries, orators and doctors at the same time, bearing witness to the multi-functionality of Manuel's courtiers. They mercilessly compete with each other to enter the emperor's 'inner circle' (τοῖς ἔνδον),

---

[31] *Pseudo-Kodinos*, 116–17, 166–7, 170–1, 178–9 and 194–203. Chalkokondyles and Sphrantzes, who give accounts of Manuel's reign, do not refer to imperial ceremonies at all, as opposed to the details found in the earlier accounts of Kantakouzenos and Gregoras.

[32] See the tables in Kiousopoulou, *Emperor or Manager*, for lists of individuals at the courts of Manuel, John VIII and Constantine XI. Forty people are mentioned in total for Manuel's court, thirteen of them are listed as *oikeioi*. On Manuel's ambassadors in particular, see Mergiali-Sahas, 'Ambassador'. See Kiousopoulou, *Emperor or Manager*, 55–80 and K. P. Matschke and F. Tinnefeld, *Die Gesellschaft im späten Byzanz. Gruppen, Strukturen und Lebensformen* (Cologne, Weimar and Vienna 2001), 160–220.

[33] *Pseudo-Kodinos*, 34–9.

enriching themselves by drafting official documents and parading their white garments – imperial gifts that signified Manuel's favour.[34]

The emperor's attitudes to the socio-economic elite and the various families it consisted of, cannot be discerned. In this regard, the sources for his reign are rather patchy and meagre. For instance, a list of his *oikeioi* exists only for the years 1399–1402.[35] Thus, it is not possible to trace the careers of these individuals. These *oikeioi* unsurprisingly include members of many prominent families, such as the Kantakouzenoi, Notarades, Goudeles and the Asanes. These families also inter-married, increasing their connectivity. Furthermore, the socio-economic elite under Manuel's rule was not only connected by blood, but was united by common interests, especially in trade. Although he was the emperor, these individuals held great power.[36] As an example, it should be remembered that members of the Goudeles family, also supporters of John VII, created a black market in grain during the blockade, placing further strain on the suffering populace. The emperor had not been able to curtail these activities, which reveals that despite the authoritative persona he liked to adopt, Manuel did not exercise great power and control over the elite – he simply lacked the political and economic means.

Mazaris and John Chortasmenos point out that Manuel chose his *oikeioi* and officials not only from the aristocracy, but also from the 'humble', that is, from those who did not possess such exalted pedigree. For instance, he frequently employed the members of the merchant Notaras family in his court; thus, it seems that he does not place a great stress on noble birth. Both authors claim that the emperor instead stressed the importance of a flair for *logoi* when selecting his *oikeoi*.[37] This peculiarity is unique to Manuel's reign, for no other Palaiologan emperor seems to have had similar criteria. Possibly, the emperor found it desirable to have individuals of a like mind around him to share his interests and to be receptive to the political messages in his texts. However, only a very few of Manuel's correspondents or collaborators seem to have held governmental posts.

---

[34] Mazaris, see especially 12–13, 22–3, 38–9 and 58–61. On Mazaris and life at the court, see M. Angold, 'Political Arts at the Late Palaiologan Court', in *Power and Subversion in Byzantium, Papers from the 43rd Spring Symposium of Byzantine Studies, Birmingham, March 2010*, eds. D. Angelov and M. Saxby (Farnham, 2013), 83–102. The presence of eunuchs can be traced until the reign of John Kantakouzenos, but it is not known whether there were any eunuchs at Manuel's court. See N. Gaul, 'Eunuchs in the late Byzantine Empire c. 1250–1400', in *Eunuchs in Antiquity and Beyond*, ed. S. Tougher (Cardiff, 2002), 199–217.

[35] Kiousopoulou, *Emperor or Manager*, 56.

[36] Necipoğlu, *Byzantium between the Ottomans and the Latins*, 190–200.   [37] Mazaris, 21.

Though a flair for *logoi* among his *oikeoi* was important, it was less so for his high-level officials and bureaucrats.

Another feature of Manuel's relationship with the elite is the 'circulation' of the officials among the political factions. The case of George Notaras is one such example. Previously an official for John V and also for Andronikos IV, he was taken on by Manuel from 1391 onwards. Similarly, Manuel Bryennios Leontaris and Demetrios Chrysoloras were officials for John VII, yet after his death, they were both also employed by Manuel. The emperor, therefore, did not hesitate to appoint those who had once served his rival nephew. His attitude, which was also probably influenced by the fact that the group of bureaucrats to choose from was rather small, was that he had to get whatever support he could from wherever he could.

Manuel as a Ruler: Some Remarks

It has been remarked that little is known of Manuel as an administrator since perhaps, there is actually little to be known.[38] Indeed, he did not make any radical changes to the already existing administrative system, and the historians narrating his reign do not offer a portrait of the emperor as an administrator. By contrast, Byzantine rulers such as Justinian I (527–65) and Alexios I Komnenos (1081–1118) are noted in the historical sources for their reforms and their governing interests. A non-Byzantine example of this type of ruler would be Frederick II (1194–1250) whose legal interests are abundantly recorded in Western sources. This was not the case for Manuel; however, a close reading of his own writings and the Venetian Senate deliberations does offer insight into the emperor's governing.

Manuel does not seem to have introduced great changes to Palaiologan governing practices, but it should also be emphasized that his political policies were varied and adapted quickly to the circumstances. As previously discussed, despite the limited agency allowed by the circumstances, the emperor did engage in serious efforts to manoeuvre around obstacles. For instance, the emperor seized on the opportunity to play the Ottoman princes against each other, and he employed this strategy with mixed success. Although he sought to downplay Italian influence in Byzantine trade, the emperor also proceeded carefully so as not to alienate these powers. He refrained from taking sides in the feuds between Venice and Genoa. After all, he often depended on both for military and economic aid.

---

[38] Barker, *Manuel II*, 408.

Still, despite petitioning Venice for help, Manuel turned a blind eye to the anti-Venetian activities of his brother Theodore in the Morea, and later, those of his own sons. He encouraged Byzantine expansion in the area, both territorially and financially. The Senate also complained that the emperor did not respect the Venetian economic privileges.[39] Further, Manuel refused to accept the Venetian claim to Tenedos and compelled Venice to adopt a more lukewarm stance in the treaty of 1406. When the Venetians delayed his return from the Morea to Constantinople in 1403, he negotiated with the Genoese to alarm the latter, and his strategy worked; the Venetians moved with more alacrity and supplied him with galleys. Likewise, in March 1406, the Venetian Senate was alarmed by a report that the emperor was planning to fortify Tenedos with the help of the Genoese. Although the report was a baseless one the concern of the Venetians indicates that they found such a manoeuvre by Manuel quite plausible.[40]

When the opportunity presented itself, the emperor also assumed the unprecedented role of a diplomat-emperor and toured European territories to seek aid. Similarly, he reached out to as many polities as possible in his quest for help, including those not in Byzantium's immediate political sphere. Manuel's diplomatic policies are echoed in a panegyric by Chortasmenos; 'he always kept them (the Ottomans) on their toes, sometimes arousing the Hungarians against them, sometimes moving the Persians against them, always fighting them with some allies'.[41] It is significant that the majority of the recorded acts of Manuel's reign pertain to embassies and foreign treaties.[42] This demonstrates his conviction that securing foreign help was the most important step in eliminating the Ottoman threat.

The Venetian Senate deliberations also reflect some of Manuel's characteristics as an administrator.[43] For instance, on one occasion, he seemed to have a preferred candidate for the appointment of a new *bailos*, and the Senate appointed the former envoy Paolo Zeno as *bailos* on Manuel's request.[44] The emperor's financial problems are the most dominant theme in the deliberations, which bears witness to the empire's increasing

---

[39] For instance, see Thiriet, *Régestes*, II, no. 1247, 66, no. 1260, 69, no. 1364, 89, no. 1948, 219. See also Chapter 5.
[40] Nicol, *Byzantium and Venice*, 349; Thiriet, *Régestes*, II, no. 1208, 56.
[41] Chortasmenos, 'Address to Manuel II', 218.
[42] See Dölger, *Regesten*, 80–112 for a list of Manuel's official acts.
[43] Thiriet, *Régestes*, II, no. 1415, 98, no. 1463, 108–9, no. 1592, 138.
[44] Thiriet, *Régestes*, II, no. 1176, 50–1.

poverty and Manuel's preoccupation with finances. One document makes it plain that Manuel often protested his poverty when he was reminded of the Byzantine debt owed to Venice.[45] He continuously petitioned the Senate for financial aid, more so than military requests, and furthermore, his complaints were almost always of a financial nature: Venetians avoiding the *kommerkion* tax, Byzantines bribing Venetians to carry their taxable merchandise and the Moreans fleeing to Venice to avoid taxation. On occasion, Manuel event sought to lay imperial claim to the inheritance of Byzantine merchants who died in Venetian territory.

While the frequency of such complaints also stems from the chiefly economic relationship between the two polities, it nevertheless indicates the importance Manuel gave to financial matters. Like his father John V and grandfather John VI before him, he tried to weaken the Venetian economic privileges at every opportunity. For instance, in 1418 the emperor imposed a tax on the wine consumed by the Venetians in Constantinople. He excused himself to the Venetian authorities by pointing out how meagre the imperial revenues were and that he was in need of money against the Ottoman threat. Despite the protests of the Senate, he even increased the tax and a year later, only made a small concession. In 1423, the Senate would moreover complain that Manuel had compelled some Jews in Constantinople to acknowledge his own authority although they were under the protection of Venice. Quite possibly, Manuel did so in order to obtain more funds.[46]

The Senate deliberations are also laced with Manuel's offers to mediate between Sigismund of Hungary and Venice. These offers were usually rejected, and yet the emperor's tenacity in this matter reveals his determination to obtain help from Venice. It can be suggested that bereft of any military or economic means, Manuel sought to enhance his political prestige by acting as a mediator. Similarly, the subject of one Senate deliberation is interesting with regards to how Manuel was perceived by others. The deliberation reflects alarm concerning Manuel's presence in the Morea, which the Senate claims, was not without danger for the region. Half of the Venetian mercenaries in the area were Greek and the Senate ordered that these soldiers to be dismissed before the emperor's arrival.[47] Quite possibly, Venice believed that these Greek soldiers might switch their loyalty to the emperor in case of a Byzantine-Venetian conflict. Yet it

[45] Thiriet, *Régestes*, II, no. 1165, 48. The original Latin is given in Iorga, *Notes et Extraits*, 137.
[46] Chrysostomides, 'Venetian Commercial Privileges', 286, 308–9; Thiriet, *Régestes*, II, no. 1916, 202.
[47] Thiriet, *Régestes*, II, no. 1578, 135.

should also be remembered that Manuel's attempts at persuasion had failed with the Thessalonians and the supporters of John VII.

As previously discussed, despite its autobiographical characteristics, Manuel's rich oeuvre offers very little insight into his actual governing practices. However, in some of his letters and the *Funeral Oration*, it is still possible to trace several of his characteristics as a ruler. To begin with, his letters reflect Manuel's understanding of the precarious situation of the empire. Tellingly, he never speaks of restoring the empire to its former glory or suggests that a bright future lies ahead. Instead the letters are adorned with bitter references to *kairos*, circumstances, which always hinder and restrict him. In a letter to Manuel Pothos, the emperor laments that he had always been forced to choose not what is more beneficial, but merely what is less harmful.[48] Indeed, a study of Manuel's reign shows that more often than not, this was the case.

In his letter collection, Manuel reflects on some of the political troubles he faced as a ruler. For instance, in 1391, he points out to Kydones that the Byzantines accompanied the sultan on his campaign only to avert even worse trials. The dangers the Byzantines faced on the campaign, according to Manuel, was nothing compared to the dangers they would face should they disobey the Ottomans.[49] The numerous sieges of Constantinople by the Ottomans prove his assessment to be true. Similarly, although Manuel was hopeful in his quest for Western aid, his letters from Europe hints that he was fully aware that Western promises could be in vain. He repeatedly stresses that the situation required deeds, and not mere promises.

In 1405, while writing to Manuel Chrysoloras about Henry IV, the emperor muses on the current state of English affairs. He also ponders the possible outcomes of securing military help.[50] Manuel agrees that the English king was indeed pressed by political troubles, but back in 1400, the emperor argues, Henry fared even worse. If the English king could promise help back then, surely he could do so now. Manuel explains that even a small gesture of military help would be of tremendous importance. First of all, he explains, the finances of the empire were so bad that any amount of money was welcome and would give the Byzantine people hope. Moreover, it would alarm the Ottomans, compelling them to reconsider any plans of attack.

Two letters in the collection deal with more concrete matters. In a letter to Manuel Chrysoloras, the emperor refers to a certain Skaranos as his treasurer.[51] Skaranos, Manuel explains, knew the financial straits the

---

[48] Letter 35.   [49] Letter 17.   [50] Letter 55.   [51] Letter 49.

empire was in, and he had a good mind and did good work. The letter indicates that Chrysoloras asked for two favours on behalf of Skaranos. These petitions cannot be discerned, but Manuel says that one of them would be granted immediately, and the other, later. This should cause no harm, he adds, as Skaranos enjoyed his goodwill (εὐμενεία).

In another letter to the future patriarch Euthymios, the emperor complains of civil unrest in the Morea – namely, the hostility of the *archontes* towards the despot.[52] He bitterly remarks upon the readiness of the Moreans to take up arms and remarks that it would have been much better if they used their arms where they should. Manuel here is referring to the absurdity of the Morean nobility fighting amongst themselves instead of joining their forces against the Ottomans. He points out to Euthymios that the Moreans being at peace with each other was of paramount importance to him. This letter is further testament to the great significance the emperor placed upon the Morea as a stronghold against the Ottomans. It also underscores his perception of local strife as the chief obstacle for resistance to the Ottomans.

The *Funeral Oration* contains some illuminating instances as well. Between the lines, the emperor expresses his opinion on European powers. The Westerners such as the English, French and the Spanish, he complains, are very slow to act. However, on occasion they are stirred to action and are capable of achieving great things.[53] These brief remarks mirror Manuel's own experiences in his quest for help from the West. Similarly, the emperor briefly discusses the Hospitallers of Rhodes, and explains that Despot Theodore ceded Corinth to them as they were in a position to protect the city: the Hospitallers were powerful, wealthy, well-connected and were also Christians. On another occasion, Manuel points out that Bayezid feared the Hospitallers as they were far stronger that the Byzantines, and knew that they could inflict harm on the Ottoman possessions near the Peloponnese.[54] While the praise he bestows on the Hospitallers stems from Manuel's desire to vindicate Theodore's sale of Corinth, it was nevertheless justified. It should also be remembered that the emperor had another reason to think highly of the Hospitallers of Rhodes: back in 1390, they had supported him during the uprising of John VII.

Manuel's lengthy efforts to offer an *apologia* for the sale of Corinth also reflects some of his policies. He argues that the sale of Corinth to the Hospitallers was a well-planned strategic move.[55] As the Byzantines were

---

[52] Letter 51. [53] *Funeral Oration*, 174–7. [54] *Funeral Oration*, 166–9, 184–7.
[55] *Funeral Oration*, 166–9.

likely to lose the city to the Ottomans, Corinth's fall would also facilitate the future conquests of adjacent cities. The sale, Manuel argues, was a pre-emptive measure. Although these explanations again seek to justify Theodore's sale, they are also sensible ones. The sale did in fact protect Corinth from falling into the hands of the Ottomans, who finally managed overrun the Morea much later. Moreover, during the blockade of Constantinople, Manuel was willing to cede the city to Venice should he be obliged to leave it. Clearly, he preferred it to be in Venetian hands rather than fall to the Ottomans. The emperor would sanction another such transfer in 1423. With Manuel's approval, his son Andronikos ceded Thessalonike to the Venetians. Once more, a Byzantine city would be given to a stronger, wealthier Christian power in order to prevent its sacking. One wonders whether the emperor resorted to this policy after his catastrophic loss of Thessalonike to the Ottomans in 1387. After all, in the 1380s, he had insisted on fighting despite the hopelessness of the situation. This stance would have resulted in the sacking of the city had Manuel's departure not enabled the citizens to surrender. In the cases of Corinth and Thessalonike in 1423, it is telling that Manuel did not urge the despots to resist at any cost, instead choosing to sanction these transfers.

Manuel's *apologia* for the sale of Corinth seems to further reveal some parallels with his own experiences as a ruler.[56] He points out that while some people grumbled that Theodore had not consulted his people on the matter, the despot had continuously sought to persuade the Moreans to fight with the Ottomans, but all of his efforts had been in vain. Moreover, some people also resented the despot's constant urging and resisting stance. Instead of letting the Moreans be yoked under the infidel, Manuel points out that by selling Corinth to the Hospitallers, Theodore had merely chosen the 'lesser evil.' All these bear a striking resemblance to the emperor's portrayal of his own experiences with the populace of Thessalonike in the 1380s, as well as that of Constantinople during the blockade.

Furthermore, Manuel's letters clearly illustrate his financial straits and are frequently interwoven with references to his pressing need for money. In Asia Minor, he minutely calculates the cost of a horse's fodder; in the Morea, the emperor extolls his restoration of the Hexamilion by noting that the people could now sell their produce at a much higher rate. In Thessalonike in the 1380s, he tells Kydones that he wouldn't have invested so much money in an embassy to the pope had he not been sure of success

---

[56] *Funeral Oration*, 194–5.

of the mission. And at another instance, he points out to Kydones that giving 100 *staters* in one payment is too much even for the emperor.[57] 'Nothing that needs to be done can be done', Manuel declares, quoting a well-known saying, 'when money is missing'.[58]

Similarly, a glance at some of his favourite metaphors may hint at two of Manuel's interests as ruler of an impoverished empire: money and merchants. The emperor's writings are strikingly adorned with coin, merchant and marketplace metaphors. While Manuel is certainly not unique in employing such metaphors, his fondness is remarkable. For instance, in the *Foundations of Imperial Conduct*, Manuel likens life to a marketplace, and people to merchants who calculate their profit and debt by their virtuous acts.[59] In the *Ethico-Political Orations*, he refers to the craft of coin- making. Elsewhere, inspired by Plato's *Phaedo*, he likens different virtues to coins of different metals.[60] When Manuel apologizes to Kydones for his silence, he compares Kydones to a person who loaned a genuine coin and did not receive the equivalent in return.[61]

In relation to his coin metaphors, it is fitting to discuss, even if briefly, some aspects of Manuel's coinage. **(Fig 8.3)** By the time he became the sole emperor, gold coinage was a thing of past. The last gold *nomisma* was struck under John V, and Manuel's own coinage consisted of silver and bronze coins. Compared to his predecessors, Manuel's coins have less metal content and their designs are more crude. In 1394/5, the emperor was forced to reduce the metal content of his coinage, but this was a trend that was already underway with the Palaiologans. On the whole, his coinage bears witness to the dire financial straits of the empire. The mints under Manuel's rule are difficult to trace. It has been proposed that two mints were in existence. Either both were in Constantinople, or

---

[57] Letter 18; Letter 12, lines 1–15; Letter 68, lines 65–6. These are a few selected examples to illustrate this point.

[58] Letter 68, lines 38–42. '. . . φημὶ τὸ δεῖσθαι μὲν τὸν καιρὸν χρημάτων ὅτι πολλῶν, ὧν μὴ παρόντων, οὐδὲν ἔστι γενέσθαι τῶν δεόντων, ὁ ῥήτωρ ἔφη. . .' This saying originated from Demosthenes, *Olynthiacs*, I, 20. However, it was also found in Aphthonios, *Progymnasmata*, 4. As discussed before, Manuel was familiar with both, however his reference to the 'rhetor' makes it more likely that he was referring to Demosthenes.

[59] *Foundations of Imperial Conduct*, col. 349, ' Ἔοικε δὲ καὶ ἀγορᾷ τὰ καθ' ἡμᾶς πράγματα, καὶ ἔξεστι πρὸς κέρδος νοῦν ἔχουσι πάντα πράττειν, πωλεῖν, ἀλλάττειν, ὠνεῖσθαι.'

[60] *Ethico-Political Orations*, 317; '. . .τὴν μεταλλικὴν . . . τὴν οἶμαι χρυσοποιϊκὴν καλομένην'. *Funeral Oration*, 216–217, 'Ἐπεί τοι καὶ δραχμαὶ πολλαί, ἂν ἐπὶ τὸ ἱστάναι τις ἐνέγκῃ, γένοιτ' ἂν τάλαντον ἰσόρροποι ἑνί που πάντως ταλάντῳ καὶ χρυσίου τάλαντον, ὕλης ὃν τιμιωτέρας πάντων ἑξῆς τῶν μετάλλων τοῖς χρηματίζεσθαι βουλομένοις, ἀτιμότερον ἂν γένοιτο τούτοις ἀργυρίου πλήθους τάλαντων.'

[61] Letter 36, lines 5–7, 'νόμισμα μὲν γάρ τις χρήσας ἀκίβδηλον ἔστιν οὗ λαβὼν οὐ τοιοῦτον ἦν ἔσχετο. . .'.

Figure 8.3 Silver hyperpyron of Manuel II, the reverse. Photo by Werner Forman / Universal Images Group / Getty Images.

one was established in Thessalonike after 1408. Some coins of *tornese* denomination also seem to have been minted in Morea under his name, but these cannot be precisely dated to a specific period of his reign.[62] While some coins have been attributed to the joint reigns of John V – Andronikos IV and John V – Manuel II, no coinage has been securely identified for the joint rule of Manuel and his son John VIII.[63]

Some Byzantine emperors could have coinage that were ideologically quite charged. For instance, the coins of Michael VIII Palaiologos alluded to the recapture of Constantinople in 1261 by depicting the Virgin with the city walls and the emperor paying obeisance to Christ. The emperor's namesake Archangel Michael was also represented as his guardian, both as an archangel and as a warrior.[64] By contrast, a study of the imagery on Manuel's coinage does not really yield any ideological insight. Design-wise, he continued to use the set iconography of his predecessors: many of his

[62] A. R. Bellinger and P. Grierson. A.*Catalogue of the Byzantine Coins in the Dumbarton Oaks Collection and in the Whittemore Collection*, vol. 5 (Washington, 1999), 214–15. Henceforth Bellinger and Grierson, *Coins*. Also see J. Baker, 'A Coinage for Late Byzantine Morea under Manuel II Palaiologos (1391–1425)', *Revue Numismatique* 162 (2006), 385–405.
[63] Bellinger and Grierson, *Coins*, 219; 7 and 200. [64] Hilsdale, *Decline*, 164–9.

coins simply depict Christ on the obverse and the emperor on the reverse. Manuel appears bust-length, full-size and sometimes, on horseback. The image of the nimbate emperor, started by Andronikos II, had by then become a standard feature of Palaiologan coinage.[65]Manuel also adhered to this tradition. Similarly, between 1391–5, he continued using his father's designs depicting St Demetrios or Sts Constantine and Helena.

There is one case of change in coinage that might be interpreted as an ideological message. In 1394/5, when he reduced the metal content of coinage, Manuel also completely changed the design of his silver half-stavrata: a bust of Christ replaced the image of St Demetrios on horseback, and the inscription on the coin was also changed. Instead of the formula *autokrator faithful in Christ*, Manuel was designated as *despotes*. Perhaps this change was carried out in order to make up space, for at the same time, the former inscription of *basileus*, had also been expanded to read *basileus of the Romans*, the longer and fuller imperial title.[66] If this were indeed the case, the emperor's decision to opt for the full imperial title may be interpreted as an attempt to assert his authority and legitimacy. Perhaps, Manuel was making a political statement against John VII and his followers, underscoring that *he* was the true emperor of the Romans.

The documents from Manuel's reign reflect the difficult circumstances he faced. As in his own letters, the word *kairos* (circumstances), is frequently employed as a means of complaint: it is always a hindrance.[67] Due to the 'changes in the affairs' and 'the anomalies of the time', immovable properties kept changing hands and were also often confiscated by the state. As the territories and the finances of the empire kept shrinking, the pool of properties at the emperor's disposal was diminished. For instance, a courtyard in Thessalonike was bestowed upon two monasteries and two individuals within a relatively short span of time. The grants were made by

---

[65] The nimbate emperor depicted the ruler with a halo or circle (nimbus) of light and glory around him.

[66] Bellinger and Grierson, *Coins*, 67, 214–15. The authors suggest that *tornesi* depicting St Demetrios might be from Manuel's reign in Thessalonike in the 1380s.

[67] Bartusis, *Pronoia*, 551–63, also notes this. The documents concerning monasteries have been edited in several monastic acts; those of Pantéleimon, Dionysiou, Docheiraiou, Protaton and Lavra. MM also has several official documents. Dennis, 'Official Documents', lists some acts that are not otherwise known. E. Schilbach, 'Die Hypothyposis der καθολικοὶ κριταὶ τῶν Ῥωμαίων vom juni 1398 (?)', *BZ* 61 (1968), 44–70 has edited a *prostagma* issued to the General Judges in 1398. See Chapter 7 for the documents Manuel issued while in Europe.

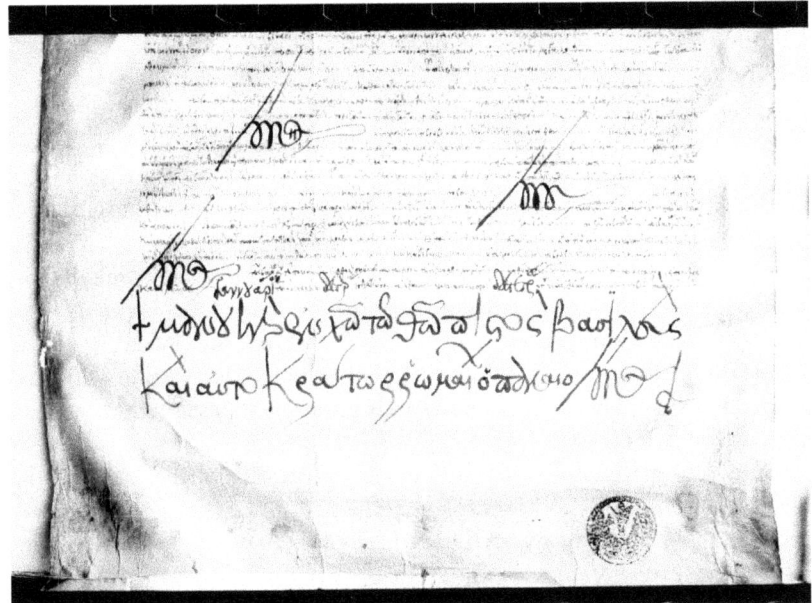

Figure 8.4 The signature of Manuel II. *Chrysobull* ratifying the ownership of the lands of the Pantokrator Monastery in Eastern Macedonia. Archives of the Pantokrator Monastery, Mt. Athos (ψ2 σ. 121–122, no. 2). Photo: Institute of Historical Research, National Hellenic Research Foundation.

three different rulers in quick succession, and unwittingly, the courtyard was given simultaneously to two monasteries.[68]

Some of these documents illuminate also, the intense mobility of Manuel's life. Several of them touch upon his travels and narrate how petitions were brought before Manuel in person when he was in Thessalonike, or how he intervened in some of the cases as he happened to be passing near the property in question.[69] Such documents would have been drafted by the imperial secretaries and later brought to the emperor. Manuel would sign them in red ink, using big letters and covering the last word in order to prevent any changes. **(Fig 8.4)** In 1394, he issued a command that the year, and not only the indiction, had to be written on all documents – a regulation that was only partially followed. This

[68] See *Actes de Lavra*, no. 163, 163–6.
[69] *Actes de Lavra*, no. 163, 163–6; *Actes de Docheiariou*, ed. N. Oikonomides (Paris, 1984), no. 52; *Actes de Dionysiou*, ed. N. Oikonomides, (Paris, 1968), no. 157, 140, all note Manuel's travels. Henceforth, *Actes de Docheiariou* and *Actes de Dionysiou*.

regulation was issued because two monasteries had presented documents claiming ownership for the same property, yet the dates were not legible. The emperor's solution was to divide the land into two equal parts.[70]

Several *prostagmata* concerning monastic properties, including the above-mentioned case with the illegible documents, indicate that Manuel heard the pleas of the monks in person and delivered the final decision.[71] His official documents also reveal quite his authoritarian side. In 1396 he issued a *prostagma* in order to secure the commemoration of his mother, a direct intervention in Church affairs. In the 1370s, as the despot of Thessalonike, he converted several monastic lands into *pronoiai*, provoking ecclesiastical protest.[72] Another *prostagma* he issued for the Monastery of Protaton shows that Manuel was also interfering with the internal management of the monastery. It has been argued that this was an unusual concern for an emperor.[73]

Some official documents from his reign present further interesting instances with regards to Manuel's governance. It has been demonstrated recently that during his sojourn in Thessalonike in 1414–15, Manuel not only issued several *prostagmata*, but also actually composed them with his own hand. These documents, consisting of one *chrysobull* and four *prostagmata*, reveal a hand that was highly accustomed to writing. The handwriting has been evaluated as being rapid, elegant and accomplished. This is highly unusual, since emperors did not draft the documents themselves, but merely signed them. Although Manuel's case was in all probability, necessitated by his travels in Thessalonike, where he possibly did not have chancery members with him, it also shows quite a personal involvement in government affairs.[74]

In addition to reflecting Manuel's concerns over the fisc, the extent of the emperor's involvement in financial affairs is also noteworthy. Not only had Manuel introduced a monetary reform in the early 1390s and had confiscated half of the monastic lands in the 1370s, he also imposed further regulations after the Battle of Ankara in 1402. For instance, after re-gaining

[70] R. J. Loenertz, 'Le chancelier impérial à Byzance au XIVe et au XIIIe siècle', *OCP* 26 (1960), 275–300 and N. Oikonomides, 'La chancelliere impériale de Byzance du 13e au 15e siècle', *REB* 43 (1985), 167–95, see especially 171. MM, II, 214; Dölger, *Regesten*, no. 3246, 82.

[71] *Actes de Lavra*, no. 163, 163–6; *Actes de Docheirou*, no. 52, 269–71.

[72] For Manuel's policy of 'pronoiarization', see Bartusis, *Pronoia*, 551–63. The term was coined by Bartusis.

[73] *Actes de Prôtaton*, ed. D. Papachryssanthou (Paris, 1975), 107–9.

[74] R. Estangüi- Gómez, 'Actes autographes de l'empereur Manuel II Paléologue conservés dans les archives du Mont Athos', in *Peribolos: Mélanges offerts à Mirjana Zivojinovic*, eds. B. Miljkovic and D. Dzeldelzic (Belgrade, 2015), 409–26. Henceforth, Estangüi-Gómez, 'Actes autographes'.

Thessalonike, he did not entirely abolish the Ottoman tax *haradj*, but compelled Thessalonians to pay its one third to the imperial treasury.[75] This move was undoubtedly not well-received by the populace, but it does reflect his attempts to strengthen the state of the treasury. During the blockade, the emperor became involved in the case of an icon that brought revenue to the owners.[76] Similarly, in 1414, when Andronikos Philanthrophenos died without an heir, Manuel took an interest in his inheritance, dividing it into three. One third went to the deceased's parents, one third to the monasteries of Athos, and the final third, the emperor transferred to the fisc.[77]

Sphrantzes presents us with one final insight into Manuel's governing. The historian claims that he turned the office of *mesazon* into a permanent position. The reasons for this decision are not clear. Of the *mesazontes* Manuel had, the names that are known to us belong to Demetrios Palaiologos Goudeles and Hilario Doria. They held office together as a pair of *mesazontes*. Increasingly, the *mesazontes* would assume more diplomatic functions. There was an internal hierarchy between the *mesazontes*, and they were probably chosen with a view to maintain the balance between old aristocratic families and the new mercantile elite.[78]

All in all, it seems that the dire circumstances of his reign, the diminished territories and the bureaucracy of his empire prompted Manuel to become a hands-on ruler on several occasions. After all, Sphrantzes even reports that Manuel supposedly claimed that the Byzantine Empire needed a manager, not an emperor.[79] This may partially have stemmed from his personality and his desire to represent himself as being completely in charge, since his writings likewise make it clear that he sought to establish himself both as a political, literary and theological authority.

An Imperial Author

Manuel's writings give us invaluable insight into his self-awareness as emperor and into the manifest importance he gave to being recognized as such. We have already discussed on many occasions how Manuel employed self-representation strategies to enhance his authority and idealize

---

[75] Necipoğlu, *Byzantium between the Ottomans and the Latins*, 341.   [76] See Chapter 6.

[77] Estangüi-Gómez, 'Actes autographes', 413.

[78] Sphrantzes, 86. Kiousopoulou, *Emperor or Manager*, 86, believes that this shows the importance Manuel gave to the organization of the state.

[79] Sphrantzes, 83.

his rule. This political use of his writings and his persona as an author-emperor is a distinctive feature of his reign, and it is not observed in other Palaiologan rulers. Clearly, besides his own enjoyment of the act of writing, he also explored writing as a political tool to advertise his opinions and position. In addition to the political messages which permeated his writings, a close reading of Manuel's metaphors and allusions underscores his desire to underline his unique status as emperor.

In a letter to Gabriel of Thessalonike, who seems to have criticized the emperor's literary activities, Manuel compares his inferiority to ancient writers with a peasant who burns his own small home in despair after seeing the imperial palace, pointing out the absurdity of such feelings of inferiority.[80] The choice of the imperial palace as an unattainable boon, is telling. In another such case, Manuel likens his position before the Virgin Mary to a person who uses an official as intermediary at the imperial palace, to gain access to the emperor.[81] This is also a very fitting metaphor when one considers the commonplace image of the Byzantine court as the earthly reflection of the heavenly court, and the role of the Virgin as the intermediary between God and humanity. Once again, this metaphor emphasizes Manuel's loftiness as emperor, indirectly comparing him to Christ, the emperor of the heavens.

Such 'imperial' metaphors even surface in the *Declamation regarding a Drunken Man*. Manuel points out that men who lack but desire children will still perceive others as blessed (εὐδαίμων), even if they themselves wear purple.[82] The imperial purple is here presented as the ultimate state of contentment. Similarly, in an early letter, Manuel tells his mother, the Empress Helena, that she ought to defer to Kantakouzenos not only because he is her father but also because of his former rank as emperor.[83] Similar sentiments can be found the emperor's remark in the *Discourse to Kabasilas* that those who sat with Manuel 'were granted this privilege', and in his emphasis in the *Dialogue with a Persian* that he was the first to be served with the platter of nuts that was circulated among the audience.[84] These vignettes, too, seek to assert the emperor's imperial authority in humiliating circumstances: first, when he had taken refuge in Lesbos; and second, during his compulsory service in the Ottoman campaign.

---

[80] Letter 52, lines 1–4.   [81] Letter 57, lines 1–5.
[82] *Declamation regarding a Drunken Man*, 275, '. . . οἱ μηδέ πῶ κατειληφότες τὸν τῶν πατέρων χορόν, τοὺς παισί κομῶντας εὐδαιμονίζοντες μᾶλλον ἤπερ αὐτούς, κἂν αὐτήν που περιβέβληνται τὴν ἀλουργίδα, κἂν τἄλλα πάντ' εὐδαίμονες ὦσι καὶ ζηλωτοί.'
[83] Letter 1, lines 20–1.   [84] *Discourse to Kabasilas*, lines 190–1; *Dialogue with a Persian*, 50.

Thus, even through metaphors, Manuel strives to enhance his imperial authority in the eyes of his audience.

He moreover often adopts the persona of the 'busy ruler'. This is true especially in the face of criticism, such as his position in the *Discourse to Iagoup*. The previously quoted letter in which Manuel gives a humorous description of the noisy palace life, is another such instance. The emperor complains about being compelled to forsake the diet prescribed by his physicians. He declares that although he was already ill and had to undertake tasks that would weaken even a healthy person, he was still compelled to carry out what was expected of his imperial rank (σχῆμα):

> .... we are a slave to the cares oppressing us rather than being the master of our own desires. All this weighs heavily on us. Nonetheless, it is consolation enough for me to keep in mind that perhaps the toil of the ruler will be of benefit to his people. They have therefore become pleasant to me, these struggles by day; and these cares by night, which keep me from my sleep and drive me to carry out my duties, cause me joy no less than sorrow. For, as it seems, sorrow does not come by itself for those who want to mix their cup, just as you 'cannot find a life without sorrow among any' of those who appear to be most blessed (τῶν εὐδαιμονεστάτων).[85]

Through a depiction of his daily life, Manuel thus paints a portrait of himself as an idealized and all sacrificing ruler. His veiled allusions to Homer and Plato further reinforce this representation. The 'cares by night' that keep the emperor awake, is possibly a reference to the *Iliad*, where Agamemnon does not sleep at night as a ruler upon whom the cares of many people have been entrusted.[86] Of all the characters in the *Iliad*, Manuel identifies himself with Agamemnon, the epitome of kingship.

Manuel also presents rulership as a mixture of joy and sorrow, a source of true blessedness (εὐδαιμονία) in the eyes of many, for as a ruler, none of these two feelings can be experienced separately. This is a reference to *Phaedo* where Socrates points out that joy and sorrow are always mixed

---

[85] Letter 44, lines 53–9. 'ὡς νῦν γε τῶν κατεπειγόντων ἡμᾶς πραγμάτων μᾶλλον ἐσμεν κτῆμα ἤπερ ἡμῶν αὐτῶν. Ταυτὶ μὲν οὖν ἐπαχθῆ. Πλὴν ἐμοὶ τὸ παραμυθούμενον ἱκανὸν ἐκεῖνο ἐνθυμουμένῳ ὡς ἴσως οἴσει καρπὸν τῷ γένει τὸ πονεῖν τὸν ἄρχοντα. ἡδεῖς μοι τοίνυν γίγνονται οἱ μεθ'ἡμέραν ἀγῶνες, καὶ αἱ τῆς νυκτὸς φροντίδες, ἅμα δὲ μὲν ἀγρυπνεῖν, ἅμα δὲ τὸ δέον ποιεῖν προξενοῦσαι, οὐχ ἧττον γε εὐφραίνουσιν ἢ λυποῦσιν. ὡς γὰρ ἔοικεν, οὐκ ἄκρατον τι πέφυκεν εἶναι τὸ λυπηρὸν κεραννύναι βουλομένοις, ὥσπερ οὐδὲ ἔστιν εὑρεῖν βίον ἄλυπον ἐν οὐδενὶ τῶν εὐδαιμονεστάτων εἶναι δοκούντων.' See also Letter 51, lines 17-8, for the same theme of neglecting food and sleep for the sake of imperial duties.

[86] Dennis has not noted these allusions, probably because they are not direct quotations. Homer, *Iliad*, Book 2, 459. Plato, *Phaedo*, 60 B–D.

together. The emperor thus identifies a bittersweet quality to the envy-provoking imperial authority and emphasizes the burdens of his rank. This self-representation functioned as an *apologia* for the supposed lack of elegance in the letter Manuel sent to Demetrios Chrysoloras; the emperor was so busy that he could not write properly. At the same time, the self-conscious display of his authorial talent is revealed even in these circumstances. Furthermore, since Demetrios Chrysoloras was serving as John VII's *mesazon* in Thessalonike, it can also be suggested that Manuel was probably aiming to promote his image as an ideal ruler there through the circulation and performance of his letter.

In accordance with traditional ideals of kingship, Manuel also envisages himself as a model for his subjects to imitate. The notion of subjects imitating their ruler is highlighted in the *Dialogue on Marriage*. The empress mother urges him to marry in order to set an example for his subjects. In a letter to Manuel Raoul, an emigré at the Latin court in Cyprus, the emperor again advocates the same idea. Raoul must imitate King James as best he can as his subject, no matter what his own personal inclinations might be. In this instance, an attentive reading makes it clear that Manuel's advice was mixed with a criticism of King James. The emperor touches upon the king's overzealous pursuit of hunting, which did not leave time for anything else. He then promptly cites the same line from the *Iliad* on kingship: ' . . . must not sleep through the night'.

Manuel mocks the notion that the king lost sleep to the hunt, when he should be doing losing sleep because of the weight of responsibility and the welfare of his subjects. This criticism becomes even more poignant when the emperor contrasts his own preoccupied state as a ruler with that of King James, and subtly portrays himself as the 'ideal' ruler.[87] Finally, a letter to Gabriel of Thessalonike, represents another such case. Gabriel seems to have disapproved of Manuel's literary endeavours and as a defence, the emperor argues that he writes in order for his subjects to imitate him, so that they do not become 'barbarians'.[88] Through his writings, Manuel sought to advertise himself as an 'ideal' ruler and attempted to bolster through *logoi*, his shaky authority as emperor.

Imperial Pastimes

Apart from his duties as emperor, Manuel enjoyed several pastimes. Again, we will turn to his oeuvre in order to gain insight into these. For example,

---

[87] Letter 32, lines 1–28.   [88] Letter 52, lines 29–36.

his writings and other sources reflect his fondness for hunting and horse-manship. This is not surprising at all. Such pastimes were to be expected in anyone of aristocratic upbringing, since hunting was also seen as military training.[89] Following this established practice, Manuel, too, stresses the importance of hunting to his son in the *Foundations of Imperial Conduct*. Yet despite the traditional and conventional nature of this advice, the emperor's language becomes markedly vivid and passionate. This change in tone can be interpreted as hinting at his more personal feelings on the issue: he fondly describes the gentle shadow of a tent, the leaves of the trees and a stream nearby, and enumerates various hunting tactics.[90]

Similarly, Manuel's writings are adorned with hunting metaphors. In the *Dialogue on Marriage*, he uses an elaborate metaphor of the hunter and the prey to describe the debate between himself and his mother. Elsewhere, while describing the necessity of education for a ruler, Manuel remarks that a noble horse does not breed with a lame mule.[91] In *On the Procession of the Holy Spirit*, he compares the use of philosophy in theology to using a horse not for hunting, but for trying to fly with the eagles.[92] And the emperor betrays great interest in a horse that Demetrios Chrysoloras had purchased, joking in his letter that Manuel himself could put the horse to a better use than his 'stay-at-home' correspondent.[93]

Cyriac of Ancona records a hunting party of Manuel's sons, John VIII and Theodore II, who set up pavilions with their courtiers to hunt with spears, dogs and falcons.[94] It is safe to assume that Manuel also enjoyed such occasions. His hunting makes appearances in various other texts: Demetrios Chrysoloras notes his love for horses and Kydones chastises him for overzealous hunting in Lemnos. In an amusing anecdote, Clavijo narrates that he was not able to see certain relics in John the Baptist in Petra because Manuel had left for a hunt and had forgotten to leave the keys with

---

[89] Kyriakidis, *Warfare*, 61–2; Angelov, 'Ideal Children', 91; A. Kazhdan, 'The Aristocracy and the Imperial Ideal', in *The Byzantine Aristocracy from IX to XIIIth Centuries*, ed. M. Angold (Oxford, 1982), 75. For some cases of perception of imperial hunting, see E. Patlagean, 'De la chasse et du souverain', *DOP* 46 (1992), 257–63.

[90] *Foundations of Imperial Conduct*, cols. 359–61 and 377.

[91] *Foundations of Imperial Conduct*, col. 352, '... μηδ' ἵππος ὑπέρθερμος τε καὶ ἰσχυρὸς ἱππέα βάναυσον ὤνησεν.'

[92] *On the Procession of the Holy Spirit*, 160, '... ὥσπερ ἂν εἴ τις κτησάμενος ἵππον ταχὺν οὐ κατατρέχειν θηρίων, ἀλλ' ἀετοῖς συνίπτασθαι βούλοιτο, οἳ ἂν τὴν πτῆσιν ἐκτείνοιεν.'

[93] Letter 43. The whole letter deals with this topic.

[94] Cyriac of Ancona, *Later Travels*, ed. and trans. E. W. Bodnar (Cambridge, MA, 2003), 53–5. He also mentions a certain Manuel from Crete, who was John VIII's falconer. *Pseudo-Kodinos*, 106–7, notes the position of *protoierakarios*, falconer, but it is unclear whether this post survived into Manuel's reign.

his wife. The Spanish traveller also boasts that the emperor sent them half
a boar he had killed on a hunt, and the *Dialogue with a Persian* records
Manuel hunting several boars.[95] Perhaps, after all, the boar was Manuel's
preferred game, and all these instances hint that the emperor entertained
a genuine passion for hunting. There is some irony in Manuel adopting the
persona of the ideal ruler in order to criticize King James of Cyprus for his
overzealous hunting, and it leaves us to ponder what his own courtiers
thought of their emperor's fondness for sport, especially in light of
Kydones' previously mentioned criticism on the subject in 1389.

Unsurprisingly, Manuel seems to have also devoted ample time to
scholarly pursuits. This tendency can be observed during his prolific
production in the 1390s and later in his European journey. Between
1403–10 Manuel again composed many works: *Clarification of a Debate
between Demetrios Chrysoloras and Antonio d'Ascoli*, the *Sermon on St Mary
of Egypt*, as well as writing the first drafts of the *Foundations of Imperial
Conduct*, the *Ethico-Political Orations* and the *Funeral Oration*. Nothing is
really known about Manuel's own personal library; however, during the
reign of his son John VIII, Pero Tafur noted the existence of a palace
library in an open space area at the palace entrance where marble blocks
served as tables and benches.[96] It contained not only books, but also board
games. Similarly, Makarios of Ankyra mentions a hall at the palace lit with
lamps and containing more than forty volumes of theological writings.[97]

Furthermore, the patriarchal library was accessible to Manuel, as well
the libraries of some monasteries, including the Chora and Saint John the
Baptist in Petra. Indeed, his friend Manuel Chrysoloras seems to have
worked in the Chora library at some point, and when visiting
Constantinople in 1422, Giovanni Aurispa studied a manuscript of
Dioscorides at the same monastery, which had been annotated and
rebound by another member of Manuel's literary circle, John
Chortasmenos.[98] It should also be noted that the emperor seems to have

---

[95] Clavijo, 34 and 44.

[96] Pero Tafur, *Travels and Adventures, 1435–1439*, trans. M. Letts (London, 1926), 80. Berger, 'Court',
11–12, believes this to be a reference to the Great Palace.

[97] V. Laurent, 'Le trisépiscopat du Patriarche Matthieu 1er (1397–1410): un grand procès canonique à
Byzance au début du XVeme siècle', *REB 30* (1972), 32–111, 42. Henceforth, Laurent, 'Le
trisépiscopat'.

[98] N. G. Wilson, 'Libraries of the Byzantine World', *GRBS* 8.1 (1967), 53–80, 54–64 and R. Nelson,
'The Italian Appreciation and Appropriation of Illuminated Byzantine Manuscripts 1200–1450',
DOP 49 (1995), 209–35, 221. More generally, see N. G. Wilson, 'Books and Readers in Byzantium',
in *Byzantine Books and Bookmen* (Washington,1975); E. Malamut, 'La monastère Saint-Jean
Prodrome de Pétra de Constantinople', in *Le sacré et son inscription dans l'espace à Byzance et en
Occident*, ed. M. Kaplan (Paris, 2001), 219–33; C. Förstel, 'Metochites and his Books between the

enjoyed a special connection with Saint John the Baptist in Petra, keeping the keys to its reliquary chests and making donations to it. The monastery also had a workshop that produced manuscripts for Manuel's imperial court, and it is reasonable to surmise that the emperor might have used their library as well.

Manuscripts certainly circulated among Manuel's literary circle. His letters indicate that he borrowed manuscripts, and also received them as gifts, such as the Plato he sent to Kydones, and the *Souda* he seems to have received from him. In his will, Kydones bequeathed a Herodotos and the Four Gospels to the emperor.[99] Another close associate of Manuel, Joseph Bryennios, had a sizeable book collection that he bequeathed to Hagia Sophia. His testament mentions grammars by Glykys, Planudes, Moschopoulos and Magistros, Aristotle's *Rhetoric, Organon, Physics* and *Nichomachean Ethics,* three *logoi* by Nikephoros Blemmydes on physics, a Ptolemy, a book on music and various books on geometry.[100] Perhaps, at some point, Manuel might have borrowed some of these works. In 1422, a member of the papal legation, Giovanni Aurispa, was given copies of Prokopios and Xenophon by 'the emperor'; it is unclear whether the emperor in question was Manuel or John VIII.[101]

Manuel speaks about neither the books he possessed, nor his reading. The only exception is in a letter addressed to Kydones where the emperor professes deep admiration for Chrysostom's 'To An Unbelieving Father', claiming that in his opinion, it surpassed all other works by the author. 'This brought me so closely in touch with him', Manuel writes, 'that I almost thought I saw the great man alive and heard him discoursing'.[102]

The emperor rarely mentions the physical environment for these pursuits. When he does so, it is always within an apologetic context vis-à-vis criticism concerning his scholarly interests. His references to writing in the

---

Chora and the Renaissance', in *The Kariye Camii Reconsidered*, eds. A. Klein, R. Ousterhout and B. Pitarakis (Istanbul, 2011), 241, 266, 244, and Chortasmenos, *Johannes Chortasmenos ca. 1370– ca. 1436/37. Briefe, gedichte und kleine Schriften. Einleitung, Regesten, Prosopographie, Text*, ed. H. Hunger (Vienna, 1969), 52–3; H. Hunger, *Schreiben und Lesen in Byzanz* (Munich, 1989) and G. Cavallo, *Lire à Byzance* (Paris, 2006), but not much discussion of the late period is found.

[99] See Chapter 6. It seems that the copy of Libanios Kydones left to Manuel Chrysoloras later found itself in the hands of Guarino of Verona after the death of the latter, Guarino, Letter 53, dated 1416, in *Epistolario di Guarino Veronese*, vol. 1, ed. R. Sabadini (Turin, 1959). Guarino remarks that it contained Chrysoloras' own marginal notes.

[100] See *Varia graeca sacra*, ed. A. Papadopoulos- Kerameus (1909), 131–2.

[101] See C. L. Stringer, *Humanism and the Church Fathers: AmbrogioTraversari* (New York, 1977), 36.

[102] Letter 25, lines 8–10, 'ὃς οὕτω με ὅλως εἰς ἑαυτὸν ἐξηρτήσατο ὡς μονονοὺ δοκεῖν ζῶντα τε αὐτὸν τὸν μέγαν ὁρᾶν καὶ διαλεγομένου ἀκούειν.'

dim lamplight in his tent in Asia Minor, or his account of his studies in the grim Tower of Anemas in the 1370s are such instances. Manuel did not cease from writing at distressing times, indeed some of his most noteworthy compositions were composed during political and personal calamities. Not only did he seek enjoyment by wielding his pen, he probably also sought to counter his troubles by permeating his text with political messages. The crushing defeat at Nikopolis, his distress during the Ottoman campaigns and his fall from grace in 1387 surely prompted Manuel to pour out his anguish on paper; as would the death of his beloved brother Theodore. Similarly, the death of Bayezid caused him to take up his pen in celebration, while playful letters from his friends provoked him to employ humour.

Manuel as Author: An Assessment

The major focus of this biography has been Manuel as an author, but as has been touched upon several times, defining literature within a Byzantine context is quite difficult.[103] The Byzantines did not even have a word that directly and exclusively corresponded to what we now define as literature. Instead, the term *logos* (word, discourse) or its plural *logoi,* was employed to describe literary, rhetorical, theological and philosophical works. Similarly, *techne* (skill), is used simultaneously for rhetorical practices, authorial style or a command of features such as allusions, metaphors or even sound harmony. Although it would be easy to classify a Byzantine letter as literary and an oration as rhetorical, what about a philosophical work composed as an elegant poem? It is also difficult to strictly categorize a theological treatise like the *Dialogue with a Persian*, which contains such remarkable literary features.

Which works of Manuel should be considered when evaluating the emperor as an author? Since the boundaries between Byzantine literary, rhetorical, philosophical and theological were blurred, the following discussion will not seek to categorize Manuel's works or to pick out the 'literary' ones. For instance, I could not leave out a discussion of *On the Procession of the Holy Spirit* on the grounds of it being a theological treatise. Indeed, many of the devices Manuel employs in his other compositions can also be found in this work. For a discussion of his authorship, therefore, I do not perceive a rigid categorization into rhetorical, philosophical or theological, as being either feasible or desirable. Instead, we will focus on

[103] See also the introduction on these following issues.

some aspects of Manuel's style across his complete oeuvre, such as his character portrayal, his allusions, imagery and use of genre.

The lack of boundaries between the rhetorical and the literary in Byzantine texts, combined with the ambiguity of distinguishing between rhetorical and literary devices, prompts me to view features such as metaphors, allusions, sound harmony or self-representation strategies as literary. To these, I would also add character portrayal, the use and combination of genres, and conveying the ideas and emotions appropriate to a given text. For me, the textual aesthetics, distinctiveness and the skill imbued in the use of such elements may also be indicative of an author's literary talent, and it is on the basis of these elements that I choose to discuss Manuel's authorship and literary merit.

So far, this biography has striven to showcase that Manuel's writings reflect a care and talent for literary aesthetics. Despite its political and self-endorsing agendas, the emperor's oeuvre should not be considered as a mere tool of political propaganda or as a receptacle of historical information. Indeed, in the Byzantine tradition, political messages were not viewed as reducing the text to a mere pamphlet. Literary aesthetics and socio-political or moral agendas were fused, not opposed to each other. Like other Byzantine authors, Manuel did not perceive the political messages in his texts as extracting from the aesthetical concerns of the work, or as a token of 'insincerity.' Although he used his works for self-promotion, this should not be interpreted as Manuel viewing his writing solely as a tool in the service of politics.

The emperor manifested a genuine passion for writing and for its aesthetic components. For instance, in many of his letters, he admits to a sense of stimulation upon receiving compositions he admired: 'I longed to write', he exclaims in one letter; in others, 'I was eager to do some writing myself . . . ', 'like a goad, your voice propelled me to write . . . '.[104] While these partially follow the *topoi*, his words also betray a fondness for putting pen to paper. Manuel's fervour is perhaps equally reflected in his strong reaction to any criticism concerning his literary activities. The most poignant examples of these are the criticism he received while in Asia Minor, the attacks of Manuel Kalekas and the complaints of Gabriel of Thessalonike. All these criticisms were met with strong resistance from Manuel, in a tone ranging from mild annoyance to full-blown polemic.

---

[104] Letter 33, lines 2–7, 'ἐπεθύμησα δὲ λόγων εὐθύς. . . προυθυμήθην μὲν οὖν τι γράψαι, πῶς οἴει, κέντρου μοι πρὸς τοῦτο τῆς σῆς φωνῆς καταστάσης. . .' I have modified Dennis' translation 'your voice was a real stimulus for me' to 'like a goad, your voice propelled me to write'.

His letters offer us some ideas on Manuel's aesthetic criteria in textual compositions, giving us a glimpse into what he appreciated as literary features. That these insights should come mostly from his letters is not surprising. Several were composed as replies to works the emperor had received, and they served as the emperor's 'feedback'. The arrangement of words, the beauty of expression, the density of ideas, the beauty of words and the syntax are a few qualities that are mentioned, as well as the ability to accomplish all these features in a few words. These were all the standard criteria in Byzantine rhetorical handbooks and essays assessing ancient authors.[105] The qualities desired by the emperor thus adhere to tradition. A passage where Manuel draws a link between music and writing is quite telling of his perception of textual composition as an act of aesthetic pleasure:

> ... those who have had their fill of sorrow and cannot even recall a melody, while others are singing, endowed with the craft of the Muses, the tunes flow spontaneously whether they will it or not; and even an old man jumps about as though he had forgotten himself, while others are dancing in rhythmic harmony.[106]

The notion of textual aesthetics also brings up the question of originality. As discussed in the introduction of this book, the meaning and importance assigned to this concept by modern scholars differs from the understanding of Byzantine authors. In the Byzantine literary tradition, following rhetorical manuals, displaying the influences of one's favoured Classical and Byzantine authors, or adorning one's work with allusions and quotations, was not perceived as a sign of 'unoriginality', nor did this render authors indistinguishable from each other. Through a study of his complete oeuvre it becomes evident that Manuel, too, displays his own style. The flow of his language, his sentence constructions, vocabulary, imagery or metaphors can be distinguished from other authors, both Classical and contemporary. Almost all of his works have unique touches of style, structural composition and in the ideas they contain.

On the whole, can Manuel be considered a talented literary figure? This biography opts for a positive answer on several grounds: while adhering to the established models, forms and practices, at times,

---

[105] Letter 33, lines 1–2, '... τὴν ἐν τοῖς ὀνόμασι καὶ τῇ συνθήκῃ λάμπουσαν ὥραν ...' and Letter 27.
[106] Letter 44, lines 71–5, '... ἢ λύπης εἶναι πεπληρωμένους μέλους οὐδὲ μέμνηται, ἄλλων δὲ ᾀδόντων μετὰ Μουσῶν ἐπιστήμης, ῥεῖ καὶ παρ' ἐκείνων τὰ μέλη μὴ βουλομένων ὥσπερ αὐτόματα, καὶ γὰρ πού τις καὶ γέρων πεπήδηκεν ὥσπερ λεληθὼς αὐτόν, ἑτέρων χορευόντων ῥυθμῷ καὶ τάξει.' I have modified Dennis' translation 'singing with true musical skill' to 'singing, endowed with the craft of the Muses'.

Manuel diverges from the traditions and introduces his own personal touches. One cannot therefore speak of him as merely following hand-books and models, or of piling one *topos* upon another. The emperor skilfully blends and combines features such as imagery, allusions, jokes or characterization into his works. The texts they adorn read as an organic whole, not as a pastiche of various literary devices. Moreover, most of these transcend mere *topoi*, as Manuel introduces his own touches to them. He thus demonstrates creativity within the established framework. As advocated by Byzantine tradition, he also always chooses what is appropriate for the occasion and the particular text. For instance, his *Discourse to the Thessalonians* opts for a more energetic and forceful style, while the style of the *Funeral Oration* is more solemn and emotional. He is thus able to vary his style to suit his purposes. Likewise, the devices he employs, such as quotations, allusions or imagery are not mere orna-ments, but usually fit in very well with the context of the text. On many occasions, these enrich the work by incorporating different layers of meaning. His letters from the Asia Minor campaign, which were filled with intelligent allusions to Homer, Aristophanes and Xenophon, are one such example. They are not mere decorations in the text, they contain veiled meanings and set forth Manuel's mood and the military atmos-phere that surrounded him.

Manuel was also a quite versatile author. His oeuvre covers a wide range of genres and he does display proficiency in them. He produced letters, orations, rhetorical exercises, poetry, theological treatises, ethico-political works, prayers, sermons, a confession and even a *kanon*. These are his surviving works; though he perhaps produced more. Although Byzantine literati often produced in multiple genres, such a wide range of different genres is rare among the emperor's literary circle, and he seldom returned to the same form. Moreover, he frequently mixed various forms and genres. Altering and combining rhetorical/literary forms and genres was an ability commended by Byzantine authors and Manuel does it well. In experimenting with combining various genres, he was also following the literary trends of the late Palaiologan era. Several of the late Palaiologan authors express an special interest in combining various genres, and yet not all authors of the period betray this tendency.[107] Similarly, of the authors who followed this trend, there are those restricted themselves to one or two experiments.

---

[107] For genre in Byzantine literature, see M. Mullett, 'The Madness of Genre', *DOP* 46 (1992), 233–43.

Manuel, on the other hand, displays a noteworthy interest in combining various genres. Thus, the emperor's *Verses to an Atheist* is an exposition of the Christian faith with complex theological material, but in political verse; the *Funeral Oration* is a blend of funerary oration, history and apology;[108] the *Discourse to Iagoup* is an epistolary discourse which functions both as a treatise on the proper study of theology and an *apologia*; his *Dialogue with a Persian* is a theological treatise written as an exceptionally lively and literary Platonic dialogue; and the *Discourse to Kabasilas* combines dialogue and epistolary discourse. It must be pointed out that these combinations should be deemed successful attempts. They read as organic wholes and not mere pastiche of different texts. Manuel's competence in several genres, combined with his further interest in combination and variation, clearly signify his talent as an author.

The emperor also displays a penchant for sound harmony and rhythm. This, too, can be interpreted as an indication of authorial talent. In the cases of the *Dialogue on Marriage* and his *ekphrasis*, Manuel's sophisticated prose rhythm and his rapprochement between prose and poetry have been noted by scholars.[109] The same tendency can be observed in many of his other works, both in prose and verse. He seems to have greatly cared for sound harmony while writing, skilfully using assonance, consonance and especially alliteration. He alters between long and shorter sentences to organize the flow of his texts. And while many of these features go unnoticed during silent reading, they can be much better appreciated when the texts are read aloud, as was intended.

With regard to his language, the emperor writes a sophisticated Attic Greek. On the whole, Manuel's Greek and syntax is difficult and elaborate, but it is not so complex that it is unreadable. He does not switch to more obscure Ancient Greek dialects or use extremely rare words. Although Manuel's language register remains very much the same throughout years and across works, he does seem to have experimented with a more complicated language in the *Discourse to the Thessalonians* as a younger man. Likewise, the Greek of *On the Procession of the Holy Spirit* is easier to read than many of his works. Perhaps, in this case, the emperor consciously employed plainer language when dealing with complex theological matters. Indeed, the use of simpler language for philosophical and

---

[108] *Funeral Oration*, 28. Leonte, 'Morea', also notes this aspect of the *Funeral Oration*.
[109] *Dialogue on Marriage*, 31–8; Davis, 'Ekphrasis', 418.

theological works was advocated by many Byzantine handbooks and authors.

The emperor's metaphors and imagery deserve special mention in any discussion of his literary merit. Although many Byzantine authors employed these devices, Manuel seems to have been especially fond of them: metaphors and imagery adorn even his theological treatise, *On the Procession of the Holy Spirit*. As previously discussed, Manuel does not merely recycle commonplace metaphors and imagery, but introduces personal touches to them, and in this he displays literary creativity within the tradition, not against it. His metaphors and imagery do not function as mere adornment but are very appropriate to the works and textual circumstances to which they belong. More often than not, they convey ideas, emotions or even other layers of meaning and are able to set the mood of a given work.

For instance, in the *Discourse to Kabasilas*, Manuel's metaphor of floating on the sea surface and his description of the harsh climate of Lesbos conveys a sense of despondency and oppression to the audience. A particularly lively scene in the *Dialogue with a Persian*, in which Manuel, the *müderris* and his entourage eat together sitting on the floor around a round table and in front of a warm fireplace, creates a visual contrast to the harsh snowstorm blowing outside their window. It juxtaposes the warm and amicable atmosphere of the *müderris'* home with Bayezid's violent outbursts in the palace where he is trapped because of the snow. Similarly, his bleak depiction of Asia Minor in the letters from the campaign of 1391, highlight Manuel's sense of hopelessness and alienation. On the whole, his imagery is especially notable for its vividness, such as in the case of his *ekphrasis*.

A key aspect of Manuel's authorship is his self-presentation and how he manipulates his self-image to suit particular circumstances. As amply discussed in this biography, he minutely crafts his self-portrait in order to achieve various goals: for political propaganda, to appeal to the audience's sympathy, to assert his status as emperor, or to defend and justify his acts. Manuel chiefly adopts the persona of an ideal, self-sacrificing and dutiful ruler; however, where appropriate, he also incorporates slight variations to this persona to further enhance his presence in the text. For instance, he can also adopt the persona of Socrates in his philosophical dialogues, or Demosthenes while speaking in front of the Thessalonians. He can be ablaze with self-defence in apologetic texts and adopt the tone of a penitent sinner in his confessions and prayers. As in the case of his self-representation, Manuel's portrayal of the others is also noteworthy. Across his oeuvre, he fashions Bayezid's image as an abominable ruler and man, lending his portrayal further depth than a stereotypical 'barbarian' sketch. In the *Dialogue on Marriage*, he fashions his mother Helena as an embodiment of practical wisdom, lending further support to his own legitimacy through his mother's voice. She also functions as a foil to the young, rash and imprudent John VII in the dialogue. Elsewhere, in his *Reply of Antenor to Odysseus*, an *ethopoiia* based on Libanios, the emperor successfully captures the craftiness and wisdom of Homer's Antenor. Above all, the *Dialogue with a Persian* also stands as a testimony to Manuel's complex and nuanced character portrayal, a trait not observed in other authors of the period. In relation to his character portrayal, his dialogues also have fictional qualities through their imaginary episodes, scenery and conversations.

Manuel is considered by some, a 'serious' author on the grounds of his high style and theological interests, and yet he actually exhibits a remarkable sense of humour and parody.[110] Even the *Procession of the Holy Spirit* is adorned with witty allusions and sarcastic remarks about the emperor's Latin opponent. The emperor's letters reflecting his polemics include some rather strange imagery: animals giving birth to large litters, people making silly noises like cicadas or leaping around like sparrows and even the imaginary transformation of his opponent into a tongue – an image influenced by Homer's term 'ten tongued'.[111]

Manuel teases his friends, and in once case praises the humour of a correspondent that provoked him to laughter and to recover from illness. He evidently appreciates and is amused by an *enkomion* of Demetrios Chrysoloras in honour of a flea that bit him.[112] Similarly, Manuel's short poem *Anacreontic Verses Addressed to an Ignorant Person* is a satirical poem based on Homer's Thersites.[113] The *Declamation regarding a Drunken Man* is a parody of an Ancient Greek courtroom, probably based on Libanios. In it a drunkard gives ridiculous eulogies to wine and disinherits his son because of the latter's sobriety. It is also worth noting that within this context, Manuel felt completely at ease having his protagonist speak about pagan sacrifices and evoking pagan deities by name. Since the genre of declamation provided him with the pretext, the emperor did not shrink from giving voice to a pagan drunkard.

---

[110] For instance, Peers, 'Ekphrasis', 208, expresses surprise at the fact that a theologically inclined figure such as Manuel could include 'pagan' influences in his ekphrasis while describing the Bacchic frenzy of the boys depicted, and without any reference to Christian texts.

[111] Letter 30 and Letters 63–6, Homer, *Iliad*, Book 2, 23–5.

[112] Letter 2 and Letter 50. Chrysoloras' composition is still unedited.

[113] *PG* 156, cols. 575–6. See Appendix 2 for the poem and a translation.

Although Manuel professes to giving great importance to authorial identity and individual style in his letters, he does not offer radically distinct ideas on authorship. Nor does he devote entire works to the questions of authorial identity or literary style. In this regard, his ideas on authorship cannot be compared, for instance, to the distinct and notable ones of a Psellos. Neither does Manuel have any discussions that resembles essays by Theodore Metochites or Photios. Similarly, he has no commentaries on Ancient authors or rhetorical manuals. He does not seem to have been interested in exploring the notion of authorship or literary/rhetorical theory. The emperor's own scattered remarks are much more commonplace. He points out to his correspondent Pothos that the audience could identify Pothos as the author of a particular work from the rhythm of the piece and the choice of words. Elsewhere Manuel claims that naming the author of a work would be paying the greatest compliment possible: remarking that a painting that was crafted by Apelles would rouse far greater admiration than saying that the work was beautiful.[114]

As might be expected, the *topos* of modesty is almost always present in the emperor's works. On the surface, Manuel never appears to be content with his compositions and always professes admiration for the ancient writers. For instance, the highest praise he can bestow on Michael Balsamon is that his work could be mistaken for that of an ancient.[115] However, a careful reading of these *topoi* reveals that Manuel was actually quite self-conscious as an author and took great pride in his compositions. He appears to have been pleased with himself on many occasions. His frequent complaints of being dulled by unpleasant circumstances actually serve to highlight the opposite. Indirectly, the emperor seeks to convey that he could still produce a multitude of elegant compositions in the face of adversity:

> ... take the case of Phidias, acknowledged as the greatest of all the ancient sculptors. Quite rightly he has always been admired for his skill, whenever he fashioned a statue from good, workable material, but we would have more cause for amazement if he showed the same skill with cheap and unyielding material ...[116]

---

[114] Letter 9, lines 1–19 and Letter 35, lines 1–12.   [115] Letter 34, lines 10–14.

[116] Letter 50, lines 38–42, '... καὶ γὰρ Φειδίας ὁ παλαιὸς κράτιστος ἀναδειχθεὶς ἐπὶ τῷ λαξεύειν, εἰκότως γε ἀεὶ τῆς ἐπιστήμης θαυμαζόμενος, ὁπότε καὶ ἐξ ἀγαθῆς καὶ ἐξ εἰκούσης ὕλης ἀνδριάντα ἤ τι ἄλλο δεδημιουργήκει προσφάτως, μᾶλλον ἂν δικαίως ἐξέπληττεν εἰ ἐξ ἀνενδότου καὶ φαύλης ἐπεδείκνυτο.' Manuel says this to praise Demetrios Chrysoloras' writing in a busy period, yet his own complaints of occupation hint that these remarks could also be applied to him.

On another occasion, the emperor suggests that Demetrios Chrysoloras would not feel that his letters were surpassed by Manuel's own sermon on the Virgin, and that the pre-eminence of the Virgin would prevent any bitter feelings.[117] The implication is of course that Manuel's sermon surpassed Chrysoloras' letters.

The emperor also discusses the question of imitation (*mimesis*). While some scholars still tend to regard imitation as 'plagiarising' or a sign of 'lack of originality', a close reading of Manuel' allusions or quotes usually reveals jokes, irony and other layers of subtle meaning that would be lost otherwise.[118] For him, and for other Byzantine writers, imitation was not a sign of banality. It was an essential part of their textual culture. The following excerpt, where the emperor defends his quotation of a letter of Libanios, is illustrative:

> ... I did not employ the word [stealing] properly, for it is not stealing to make some use of the writings of the common teachers, but justified borrowing ... Like a public well, those men offered themselves and the results of their efforts to everyone, so that those drinking from it are not thieves, but fulfil the very purpose for which it had been dug.[119]

The emperor similarly expresses a positive view as far as imitation of contemporary authors is concerned. He writes that the beauty of the letters he receives invite him to imitation: 'for each person imitates what he admires'.[120] Manuel on occasion recycled literary features in his own works as well; a practice that can also be observed in the works of other Byzantine authors. For instance, he borrows the spring imagery from his *ekphrasis* in his *Epistolary Discourse to Ivankos*, while the *Dialogue with the Persian* and the *Epistolary Discourse on Dreams* share the same imagery of a fireplace. Similarly, the *Declamation regarding a Drunken Man*, the

---

[117] Letter 61, lines 13–14.

[118] For imitation in Byzantium, see H. Hunger, 'On the Imitation (ΜΙΜΕΣΙΣ) of Antiquity', *DOP* 23/24 (1969/70), 15–38. For imitation and originality, see A. R. Littlewood (ed.) *Originality in Byzantine Literature, Art and Music*, ed. A.R. Littlewood (Exeter, 1995), especially A. Kazhdan, 'Innovation in Byzantium', 1–14 and R. Browning, 'Tradition and Originality in Literary Criticism and Scholarship', 17–28. Also, see T. J. Miller, *Poetic License: Authority and Authorship in Medieval and Renaissance Contexts* (New York and Oxford, 1986), 3–5, 9–12, 35 for imitation and the authority of past authors in Western Europe.

[119] Letter 50, lines 21–6, '... ἀλλὰ γὰρ οὐχ ὑγιῶς ἐχρησάμην τῇ λέξει. Οὐδὲ γὰρ κλέπτειν ἂν εἴη τὰ τῶν κοινῶν διδασκάλων εἰ τούτοις γέ που τις χρῷτο, ἀλλὰ λαμβάνειν αὐτὰ δικαίως, οὐδ' ἀλλότρια τίνι νομίζειν ἐκεῖνα ἃ τις ἔδωκει τοῖς πᾶσιν εἶναι. Φρέαρ γὰρ αὐτοὺς ἐκεῖνοι καὶ τοὺς ἑαυτῶν πόνους ἅπασι προὔθηκαν, ὅθεν οὐ φῶρες οἱ πίνοντες, αὐτό γε τοῦτο πάντως ποιοῦντες ἐφ' ᾧ τὸ φρέαρ διορώρυκται.'

[120] Letter 44, lines 75–7, '... μιμεῖται δὲ ἕκαστος ὃ θαυμάζει...'; Letter 45, lines 111–19.

Foundations of Imperial Conduct and the *ekphrasis* share the same imagery of a flowery meadow.[121]

Ultimately, Manuel should not be regarded as an emperor who happened to wield a pen and who left us many historical sources as a happy coincidence. Although he did employ writing as a means of political advertisement and legitimation, there is ample evidence that he also enjoyed writing for aesthetic reasons; the two were not mutually exclusive. As an author, he was able to distinctly express ideas and convey emotion through his works. His blending of various forms and genres, sound harmony, imagery, metaphors and distinctive character portrayals are all quite noteworthy. As an author of considerable talent, his works deserve study for their literary merit, and not just as historical sources.

An Upsurge of Tribulation: 1407–16

A tragic event in 1407 impelled the emperor to seek solace again in writing. After a long illness and having adopted the monastic habit, Manuel's beloved brother Theodore died in Mistra. Manuel would compose his famous *Funeral Oration* to mark the occasion. The work would be later revised on several occasions up until 1416. Theodore passed away childless. Despite his profound sorrow, the affairs of the empire demanded Manuel's immediate attention. His brother's death necessitated the appointment of a new despot and required Manuel's presence to impose order in the troubled region. The emperor left his capital in the autumn of 1407 and sailed to the Morea.[122]

Morea, one of the last remaining bastions of the Byzantine Empire, presented the emperor with great challenges. His late brother Theodore had been forced to contend with incessant Ottoman plundering raids, Venetian demands, the hostility of the Navarrese and various other Latin principalities. Furthermore, the region was home to an aristocracy whose members were especially opposed to imperial authority and displayed strong centrifugal tendencies. Displeased with Theodore's centralizing policies, some of the *archontes* even switched to Bayezid's side. The despot's

---

[121] Davis, 'Ekphrasis', 411 and Letter 45, lines 175–90; *Dialogue with a Persian*, 8, and *Discourse on Dreams*, 239–40; *Declamation Regarding a Drunken Man*, 304 and *Foundations of Imperial Conduct*, col. 332.

[122] Iorga, *Notes et Extraits*, 1, 160 and Thiriet, *Régestes*, nos. 1290 and 1291, 74–5 note Manuel's request for an escort galley for his journey. Schreiner, *Kleinchroniken*, Chronik 33/24 and Chronik 33/24 record Manuel's arrival in November 1407. Sphrantzes, 8–9; Doukas 138–9 and Chalkokondyles, 356–9 report the death of Theodore I and the installment of Manuel's son Theodore II as the new despot.

sale of Corinth to the Hospitallers had further estranged the local population. Thus, the instability of the Morea and the weakness of the imperial
authority in the region prompted Manuel to take the matters in his own
hands.

The emperor's second son, Theodore, had already been in Mistra for
several years, and after the emperor formally installed him as the new
despot of Morea he stayed for the autumn.[123] That the emperor went to
Morea in person to install his son, demonstrates the importance he gave to
order in the region and to intervening personally in the more remote
corners of his diminished empire. Again, this assertion of his personal
presence in Morean and later, in Thessalonian affairs, is a characteristic
unique to Manuel. He had previously sojourned years in Europe, and now,
he would travel in his own territories. While in Mistra, one can imagine
that the emperor paid many visits to Theodore's tomb in the
Brontocheion, and there, on a fresco, Manuel would have seen twin images
of his beloved brother, dressed in both imperial and monastic garb.[124]

Another death occurred in the September of 1408 when Manuel's
nephew John VII passed away in Thessalonike. He was only thirty-eight
years old, and his infant son Andronikos had long since predeceased him.[125]
Thus passed away Manuel's great rival for the throne. John VII's claim was
not invalid; his rebellious father had been the elder son, and despite the
turmoil he provoked in his quest for the throne, John was not only
a popular ruler in Thessalonike, he had also successfully defended
Constantinople for four and a half years in his uncle's absence. And yet
the emperor never seems to have fully trusted his nephew. After all, his
nephew had deposed John V and violently opposed Manuel for many
years. Furthermore, the historian Chalkokondyles also notes John VII's
dealings with Bayezid against his uncle. However, he does appear to have
been peaceful after obtaining Thessalonike and Thessaly to rule.
Ultimately, all the depictions of John and his motives come from
Manuel himself. John's side of the story remains obscured.

---

[123] Thiriet, *Régestes*, II, no. 1282, 73 notes the installment of Theodore II.
[124] D. Zakythinos, *Le despotat grec du Morée. Vie et institutions* (Athens, 1953; reprinted London, 1975),
   164, for Theodore's burial place.
[125] Sphrantzes, 6–7; Doukas, 112–13; Schreiner, *Kleinchroniken*, Chronik 7/27; Dölger, *Regesten*, 77, no.
   3209; and Mioni, 'Cronaca', no. 28. See Dölger, 'Johannes VII'; G. T. Dennis, 'John VII
   Palaiologos: A Holy and Just Man', in *Byzantium State and Society: In Memory of Nikos
   Oikonomides*, ed. A. Avramea, A. E. Laiou and E. Chrysos, (Athens, 2003), 205–17 and Ganchou,
   'Autour de Jean VII', 367–85, for assessments of John VII. The last two articles emphasize that John
   was popular in Thessalonike, and that he did actually defend Constantinople for four years. Thus,
   they represent a more favourable picture of John VII as opposed to Dölger.

Whatever his feelings towards John might have been, Manuel refrained from speaking ill of his estranged nephew, and after John's death, he would later delete all his insults from the *Dialogue on Marriage*. As with the aftermath of Theodore's death, Manuel went to Thessalonike in person after John VII died to install his third son Andronikos as the despot of the city. Nothing much can be gleaned about Andronikos, but we are told that as a grown man, he was reported by various sources as being in very poor health, but during the period of Andronikos' age of minority, Demetrios Laskaris Leontaris was put in charge. Thus, following partially in the footsteps of his father, John V, the emperor appointed his sons to positions of power in the key regions of the empire, taking personal control of matters and installing his son in person. Symeon of Thessalonike mentions that the emperor had to deal with some turbulence (ταραχή) in the city.[126] Perhaps, the remaining supporters of John VII were causing minor unrest, but, Andronikos' installation in Thessalonike served as a political message to the faction of the deceased John VII: the city – and the empire – now belonged entirely to Manuel and his line. An image commissioned later by Despot Andronikos in 1416 underscores this idea. It depicted Manuel in full imperial regalia with Thessalonike in the background, clearly in homage to his father as the legitimate ruler of the empire and more specifically of Thessalonike. Sadly, this image is now lost and is only known to us though a description in a poem by Makarios Makres, which was composed to celebrate the work.[127]

Emperor and the Church

After an absence of a year, Manuel finally left Thessalonike to return to his capital in early 1409. More turbulence awaited the emperor in Constantinople. An ecclesiastical dispute erupted in 1409. It concerned the investiture of Patriarch Matthew whose opponents claimed was guilty of 'trisepiscopacy', occupying three episcopal seats in succession. Matthew was furthermore accused of collaborating with the Ottomans during the

---

[126] Barker, *Manuel II*, 279–80. For the turbulence, see Symeon of Thessalonike, 'Oration on Saint Demetrios', 122. For Andronikos' illness, see Doukas, 247; Chalkokondyles, 338–9; Schreiner, *Kleinchroniken*, Chronik 22/32.

[127] See S. Kapetanaki, *An Annotated Critical Edition of Makarios Makres' Life of St Maximos Kausokalyves, Encomion of the Fathers of the Seven Ecumenical Councils, Consolation to a Sick Person, or Reflections for Endurance, Verses on the Emperor Manuel II Palaiologos, Letter to Hieromonk Symeon, A Supplication on Barren Olive Trees*, ed. S. Kapetanaki (PhD thesis, University of London, 2001), 254, for an edition of the poem. Henceforth, Kapetanaki, Makarios Makres.

blockade and thus, it was argued that his investiture was uncanonical and utterly void. While Manuel had been away in Europe, several ecclesiastics had persevered in disputing the legitimacy of the patriarch. This dispute had been going on since 1396, almost immediately after the patriarch had been invested. Together with Matthew of Medea, Makarios of Ankyra was one Patriarch Matthew's most ferocious adversaries. He argued not only that Matthew's investiture was uncanonical and void, but also that he had ascended to the throne chiefly thanks to Manuel, protesting that the emperor had disregarded the canons in order to promote his favoured candidate. During the synod of 1396, however, the majority of the prelates confirmed Patriarch Matthew's legitimacy. Lacking supporters, Makarios was briefly suspended from priesthood; his polemical stance and refusal at reconciliation contributed greatly to this punishment. It is probable that Manuel took Makarios to Europe with him in order to prevent him from stirring up further trouble in his absence.[128]

The dispute would not end there; the whole affair further escalated around 1402 during Manuel's absence, and during John VII's regency, five years after his investiture, Matthew was deposed.[129] It should be noted that these accusations and the deposition were, at least partially, political motivated. While Patriarch Matthew was regarded as Manuel's 'man', some of his opponents were close to John VII. Almost immediately upon his return, Manuel restored the patriarch to his office in 1403. Such changes were not unusual: Andronikos IV filled the vacant office with his own candidate during his coup in 1376; when John V regained the throne, he appointed a new patriarch; thus, John VII and Manuel were simply repeated the same pattern in deposing, and then restoring Patriarch Matthew to his office. In Byzantium, ecclesiastical and political affairs were often intertwined, and Manuel's reign was no exception.

The synod convoked in 1403, and presided over by Manuel in person, restored Matthew to the patriarchal office. Although Makarios of Ankyra and Matthew of Medea seemed placated initially, they carried on with their campaign against the patriarch. Makarios composed pamphlets calling the

---

[128] G. T. Dennis, 'The Deposition and Restoration of Patriarch Matthew I, 1402–1403', *BF* 2 (1967), 101, reprinted in *Byzantium and the Franks, 1350–1420* (London, 1982), Study VI. Henceforth, Dennis, 'Matthew I'.

[129] The following account of this ecclesiastical controversy is discussed in detail by V. Laurent, 'Le trisépiscopat' and to a lesser extent by Dennis, 'Matthew I', 100–6.
    Their sources are the Synodal Tome of 1409 and the Apology of Makarios of Ankyra, which remain unedited. Laurent and Dennis provide editions of many relevant passages from these texts. Schreiner, *Kleinchroniken*, Chronik 12/13 notes this ecclesiastical controversy, but only names the bishop of Gothia as the opposing party.

patriarch *archontoepiskopos* (ἀρχοντοεπίσκοπος) and *chrysobullatos* (χρυσοβουλλάτος); respectively 'ruler-made bishop' and 'the chrysobulled one'. These newly coined words were fierce protests against the emperor's intervention in the affair.[130] Makarios, who in his treatises, had previously emphasized the emperor's rights in convoking an ecumenical council, now protested vehemently against imperial intervention: the emperor was acting uncanonically and had no right to involve himself in ecclesiastical matters. Makarios also protested that the emperor had dictated the terms to the synod and was both the judge and the judged party.[131] His apology, which preserves Manuel's addresses in loose paraphrases, represents the emperor as extremely autocratic, almost tyrannical. Variants of *horizein* (ὁρίζειν) dominate the text and interjections such as 'I now manifestly *order* you ... ' and 'you force me to *order* .... ' are quite frequent. However, Makarios'a own arguments were also problematic, especially the ones disputing the legitimacy of the synod convoked by the emperor. Although the emperor's exact rights over the Church were sometimes contested, Manuel's acts in the affair of Patriarch Matthew had ample precedent.[132]

As mentioned, the whole affair erupted in 1409 when a pamphlet written by Makarios against the patriarch fell into Manuel's hands. The emperor hoped that Makarios would reform and sent him several chastising imperial orders, but he refused any attempt of reconciliation and continued his raging polemics against Patriarch Matthew. It was in 1409, upon the discovery of several more pamphlets that also contained insults towards Manuel personally, that the emperor convoked another synod. Makarios of Ankyra and Matthew of Medea were duly deposed and excommunicated, and Makarios was confined at a monastery either at an island or in Constantinople, at the emperor's discretion.

The personal aspect of this affair has not been thoroughly discussed. Manuel had indeed been patient with Makarios for a long time, always inviting him to reconciliation, but he drastically changed his stance in 1409. Though it is probable that the harsh punishment at least partially stemmed from Makarios' personal attacks on Manuel, the dispute had been ongoing since 1396. So why did the emperor choose to penalize

---

[130] See Laurent, 'Le trisépiscopat', 77 and 89 for excerpts from Makarios containing these coined insults.

[131] Dennis, 'Matthew I', 105, n. 24: '...οὕτω κἂν τῇ εἰς τὸ παλάτιον συνόδῳ αὐτὸς ἦν καὶ ὁ κρινόμενος καὶ ὁ κρίνων.' By 'the judged party', Makarios is referring to the fact that it was Manuel who convoked the synod and had complaints against him.

[132] Laurent, 'Le trisépiscopat', 97, 109–10 and Makarios of Ankyra, *18–9.

Makarios at that particular moment? I would argue that the insults and the explicit criticism directed towards Manuel were probably the last straw. The emperor had made it clear during the earlier dispute with Manuel Kalekas, that he would not tolerate criticism. Not only did he attack Kalekas in a discourse, he also turned a deaf ear to Kalekas' subsequent pleading over the years. Now, Manuel turned his anger upon Makarios. Like that of Kalekas, this episode is illuminating since it once again reveals the emperor's tendency to flare up when confronted with criticism.

Despite his piety, Manuel had numerous clashes with the Church. These clashes are not isolated cases, nor can they be condensed into one single period, they are recurrent throughout his reign. The emperor's desire to dominate and control ecclesiastical affairs seems to have been a constant since his younger days; it does not appear suddenly at a given point in his reign. His confiscation of the monastic properties in Thessalonike in the 1380s and his intervention with a *prostagma* to ensure the commemoration of his mother in 1396, are two episodes that had elicited protest from ecclesiastics. After the Makarios affair, in 1416, Manuel also would provoke a confrontation with his friend the Patriarch Euthymios by personally appointing the Metropolitan of Moldavia without convoking a synod. Further controversy would be averted only by the patriarch's death.[133] It is telling that in all cases Manuel got his wishes and, with the exception of Euthymios, the clergymen who confronted the emperor faced consequences. Ultimately, Manuel also seems to have wreaked vengeance on anyone contesting his authority. In 1409, he was stirred into taking action after Makarios insulted him. His four surviving letters to Makarios are laced with a myriad of insults and indicate that Manuel took the whole affair very personally.[134]

Were his interventions in various ecclesiastical affairs uncanonical? Was Manuel's claim of imperial rights over the Church illegitimate? These are difficult questions to answer.[135] The issue of imperial rights over the Church was a 'grey area', and conflicting opinions existed concerning the emperor's exact position. Indeed, imperial involvement in ecclesiastical matters was a matter of continuous dispute throughout Byzantine history.

---

[133] Laurent, 'Le trisépiscopat', 96; S. Runciman, 'Manuel II and the See of Moldavia', in Καθηγήτρια: *Essays Presented to Joan Hussey for her 80th Birthday*, ed. J. Chrysostomides, (Camberley, 1988), 515–20. Sylvester Syropoulos, *Mémoires*, ed. and trans. V. Laurent (Rome, 1971), 102–3 is the only author to mention this controversy. Henceforth, Syropoulos and Runciman, 'Manuel II and the See of Moldavia'

[134] These letters will be analysed in Chapter 9.

[135] On this issue, see especially Macrides, 'Emperor and Church', also Laurent, 'Le trisepiscopat', 90–4, Angelov, *Imperial Ideology*, 358–72, Makarios of Ankyra, *48–50.

However, both secular and canon law explicitly granted the emperor many rights. For instance, the Acts of the Fourth Ecumenical Council (870) stipulate that primacy in the synods belonged to the emperor, and not to the patriarch. As a visual demonstration of this, the emperor and the delegates sat in the middle the assembly, while the patriarch and the prelates were seated on the sides.

The emperor, or his chosen delegates, had the right to convoke synods, and imperial delegates could also act as judges in disciplinary cases. All church canons needed imperial signature to become valid. Similarly, Justinian's *Novels* stated that the emperor could legislate laws that would wholly apply to the Church. He was likewise entitled to oversee the observance of imperial decrees pertaining to ecclesiastical matters, as well as those of the sacred canons. Famed commentators of canon law, Theodore Balsamon (twelfth century) and Demetrios Chomatenos (thirteenth century), also gave the emperor extensive rights over the Church. For instance, the latter stated that the emperor had the right to move newly appointed bishops from their sees, or to transfer bishops between sees and preside over synods. As we will shortly discuss in more detail, all these rights given to the emperor seemed to lend support to Manuel's actions – or at least to most of them.

These rights stemmed from the quasi-sacerdotal persona of the emperor.[136] A Byzantine ruler had a mixed persona of a layman and quasi-priest, and his anointment at the coronation invested the emperor with priestly qualities. He boasted the ecclesiastical titles *epistomonarches* and *depoutatos* and had sacerdotal rights in the liturgy. Although none were allowed to enter the sanctuary without holding a priestly rank, his quasi-priestly persona gave the emperor the right to enter the sanctuary and offer gifts to God. Recent studies have suggested that imperial authority over the Church declined during the Palaiologan era, and that emperors did not exert as much influence over the Church as before. However, a recent study demonstrates that this claim does not hold true. In their correspondence with the emperor, metropolitans still referred to themselves as the *douloi*, servants, of the emperor. Likewise, the emperor employed them as his *douloi*, sending them to embassies and appointing them to other such tasks.

The Palaiologan patriarchs, too, often turned to the emperors to resolve ecclesiastical matters. For instance, in the thirteenth century, Patriarch Athanasios called on Andronikos II to expel the provincial bishops residing

---

[136] Angelov, *Imperial Ideology*, 358–60 and G. Dagron, *Emperor and Priest: The Imperial Office in Byzantium* (Cambridge, 2003).

in Constantinople. He also asked the emperor to put the Metropolitan of
Cyzicus, accused of simony, to trial.[137] Similarly, in 1411, when a territorial
dispute arose between the patriarchate and the autocephalous
Archbishopric of Ohrid, the patriarch turned to Manuel for help.
Relying on a *chyrsobull* issued by Michael VIII, the emperor confirmed
that the diocese under question was bound to Adrianople and was hence
under patriarchal control. He issued a *prostagma* as to the same effect, and
his decision was approved by the holy synod.[138]

As in the earlier periods of Byzantine Empire, Palaiologan emperors still
exerted great influence in the selection of the patriarch. More often than
not, the emperor's preferred candidate was chosen. The patriarch might
anoint the emperor at his coronation, but it was the emperor who 'created'
the patriarch. Pseudo-Kodinos' depiction of the coronation of the patriarch is illustrative of this dynamic. Although the patriarch is not compelled
to kiss the feet of the emperor, the latter's throne is higher. Moreover, the
imperial throne is set up even higher than usual, further underscoring
imperial ascendancy over the patriarchal throne.

Thus, Manuel did enjoy rights and privileges in ecclesiastical affairs.
And although his involvement in ecclesiastical affairs was criticized on
several occasions, the emperor's actions had ample precedent. For instance,
although Makarios of Ankyra and Syropoulos criticized Manuel for exert-
ing influence in patriarchal investiture and pushing forward his own
candidate, many emperors resorted to this practice.[139] One could always
dispute imperial involvement in the election of a patriarch as having no
basis in the canon law, but it was an established practice. It is true that no
canon explicitly granted the emperor the right to choose the patriarch;
however, emperors were always highly influential in the process.
Consequently, Manuel's own involvement in the case of Patriarch
Matthew and later, Patriarch Joseph, was nothing out of the ordinary,
however unwelcome it might have been to some.

With regards to the legitimacy of the synods convoked by Manuel, many
sources sanctioned his actions. Acts of the Fourth Ecumenical Council,
and the jurists Balsamon and Chomatenos all explicitly state that the

---

[137] For the Church in Late Byzantium, see Angelov, *Imperial Ideology*, 351–416 and more generally,
D. Nicol, *Church and Society in the Last Centuries of Byzantium* (Cambridge, 1979). See Macrides,
'Emperor and Church' for this new interpretation.

[138] G. Prinzing, 'Emperor Manuel II and Patriarch Euythmios II on the Jurisdiction of the Church of
Ohrid', in *Le Patriarcat oecuménique de Constantinople et Byzance hors frontières (1204–1586)*, eds.
M. H. Blanchet, M. H. Congourdeau and D. I. Mureşan (Paris, 2014), 243–71.

[139] See Macrides, 'Emperor and Church', and Angelov, *Imperial Ideology*, 359–60; Laurent, 'Le
trisepiscopat', and Syropoulos, 101–5.

emperor had the right to convoke synods and to preside over them. Furthermore, secular authorities such as *archontes* and the emperor's *oikeoi* could be present at these synods. During the reign of John V, in the 1380s, these rights were confirmed in an official document.[140] In 1409, however, Makarios refused the legitimacy of the synod restoring Patriarch Matthew on the grounds that it had been convoked and presided over by the emperor. Similarly, Syropoulos criticized Manuel for convoking a synod in 1416 after the death of Patriarch Euthymios and also noted the presence of secular authorities in the synod: *archontes*, such as Demetrios Chrysoloras and the *mesazon* Goudeles. He disapprovingly mentions that they all supported the emperor. Despite the complaints of Makarios of Ankyra and Syropoulos, the above-mentioned texts lent support to Manuel's actions. It is clear, however, that the emperor's right was still debated and disputed by many.

Manuel's appointment of the Bishop of Poleanina as the Metropolitan of Moldavia was more problematic.[141] While returning from Morea in 1416, the emperor met with the Bishop of Poleanina in Thessalonike. As the see of Moldavia had recently come vacant, Manuel appointed the bishop as the new metropolitan, duly sending him to Constantinople. He did not consult anyone in this, however, and it has been proposed that the emperor's decision was partially politically motivated by a wish to strengthen the Byzantine influence in the Balkans. Although the sees of Wallachia and Moldavia were not under the direct control of the patriarchate, they were of great significance to the empire. Through a Byzantine metropolitan, the emperor could exert influence in the area and even attract new allies. Manuel seems to have embraced this appointment as a important political opportunity.

When Patriarch Euthymios and the synod fervently contested this appointment as uncanonical, Manuel reminded them of the imperial rights dictated in the document of 1380/2. According to this document, the emperor had the right to transfer bishops between sees, keep them in Constantinople or send them to their sees, and he could select a metropolitan among three candidates proposed to him. It must be pointed out that the right to promote a bishop to metropolitan – what Manuel did – is not explicitly granted in this document, and it represents more of a 'grey' area. Thus, the document on which the emperor relied did

---

[140] See above. This document of 1380s is edited, translated and discussed in V. Laurent, 'Les droits de l'empereur en matière ecclésiastique: L'accord de 1380–82', *REB* 13 (1955), 5–20. Also see P. Guran, 'Patriarche hesychaste et empereur latinophrone. L'accord de 1380', *RESEE* 39 (2001), 53–62.

[141] Laurent, 'Le trisépiscopat', 96; Runciman, 'Manuel II and the see of Moldavia'.

not support his actions. The affair over the see of Moldavia was resolved rapidly as Patriarch Euthymios, the chief opponent of Manuel's decision, died soon afterwards. 'I admire him', Syropoulos writes on Manuel, 'but only this one single act, I cannot praise.'[142]

On many occasions, Manuel's involvement in the Church had documentary support and precedent. In this regard, the writings of Symeon of Thessalonike and Makarios of Ankyra that protest against imperial intervention, should not be interpreted as indicating a weakening of imperial authority over the Church. These two churchmen were attempting to show that the emperor was subject to the Church, though practice indicated otherwise.[143] Scholars have also often noted the 'conflicting' attitudes of Makarios on this issue. Although in 1409 he fervently rejected the imperial authority in ecclesiastical matters, he professed otherwise in his treatise on the procession of the Holy Spirit. There, Makarios claimed that his anointment made the emperor a bishop and a teacher of the faith and that he was the supreme governor and protector of the Church. Only the emperor had the power to convene ecumenical councils.[144] This change of attitude in Makarios should not be seen as a contradiction, but rather as the outcome of the very different contexts of the two cases. In 1409, he rejected Manuel's authority because he was opposed to Patriarch Matthew; in his treatise against the Latins, he extols imperial authority over the Church only because he seeks to demonstrate that the emperor is superior to the pope. Only the Byzantine emperor can convene a Church council, Makarios argues, and not the Latin pope. In each text, Makarios presented the arguments that suit his particular goals.

However, Manuel also seems to have been too insistent on exercising his imperial privileges over the Church. In 1416, he did not allow the synod to elect a new patriarch before having the rights of 1380/2 confirmed.[145] His reign also reveals a pattern of continuous clashes with ecclesiastics. Furthermore, the disputes of 1409 and 1416 are not isolated events. Although the emperor did have rights over the Church, Manuel seems to have been too involved in ecclesiastical affairs, and at times, a little too forceful as well. It was perhaps the insistence and the frequency of his

---

[142] Syropoulos, 104–5, "Ἐγὼ δὲ πάντα τὰ τοῦ θαυμαστοῦ βασιλέως θαυμάζων οὐδὲ ἱκανὸν ἐμαυτὸν κρίνων πρὸς τοὺς ἐπαίνους ἐκείνου, ἐν τοῦτο καὶ μόνον ἐπαινεῖν οὐκ ἔχω. ἀνάξιον γὰρ τῆς ἀρετῆς καὶ τῆς σοφίας καὶ τῆς συντετριμμένης ἐκείνου καρδίας ἡγοῦμαι, τὸ δουλεία ὑποβαλεῖν τὴν ἐκκλησίαν Χριστοῦ καὶ ἐξ ἐκείνου οὕτως καὶ τοὺς ἐξῆς αὐτὴν διασέχεσθαι.'

[143] Macrides, 'Church'. For Symeon of Thessalonike's works, see De Sacro Templo, PG 155, cols. 305–60, col. 352; De Ordinatibus, PG 155, cols. 361–468, cols. 416 and 444.

[144] Makarios of Ankyra, 48–9, 365–72.   [145] Syropoulos, 104–6.

intervention that irked people like Symeon of Thessalonike and Syropoulos. For instance, Manuel could have easily averted trouble in 1416 by at least consulting the patriarch – his literary collaborator – before appointing the metropolitan of Moldavia. The fact that he delayed the election of a new patriarch until he had his imperial rights confirmed, also demonstrates the importance Manuel gave to asserting his control over the Church. Further, he not only advertised himself as a learned theologian, but also sought to lend sanctity to Orthodox doctrines and Palamism through his emperor-author persona. His insistent involvement in ecclesiastical affairs therefore reflects Manuel's desire to extend his imperial power to the Church.

Ottoman Threat Renewed

The ecclesiastical controversy caused by Makarios was not the sole problem the emperor would face in these years. By 1409, the situation on the once calm Ottoman front was becoming increasingly fraught. The emperor had taken full advantage of the disintegration of the Ottoman Empire to regain some lost land and political prestige. He was no longer an Ottoman vassal, but almost an equal to the Ottoman rulers. In 1403 Manuel signed a treaty with Bayezid's elder son, Süleyman, nominally accepting him as the heir to the Ottoman throne. However, a few years later the power dynamic among the Ottoman princes had shifted dramatically: Isa was dead, Musa had gathered a large group of supporters and Mehmed had reached maturity, joining in the fight for the throne.[146] The emperor now had three claimants

---

[146] The following simplified account of the Ottoman civil war is from Kastritsis, *Sons of Bayezid*, especially 124–43. Also E. Zachariadou, 'Süleyman Çelebi in Rumili and Ottoman Chronicles', *Der Islam* 60 (1983), 268–96, re-printed in E. Zachariadou, *Studies in Pre- Ottoman Turkey and the Ottomans* (Aldershot, 2007), Study XI. The most important Ottoman account of the civil war is Ahval-i Sultan Mehmed bin Bayezid Han, published first as *Ruhî Tarihi*, ed. H. E. Cengiz and Y. Yücel, *Belgeler* 14–18 (1989–1992), 359–472. See now also D. Kastritsis, *The Tales of Sultan Mehmed, Son of Bayezid Han, Annotated English Translation, Turkish Edition and Facsimiles of the Relevant Folia of Bodleian Marsh 313 and Neşri Codex Menzel* (Cambridge MA, 2007). Henceforth, Kastritis, *The Tales of Sultan Mehmed*. The later Ottoman chroniclers seem to have relied on this work for their account of the civil war. Aşıkpaşazade, 109–14, omits all references to the Byzantine involvement. Neşri, 426–517, gives a more detailed account and refers to the Byzantine support of various princes. *Anonymous Tevârîh*, 51–6, also narrates the events.

The Byzantine sources who deal with the Ottoman civil war are Doukas, 112–13, 122–3, 126–35; Chalkokondyles, 278–89; Sphrantzes, 8–9; Schreiner, *Kleinchroniken*, Chronik 97, 2–3; Chronik 96/2; Chronik 72a/ 13–6. Konstantin the Philosopher, 23–35, narrates some episodes of the civil war. Ibn Arabshah, 186–7, mentions the fights among Bayezid's sons. Clavijo, 26, refers to the events after Isa's death.

to deal with. By 1409–10, Musa had gathered a large body of *akıncı*, raider troops, which he had attracted on the account of his aggressive territorial policies. Musa's policies were rather similar to those of his father Bayezid: both had aggressive conquest designs and both were much more favourably disposed to the cause of the *akıncıs*, the raiders.[147]

In an attempt to play the brothers against each other, Manuel invited Musa to cross to Thrace. The emperor also reached out to Mircae of Wallachia to support Musa.[148] Manuel perhaps thought that setting the brothers against each other would further weaken the Ottomans and prevent their unification; however, he gravely misjudged Musa's aggressive and expansionist policy. The emperor's move proved a disastrous. Musa soon turned to plundering Byzantine and Balkan territories, and in response, Manuel allied with Süleyman and transported him across the Bosphorus. In June of 1410, Süleyman defeated Musa at the Battle of Kosmidion, just outside the walls of Constantinople.[149] The victory was short-lived, however, and in 1411, Musa triumphed and had his brother strangled. Soon after, he turned his wrath on Manuel and Byzantium for their support of Süleyman, attacking Thessalonike, Constantinople and Selymbria. By August 1411, once more, Constantinople found itself under Ottoman attack. Manuel's plot had utterly backfired.

The Ottoman attacks in 1411 under Musa Çelebi were not as crippling as Bayezid's long blockade between 1394–1402 had been. Nevertheless, the genre in which Manuel chose to compose on this occasion is telling of the despair he must have felt[150]: a *kanon* to beseech the Virgin.[151] Perhaps old age and a growing interest in theology also contributed to this choice. The language of the *kanon* reflects a sense of urgency; 'help us now' and 'do not delay' are frequent pleas, as are words indicating misfortune. Manuel also relinquishes his traditional role as the helmsman of the state ship. Instead, he indicates that the tiller is now in the Virgin's hands. The emperor sent the *kanon* to Gabriel of Thessalonike and to the Protos of Mount Athos. Manuel relied on his imperial status and commanded that his *kanon* be sung in the oratories one day of the week, in yet another subtle attempt to

---

[147] Kastritsis, *Sons of Bayezid*, 9–10.

[148] Musa married a daughter of Mircea. However, Mircea later become hostile to Byzantium, perhaps on the grounds that Manuel had supported an obscure pretender to the Wallachian throne; a claim that is made by Chalkokondyles. See Kastritsis, *Sons of Bayezid*, 137–9 and Mureşan, 'Trois empereurs', 67–9.

[149] Kastritsis, *Sons of Bayezid*, 150–1 points out that the battle was probably visible from Blachernai; thus, Manuel might have even witnessed it with his own eyes.

[150] Kastritsis, *Sons of Bayezid*, 170, points out that these were attacks as opposed to a continuous siege.

[151] *Lettres de l'empereur Manuel Paleologue*, ed. E. Legrand (Amsterdam, 1962), 94–102.

assert his authority over the Church. Although Manuel composed the text of the hymn afresh, its melody, the *eirmos*, was that of another *kanon*; in short, he wrote the words but not the music; this was a widespread practice in composing *kanons*.[152] Manuel's *kanon* is quite long and its language is rather complicated. Upon careful reading, one can identify Manuel's authorial style in his hymn, such as his vocabulary, imagery and syntax.

In the letter accompanying the *kanon*, the emperor asks the Virgin to intercede with Christ directly on his behalf. He likens his situation to people who do not have access to the emperor and ask intermediaries at the imperial palace to plead on their behalf.[153] Even this metaphor highlights Manuel's consciousness of his imperial dignity and his desire to convey it to his ecclesiastical correspondents. He indirectly compares Christ and the emperor. Still, his choice of the Virgin as the addressee of the *kanon* is historically fitting. The Virgin was both the intermediary between God and humanity, and the protector of Constantinople. In the *kanon*, Manuel calls the city her province and alludes to her 'former favours'. Perhaps, this was a reference to the miraculous lifting of the blockade in 1402. The emperor also draws links between Musa and Bayezid, *the other khan* who laid siege to Constantinople. At the end of the *kanon*, Manuel prays that the Virgin may destroy Musa as she destroyed his father.

Manuel would soon get his wish. Constantinople was relieved of the Ottoman attacks as Musa turned his attention to Selymbria and then to Serbia. Manuel attempted to further distract him by sending Orhan, a hostage Ottoman prince, to Thessalonike as yet another contender for the Ottoman throne. However, Musa prevailed again and had Orhan strangled. Ever vigilant, the emperor then allied with Mehmed Çelebi. This time, the Ottoman chronicler Aşıkpaşazade does not refrain from admitting the Byzantine involvement, writing that Mehmed sent Fazlullah to Manuel, a judge who was on friendly terms with the emperor. As narrated also by other Ottoman sources, the Byzantines provided troops for Mehmed, but Manuel excused himself by pleading old age.[154] In July 1413, aided by Byzantine and Serbian troops, Mehmed defeated

---

[152] I thank Prof. Stig Frøyshov for his generous help and for our discussions on this work. He identified the *eirmos* as that of a *kanon* by John the Monk, probably John of Damascus. See, Εἱρμολόγιον, ed. S. Eustratiades (Chennevières sur Marne, 1932), 159–60.

[153] Letter 57 to Gabriel of Thessalonike and the protos of Mount Athos.

[154] Kastritsis, *The Tales of Sultan Mehmed Han*, 36–7; Aşıkpaşazade, 114; Neşri, 506–7. Although the Ottoman chroniclers report that Manuel excused himself from the battle on account of his age, two years later in 1415, he would personally launch a brief campaign against Giorgio Gattilusio on Thasos. Nevertheless, aged sixty-three in 1413, Manuel was old by the standards of his time.

Musa at the Battle of Çamurlu near Sofia, and after ten years, the Ottoman state was once more united under a single ruler.

During this period, Manuel tried to play all the aspirants against each other and to secure support from various Balkan states.[155] Although his manoeuvres bought time for the Byzantine Empire, they eventually failed to prevent the unification of the Ottoman state. Had military help arrived from Europe as Manuel hoped for, it might have been possible to eliminate all Ottoman contenders one by one, but it was not to be, by 1413, some of the former prestige of the Byzantine Empire was restored – chiefly through good fortune. Thanks to the Ottoman defeat at Ankara, Manuel not only regained land, he had become a political equal to the Ottoman rulers, and for a long time managed to preserve equilibrium on the Ottoman front. Yet, his decision to lend support to Musa was a misjudged one. Ultimately, in his attempts to eliminate the threat of Musa, he helped Mehmed to strengthen his own position, though, of course, the Ottoman Empire might have eventually been united without Manuel's schemes. Though Mehmed swore an oath of peace to Manuel, it was more of a personal bond between the two rulers rather than a long-lasting agreement, and the emperor was deeply aware of it and would never stop seeking protection against the Ottomans.

A project that Manuel carried out in 1415 tells us a great deal about his awareness of the political situation. In March, he led a brief military excursion against the Genoese lord Giorgio Gattilusio, who had invaded Thasos. The emperor then sailed once again to the Morea. There, in less than a month, he renovated the Hexamilion, the famous defensive wall of the Peloponnese. The renovated wall was supposed to serve the double function of keeping the Ottomans at bay and taming the unruly locals. In a letter, the emperor points out that the restoration had been carried out against the will of the Ottomans: Mehmed was extremely displeased. However, the sultan was unable to do anything at the time, as he was pressed by other affairs.[156]

---

[155] Ibn Arabshah, 185, points out that after the disintegration of the Ottoman Empire, the Christians had become bold since the Muslims needed their help.

[156] Barker, *Manuel II*, 300; Mazaris, 80–1. Manuel addressed two harsh letters to Gattilusio, Letters 58 and 59. Mioni, 'Cronaca', no. 35. On Manuel's restoration of the Hexamilion, Barker, *Manuel II*, 298–318, and Barker, 'On the Chronology of the Activities of Manuel II Palaeologus in the Peloponennesus in 1415', *BZ* 55 (1962), 39–55. Sphrantzes, 10–11; Chalkokondyles, 302–5; Mazaris, 66–80; Isidore of Kiev, 'Pangeyric', 165–6; Plethon, 'Address to Manuel Palaiologos on the affairs of the Peloponesse', ed. S. P. Lampros, *ΠΠΠ*, III, 246–5, 250. Henceforth, Plethon, 'Address to Manuel'. Schreiner, *Kleinchroniken*, Chronik 33/26–27; 32/33; 22/ 24; 35/6; 40/1; 42/5. Letter 68, lines 198–214. Konstantin the Philosopher, 16, also notes the restoration of the Hexamilion.

Falling into his usual pattern, Manuel imposed a tax upon the Moreans for the guarding of the wall. He also petitioned Venice for financial contributions, but without success.[157] In November 1417, Manuel would even successfully ask the pope for indulgences to be granted for those who contributed to the defence of the Hexamilion. His reaching out to the pope indicates the importance of this project for Manuel.[158] Originally built by Theodosios II, the Hexamilion extended from the Isthmus of Corinth to the Saronic Gulf and was slightly shorter than six miles and adorned by a total of 133 towers. The Isthmus had been deemed a suitable place for defence since Antiquity because of its natural position. Although panegyrics exalt the emperor for the restoration, the work itself cannot have been extensive since it was completed in a very short time. Furthermore, the archaeological evidence points to a limited restoration. For instance, one particular case indicates an extension of a diagonal wall, a very limited renovation attempt.[159] Despite Manuel's pride in his achievement and the extolling of the panegyrists, only minor works were carried out.

Still, the restoration of the wall meant that not only was the land defended against the Ottomans, but also that the despot gained in power vis-à-vis the Morean *archontes*. Moreover, the newly imposed tax displeased the locals greatly; some even fled to Venice to avoid payment.[160] Manuel's taxation policies had already backfired both in Thessalonike and during the blockade of Constantinople; the fact that he took the risk again in Morea reveals his dire need of money. However unpopular, additional taxation was the only way in which the emperor could improve the empire's finances. Nonetheless, a revolt against Manuel broke out, and resorting to arms, the emperor quickly crushed the rebellion in 1416. Mazaris notes that Manuel had to grant favours to the leaders of the rebellion, suggesting that the emperor was compelled to a degree, to give in to the *archontes*.[161] Despite his military victory and the Hexamilion, imperial authority was still insecure in the Morea.

That the uprising had affected Manuel deeply is evident in a long letter addressed to his spiritual fathers David and Damianos on the events.

---

[157] D. Zakythinos, *Le despotat grec du Morée. L'histoire politique.* (Athens, 1953; reprinted London, 1975), 237. Henceforth, Zakythinos, *Le despotat*. The tax was called βιγλιστικόν. For Manuel's requests to Venice: Iorga, *Notes et Extraits*, 232–3 and 239–240; Thiriet, *Régestes*, 11, nos. 1583 and 1592, 136–8. In 1417, Venice promised to help defend the Hexamilion should the need arise; Iorga, *Notes et Extraits*, 1, 258–9 and Thiriet, *Régestes*, 11, no. 1635, 150.

[158] Barker, *Manuel II*, 325; Raynaldus, *Annales Ecclesiastici*, vol. 27, no. 17, 475.

[159] T. E. Gregory. Isthmia, V, *The Hexamilion and the Fortress* (Princeton, 1993), 2–4, 19 and 41–4. Henceforth, Gregory, *Hexamilion*.

[160] Thiriet, *Régestes*, 11, no. 1592, 138–9.   [161] Mazaris, 84.

A careful reading unsurprisingly reveals the letter's function as an *apologia* for Manuel's Hexamilion project.[162] The opening of the letter, a description of a storm that almost shipwrecked the emperor, sets the tone for an account wherein a self-sacrificing Manuel overcomes dangers and plots.[163] Ingratitude is the word that the emperor employs the most in the letter. He had given the Moreans peace and freedom, he complains, but they repaid him by undermining his effort. In an interesting twist, Manuel divides the Moreans into three hierarchical groups: those who fully co-operated, those who were uncertain, but still joined in the efforts, and finally, those who opposed him.

Not all were equally guilty, the emperor argues. Those who doubted the efficiency of the undertaking could be easily pardoned as even he himself had doubts in the beginning. As might be expected, the co-operative group consists of 'men of right reasoning' and the opposing group are labelled as going 'mad under the sunlight'.[164] The 'good' group of people emerge as those who support their emperor, and Manuel highlights the irony that the lowest in this hierarchy, the rebellious *archontes*, are also the highest in actual rank. He promptly ends his letter by claiming that God did not allow their malice to succeed and would still show the rebels mercy. Thus, God sides manifestly with Manuel and renders his cause a just one, while His clemency towards the *archontes* mirrors that of the emperor.

The Hexamilion is one of the chief episodes in Manuel's reign, which is reported both in chronicles and other texts.[165] While he boasted that the task's magnitude and difficulty required none other than God's hand, the literati joined him in representing the restoration as a magnificent deed.[166] Unsurprisingly, none of them mention that the project had been envisaged by the late Despot Theodore. Demetrios Chrysoloras goes so far as to claim that a novel building technique that combined wood and stone, was employed; however, this statement cannot be confirmed by any other source.[167] All authors of the period naturally side with Manuel concerning

---

[162] Letter 68.

[163] This does not mean that the storm was merely fiction, but Manuel's choice to open the letter with this episode, as well as linking it to the troubles he experienced in the Morea, is clearly a stylistic device.

[164] Letter 68, lines 100–25.

[165] Bessarion, 'Monody', 287; Demetrios Chrysoloras, 'Synkrisis', 239–44; Chortasmenos, Letter 45, 201–6; Mazaris, 64–9, 80–1; Manuel Chrysoloras, *Discourse on the Funeral Oration*, 114–15.

[166] Letter 68, lines 194–5.

[167] See Chrysostomides, *Monumenta Peloponessica*, no. 157, 309 and no. 361, 181; Thiriet, *Régestes*, i, no. 864, 204, no. 897, 211; ii, no. 1017, 18 for Theodore's requests to Venice for help concerning the Hexamilion project. Demetrios Chrysoloras, 'Synkrisis', 243–4.

the rebellion in 1416, and Manuel Chrysoloras even warns that the emperor's benevolence had its limits: first, he had shown benevolence by restoring the walls, but then he had then resorted to war to stifle the uprising.[168] The Hexamilion project is on the whole, portrayed as a significant undertaking during Manuel's reign.

Plethon seized on the renovation as an opportunity to propose his famous scheme for the Peloponnese. He envisioned a government modelled on Ancient Sparta, where the Morea would become completely self-sufficient and not dependent on foreign pay. Because of the original political reforms that are proposed and Plethon's popularity among modern scholars, this text and other addresses to Manuel have been analysed many times. However, with regard to Plethon's proposals, it should be taken into account that the emperor did not have much authority in the region. Even the minor restoration of the Hexamilion caused a rebellion by the *archontes*. Furthermore, various Latin powers, especially the Venetians, had interests in the Morea and were active participants in its politics. Even if Manuel had tried to implement the reforms proposed by Plethon and attempted re-organize the Morean social structures, it is probable that neither the Moreans, nor the Venetians would have allowed such drastic changes.[169] However interesting and original Plethon's proposals may have been, they would be too difficult to implement in reality.

The emperor himself criticized the Moreans quite harshly. His *Funeral Oration* to his brother Theodore is also a brief history of the Morea, in which of course, Manuel is a key actor. Although in 1408/1409, Manuel seems to have delivered a shorter oration in the Morea, the actual *Funeral Oration* was delivered by Isidore of Kiev and Theodore Gazes around 1415. The identity of the audience is unknown, but it must have consisted of the *archontes* and the ecclesiastics.[170] In the oration, the emperor blames the

---

[168] Demetrios Chrysoloras, 'Synkrisis', 244.

[169] Plethon, 'Address to Manuel', 248–52. On the addresses, see C. M. Woodhouse, *George Gemistos Plethon* (Oxford, 1986), 92–8; W. Blum. *Georgios Gemistos Plethon. Politik, Philosophie und Rhetorik im spätbyzantinischen Reich* (Stuttgart, 1988), 36–44; V. Hladký, *The Philosophy of Gemistos Plethon: Platonism in Late Byzantium, Between Hellenism and Orthodoxy* (Farnham, 2014), 11 and T. Shawcross, 'A New Lykourgos for a New Sparta: George Gemistos Plethon and the Despotate of the Morea', in *Viewing the Morea: Land and People in the Late Medieval Peloponnese*, ed. S. Gerstel (Washington DC, 2013), 419–52.

[170] The 'history' aspect of the *Funeral Oration* has also been noted by Leonte, 'Morea' and Leonte, *Rhetoric in Purple*, 243–89. See *Funeral Oration*, 30–31, Manuel Chrysoloras, *Discourse on the Funeral Oration*, 47 and the letter of Isidore of Kiev in W. Regel, *Analecta byzantino-russica* (Petrograd, 1891), Letter 8, 65–69. See also D. A. Zakythinos, 'Μανουὴλ Β'ὸ Παλαιολόγος καὶ ὁ καρδινάλιος Ἰσίδορος ἐν Πελοποννήσῳ', *Mélanges Octave et Melpo Merlier*, III (=Collection de l'Institut Français d'Athènes, 94), (Athens, 1957), 45–67.

Moreans for co-operating with the Ottomans, and the conversion of some Moreans to Islam is the major theme.[171] Manuel ponders whether to call them barbarians or Romans.[172] And he notes with satisfaction that these Morean converts failed to convince the Ottomans of their sincerity in joining them, and are viewed by the Ottomans with suspicion for having spurned their life-long beliefs and customs in favour of foreign ones. This idea that a person could not (and should not) leave the faith and the customs to which he had been born, accords with the views expressed by Manuel in the *Discourse to Iagoup* and the *Dialogue with a Persian*. This example further indicates Manuel's inflexible outlook. As in the case of his other two works, the *Funeral Oration* envisions identity as a blend of religion, ethnicity and customs.

The *Funeral Oration*: Idealizing One's Reign

A unique blend of funerary oration and history, the *Funeral Oration* is one of Manuel's most well-known works, and arguably his most studied.[173] In it, Manuel manipulates the historical narrative of the oration in order to pursue his own literary and political agenda, which acquires further significance when one considers that the work was actually performed before a Morean audience. Like many of his writings, the *Funeral Oration* was also a vehicle through which Manuel conveyed political messages and attempted to enhance his authority among his Morean subjects.[174]

As has been noted by previous scholars, the blending of the genres of funerary oration and history, was indeed an innovative approach to a traditional format. Manuel himself seems to have shown an awareness of and perhaps pride in the novelty of his approach. For instance, he points out that giving an even more detailed narrative was a historian's task.[175] It has been convincingly argued many times that the *Funeral Oration* is an apology for Theodore's rule in the Morea.[176] I will not summarize these

---

[171] On the cooperation of the Moreans with the Ottomans and their resistance to central authority, see Necipoğlu, *Byzantium between the Ottomans and the Latins*, 259–83.

[172] Due to the mixed ethnic make-up of the Morea, Mazaris, too, calls them barbarians; they are not Hellenes, but Tzakonians, 64–9. Of course, his critique also stems from their disobedience to Manuel, to whom the text was addressed. For Morea's ethnic make-up, see Zakthinos, *Le Despotat* I, 3–4, 16–17, 32; *Funeral Oration*, 126–9. Page, *Byzantine Identity*, 243–66, especially 255 for identity in the *Funeral Oration*.

[173] Another contender for this ranking is the *Dialogue on Marriage*.   [174] See also Leonte, 'Morea'.

[175] *Funeral Oration*, 96–7. The audience also seems to have noted this, see Manuel Chrysoloras, *Discourse on the Funeral Oration*, 71, 114–15.

[176] Leonte, 'Morea', Chrysostomides, *Funeral Oration*, 28.

previous studies, but instead add a few more dimensions to these arguments. For instance, the *Funeral Oration* can also be interpreted as an *apologia* for Manuel. He was, after all, a direct participant in his brother's policies. Although Theodore is the hero of the *Funeral Oration*, the text is also equally about Manuel, and the emperor's presence, both political and textual, is always felt in the narrative.[177]

This 'double' apology can be observed especially in the episode of Theodore's sale of Corinth to the Hospitallers. As despot of Morea, Theodore had carried out the sale with Manuel's consent. Although the sale of Corinth was also the emperor's responsibility, in his narrative, Manuel claims that this decision was fully supported by their mother. As in *the Dialogue on Marriage*, the approval of Empress Helena lends sanctity to political decisions. Manuel also explains his brother's reasoning: he chose the Hospitallers as a 'lesser evil', and accepted a small diminution in his possessions for a future increase.[178] These explanations suggest that the emperor sought to excuse his own sanction of the sale as well.

Moreover, Manuel argues that there was a ploy to deceive the Ottomans behind Theodore's decision, and his true intention was to get Corinth back as soon as possible. In order to clear his brother of any wrongdoing, Manuel then goes on to argue that deceit can be forgiven if it leads to a greater good. In short, the goal justified the means. This provides a stark contrast to his stance in the *Dialogue on Marriage* and in a letter addressed to Demetrios Chrysoloras, where in relation to John VII, he protests that deceit is unforgivable under any circumstance. That he went to such lengths to redeem the sale of Corinth, may therefore be interpreted as an attempt to clear himself of blame.

Manuel's mixture of the genres of history and funeral oration allowed him to impose his own presence on events, thereby strengthening the 'double' apologetic aspect of the text. Manuel was selective in his historical narrative, and while he claims that this was to aid the narrative flow, it also served his own narrative goal of representing his actions in the best light possible. For instance, he skips the *genos* part of the oration, excusing himself by claiming that Theodore's great virtue nullified the need. This omission allows him to pass over the reign of his father, John V, however, and by extension the fact that he was a mere second son who was not destined for the throne.[179] Similarly, although it would have helped to

---

[177] For Manuel's narrative strategies in the *Funeral Oration*, see Leonte, 'Morea'.

[178] *Funeral Oration*, 170–9.

[179] *Funeral Oration*, 78–81. Leonte, *Rhetoric in Purple*, 262–3, 280 also notes this omission and its political significance.

highlight his alliance with Theodore, Manuel passes over his own rule in
Thessalonike and the re-establishment of Andronikos as heir.[180] Again,
these were episodes that risked tarnishing his idealized image. In contrast,
Manuel expands upon the Serres gathering in 1394, elaborating especially
on Bayezid's murderous schemes. By placing such great emphasis on this
event, Manuel was evidently attempting to clear himself of blame for
bringing about the blockade of Constantinople.[181]

On the other hand, the emperor inserts several non-Morean events into
the narrative in order to draw attention to his own person and to represent
himself as a self-sacrificing ruler. His reference to his European journey and
his laments for the dangers he faced, can be interpreted as one such
instance.[182] All in all, Manuel always emerges as a central figure in any
political decision taken. He is not only a major figure in Theodore's Morea,
but even participates in his parents' secret discussion in the Tower of
Anemas in 1373. Thus, in the text, Manuel depicts himself as a figure of
authority, both as a speaker and a decision maker, and he carefully shapes
the narrative to represent an idealized version of the history of his own rule.

Similarly, it can be proposed that Theodore's portrayal in the *Funeral
Oration* also allows Manuel to dominate the text. The emperor depicts his
brother almost as a younger 'self' in many respects, and Theodore is
represented as always acting out of obedience to Manuel in critical
moments. In the episode of the Tower of Anemas, 'As he would be in
other cases, he was persuaded by me', Manuel points out, 'and said he
would do what I wanted'.[183] Theodore's complete obedience to his brother
is an underlying theme; he is directed and controlled by Manuel. Likewise,
the notion that Manuel and Theodore were 'one' is also a major theme in
the oration. Significantly, the emperor points out that to praise Theodore
is actually to praise his own self, as they were one in everything.[184] With this
comment, albeit while bestowing praise on Theodore, Manuel also appro-
priates his brother's successes. While this depiction highlights the especially close bond between the brothers, it also helps to draw the emperor
into the foreground of Morean politics. Theodore's rule in the Morea thus
almost becomes a small 'branch' of Manuel's rule as the emperor.

Finally, a close reading suggests that Theodore's portrayal also corresponds closely to the Aristotelian ideals promulgated in Manuel's ethico-

---

[180] *Funeral Oration*, 108–9.   [181] See Chapter 5.   [182] *Funeral Oration*, 162–3.
[183] *Funeral Oration*, 106–7, ' Ἀλλ' οὕτω πάλιν οἷς ἂν γνοίην ἐπείθετο, ὡς ἀρκοῦν εἶναι καὶ νεῦσαι, καὶ
ἔφη πράξειν ὃ θέλοιμι. . . .'
[184] *Funeral Oration*, 218–19.

political thought, especially those of the *Foundations of Imperial Conduct* and the *Ethico-Political Orations* (1410–16). Both works were in progress as Manuel was composing the *Funeral Oration*. We have already discussed how Manuel employed Aristotelian concepts in his *Discourse to the Thessalonians* and the *Dialogue with a Persian* while fashioning his portrayal of the Ottomans. The existence of an ethical framework in the *Funeral Oration* also seems to have been noticed by Manuel Chrysoloras, who notes Manuel's preoccupation with ethics and virtue.[185] Moderation (τό μέτρον, μετριότης), emerges as a key feature in the emperor's ethico-political works; it is identified as Theodore's chief virtue in the *Funeral Oration* and is much emphasized throughout the narrative. Manuel even claims that Theodore collected maxims on moderation.[186] In a node to Aristotelian ethics, Theodore is also described as possessing the mean of all human characteristics: he is halfway between gentleness and severity, frugality and generosity.[187]

Again, as in Manuel's ethico-political thought, choice (προαίρεσις) becomes a significant concept in the *Funeral Oration*. Theodore sacrifices himself for the Moreans by choice.[188] His sale of Corinth is explained by a borrowing from the *Nicomachean Ethics*: Theodore is like a sailor who has to throw his cargo into the sea to avoid sinking. Thus, Manuel surmises, as in the case of Aristotle's sailor, Theodore's deed can be categorized neither as voluntary nor involuntary, and thus he cannot be blamed.[189] Furthermore, as in the *Dialogue with a Persian*, Manuel contrasts the Life of Pleasure and the Life of Virtue, and Theodore is portrayed as following the latter.[190] Finally, his brother displays other qualities put forth by Manuel in his ethico-political works. The despot trusts in others, he values time and never wastes it; for once lost, time cannot be gained.[191] Even in prosperity, he watches out for tempests as he knows that fortune delights in changes.[192] These are all maxims that adorn the emperor's ethico-political works, and ultimately, Manuel relies on a chiefly Aristotelian framework for his character portrayal of Theodore, fashioning his image to promote to his own political and ethical ideals.

---

[185] Manuel Chrysoloras, *Discourse on the Funeral Oration*, 93; E. Nuti, 'Manuel Chrysoloras' Περί τοῦ Βασιλέως λόγου: Genre, Aims, Content, and Sources', *GRBS* 56 (2016), 164–97.
[186] *Funeral Oration*, 92–3.
[187] *Funeral Oration*, 87–9. Aristotle, *Nicomachean Ethics*, I, v-vi; x, vi-viii. This has not been noted by the editor of the text.
[188] *Funeral Oration*, 154–5.
[189] *Funeral Oration*, 171–2, Aristotle, *Nicomachean Ethics*, II, ii; v-vi; especially vii.
[190] *Funeral Oration*, 108–9.   [191] *Funeral Oration*, 75–6, 92–3.   [192] *Funeral Oration*, 88–9.

The *Funeral Oration* is a manifestation of genuine affection on Manuel's behalf. His choice to embed political messages in his narrative should not be interpreted as a sign of insincerity. His emotive language in the oration was probably not a mere rhetorical ploy but truly heartfelt. The very fact that Manuel composed such a lengthy funerary oration may be taken as an indication of the great effect Theodore's death had on him. That the oration clearly had a very strong political agenda also must have prompted Manuel to devote a great deal of time and care to the work. Yet the *Funeral Oration* should not be considered purely as a text of political propaganda, but as a work blending political agenda and deep affection. Though it may be a testament to Theodore's and Manuel's policies in the Morea, it is also a testament to brotherly love and devotion.

The empress mother and Theodore are the only family members that figure in Manuel's compositions. However, the lengthy *Funeral Oration* is entirely about Theodore, and another major work, the *Dialogue with a Persian*, is also dedicated to him. Manuel had spent his whole life with Theodore, his *other self*, as he describes his brother in the oration and in one of his letters.[193] All his life, amidst a family torn by strife, he received political and personal support from his brother. In the 1380s, having broken off with his entire family, it was Theodore with whom he allied. It was also with Theodore that Manuel originally planned to take refuge after his escape from Thessalonike, and during his European journey, he had committed his family to Theodore's care. His death thus deprived Manuel of a major source of personal support.

In the *Funeral Oration*, the emperor lamented the passing away of his entire family. Although his lamentation conforms to the established rhetorical practices, it also rings true. Manuel was now in his sixties, and he had struggled with instability all his life. From this point onwards as he grew older and lonelier, the emperor would seek solace in writing, especially in writing theological and devotional texts:

> It was fitting and better that I should die before you who were the younger. But you overtook me, (would that it had never happened), and I, as it seems, who claimed to be inseparable from you, were proved wrong. Leaving your body on earth you went to God while I still live here.[194]

---

[193] Letter 13; see Chapter 3.

[194] *Funeral Oration*, and 240–1, "Ἔδει γὰρ καὶ βέλτιον ἦν ἐμοὶ μὴ σοῦ τοῦ νεωτέρου γενέσθαι δεύτερον πρὸς τὸ μεταστῆναι τῶν τῇδε. Ἀλλ' ἔφθασας γε ἡμᾶς ὡς οὐκ ὤφελε, καὶ ἡμεῖς, ὡς ἔοικεν, ἀχώριστοί σου λέγοντες ἔσεσθαι, ἠλέγχθημεν ψευδόμενοι. Αὐτὸς γὰρ ᾤχου πρὸς θεὸν ἀφεὶς τὸ σῶμα τῇ γῇ, ἡμεῖς δ' ἐνταῦθα διατρίβομεν ἔτι.'

CHAPTER 9

The Protean Emperor

.... how you practice rhetoric while ruling, and while practicing rhetoric, you rule excellently; like Plato, you philosophize and while philosophizing, you pronounce most rhetorical speeches . . . .'[1]

Manuel's life between 1410–16 was dominated by a flurry of writing. Along with the famous *Funeral Oration*, these years witnessed the creation of many works, but now ethico-political compositions would be the dominant theme in his oeuvre. After his return from the West in 1403, Manuel set to work upon two of his most extensive compositions: *Foundations of Imperial Conduct* and the *Ethico-Political Orations*. By 1410, the *Foundations* and at least six of the orations were composed. Evidence suggests that the revised and 'published' versions of these texts were circulating in courtly circles by 1416.[2] These two works can be treated as a culmination of Manuel's ethico-political thought, traces of which we previously saw in his orations and dialogues.[3]

The *Foundations of Imperial Conduct*

Of the two compositions, the earlier one, the *Foundations*, also has the distinction of being one of the last Byzantine specimens of the so-called

---

[1] Polemis, 'Anonymous Panegyric', 710, lines 105–7, '. . . πῶς καὶ βασιλεύων ῥητορεύεις, καὶ ῥητορεύων, βασιλεύεις ὅ τι κάλλιστα, καὶ μετὰ Πλάτωνος φιλοσοφεῖς, καὶ φιλοσοφῶν δημηγορεῖς ῥητορικώτατα.'

[2] *Foundations of Imperial Conduct* is edited in *PG* 156, cols. 315–81 and also S. Nicolae, *Manuel Paleologul, Sfaturi pentru educaţia împărătească*, Academia Romaniae, Institutum Studiorum Europae Meridionalis-Orientalis, Scriptores Byzantini X (Bucarest, 2015), 62–162. See also C. Billò, 'Note al testo dei Praecepta Educationis Regiae di Manuele II Paleologo', *Medievo Greco* 1 (2001), 23–8. For the dating of the *Foundations* and the *Ethico-Political Orations*, *Ethico-Political Orations*, 46–52. It is also convincingly demonstrated that the *Foundations* were composed earlier than the *Ethico-Political Orations*.

[3] Kakkoura proposes that the term 'ethico-political' is suitable to describe the work since it combines moral advice and political theory, as was Manuel's aim. *Ethico-Political Orations*, 34. The *Foundations* is also, then, an ethico-political work.

mirror of princes genre. These were advisory texts addressed to rulers concerning the best conduct in both private and public spheres.[4] Although *mirror of princes* was not a term used by the Byzantine authors, it will be used here for the sake of convenience, in order to distinguish these texts from other forms of advisory literature. Across centuries, many specimens of *mirror of princes* are found in Byzantium, some well-known examples being Agapetos in the sixth century, Pseudo-Basil in the ninth century, and Nikephoros Blemmydes and Thomas Magistros in the fourteenth century.[5] However, Manuel is in a rare position as an emperor who authored a work in this genre.[6]

Let us briefly set forth then the main features of Manuel's *mirror*. *The Foundations* is organized into 100 chapters, *kephalia*. This form was employed by many Byzantine writers for theological or philosophical treatises. For instance, both Agapetos and Pseudo-Basil composed their *mirrors* as chapters. In Manuel's work, as in these two *mirrors*, an acrostic is formed with the first letter of each chapter.[7] Structure-wise, his work is coherent; discussions of similar topics are grouped together and there are repeats to stress particularly important points. It has been recently demonstrated that Manuel combines the gnomic tradition with Classical authors and the Church Fathers. The emperor acknowledges

---

[4] There are also other advisory texts contemporary to the *Foundations*, as well as later ones, such as Plethon's addresses to Manuel and the Despot Theodore. However, these advisory texts can be called 'integrated mirrors' instead of independent, fully composed *mirrors of princes*. Manuel's work, however, is a 'complete' and 'independent' *mirror of princes*, advising the ruler on all aspects of governing and private conduct.

[5] For discussions of *mirror of princes* in Byzantium, see the following. Mostly, Manuel is absent from the discussions or is quickly dismissed. If his composition is discussed, the emphasis is on the chapters relating to his advice concerning the Church. P. Odorico, 'Les miroirs des princes à Byzance. Une lecture horizontale', in *L'éducation au gouvernement et à la vie: la tradition des régles de vie de l'Antiquité au Moyen Age. Colloque International Pise, 18 et 19 Mars 2005*, ed. P. Odorico (Paris, 2009) 223–46; I. Ševčenko, 'Agapetos East and West. The Fate of a Byzantine Mirror of Princes', *RESEE* 16 (1978), 1–45. Henceforth, Ševčenko, 'Agapetos'. P. Henry III, 'A Mirror for Justinian: The *Ekthesis* of Agapetos', *GRBS* 8 (1967), 381–408; A. Markopoulos, 'Autour des chapitres de Basile Ier', in *Εὐψυχία. Mélanges offerts à Hélène Ahrweiler*, eds. M. Balard, et al.,vol. II (Paris, 1998), 469–79; G. Prinzing, 'Beobachtungen zu integrierten Fürstenspiegeln der Byzantiner', *JÖB* 38 (1988), 1–31; K. Paidas. *Η Θεματική των Βυζαντινών Κατόπτρων Ηγεμονίας της Πρώιμης και Μέσης Περιόδου (398–1085)* (Athens, 2005); K. Paidas,*«Κάτοπτρα Ηγεμόνος» της Ύστερης Περιόδου (1254-1303): Εκφράσεις του Βυζαντινού Βασιλικού Ιδεώδους* (Athens, 2006); W. Blum, *Byzantinische Fürstenspiegel: Agapetos, Theophylakt von Ochrid, Thomas Magister* (Stuttgart, 1981); Angelov, *Imperial Ideology*, 12, 92, 184–91, 223–4, 254, 392 and 419.

[6] The ninth-century *mirror*, the so-called Pseudo-Basil, was thought to be authored by Basil I, but was in possibly written by the Patriarch Photios. See the article by Markopoulos in footnote 5.

[7] It reads: Βασιλεὺς Μανουὴλ πατὴρ βασιλεῖ Ἰωάννῃ υἱῷ, καρπὸν τῆς ἐμῆς ψυχῆς ὁποιασοῦν, τροφὴν τῇ σῇ ψυχῇ ἀκμαζούσῃ, δίδωμι δηλονότι. ἧ ὁ θεὸς εἴη κοσμήτωρ.

this blending in his prefatory letter.[8] Although Manuel names Isokrates and Dio Chrysostom as models for this genre, the *Foundations* does not reflect the strong influence of either. A comparison reveals some vague similarities with Isokrates' advice in *To Nicocles* concerning topics such as education, choice of friends, loyal service and flattery, mastering desires and combining courtesy with dignity. However, these constitute such commonplace advice that it is not possible to conclude definitively whether Isocrates was Manuel's inspiration.

Both the work itself and the prefatory letter are addressed to Manuel's son and heir, John VIII. Yet probably, as was the case for his other works, he was targeting a wider audience; the *Foundations* might even have been intended to be performed in a *theatron*. Certain panegyrics addressed to Manuel refer to the *Foundations*, indicating that the work was known by the literati of the period. The *Foundations* and the *Ethico-Political Orations* have recently attracted extensive study, especially with regard to their textual structures, manuscript traditions and reflections of imperial ideology.[9] This discussion will discuss the chief ethico-political ideas that Manuel puts forth and will link them to his previous compositions. Once more, we will also focus on the emperor's self-representation strategies.

In the *Foundations*, Manuel refers to John as a boy, *meirakion*, indicating that he was a youth at the time of the composition.[10] By 1411 John had married Anna of Moscow, and by 1414, he was already acting as a regent during his father's absence. Although the exact date of his proclamation is not known, by that time, John was already co-emperor.[11] Similarly, in 1416–17, he would be sent to the Morea and was also involved in the transport of the Ottoman pretender, Mustafa. Together with his brother Theodore, John also contended with the Prince of Achaia, Centurione Zaccaria, and sought to expand Palaiologan power in the peninsula.[12] John appears more frequently in the sources after this date. This is not surprising as by then John was gaining in political influence. Little is known about him as a young boy or about his relationship with his father, but Manuel had been travelling in Europe for almost four years during his childhood, as

---

[8] Leonte, *Rhetoric in Purple*, 155–6, 165 makes these observations.

[9] See the dissertations by Leonte and Kakkoura.

[10] In later editions, the term is replaced by ἀνήρ, indicating John's advancing age. *Ethico-Political Orations*, 47–8.

[11] John appears dressed as an emperor in the manuscript of Pseudo-Dionysios that Manuel had sent to the cathedral of Saint Denis in 1407. The inscription on the illumination refers to him as emperor. See Chapter 7.

[12] Barker, *Manuel II*, 344–5; Doukas, 133–5, 346–7.

well as within his territories. Ultimately, he was absent for long periods of time.

What was Manuel's influence on his six sons, two of whom would go on to become emperors? Given his frequent absences and political preoccupations, the emperor could not have spent much time with them. For several years, his son Theodore even lived in Mistra with his uncle. The emperor later sent his other sons to the Morea as well. In a letter dated to the mid-1390s, Manuel appointed a certain Theodore Kaukadenos as tutor for his daughter and two sons.[13] The boys in question must have been John VIII and Constantine, the first son by this name who died in infancy. As for the unnamed daughter, she must have been the same girl who died and was buried in Monemvasia.[14] The letter reveals the importance Manuel placed upon his sons' education. This is hardly surprising for an emperor, especially an erudite one like Manuel, who also, notably, included his daughter in the imperial classroom and did not seem to discriminate between boys and girls in terms of education.

Apart from this one instance, his sons are not discussed in any of Manuel's writings. Even John VIII is the addressee of the two ethico-political works only by virtue of being the heir, and nothing intimate can be gleaned from the texts. The only hints of his relationship with John are found in Sphrantzes, who in his bias, highlights the contrast between the reckless attitude of John with the wisdom of Manuel. Like Manuel, John and Theodore seem to have been very fond of the hunt and they often figure in sources as hunters. Theodore II, the despot of Morea, did become a significant patron for the literati in Mistra and nurtured the intellectual life of his despotate. Though he was interested in scholarship, he did not become an avid author like his father. The future emperors, John VIII and Constantine IX, would also offer the literati some patronage, but would not display a remarkable interest in scholarly pursuits.[15]

Syropoulos and Sphrantzes narrate a peculiar episode concerning Demetrios, the emperor's fifth son.[16] In 1421/22, Demetrios fled to Pera where, Sphrantzes adds, he intended to submit to the Ottomans. However, the young despot changed plans and instead attempted to go to the court of Sigismund of Hungary; although his parents summoned him back,

---

[13] Letter 27, lines 13–6.   [14] See Chapter 7.
[15] Sphrantzes, 28–9, mentions John being at the hunt when an envoy from Hungary arrived. Ghillebert de Lannoy, 65, notes that John VIII took him to hunt on various occasions in 1422. Pero Tafur also narrates a hunting party with John VIII and Theodore II, see Chapter 8.
[16] Syropoulos, 112–14; Sphrantzes, 24–5. Schreiner, *Kleinchroniken*, Cronik13/8–9 also reports the incident.

Demetrios disobeyed and the imperial couple was forced to authorize his visit to the Hungarian court. Demetrios travelled to Hungary, accompanied by Matthew Asan and would later marry Asan's daughter. These accounts are intriguing, as they portray Demetrios as disobedient to Manuel. After the death of John VII's death, he would also compete with his elder brother Constantine XI for the throne, and in the Morea, he would strive against his younger brother Thomas. These depictions of Demetrios thus have a ring of truth to them.[17]

Ultimately, we can draw no clear portrait of Manuel as a father. While addressing John in the prefatory letter to the *Foundations*, Manuel represents himself as an ideal father, teacher and emperor. By combining the personae of teacher and father, Manuel mingles authority with fatherly affection. The emperor begins the letter by speaking about his journey to Europe: 'I sailed away', he writes, 'leaving you (John) in the Peloponnese. Oh, how my heart grieved!'[18] Elsewhere, he professes that his love for John exceeds that of any father's love for his son. Both in the letter and the work, direct addresses to John as 'dearest' are found, creating a sense of intimate dialogue between father and the son. Yet despite these protestations of affection, nothing intimate can be gleaned from the text. Manuel's adopted persona of a loving father only serves to further burnish his self-image as an ideal emperor and an exceptionally affectionate and devoted father.

Subtly, the emperor sets himself as an example for his son to follow. For instance, in a modesty *topos*, he suggests that John can learn from his mistakes. The implication that John should take Manuel's good habits and virtues as his example is a theme throughout the *mirror*. Moreover, the emperor emphasizes his unique position as a ruler who penned an advisory text. Isokrates and Dio Chrysostom were great authors, Manuel argues, but they had to refrain from giving advice in order not to appear too bold. The implication is, of course, that as the emperor Manuel faced no such dilemma. He also underscores that he has personal experience of what it means to rule. The same insistence is also found in the *Ethico-Political Orations*, where Manuel reminds his audience that he had the necessary experience in life both as a mature man and as emperor.[19] Even from the

---

[17] Many years before, Manuel's younger brother Michael sought the Trapezuntine throne. Manuel's sons governed the following: Theodore was the despot of Morea, Andronikos the despot of Thessalonike, while Constantine had lands around the Black Sea. Later, Demetrios would rule Lemnos, and John VIII, as the heir, acted on his father's behalf in Constantinople, as well as being sent on various missions.

[18] *Foundations of Imperial Conduct*, col. 313, Ἐν Πελοποννήσῳ σε λιπών, ἐξ Ἰταλίας ἐρχόμενος (ὦ πῶς ἐνεγκεῖν ἐδυνήθην;)....'

[19] *Foundations of Imperial Conduct*, col. 317.

start, he embraces the persona of an authoritative emperor-author and
seeks to emphasize his unique imperial rank: he is not just any author or
father.

This teacher-advisor-emperor version of Manuel is always present in the
Foundations and *the Ethico-Political Orations*.[20] In the latter work, he points
out that he corrects mistaken notions not only for the benefit of John, but
also because it suits his imperial rank (σχῆμα).[21] In the *Foundations* and the
Ethico-Political Orations, Manuel takes pains to communicate his imperial
authority to the audience. In a *topos*, he emphasizes that the emperor, too, is
a mortal man while also drawing attention to the distinctiveness of the
imperial rank: 'Everything is the same *except* your rank', he says, and 'you
have nothing more than them *except* your rank … '.[22] Manuel implicitly
flaunts the uniqueness of imperial authority; he and John do possess something that their subjects lack.

Moreover, as seen in his letters, Manuel strives to highlight the difficulties of rulership. That the ruler has public cares day and night is a Homeric
theme employed in the *mirror*. An emperor must likewise seek 'the good'
(τὸ καλόν), since people will be led by his decisions; this is possibly yet
another allusion to the *Iliad*.[23] Crucially, because the audience knows that
the author is the emperor, Manuel's advice alludes to his own troubles and
responsibilities. Not only does he offer advice to his heir, he once again
promotes a vision of himself as the ideal, dutiful emperor.

With regards to its contents, the *mirror* advocates ideals that are
a fusion of the teachings of the Church Fathers and Plato. Aristotle's
Nicomachean Ethics is an especially dominant influence. The advisory
topics include the search for the best way to live, voluntary and involuntary deeds, choice, moderation and humility, hopefulness, education,
perseverance, piety, and magnanimity. More specific advice on military
matters, handling slander and choosing worthy advisors, is also offered.

---

[20] Leonte, *Rhetoric in Purple*, 192–243, also argues that Manuel adopts the persona of a teacher in his
ethico-political works. He does not focus on self-representation or Manuel's insistence on his
imperial rank, but on the didactic voice in the work. Leonte classifies Manuel's advisory texts
into three groups: the deliberative voice, the dialogic voice and the didactic voice. As Manuel
directly counsels his son and acts as a teacher, the *Ethico-Politcal Orations* are listed under the
didactic voice.

[21] *Ethico-Political Orations*, 385.

[22] *Foundations of Imperial Conduct*, cols. 324 and 352, 'Μᾶλλον δὲ σύνδουλος, καὶ ἀδελφός, καὶ
ὁμότιμος, πλὴν τοῦ σχήματος …' and '… μηδὲν πλέον ἔχων ἢ σχῆμα … '.

[23] *Foundations of Imperial Conduct*, col. 331, 339, 335–57, 359, 369. *Foundations of Imperial Conduct*, col.
331, 339, 335–57, 359, 369. "Μᾶλλον δὲ σύνδουλος, καὶ ἀδελφός, καὶ ὁμότιμος, πλὴν τοῦ σχήματος…'
and '…μηδὲν πλέον ἔχων ἢ σχῆμα…' Homer, *Iliad*, Book 2, 60-62. See also Letter 32, where
Manuel quotes Homer verbatim on this theme.

Overall, the emperor's advice is firmly rooted in the ideas found in previous *mirrors* and other rhetorical texts dealing with imperial power. Issues discussed by Manuel, such as rule by divine right, the importance of generosity, philanthropy, self-control and altruism, the philosopher-king, peace and war, are all commonplace.[24] On the whole, despite Manuel's rare status as an author-emperor, the *Foundations* is mostly a tradition-bound work.

The emperor seems to have relied on Agapetos as a model. Not only does he use the same form of *kephalia* as Agapetos, but some of his advice, such as the good use of time and the irreversibility of time, also closely resembles Agapetos' arguments. Furthermore, some chapters seem to betray Agapetos' linguistic influence.[25] Manuel's choice of Agapetos as model, in itself, is a distinctive feature of his work. While he may have relied on a model to compose his own text, it is notable that he opted for this sixth-century *mirror* over of any of the others. True, Agapetos' well-known *mirror* was widely circulated and copied over the centuries, but not all Byzantine authors who wrote advisory works relied on it. Certainly, Manuel's own contemporaries do not display the same degree of interest in Agapetos as the emperor himself did.

A comparison of Manuel's *mirror* with works by Agapetos, Pseudo-Basil, Nikephoros Blemmydes and Thomas Magistros demonstrates that many of Manuel's ideas were shared by these authors.[26] For instance, Manuel's discussions about the emperor receiving the sceptre from God and the necessity to imitate God, are very prominent especially in Agapetos and in Pseudo-Basil.[27] Like Manuel, all four authors place great importance on

---

[24] Angelov, *Imperial Ideology*, 184–97. For a general discussion of peace and war in *mirrors of princes*, see J. Munitiz, 'War and Peace Reflected in some Byzantine Mirrors of Princes', in *Peace and War in Byzantium. Essays in Honour of George T. Dennis*, eds. T. Miller and J. Nesbitt (Washington DC, 1995), 50–61.

[25] On Agapetos, see Angelov, *Imperial Ideology*, 186 and Ševčenko, 'Agapetos'. Agapetos' chapters 1, 4, 12, 18, 22, 26 and 35, seem to have been especially influential on Manuel. Agapetos' work is edited in Agapetos the Deacon, *Der Fürstenspiegel für Kaiser Iustinianos*. ed. R. Riedinger (Würzburg, 1994). Henceforth, Agapetos. Ševčenko, 'Agapetos', 8–9, also points out several parallels between Manuel and Agapetos.

[26] I have chosen these four specimens, as Agapetos and Pseudo-Basil were widely copied, while Magistros and Blemmydes were Late Byzantine authors, like Manuel. See K. Emminger, *Studien zu Griechen Fürstenspiegel*, III, (Munich, 1906–1913), 50–71 for Pseudo-Basil, *Magistros. La Regalità*. ed. P. Volpe Cacciatore (Naples, 1992) for Thomas Magistros ; and *Des Nikephoros Blemmydes' Βασιλικὸς Ἀνδριάς und dessen Metaphrase von Georgios Galesiotes und Georgios Oinaiotes*, eds. H. Hunger and I. Ševčenko (Vienna, 1986) Henceforth, Pseudo-Basil, Magistros and Blemmydes.
On commonplace ideas found in advisory texts and panegyrics, see Angelov, *Imperial Ideology*, 78–94; and F. Dvornik, *Early Christian and Byzantine Political Philosophy, Origins and Background*, 2vols. (Washington DC, 1966)

[27] Agapetos, 26, 28, 50; Pseudo-Basil, 53, 56; Blemmydes, 46.

justice and lawful rule.[28] His advice on the necessity of mastering pleasures, and distinguishing between good advisors and flatterers are again shared by all these authors.[29] Finally, as in Manuel's *mirror*, Blemmydes also advocates the notion of a philosopher-emperor.[30] Thus, in many instances, the emperor's work recycles ideas found in other Byzantine examples of the genre.

Despite his adherence to tradition, Manuel's work still has features that are distinguishable from these other four authors. Although his more unique touches have been largely neglected by scholars, these two advisory works still offer insight into Manuel's own ideas on rulership and ethics. For example, several of the emperor's remarks are intriguing and seem to suggest a personal insight. For instance, he advises his son to have patience and faith in God when he is slandered and falsely blamed by his subjects; moreover, he reminds John that as emperor, the bad deeds carried out by his servants would be ascribed to him.[31] These do seem to reflect Manuel's own experiences, especially during the blockade of Constantinople. Similarly, though the advice that wealth is desirable solely for the benefit of the emperor's subjects, is a commonplace idea shared by Agapetos, Pseudo-Basil, Magistros and Blemmydes, comparison reveals Manuel's treatment of this subject to be far more extensive.[32] Perhaps, this difference can be interpreted as stemming from the financial constraints he personally experienced as a ruler. After all, economic turmoil had made Manuel into an emperor who could not afford to ignore all aspects of finance.

Similarly, although the importance of ruling willing subjects is emphasized in Agapetos and Pseudo-Basil, Manuel's own emphasis on this issue is remarkable. His advice, here may also be a reflection of his own life experience. Following the tradition notion, Manuel argues that if his subjects are unwilling, the emperor will not be able to rule effectively.[33] And it is worth noting that in the civil wars Manuel endured between himself, his father, his brother and nephew, the outcome was usually decided by the support of the populace. Manuel therefore knew just how crucial his subjects' approval could be. Similarly, like Agapetos, Manuel argues that only thing that cannot be recovered is time,[34] though he enigmatically adds that wealth, success and

---

[28] Agapetos, 42; Pseudo-Basil, 61, 66; Magistros, 35; Blemmydes, 62.

[29] Agapetos, 32, 36, 40; Pseudo-Basil, 55, 57–8, 69; Magistros, 32–3, 59–60; Blemmydes, 58.

[30] Blemmydes, 44.   [31] *Foundations of Imperial Conduct*, cols. 343–4, 367–8.

[32] Agapetos, 56; Pseudo-Basil, 52, 59, 61–2; Magistros, 5–54; Blemmydes, 64. *Foundations of Imperial Conduct*, cols. 327–9, 361.

[33] Agapetos, 48; Pseudo-Basil, 66. The issue of the people's support and legitimacy has been discussed in A. Kaldellis, *The Byzantine Republic* (Cambridge MA, 2015), but the case of Manuel is not included.

[34] Agapetos, 30.

even the *throne* can be recovered.[35] This notion of a recoverable throne is unique to Manuel, and can perhaps be interpreted as a reflection of his own loss and regaining of power.

The contrast between tyranny and legitimate rule was also a widespread theme in the genre. And here, yet again, Manuel's own arguments in the *Foundations* include some unusual aspects. He does conform to tradition in his acknowledgement that legitimate rule relies on laws and not on the arbitrary will of the ruler, but he nevertheless suggests that these two forms actually resemble each other and admits to being unsure how much a tyrant and an emperor really differ from each other.[36] It is tempting to contemplate the parallels between these remarks and the accusations of tyranny levelled at Manuel; one prominent instance of this being rule in Thessalonike. Thus, the *Foundations* manifest some personalized insights.

The chapters in the *Foundations* on the relationship between the Church and the emperor are notable parts of the emperor's work. Other *mirrors* do not dedicate much attention to this issue. This addition in the *Foundations* clearly stems from Manuel's own dealings in ecclesiastical affairs. He advises John: 'You should lead the Church before everyone else, who leads you before everyone else ... '. Here, Manuel is clearly attempting to assert imperial authority over the Church, and this idea is strengthened when we recall that the work was not solely addressed to John but was circulated among the literati. This claim of authority was thus equally directed towards the members of the imperial court, the literati and the ecclesiastics; perhaps especially to dissidents like Symeon of Thessalonike.

In addition to claiming imperial authority over the Church, Manuel envisions it as a bulwark and a haven. It is, he adds, a defensive weapon against the storms of opposing arguments; the Church could scare away every arrogant tongue.[37] More significantly, the emperor advises his son to 'correct' those erring tongues if possible, otherwise be content to merely observe their folly. Manuel advocates the idea that heretical or dissident beliefs should be dealt by the emperor, not solely by the patriarch or the clergy. Once more, he proposes direct imperial intervention in Church affairs and matters of dogma.

---

[35] *Foundations of Imperial Conduct*, col. 360, "Χρήματα μὲν γάρ, καὶ δόξαν, καὶ θρόνον, καὶ τὰ τοιαῦτα, ἔνεστιν ἀποβαλόντα ἀνακαλέσασθαι, καὶ μετὰ προσθήκης ἐπανακτήσασθαι εἰ καὶ μὴ πάνυ ῥᾴδιον... '.

[36] *Foundation of Imperial Conduct*, col. 373, Ἐοικέναι γὰρ δοκεῖ τὸ βασιλεύειν τῷ τυραννεῖν. Διίστασθον δὲ ἀλλήλων, ὅσον οὐδ' εἰπεῖν εὐχερές.'

[37] *Foundations of Imperial Conduct*, col. 325, 'Σὲ πρὸ πάντων ἄγειν δεῖ τὴν σε πρὸ πάντων ἄγουσαν Ἐκκλησίαν, πάντα σοί μετὰ Θεὸν γιγνομένην....'

As we discussed earlier on, prompted both by his desire to exert stronger authority as emperor, as well as his own interest in theology, Manuel frequently sought to assert imperial authority over the Church. Yet, although Makarios of Ankyra and Symeon of Thessalonike protested against his involvement in Church affairs, his conduct had precedent across Byzantine history and was not entirely without basis.[38] Manuel's unique insistence in the *Foundations* on the emperor's right – and duty – to lead the Church, reveals the importance he gave to having his imperial prerogatives recognized. The undisputed confirmation of these imperial rights was indeed a major concern to him.

In these *kephalia*, Manuel's language is moreover flooded with military metaphors. While such battle and weapon imagery might reflect the literary influence of the Psalms, it can also be interpreted as reflecting his stance on ecclesiastical matters. In relation to his wording of 'arrogant tongues', it is interesting to note that Manuel displays a fondness for employing tongue-related imagery in his works with polemical undertones. In two prominent examples, in his Anacreontic verses, he imagines ripping out the tongue of his opponent from its root. In a letter, Manuel envisions Makarios of Ankyra transforming into a tongue.[39] Again, he employs his 'tongue' imagery within a polemical atmosphere in the *Foundations*.

As in the case of the emperor and the church, whenever Manuel introduces some personal touches to traditional ideas, he does his best to emphasize these to his audience. His insistence indicates that the emperor wished for some recognition as a thinker as well. The most striking instance concerns the scheme of cardinal virtues. Manuel does not limit the cardinal virtues to wisdom, bravery, temperance and justice, but adds love (ἀγάπη) and moderation (μετριότης) to the list, insisting that the number of virtues should be six, not four.[40] The insistance on this contrast between his own scheme and the four cardinal virtues suggests that Manuel was aware of his slight departure from the tradition.[41] While other authors could also highlight different virtues and alternate the number of the cardinal virtues, this 'six virtue' scheme with the addition of love and moderation is unique to Manuel.[42]

---

[38] See Chapter 8.

[39] See Appendix 2 and Letter 65, lines 6–7. 'ἀλλὰ καὶ ὅλος μεταβαλὼν ἐς γλῶτταν ἀκριβέστατα καὶ φωνήν. Οὔκουν σοι τοιαύτης πιθανότητος μέτεστιν.' In his homily concerning Manuel's confiscation of monastic properties in Thessalonike, Isidore Glabas also states that he would continue to defend the rights of the Church, even if *one* would threaten to cut out his tongue. See Chapter 3.

[40] On the four cardinal virtues, see Angelov, *Imperial Ideology*, 52–3.

[41] *Foundations of Imperial Conduct*, col. 365.

[42] For instance, Theodore II Laskaris envisioned three cardinal virtues: zeal, truthfulness and mildness. Angelov, *Imperial Ideology*, 93.

His choice of moderation as one of the cardinal values clearly stemmed from the Aristotelian notion of moderation and the 'golden-mean'. As love was moreover considered a Christian virtue, its inclusion among the cardinal virtues also demonstrates the influence of Christianity on Manuel's ethico-political outlook. A few chapters later in the *Foundations,* he again refers to the cardinal virtues as being six in total. Manuel ultimately adopts his own group of cardinal virtues and expects his audience to do the same.[43] He proudly claims that although the four cardinal virtues scheme is a firmly established one, *he himself* does not wish to exclude love and moderation.

Manuel's reliance on *Nicomachean Ethics* is a significant, yet hitherto undiscussed feature of the *Foundations.* This extensive reliance on Aristotelian ethics is also unique to Manuel's *mirror.* it is entirely absent in Agapetos, Pseudo-Basil, Magistros and Blemmydes. As the suitability of Aristotelian ethics to Christianity made it extremely popular among Byzantine scholars, Manuel's reliance on this text is not surprising; however, its extent is notable.[44] The *Foundations* opens with a discussion of different ways of life and the search for the best life, also an important topic in Aristotle.[45] As in Aristotle, to lead a good, virtuous life, *eu zen,* and to search for true happiness, *eudaimonia,* are the key points for Manuel's discussions.[46] As argued previously, the emperor often referred to these Aristotelian notions in his orations and dialogues. In the *mirror,* Manuel devotes much space to Aristotle's ideas on voluntary and involuntary actions, moderation and choice (προαίρεσις).[47]

The emperor attributes great importance to choice: building upon Aristotle, Manuel argues that choice is the most crucial element of an individual's life, since it is through choice that one differentiates between lifestyles and takes action, good or bad. Choice is the only thing that

---

[43] *Foundations of Imperial Conduct,* col. 373.
[44] For the following discussion of *Nicomachean Ethics,* these articles have been relied upon; J. O. Urmson, 'Aristotle's Doctrine of the Mean', *American Philosophical Quarterly* 10.3 (1973), 223–30; P. Losin, 'Aristotle's Doctrine of the Mean', *History of Philosophical Quarterly* 4.3 (1987), 329–41; T. H. Irwin, 'Aristotle on Reason, Desire and Virtue', *The Journal of Philosophy* 72.17 (1975), 567–78; C. Chamberlain, 'The Meaning of Prohairesis in Aristotle's Ethics' *Transactions of the American Philological Association,* vol. 114 (1984), 147–57. For Aristotle in Byzantium, see in general C. Barber and D. Jenkins (eds.) *Medieval Greek Commentaries on the Nicomachean Ethics,* (Leiden, 2009), especially, L. Benakis, 'Aristotelian Ethics in Byzantium', 63–9; K. Oehler, 'Aristotle in Byzantium', *GRBS* 5.2 (1964), 133–46.
[45] *Foundations of Imperial Conduct,* cols. 319–22.
[46] Aristotle, *Nicomachean Ethics,* I, i, iii–vii for the discussion of the lives and *eudaimonia.*
[47] Aristotle, *Nicomachean Ethics,* II, ii and vi on moderation; III, i–ii for voluntary/involuntary deeds; III, i–iv for choice (προαίρεσις). On free will in Byzantine philosophy and the patristic tradition, see Telfer, 'Autexousia'; L. Benakis, 'Ἐλευθερία καὶ ἀναγκαιότητα στην Βυζαντινή φιλοσοφία', Δωδώνη 25 (1996), 203–20.

distinguishes people from one and the other, leading to a path of virtue or vice.[48] In this regard, Manuel also modifies an ancient saying: 'there is no misfortune that cannot be borne by man.' Yet while the poet attributes this to human nature, the emperor attributes it to *choice*.[49] Choice was also a significant concept in Christian thought, and Manuel's ethico-political outlook also conforms to Christian ideals. Furthermore, drawing on the Patristic tradition, Manuel points out that every human being has a will and is thus capable of making choices. While the discussion of will itself as a distinct faculty is absent in Aristotle, it was a major concept in Christian thought. Manuel thus supplies this argument on free-will from Christian thought, conventionally fusing these two traditions.[50]

Manuel's extensive discussion of moderation (μεσότης, μετριότης) and avoiding extremes (ἀκρότητας) also relies heavily on Aristotle.[51] As shown, the emperor goes so far as to add moderation to the cardinal virtues. Even Manuel's final verdict on the best life follows the principle of moderation; significantly, Manuel does not choose a life of strict virtue as opposed to the life of pleasure, but opts for the mean – a virtuous life with also a share of pleasure.[52] This extent of Manuel's discussions of Aristotelian ethics sets the work apart from other *mirrors*. *Nicomachean Ethics* was indeed popular among Byzantine authors, but not all works relied on it, and certainly not to the same extent as Manuel. Over his life, one observes that the emperor's ethico-political thought was greatly shaped by Aristotle, but it must also be stressed that Manuel does not add any new dimensions to these Aristotelian notions.

The *Ethico-Political Orations*

As a continuation of the *Foundations*, Manuel composed a longer and far more detailed work, the *Ethico-Political Orations*.[53] This work is also

---

[48] *Foundations of Imperial Conduct*, col. 321.
[49] *Foundations of Imperial Conduct*, col. 361. I have not been able to identify the saying, especially since, as he also points out, Manuel rephrased it.
[50] The notion of will in Christian thought was especially discussed by John of Damascus, who integrated the concept of will as a distinct human ability to Aristotle's discussion of voluntary and involuntary actions. See M. Frede, 'John of Damascus on Human Action, the Will and Human Freedom', in *Byzantine Philosophy and its Ancient Sources*, ed. K. Ierodiakonou (Oxford, 2002), 63–97, especially 64–5. Henceforth, Frede, 'John of Damascus'.
[51] Aristotle, *Nicomachean Ethics*, especially II, ii and vi.
[52] *Foundations of Imperial Conduct*, cols. 319, 333, 367, 372–3.
[53] Kakkoura points out that the initial stages of the composition fall between 1403–10, but the work was certainly composed after the *mirror*. Like the *Foundations*, it seems to have been circulated at the latest by 1416, *Ethico-Political Orations*, 47–9. On the comparison between the sermon on St Mary of Egypt and the sixth oration, see E. Kaltsogani, 'Zur Entstehung der Rede des Manuel II Palaiologos

composed for John VIII, who once more, is positioned as his father's student.[54] The orations deal with education, pleasure, voluntary and involuntary action, love and humility. Manuel thus expands upon the earlier themes of the *Foundations*, but also incorporates the Christian virtue of humility into his former discussions. A recent study has shown that the *Ethico-Political Orations* also possesses an interesting rhetorical structure. The work is a synthesis of elements from *mirror*, letter, *erotapokrisis* and homily. Moreover, the seven orations each represent a different rhetorical genre, such as protreptic, philosophical, homiletic and panegyric, together forming a diatribe.[55] This structure exemplifies Manuel's interest in combining various genres.

Once more, the emperor's ethico-political thought comes across as a fusion of Plato, Aristotle and the Fathers.[56] It is difficult to establish a direct link between Manuel and another author as far as Christian sources are concerned, since many ideas were shared by multiple authors and borrowed from each other. It has been proposed that he may have relied upon John of Damascus and Nemesios of Edessa.[57] However, these influences are difficult to untangle, since John of Damascus himself also relied on Nemesios of Edessa. All in all, it is unclear precisely which ideas Manuel borrowed from specific authors. The emperor's work does not reveal significant textual parallels with any particular author.[58] While, as in the *Foundations*, the ideas presented by Manuel adhere on the whole, to tradition, the *Ethico-Political Orations* do contain some personal touches.[59]

Like the *Foundations,* the orations seem to reflect some of Manuel's own experiences.[60] The first oration possibly contains a reminiscence about

---

auf die Heilige Maria von Ägypten (BHG 1044c)', *Parekbolai* 1 (2011), 37–59. Henceforth, Kaltsogani, 'Zur entstehung der Rede des Manuel II Palaiologos'.

[54] In a rare instance, Manuel highlights John's progress in the regular classroom. He points out that John could now appreciate an allusion to Aristophanes since his teacher had recently initiated him in the work of the playwright, *Ethico-Political Orations*, 335.

[55] Leonte, *Rhetoric in Purple*, 192–243, convincingly argues that Manuel used different genres for the orations and that the whole work formed a diatribe. A diatribe is a set of lectures on a moral theme, characterized by vivid language and guiding the reader through successive stages of moral development.

[56] For these observations, see *Ethico-Political Orations*, 47–9, 35, 38. Kakkoura considers the possibility that Manuel might have relied upon the paraphrase of *Nicomachean Ethics* commissioned by his grandfather John Kantakouzenos, but points out a lack of evidence. As will be discussed below, Manuel seems to have been familiar with the work itself, which is not surprising given the popularity of Aristotelian ethics in Byzantium.

[57] Kakkoura, *Ethico-Political Orations*, 78.

[58] On John of Damascus' reliance on Nemesios of Edessa, see Frede, 'John of Damascus', 65.

[59] *Ethico-Political Orations*, 187.

[60] In an intriguing remark, Manuel claims to have seen people hated by their parents because of their actions, perhaps reminiscence of his rebellious brother Andronikos; *Ethico-Political Orations*, 427;

Manuel's unpopularity in Thessalonike and the subsequent loss of the city. 'When a city is divided', the emperor writes, 'all is lost.'[61] Manuel also incorporates political remarks affirming the legitimacy of his rule. These can be interpreted as being directed against his nephew John VII, who was still alive during the earlier stages of the composition. Tellingly, the emperor underlines to his own son John VIII that as co-emperor he inherited the status of emperor from his father.[62] Throughout the work, John VIII is represented as Manuel's legitimate successor; that is, Manuel and John are not just any father and son but an emperor and his successor. To emphasize this, Manuel frequently addresses John as co-emperor (συμβασιλεῦ). Across the text, John VIII and his father are thus advertised as the legitimate possessors of the Byzantine throne.

Similarly, the last passages of the seventh oration are politically very charged. In one striking instance, Manuel compares his throne to that of Moses, on which the Pharisees sat. The emperor goes so far as to claim that his throne was greater than that of Moses. Here, Manuel does not refer to the throne in impersonal terms. Instead, he continuously employs the first person singular in order to emphasize his ownership of the throne. This sense is further strengthened by remarks such as; 'the throne on which I am now sitting . . . .'[63] The orations not only offer John VIII moral advice, they also function as political propaganda, asserting his status as the legitimate successor and advertising Manuel's imperial authority.

As for their contents, although the orations deal with various topics a few themes stand out in the extensive treatment they receive. One such central theme in the orations is fortune (τύχη) and its role in human affairs. We have previously traced the same concern with fortune in Manuel's earlier works, the *Panegyric to John V* and the *Dialogue with a Persian*.[64] But in the orations, Manuel expands upon the case of Xerxes and the Greeks to illustrate his arguments. This is not a surprising choice since in other

---

Kakkoura also makes this connection, 144. Yet it is not possible to pursue this argument further, as the remark is too vague.

[61] *Ethico-Political Orations*, 334; Kakkoura also makes this connection, 66–7.

[62] *Ethico-Political Orations*, 326 and 470, 'πάντα δεύτερα ἦγε, καὶ βασιλείαν αὐτήν, κλῆρον δικαιότατον, ἐκ πατρὸς αὐτῷ κατελθοῦσαν μεγίστην οὖσαν.'; '. . . ὦ συμβασιλεῦ τε παῖ. . .'. At least six of the orations had been composed by 1410. John VII died in 1408, thus it is quite possible that he was alive at the initial stages of the composition.

[63] *Ethico-Political Orations*, 472–3, 'Κάθημαι γὰρ δὴ καὶ αὐτὸς . . . Ἡ δὲ δὴ καθέδρα, ἐφ' ἧς ἔγωγε νῦν . . . "Ωστ' ἐγὼ μὲν ὅπερ εἶπον, ἐπὶ τοῦ θρόνου κάθημαι, τοῦ τὸν θεὸν εἰκονίζοντος, οἱ δὲ ἱερεῖς τε καὶ Φαρισαῖοι, ἐπὶ τῆς Μωσέως καθέδρας. Αὔτη δέ, τῆς ἡμετέρας ἐλάττων, καὶ μοῦ μηδεὶς καταγνώτω τόλμης, μηδ' αὐθαδείας. Οὐ γὰρ ἐμαυτὸν πρὸς τὸν θεόπτην συγκρίνω —πόθεν; ἄπαγε- τὰς δὲ καθέδρας ἁπλῶς . . . ἀλλ' ἡ βασιλεία ἀμείνων ἡγεμονίας.'

[64] Especially the *Dialogue with a Persian* and the *Panegyric to John V*.

works, the emperor discusses the success of the Ottomans as an outcome of mere fortune.[65] Here, Xerxes' portrayal is especially reminiscent of that of Bayezid. His arrogance is strongly emphasized; he suffers as he is unable to change and moderate his nature. That the Persians are equated conventionally with present day Ottomans also becomes quite clear as Manuel refers to them as a *genos* bereft of *paideia* and remarks that the Athenians did not merely ward the Persians off their lands, but also from all things *Hellenic*.

The emperor argues that success such as that of the Ottomans is ascribable to good fortune and not to virtue; in other words, it is not real *eudaimonia*. Once more, as in the *Panegyric to John V* and the *Dialogue with a Persian*, Manuel uses *eudaimonia* not in the sense of mere prosperity or happiness, but as a philosophical concept, a perfect state attained through the constant practise of virtue. The outlook displayed here is identical to the one found in Manuel's discussions of the Ottomans' success in the *Dialogue with a Persian*. In this instance, Manuel also explicitly refers to the wheel of fortune. However, significantly, Manuel uses the notion of thewheel of fortune only to discuss the pagan Athenians and the Persians. Christianity and perseverance in faith is only ever discussed within the framework of virtue and *eudaimonia*. As in the *Dialogue with a Persian*, Manuel deliberately associates the agency of fortune only with the pagans and the Ottomans, while the successes of the Christians are assigned to virtue and perseverance in God.[66] Ultimately, through his discussions of fortune, the emperor seeks to downplay the Ottoman victories and to instil hope for a Byzantine 'revival'.

Another key theme in the orations is virtue. Manuel focuses on virtues as leading to *eudaimonia*. He is, once more, clearly following *Nicomachean Ethics*, where this discussion is a central topic. As in the *Foundations*, the discussion of the four cardinal virtues is omitted in the emperor's orations. Instead Manuel devotes an entire oration to two particular virtues: humility and love. In the *Foundations*, he advocated that two virtues especially, moderation and love, were crucial in order for one to succeed in outer and inner matters. Now, in the *Ethico-Political Orations*, he proposes love and

---

[65] *Ethico-Political Orations*, 319–30. After the defeat of Bayezid by Tamerlane, many panegyrists at Manuel's court also used the case of Xerxes' defeat against the Greeks as a parallel to the Ottomans; but none is as detailed as Manuel. Manuel refers to the story as being from a history. Kakkoura notes that the working copy of the text names Xenophon, but that Manuel's narration is closer to that of Herodotos, *Ethico-Political Orations*, 43. Within this context, it is worth adding that by that date (1403–10), Manuel was already in possession of a Herodotos, one left to him by Kydones in his will, see Chapter 6.

[66] *Ethico-Political Orations*, 340.

humility (*tapeinosophrosyne*) as the two most important virtues. Thus, the emperor exchanges moderation for humility.

One reason as to why Manuel opted not to treat moderation as a separate virtue in the *Ethico-Political Orations*, might be that he had already devoted extensive discussions to it. It is such a key theme in the orations that moderation is embedded into every action, choice and virtue. Moreover, love, the second virtue he chose to emphasize in both works, was a Christian one. By substituting the Aristotelian notion of moderation with another Christian virtue, humility, Manuel increases the role of Christian thought in the *Ethico-Political Orations*. Indeed, the dominance of Christian thought is felt throughout Manuel's entire work, especially in the sixth oration. In this regard, it is worth noting that, Manuel's sermon for St Mary of Egypt and this oration are modified versions of the same text; the sermon is woven around St Mary's humility.

In the sixth oration, the emperor argues that humility is above all virtues. The emperor's discussion of humility here betrays the influence of John Climacus. Moreover, some other parallels between the two can also be seen concerning their general treatment of virtue.[67] Manuel argues, however, that humility and love are equal to each other and envisions a circle of virtues in which humility is the starting point and love the ending point. Consequently when one returns to the original starting point, love and humility are equal. Again, instead of the four cardinal virtues, the emperor adopts a scheme of virtue that is strongly influenced by Christianity as opposed to ancient philosophy. In the orations, Manuel seems to have further developed his own scheme of virtues by the inclusion of this circular arrangement.

Yet another significant topic in *Ethico-Political Orations* is pleasure. Manuel devotes two complete orations to this issue. The first is based on the traditional view that pleasure is bad and should be completely shunned; however, in the second, the emperor combats this view. For Manuel, pleasure is good as long as it is partaken with moderation. In the *Foundations*, too, Manuel had opted for a life of virtue with moderate amounts of pleasure; that is, not a complete avoidance of pleasure. This argument of pleasure in moderation, was already an established view that was advocated by several Christian authors, including Maximos the Confessor.[68]

---

[67] *Ethico-Political Orations*, 175. John Climacus, *Scala Paradisi*, PG 88, cols. 631–1161. Kakkoura argues that chapters 22, 23 and 25 of John Climacus have some similarities with Manuel, an observation that I agree with.
[68] *Ethico-Political Orations*, 100–1.

Manuel suggests that it is excess (ἀκρασία) which makes pleasure bad. Once more, moderation becomes a significant theme for the emperor. Undesirable outcomes are not due to the pleasure itself, he argues, but to human agency. If all things come from God, Manuel goes on, and all things are good in their essence, then pleasure, too, is good in its essence.[69] It is only through human excess that pleasure becomes sullied. Manuel's claim that all things are good in essence is also reminiscent of the discussions in the *Clarification of a Debate between Demetrios Chrysoloras and Antonio d'Ascoli*, composed c. 1410. Here, the emperor proposes that as a creation of God, Judas was good in essence. He betrayed Christ not because he was bad by nature, but through choice (*proairesis*).[70] This outlook as regards choice and moderation is manifested across the emperor's works.

Finally, as seen in the *Foundations*, Aristotelian concepts of choice and voluntary/involuntary deeds form other dominant thread of discussion. Manuel openly acknowledges his debt to Plato and especially to Aristotle here. This clear acknowledgement is a unique occurrence in his works.[71] Again, in the *Ethico-Political Orations*, Manuel emphasizes choice as the sole distinguishing feature among people. Following Aristotle's view, he divides deeds into two categories of voluntary and involuntary action.[72] Again, following Aristotle, Manuel discusses a third category of mixed actions, which can be classified as neither voluntary or involuntary. On this occasion, the emperor also coins the term *miksoekousia* (μιξοεκούσια) for this unnamed Aristotelian category.[73] This is the one small contribution that Manuel makes to Aristotle's ethics and he proudly draws attention to

[69] *Ethico-Political Orations*, 350–1, 368, 383, 385–6, 395, 403 for some important points.

[70] F. Tinnefeld, 'Es wäre gut für jenen Menschen, wenn er nicht geboren wäre: Eine Disputation am Hof Kaiser Manuels II. über ein Jesuswort vom Verräter Judas. Einleitung, kritische Erstedition und Übersetzung (I)', in Ἀνδριάς. *Herbert Hunger zum 80. Geburtstag, JÖB* 44 (1994), 421–30; F. Tinnefeld, 'Es wäre gut für jenen Menschen, wenn er nicht geboren wäre: Eine Disputation am Hof Kaiser Manuels II. über ein Jesuswort vom Verräter Judas. Einleitung, kritische Erstedition und Übersetzung (II)', *JÖB* 45 (1995), 115–58. Henceforth, *Clarification*.

[71] *Ethico-Political Orations*, 354. A passage in the *Funeral Oration* also demonstrates Manuel's first-hand knowledge of the *Nicomachean Ethics*, where the emperor borrows Aristotle's example of a sailor being forced to throw the cargo of a sinking ship into the sea. *Funeral Oration*, 170–1, 'καὶ ἑῴκει ταῦτα πράττων τοῖς σφοδρῷ ληφθεῖσι κλύδωνι, οἳ ταῖς ἑαυτῶν χερσὶ πολλὰ τῶν ἀγωγίμων ἀποβαλλόμενοι κέρδος τὴν ζημίαν ἡγοῦνται, οὐχ ἁπλῶς τῷ πράγματι χαίροντες, ἀλλ' ἵνα μὴ τὸ πᾶν ἐθέλοντες ἔχειν, τοῦ καιροῦ πρὸς τοὐναντίον βιαζομένου, τὸ πᾶν κακῶς ἀπολέσωσιν.' Aristotle, *Nicomachean Ethics*, III, i, 5–8.

[72] Kakkoura points out that will (αὐτεξουσία) is absent here, as opposed to the *Dialogue with a Persian*, 80. See *Ethico-Political Orations*, 87.

[73] *Ethico-Political Orations*, 358, see below for the translation of this passage. Aristotle, *Nicomachean Ethics*, III, i, 5–8.

his 'innovation': 'Let us coin a name, let us innovate a little something . . . ' he declares. Apart from these discussions, references to these two categories of voluntary/involuntary action and choice are scattered throughout the work, underscoring Manuel's examples.

For instance, Xerxes is depicted as a tyrant because he rules over an unwilling nation; however, he cannot command the conscience (γνώμη) because it stems from the soul. Since people are chiefly soul, Xerxes is not actually ruling over them, as he cannot rule their souls.[74] Similarly, if a *genos* does evil in obeying a tyrant, Manuel argues that it is still a voluntary action.[75] Significantly, the emperor does not assign this situation to the third category in Aristotle, which consists of deeds that were forced or compelled by the situation and the person carries out involuntarily. Since he conventionally characterizes Persian rulers and the Ottoman sultan as tyrants, perhaps Manuel's above-mentioned categorization served to vilify the Ottomans, who are represented as voluntarily obeying the 'evil' wishes of their rulers.

Manuel as a Thinker

The *Foundations of Imperial Conduct* and the *Ethico-Political Orations* are not merely advisory works, they are also the two works where Manuel focuses on the notion of rulership and offers personal insight into what it meant to be the emperor. It was after his return from Europe, especially between 1410–16, that he wrote these compositions which directly pertain to the imperial office. Similarly, his Letter 44 where he reflects on the burdens of rulership, dates to these years. Previously, apart from remarks scattered across various works, the emperor did not really focus on the imperial office *per se* in his writing. One can attribute Manuel's increasing preoccupation with the imperial office both to his growing maturity as emperor, and to his need to prepare his heir for rulership. After all, Manuel had by then reigned as sole emperor for at least ten years; even longer while composing the *Ethico-Political Orations*. He had witnessed much and was a seasoned ruler: as a man over fifty, he had accumulated significant experience. He was thus at a time in his life, where he might have wished to reflect more on the nature, duties and burdens of the imperial office.

Similarly, his son John VIII was now of an age to receive serious instruction on rulership; advisory texts were needed. Instead of having his son study older works or hiring tutors to compose such texts for him,

---

[74] *Ethico-Political Orations*, 330.   [75] *Ethico-Political Orations*, 357.

Manuel personally penned advice for John. Not only was Manuel a writer, but as he often stressed in these works, he himself knew what it meant to be the emperor and was therefore in an ideal position to author advisory texts addressed to a future ruler. He seems to have embraced the opportunity. The emperor, moreover, took the opportunity to lace both works with many political messages that lent legitimacy to his own rule and allowed him to further advertise himself as ruler.

It can be argued that The *Ethico-Political Orations* represent the culmination of Manuel's ethico-political thought previously traced in his orations and dialogues. As early as the 1380s, the *Discourse to Thessalonians* manifested that Aristotelian notions of choice and involuntary/voluntary deeds were central notions in the emperor's thought. The *Ethico-Political Orations* is the work in which Manuel elaborates on his ideas as a whole, connected thought system. While Manuel also wrote two short advisory works on similar issues, *Address as if from a Benevolent Ruler to his Subjects* and *Admonitions Leading to Brevity and Peace in the Councils*, the *Ethico-Political Orations* is his most extensive work concerning ethical philosophy.[76]

As the emperor, Manuel was in a rare position to author texts addressed to a future ruler. However, apart from a few personal insights, he does not advocate ideas that truly break from the tradition. He has no new theories on issues such as the nature of kingship, the relationship between the ruler and his subjects, or on government. The same holds true for his dealings with ethical philosophy. Manuel displays a life-long interest in the main philosophical principles and concepts of *Nicomachean Ethics*, such as moderation, choice, *eudaimonia* and voluntary/involuntary deeds, and he enriches these discussions with Christian sources; however, apart from some personal insight, the emperor does not offer any significant contributions or alterations to these debates. Instead he chiefly produces an amalgam of Aristotelian and Christian thought, albeit an erudite and extensive one.

Still, we must tread carefully here: Manuel, like the majority of the Byzantine literati, produced philosophical texts that were based on earlier models and authors. It was not unusual to add to, modify and vary ideas found in the existing body of scholarship; this was an important part of the Byzantine scholarly heritage. Although he wasn't an extremely distinctive thinker with highly unusual ideas, Manuel did

---

[76] These two short works cannot be dated, but perhaps they might have been composed around the same time as with the *Foundations* and the *Ethico-Political Orations*. See Appendix 3 for a translation of the *Address as if from a Benevolent Ruler* and Appendix 6 for the transcription and translation of the *Admonitions*.

display some originality in his ethico-political works within the tradition. For instance, his decision to select Agapetos and *Nicomachean Ethics* as models was a choice that distinguished him from many of his contemporaries. Likewise, both in the *Foundations* and the *Ethico-Political Orations*, Manuel again consciously selected from and further embellishing commonplace notions and advice. He did not merely reproduce earlier authors, but instead focused on several themes that were of particular interest to him, expanding upon and introducing variations to pre-existing ideas. These are all active choices that he made as a thinker and an author. Manuel's discussions of the Church and imperial power, the heavy emphasis he placed on financial matters, his preoccupation with choice and moderation, are all examples of these processes. The emperor's selections regarding his sources, models and themes set his work apart from those of his contemporaries, and his personal and more practical insights about ruling also render his compositions worthy of notice. His devising of a scheme of six cardinal virtues is yet another instance that is peculiar to him. Moreover, between these two compositions, one can observe some changes in Manuel's thinking. For instance, although he first envisions the six cardinal virtues in the *Foundations*, he later discards moderation as a virtue in the *Ethico-Political Orations*, replacing it with humility. Similarly, it is in this later work that the emperor introduces the idea of a circular chain of virtues.

As regards the emperor's stance on philosophy, Manuel's especial interest and reliance on *Nicomachean Ethics* probably stemmed from its malleability and compatibility with Christian ideas. Notions of choice and voluntary action were, after all, significant aspects of Christian thought. The emperor further enriches these discussions with the notion of free will; again, an idea borrowed from Christian thought. Thus, Manuel opted for an ethico-political thought that conformed and was also shaped by Christianity. In the *Foundations* and the *Ethico-Political Orations*, for instance, Manuel stays within the boundaries he set for himself in the *Discourse to Iagoup* in the 1390s: that philosophy should be concerned only with *this* life, addressing only political and moral issues.[77]

Manuel's two works deal with only ethical and political philosophy, steering clear from its other branches. There are no discussions of nature, physics or metaphysics, and while his other writings show a familiarity with Platonic idealism and Aristotelian logic, these had no influence on his philosophy. Nor did Manuel ever pen a commentary on an Aristotelian or

---

[77] *Discourse to Iagoup*, 342 and *Procession of the Holy Spirit*, 18.

neo-Platonic treatise. Even his *Discourse on Dreams*, despite discussing Platonic notions of the soul, was still dominated by Christian interpretations: the soul cannot prophesize in dreams and only holy men can prophesize.[78] Although he lived in an era of great interest in other branches of philosophy, and was in contact with figures such as Demetrios Kydones, Plethon and Bessarion, Manuel did not follow in their footsteps. His own interests and thought ultimately remained firmly rooted in the traditions of Orthodox Christianity.

Manuel's Manuscripts

As they bear witness to Manuel's collaboration with members of his literary circle, these two ethico-political works also necessitate some discussion of the production of Manuel's manuscripts. In the past decade, Manuel's manuscripts have received extensive studies, enriching our understanding of his works.[79] The great majority of Manuel's works survive in several manuscripts, yet all date to the later years of his reign. While some of his works were copied after his death, the emperor had his works collected in several manuscripts, personally supervising the process. The manuscript copies often represent different stages of the texts and demonstrate that like many other Palaiologan authors, Manuel made extensive revisions.[80] For instance, the *Funeral Oration* survives in six different stages.[81] At one point, Manuel even seems to have crossed out the *Dialogue on Marriage* from the Par. gr. 3041.[82] Two of these manuscripts, Par. gr. 3041 and Vat. gr. 632, contain his autograph corrections. The fourth oration of the *Ethico-Political Orations* in Vat. gr. 632, is also written by the emperor himself.[83] The manuscripts also reveal the evidence of multiple hands, some of which are not identifiable. For instance, Vat. gr. 632, contains as many as eighteen different hands. Those hands that can be identified belong to Makarios Makres, Joseph Bryennios, George Scholarios and Isidore of Kiev, who was

---

[78] *Discourse on Dreams*, 246, '... ἀεὶ φανέν τι παρὰ θεοῦ, ἐγρηγορόσι τε καὶ καθεύδουσιν, ἀγαθοῖς τε ἀνδράσι καὶ μὴ τοιούτοις, ὧν τοσαῦτα τὰ παραδείγματα καὶ τοῖς ἅπασι γνῶμαι ὡς εἶεν ἂν περίεργον ἀριθμεῖν. Ἀλλὰ καὶ τὸ φθονερόν τε καὶ πονηρότατον πνεῦμα ... ψεύδεται δὲ νῦν μὲν ἑκόν, νῦν δὲ ἄκον ἀπατηθέν.' See Alfagame, 'La epístola'.

[79] Concerning the dating and the production of Manuel's manuscripts, I rely on the introductions of the dissertations of Dendrinos and Kakkoura, *Procession of the Holy Spirit* and *Ethico-Political Orations*.

[80] Dennis, *Letters*, xvi–xxvi; *Procession of the Holy Spirit*, xli–xcii; *Ethico-Political Orations*, 210–42.

[81] *Funeral Oration*, 30–1. [82] *Dialogue on Marriage*, 13–20.

[83] *Ethico-Political Orations*, 210. While Manuel's hand has long been detected in Par. gr. 3041, Kakkoura is the first person to identify Manuel's hand in Vat. gr. 632.

Manuel's chief copyist for many of these manuscripts, and many of these cases also indicate Manuel's oral collaboration with the copyists.[84]

The fact that several prominent members of the emperor's literary network were involved in the production of his manuscripts formed another means for Manuel's works to circulate among the literati. In one instance, Makarios Makres even included several works of the emperor with some of his own: in Vat. gr. 1107 and Vat. gr. 632, containing Manuel's *Ethico-Political Orations*. This manuscript was probably owned by someone in the emperor's circle, though the fair manuscript copies, as opposed to the draft, working copies, were probably intended for the imperial house. In this regard, it should be noted that four luxury manuscripts copied by Manuel's chief copyist, Isidore of Kiev, consisting of Vat. Barb. gr. 219, Vat. gr. 1619, Vindob. phil. gr. 98 and Cryptensis 161, form the complete collection of the emperor's oeuvre. He seems to have strived towards a complete, imperial-quality edition of his works, that would stand as a monument to his persona as an emperor-author. After the fall of Constantinople, several of these manuscripts, such as Vat. Barb. gr. 219 and Vindob. phil. gr. 98, passed into the hands of the famous collector Cardinal Bessarion.

These manuscripts bear witness to Manuel's self-construction as an author: they were carefully corrected, arranged and collected in manuscripts, and he himself was heavily involved in the process. Thus, the emperor's authorial persona and his surviving works are not the products of mere chance or of later copyists, they are the direct result of the emperor's own self-construction: he chose which works would survive and in which format, and indeed what sort of an authorial image he wished to project to his readers and posterity. Both the process and the products were meticulously planned. It is also clear that the emperor cared deeply

---

[84] *Funeral Oration*, 36–7; *On the Procession of the Holy Spirit*, xli–xcii; Ch. Dendrinos, 'Co-operation and Friendship among Byzantine Scholars in the Circle of Emperor Manuel II Palaeologus (1391–1425) as reflected in their Autograph Manuscripts', Paper presented at International Colloquium Unlocking the Potential of Texts: Interdisciplinary Perspectives on Medieval Greek, organized by the Centre for Research in the Arts, Social Sciences and Humanities, University of Cambridge, 18–19 July 2006, Cambridge, United Kingdom, 18/07/06 – 19/07/o. Henceforth, Dendrinos, 'Co-operation'. Also see Dendrinos, 'Palaiologan Scholars at Work: Makarios Makres and Joseph Bryennios' Autograph', in *From Manuscripts to Books: Proceedings of the International Workshop on Textual Criticism and Editorial Practice for Byzantine Texts* (Vienna 10–11 December 2009). eds. A. Giannouli and E. Schiffer (Vienna, 2011), 23–51, especially for the cases of Manuel, Makarios Makres and Joseph Bryennios. For possible links between Manuel's manuscripts and the Monastery of John Prodromos in Petra, see D. de Matons-Grosdider and C. Förstel, 'Quelques manuscrits grecs liés à Manuel II Paléologue', in *Proceedings of the 6th International Symposium on Greek Paleography, Drama, Greece, 21–27 September 2003*, vol. 1 (Athens, 2008), eds. B. Atsalos and N. Tsironis, 375–86.

about the reception and the longevity of his oeuvre, seeking to correct and polish his works, and to circulate these versions among the literati as an advertisement for the authorial identity he created.

The emperor's preoccupation with the production of his manuscripts dates to the later years of his reign. This is not surprising. After all, not only did he enjoy relative tranquillity post-1402, at least for some years, he had also produced a sizeable oeuvre until that point. Upon his return from Europe, Manuel also penned several significant works up to 1416. By this time, Manuel was a much older and more mature author-emperor, and the time was ripe for him to create and organize a collection of his works. Thus, it is reasonable to suggest that the production of the manuscripts of his works peaked in these later years. It is also probable that through his manuscripts Manuel sought to bequeath his oeuvre to posterity as an enduring monument to his role as an author-emperor. The fact that he had his complete works organized into four luxury manuscripts also supports this: the emperor wished to have an 'omnibus Manuel', both for his contemporaries and the future generations.

Manuel's manuscripts are not illuminated except for his famous portrait in Par. suppl. gr. 309. (**Fig 9.1**) However, this portrait, too, is illustrative of the authorial persona he wished to project. It depicts him in full imperial regalia: he is present not as an ordinary author, but as the emperor. This portrait should not be seen as merely an adornment to the manuscript, but rather as a 'visual' assertion of Manuel's status as author-emperor. Moreover, the choice of work for this portrait is also suggestive. The image accompanies the *Funeral Oration*, arguably the most politically charged piece among Manuel's entire oeuvre. The *Funeral Oration* is almost a 'mini-history' of his reign, and a highly idealized one at that. It is thus an extremely fitting work in which to incorporate this imperial portrait.

Manuel's Literary Network

In addition to organizing *theatra* and offering patronage to the literati, Manuel also specifically sent many of his compositions to the members of his literary circle, often accompanied by letters. Behind the *topoi* of modesty, these letters are a testament to Manuel's pride in his authorship. A look at the chronology of the emperor's letters show that post-1402, especially after 1410, he shared his works more frequently and intensely with the literati. Before that time, only Demetrios Kydones seems to have received works. This change probably stemmed from the increasing literary productivity of the emperor after 1402, and again, especially between

Figure 9.1 Portrait of Manuel II. Paris, Bibliothèque nationale, Parisinus
supplèment grec 309. Granger Historical Picture Archive / Alamy Stock Photo.

1410–16. Perhaps, it can also be interpreted as a growing interest in having
his works circulated among the literati. After the eight-year long blockade
of Constantinople and another few years on his European journey, the
emperor's desire and opportunities in this venture may have increased. By
1410, his rival claimant John VII was also dead, and once Manuel's
territories and position as emperor were more secure – however tenuously
so – he may have found more opportunities to share his work with the

literati. As a more mature man and emperor, he may have also felt a stronger desire to form links with the literati and to advertise his works and views more confidently. Further, through circulation and feedback, Manuel may have also wished to polish and prepare his works in order to be 'published' in his luxury manuscripts, as 'final' versions.

Manuel sent the *Discourse to the Thessalonians* and *Dialogue on Marriage* to Kydones in 1383 and 1396 respectively. In 1416, he sent the *Sermon on the Dormition* to Demetrios Chrysoloras and in 1410, the *Sermon on St Mary of Egypt* to Gabriel of Thessalonike.[85] Manuel Chrysoloras received the *Funeral Oration* around 1410,[86] and in 1411, he sent his *kanon* to Gabriel of Thessalonike. Manuel's spiritual fathers, David and Damianos received the *Confession* around 1416, and were also asked to add corrections as they saw fit and to show it to Makarios Makres. The anonymous vita of Makarios Makres also narrates that the emperor often sent his works to Makarios.[87] Manuel Chrysoloras' student, the Italian scholar Guarino of Verona received two compositions: the *Funeral Oration* and the *Foundations of Imperial Conduct*.[88]

Similarly, in 1410, the Patriarch Euythmios was sent the *Clarification of a Debate between Demetrios Chrysoloras and Antonio d'Ascoli*. In the accompanying letter, employing a Platonic notion, Manuel claims that the work was not only his 'child', but also that of Euthymios who could add and remove as he wished.[89] Manuel Chrysoloras, too, was instructed to add and remove from the *Funeral Oration* as he wished.[90] Significantly, both men replied that the emperor's compositions were so perfect that their corrections were not needed; Chrysoloras tellingly likens his corrections to patching a *purple* garment with rags.[91] Manuel's imperial status and authority was thus still very much felt in his literary collaborations. His correspondents probably said what he wanted to hear: no critical replies or

---

[85] Letters 11, 62, 61 and 52.   [86] Letter 56.
[87] Dendrinos, 'Co-operation', 4–5. For the *Confession*, see Chapter 10.
[88] Letter 60. Leonte, *Rhetoric in Purple*, 144, and Dennis, *Letters*, 168, argue that the notes in the margins of Vat. gr. 1619 ff. 188–210v indicate that this text of the *Foundations* had been sent to Guarino for corrections and comments. See also A. Rollo, 'A proposito del Vat gr 2239: Manuele II e Guarino', *Νέα Ρώμη* 3 (2006), 375–88 and P. Schreiner, 'Ein seltsames Stemma. Isidor von Kiev, die Leichenrede Kaiser Manuels auf seinen Bruder Theodoros und eine moderne Ausgabe', in *Lesarten: Festschrift für Athanasios Kambylis zum 70. Geburtstag. Dargebracht von Schülern, Kollegen und Freunden*, eds. I. Vassis et al. (Berlin- New York, 1998), 211–25 for Schreiner's discovery of a new text of the *Funeral Oration* in Vat. gr. 2239, which seems to have been the copy that Manuel sent to Guarino of Verona.
[89] Letter 54, lines 1–8.   [90] Letter 56, lines 29–31.
[91] Manuel Chrysoloras, *Discourse on the Funeral Oration*, 126, '... ἅμα θρασὺ καὶ ἀπᾶδον ῥάκια καταχρύσοις ἱματίοις παραρράπτειν.' Euthymios' reply is published by Tinnefeld as an appendix to the *Clarification*, 151.

evaluations of Manuel's work by any of the literati survive, only praise and admiration. Despite Manuel's collaboration with the foremost literati of his day, he remained the emperor and not a *primus inter pares* among his literary circle.

His self-representation as an author-emperor and his close networking with the literati should not be interpreted as Manuel having an 'egalitarian' stance or as seeking political advice. In all of his works, he strives to assert his authority and superiority as emperor. He defends, legitimizes and idealizes himself and his policies, and his views are asserted rather than presented as being open to contestation. Similarly, as a theologian-emperor he also seeks to impose his own theological stance – Orthodoxy and Palamism – and to lend them political sanction. Manuel thus primarily employed his literary network and *theatra* to disseminate his own views, and not to have open discussions regarding politics or religion. While the opinions of the elite and the general populace could indeed be influential in the late Palaiologan era, there is no indication that Manuel sought to become a *primus inter pares* among the literati or that he was influenced by their advice and opinions in the governing of the empire. On the contrary, he did not heed the Plethon's advice and plans for the Morea, nor did he share Demetrios Kydones and Manuel Chrysoloras' political stances. Even in the *Foundations*, despite paying lip service to common-place advice that a ruler should listen to counsel and not carry act before being advised, Manuel points out that the emperor should not wholly subject himself to councils.[92]

One should therefore not interpret Manuel's author-emperor persona and his bonds with the literati as a sign that he wished to encourage open debates about his politics. The emperor did not seek political advice through his works, nor did he attempt to incorporate the literati and their opinions into his government. A comparison of the lists of his government officials and bureaucrats, and members of his network, is further illuminating in this regard. Apart from his ambassador Manuel Chrysoloras and John VII's *mesazon* Demetrios Chrysoloras, there are no surviving letters to individuals who were at the heart of Byzantine political affairs.[93] In this regard, it is telling that the emperor also adopts the role of an authority figure in compositions addressed to other people. It is always his own ideas and views that dominate. For instance, in the *Clarification of a Debate*

---

[92] *Foundations of Imperial Conduct*, cols. 373–4.
[93] Some officials, such as Iagaris, Antiochos and Demetrios Skaranos, are each once mentioned in Manuel's correspondence, but only in passing.

between Demetrios Chrysoloras and Antonio d'Ascoli, Manuel 'clarifies' and gives the final verdict on the debate. While Manuel collaborated with the cherished members of his literary circle, his imperial rank is still very much felt in this process of collaboration: he is always the superior figure as the emperor, and there is no indication that he wished to be perceived as an equal.

Finally, it must be pointed out that as far as his theological compositions were concerned, Manuel chose to collaborate only with people who shared his own stance, such as Makarios Makres, Joseph Bryennios and the Patriarch Euthymios. In contrast, Demetrios Kydones and Manuel Chrysoloras received philosophical dialogues and orations. Although the emperor shared his theological oeuvre only with the like-minded, he was still able to value the friendship and scholarly abilities of people who held different beliefs. As previously mentioned, his circle not only included Orthodox and Palamites, but also anti-Palamites and Latin converts. This may not have solely arisen from some aspect of character, but possibly also from a desire to unite these different views under his imperial patronage.

In addition to the *Foundations*, Manuel sent his *Funeral Oration* to Guarino of Verona in Constantinople, suggesting that it could be translated into Latin or Italian.[94] He also sent his *Ethico-Political Orations* to Alexios III of Trebizond.[95] These two not only reflect the high regard Manuel had for his own oeuvre, but also his desire to project his emperor-author image into foreign literary circles. His selection of works strengthens this interpretation. All of these texts, especially the *Funeral Oration*, are very politically charged. The emperor seems to have selected the works that had a conspicuous political flavour amd would best advertise his reign. For instance, although it was composed as a response to a French monk, Manuel does not seem to have attempted to have his treatise on the Procession circulated abroad or translated into Latin. After all, despite its engagement with Latin theology and its potential interest for a foreign audience, the treatise does not have the same political undertones as the works mentioned above .[96]

Manuel does not seem to have really taken advantage of his contacts with Western scholars. Not only did he fail to forge bonds with Italian

---

[94] Letter 60, lines 15–17, 'φανέρου τε οἷς ἂν γνοίης καὶ πρὸς τὴν Λατίνων φωνήν, εἰ δὲ βούλει, τὴν ἰδίαν τοῦτο μεταβάλλειν ἀξίου.' Guarino, Letter 94.

[95] Letter 53.

[96] Furthermore, although Manuel did not shrink from manifesting his disagreements concerning some aspects of Latin theology and the papal supremacy, having this treatise translated into Latin could pose the risk of rendering the emperor 'polemical' and hostile in the eyes of a Latin audience.

scholars during his journey, he also does not seem to have engaged in particularly close relations with those residing in Constantinople. That he sent two of his works to Guarino of Verona, indicates Manuel's high regard for this Italian scholar. Yet nothing beyond this can be discerned about their relationship.

The emperor does not seem to have engaged with the humanist outlook of Guarino of Verona and Giovanni Aurispa, both of whom, at some point, resided in Constantinople. Despite his own scholarly interests, he also did not really adopt Manuel Chrysoloras' stance of seeking political help by advertising Byzantine learning in Europe. The emperor probably sent the *Funeral Oration* to Guarino in the hopes that the latter might translate it, and even suggests as much. This hints at Manuel's desire to reach out to a wider audience in Italy and Europe, and not just to a few scholars who could read Greek. Although Manuel probably intended to advertise his rule and erudition to a European audience – the *Funeral Oration* is after all almost a condensed history of his reign – this attempt is an isolated instance and the emperor does not seem to have pursued it further. Apart from this, Manuel did not endeavour to personally reach out to the West through his works. As for the *Funeral Oration*, Guarino did pass it onto Ambrogio Traversari, but its immediate circulation seems to have ended there.

Praise and Criticism: Works Addressed to Manuel

Within the context of the emperor's relations with the literati, it is now fitting to discuss the works addressed to Manuel. Although the particulars cannot be discerned, the fact that Manuel offered patronage to the literati is evinced by the works and letters addressed to him; indeed, one panegyric also claims that he promoted schools and teachers.[97] The emperor was also in contact with John Chortasmenos, Plethon and perhaps Bessarion, though he does not seem to have formed any close bonds with them, although the latter wrote a funeral oration for Manuel and obtained several of the emperor's manuscripts. Chortasmenos addressed some works to Manuel, and Plethon wrote a preface to the *Funeral Oration*. Manuel's reign boasted many talented scholars, which suggests that his patronage and promotion of learning may have contributed to a efflorescence of scholarship.

Seven laudatory works were addressed to Manuel between 1408 and 1417. Although these do not include Isidore of Kiev's oration addressed to

---

[97] See below.

John VIII in 1429, it will be considered here, as it contained lengthy sections on Manuel.[98] As in the case of his manuscript production and the intense circulation of his works, courtly panegyric had a surge in the later years of his reign. The laudatory works addressed to him also coincided with a period of several minor achievements by the emperor, such as the territorials gains after the Battle of Ankara, Manuel's manipulation of the Ottoman civil war, the renovation of the Hexamilion and the quelling of the Morean rebellion. It is reasonable, therefore, that the literati addressed panegyrics to the emperor in the same time frame as these events. Thus, these later years of Manuel's reign saw an upsurge in courtly panegyric, especially when compared to the reign of his father John V, who was uninterested in *logoi*. Although the exact occasions for the composition of these laudatory works are not known, they do indicate that Manuel offered significant patronage to the literati.

A very interesting aspect of these panegyrics is the authors' insistence on Manuel's multi-faceted rule and their echo of his own self-representation. For instance, Manuel's self-representation as a teacher in his ethico-political works was duly picked up by figures such as Isidore of Kiev, Manuel Chrysoloras, Demetrios Chrysoloras and Chortasmenos, who reflected back Manuel's self-representation in order to flatter the emperor.[99] An anonymous panegyric, written in the same vein, also claims that he installed new teachers in Constantinople and promoted schools.[100] Moreover, two literati not only allude to Manuel's self-representation, but also directly imitate the emperor's ethico-political works. Chortasmenos echoes the acrostic of the *Foundations* while Demetrios Chrysoloras

---

[98] These are Dendrinos, *Anonymous Oration*; Isidore of Kiev, 'Panegyric'; Bessarion, 'Monody'; Demetrios Chrysoloras, *Hundred Letters*, ed. F. Bizzaro. *Demetrios Chrisolora, Cento Epistole a Manuele II Palaeologo* (Naples, 1984); Demetrios Chrysoloras, 'Synkrisis'; Manuel Chrysoloras, *Discourse on the Funeral Oration*; Chortasmenos, 'Address to Manuel II'; Makarios Makres, 'Monody on Manuel Palaiologos', ed. A. Sideras, *Unedierte byzantinische Grabreden* (Thessalonike, 1985), 301–7 and Polemis, 'Anonymous Panegyric'. Henceforth, Demetrios Chrysoloras, *Hundred Letters*; Makres, 'Monody'.

Hundred Letters and *Discourse on Funeral Oration* can be considered panegyrics because of their laudatory content. Ioannis Polemis convincingly argues that the anonymous oration edited by Dendrinos is not a funeral oration, but a panegyric. See Polemis, 'Anonymous Panegyric'. See also O. J. Schmitt, 'Kaiserrede and Zeitgeschichte im späten Byzans: Ein Panegyrikos Isidors von Kiew aus dem Jahre 1429', *JÖB* 48 (1998), 209–42.

[99] Leonte, *Rhetoric in Purple*, 186–7, 356, also discusses Manuel's representation as teacher in the panegyrics. Isidore of Kiev, 'Panegyric', 210; Demetrios Chyrsoloras, 'Synkrisis', 233; Bessarion, 'Monody', 286; Manuel Chrysoloras, *Discourse on the Funeral Oration*, 130. Demetrios Chrysoloras, *Hundred Letters*, kephalion on 63; Chortasmenos, 'Address to Manuel II', 222–3; also, his Letter 49, 204–5.

[100] Polemis, 'Anonymous Panegyric', 709, emphasizes Manuel's love for education, claiming that he installed new teachers in Constantinople.

imitates the structure of the same text in his *Hundred Letters*, as well as making explicit allusions to the advice given by Manuel.[101] They possibly aimed at flattering the emperor by imitating his works as 'models'.

Furthermore, the panegyrists mirrored Manuel's self-representation not only as a teacher, but also as a multi-faceted ruler: a statesman, a soldier, an author, a philosopher and a theologian. Once more, his representation in panegyrics conforms to his own projected self-image. For instance, Manuel's fervour for scholarly pursuits seems to have caused the literati to take up the commonplace Platonic ideal of the philosopher-king with greater frequency, and it appears in almost all of the panegyrics.[102] Manuel is portrayed as an example to his subjects in his learning and as a lover of *logos* above all things; he wears the purple of *logoi* and is also crowned by them. Moreover, the panegyrists emphasize the versatility of the emperor, claiming that he was equally competent in rhetorical, philosophical and theological compositions.[103] Demetrios Chrysoloras especially elaborates on this theme, pointing out that the emperor wrote verses, letters, chapters, *ekphraseis*, as well as composed treatises against both the Latins and the Turks. He also noted that some of these works were ethical, while some were laments: these are clearly references to Manuel's ethico-political works and the *Funeral Oration*.[104]

While they expanded upon Manuel's scholarly pursuits, the panegyrists also gave equal importance to his other skills as emperor. In accordance with the traditions of imperial panegyric, he is portrayed as a skilled commander. The rebellion against the building of the Hexamilion and the sieges he endured are the episodes which form the basis of this portrayal.[105] Although this depiction is a conventional one, in Manuel's case, it also corresponds to the reality; he was indeed quite active militarily. Similarly, other aspects of the emperor that the panegyrists focused on were his diplomatic efforts.[106] His exploitation of the Ottoman fragmentation is

---

[101] Chortasmenos, 'Address to Manuel II', 222.

[102] For the notion of philosopher-king in imperial ideology, see Angelov, *Imperial Ideology*, 184–97.

[103] Demetrios Chrysoloras, *Hundred Letters*. See *kephalia*, 40, 49, 76, 97 and 98. The text is a notable exception in having no references to Manuel's interest in theology. Bessarion, 'Monody', 287; Demetrios Chrysoloras, 'Synkrisis', 229–32; Polemis, *Anonymous Oration*, 707–9; Makres, 'Monody', 303–5; Dendrinos, *Anonymous Oration*, 448–9.

[104] Demetrios Chrysoloras, 'Synkrisis', 229–32. He also claims that Manuel composed works on nature. Was this an exaggerated claim, or was there such a work by Manuel that was eventually lost? Perhaps this was a reference to Manuel's *Discourse on Dreams*, where he also discussed the natural processes of the human body in relation to dreams.

[105] See Mazaris, 80–1; Bessarion, 'Monody', 286–7; Demetrios Chrysoloras, 'Synkrisis', 225 for some examples.

[106] Chortasmenos, 'Address to Manuel II', 218–19; Makres, 'Monody', 306–7; Isidore of Kiev, 'Panegyric', 214–15.

extolled and his attempts to seek various allies is similarly lauded.[107] Although the depiction of the emperor as a philosopher and a seasoned soldier was commonplace in panegyrics, it can be argued that Manuel's scholarly pursuits and tumultuous reign gave the orators a reason to further expand upon these traditional ideas.[108] Ultimately, the panegyrists fuse commonplace ideological notions with the realities of his reign.

Significantly, the panegyrists do not discuss these aspects of Manuel separately, but prefer to underscore his uniqueness in combining all these talents. This, again, corresponds to the image of a multi-faceted, all-authoritative emperor that he desired to project. The panegyrists emphasize that the emperor was a ruler, a warrior, a philosopher and a rhetor at the *same time*. Chortasmenos, for instance, claims that Manuel has a two-fold soul, one part of which deals with *logoi*, and the other with war and hunting. In his monody, Bessarion calls him an emperor, warrior and rhetor, like the ideal Homeric king, but, Bessarion points out that since Manuel rises above the Homeric formula, he felt compelled to add 'rhetor' to describe him.[109]

On the whole, the literati seem to have uncritically reflected back Manuel's own self-representation, portraying him as the all-authoritative, multi-talented emperor he aspired to be. Although Manuel may have sought to project this image in order to enhance and extend his feeble authority over many spheres – political, scholarly, theological and ecclesiastical – it may have also partially stemmed from his personality. Not only did he possess multiple talents and interests, he also appears to have been rather conscious of this fact.

Manuel's responses to these panegyrics are unknown, but a few of his letters offer a glimpse into his reactions to praise. One such letter, written between 1403 and 1410, is a reply to an *ethopoiia* of the emperor by Demetrios Chrysoloras a composition that is now lost. Employing the *topos* of modesty, Manuel points out that others may criticize Chrysoloras and he should therefore moderate his extravagant praise of the emperor.[110]

---

[107] Chortasmenos, 'Address to Manuel II', 218, '... τοὺς τέως ἀλαζόνας περὶ ἑαυτῶν παρεσκεύαζες, νῦν μὲν Παίονας αὐτοῖς ἐπεγείρων, νῦν δὲ Πέρσας κινῶν κατ' αὐτῶν, ἄλλοτε ἄλλους ἐκείνοις ἐκπολεμῶν.'

[108] On these aspects of panegyrics, see Angelov, *Imperial Ideology*, 184–97. See also N. Radošević, 'The Emperor as the Patron of Learning in Byzantine basilikoi logoi', in *Το Ελληνικόν: Studies in Honor of Speros Vryonis Jr*, vol. 1, eds. J. S. Langdon et al. (New Rochelle, New York, 1993), 267–88.

[109] Chortasmenos, 'Address to Manuel II', 223; Bessarion, 'Monody', 287; Dendrinos, *Anonymous Oration*, 449; Manuel Chrysoloras, *Discourse on Funeral Oration*, 61, 64–5; Polemis, 'Anonymous Panegyric', 710.

[110] Letter 46.

In another letter dealing with the same issue, Manuel claims that no praise will move him to forget his own self, and that the praises of Chrysoloras are those of a lover since they are biased.[111] However, behind these *topoi* of modesty, the letters hint at the emperor's pleasure. That Manuel did enjoy such praise is evident from the sheer number of panegyrics and other writings produced for him. After all, none would have been written had the emperor really disliked receiving them.

While his responses to praise are obscured by *topoi* of modesty, his strong reaction to criticism make it plain that Manuel was quickly roused to anger, especially when his self-perception as an accomplished author-emperor was challenged. This previously unexplored aspect of Manuel actually provides more insight into his self-perception than his responses to praise. Perhaps the most poignant case illustrating this trait is the emperor's polemic with Manuel Kalekas in 1396. Kalekas' criticism of his theological interests caused Manuel to pen a lengthy *apologia*, attacking Kalekas in return. While he had originally claimed that the emperor should merely be concerned with state affairs, Kalekas' tone in his letters asking forgiveness, is noticeably different. On those occasions, Kalekas heaps praise on Manuel's literary abilities and diverse scholarly interests, also marvelling at how competent the emperor was at *all* aspects of ruling. It is clear that Kalekas hoped to obtain forgiveness by nourishing the wounded ego of the emperor and reflecting back his projected image of a multi-faceted emperor. Over the years, Kalekas' letters become increasingly pleading, asking both for forgiveness and for a safe conduct to Constantinople, as well as imploring for replies. We can infer that Manuel never replied and never forgave Kalekas.[112]

Another such critic was Makarios of Ankyra. The letters Manuel addressed around 1409 to Makarios, whose name seems to have been removed later as the addressee for reasons of propriety, reveal much about the anger he felt over Makarios' criticisms concerning his ecclesiastical involvement.[113] The letters contain strong language: Makarios is called a madman, a bad, shameful and overbearing person who has abused the times in order to enrich himself by bribes. This flurry of insults reveals the extent of the emperor's rage. Further, Manuel narrates how the *theatron* jeered at Makarios' letters, adding that he himself refrains from insulting

---

[111] Letter 48.   [112] See Kalekas, Letters 28, 29, 34, 39. Also Apologia 1, 309, addressed to Manuel.
[113] Letters 63–6, also Chapter 8. See also G. T. Dennis, 'Four Unknown Letters of Manuel II Palaeologus', *Byzantion 36* (1966), 35–40, reprinted in G. T. Dennis, *Byzantium and the Franks, 1350–1420* (London, 1982), Study VII.

Makarios for the sake of his imperial rank (σχῆμα). With regards to their content and language, however, the letters are extremely insulting.

Some other compositions by the emperor can be connected to such disputes. One such case is his *Anacreontic Verses Addressed to an Ignorant Person*.[114] The work cannot be dated, but in it Manuel addresses a certain 'foolish' person, who babbles like Thersites and disturbs everyone; he would not stop even if his tongue were to be ripped out. Like Odysseus with Thersites, the emperor dreams of bashing his opponent over the head with a stick. This tongue imagery can also be found in other 'polemical' writings by Manuel, while the reference to Thersites may perhaps be linked to the letter addressed to Makarios. Although Thersites was the stock type of fool in Byzantine textual tradition, Manuel does not refer to him except in these two instances. Moreover, it is worth noting that in the *Iliad*, Odysseus does not hit Thersites only because he babbles, but also because he criticizes Agamemnon, the epitome of kingship. In this instance, it is tempting to link Manuel's references to Thersites with Makarios. Yet the poem and Makarios cannot be linked with certainty.

An undated missive in Manuel's collection, addressed to a an 'ignorant' person, also seems to be another such polemical letter. It is probably not a rhetorical exercise, but an actual letter. His style in his *ethopoiia* and his declamation is distinctly different from this letter. Again, as in case of Makarios, the language is insulting, and the *theatron* is depicted as jeering.[115] Although the letter cannot be precisely dated, its position in the collection would put it in the late 1390s; it may have been addressed to Kalekas.[116] All these cases reveal a different side to Manuel. In his sensitivity to criticism, the emperor did not refrain from resorting to strong language and engaged readily in polemics. His aversion to criticism was rooted in his desire to assert his imperial authority and superiority as emperor. Although a degree of intolerance can be expected of a medieval ruler, the pronounced personal nature of Manuel's intolerance suggests that may have been a character trait.

One final case concerns some critical remarks made by Demetrios Chrysoloras and his *Hundred Letters*. Written around 1417, the *Hundred Letters* is an apology to the emperor which imitates the structure of the *Foundations* and echoes some of the emperor's advice. The exact nature of Chrysoloras' offences and the reasons for Manuel's dissatisfaction cannot

---

[114] Appendix 2.   [115] Letter 28.

[116] As in the case of Makarios of Ankyra, Manuel seems to have later removed the name of the addressee. The 'ignorant' person in this letter has a preoccupation with the 'truth' and aspires to be an athlete in this contest. This depiction corresponds to Kalekas' language in his two apologies.

be discerned. Chrysoloras merely refers to his 'failure to acknowledge the loftiness of the emperor' and names Demetrios Laskaris Leontaris, adviser of the despot Andronikos in Thessalonike, as bringing forth these accusations. The text also hints that Chrysoloras had been banished from Manuel's presence.[117] The tone of the work is very imploring; almost every 'letter' ends with a plea for forgiveness. Like Kalekas, Chrysoloras represents Manuel as a well-rounded emperor and author, though it can be argued that this portrayal of the emperor as a multi-faceted ruler in addition to the imitation of the *Foundations* was intended to flatter and thereby obtain forgiveness.

Demetrios Chrysoloras implores the emperor to be gentle and forgiving, and not to give way to anger. He echoes the emperor's advice in the *Foundations* on the importance of philanthropy and imitating God's forgiveness, cleverly reminding Manuel of his own advice.[118] His insistence, along with case of Kalekas, suggests that the emperor could be roused to anger by criticism. In this regard, Mazaris also makes a passing reference to Manuel's anger. However, as the text was intended to be a satire, also probably performed in Manuel's presence, this remark seems to have been a playful one.[119] Eventually, Chrysoloras' offence does not appear to have been as wounding as the Kalekas' critique. Thanks to his friendship with the emperor and his witty *apologia*, he was soon forgiven, and Manuel replied to the *Hundred Letters* with praise.[120] Undoubtedly, he was pleased by the imitation of his own work and the careful flattery.

A Dissident Son? Manuel and John VIII

For Manuel, dissident voices among the court circle were easy to deal with either through punishment or forgiveness. The affair of Chrysoloras, for instance, was easily settled in 1417. Yet by 1420, Manuel seems to have had another dissident voice at his court: that of his son John VIII. John was now in his twenties and no longer the eager young student represented in the ethico-political works. In 1414, John married Anna of Moscow. It is

---

[117] Demetrios Chrysoloras, *Hundred Letters*, 40–1, ' ἄριστε βασιλεῦ, Λεοντάρης ἡμῖν ἔγραψεν ὁ καλὸς καὶ ὠνείδιζεν ὡς ἀπρεπῆ τῷ καλῷ γράψασι βασιλεῖ … Λεοντάρης ἡμῖν ἀπαιδευσίαν εἰς τὸ σὸν ὕψος ὁ καλὸς ἐγκαλεῖ, τόδε μανίαν τις ἂν ἔχοι τεκμηριώσασθαι μᾶλλον οὐχ ἕτερον.' In his *Synkrisis*, Demetrios Chrysoloras also claims that the emperor was gentle in punishment, he would merely chastize the offender and order him not to come into his presence. Demetrios Chrysoloras, 'Synkrisis', 227–9.

[118] Demetrios Chrysoloras, *Hundred Letters*, see *kephalia* 26, 33, 34, 46, 47, 53, 54; the last two are very poignant.

[119] Mazaris, 38–9.   [120] Letter 61.

significant that on the magnificent *sakkos* sent to Moscow to commemorate the marriage, while Anna is depicted with her parents, John is portrayed alone. He is represented to the Muscovite audience as an emperor and political figure in his own right, without the 'visual' authority of his father. His appearance without Manuel may be taken as an indication of John's growing importance as co-emperor and that his maturity was further cemented by his marriage.[121] Around 1416, Manuel sent John to the Morea to help his second son Theodore to rule the despotate. Upon his return in 1418, John found out that his wife Anna of Moscow had died from the plague.[122] Manuel once more set himself the task of finding a suitable bride for his heir, and this time also for his second son Theodore. The emperor turned to the pope in his search for candidates, and in 1420, negotiations took place with the papacy. In the summer, the imperial ambassador Eudaimonioannes escorted Sophia of Monferrat and Cleope Malatesta to their bridegrooms.

In these marriage negotiations, Manuel departed from his earlier choices of Orthodox brides in the case of both his own marriage and John's first marriage. Significantly, the emperor was now willing to choose Catholic brides for his sons, and both women would be allowed to keep their faith. This decision was perhaps influenced by the ongoing debates regarding the church union and a desire to appeal to the West in order to secure help against the Ottomans. It also demonstrates that the emperor did not view the continuous discussions with the papacy as merely keeping up appearances in order to get military help, but also that he was earnest in his efforts despite his opposition to concluding a union on Latin terms. Matrimonial alliances with the West were much more likely to bring political benefits than Balkan ones like that forged with his late father-in-law the Serbian lord Constantine Dejanović. Not only was Manuel's choice of Italian, Catholic brides for his sons a gesture of goodwill and rapprochement with the papacy, but both women also came from reasonably well-connected, wealthy families.

The marriage of John and Sophia was duly celebrated in January 1421, though unfortunately, it would not be a happy one. John was also finally crowned as co-emperor.[123] It can be no coincidence that it is at this time that John begins to appear in the sources as a decision maker. He still

---

[121] Hilsdale, *Decline*, 292–4.   [122] Sphrantzes, 12–13; Schreiner, *Kleinchroniken*, Chronik 97/4.
[123] John VIII had already been proclaimed co-emperor by 1408 but was not crowned, see Sphrantzes, 14–15 and Syropoulos, 106–7. Doukas, 237 and Chalkokondyles, 340–1, narrate that both marriages were unhappy ones. Doukas especially elaborates on Sophia's ugliness and John's repulsion. For the dating of the coronation and the marriage, see F. Dölger, 'Die Krönung Johannes VIII zum

appears to have been deferential to his father at least on some subjects, since he did not repudiate Sophia as long as the latter lived, but as soon as his father died John allowed her to leave Byzantium. Still, concerning the empire's relations with the Ottomans, John seems to have held differing views from his father.

Despite the relative equilibrium reached with Mehmed for ten years (1410–20), Manuel never ceased in his seearch for help against the Ottomans. He knew very well, that the peace was only a temporary one. After 1410, his diplomatic efforts with the West intensified. He constantly corresponded with Venice, Genoa, Sigismund of Hungary and the papacy and agitated to form an anti-Turkish league.[124] Back in 1410, the emperor had sent Manuel Chrysoloras to Europe to visit some Italian cities, France and England. The discussions Chrysoloras participated in revolved around the theme of the church union, and in 1414 Chrysoloras attended the Council of Constance. These negotiations brought no concrete results, yet the discussion at the Council of Constance was to form the basis for the Council of Florence in 1439.[125] When Manuel Chrysoloras died in 1415, a significant blow was dealt to Manuel. Not only had he lost a skilled diplomat, but also a cherished literary collaborator and friend.

According to the narratives of Sphrantzes, Chalkokondyles and Doukas, John seems to have adopted a more aggressive stance towards the Ottomans, taking advantage of an Ottoman pretender to the throne. By 1417, he had already transported Mustafa, a son of Bayezid in Byzantine custody, to Mistra. The Ottoman sources all call this Mustafa a pretender, a false (*düzmece*) one, as does Symeon of Thessalonike; however, Mehmed's great concern in ensuring that Manuel continue to hold Mustafa a prisoner and not release him, indicates that he may have truly been Bayezid's son. It is in this light that one must understand the Ottoman chronicles narrative that Mustafa, the son of Bayezid, went missing after the Battle of Ankara. The Persian source on Tamerlane, Ibn Arabshah reports the same, but as no source reports his death, it is

---

Mitkaiser', *BZ* 36 (1936), 318–19. See also Schreiner, *Kleinchroniken*, Chronik 9/48; 22/32; 38/3; 100/6 and Mioni, 'Cronaca', no. 36.

[124] On the proposed anti-Turkish league; Thiriet, *Régestes*, 11, nos. 1592, 138; 1599, 140 and 1635, 150. These letters addressed to Sigismund are published in German translation in *Kaiser Manuel II Palaiologos: Dialog über den Islam und Erziehungsratschläge*, trans. W. Baum and R. Senoner (Vienna, 2003), 157–66.

[125] Barker, *Manuel II*, 322 and Gill, *The Papacy*, 20–39. See Barker, *Manuel II*, 322–36 for a political narrative of these years. As the events relating to the Council of Constance have been researched extensively, they will not be repeated here. See Gill, *The Papacy*, 20–1 for Manuel and the Council of Constance.

not inconceivable that the 'lost' Mustafa eventually appeared to challenge his brother for the throne.[126]

As John was on a mission for Manuel and was not yet crowned in 1417, this Mustafa was probably transported to Mistra on Manuel's directive, not John's; but, around 1420, John's stance seems to have changed. Sphrantzes narrates an episode in 1421, when a rumour spread that the sultan was coming to conquer the city. Several *archontes* and ecclesiastics urged Manuel to take action, who in return replied that he would not betray his oath. The rumour was a baseless one, and the Byzantine emperor and the sultan dined in peace.[127] This episode is illuminating in that it reveals that, although John is not explicitly named, a divergent faction was already present at the court.

Soon after this episode reportedly took place, Mehmed died and a heated debate on the question of Ottoman succession arose in the Byzantine court. According to Chalkokondyles and Sphrantzes, Manuel wished to allow Murad, son of Mehmed, to succeed, as had been agreed. He found any meddling in Turkish affairs to be dangerous at the moment. John and his faction, on the other hand, were in favour of supporting Mustafa against Murad in order to throw the Ottomans into chaos.[128]

The Byzantines ultimately opted to support Mustafa against Murad, and in September of 1421, John VIII personally helped the pretender to take Gallipoli. Although the Ottoman sources omit the role of the Byzantines in the affair, Sphrantzes, Doukas, and the traveller Ghillebert de Lannoy narrate its early stages. They claim that the Byzantines launched Mustafa – a son of Bayezid – against Murad. The pretender was transported to Gallipoli. As a reward for this support, Mustafa was expected to hand Gallipoli over to the Byzantines. Byzantine sources do not explicitly state this prior agreement, but their explicit references to Mustafa's refusal to hand over Gallipoli, combined with de Lannoy's account, suggest that this indeed had been agreed upon.[129]

Manuel's exact role in this affair is not clear; his surviving letters do not extend to this period and Sphrantzes, Chalkokondyles and Doukas all attempt to distance the old emperor from the event. Sphrantzes narrates that Manuel told his son to do as he wished since he himself was old and

[126] Sphrantzes, 10–11. See also Ferhan Karlidökme Mollaoğlu, '"Düzmece" olarak anılan Mustafa Çelebi ve Bisans (1415–1416/17)', *Ankara Üniversitesi Dil ve Tarih-Coğrafya Fakültesi Dergisi*, no 49/ 2 (2009), 173–85. Symeon of Thessalonike, 'Oration on St Demetrios', 49–50; Aşıkpaşazade, 106; Neşri, 350–2; *Anonymous Tevârih*, 50.

[127] Sphrantzes, 14–7.   [128] Chalkokondyles, 364–77; Sphrantzes, 18–19.

[129] Sphrantzes, 20–1; Doukas, 180–1; Ghillebert de Lannoy, 566–7.

near death; he left the affair entirely in John's hands. While giving an account of these events, Chalkokondyles contrasts John's youth and ambition with Manuel's wisdom. Similarly, Doukas claims that Manuel gave his support to Mustafa only upon Murad's refusal to hand over his brothers to Byzantium as indicated by the will of Mehmed. Doukas, too, represents the Mustafa affair as being directed by John alone. Manuel is frequently described as being old, ill, bedridden and having left the government to John.[130]

It is possible that the historians were deliberately trying to distance Manuel, whom they viewed positively, from this affair. After all, they knew in hindsight that it would end in disaster for the Byzantines. In this regard, Sphrantzes' account has already been noted for his bias against John VIII; indeed, the historian often compares him unfavourably to his father. The historians' depictions of this episode may have also partially stemmed from a desire to distance the 'wise' emperor from the event, and to lay the blame for the fiasco on the young, 'rash' and 'inexperienced' John. However, it would be too much of a coincidence that all three historians had similar narrative goals and were thus completely distorting events. As it often is, the reality may have been somewhere in between: it is more likely that whatever his initial misgivings, Manuel eventually accepted his son's decision, if not wholeheartedly, and actually lent his support to the scheme.

Whatever his original stance may have been in the beginning, in the end, the decision was carried out with Manuel's consent and should not be ascribed to John alone. Despite the picture of 'retirement' that emerges from the historians narrating this episode, all political decisions until his death were carried out either by Manuel, or with his consent. The historians depict him as making political decisions also after this Mustafa affair, even ceding Thessalonike to Venice in 1423 with his consent. Thus, the notion that the scheme was carried out against Manuel's will and that he had nothing do with it, is not a tenable one. Moreover, while these Byzantine historians portray the Mustafa affair as a rash move, it very much aligned with Manuel's own divide-and-rule policy during the Ottoman civil war. Ten years previously, this divide-and-rule policy had worked for quite some time, eventually leading to an extended period of peace. Murad's youth also strengthened the Byzantines' hand, but ultimately, the decision and the outcome of the Mustafa affair were still Manuel's responsibility and should not be assigned solely to John VIII.

---

[130] Sphrantzes, 18–19; Doukas, 172–3, 228–9, 232–5.

The Byzantines were sorely disappointed in Mustafa, who refused to hand over Gallipoli. In 1422, he crossed to Anatolia and was defeated by Murad then fled to Rumelia. By the summer of 1422, Murad crossed to Rumelia where he had Mustafa strangled.[131] Mustafa did not last even a year against Murad, and he would be remembered as 'False' Mustafa, not as a son of Bayezid but as a pretender created by the emperor to complicate the Ottoman power dynamic[132] Murad's response to the Byzantines was a swift one. In July 1422, he laid siege to Constantinople, and this would be the third – and the last – Ottoman siege Manuel was to witness.

---

[131] Sphrantzes, 20–1, Doukas, 184–5. Schreiner, *Kleinchroniken*, Chronik 53/21. Also see Barker, *Manuel II*, 359.

[132] However, Doukas narrates that even among the Byzantines, rumours existed that he was a false pretender, he claims that he actually was Bayezid's son; Doukas, 228–9.

CHAPTER 10

Exchanging Empires

He exchanged the earthly empire for the heavenly one, pain for apathy, fortune for true happiness . . .[1]

The siege of Constantinople in 1422 by Murad II would be a brief one. Yet it was a serious enough threat for Manuel to appeal to the West for help.[2] As had been the case for the past three decades, the Venetian Senate expressed its support, but offered no concrete assistance.[3] The emperor tried to mollify the sultan with embassies, but all of his attempts were declined. A dramatic event took place during these peace negotiations. One of the Byzantine envoys, Theologos Korax, was accused of treachery by the Byzantines upon the discovery of several luxury items among his possessions. He was suspected to have received these from the sultan, as bribes. Korax was dragged before Manuel by an enraged mob.

At the time, Manuel was residing in the Peribleptos Monastery. The emperor wished to subject Korax to a fair trial, but to no avail: the envoy was lynched by an angry mob.[4] This story reveals much about the volatility of the circumstances. The siege was only lifted about two and a half months later, when the Byzantines succeeded in defeating the Ottomans before the land walls.[5] The troops were led by John VIII; Manuel, aged seventy-two and in declining health, was no longer able to command.

---

[1] Makarios Makres, 'Monody', 307, 'ὅς γε τῆς ἐν γῇ βασιλείας ἠλλάξατο τὴν οὐρανίον καὶ παθῶν ἀπάθειαν καὶ τύχης εὐδαιμονίαν. . . .'

[2] For accounts of this siege, see Sphrantzes, 22–3; Chalkokondyles, 382–3 and Doukas 228–9, also Schreiner, *Kleinchroniken*, Chronik 13/2–4 and Mioni, 'Cronaca', no. 39. Doukas claims that Manuel resided in the Peribleptos because of a plague, while Sphrantzes makes no mention of this. Barker, *Manuel II*, 360–83, includes a detailed political account of these last years of Manuel's reign, but he too is constrained by the lack of sources for this period.

[3] Iorga, *Notes et Extraits*, II, 323–5; Thiriet, *Régestes*, II, nos. 1854 and 1855, 197.

[4] Doukas, 228–9. This episode is discussed by Necipoğlu, *Byzantium between the Ottomans and the Latins*, 143–4, who argues that the rumours about Korax were probably true.

[5] A detailed account of this confrontation and the preparations for it are found in Kananos' narrative on the siege; John Kananos, *Ioannis Canani De Constantinopolitana Obsidone Relatio. A Critical*

The reasons for this swift lifting of the siege are unclear. The Byzantine victory on 22 August was certainly a decisive factor, but there may have been another reason for Murad II's sudden withdrawal. During the siege, Manuel seems to have contacted yet another Mustafa, this time one of Murad's brothers, a young boy who was residing in Anatolia with his tutor. Again, the emperor attempted to play one Ottoman contender against the other. The following picture emerges from both Byzantine and Ottoman sources, although the latter omitted the Byzantine involvement in the affair.[6] In October, after the siege, Mustafa was received in Constantinople. He was subsequently married to a great-niece of Manuel by his half-sister Zampia Doria.[7] Manuel's plan was probably to use Mustafa as a threat against Murad in the future, should the need arise. Around the same time, papal legates, Antonio da Massa, Giovanni Aurispa and Francesco Filelfo, were also present in the city for discussions concerning the long desired Church union.[8] On 16 September, Manuel had already received this legate, and he was expected to do so again in October. However, on the day of Mustafa's arrival, disaster struck the Byzantine court. The emperor had a stroke.

Turbulence Takes its Toll

We cannot discern the particulars of the emperor's illness. Byzantine chronicles and histories reporting Manuel's call it *hemiplexia* (ἡμιπληξία), a term that Byzantine authors used to refer to a stroke that left only one side of the body paralysed. The term *apoplexia* (ἀποπληξία) described a total paralysis; however, the use of these terms was also not always consistent. Byzantine medical authors demonstrate some knowledge on strokes. For instance, many were aware that it originated from the head and caused paralysis and loss of speech.[9] Advanced age and stress are both risk factors for a stroke, and

---

Edition, with English Translation, Introduction and Notes of John Kananos' Account of the Siege of Constantinople in 1422 ed. and trans A. M. Cuomo (Leiden and Berlin, 2016).

[6] Chalkokondyles, 386–9; Sphrantzes, 22–3; Schreiner, *Kleinchroniken*, Chronik 13/5, 91/10 and Doukas 228–9, the latter being the most detailed narrative. Barker, *Manuel II*, 366–7, proposes that Manuel's contacts with Mustafa caused Murad II great alarm, and that this was a strong reason as to why the siege was lifted so swiftly. Aşıkpaşazade, 134–7; Neşri, 567–73 and *Anonymous Tevârîh*, 63–4.

[7] That it was this young Mustafa who was married into the imperial family, and not the older, the so-called False Mustafa, is proposed by Ganchou, 'Zampia'. He also discusses in detail the identity of the bride, concluding that she was the great niece of Manuel, and not a granddaughter.

[8] Gill, *The Papacy*, 37; G. Patasci, 'Joseph Bryennios et les discussions sur un council d'union (1414–1431)', *Κληρονομία* 5 (1973), 73–96, 83 and Raynaldus, *Annales Ecclesiastici*, vol. 27, 522–3. Henceforth, Patasci, 'Bryennios'.

[9] A TLG search for ἡμιπληξία yields fourteen results, mostly from medical authors and historians. For instance, Paul of Nicaea, a seventh-century author, defines *hemiplexia* as the paralysis of either the right or the left side of the body, while *apolexia* caused a full paralysis, loss of speech and also loss of hearing, but

at age seventy-two and under the dire stress of the Ottoman blockade, Manuel was at risk.

The stroke was apparently so serious that some Western reports mistakenly claimed that Manuel had died.[10] During Manuel's incapacity, the papal legate and Mustafa were dealt with by John VIII. On 19 October, a public synod took place in the Church of Saint Stephen, and between September and November, Joseph Bryennios delivered his orations on the union at the palace.[11] The choice of Bryennios as a spokesperson is significant as he was against a Church union on Latin terms. No doubt, this choice had been predetermined by Manuel, who was also a friend of Bryennios. While not polemical, Bryennios' orations oppose the Latin arguments. Another such insight comes from Syropoulos who reports that Bryennios claimed to have found an 'unassailable' argument for the defence of the Orthodox stance on the Procession.

Ultimately, Bryennios aimed at a refutation of the Latin arguments.[12] Although Manuel desired a union for political reasons, he crucially chose a representative who was not a pro-Latin, but who shared his own stance: seeking a union that did not compromise Orthodox doctrines. Manuel, too, wished to conclude a union based on his own theological stance and would not give up his own beliefs. The emperor probably also feared that such a union would only further divide the Byzantine society. This

---

not fever, see *Paolo di Nicea, Manuele Medico*, ed. A. M. Ieraci Bio (Naples, 1996), 45–231, 124. See also J. Lascaratos and V. Manduvalos, 'Cases of Stroke on the Throne of Byzantium', *Journal of the History of the Neurosciences* 7.1 (1998), 5–10. Henceforth, Lascaratos, 'Stroke'.

[10] The mistaken Western reports are noted by Barker, *Manuel II*, 367, n. 119. They are respectively a Venetian report and a papal document. Iorga, *Notes et Extraits*, I, 335–6, n. 4; Raynaldus, *Annales Ecclesiastici*, vol. 27, no. 26, 556. Barker believes that Marino Sanudo, a Venetian chronicler, also mistakenly reports Manuel as being dead. However, the chronicle merely says that John VIII had been crowned as emperor during his father's lifetime. It still refers to Manuel as the old emperor; '… l'Imperador Calogiani da Constantinopoli, fiol de l'Imperador vechio Manolli, incoronado in vitta del padre…'. Marino Sanudo il giovane, *Vita dei Duchi (1423–1474)*, ed. A. Caraccioio Ardco (Venice, 1999), vol. 1, 16. Henceforth, Sanudo.

[11] Sphrantzes, 22–3; Doukas, 234–5; Syropoulos, 112–13; and Schreiner, *Kleinchroniken*, Chronik 13/7. Barker, *Manuel II*, 367, n. 119, believes that Sphrantzes claims that Manuel had the stroke after breakfast, while the chronicle claims that it happened at midday. However, it is also possible that Sphrantzes used *ariston* to refer to a meal eaten during daytime as opposed to its more specific meaning as breakfast. In Byzantine usage, in general, the term had lost its original meaning and was used to denote any meal, see ODB, 1, 170. Moreover, before the stroke episode, Sphrantzes also narrates how Mustafa, who came to pay homage to the emperors, was received by them. The plural indicates Manuel's presence. While Barker interprets this episode as merely indicating Mustafa's arrival in order to pay homage, Sphrantzes also notes the admiration of Manuel by Mustafa's entourage, which suggests that they indeed saw Manuel.

[12] Patasci, 'Bryennios', 79–87, 91–3; Syropoulos, 120. Kolbaba, 'Repercussions', 67, points out that the 'unassailable' argument of Gregory of Cyprus, although a significant theological achievement, left no room for mutual negotiation and compromise between the two churches.

sentiment is echoed by Sphrantzes, in his well-known account of Manuel's advice to his son: John was to engage in discussions to obtain help, but never to commit himself to a union. It would only cause social tension.[13] At the end of the discussions in autumn 1422, the Byzantines handed the papal legate their written response. They refused the Roman primacy and submission to the papacy on doctrinal issues, and consequently, no union was reached.[14].

Meanwhile, the young Mustafa fared even worse than the previous pretender. Sometime in the autumn, he crossed to Anatolia with Byzantine help, but only a few months later, in spring 1423, he was betrayed by his own tutor and strangled.[15] Interestingly, unlike in the case of the previous Mustafa, Byzantine historians assign this scheme to Manuel himself, and not to John VIII. As discussed earlier, the historians condemned the False Mustafa affair and held John VIII responsible for it; however, they refrained from passing judgement on Manuel's support for the young Mustafa, though they knew that this second attempt was as rash as the first had been and would end as badly.

The historians portrayed Manuel's scheme as a mark of his wit and political flair, but in reality, the False Mustafa affair and the backing of this younger Mustafa were very similar political moves as regards both process and result. In the case of the second Mustafa, Doukas claims that Manuel devised the scheme(σοφίζεσθαι) from his sickbed, and he portrays this plot as an act of masterly guile by the ailing but still shrewd emperor. One possible explanation for this could be that the historians perceived this second plot as a means of remedying the siege. Indeed, their narratives describe the siege as a misfortune which the Byzantines – that is, John VIII – brought upon themselves through their support of the first Mustafa. Manuel is here depicted as having to support a pretender in order to distract the sultan from the siege, while John VIII is painted as having unnecessarily muddied the waters. Regardless of how the historians sought to portray this intrigue, the second plot brought Murad's vengeance down upon the empire: the sultan would raid Thessalonike and the Peloponnese, and the final Turkish-Byzantine treaty was very unfavourable for the

---

[13] Sphrantzes, 116. Biased against John VIII, Sphrantzes 'reports' this advice to underline the problematic aspects of John's acceptance of the union in Florence. John is represented as not following his father's 'wise' stance. Yet Sphrantzes' account also fits in well with Manuel's outlook.

[14] See V. Laurent, 'Les préliminaires du concile de Florence. Les neuf articles du pape Martin V et la réponse inédite du patriarche de Constantinople Joseph II', *REB* 20 (1962), 5–60, for the response of the Byzantines.

[15] See above for the sources. The fate of Mustafa's wife is unknown.

Byzantines. That the historians overlook these outcomes in their narratives, can once more be interpreted as a bias in favour of Manuel and against John VIII.

Significantly, even after Manuel's stroke, the historians portray him as politically active. They do emphasize his fragile state by pointing out that he was ill and bedridden, but was at least able to converse and seemed to have partially recovered. Sphrantzes especially reports several conversations and narrates how the emperor distributed his clothes before his death.[16] The monody on Manuel by Bessarion also alludes to the long duration of the emperor's illness.[17] Further, although in September 1424, it was John VIII who signed the Byzantine-Venetian treaty, the Venetian Senate resolutions continue to consider Manuel as the senior emperor until his death.

For instance, concerning the case of a mistreatment of some Venetian merchants, the envoy is instructed to pass over John VIII and directly see the 'old' emperor. He was to threaten Manuel with immediate military action should he not resolve the situation. This reveals that Manuel was still perceived as the final and more significant decision maker. Another deliberation, dated July 1424, instructs the *bailos* to visit the 'old' emperor in person, which demonstrates that Manuel was still able to engage in political discussions. However, the document also seems to foresee the possibility of him being unable to receive the petition in person. It is noted that as a second option, the *bailos* could see Manuel's representative.[18] Therefore, although he was ill, the emperor still took an active part in policymaking.

Mustafa's death did not end the hostilities between the Ottomans and Byzantium.[19] In May 1423, Murad's general, Turahan, raided the Peloponnese. The Hexamilion, Manuel's cherished achievement, was reduced to ruins.[20] The Ottomans also attacked Thessalonike, and the city was in such a desperate state that the young despot Andronikos had to cede the city to the Venetians to protect it. A move to which the emperor gave his consent.[21] The city where Manuel had his first taste of ruling, and

---

[16] Some of the terms used are *asthenos* (ἀσθενός) and *katoikitos* (κατοικίτος). Sphrantzes, 24–5. A brief article in a medical journal claims that Manuel must have lost his powers of speech. However, this statement is based on an erroneous reading of Bessarion's monody, see D. Vassilopoulos and E. Poulakou-Rebelakou, 'The Three Last Years of Manuel II Paleologus' Reign Between Two Stroke Attacks, Aphasia or Not?', *Historical Neuroscience* 20 (2011), 277–83.

[17] Bessarion, 'Monody', 284–5. [18] Thiriet, *Régestes*, 11, no. 1948, 219.

[19] A Venetian deliberation dated to spring 1423 still mentions the possibility of another attack on Constantinople. Iorga, *Notes et extraits*, 1, 336–7; Thiriet, *Régestes*, II, no. 1885, 204.

[20] Sphrantzes, 24–25; Schreiner, *Kleinchroniken*, Chronik 32/37, 33/34, 36/15, 72/5.

[21] On the negotiations, see Iorga, *Notes et extraits*, I, 343; Thiriet, *Régestes*, 11, no. 1905, 204; no. 1892, 205–6; no. 1897, 207; also, Chalkokondyles, 396–7, Schreiner, *Kleinchroniken*, Chronik 22/33, 34/1, 38/8, 39/4. Necipoğlu, *Byzantium between the Ottomans and the Latins*, 102–4.

which he had defended so vigorously in the 1380s, had now left Byzantine hands.

At this point, the emperor was too old to be personally active in diplomacy. Now, it was John VIII's turn to travel to various European courts. Like his father some twenty years previously, John would seek allies against the Ottomans. Having appointed his brother Constantine as regent, John left in the summer of 1423. He visited Venice, Milan and Mantua; the next summer, John was in Hungary to negotiate with Sigismund. It should be pointed out that John followed a very similar route to that of his father, excepting France and England. Both Sigismund and the Visconti rulers of Milan had been brought into the picture by Manuel, and John built upon the contacts and alliances that his father had fostered.

In November 1424, John returned empty-handed. Unlike that of his father, his journey did not stir great excitement in Europe. This was probably due to the fact that he did not visit France and England and that a visit to Italy by a second Byzantine emperor was no longer a novel event.[22] While John was away, negotiations with Murad continued. Loukas Notaras and Sphrantzes were sent to the sultan on an embassy as a final attempt, and thanks to their efforts, on February 1424, a treaty finally was signed.[23] The results, however, were a far cry from the terms of 1403: the Byzantines lost all the territorial concessions that they had received from Mehmed, and they agreed to pay tribute.[24] Whatever little success the emperor had achieved during his reign was now permanently lost.

Towards the End: An Assessment of Manuel's Reign

The treaty of February 1424 is the last significant political act of Manuel's reign. His final year remains in shadows in all respects, both personally and politically. His surviving correspondence ends around 1417 and other writings cannot be securely dated to the period of the 1420s. Thus, Manuel's feelings about the final outcome of his Ottoman policies cannot be traced. He had struggled to keep the Ottomans at bay ever since his accession to the throne, and only Tamerlane's victory over Bayezid had saved the empire, albeit temporarily. In the aftermath the emperor had

---

[22] Sanudo, 16–19; Syropoulos, 112–13; Iorga, *Notes et Extraits*, 1, 349–50; Schreiner, *Kleinchroniken*, Chronik 13/10, 34/2; and Mioni, 'Cronaca', no. 41.

[23] Sphrantzes, 24–25.

[24] Dölger, *Regesten*, nos. 3412–14, 112; Chalkokondyles, 396–397; Sphrantzes, 26–7; Schreiner, *Kleinchroniken*, Chronik 13/11, 22/35 and Mioni, 'Cronaca', no. 42.

managed to claw back some land and restore some of the empire's political prestige, but in 1424, all his efforts were drastically undone.

Manuel's reign is characterized by periods of conflict and peace with the Ottomans. The end of his reign saw a return to the original state; thus, his rule can be seen almost as a cycle. Could he have prevented the advance of the Ottomans and restored the empire to its former glory after all? In all fairness, Manuel did make several political moves that can be considered rash. His independent reign in Thessalonike, his disobedience to Bayezid in 1394 and his support of the two Ottoman pretenders, eventually brought harm to the empire; however, it is fair to note that the bleak circumstances left the emperor with very little room to manoeuvre.

Manuel was aware of the dangers posed by the Ottomans, and he strove endlessly to obtain help to stand against them. Although he never engaged in a military offensive against the Ottomans after his loss of Thessalonike in 1387, he was not completely submissive. Even when relations between the two empires seemed to be tranquil, Manuel was never at ease and frequently devised schemes he hoped would eliminate the Ottoman threat. Throughout his reign he remained vigilant in face of the obstacles and persevered to save his realm. He tried every solution he could find and knocked on every door for help. At the start of his reign, the empire was already dependent on Western help, both militarily and financially, and it was not possible for Manuel to raise the required troops or funds from his own meagre resources. More often than not, however, foreign assistance was not forthcoming. Under duress, the emperor always resorted to additional taxation and confiscation, and this is a pattern that can be observed during his despotate in the 1370s, his rule in Thessalonike, the blockade of Constantinople and the restoration of the Hexamilion. Although these were logical measures, yet they also caused tension between Manuel and his subjects. The existence of an alternative emperor, John VII, further complicated matters.

Despite being largely driven by circumstances Manuel did display some initiative as a ruler and was not reduced to a totally passive role. He desperately tried to improve the empire's finances and did all he could to relieve its dire financial straits, which he perceived – quite astutely as it turns out – to be the chief obstacle faced by the empire. He also did not merely petition Venice for help but endeavoured to come up with offers that might interest or tempt them to lend their assistance. To this end, Manuel offered relics, islands, meditation with Sigismund. He also sanctioned the sale of Corinth to the Hospitallers, and supported Theodore and his own sons to defend the Byzantine interests in the Morea. Back in

1396, together with Sigismund of Hungary, Manuel even assembled a crusading army. Similarly, in the Morea, managed to assert some imperial authority over the rebellious *archontes*.

The emperor, moreover, reached out to a wider political sphere, such as Spanish rulers, France and England, and even Denmark, visiting Western courts in person to state his case. All Western political powers had their own internal troubles at the time; moreover, they also had no real incentive to help Byzantium. With regards to a Church Union, while Manuel wished to conclude the union without compromising any Orthodox doctrines, the papacy had its own conditions. As previously discussed, like many of his contemporaries, the faith of his empire and own self was not something Manuel was willing to compromise for political benefit. Furthermore, it should be remembered that both the Council of Lyons in 1274 and the Council of Florence in 1439 brought little benefit to the empire. They merely acerbated social tensions. It is very likely that even if Manuel had given into all the demands of the papacy and concluded a union, no significant benefit would have materialized for the Byzantine Empire.

Although Bayezid's death was a severe blow to the Ottoman Empire, even a single contender like Musa Çelebi was still able to challenge the Byzantium. This demonstrates how vulnerable the Byzantine Empire was at this time. Manuel's policies during the Ottoman civil war bought some time for his empire. By playing one prince against the other, he delayed the unification of the Ottoman realm, and for some time, he was able to divert the princes' attention away from Byzantine territories. However, in order to eliminate Musa, Manuel was also compelled to support Mehmed, and eventually, in an ironic twist, his actions helped Mehmed to unite the Ottoman polity. His further attempts to manipulate Ottoman pretenders had mixed success. In Morea, for instance, his restoration of the Hexamilion kept the Ottomans at bay for some time. It was the lack of financial resources and manpower that led to the wall's eventual destruction. Manuel's Ottoman policies can be characterized neither as a resounding success, nor as an abject failure. He probably achieved as much as was possible under the dire circumstances and arguably extended the life of the empire. His reign also witnessed several minor achievements, including the territorial gains of 1403, the restoration of the Hexamilion and the quelling of the Morean rebellions.

Ultimately, circumstances played a major role in the fate of the empire, and the emperor's writings also betray this sense. Although Manuel denied the agency of fortune in his ethico-political writings, the narratives of the

Funeral Oration and the *Discourse to Iagoup* are laced with laments on the subject of fortune. In the *Dialogue with a Persian*, fortune once again forms a leitmotif in the discussion of the suffering of the Byzantines. As commonplace as Manuel's words may have been, they nevertheless ring true. In a letter dating to 1398, the emperor complained that he his fate had been to choose not the best option, but the least harmful. This insight characterizes his reign.[25]

The Old Emperor

Nothing more is heard of Manuel after the treaty of 1424. The only hints we have are the conversations of the 'bedridden' emperor alluded to in Sphrantzes. The textual sources from the period open an intriguing window into the perception of Manuel's advanced age. Both Sphrantzes and Doukas dwell on his advanced years and illness, and even the Venetian documents describe Manuel as the 'old emperor'. While this designation is partially used to differentiate between the old, ailing father, and the young emperor, Manuel's age of seventy-five was indeed very advanced for the period. Ages above seventy were rarely encountered. Even in narratives dealing with the 1410s, the Ottoman chronicles and the *Chronicle of Kefalonia* refer to Manuel, then in his sixties, as being old (gayet pîr and γέρων).[26]

He similarly becomes 'the old emperor' (l'Imperador vechio Manolli) for the Venetian chronicler Sanudo.[27] While visiting Constantinople in 1422, Ghillebert de Lannoy designates Manuel 'the old emperor' (le vieux) also, since he saw both Manuel and his co-emperor John VIII. Tellingly, it is John VIII who takes Ghillebert hunting. Aged seventy-two, Manuel no longer hunted, though it had been once, one of his favourite pastimes.[28] All things considered, the emperor's rather unusual life span seems to have made an impression on his contemporaries.[29]

---

[25] Letter 35, lines 17–19, '... ἀλλ' ἐπεί σχεδόν μοι ὥσπερ τις κλῆρος ἄνωθεν κάτεισιν οὐκ ἀπό τῶν ὠφελίμων τό κρεῖττον ἀλλ' ἀπό τῶν βλαβερῶν τό ἧττον ἐκλέγεσθαι....'
[26] Kastritsis, *The Tales of Sultan Mehmed*, 36–7; Neşri, 506–7, and G. Schirò, 'Manuel II Paleologo incorona Carlo Tocco despota di Gianina', *Byzantion* 29/30 (1959/60), 209–30, 229.
[27] Sanudo, 16. [28] Ghillebert de Lannoy, 65.
[29] See A. M. Talbot, 'Old Age in Byzantium', *BZ* 77 (1984), 267–78, who points out that statistics demonstrate that very few people lived beyond the age of fifty. Ages over seventy were considered as 'extreme' old age by the Byzantines. For representations of old age in Byzantine literature in the twelfth century, see E. Papadapoulou, 'Περί της ηλικίας καί του γήρατος από τη γραμματεία του ενδέκατου καί δωδεκάτου αιώνα', *Byzantina Symmeikta* 17 (2005), 131–98. It is also argued that the greater the age of an old person, the more likely that the authors would emphasize it.

The historians Chalkokondyles, Doukas and Sphrantzes all elaborate on Manuel's failing health in the 1420s. His *Sermon on the Dormition* (c. 1416) and a confession he penned for his spiritual fathers, contain further hints that the emperor had fallen seriously ill around 1414–16. The *Confession Addressed to his Spiritual Fathers Monks David and Damian* was intended for those wishing to purify themselves before Holy Communion. The *Confession*, its accompanying letter, and the *Morning Prayers* have been shown to form a *diatribe*.[30] The severity of Manuel's illness becomes evident when one considers that the emperor penned two lengthy theological compositions in thanksgiving for his recovery around 1416, but it is not clear whether these compositions concerned a single bout of illness or multiple ones. In the letter accompanying the confession, Manuel indicates that he was ill around 1414. He also seems to have worked on the confession for almost two years; however, it is unclear whether the *Sermon on the Dormition* also took two years to complete. As it also refers to his recovery from a grave illness, either the sermon was composed during the same illness as that of the confession, or was written about a second, later episode of ill-health. It is more probable that both texts deal with the same instance.

Several possibilities have been suggested regarding Manuel's illness around 1414.[31] In the above-mentioned confession and accompanying letter, Manuel speaks of gastric and bone pain, fever and foul-smelling ulcers. Although many of these are also literary motifs borrowed from the Psalms and thus cannot be as interpreted as definitive evidence to identify Manuel's illness, one theory is that the emperor may have been suffering from an episode of acute gout. The reason for this surmise is that during this period of illness he was accompanied by Demetrios Pepagomenos, an *apogrepheus* (censor) and a doctor specializing in gout, on a trip to Mistra. Furthermore, Manuel's father John V and his son John VIII also suffered from gout, and it is possible that Theodore I and Theodore II, too, suffered from the malady. In his medical treatise, Pepagomenos stated that he treated gout with colchine, which can cause gastrointestinal pain in high doses. On the other hand, Manuel may have been suffering from

---

[30] See footnote 31.

[31] I thank Charalambos Dendrinos for allowing me an early access to this article, where he puts forward these theories on Manuel's illness; Ch. Dendrinos, 'Emperor Manuel II Palaeologus' Unpublished Letter to his Spiritual Fathers David and Damianos', in *Bibliophilos: Books and Learning in the Byzantine World*, eds. Ch. Dendrinos and I. Giarenis, Byzantinisches Archiv (in press). Henceforth, Dendrinos, 'Unpublished letter'. The article contains a critical edition of the letter accompanying Manuel's *Confession*.

another illness known as Familial Mediterranean fever which presents similar symptoms and was also treated by colchine.

Mazaris likewise mentions an epidemic outbreak that wreaked havoc in Constantinople in early 1414.[32] He labels this epidemic as some sort of flu and describes the symptoms as fever, fatigue/paralysis of limbs and spots on the skin. These also conform to Manuel's own references to his illness, and thus it is possible that the emperor was suffering from a very serious flu or Dengue fever attack. Of course, there is no way to conclusively prove any of these theories, but what we do know is that his confession and accompanying letter indicate that Manuel's health was already failing around 1414, eight years before his final stroke.

It would seem that advancing age and feeble health increased the emperor's preoccupation with religion. As the 1410s progressed, one can observe that his compositions leaned increasingly towards religious writings, such as homilies and prayers. In his narrative corresponding to the 1420s, Doukas does not merely portray Manuel as being old and feeble. In several passages, he remarks that the emperor had by then devoted himself entirely to theological writings.[33] However, no theological work by the emperor, or, for that matter, any work, can be securely dated to that period. While Manuel turned his attention to theology more intensely in his later years, his sermons, the confession addressed to his spiritual fathers, and his prayers, all date to around 1410–16. Perhaps during this period Manuel occupied himself with theology simply by revising some of these works and reading other theological texts, or perhaps Doukas may have mistakenly attributed some of his earlier compositions to this period.

On the whole, Doukas does not miss the mark in noting that Manuel became even more pious in his later years. As discussed previously, it is not really possible to make any accurate assessment of the changes to his literary network; however, it appears that with age, monks increasingly formed the emperor's intellectual company of choice. For instance, Mazaris claims that the monks of Xanthopouloi were quite influential with Manuel in later life. Indeed, a certain Makarios from this monastery, who was also Manuel's spiritual father, was among the executors of the emperor's will. Joseph Bryennios, yet another theologian, was not only Manuel's collaborator in

---

[32] Mazaris, 2–4; Dendrinos, 'Unpublished letter', 3–10. Dendrinos also points out that in 1414 there had been an outbreaking of an epidemic, probably of severe flu, in France and Russia.

[33] Doukas, 228–9.

his works, but was also named an executor of his will.[34] From 1410 onwards especially, Manuel began to regularly collaborate on theological works with figures such as the Patriarch Euthymios, Gabriel of Thessalonike, Demetrios Chrysoloras and more notably, Makarios Makres and Joseph Bryennios. The emperor's final decade thus bears testimony to a growing inclination towards ecclesiastics and theologians as literary companions.[35]

During 1422, Manuel asked Bryennios to deliver sermons on the Trinity at the palace. During his soujourn in Thessalonike in 1416, the emperor had personally visited his spiritual fathers, the monks David and Damian, and also addressed them in two lengthy letters (in 1415 and 1416) and in the *Confession*.[36] Furthermore, Manuel invited Makarios Makres to Constantinople several times.[37] While his circle always included people with theological interests, as he grew older, Manuel reached out increasingly to monastic circles, a reflection of his growing piety. The emperor's theological interests paved the way for this inclination. A careful reading demonstrates that his writings also slowly became predominantly theological; even the *Ethico-Political Orations* are remarkably preoccupied with Christian thought, and with sin and repentance.

Around the same time, the emperor appears to have also become increasingly preoccupied with illness, repentance and especially with death. These new themes dominate his sermons, prayers and various other writings. Even the *Funeral Oration* includes almost a mini treatise on death at the very end. Although this section in the oration is not really connected to Theodore's death per se, it reflects Manuel's thoughts on death as a natural and philosophical phenomenon.[38] References to illness, sin and death were common in the above-mentioned genres; they were *topoi*. Yet it is also significant that such genres and themes appear in this particular period of Manuel's life, around 1416, when he had recovered from a significant illness, and not earlier on.

---

[34] Mazaris, 20–1. Makarios of the Xanthopouloi, who was also Manuel's spiritual father, is not identical to Makarios Makres, who was then the *hegoumenos* of the Pantokrator. Sphrantzes claims that this Makarios was formerly Jewish, Sphrantzes, 32–3.

[35] He collaborated with Euthymios on the *Clarification of a Debate*, he sent the sermons on *St Mary of Egypt* and the *Dormition* to Gabriel of Thessalonike and to Demetrios Chrysoloras. For his collaboration with Makres and Bryennios, see Dendrinos, 'Co-operation'.

[36] Dr Charalambos Dendrinos kindly gave me his own edition of the *Confession* based on Cyrptensis 161, ff. 12–65v, Par. suppl. gr. 1018, ff. 6v–53v and Pontificio Collegio Greco di S. Atanasio, cod. II, ff. 9–69v. Henceforth, *Confession*. An edition of the work has by then appeared; S. D. Lamprou, Μανουὴλ Β΄ Παλαιολόγου Πρὸς τὸν ἑαυτοῦ πνευματικόν. Εἰσαγωγή – Ἔκδοση (Thessalonike, 2018). This work came to my notice too late and was unavailable to me. Thus, I rely on Dr Dendrinos' edition. Letter 68 and Dendrinos, 'Unpublished letter' for these two letters.

[37] Kapetanaki, *Makarios Makres*, 13–15 and Argyriou, *Makres*, 190, 206–7.

[38] *Funeral Oration*, 246–56.

Sermons, Prayers and Confessional Works

Among these compositions are Manuel's four surviving sermons.[39] While the dating of the two sermons on the *oikonomia* and the providence of the Lord and on John the Baptist cannot be determined with certainty (before 1417), the ones on Mary of Egypt and the Dormition date respectively to c. 1410 and 1416.[40] As Manuel seems to have focused more on sermons and confessional works after the 1410s, one can surmise that the other two sermons date to the same years. Other religious works dating approximately to the same period are the *Morning Prayers*, the *Confession to his Spiritual Fathers* (both c. 1416) and a poem, *Chapters of Compunction*.[41] Manuel began composing the *Confession* after his illness around 1414 and sent the work to his spiritual fathers David and Damianos in 1416. Despite its private confessional tone, the *Confession* was probably again intended for circulation.[42] Similarly, one can assume that Manuel also circulated the *Morning Prayers*: it formed a *diatribe* along with the *Confession* and its accompanying letter.[43] Since these works display an intense preoccupation with death, sin and repentance, we will now explore them in relation to Manuel's final years, offering some preliminary remarks pertaining to their contents and literary features.

Like many of his other compositions, Manuel circulated at least two of his sermons. Those on St Mary of Egypt and the Dormition were sent to

[39] Since some scholars prefer to call informal, delivered 'on the spot' addresses 'homilies', and the more formal, prepared and more difficult ones 'sermons', I have opted to refer to Manuel's compositions as sermons. On this issue, see M. Cunningham, 'Preaching and Community', in *Church and People in Byzantium, 20th Spring Symposium of Byzantine Studies, Manchester 1986*, ed. R. Morris (Birmingham, 1990), 29–47. Henceforth, Cunningham, 'Preaching and Community'.

In my discussion of the sermons, I have relied on the following basic bibliography: Cunningham, 'Preaching and Community'; Th. Antonopoulou, 'Byzantine Homiletics: An Introduction to the Field and its Study', in *A Catalogue of Byzantine Manuscripts in their Liturgical Context*, eds. K. Spronk, G. Ruwhorst and S. Royé (Brepols, 2013),183–98; and W. Meyer, 'Homiletics', in *The Oxford Handbook of Early Christian Studies*, eds. S. Ashbrook Harvey and D. G. Hunter (Oxford, 2008), 565–79.

[40] *Sermon on the Dormition*, ed. M. Jugie, *Homelies Mariales Byzantines, Patrologia Orientalis*, 16, cols. 119–42; *Sermon on Oikonomia and the Providence of the Lord*, ed. S. Lamprou, 'Περὶ τῆς οἰκονομίας καὶ προνοίας τοῦ Κυρίου ἀνέκδοτος λόγος τοῦ αὐτοκράτορος Μανουὴλ Β´ Παλαιολόγου', Θεοδρομία 4 (2014): 488–30; *Sermon on John the Baptist*, ed. C. Billò, 'La Laudatio in S. Iohannem Baptistam di Manuele II Paleologo', *Medioevo Greco*, 2 (2002), 49–63. Henceforth, *Sermon on the Dormition* and *Sermon on the Providence of the Lord*.

Sermon on St Mary of Egypt is found in Vat. gr. 632, ff. 336–50v and Vat gr. 1619, ff. 15–29v.

[41] The *Morning Prayers* is found in *PG* 156, cols. 563–74. Henceforth, *Morning Prayers*. See cols. 575–6 for the *Chapters on Compunction*.

[42] David was the *hegoumenos* of Nea Mone in Thessalonike and the superior of Makarios Makres, see V. Laurent, 'Ecrits spirituels inédits de Macaire Choumnos', Ἑλληνικά 14 (1955), 40–86, 52; Argyriou, *Makres*, 197–8.

[43] See Dendrinos, 'Unpublished letter'.

Gabriel of Thessalonike and Demetrios Chrysoloras respectively.[44] The sermons themselves make frequent references to a *theatron* and contain many suggestions that they were performed. Consequently, these sermons are not among the so-called 'desk-homilies' but were actually delivered.[45] Already seeking to assert authority in all spheres of politics and ecclesiastical affairs, the emperor now also adopted the persona of a preacher. His sermons have earned Manuel a rare place in Byzantine history as one of the very few preaching emperors. Other notable examples include Constantine I and Leo VI. Unlike Leo VI, Manuel produced a very small number of sermons; his general literary output is also much broader, but his style is also more elevated and his discussions much more theologically charged. While Leo VI was later criticized for his style, no comments survive in Manuel's case.[46] Yet this line of imperial preachers suggests a connection between Manuel and this tradition.

Was Manuel imitating these emperors as models of imperial preachers? Leo VI took another emperor-preacher, Constantine the Great, as his model and his court ideology contained strong Constantinian references. But this kind of political emulation is absent in Manuel's court, nor does he ever mention these two emperors. It would be safe to assume therefore that the emperor did not preach in order to imitate Constantine or Leo. Yet through his preaching, he certainly sought to present himself as a theological authority, and to assert authority over the Church, possibly turning to sermons as a part of his much broader literary and scholarly interests. One also should consider that many of the literati in his circle, even laymen, composed sermons. These included Gabriel of Thessalonike, Nicholas Kabasilas, Joseph Bryennios, Demetrios Chrysoloras and the deceased Demetrios Kydones. Sermons were thus authored by many in the emperor's circle. Although Manuel undoubtedly adopts the persona of an 'emperor-preacher' in his sermons, one must refrain from placing too much emphasis on the imperial preaching model. Instead, we must contextualize Manuel's sermons within his own milieu.[47]

On the whole, the language of his sermons is complicated, and the compositions are quite long. The target audience is clearly the literati and

---

[44] Letters 52 and 61.

[45] 'Desk homily' is a term used to designate a homily that had been written solely for private reading and was not actually intended for performance. For the term and the difficulty of distinguishing between these and delivered works, see Cunningham, 'Preaching and Community'.

[46] For an in-depth analysis of Leo VI's homilies, see Th. Antonopoulou, *The Homilies of Leo VI* (Leiden, 1997), especially 35 for the posthumous critique of Leo's style.

[47] While he may not be imitating Leo or Constantine, Manuel's sermons do have political messages. This will be discussed below.

those present in the palace, where they were performed. Manuel's language in preaching is on the same level of complexity as his other works. It resembles the high style of Nicholas Kabasilas' sermons rather than the 'lower' register of his other contemporaries, such as Isidore Glabas and Gabriel of Thessalonike who had to address a much wider audience. The language of Manuel's confessional works is also complex and elevated.

Manuel's sermons lack both narration and dialogue. In the *Sermon on the Dormition*, the emperor even points out that he will purposefully refrain from narration.[48] Moreover, in contrast with his other theological works, Manuel's sermons also frequently omit Classical allusions and his usual imagery. Manuel's sources are chiefly Scriptural, and as expected the emperor also makes several references to the Church Fathers. Instead of dialogues and narrations in his sermons, Manuel engages in theological discussions and heavily emphasizes moral exhortations until his sermons resemble treatises on issues of morality. This resemblance is also reinforced by the fact that the *Sermon on St Mary of Egypt* and sixth oration of the *Ethico-Political Orations* are modified versions of the same text.[49] Content wise, while this sermon focuses on sin and penance, the one on John the Baptist extolls him as the forerunner of Christ. The *Sermon on the Dormition* and the *Sermon on the Providence of the Lord* have more theological discussions compared to the other two, and their literary features also deserve especial mention.

The *Sermon on the Providence* focuses on the mystery of the Incarnation and deliverance of humanity by means of Christ's sacrifice. The text reveals an intense preoccupation with Christ's death and sacrifice. Not only does this parallel Manuel's preoccupation with death in his *Confession*, prayers and the *Sermon on the Dormition*, it also stems from the occasion: the work was performed on the Holy Saturday, marking the entombment of Christ.[50] God's goodness and clemency, through which the human race is ultimately delivered, is a major theme of the sermon. The emperor also stresses the significance of the human role in deliverance. Human will and choice (προαίρεσις) are crucial for deliverance, he argues, albeit with divine help. God created him, giving him reason (λόγος) and free will

---

[48] *Sermon on the Dormition*, col. 120. See also M. Cunningham, 'Dramatic Device or Didactic Tool? The Function of Dialogue in Byzantine Preaching', in *Rhetoric in Byzantium, Papers from the 35th Spring Symposium of Byzantine Studies*, ed. E. Jeffreys (Aldershot 2003), 101–16.

[49] See Kaltsogani, 'Zur Entstehung der Rede des Manuel II Palaiologos'. Since this oration was analysed in Chapter 9, the sermon will not be discussed here again.

[50] *Sermon on the Providence of the Lord*, 502, ᾿Αναγινώσκεται δὲ τῷ Μεγάλῳ Σαββάτῳ πρὸ τοῦ ἐπιταφίου κανόνος.'

(αὐτεξουσία), the emperor exclaims.[51] For instance, Manuel points out that committing evil and sin are voluntary deeds that allow God to be able to mete out justice. Any divine punishment in turn, is for the benefit of humanity.

Likewise, the Christian notion of free will is frequently employed throughout the sermon.[52] The emperor points out that the Incarnation came into being through free will and choice: both Christ and the Virgin Mary participated voluntarily in the Incarnation, the greatest good of humanity. The same ideas are also found in the *Sermon on the Dormition*. The emperor's life-long interest in the notions of freewill, choice and voluntary/involuntary deeds surfaces in his sermons as well. Although notions such as sin being a product of free will and the voluntary nature of the Incarnation, were already fundamental Orthodox arguments, Manuel's own focus on choice and free will is still noteworthy.[53]

Style wise, the *Sermon on the Dormition* is perhaps the most remarkable of these works. Unlike the other three sermons, it boasts several Classical allusions, notably to Aphthonios, Homer and the Platonic *Phaedo*. Contrary to the other 'unadorned' sermons, the emperor employs metaphors and imagery. Thus, the literariness of this particular sermon is more pronounced. The *Dormition* is theologically interesting as well, since many debates were attached to the person of the Virgin concerning her nature, her conception and the Dormition. These were all central questions in Christian theology and Manuel expresses his opinions on each of them.[54] In this regard, the volume of Marian sermons in Byzantium is exceptionally bulky. Many of Manuel's contemporaries also produced sermons and theological works concerning the Virgin, and the ideas Manuel expresses on these debates were shared by many authors.

Throughout this sermon, as well, Manuel places a great emphasis on choice (προαίρεσις). As the Virgin was a voluntary participant in the Incarnation, Manuel argues, choice is the reason behind the mystery.[55]

---

[51] *Sermon on the Providence of the Lord,* 505, 'Καὶ δὴ τρισί με τούτοις τιμήσας, τῷ πλάσαι, τῷ λόγῳ κοσμῆσαι, τῷ ἀναδῆσαι/ τελευτῶν αὐτεξουσιότητι . . .'.

[52] On free will in Christian thought, see Telfer, 'Autexousia'.

[53] Meyendorff, *Byzantine Theology,* 143–6.

[54] See A. Wenger, *L'assomption de la T. S. Vierge dans la tradition Byzantine du VIe au Xe siècle. Etudes et documents* (Paris, 1955); M. Jugie, *La mort et l'assomption de la Très Sainte Vierge* (Rome, 1944); Dvornik, 'The Immaculate Conception'; See H. M. O'Carroll, *A Theological Encyclopedia of the Blessed Virgin Mary* (Eugene, Oregon, 1991), 119 for the views of Kydones, Manuel Chrysoloras and Demetrios Chrysoloras. M. Jugie, 'Le discours de Demetrius Cydonès sur l'Annonciation et sa doctrine sur l'Immaculée Conception', *Echos d'Orient* 17 (1915), 97–106. Henceforth, Jugie, *La Mort et l'assomption.*

[55] *Sermon on the Dormition,* col. 124.

Again, the emperor's life-long preoccupation with choice is woven into his discussions of the Incarnation. He also devotes much space to the issue of the Virgin's humanity and purity: she is chosen by God for her purity and perfect virtue, being free from sin, and her body was also not subjected to it after her death. Once more, these questions and arguments prevailed in many Byzantine Marian sermons, and Manuel strictly follows the traditional Orthodox arguments.

A more interesting debate deals with the precise status of the Virgin: whether she ranked above or below the angels, was a widespread discussion. She is close to God because of the Incarnation, the emperor points out, but Manuel also cautions reserve concerning her status: only God is above the bodiless, he argues. The emperor expresses his doubts as to whether she should be considered above the Cherubim and the Seraphim. Directly addressing the Virgin, he exclaims that she would not compete with the angels for the first place: let us observe the mean (τὸ μέτριον) in her worship, the emperor concludes, for only God knows her exact status. He thus refrains from ranking the Virgin Mary above the angels.[56] Elsewhere in the sermon, Manuel presents discussions relating to her mortality. He points out that despite being the mother of Christ, it was natural that the Virgin had to die. After all, she was mortal and would also desire to be reunited with her son. Moreover, even Christ, the Son in the Holy Trinity, submits to death in order to deliver the human race from sin; though he is life itself, Christ's death is needed to ignite the hope of unending life for humanity.

The Assumption of the Virgin Mary is another significant debate that Manuel touches upon. Many divergent thoughts existed on the question on the Assumption among Byzantine theologians. These examined whether both the soul and the body were elevated, the precise moment this elevation occurred, and whether Mary would still be resurrected at the Resurrection. After the eighth and the ninth centuries especially, many theologians supported the notion that her body was elevated to heaven and that her shroud remained empty.[57] Manuel does not enter into lengthy discussions concerning whether Mary's body was elevated to heaven or not,

---

[56] *Sermon on the Dormition*, cols. 110–12, 'Τὸ γὰρ ὑπερκεῖσθαι τῶν ἀσωμάτων διὰ τὴν φύσιν, μόνου σαφῶς δηλαδὴ τοῦ παραγαγόντος τὸ σύμπαν ἐκ τοῦ μηδαμῇ μηδαμῶς ὄντος. Σὺ δὲ ταῖς τάξεσι τῶν ἀγγέλων τῆς οὐσίας ἕνεκα ὑπὲρ πρωτείων οὐκ ἂν ἐρίσαις, τοῦ σοῦ προπάτορος μεμνημένη . . .'. See B. E. Daley. *On the Dormition of Mary: Early Patristic Homilies* (Crestwood N.Y, 1997) and B. E. Daley, 'At the Hour of our Death: Mary's Dormition and Christian Dying in Late Patristic and Early Byzantine Literature', *DOP* 55 (2001), 71–89, 86, and Dvornik, 'Immaculate Conception', 93–6.

[57] Daley, 'Death', 86.

and he similarly skips over precisely when this elevation occurred.[58] Instead he merely claims that in heaven, she saw Christ with the eyes of her immortal soul, and elsewhere mentions in passing that both her soul and body were elevated. Although it seems that Manuel accepted the Assumption of the body of the Virgin, he does not dwell on the issue.[59]

The emperor's preoccupation with death in these two sermons is also rather striking. This interest stems partially from the topics of the sermons. Yet this theme also appears in Manuel's oeuvre around the same time as his recovery from a grave illness in 1416. The *Dormition* is especially noteworthy in this context. Here, death is not examined with regard to the theological debates concerning the Assumption, or sin and salvation, but as a natural and a philosophical phenomenon. In Manuel's work, the theme of death dominates the entire sermon. We call this event – the separation of the soul from the body – death, Manuel explains in the *Sermon on Dormition*, but it is only the name that terrifies people.[60] It is not death itself, he continues, but the fear of the unknown that disturbs people, and everything dies – even the barbarians accept it. Following the model of the Platonic *Phaedo*, Manuel also argues that death is actually desirable for philosophers, since their soul is freed from bodily chains and escapes from the inevitable sorrows of life.[61] Eventually, Manuel invites the audience not to mourn, but to celebrate the Virgin's death, because she had overcome death by her virtue. Thus, Manuel believes that virtue is humanity's one defence against the fear of death.[62] This exhortation not only aimed at consoling the audience in the face of mortality, but possibly also the recently recovered author himself.[63]

The sermons on the providence of the Lord and the Dormition are also remarkable with regard to Manuel's self-representation. As always, he seeks to enhance his imperial and textual authority, and he carefully hints at his imperial status. Even in preaching to the palace audience, Manuel portrays the role of the emperor as being responsible for the faith of his subjects.

---

[58] See Jugie, *La mort et l'assomption*, 188–9, 250–67.

[59] Jugie and Dvornik propose that Manuel's stance on the Assumption could have been influenced by the Franciscans; *Sermon on the Dormition*, col. 117 and Dvornik, 'Immaculate Conception', 111. However, Dendrinos proposes that Manuel's position originates in the Orthodox teachings, *On the Procession of the Holy Spirit*, 383. See Dendrinos, *On the Procession of the Holy Spirit*, 21, for Manuel's reference to the difference between the Franciscans and the Dominicans.

[60] *Sermon on the Dormition*, cols. 119–20 and 138.

[61] *Sermon on Dormition*, col. 127. This outlook is also found in the *Funeral Oration*, whose revisions he finished around the same time, c. 1416, *Funeral Oration*, 246–56.

[62] *Sermon on the Dormition*, cols. 136–7.

[63] On the perception of death in Byzantium, see G. T. Dennis, 'Death in Byzantium', *DOP* 55 (2001), 1–7.

This can be interpreted as a subtle statement to the ecclesiastics that Manuel had authority over matters of faith. For instance, in these sermons the emperor is especially preoccupied with the royal imagery of the Virgin and Christ. Manuel implicitly draws parallels between himself, the earthly emperor, and the Emperor Christ. Although Christ was often referred to as emperor of the heavens, Manuel's own insistence on this epithet is rather striking. Similarly, he points out that as a rational human being, God set him to rule over the other creations. His choice of the verb to rule, *basileuein*, also brings to mind Manuel's status as *basileus*.[64]

His confessional works are similarly interwoven with many allusions to Manuel's imperial rank. Although the confessional and liturgical texts elicited the suppression of the author's identity and sometimes even encouraged anonymity, Manuel did not let go of his imperial status. He is no ordinary penitent sinner, but again, dominates the text as the emperor. Hence, Manuel's desire to enhance his imperial authority causes him to step away from tradition in his confessional works. For instance, in the *Morning Prayers*, Manuel gives thanks to God for his beneficence in both private and public affairs (ἰδίᾳ καὶ κοινῇ) and stresses the public nature of his imperial office. Similarly, he addresses Christ as emperor and continuously draws subtle parallels between Christ and himself through the parable of the Good Shepherd.[65] In the shorter, second prayer, Manuel tellingly prays for divine help in leading himself and his *subjects* in life. Here once again he makes a subtle imperial allusion. The emperor was often portrayed as a helmsman in Byzantine panegyrics, a *topos* that Manuel was himself very fond of.[66] These same tendencies are found in the *Confession*, where Manuel gives thanks for God's grace not only towards the *genos*, but also towards the author, himself.[67] The emperor then strives to reinforce his status as emperor through parallels between David's confession and his own.[68] In short, Manuel weaves the text around his imperial office as he does in so many other instances.

---

[64] *Sermon on the Providence of the Lord*, 505.

[65] *Morning Prayers*, cols. 569 and 573. In 1392, during Manuel's coronation, the parable of the Good Shepherd had been read as imperial propaganda against John VII, see Chapter 5.

[66] The text is edited in *PG* 156, cols. 574–6. See Appendix 4 for a translation.

[67] *Confession*, Cyrptensis 161 f. 11v, '... οὐ μόνον κοινῇ τὴν ὑπὲρ τοῦ γένους, ἀλλὰ δὴ καὶ τὴν ἰδίαν γεγενημένην (ἀγαθότητα) ὑπὲρ αὐτοῦ γεγραφότος...'.

[68] *Confession*, Cryptensis 161 f. 15v, 'ὁ δὴ Δαυίδ, πάντα μὲν θαυμάσιος ὤν, ὀλίγα δ' ἄττα προσκεκρουκώς, οὐκ ἐτόλμησεν. Οὐ γὰρ ἁπλῶς ἠξίωσεν εἰπεῖν, μὴ ἐλέγξῃς μὴ δὲ παιδε ὑσῃς με.' See Angelov, *Imperial Ideology*, 127–31, for uses of David in imperial ideology in the Nicaean and early Palaiologan periods. David appears less frequently in panegyrics in the later period.

Apart from these allusions to his status as emperor, Manuel embraces the persona of a penitent sinner in his confessional works and prayers. He is intensely concerned with sin and repentance, as well as with illness, old age and death.[69] The persona of the penitent sinner, and the emphasis on the human capacity for sin and repentance were fundamental features of Byzantine liturgical works.[70] Thus, Manuel adopts the traditional attributes of the genre. Yet while these were conventional themes, once more it is telling that both these genres and themes appear in Manuel's old age, and not earlier. In the *Confession*, while pondering on his sins while he first addresses his spiritual fathers before conversing directly with God, the emperor also gradually moves from the royal 'we' to the first person singular. This has further significance as a sign of Manuel's transformation into a humble, penitent sinner. 'I was, am and will be unworthy', he admits, exclaiming in another passage, 'I tremble, shiver and am afraid ... '.[71]

Manuel adopts the same persona of the penitent sinner in his short poem, *Chapters of Compunction*. Using extensive biblical allusions, he laments that he had been distanced from God through his sins; he is ravaged by illness and enflamed by his conscience. Manuel weeps, stripping himself naked willingly because of his *akrasia*, immoderation. The emperor even incorporates his fixation with choice and moderation into this poem. He begs to be cloaked by Christ and bemoans his excruciating thirst. All of these, the cloak, the thirst and the breadcrumbs, are allusions to the New Testament. Referring to the Gospel of Matthew, Manuel moreover assumes the persona of the rich man, but he adds a twist by also placing himself in the position of the beggar pleading for crumbs. As a penitent emperor, the rich man and the beggar parable was a quite fitting one for Manuel. He is the rich man because of his imperial rank, but he also wishes to be identified with the good beggar.

The *Morning Prayers* focus on the same theme. The tone is very intimate and pleading, interjections such as 'woe to me' or 'alas', are frequent. Once more, also following the *topoi* of the genre, Manuel refers to his illnesses, to his burning, inflamed wounds and his trembling marrow. No peace was left in his bones. While the former is clearly a metaphor for his sinful soul,

---

[69] For repentance in early Byzantine theology, see A. Torrance. *Repentance in Late Antiquity. Eastern Ascetism and the Framing of the Christian life c. 400–650 CE* (Oxford, 2013), 158–76. For confessional literature in the Middle Ages as an expression of selfhood, see A. Gurevich, *The Origins of European Individualism* (Oxford, 1995), 114–15, 131.

[70] For a discussion, see D. Krueger, *Liturgical Subjects. Christian Ritual, Biblical Narrative and the Formation of the Self in Byzantium* (Philadelphia, 2014), especially 1–29.

[71] *Confession*, Cryptensis 161 f. 15, 'Τρέμω, φρίττω, δέδια...'; 17v, 'ἀχρεῖος γάρ εἰμι, καὶ ἦν, καὶ ἐξῆς ἔσομαι.'

the latter is also reminiscent of a physical illness. 'I grew old among my enemies', the emperor bewails, 'despised, trampled under their feet . . . .'[72] The *Morning Prayers* closes with Manuel's pleading for deliverance before his death, 'as', he remarks, 'perhaps it is imminent now.'[73]

The End of an Era

Manuel's foresight in the *Morning Prayers* came true on 21 July 1425. Having become the monk Matthew a few days earlier, the emperor succumbed to his long illness.[74] He was buried in the Monastery of the Pantokrator on the same day amidst much wailing and expressions of grief from the people of the city; such mourning, Sphrantzes and Bessarion rhetorically exclaim, had never been witnessed before.[75] Shortly before his death, Manuel had dictated his will to Sphrantzes. The late emperor's wishes were carried out by Sphrantzes, Joseph Bryennios and a certain Makarios from the Xanthapouloi, who was Manuel's spiritual father. He left each of his sons some of his personal valuables and the rest was divided into four. The first portion was reserved to pay for memorial rites for Manuel and his relatives; the remaining three portions were distributed respectively among the poor, the doctors and Manuel's fellow monks.[76] Empress Helena would later be interred next to the emperor. Their son Theodore II, despot of Morea, would embellish the tombs with gilded slates around 1435, accompanied by a set of textiles depicting Manuel and Helena in both imperial and monastic garbs. Bessarion's verses on the same topic were probably commissioned for these textiles; sadly no trace of the tombs survives today.[77]

---

[72] *Morning Prayers*, col. 565.

[73] *Morning Prayers*, col. 568, '. . . ὥσπερ πρὶν εἰς γῆν ἀποστρέψαι θανάτῳ, ἐγγὺς νῦν ἔστι ἴσως. . . .'

[74] Sphrantzes, 30–1; Doukas, 236–7; Schreiner, *Kleinchroniken*, Chronik. 7/28; 13/14; 22/23 and Mioni, 'Cronaca', no. 43. Chalkokondyles omits Manuel's death. Bessarion, 'Monody', 284, mentions Manuel becoming the monk Matthew. A poem also deals with Manuel's imperial and monastic σχῆμα, 'Anonymous Verses to Manuel and Helena Palaiologos,' ed. S.P. Lampros, *ΠΠ*, III, 281–3. For the Pantokrator's function as the burial site of several imperial personalities, see *The Pantokrator Monastery in Constantinople*, ed. S. Kotzabassi (Leiden and Berlin, 2013), especially 57–70.

[75] Bessarion, 'Monody', 285. It is possible that Bessarion delivered an informal speech and later wrote a more elaborate version. His references to 'this tomb here' (τόνδε τὸν τάφον) seem to be indicating actual spatial presence, but they could also be an allusion to Pericles' funeral oration in Thucydides.

[76] Sphrantzes, 31–2. It is not known with which monastery Manuel was affiliated as a monk. It could have been the Pantokrator, where Makarios Makres was *hegoumenos* and where Manuel was eventually buried. It could also have been the monastery of the Xanthopouloi, with whose monks Manuel seemed to be close. Finally, it could have been the Peribleptos, where Doukas claims Manuel resided during an epidemic around 1422.

[77] N. Melvani, 'The Tombs of the Palaiologan Emperors', *BMGS* 42, 2 (2018), 237–60, 247–9.

At the time of his death, Manuel was seventy-five years old. It was an impressive age for the time. He had ruled the empire for nearly forty years. His near contemporary historians Doukas and Sphrantzes would craft his image as a wise, brave, dignified and pious ruler. Even Chalkokondyles, who criticizes other Palaiologoi, has nothing negative to say about Manuel.[78] The empire that Manuel fought so hard to preserve would fall only twenty-eight years after his death, and with it the tradition of Byzantine history writing would come to a halt; Manuel's memorial thus ended with these above-mentioned historians. At this point, his legacy becomes obscure. Of his surviving sons, Andronikos died young in 1429; John VIII would die childless; the despot of Morea, Theodore II, would only have a daughter, and this grand-daughter, Helena Palaiologina, would become the queen consort of Cyprus;[79] Constantine XI would become famous as the last martyr-emperor of Byzantium, perishing without issue; and Demetrios would submit to the Ottomans with his only child, another Helena predeceasing him.

Manuel's youngest son, Thomas, would go to Rome and the last claimants to the Byzantine throne would spring from his line. After Thomas' death, his children were brought up in Rome by the pope, and their upbringing was supervised by Cardinal Bessarion. In an ironic twist, Manuel's namesake grandson by Thomas submitted to the Ottomans and served the sultan. Thomas' daughter Helena Palaiologina married the Serbian lord Lazar Branković and had three daughters. Yet another daughter, Zoe Palaiologina married the Grand Prince of Muscovy, Ivan III, and through her, Manuel became the great-great grandfather of the Russian Tsar Ivan the Terrible. Manuel's grandson Andreas Palaiologos became the last claimant to the title of emperor of Byzantium. He died in Rome in 1502 and was buried in St Peter's basilica alongside his father. Upon his death, he bequeathed his imperial title to the Catholic monarchs Isabella of Castile and Ferdinand of Aragon. They never used it.[80]

What was the legacy Manuel bequeathed to the Byzantine Empire? Since the empire fell only twenty-eight years later, this is a difficult issue to trace. However, Manuel's influence may still be observed during the reigns of the two last emperors – both his sons.[81] In their Western policies,

---

[78] Doukas, 236–7; Sphrantzes, 20–2. A short chronicle would also record Manuel as the pious and the holy emperor, probably also thanks to his adoption of the monastic habit. Schreiner, *Kleinchroniken*, Chronik 7/13.

[79] See Nicol, *Last Centuries*, 399–401; for Manuel's descendants.

[80] For Andreas' life, see Harris, J. Harris, 'A worthless prince? Andreas Paleologus in Rome — 1464–1502', *OCP* 81 (1995), 537–54.

[81] See Nicol, *Last Centuries*, 345–70, for the events of these reigns.

both John VIII and Constantine XI built upon their father's example. They, too, petitioned the West for help, and Constantine even continued Manuel's Aragonese relations. Like Manuel, John also sought to defeat the Ottomans via a crusade, and like Nikopolis, the Crusade of Varna (1444) would fail. Moreover, as he had done in 1423, as emperor, John VIII visited Italy again in person. After Manuel, he became the second traveller-emperor, and although he did not travel as extensively as his father, John arguably followed Manuel's example.

Similarly, John VIII's participation in the Council of Florence stemmed from Manuel's earlier negotiations with the papacy. Manuel had been averse to a one-sided union, but it was his dealings with Rome that paved the way for those of John VIII. On the Ottoman front, both John and Constantine continued their father's schemes of lending support to various pretenders. In the Morea, they strove to keep Hexamilion functioning, but without financial resources and foreign help, the Ottomans breached the walls more than once. The emperor was ultimately proved to be correct and astute concerning the significance he attributed to the financing of these defences.

As an author, Manuel's works retreated into shadows. No Byzantine author seems to have relied on Manuel as a source or even as an influence. Several of his manuscripts ended up in the library of Bessarion after the fall of Constantinople, but the emperor does not seem to have enjoyed much renown in humanistic circles. It is difficult and fruitless to speculate as to whether Manuel would have remained a celebrated author had the empire not fallen so quickly after his death. His manuscripts chiefly ended up in Italy, and although several of his works were copied in subsequent centuries, Manuel was mostly forgotten. In Constantinople, and to an extent, in Mistras, he supported scholars and literati, organizing *theatra* and, supposedly, even encouraging the spreading of learning through schools. He corresponded and collaborated with many of the famed literati of the period and certainly contributed to the literary and scholarly life of the Byzantine Empire.

Although the emperor himself displayed little interest in humanism at the dawn of the Renaissance, scholars connected to Manuel's literary circle spread Greek learning in the Morea and in Italy. He sent Manuel Chrysoloras to Europe for diplomatic missions, and Plethon, Isidore of Kiev, Manuel Chrysoloras and Bessarion had all been in contact with Manuel: they dedicated works to him, worked on his manuscripts and even wrote prefaces for the *Funeral Oration*. Because the emperor, to an extent, acted as their literary patron, it is possible to say that, very indirectly, Manuel did contribute to the Byzantine role in the Renaissance.

Living during a period of time that saw the end of the Byzantine Empire, the rise of the Ottomans and the flowering of the Renaissance, Manuel witnessed a fascinating period in history. He was himself no less intriguing as both a ruler and as an author. As emperor, Manuel was constantly constrained by the challenges posed by the times in which he lived, and though he was often swept along with the tide, he always persevered in his attempts to safeguard his empire. It was these very same circumstances that also inspired him to pen the many remarkable compositions which would eventually preserve his name across the ages. Had Manuel been born in another time, the *Dialogue with a Persian* might never have come into existence. Throughout his life, he witnessed defeats, turmoil, family betrayals and personal losses, but his life was also a testament to brief victories, abundant literary achievement, and the forging of cherished bonds with family and friends. As envisioned in his beloved *Phaedo*, Manuel's life, too, was a mixture of joy and grief – though perhaps, the latter had been more dominant. A saying of Aphthonios, often quoted by Manuel, tells us that a life free from sorrows is indeed nowhere to be found: this maxim above all others is a fitting summary of Emperor Manuel's life.

Conclusion

Manuel II Palaiologos had a tumultuous but rich life. At the crossroads of Byzantine, Ottoman and Western medieval history, he witnessed many significant events and moments, and his path crossed with many celebrated historical figures. This biography sought to depict Manuel II Palaiologos as a multi-faceted ruler and author by tracing his life from childhood to his death and focusing on his person instead of the history of his reign. In order to achieve this goal, this book has explored Manuel's complete oeuvre for the first time, discussing some aspects of his literary style, his self-representation, his portrayal of characters and the various messages that he imbedded into his work. Through his writings and other sources, I have attempted to gain insight into Manuel's thoughts and feelings, as well as his reactions to events, the environment and the people around him. This book has attempted to portray Manuel as a personality by offering the reader glimpses of *him* as opposed to providing yet another narration of the events of his reign.

In his oeuvre, Manuel did not aim to represent his life as accurately as possible or to offer information to his audience about political events. Rather, the emperor's writings were moulded and polished carefully; they represent Manuel and the events in his life as he wished his audience to perceive them. Thus, one of the major themes of this study has been Manuel's self-representation and the autobiographical aspects of his works. From his youth onwards, the emperor sought to offer an idealized self-image to his audience: he promoted his political stance, advertised his rule, defended his deeds and offered apologies for his criticized policies. His self-representation and autobiographical digressions were meticulously fashioned to achieve these textual goals.

Especially after becoming the sole emperor, Manuel sought to enhance his political authority through his writings, where, significantly, the emperor always assumes the superior position. In his works he insists upon the loftiness and uniqueness of his status as emperor, never representing himself as a *primus inter pares* in either politics or scholarly collaboration. Manuel also attempted to assert himself not only as a political, but also as a theological and literary authority. Arguably, he wished to exert authority over all these spheres: political, religious and literary. By insisting upon employing these textual strategies and presenting himself as a multi-faceted ruler, Manuel sought to both conceal and bolster his feeble authority as emperor. Lacking in any concrete political and socio-economic power, he resorted to writing as a means of political expression. This makes him unique among the Palaiologan emperors. This insistence on his wide-ranging authority might have partially stemmed from his personality: Manuel indeed appears to have been a figure with multiple interests and talents.

The autobiographical aspects of the emperor's oeuvre also allow us a glimpse into his personality and life. Through an analysis of his works, we have traced his thoughts and feelings on significant events: the civil strife he witnessed, his humiliating experiences with the Ottomans, the deaths of beloved ones, his stance towards marriage, political and military defeats. Similarly, we have discussed his relationship with various family members, and with friends and foes. Likewise, his feelings towards his mother, his brother, his mentor Kydones and his nemesis Bayezid can be traced in the lines he penned. In this regard, this biography highlighted the importance of not exaggerating Kydones' influence on Manuel's person and reign. Moreover, a close reading of several of his letters, such as the *Discourse to Iagoup,* indicates that Manuel had little tolerance for criticism and was prone to flare-ups and polemic. The emperor's preferred pastimes, such as his scholarly occupations, hunting and horsemanship, can likewise be discerned in his writings, and are even reflected in the imagery and metaphors he employed.

Manuel II Palaiologos was a significant writer, not just because he was an emperor-author, but also because he was a gifted one. His writings can (and should) be used as historical sources through careful and nuanced analysis. However, they also deserve study not only on the grounds that their author was an emperor, but also for their own literary merit. Manuel has mostly been overshadowed by figures such as Demetrios Kydones or Manuel Chyrsoloras as an author of the fourteenth and fifteenth centuries. Yet more than being considered an emperor who merely happened to wield a pen, Manuel was a productive and versatile author who produced more than thirty-three surviving works; letters, orations, sermons, theological and ethico-political treatises, dialogues, poems, prayers, rhetorical exercises, a *kanon* and a *mirror.* He furthermore experimented with blending various genres, such as the blending of history and funeral oratory in the

Funeral Oration, poetry and theology in his *Verses Against an Atheist*, epistolography and Platonic dialogue in the *Discourse to Kabasilas*. It can be argued that, while many Palaiologan authors produced in multiple genres, Manuel's versatility, as well as the sheer volume of his output, surpasses that of his contemporaries.

This biography has advocated for Manuel's as an author of considerable literary merit. Across his oeuvre, one can trace a consistent interest in the literary aspects of writing, regardless of the genre or the goals of the work. He paid close attention to sound harmony, for instance, and even *On the Procession of the Holy Spirit* is adorned with lively and at times, amusing, imagery. Furthermore, the *Dialogue with a Persian*, as argued, can be understood as a rapprochement between the literary and the theological. In short, Manuel's imagery and metaphors are vivid, varied and quite distinctive. He does not merely follow the *topoi* but introduces his own touches. Manuel also embedded subtle political statements, philosophical digression and jokes into his metaphors, allusions and imagery. Through an analysis of his allusions, imagery, metaphors and self-representation, it is possible to read many layers of meaning into his work that might otherwise remain otherwise lost to the modern reader. It is a delight to peel off these multiple, intricate layers of meaning. Thus, a close reading of his works allows Manuel and his representation of the events to emerge as complex and engaging, enabling the reader to gain new insights. With regards to his language, Manuel's Attic Greek is elevated, but it very rarely becomes unnecessarily complicated so that the meaning is lost.

Manuel's self-representation and character portrayal deserve special attention for their complexity and nuance. His self-representation was always adapted to the genre and the context. He could be the 'innocent victim' in the *Discourse to Kabasilas*, the teacher in his ethico-political works, a Socrates-like figure in his dialogues and a penitent sinner in his liturgical and homiletic compositions. Yet in all contexts he never failed to underscore his imperial status and authority. His portrayal of others is equally noteworthy. Often, Manuel fleshed out the figures that graced his works, be it the Ottoman sultan, his mother Helena or his opponents. He seems to have employed an ethical framework to colour these depictions, especially relying on Aristotelian philosophy. The Ottomans in the *Dialogue with a Persian* are not represented as stereotypical 'barbarians', their depiction is complex and multi-layered. Arguably, on account of its lively dialogue, witty jokes, everyday life anecdotes and character depiction, *Dialogue with a Persian* can be considered both a literary and a theological work.

As Manuel II Palaiologos wrote many philosophical and theological works, he is a part of Byzantine philosophical and theological studies. Despite his association with figures such as Demetrios Kydones, Manuel Chrysoloras and even Plethon, however, Manuel did not display any interest in their theological or philosophical outlook. He, was even, to a degree, tolerant of their different stances. Remarkably, Manuel's extensive travels and contacts with Italian scholars did not influence his thought either. His own literary, philosophical and theological interests did not conform at all to those of humanist scholars, and the emperor remained a firm Orthodox throughout his life, even displaying Palamite tendencies. Overall, he exhibits remarkable theological erudition, steadfastly defending the traditional Orthodox study of theology and opposing syllogisms and the use of philosophy in theology. Moreover, he sought to differentiate clearly the boundaries between philosophy and theology. Defining philosophy as a branch concerned with the affairs of 'this world', Manuel confined his interests to ethical and political philosophy, and in this way sought to defend the Orthodox theological stance vis-à-vis the pro-Latins and Catholic converts. Albeit offering no novel interpretations, his fascination with Aristotelian ethics can be traced across his life. Ultimately, despite witnessing the early phases of the Italian Renaissance and the flourishing of Byzantine scholarship, as a thinker and a scholar, Manuel remained mostly bound by earlier conventions.

Manuel's life is also fascinating by virtue of his being one of the last rulers of Byzantium during times of political and socio-economic upheaval. This raises the question of whether or not Manuel might have 'saved' the Byzantine Empire and prevent its fall. This biography leans heavily towards the negative. Historical events and their outcomes are not solely determined by people but also by the circumstances in which they find themselves. During Manuel's reign, more often than not, it was not the emperor, but the circumstances that influenced the decisions and the outcomes.

By the 1350s, Byzantium was already too weak to challenge the growing Ottoman Empire on its own. Bereft of military and economic power, it required significant help from Western Europe. Like his father, John V, Manuel turned to Europe for help; however, European powers were usually too involved in their own problems to send concrete military or economic assistance, and furthermore, had no real incentive to help Byzantium. With regards to a church union, the emperor was cautious and remained firm in his Orthodox stance. One can hardly blame him for his lack of enthusiasm for a union with the Latin church: the bleak outcomes of the Council of Lyon, the Council of Florence and the conversion of John V, hint that a union concluded under Manuel was also unlikely to bring any benefit. Moreover, while the emperor wished to conclude a union on Orthodox terms, the papacy posed its own terms to the Byzantines. Such an outcome was likely to increase the tensions in the Byzantine society.

Similarly, as is abundantly reflected in his writings, Manuel faced difficulties as far as socio-economic realities were concerned. The fisc was all but empty, and the emperor was heavily in debt to the Venetians. The wealthy continuously oppressed the poor and looked out for their own interests, as can be seen in the grain black market they created during the blockade. The Morean *archontes* rebelled frequently, and in the 1380s the Thessalonians even opted for surrendering to the Ottomans. Manuel's weak authority prevented him from solving these social and economic problems definitively. For the majority of his reign, his authority was furthermore undermined by the existence of an alternative emperor in the person of John VII. The territorial gains of 1403 and the period of peace between 1403–10 were achieved only thanks to the defeat of Bayezid at the hands of Tamerlane.

A close reading of Manuel's own writings, official documents and the Venetian Senate deliberations offers insight into his governance. Although driven by the circumstances, the emperor fervently sought to overcome obstacles: he did not merely petition Venice for help, he strove to come up with offers that might interest them, and when the opportunity presented itself, he toured Europe in person to seek aid. Manuel's chief concern appears to have been the empire's finances. He resorted to every strategy to increase his feeble economic means, and all documents reflect this intense preoccupation with money and ways in which it might be obtained. The emperor's writings are likewise adorned with money related metaphors. Beginning with his despotate in the 1370s, one can trace patterns of taxation and confiscation across Manuel's reign; he always resorted to such strategies under dire circumstances. Considering that many problems, such as social strife, siege defences and the ultimate fall of the Hexamilion stemmed from a lack of resources, Manuel was astute in the importance he attributed to finances.

The emperor also appears to have been quite personally involved in many aspects of governing. He composed documents in his own hand, personally addressed monastic disputes and frequently travelled across his territories to handle matters in person. He meddled in the internal affairs of a monastery and sought to establish authority over the Church. While this was also necessitated by scaling back the bureaucracy, it also reveals a controlling streak in Manuel's character. Perhaps, as he wished to project the image of a multi-faceted ruler, he also desired to be directly involved in many aspects of governing.

Manuel was instrumental in several events and decisions of his reign, and he exercised some influence on the changes that impacted the region. The outcomes did not always conform to his intentions, however: it was his rule in Thessalonike, for instance that led to the city's capture by the Ottomans in 1387. He succeeded in recovering the city and some land from the Ottomans in 1403 only to lose them again later. He lent support to his brother Theodore's rule in the Morea and sanctioned the sale of Corinth to the Hospitallers. He quelled John VII's rebellion in 1390 and those of the Moreans in 1416. Along with Sigismund of Hungary, he took part in the formation of the ill-fated Crusade of Nikopolis. Manuel was an especially influential actor in the Ottoman civil war, playing one brother against the other, and though his support of Mehmed enabled the latter to unite the empire, the emperor successfully took advantage of the Ottoman interregnum to regain land and some of the empire's political prestige. On the cultural front, he supported many Byzantine scholars and championed Orthodoxy, as well as, to an extent, Palamism. After 1402, especially, he contributed greatly to the scholarly and literary life of Byzantium by organizing *theatra*, offering patronage, and corresponding and collaborating with many literati.

Despite Manuel's efforts to safeguard Byzantium, some of his actions did indeed cause harm to the empire. He certainly was not as 'irreproachable' as his writings suggest. For instance, his separatist rule in Thessalonike during the 1380s was an act of defiance and revenge towards his father John V, since Manuel established himself in Thessalonike for essentially personal reasons and for his own glory. While his persistent efforts to save the city from the Ottomans served the empire's interests, they also served his own ambitions. After all, should the city fall he too would lose everything. Although it probably served as no more than a pretext for the sultan, it was Manuel's disobedience to Bayezid that triggered the devastating blockade of Constantinople. Similarly, although the economic situation demanded it, Manuel's imposition of new taxes and confiscations often backfired. These policies only diminished the emperor's popularity and increased the plight of the poor citizens. Moreover, although Sphrantzes and Doukas place the blame for the so-called False Mustafa affair on John VIII, it must not be forgotten that Manuel was still the senior ruler at the time. Even if he was not the one to conceive the idea, the decision was still carried out with his consent. Finally, as both his writings and sources testify, Manuel sought to control the Church. In the process, he did not refrain from engaging in heated polemics. Indeed, his rule reveals a pattern of continuous episodes of conflict with ecclesiastics.

Almost 600 years after his death, Emperor Manuel II Palaiologos' life remains fascinating. It is a tale of intrigue, loss and turbulence; but it is also one of commitment, perseverance and creativity. Not only does Manuel deserve a place in Byzantine literary history as a talented author, his biography also offers a window into his world. As a ruler, he played a part in some of the crucial changes taking part in the fourteenth- and fifteenth-century Mediterranean. Ultimately, Manuel's influence did not really extend much beyond his own times, but throughout his lifetime he was a significant political and literary figure. Living in times of rapid socio-political change, and in the company of figures such as Demetrios Kydones, Bayezid I, Charles VI, Jean de Berry and the Italian humanists, he bore witness to the end of Byzantium, the rise of the Ottomans and the beginnings of the Italian Renaissance. It was in such a world that Manuel lived, ruled and wrote.

The Complete Oeuvre of Manuel II Palaiologos[1]

Letters (sixty-six surviving items)	late 1370s–1417
Discourse to the Thessalonians (Advisory Discourse to the Thessalonians when They were Besieged)	1383
Epistolary Discourse to Kabasilas	summer 1387
Panegyric to John V Palaiologos (Panegyric to his Father on the Occasion of his Recovery)	1390
Dialogue with a Persian	1392–9
Epistolary Discourse to Alexios Iagoup	1396
Dialogue on Marriage	c. 1396
Epistolary Discourse on Dreams to Andreas Asan	c. 1396–9 (?)
Verses to an Atheist	c. 1396 (?)
Anacreontic Verses to an Ignorant Person	c. 1396 or c. 1409 (?)
On the Procession of the Holy Spirit	c. 1400
On the Order in the Trinity	after the Procession
Ekphrasis on a Tapestry in the Louvre	1400–2
Ethopoiia on Tamerlane	c. 1402
Psalm on the Fall of Bayezid	c. 1402
Funeral Oration on his Brother Theodore	1407–16
Clarification on a Debate between Demetrios Chrysoloras and Antonio d'Ascoli	1409/10
Epistolary Discourse to Ivankos	1410
The Sermon on St Mary of Egypt	c. 1410
The Foundations of Imperial Conduct	c. 1410
Seven Ethico-Political Orations	1410–16
Supplicatory Kanon to the Virgin	1411
Sermon on the Dormition	c. 1416
Sermon on Oikonomia and the Providence of the Lord	1410–16?
Sermon on John the Baptist	1410–16?
Confession Addressed to his Spiritual Fathers, Monks David and Damian	c. 1416
Letter accompanying the Confession	c. 1416

[1] See the bibliography for the manuscripts and the editions of these works. These dates have been proposed by the editors of Manuel's oeuvre.

(*cont.*)

Morning Prayers	c. 1416
Another Short Morning Prayer	c. 1416
Verses of Compunction	1416–20?
Admonitions Leading to Brevity and Peace in Councils	?
Reply of Antenor to Odysseus	?
Declamation regarding a Drunken Man	?
Address as if from a Benevolent Ruler to his Loyal Subjects	?
Prayer for Those in Peril or Simply at Sea	?

APPENDIX 2

Τοῦ βασιλέως κυροῦ Μανουὴλ τοῦ
Παλαολόγου στίχοι Ἀνακρεόνατειοι πρός
τινα ἀμαθῆ καὶ πλεῖστα φληναφοῦντα.[1]

Ἀκριτόμυθε Θερσίτα,
Ὃς βοᾷς μὲν μάλιστα γε,
Σιωπᾷς δὲ ἥκιστα γε,
Πῶς σέ τις παύσῃ ληροῦντα,
Φλυαροῦντα, φληναφοῦντα,
Καὶ μὴ ῥάβδῳ σου συνθλάσῃ
Τὸ κρανίον εὖ ποιήσας;
Ἐὰν γάρ τίς σου τὴν γλῶσσαν
Πρόρριζον ἐξανασπάσῃ,
Ἀλλὰ σὺ καὶ ταύτῃ πλέον
Παρελθὼν διενοχλήσεις,

Καὶ φωναῖς ἀσήμοις αὖθις
Οὐκ ἀνέξεις· ὡς γλωττίζων
Ἕρδες κόρακας τὸ τάχος,
Οὐδὲ γὰρ ἀνέχομαι σου.

Anacreontic verses of Emperor *Kyr*
Manuel Palaiologos to an ignorant
person who excessively prattles.

O babbling Thersites,
you who shout above all,
yet are silent the least of all,
how could one stop you,
flaky, foolish and prattling?
And would he not do well
to crush your skull to pieces with a rod?
For even if one would tear away
your tongue utterly by its root,
even then, coming to us,
you would still make more nuisance with
    your tongue,
and from base blubbering,
you would not cease. Since in billing,
you surpass easily the crows,
I cannot endure you.

[1] *PG* 156, cols. 575–6.

Address as if from a Benevolent Ruler to his Loyal Subjects who are in the Prime of their Lives

Since I have always wished what is beneficial to you and have sought it by all means, I thought it necessary to briefly give you these counsels as if giving a gift. Since it is as if innate in humankind to strive to succeed in 'outer matters', one also should consider success in 'inner matters' useful – the former follows the latter. For if you are good man and wish to climb up to the top in public honours, in all things, pursue things in which you may be zealous with serious deeds. In all circumstances show yourself as not less ready than as faithful. So then, if you wish to obtain true happiness (*eudaimonia*), avoid slackness, easiness and sleeping lazily on soft beds. For a careless, laid back and feeble man can never do well. Instead, pursue the things which you know lift up many people from ill to bright fortunate. Despise wishing to eat in as a lazy man; know this to be the job of drones who can never do well and in contrast, that for bees, producing is a law of nature. Certainly, merely taking without producing befits those who always hold their hands at their sides. This habit is likely to belong to damaging and indolent people. Those who have strength of body, youth and health, are worthy of great accomplishments and drive away those things conducted by many people; these people prove themselves to be noble men on behalf of their *genos*, fatherland and their ruler. By doing so, my dearest subject, with the help of God, you will easily obtain what is sought after. And if you don't take something immediately, ask for it. Neither show anger (for it is mean-spirited), nor surrender to the flow of things (for it is feeble). Instead, hold on to your goal tightly, braced with good hopes, and most importantly, show yourself to be a true man by adding greater things to your former zeal and eagerness. Your affairs will be in accordance with reason when you are zealous and hold on tightly to the necessary things. Then, surely, having devoted yourself to these things, you will come to success through them, not least through God, who has in His will, the governing power in all things.[1]

[1] *PG* 156, cols. 562–4.

Another Morning Prayer

I give thanks to you, God and Father, along with your only-begotten Son and your all-holy Spirit, since you have tolerated and overlooked the magnitude of my manifold sins, you have deemed me worthy to behold the sunlight and my mind, darkened with passions, to be led away from sunlight your perception, the true and everlasting light. You have granted me to pour forth my supplication to you, to relate you my afflictions and desires to you, who announced that He is with us who are still speaking and to open to those who knock the door.

Grant me, o all-benevolent Lord, that I be without care in the future, having entrusted the tillers of my life to you, the good helmsman. May my soul be attached behind you, so that your right hand may receive me in return. Guide me in your path and I will journey in your truth. Teach me how I should lead myself in life, and those under me. Fix your righteous fear firmly in the heart of your servant. By this fear, direct me to gape at your love, or rather at you, the height of all desires, being love yourself. Deem me worthy to turn away from all evil and show me to be forth as the doer of your commandments through the intercession of your only-begotten Son and our Saviour, Jesus Christ. Amen.[1]

---

[1] *PG* 156, cols. 574–6.

Ethopoiia *on Tamerlane*

What words would the leader of the Persians and the Scythians say to the tyrant of the Turks, who spoke boastingly and arrogantly, and was unendurable because of his threats when his affairs were good yet became the opposite after his defeat.

It seems that, desired for long, to wage war is hostile in its nature since the very start. One who is moved by such a nature cannot restrain himself from trying to cause suffering at all times. And you, during the times when your affairs progressed according to your wishes, and when you were trying to oppose my affairs with impostures and insults (for they were not mightier than deeds), already, your brow was lifted high and your empty insolence did not cease. Least of all, even now you are hatefully stationed to us, in another manner. For wailing after your defeat (you had not discovered that that this life was full of reflux, nor had you expected, as the affairs clearly show, that your good fortune would change – indeed the affairs are accustomed to do so, it is neither unlikely nor impossible), you belittle my brave deeds. Indeed, you bite no less than before by further casting off your pride. I believed that I had won a bright reputation that would endure since I overcame an illustrious man, greatly accomplished in virtue. Yet you show this glory to be untrue by pouring shame over yourself and showing yourself to be a man easily provoked in the matters in which you cannot bear human misfortune. Therefore, your victories are assigned to fortune, not to virtue. And now, you fall upon and ravage my successes, turning the glory upside down, reversing my former opinion of you. If I did not overcome a noble man, then how I shall be perceived as noble through this glory? So, let the gold go away, let all the spoils and your great wealth, gathered from many places, go away since the glory I longed for is absent. This desire of glory had led me, in my old age, from the ends of the world onto you. And now, I see that my toils have been cheated.

Appendix 6

Τοῦ αὐτοῦ ἅτινα συντομίαν ἄγει καὶ εἰρήνην ἐν ταῖς βουλαῖς[1]

Μὴ ἀνακόπτειν ἀρξάμενον.

Μὴ μέμφεσθαι περὶ λέξιν.

Μὴ λέγειν τὰ παρ' ἄλλων λεχθέντα ἀλλὰ προστιθέναι ἢ ἀφαιρεῖν.

Μὴ λέγειν περὶ τῶν ἑπομένων πρὸ τοῦ τὴν καθόλου δόξαν στερχθῆναι.

Μὴ διαλέγεσθαι πρὸς πρόσωπον ἀλλὰ ἁπλῶς λέγειν τὰ δοκοῦντα.

Μὴ πολυπλασίαξειν τὸ κυρωθέν.

Μὴ λέγειν ἑτέραν βουλὴν πρὸ τοῦ τήν λαληθεῖσαν λαβεῖν τέλος.

Some advice by him (Manuel II Palaiologos) that lead to brevity and peace in councils

Do not interrupt one who has begun speaking.

Do not accuse someone for their words.

Do not repeat things already said by the others, but add or subtract from these words.

Do not speak about consequences before the heart of the actual matter has been agreed upon.

Do not engage in conversations, but rather state plainly what you think.

Do not repeat what has been confirmed.

Do not offer another piece of advice before the advice being offered at the moment is finished.

---

[1] Transcribed from Vat. Barb. gr. 219, ff. 90v. First edition in Leonte, *Rhetoric in Purple*, 163–164.

The Early Death of Three of Manuel's Children

In addition to his surviving sons, Manuel had another son named Constantine and two unnamed daughters, who all died young. These three children are mentioned by Sphrantzes and a *chrysobull* of Manuel dated to September 1405, confirming an earlier *argyrobull* issued by the Despot Theodore to commemorate the memories of these children. They died young and were buried in Monemvasia, in Helikobounon.[1]

In his narrative, Sphrantzes places these deaths in 1403–13. Manuel's *chrysobull* merely indicates that 1405 was *terminus ante quem*. So the window for these deaths may be taken as 1403–5. However, a close reading reveals that the relevant passage in Sphrantzes is not arranged chronologically, but thematically. It moreover has confusions that pertain to dating. Hence, his dating of the deaths to 1403–13 should not be taken at face value. As for *argyrobull* that had preceded *the chrysobull* of 1405, there is no indication that the two were issued in quick sequence. The *argyrobull* could have been issued years before Manuel's confirmatory *chrysobull*. Moreover, placing the deaths around 1405 would mean that Constantine, the elder son, and Constantine XI were probably alive at the same time. This would mean that there were simultaneously two sons of the same name, which is not likely. Finally, if the three children had died closer to 1405, or at any rate, after Manuel's return from Europe in 1403, it would mean that they were left behind in the Morea, while their siblings were taken to Constantinople with their parents. Instead, I would like to suggest the possibility that these children might have died when Manuel was away in Europe, between 1400–3.

Sphrantzes names the boy who died young as Constantine, the emperor's second son. He is not to be confused with the future Constantine

---

[1] Sphrantzes, 6–7, who also records the birth and death of another son Michael. See MM, V, 168–70 for the *chrysobull*. Barker, *Manuel II*, 475, merely points out that these might be Manuel's illegitimate children, without discussing their deaths. Schreiner, 'Untersuchungen', 290–3, does discuss these children. However, the author merely points out that they must have been dead before September 1405, the date of the *chrysobull*.

XI, who was Manuel's fourth surviving son. Thus, after John VIII, he was the second eldest and was older than Theodore II. In a letter dating to the mid-1390s, Manuel appointed Theodore Kaukadenos as a tutor to his two sons and a daughter.[2] This letter cannot be precisely dated, but its placement in the collection would date it to the mid- to late 1390s. In this regard, it should be pointed out that very few letters are out of sequence in the collection. The letters that are chronologically misplaced are either epistolary discourses or letters accompanying literary works that Manuel sent to the members of his circle. Thus, they are 'special' letters. There is no reason to date the letter to Kaukadenos to a much later period; it probably indeed belongs to the mid-1390s. While George Dennis proposes that the sons referred to in this letter should be John VIII and Theodore II, it is likely in light of Sphrantzes' narrative and the *agyrobull*, that they were John and Constantine, the first son by this name.

The relevant passage in Sphrantzes concerns the years 1403–13 and mentions the deaths of the three children towards the end of the section. However, the event might have been narrated at this point for reasons of thematic coherence, and not because the deaths indeed occurred in 1403–13. An attentive reading reveals that the passage in question is not strictly chronological, but instead is organized thematically. Many of the events mentioned are also not dated. The narration of the political events of 1403–13 is sandwiched between two episodes regarding imperial children. The first is the birth of Constantine XI in 1405 and the second (which is undated) is the death of the three children and the births of Manuel's subsequent children.[3] The middle part narrating the political events of 1403–13, *preceded* by Constantine XI's birth in 1405, is also not in a strict chronological order. After the narration of the events of 1411–13, Sphrantzes starts reporting the deaths of the children and the births of the others. He also mentions the birth of a certain Michael, who seems to have died shortly after his birth. However, as evinced by the *chrysobull* of Manuel, the death of the three children buried in Monemvasia occurred before September 1405 at the latest.

Sphrantzes also seems to have arranged these entries 'thematically'. The birth of Constantine in 1405 and the deaths/births of the children are narrated separately from the political events of 1403–13. Sphrantzes' account of the events starts with the birth of Constantine XI. Clearly, as the last emperor of Byzantium and Sphrantzes' much esteemed patron, the historian found his birth rather significant – both for the empire and for

[2] Letter 27. [3] Sphrantzes, 6–7.

himself. He chose to narrate this birth immediately after Manuel's return about two years earlier, even before the political events. It is noteworthy that he recorded the birth in a separate entry. He did not mix the birth with the political events of 1403–13 or the account of the other children. When narrating the deaths of the children after his account of political events, Sphrantzes blends their story with the birth and death of Michael in Constantinople, and the subsequent births of Demetrios and Thomas. In this regard, the deaths of two imperial girls and a second son (already with several brothers) were not of great significance neither for the empire nor for Sphrantzes. The same holds true for the birth of the two younger sons who never become emperors, and also for Michael. All these children appear together not necessarily because the events took place around the same time, but because they formed a group as the 'less significant' imperial children. The exclusion of Constantine XI from this group further supports this 'thematic' arrangement.

Sphrantzes does not narrate any events prior to Manuel's return (with the exception of Bayezid's defeat), so it is possible that he simply included these deaths in the section where he introduces the subsequent imperial children. Furthermore, Sphrantzes altogether skips the birth of Andronikos, the future despot of Thessalonike. This son was born during Manuel's absence. Thus, not only is Sphrantzes' chronology a bit confused, he is also not totally accurate. Overall, Sphrantzes' approximate placement of these children's deaths around 1403–13 need not be taken very literally. They may have very well died before 1403, when their father was away in Europe. It is only upon Manuel's return that Sphrantzes' chronicle starts, and he may have simply opted to report these deaths in his account of the 'lesser' imperial children.

The three children might have died far earlier than 1405. First of all, the exact time period between Theodore's undated *argyrobull* and Manuel's subsequent *chrysobull* in September 1405 is not known. There is no evidence that they were issued in quick sequence; Theodore's bull might have been issued much earlier than 1405. Moreover, Sphrantzes mentions that the future Constantine XI was born on 8 February 1405. Unless the first Constantine died in January or the first days of February 1405, this would mean that there would be two sons named Constantine simultaneously, which in unlikely. The first Constantine must have died before the birth of the younger Constantine. Either he indeed died only one month before the birth of Constantine XI or he died well before 1405. Finally, the illumination of the imperial family in the Pseudo-Dionysios manuscript depicts only John, Theodore and Andronikos. The illumination was produced between 1403–5; the absence of the first Constantine indicates that he was dead by then.

The fact that these children were buried in Monemvasia indicates that they also died there, and not in Constantinople. Sphrantzes' account confirms that they died in Monemvasia. As all three children seem to have died round the same time, it is highly probable that they fell victim to some sort epidemic illness. If the three children indeed died post-1403, it would mean they were in the Morea while their mother and other siblings were in Constantinople. Perhaps, as the second son, Constantine had been designated as the future despot of Morea (a position later taken by the next brother, the future Theodore II) and would be brought up by his uncle Theodore I. This would later be the case for Theodore II. However, why would the two girls also have been sent to the Morea? If these children died after 1403, it makes more sense that they should have been in Constantinople, with their parents.

The notion that these children died when Manuel was away in Europe, during the years 1400–3 is plausible. All of the imperial children had been left in Monemvasia with the empress during the emperor's absence during 1391–1403. Venetian Senate resolutions and other sources do not give the names or the numbers of the children. Doukas refers to only John VIII and Theodore II.[4] He is not aware of the existence of these children that died young. Doukas claims that all children had been born after Manuel's return from Europe and hence, he names John and Theodore as the only imperial children born at the time of Manuel's journey. However, Manuel's own Letter 27 clearly indicates otherwise – the first Constantine and at least one daughter were born in the 1390s. It is indeed logical that all of the imperial children were together in the Morea with their mother. Certainly, Constantine and his two sisters must have accompanied their mother and siblings to the Morea. It makes no sense that only John and the third son, Theodore, accompanied their mother, leaving the other children behind in Constantinople.

Had the three children died during the two months when their father was in the Morea while waiting for transport to Constantinople, their deaths would have been probably mentioned by at least some sources. Moreover, Manuel could have probably issued a *chrysobull* right there in the Morea, without the need for Theodore's *argyrobull*. However, if the children perished during their father's absence in 1400–3, this would explain why they died and were buried in Monemvasia, and not in Constantinople.

---

[4] Doukas, 56.

After his return from Europe in 1403, Manuel confirmed Theodore's *argyrobull* in 1405. What compelled Manuel to confirm the earlier act is unclear: an *agyrobull* from a despot did not necessarily need a *chrysobull* from the emperor to become valid or to have force. Manuel either desired to lend further authority to the previous document or to address a confusion/mismanagement regarding the commemorations. The *chryso-bull* states that it confirmed and gave force to the earlier *argyrobull*.

With regard to the deaths of his children, the portrayal of Manuel by the Western chroniclers is rather intriguing – he is said to have been dressed head-to-toe in white.[5] The late Byzantine ceremonial manual of Pseudo-Kodinos states that white clothes were the mourning apparel of the emperor, especially for close relatives. During Manuel's reign, as the evidence for mourning in white is lacking and the Western sources portray him as wearing white, it is thought that this practice was no longer extant.[6] However, a possibility exists that Manuel was truly wearing white to signify mourning if his three children had died in Monemvasia when he was away in Europe. The matter is complicated by the fact that his son John VIII is also later reported to be wearing white. However, John VIII is not reported as wearing head-to-toe white, but red and white.[7] Ultimately this theory concerning Manuel's white clothing cannot be conclusively proven, but it is a plausible one.

---

[5] *Chronique de Saint Denis*, III, 756–7 and Adam of Usk, 353–56, 6–7.
[6] Pseudo-Kodinos, 262–6 and 335.
[7] Pseudo-Kodinos, 355. For John VIII, see J. Gill, *The Council of Florence* (Cambridge, 1959), 183–4, where the author translates the Italian chronicle narrating the emperor's clothing.

Glossary

Archon (pl. archontes): term denoting a nobleman or magnate, also used for provincial governors and to denote the elite in general

Argyrobull: an imperial decree issued by a despot, named after the silver seal accompanying the document

Bailos: representative of the Venetian community in Constantinople

Basileia: empire

Basileus: emperor

Chrysobull: an imperial decree issued by the emperor, named after the golden seal accompanying the document

Despot: Byzantine imperial title, usually given to the sons of the emperor

Ekphrasis: a written description of a person, place, building, object or even the weather; an exercise in progymnasmata (see below)

Energeia: Greek term denoting God's energies; as a rhetorical term, it means vividness

Enkomion (pl. enkomia): panegyric, also an exercise in progymnasmata (see below)

Ethopoiia: characterization or a character study; an exercise in progymnasmata (see below)

Eudaimonia: Aristotelian concept of perfect flourishing and contentment that is achieved through virtue

Genos: race, nation, clan

Hegoumenos: abbot of a monastery

Hyperpyron (pl. hyperpyra): Byzantine coinage introduced in the 11th century, originally used to refer to gold coinage, the term is gradually also used for silver coins

Hypostasis (pl. hypostases): Greek term used to denote the three persons of the Trinity; Father, Son and the Holy Spirit

Indiction: a chronological system consisting of a fifteen-year cycle, used in Byzantine chronicles, histories and documents

Logos (pl. logoi): word, reason, logic, also used to denote any kind of text; in plural, broadly refers to textual and scholarly spheres

Mesazon (pl: mesazontes): chief minister, increasingly assumes more diplomatic functions

Oikeios (pl. oikeioi): court title, a familiar of the emperor

Oikoumene: Byzantine concept that denotes the 'civilized' world

Ousia: Greek term for God's essence

Paideia: education and cultural knowledge, especially in Greek language, rhetoric and literature

Palamism: a theological system based on the teachings of Gregory Palamas (1296–1359), its central tenet is a distinction between God's essence and energies. Palamism proposes that while God's essence is wholly unknowable, man can know God through his energies; through participating in God's energies, man can reach a mystical union with God.

Patris: fatherland

Podesta: the governor of the Genoese colony in Pera

Polis: city, often used to refer to Constantinople when used with the definite article

Progymnasmata: set of rhetorical exercises, frequently studied during secondary education

Pronoia: system of granting state income to individuals and institutions, such as income from land, tax collection or water and fishing rights

Prostagma (pl. prostagmata): a document issued by the imperial chancery, concerning administrative issues, grants and privileges

Relic: body remnants or objects associated with a saint

Schema: original meaning scheme, plan or device, also means rank

Syllogism: deductive reasoning, a logical argument the conclusion of which is supported by two premises; e. g. all humans are mortal; Socrates is human, therefore Socrates is mortal.

Taxis: Byzantine concept of a harmonious and natural hierarchical order in all spheres (e. g. society, the Church, foreign peoples or entities)

Theatron (pl. theatra): a literary gathering where works are performed and evaluated

Theios: uncle, either by birth or through marriage

Topos (pl. topoi): commonplace idea, expression or literary usage

Bibliography

Manuscripts

Par. gr. 3041
Vat. Barb. gr. 74
Vat. Barb. gr. 219
Vat. gr. 1619

I. Primary Sources

i. The Writings of Manuel II Palaiologos

Address as if by a Benevolent Ruler to his Subjects, *PG* 156, cols. 562–4.

Admonitions Leading to Brevity and Peace in Councils, Vat. Barb. gr. 219, f 90v; transcription and translation in Appendix 6.

Advisory Discourse to the Thessalonians when They Were Besieged, ed. B. Laourdas, 'Ὁ συμβουλετικὸς πρὸς τοὺς Θεσσαλονίκεῖς τοῦ Μανουὴλ Παλαιολόγου', *Μακεδονικά* 3 (1955), 290–307.

Anacreontic Verses to an Ignorant Person, *PG* 156, cols. 575–6.

Another Morning Prayer, *PG* 156, cols. 574–6.

Clarification of a Debate between Demetrios Chrysoloras and Antionio d'Ascoli, ed. F. Tinnefeld, 'Es wäre gut für jenen Menschen, wenn er nicht geboren wäre: Eine Disputation am Hof Kaiser Manuels II. über ein Jesuswort vom Verräter Judas. Einleitung, kritische Erstedition und Übersetzung (I)', in *Ἀνδριάς. Herbert Hunger zum 80. Geburtstag, JÖB* 44 (1994), 421–30; F. Tinnefeld, 'Es wäre gut für jenen Menschen, wenn er nicht geboren wäre: Eine Disputation am Hof Kaiser Manuels II. über ein Jesuswort vom Verräter Judas. Einleitung, kritische Erstedition und Übersetzung (II)', *JÖB* 45 (1995), 115–58.

Confession addressed to his Spiritual Fathers on the Occasion of His Recovery from a Serious Illness, ed. S. D. Lamprou, *Μανουὴλ Β΄ Παλαιολόγου Πρὸς τὸν ἑαυτοῦ πνευματικόν. Εἰσαγωγή – Ἔκδοση* (Thessalonike, 2018).

Declamation regarding a Drunken Man, ed. J. Boissonade, *Anecdota Graeca* II, (Paris, 1844; repr. Hildesheim, 1962), 274–307.

Dialoge mit einem Muslim, 3 vols, ed. and trans. K. Förstel (Würzburg, 1995).

Dialoge mit einem Perser, ed. E. Trapp (Vienna, 1966).

Dialogue with the Empress Mother on Marriage, ed. and trans. A. Angelou (Vienna, 1991).

Dialogum de Matrimonio, ed. C. Bevegni (Catania, 1989).

Ekphrasis on a Tapestry in the Louvre, ed. and trans. J. Davis, 'Manuel II Palaeologus' A Depiction of Spring in a Dyed, Woven Hanging', in *Porphyrogenita: Essays on the History and Literature of Byzantium and the Latin East in Honour of Julian Chrysostomides*, in Ch. Dendrinos et al. (eds.) (Aldershot, 2003), 411–21.

Entretiens avec un Musulman, 7e controverse, ed. and trans. Th. Khoury (Paris, 1966).

Epistolary Discourse to Alexios Iagoup, ed. Ch. Dendrinos. *An Annotated Critical Edition* (editio princeps) *of Emperor Manuel II Palaeologus' treatise On the Procession of the Holy Spirit* (PhD dissertation, Royal Holloway and Bedford New College, University of London, 1996), 326–73.

Epistolary Discourse on Dreams to Andreas Asan, ed. J. Boissonade, *Anecdota Nova*, 11 (Paris, 1844), 239–50.

Ethopoiia on Tamerlane, ed. E. Legrand, *Lettres de l'empereur Manuel Paléologue*, (Amsterdam, 1962), 103–4.

Foundations of Imperial Conduct, *PG* 156, cols. 313–84; ed. S. Nicolae, *Manuel Paleologul, Sfaturi pentru educaţia împărătească*, Academia Romaniae, Institutum Studiorum Europae Meridionalis-Orientalis, Scriptores Byzantini x (Bucharest, 2015), 62–162.

Funeral Oration to His Brother Theodore, ed. and trans. J. Chrysostomides (Thessalonike, 1985).

Kaiser Manuel II Palaiologos: Dialog über den Islam und Erziehungsratschläge, trans. W. Baum and R. Senoner (Vienna, 2003).

Lettres de l'empereur Manuel Paléologue, ed. E. Legrand (Amsterdam, 1962).

The Letters of Manuel II Palaeologus, ed. and trans. G. T. Dennis (Washington DC, 1977).

Letter to his Spiritual Fathers David and Damian, ed. Ch. Dendrinos. 'Emperor Manuel II Palaeologus' Unpublished Letter to his Spiritual Fathers David and Damianos, *Bibliophilos: Books and Learning in the Byzantine World*, eds. Ch. Dendrinos and I. Giarenis, Byzantinisches Archiv (in press).

Morning Prayers, PG 156, cols. 564–74.

On the Order in the Trinity, ed. Ch. Dendrinos. *An Annotated Critical Edition* (editio princeps) *of Emperor Manuel II Palaeologus' treatise On the Procession of the Holy Spirit* (PhD thesis, Royal Holloway and Bedford New College, University of London, 1996), 318–25.

On the Procession of the Holy Spirit, ed. Ch. Dendrinos. *An Annotated Critical Edition* (editio princeps) *of Emperor Manuel II Palaeologus' Treatise On the Procession of the Holy Spirit* (PhD thesis, Royal Holloway and Bedford New College, University of London, 1996), 1–317.

Panegyric to John V Palaiologos, ed. J. Boissonade, *Anecdota Graeca, 11* (Paris, 1844; repr. Hildesheim, 1962), 223–45.

Prayer for those in Peril or Simply at Sea, Par. gr. 3041 f 127 v; Vat. Barb. gr. 219, ff 91 v-92.

Psalm on the Fall of Bayezid' ed. E. Legrand. *Lettres de l'empereur Manuel Paléologue*, (Paris 1893; Amsterdam, 1962), 104.

Reply of Antenor to Odysseus, ed. J. Boissonade, *Anecdota Graeca*, II (Paris, 1844; repr. Hildesheim, 1962), 308–9.

Sermon on the Dormition, ed. M. Jugie. *Homelies Mariales Byzantines, Patrologia Orientalis*, 16, cols. 119–42.

Sermon on Oikonomia and the Providence of the Lord, ed. S. Lamprou, "Περὶ τῆς οἰκονομίας καὶ προνοίας τοῦ Κυρίου ἀνέκδοτος λόγος τοῦ αὐτοκράτορος Μανουὴλ Β' Παλαιολόγου," *Θεοδρομία* 4 (2014): 488–30.

Sermon on John the Baptist, ed. C. Billò, 'La laudatio in S. Iohannem Baptistam di Manuele II Paleologo', *Medioevo Greco*, 2 (2002), 49–63.

Sermon on St Mary of Egypt, Vat. gr. 1619 f 15–29v; Vat. gr. 632 f 336–50v.

Seven Ethico-Political Orations, ed. C. Kakkoura, *An Annotated Critical Edition of Emperor Manuel II Palaeologus' "Seven Ethico-political Orations"* (PhD thesis, Royal Holloway, The University of London, Royal Holloway, 2013).

Supplicatory Kanon to the Virgin, ed. E. Legrand. *Lettres de l'empereur Manuel Paléologue*, (Paris 1893; repr. Amsterdam, 1962), 94–102.

Verses Against an Atheist, ed. I. Vassis, 'Οἱ ανέκδοτοι στίχοι προς άθεον άνδρα του Μανουὴλ Β' Παλαιολόγου', *Βυζαντινά* 32 (2012) 37–100.

Verses on Compunction, *PG* 156, cols. 575–6.

ii. Byzantine literati

Agapetos the Deacon. *Der Fürstenspiegel für Kaiser Iustinianos*, ed. R. Riedinger (Würzburg, 1994).

Anonymous Narrative of Siege of Constantinople, ed P. Gautier, 'Un récit inédit du siège de Constantinople par les turcs (1394–1402)', *REB* 23 (1965), 100–17.

Anonymous Oration, ed. Ch. Dendrinos, 'An Unpublished Funeral Oration on Manuel II Palaeologus († 1425)', in *Porphyrogenita: Essays on the History and Literature of Byzantium and the Latin East in Honour of Julian Chrysostomides*, Ch. Dendrinos et al. (eds) (Aldershot, 2003), 423–57.

Anonymous Panegyric, ed. I. Polemis, 'Two Praises of the Emperor Manuel II Palaiologos: Problems of Authorship', *BZ* 103 (2010), 699–714.

'Anonymous Verses to Manuel and Helena Palaiologos', ed. S. P. Lampros, *ΠΠ*, III, 281–3.

Argyropoulos, John. 'La comédie de Katablattas. Invective byzantine du XVe siècle', eds. P. Canivet and N. Oikonomides, *Δίπτυχα* 3 (1982–83), 5–97.

Bessarion. 'Monody on Manuel Palaiologos', ed. S. P. Lampros, *ΠΠ*, III, 284–90.

Blemmydes, Nikephoros. *Des Nikephoros Blemmydes βασιλικὸς Ἀνδριὰς und dessen Metaphrase von Georgios Galesiotes und Georgios Oinaiotes*, eds. H. Hunger and I. Ševčenko (Vienna, 1986).

Bryennios, Joseph. Ἰωσὴφ τοῦ Βρυεννίου μετά τινος Ἰσμαηλίτου Διάλεξις', ed.
A. Argyriou, *EEBΣ* 35 (1966–1967), 141–95.

Testament, ed. A. Papadopoulos- Kerameus, *Varia Graeca Sacra* (Leipzig, 1975),
131–2.

Ἰωσὴφ Μοναχοῦ τοῦ Βρυεννίου τὰ Εὑρεθέντα, 2 vols, ed. E. Voulgares (Leipzig
1768, Thessalonike, 1991).

Chrysoloras, Demetrios. *Demetrios Chrisolora, Cento Epistole a Manuele II
Palaeologo*, ed. F. Bizzaro (Naples, 1984).

*An Annotated Critical Edition of Demetrios Chrysoloras' Dialogue on Demetrios
Kydones' Antirrhetic Against Neilos Kabasilas*, ed. V. Pasiourtides (PhD thesis,
Royal Holloway, University of London, 2013).

'Action de grâces pour l'anniversaire de la bataille d'Ankara (28 juillet 1403)', ed.
P. Gautier, *REB* 19 (1961), 340–57.

'*Synkrisis* of the Emperor of Today and Ancient Emperors', ed. S. Lampros, *ΠΠ*,
III, 222–45.

Chrysoloras, Manuel. Τοῦ Χρυσωλορᾶ Σύγκρισις Παλαιᾶς καὶ Νέας Ῥώμης', ed.
C. Billò, *Medioevo Greco* 0 (2000), 1–26.

*Manuel Chrysoloras and his Discourse Addressed to the Emperor Manuel II
Palaeologus*, eds. C. G. Patrinelis and D. Z. Sophianos (Athens, 2001).

Chortasmenos, John. *Johannes Chortasmenos ca. 1370- ca 1436/37. Briefe, Gedichte
und kleine Schriften. Einleitung, Regesten, Prosopographie, Text*, ed. H. Hunger
(Vienna, 1969).

Εἱρμολόγιον, ed. S. Eustratiades (Chennevières sur Marne, 1932).

Glabas, Isidore. Ἰσιδώρου Ἀρχιεπισκόπου Θεσσαλονίκης Ὁμιλίαι εἰς τὰς Ἑορτὰς
τοῦ Ἁγίου Δημητρίου, ed. B. Laourdas (Thessalonike, 1954).

Ἰσιδώρου Γλαβᾶ Ἀρχιεπισκόπου Θεσσαλονίκης Ὁμιλίες, 2 vols, ed.
B. Ch. Christophorides (Thessalonike, 1992–1996).

'Ἰσιδώρου μητροπολίτου Θεσσαλονίκης, ὀκτὼ ἐπιστολαὶ ἀνέκδοτοι', ed.
S. Lampros, *Νέος Ἑλληνομνήμων* 9 (1912), 343–414.

Συμβολὴ εἰς τὴν ἱστορίαν τῆς Θεσσαλονίκης. Δύο ἀνέκδοτοι ὁμιλίαι Ἰσιδώρου
ἀρχιεπισκόπου Θεσσαλονίκης', ed. C. N. Tsirpanlis, *Θεολογία* 42 (1971),
548–81.

Gregoras, Nikephoros. 'Nikephoros Gregoras, Dankrede an die Mutter Gottes', in
Texts and Studies in Neoplatonism and Byzantine Literature, ed.
L. G. Westerink, (Amsterdam, 1980), 229–41.

Isidore of Kiev. 'Panegyric for Manuel and John VIII Palaeologos', ed. S.
P. Lampros, *ΠΠ*, III, 132–99.

'Letter 8, addressed to Manuel II Palaiologos', ed. W. Regel. *Analecta byzantino-
russica* (Saint Petersburg, 1891), 66–9.

John Climacus. *Scala Paradisi*, PG 88, cols. 631–1161.

John of Damascus. *Dialectae sive capita philosophica*, ed. B. Kotter. *Die Schriften
des Iohannes von Damaskos*, I (Berlin, 1969).

Kabasilas, Nicholas. 'Nicolas Cabasilas' panegyrics inédits de Matthieu
Cantacuzene et d'Anne Paléologine', ed. M. Jugie, *Izvetija Russkago
Archeologiceskago Instituta v Konstantinopole, xv*, (1911), 112–21.

Kalekas, Manuel. *Correspondance de Manuel Calécas*, ed. R. J. Loenertz (Vatican, 1950).

Kananos, John. *Ioannis Canani De Constantinopolitana Obsidone Relatio. A Critical Edition, with English Translation, Introduction and Notes of John Kananos' Account of the Siege of Constantinople in 1422* ed. and trans A. M. Cuomo (Leiden and Berlin, 2016).

Kantakouzenos, John. *Four Apologies and Four Orations Against Isla*m, PG 154, cols. 371–692.

Ioahannis Cantacouzeni refutationes duae Prochori Cydonii et Disputatio cum Paulo Patriarcha Latino epistulis septem tradita. eds. E. Voordeckers and F. Tinnefeld. (Brepols, 1987).

Kydones, Demetrios. *Démétrius Cydonès Correspondance*, 2 vols, ed. R. J. Loenertz (Rome, Vatican City, 1951–1960).

'Oratio pro Subsidio Latinorum', *PG* 154, cols. 961–1008.

'Oratio ad Iohannem Palaeologum', ed. R. J. Loenertz, *Démétrius Cydonès, Correspondance*, I (Vatican City, 1956), 10–23.

'The Monody of Demetrios Kydones on the Zealot Rising of 1345 in Thessaloniki', ed. and trans. J. W. Barker, in Μελετήματα στὴ Μνήμη Βασιλείου Λαούρδα (Thessalonike, 1975), 285–90.

Magistros, Thomas. *Magistros. La Regalità.* ed. P. Volpe Cacciatore (Naples, 1992).

Makarios of Ankyra. *Treatise Against the Errors of the Latins*, ed. C. Triantafyllopoulos, *An Annotated Critical Edition of the Treatise Against the Errors of the Latins by Makarios, Metropolitan of Ankyra (1397–1405)*, 2 vols (PhD thesis, Royal Holloway, University of London, 2009).

Makarios Makres. *Macaire Makres et la polémique contre l'Islam*, ed. A. Argyriou (Vatican City, 1986).

Μακαρίου τοῦ Μακρῆ Συγγράμματα, ed. A. Argyriou (Thessalonike, 1996).

'Monody on Manuel Palaiologos', ed. A. Sideras. *Unedierte byzantinische Grabreden* (Thessalonike, 1985), 301–7.

An Annotated Critical Edition of Makarios Makres' Life of St Maximos Kausokalyves, Encomion of the Fathers of the Seven Ecumenical Councils, Consolation to a Sick Person, or Reflections for Endurance, Verses on the Emperor Manuel II Palaiologos, Letter to Hieromonk Symeon, A Supplication on Barren Olive Trees, ed. S. Kapetanaki (PhD thesis, University of London, 2001).

Maximos Confessor. Περὶ Θεολογίας καὶ τῆς Ἐνσάρκου Οἰκονομίας Υἱοῦ τοῦ Θεοῦ, *PG* 90, 1083–176.

Mazaris. *Journey to Hades: Or Interviews with Dead Men About Certain Officials of the Imperial Court*, ed. and trans. J. N. Barry et al. (Buffalo, NY, 1975).

Metochites, Theodore. *Theodore Metochites' Poems to 'Himself': Introduction, Text and Translation*, ed. and trans. M. Featherstone (Vienna, 2000).

Theodore Metochites on Ancient Authors and Philosophers. Semeioseis gnomikai 1–16 & 71, ed., trans. and notes K. Hult (Gothenborg, 2002).

Palamas, Greogory. 'La captivité de Palamas chez les Turcs, dossier et commentaire', ed. A. Philippides-Braat, *TM* 7 (1979), 109–221.

The One Hundred and Fifty Chapters, ed. and trans. R. E. Sinkewicz (Toronto, 1988).

The Triads, ed. with an introduction J. Meyendorff, trans. N. Gendle (New Jersey, 1983).

Paul of Nicea. *Paolo di Nicea, Manuele Medico*, ed. A. M. Ieraci Bio (Naples, 1996).

Pseudo-Basil. *Studien zu den griechishen Fürstenspiegeln*, III, ed. K. Emminger (Munich, 1906–1913), 50–71.

Pseudo-Kodinos. *Traité des offices*. ed. and trans. J. Verpaux (Paris, 1966).

Pseudo-Kodinos and the Constantinopolitan Court: Offices and Ceremonies, ed. and trans. R. J. Macrides, J. A. Munitiz and D. G. Angelov (Ashgate, 2013).

Plethon, Gemistos. 'Monody on Helena Palaiologina', ed. S. P. Lampros, *ΠΠ*, III, 266–80.

'Address to Manuel Palaiologos on the Affairs of the Peloponesse', ed. S. P. Lampros, *ΠΠ*, III, 246–65.

'Address to Manuel Palaiologos', ed. S. P. Lampros, *ΠΠ*, III, 309–312.

Potamios, Theodore. 'The Letters of Theodore Potamios' ed. and trans. G. T. Dennis, in *Byzantium and the Franks, 1350–1420*, ed. G. T. Dennis (London, 1982), 1–40.

Scholarios, Gennadios. 'Consolatory Oration to the Emperor Constantine on the Death of his Mother', in *Georgios Scholarios. Oeuvres complètes*, eds. L. Petit, A. Siderides and M. Jugie, vol. I, (Paris, 1928), 262–70.

Symeon of Thessalonike. *Τὸ Λειτουργικὸν Ἔργον Συμεὼν τοῦ Θεσσαλονίκης*. ed. I. Phountoules (Thessalonike, 1966).

Τὰ Λειτουργικὰ Γράμματα. ed. I. Phountoules (Thessalonike, 1968).

Politico-Historical Works of Symeon Archbishop of Thessalonica (1416/17 to 1429), ed. D. Balfour (Vienna, 1979).

De Sacro Templo, PG 155, cols. 305–60.

De Ordinatibus, PG 155, cols. 361–468.

Syropoulos, Sylvester. *Mémoires*, ed. and trans. V. Laurent (Rome, 1971).

iii. Byzantine Histories and Chronicles

Chalkokondyles, Laonikos. *The Histories*, ed. and trans A. Kaldellis (Cambridge MA and London, 2014).

Chronicle of Epiros, ed S. Cirac Estopañan. *Bizancio y España. El Legato de la Basilissa Maria y de los Déspotas Thomas y Esaú de Joannina* (Barcelona, 1943).

Chronicle of Kephalonia, ed. G. Schirò. 'Manuel II Paleologo incorona Carlo Tocco despota di Gianina', *Byzantion* 29/30 (1959/60), 209–30.

Doukas. *Historia Byzantina*, ed. V. Grecu (Bucharest, 1958).

Decline and Fall of Byzantium to the Ottoman Turks. An Annotated Translation of "Historia Turca-Byzantina, trans. H. J. Magulias (Detroit, 1975).

Ecthesis Chronica and Chronicon Athenarum, ed. S. P. Lampros (London, 1902).

Byzantine Historia, ed. L. Schopen, 3 vols (Bonn, 1853).

Kantakouzenos, John. *Historiarum Libri IV*, ed. L. Schopen, 3 vols. (Bonn, 1828–1832).

The History of John Kantakouzenos, Book 1. Edition, Translation and Commentary, ed. and trans. R. H. Trone (PhD thesis, The Catholic University of America, 1979).

An Annotated Translation of Emperor John VI Kantakouzenos, History, Book III, ed. and trans. B. McLaughlin (PhD thesis, Royal Holloway, University of London, 2018).

Makhairas, Leontios. *Leontios Makhairas. Recital Concerning the Sweet Land of Cyprus Entitled 'Chronicle'.* ed. R. M. Dawkins, (Oxford, 1932), 2 vols.

Mioni, E. 'Una inedita cronaca bizantina dal Mar. gr. 595', *Rivista di Studi Bizantini e Slavici* 3 (1981), 71–88.

Panaretos, Michael. Μιχαὴλ τοῦ Παναρέτου Περὶ τῶν Μεγάλων Κομνηνῶν, ed. O. Lampsides (Athens, 1958).

Schreiner, P. *Die Byzantinische Kleinchroniken*, 3 vols (Vienna, 1975).

Sphrantzes, Georgios. *Cronaca*, ed. and trans. R. Maisano (Rome, 1990).

iv. Western and Slavic Sources

Adam of Usk. *The Chronicle of Adam Usk, 1377–1421*, ed. C. Given-Wilson. (Oxford, 1997).

Annales Mediolanenses, ed. L. A. Muratori, *RIS* 16 (Milan, 1730).

Bertrandon de la Brocquière. *Le voyage d'outremer*, ed. C. H. A. Schefer (Paris, 1892).

Bulgarian Chronicle, ed. J. Bogdan, 'Ein Beitrag zur bulgarischen und serbischen Geschichtsschreibung', *Archiv für slavische Philologie* 13 (1891), 481–543.

Caresini, Rafaino. *Chronica AA. 1343–1388*, ed. E. Pastorello, *RIS* 12/2 (Bologna, 1923).

Caroldo, 'Studies on the Chronicle of Caroldo, with special reference to the history of Byzantium from 1370 to 1377', ed. J. Chrysostomides, *OCP* 35 (1969), 123–82, re-printed in J. Chrysostomides, *Byzantium and Venice 1204–1453*, eds M. Heslop and C. Dendrinos (Farnham, 2011), Study II.

Chinazzo, Danielo. *Cronoca della Guerra di Chioggia*, ed. L. A. Mutatori (Milan, 1864).

Clavijo, Ruy González de, *Embassy to Tamerlane*, trans. Guy Le Strange (London, 1928).

Cyriac of Ancona, *Later Travels*, ed. and trans. E. W. Bodnar (Cambridge MA, 2003).

de Mézières, Philippe, *The Life of Saint Peter Thomas*, ed. J. Smet (Rome, 1954).

Eulogium (Historiarum sive Temporis): Chronicon ab orbe condito usque ad annum Domini M.CCC.LXVI, a monacho quondam Malmesburiensi exaratum. ed. F. S. Haydon, London, 1863), III, Continuatio Eulogii.

Gataro, Andrea. *Historia Padovana 1311–1506*, ed. L. A. Muratori, *RIS* 17 (Milan, 1730).

Ghillebert de Lannoy. *Oeuvres de Ghillebert de Lannoy, voyageur, diplomate et moraliste*, ed. Ch. Potvin (Louvain, 1878).

Guarino of Verona. *Epistolario di Guarino Veronese*, vol 1, ed. R. Sabadini, (Turin, 1959).

Ignatius of Smolensk. *The Journey to Constantinople*, ed. and trans. G. P. Majeska, *Russian Travelers to Constantinople in the Fourteenth and Fifteenth Centuries* (Washington DC, 1984), 76–113.

Inventoires de Jean duc de Berry (1401–1416), 2 vols, trans. and annotated J. Guiffrey (Paris, 1894).

Jean Juvenal des Ursins. *Histoire de Charles VI*, ed. J. F. Michaud and J. J. F. Poujoulat, *Nouvelle collection dés mémoires pour servir à l'histoire de France*, vol. 2 (Paris, 1836).

Konstantin the Philosopher, ed. and trans. M. Braun, *Lebensbeschreibung des Despoten Stefan Lazarevics* (The Hague, 1956).

Le livre des faits du bon messire Jehan Le Maingre, dit Bociquaut, Mareschal de France et gouverneur de Jennes, ed. D. Lalande. (Geneva, 1985).

Pintoin, Michel. *Chronique du Religieux de Saint-Denis concernant le Regne de Charles VI de 1380 à 1422*, ed. and trans. L. Bellaguet, in *Collection de documents inédits sur l'histoire de France*, vol. 2 (Paris, 1840).

Sanudo, Marino. *Vita dei Duchi (1423–1474)*, ed. A. Caraccioio Ardco (Venice, 1999), vol. 1.

Schiltberger, Johannes. *The Bondage and Travels of Johann Schiltberger, 1396–1427* ed. and trans. J. B. Telfer (London, 1879).

Stella, Giorgio. *Annales Genuenses*, ed. G. Petti Balbi (Bologna, 1975).

Tafur, Pero. *Travels and Advantures, 1435–1439*, trans. M. Letts (London, 1926).

The London Chronicles, ed. M. R. McLaren. *The London Chronicles of the Fifteenth Century: A Revolution in English Writing* (Cambridge, 2002).

Tuetey, A. *Journal de Nicolas de Baye, greffier du parlement de Paris, 1400–1417*, vol. I (Paris, 1885).

Walsingham, Thomas. *Historia Anglicana*, II, ed. H. T. Riley (London, 1864).

Vita Ricardi Secundi, ed. G.B. Stow (Philadelphia, 1977).

Zeno, Iacobo. *Vita Caroli Zeni*, ed. N. Zanichelli (Bologna, 1940).

v. *Classical and Hellenistic Greek Authors*

Aeschylus. *Persians; Seven against Thebes; Suppliants; Prometheus Bound*, trans. A. H. Sommerstein (Cambridge, 2009).

Aphthonios. *Progymnasmata*, ed. H. Rabe (Leipzig, 1926).

Aristophanes. *Frogs; Assemblywomen, Wealth*, ed. and trans J. Henderson, (Cambridge, 2002).

Aristotle. *Nicomachean Ethics*, trans. H. Rackham (Cambridge, 1934).

Demosthenes. *Phillipics; Olynthiacs; Minor Orations 1–17 and 20*, trans. C. A. Vince and H. J. Vince (Cambridge, 1930).

Hermogenes. *Opera*, ed. H. Rabe (Leipzig, 1913; reprinted 1969).

Homer. *Iliad*, trans. A. T. Murray, 2 vols (London, 1999).

Libanios. *Declamationes I- XII*, vol. v, ed. R. Foerster (Leipzig, 1909).

Plato. *Euthyphro; Apology; Crito; Phaedo; Phaedrus*, trans. H. N. Fowler (Cambridge, 1914).

vi.   Ottoman and Other Oriental Sources

Anonymous. *Tevârîh-i Âl-i Osman*, ed. F. Giese, re-ed. N. Azamat (Istanbul, 1992).

Aşıkpaşazade. *Âşıkpaşazâde Tarihi (1285–1502)*, ed. N. Öztürk (Istanbul, 2013).

Gazavât-ı Sultan Murad b. Mehemmed Han: İzladi ve Varna Savaşları (1443–1444) Üzerinde Anonim Gazavâtname, eds. H. İnalcık and M. Oğuz (Ankara, 1989).

Ibn Arabshah. *Timur the Great Amir*, trans. J. H. Sanders (London, 1936).

Ibn Battuta. *The Travels of Ibn Battuta: A.D 1325–1354*, 2 vols, eds. and trans. C. Defremery and B. R. Sanguinetti (Cambridge, 1962).

Neşrî. *Kitâb-ı Cihan-nümâ*, 2 vols, eds. F. R. Unat and M. A. Köymen (Ankara, 1949–1957).

Ruhî Tarihi, ed. H. E. Cengiz and Y. Yücel, *Belgeler* 14–18 (1989–1992), 359–472.

The Tales of Sultan Mehmed, Son of Bayezid Han, annotated English translation, Turkish edition and facsimiles of the relevant folia of Bodleian Marsh 313 and Neşri Codex Menzel, ed. and trans D. Kastritsis (Cambridge MA, 2007).

vii.   Document Collections and Diplomatic Editions

Actes de Dionysiou, ed. N. Oikonomides (Paris, 1968).

Actes de Docheiariou, ed. N. Oikonomides Paris, 1984).

Actes de Lavra, III, De 1329 à 1500. eds. A. Guillou, P. Lemerle, D. Papachryssanthou, and N. Svoronos (Paris, 1979).

Actes de Saint-Pantéléèmôn, ed. V. Kravari (Paris, 1982).

Actes de Prôtaton, ed. D. Papachryssanthou (Paris, 1975).

Actes du Pantocrator, ed. V. Kravari (Paris, 1991).

Baronius, C. and Raynaldus, O. *Annales Ecclesiastici*, vols. 25–27 (Bar-le-Duc, 1872–1880).

Belgrano, L. T. 'Studi e documenti sulla Colonia Genovese di Pera (Prima serie),' *Atti della Società Ligure di Storia Patria* 13, 2 (1877), 97–317.

Chrysostomides, J. *Monumenta Peloponnesiaca: Documents for the Study of the Peloponnese in the 14th and 15th Centuries* (Camberley, 1995).

Darrouzes, J. *Les régestes des actes du patriarchat de Constantinople*, 1/6 (Paris, 1979).

Dölger, F. *Regesten der Kaiserurkunden des oströmischen Reiches von 565–1453*, 5: Regesten von 1341–1453 (Munich, 1965).

Iorga, N. *Notes et extraits pour servir à l'histoire des Croisades au XVe siècle*, vol. 1 (Paris, 1899) et seq.

'Venetia in Marea Neagra', *Analele Academiei Romane, Memoriile Sectiunii Istorice*, II, 36 (1913–14), Pt. 1, 1043–70; Pt. 2, 1071–188: documents, 1058–70, 1093–118.

Issues of the Exchequer; Being a Collection of Payments Made Out of His Majesty's Revenue, from King Henry III to King Henry VI Inclusive, ed. F. Devon, (London, 1837).

(Memorials of the Reign of King Henry IV). Official Correspondence of Thomas Bekynton, Secretary to King Henry IV, Bishop of Bath and Wells. ed. G. Williams, (London, 1872), vol. 1.

Miklosich, F. and Müller, W. *Acta et diplomata graeca medii aevii sacra et profana*, 6 vols. (Vienna, 1860–90).

Proceedings and Ordinances of the Privy Council of England, I, ed. H. Nicolas (London, 1834).

Rubió I Lluch, A. *Diplomatari de l'Orient Català (1301–1409)* (Barcelona, 1947).

Royal and Historical Letters During the Reign of Henry the Fourth, King of England, and of France, and of Lord of Ireland, vol. 1, AD 1399–1404, ed. F. C. Hingeston, (London 1860).

Theiner, A., and Miklosich, F. *Monumenta spectantia ad unionem ecclesiarum graeca et romana* (Vienna, 1872).

Thiriet, F. *Régestes des délibérations du sénat de Venise concernant la Romanie*, 3 vols (Paris, 1958).

Thomas, G. M and Predelli, R. *Deputazione di storei patria per le Venezie. Diplomatarium Veneto-levantinum 1351–1454* (Venice, 1880–99; repr. Cambridge, 2012).

Secondary Sources

Abulafia, D. *Frederick II: A Medieval Emperor* (Oxford, 1999).

Agapitos, P., Metse, E. and Hinterberger, M. Εἰκών καὶ λόγος: ἐξι βυζαντινές Περιγραφές Ἔργων Τέχνης (Athens, 2006).

Akışık, A. 'Praising A City: Nicea, Trebizond and Thessalonike, in *Journal of Turkish Studies, In Memoriam Angeliki E. Laiou*, eds. N. Necipoğlu and C. Kafadar, (Leiden, 2011), 1–25.

Self and Other in the Renaissance: Laonikos Chalkokondyles and Late Byzantine intellectuals (PhD thesis, Harvard University, 2013).

Alderson, A. D. *The Structure of the Ottoman Dynasty* (Oxford, 1956).

Alexandrescu-Dersca, M. M. *La campagne de Timur en Anatolie (1402)* (Athens, 1956).

Alfageme, I. R. 'La epístola περὶ ὀνειράτων de Manuel Paleólogo', *Cuadernos de filología clásica* 2 (1971), 227–55.

Anastasjević, D. 'Jedina vizantijska carica Srpkinja', *Brastvo* 30 (1939), 26–48.

Andreeva, M. A. 'Zur Reise Manuels II. Palaiologos nach West-Europa', *BZ* 34 (1934), 37–47.

Andriopoulou, S. *Diplomatic communications between Byzantium and the West under the Palaiologoi* (1354–1453) (PhD thesis, The University of Birmingham, 2010).

Angelou, A. D. 'Who am I? Scholarios' answers and the Hellenic identity', in *Φιλέλλην: Studies in Honour of Robert Browning*, eds. C. Constantinides, N. Pamagiotakes et al (Venice, 1996), 1–19.

Angelov, D. G. *Imperial Ideology and Political Thought in Byzantium, 1204–1330* (Cambridge, 2007).

'Emperors and Patriarchs as Ideal Children and Adolescents: Literary Conventions and Cultural Expectations' in, *Becoming Byzantine: Children and Childhood in Byzantium*, eds. A. Papaconstantinou and A. M. Talbot (Washington, 2009), 85–125.

'Three Kinds of Liberty as Political Ideals in Byzantium, Twelfth to Fifteenth Century', in *Proceedings of the 22nd International Congress of Byzantine Studies*, 1: *Plenary Sessions* (Sofia, 2011), 311–31.

The Byzantine Hellene: The Life of Emperor Theodore Laskaris and Byzantium in the Thirteenth Century (Cambridge, 2019).

Angold, M. 'The Autobiographical Impulse in Byzantium', *DOP* 52 (1998), 225–57.

'Autobiography and Identity: The Case of the Later Byzantine Empire', *BSl* 60 (1999), 18–32.

'The Decline of Byzantium seen through the Eyes of Western Travellers', in *Travel in the Byzantine World, Papers from the 34th Spring Symposium of Byzantine Studies, Birmingham, April 2000*, ed. R. J. Macrides (Aldershot, 2002), 213–23.

'Political Arts at the Late Palaiologan Court', in *Power and Subversion in Byzantium, Papers from the 43rd Spring Symposium of Byzantine Studies, Birmingham, March 2010*, eds. D. Angelov and M. Saxby (Farnham, 2013), 83–102.

Antonopoulou, Th. *The Homilies of Leo VI* (Leiden, 1997).

'Byzantine Homiletics: An Introduction to the Field and its Study', in *A Catalogue of Byzantine Manuscripts in their Liturgical Context*, eds. K. Spronk, G. Ruwhorst and S. Royé (Brepols, 2013), 183–98.

Ariantzi, D. (ed.) *Coming of Age in Byzantium: Adolescence and Society* (Leiden and Berlin, 2017).

Atiya, A. S. *The Crusade of Nicopolis* (London, 1934).

Autrand, F. *Charles VI, La folie au pouvoir* (Fayard, 1986).

Avramea, A. 'Land and Sea Communications, Fourth to Fifteenth Centuries', *EHB*, 57–90.

Babinger, F. *Mehmed II Conqueror and his Times*, trans. R. Manheim (Princeton, 1994).

Baker, J. 'A Coinage for Late Byzantine Morea under Manuel II Palaiologos (1391–1425)', *Revue Numismatique* 162 (2006), 385–405.

Bakirtzis, Ch. 'The Urban Continuity and the Size of Late Byzantine Thessalonike', *DOP* 57 (2003), 35–64.

'The Practice, Perception and Experience of Byzantine Fortification', in *The Byzantine World*, ed. P. Stephenson (New York, 2010), 352–71.

Balivet, M. *Byzantins et Ottomans: relations, interaction, succession* (Istanbul, 1999).

'Le soufi et le basileus: Haci Bayram Veli et Manuel II Paléologue', *Medievo Graeco* 4 (2004), 19–31.

Barber, C. and Jenkins, D. *Medieval Greek Commentaries on the Nicomachean Ethics*, (Leiden, 2009).

Barber, C. and Papaioannou, S. (eds.) *Michael Psellos on Literature and Art: A Byzantine Perspective on Aesthetics*, (Indiana 2017).

Barker, J. W. 'John VII in Genoa: A Problem in Late Byzantine Source Confusion', *OCP* 28 (1962), 213–88.

'On the Chronology of the Activities of Manuel II Palaeologus in the Peloponennesus in 1415', *BZ* 55 (1962), 39–55.

Manuel II Palaeologus (1391–1425): A Study in Late Byzantine Statesmanship (New Brunswick, 1969).

'The Problem of Appanages in Byzantium during the Palaiologan Period', *Byzantina 3* (1971), 103–22.

'Byzantium and the Hospitallers, 1306-1421', in *Bisanzio, Venezia e il Mondo Franco-Greco (XIIe–XVe s.)*, eds. C. Maltezou, P. Schreiner (Venice, 2002), 41–64.

'Late Byzantine Thessalonike: A Second City's Challenges and Responses', *DOP* 57 (2003), 5–30.

Bartusis, M. *Land and Privilege in Byzantium: The Institution of Pronoia* (Cambridge, 2012).

Bates, D. et al. (eds.) *Writing Medieval Biography* (Woodbridge, 2006).

Beaton, R. *The Medieval Greek Romance* (Cambridge, 1989).

Beck, H. G. *Kirsche und theologische Literatur im byzantinischen Reich* (Munich, 1959).

Benakis, L. Ἐλευθερία καὶ ἀναγκαιότητα στην Βυζαντινὴ φιλοσοφία', Δωδώνη 25 (1996), 203–20.

'Aristotelian Ethics in Byzantium', in *Medieval Greek Commentaries on the Nicomachean Ethics*, eds. C. Barber and D. Jenkins (Leiden, 2009), 63–9.

Berger, A. 'The Byzantine Court as Physical Space', in *The Byzantine Court. Source of Power and Culture. Papers from the Second Sevgi Gönül Symposium, Istanbul 21–23 June 2010*, eds. A. Ödekan, N. Necipoğlu and E. Akyürek (Istanbul, 2013), 3–12.

Berger de Xivrey, J. 'Mémoire sur la vie et les ouvrages de l'empereur Manuel Paléologue', *Mémoires de l'Institut de France, Académie des Inscriptions et des Belles Lettres* xix, 2 (Paris, 1853).

Bernicolas-Hatzapoulos, D. 'The First Siege of Constantinople by the Ottomans (1394–1402) and its Repercussions on the Civilian Population of the City', *Byzantine Studies* 10/11 (1983), 39–51.

Bevegni, C. 'La lettera ad Alessio Iagoup di Manuele II Paleologo: una rilettura del Par. gr. 3041', *La Parola del Passato 233* (1987), 103–8.

Billò, C. 'Note al testo dei Praecepta Educationis Regiae di Manuele II Paleologo', *Medievo Graeco* I (2001), 23–8.

Biriotti, M. 'Introduction: Authorship, Authority, Authorization', in *What is an Author?*, eds. M. Biriotti and N. Miller (Manchester and New York, 1993).

Black, J. *Absolutism in Renaissance Milan* (Oxford, 2009).

Blondell, R. *The Play of Character in Plato's Dialogues* (Cambridge, 2002).

Blum, W. *Byzantinische Fürstenspiegel: Agapetos, Theophylakt von Ochrid, Thomas Magister* (Stuttgart, 1981).

  Georgios Gemistos Plethon. Politik, Philosophie und Rhetorik im spätbyzantinischen Reich (Stuttgart, 1988).

Bourbouhakis, E. 'Rhetoric and Performance', in *The Byzantine World*, ed. P. Stephenson (Oxford and New York, 2010), 175–87.

Brauer, M. 'Politics or Leisure? A Day in the Life of King Charles V of France (1364–80)', *The Medieval History Journal* 18, 1 (2015), 46–63.

Brickhouse, T. C. and Smith, N. D. *Plato's Socrates* (New York, 1994).

Brown, P. *Augustine of Hippo: A Biography* (London, 1967).

  Power and Persuasion in the Late Antiquity (Madison, 1992).

Browning, R. 'Homer in Byzantium', *Viator* 6 (1975), 15–33.

  'Enlightenment and Repression in Byzantium in the Eleventh and the Twelfth Centuries', *Past and Present* 69 (1975), 3–29.

  'Tradition and Originality in Literary Criticism and Scholarship', in *Originality in Byzantine Literature, Art and Music*, ed. A. R. Littlewood (Exeter, 1995), 17–28.

Bryer, A. A. M. 'Greek Historians on the Turks: The Case of the first Byzantine-Ottoman Marriage', in *Writing of History in the Middle Ages: Essays Presented to R. W. Southern*, eds. R. H. C. Davis and J. M. Wallace-Hadrill, (1981), 471–93.

Buckler, G. 'Byzantine Education', in *Byzantium: An Introduction to East Roman Civilization*, eds. N. H. Baynes and H. St. L. B. Moss (Oxford, 1948), 204–7.

Buettner, B. 'Past Presents: New Year's Gifts at the Valois Courts, ca. 1400', *The Art Bulletin*, 83, no. 4 (December 2001), 598–625.

Burke, S. *The Death and the Return of the Author: Criticism and Subjectivity in Barthes, Foucault and Derrida* (Edinburgh, 1998).

Calofanos, G. 'Manuel Palaiologos: Interpreter of Dreams?', in *Manzikert to Lepanto: the Byzantine World and the Turks (1071–1571). Papers Given at the 19th Spring Symposium of Byzantine Studies, March 1985=BF 16* (1991), eds. A. M. Bryer and M. Ursinus, 447–55.

Cameron, A. *Arguing It Out: Discussion in Twelfth-Century Byzantium* (Budapest, 2016).

Cameron, A. and Gaul, N. (eds.) *Dialogues and Debates from Late Antiquity to Late Byzantium* (London and New York, 2017).

Cammelli, G. *I dotti Bizantini e le origini dell'Umanesimo, I, Manuele Crisolora* (Florence, 1941).

Cavallo, G. *Lire à Byzance* (Paris, 2006).

Çelik, S. 'The Emperor, the Sultan and the Scholar: The Portrayal of the Ottomans in the *Dialogue with a Persian* of Manuel II Palaiologos', *BMGS* 41 2 (2017), 208–28.

Chamberlain, C. 'The Meaning of Prohairesis in Aristotle's Ethics', *Transactions of the American Philological Association* vol. 114 (1984), 147–57.

Champollion-Figéac, A. *Louis et Charles, Ducs d'Orléans, leur influence sur les arts, la littérature et l'espirit de leur siècle* (Paris, 1844), 3 vols.

Chapin Lane, F. *Venetian Ships and Shipbuilders of the Renaissance* (Baltimore, 1934).

Charanis, P. 'Internal Strife in Byzantium during the Fourteenth Century', *Byzantion 15* (1940–1941), 208–30.

'The Monastic Properties and the State in the Byzantine Empire', *DOP* 4 (1948), 53–118.

Chrysostomides, J. 'John V Palaeologus in Venice (1370–1371) and the Chronicle of Caroldo: a Re-interpretation, *OCP 31* (1965), 46–84, re-printed in J. Chrysostomides, *Byzantium and Venice 1204–1453*, eds M. Heslop and Ch. Dendrinos (Farnham, 2011), Study I.

'Venetian Commercial Privileges under the Paleologi', *Studi Veneziana* 12 (1970), 267–356, re-printed in J. Chrysostomides, *Byzantium and Venice 1204–1453*, eds M. Heslop and Ch. Dendrinos (Farnham, 2011), Study III.

Clanchy, M. *Aberlard. A Medieval Life* (Oxford, 1997).

Crosby, M. *L'abbaye de S. Denis* (Paris, 1953).

Colenbrander, H. Th, 'The Limbourg Brothers, the 'Joyaux' of Constantine and Heraclius, the Très Riches Heures and the Visit of the Byzantine Emperor Manuel II Palaeologus', in *Flanders in a European Perspective. Manuscript Illumination Around 1400 in Flanders and Abroad. Proceedings of the International Colloquium of Illuminated Manuscripts, Leuven 7–10 September*, eds. M. Smeyers and B. Cardon (Leuven, 1995), 171–84.

Constantinides, C. N. *Higher Education in Byzantium in the Thirteenth and Early Fourteenth Centuries, 1204- ca. 1310* (Nicosia, 1982).

'Teachers and Students of Rhetoric in the Late Byzantine Period', in *Rhetoric in Byzantium: Papers from the 35th Spring Symposium of Byzantine Studies, Exeter College, the University of Oxford, March 2001*, ed. E. Jeffreys (Ashgate, 2003), 39–53.

Contos, L. C. 'The Essence-Energies Structure of Saint Gregory Palamas with a Brief Examination of its Patristic Foundation', *The Greek Orthodox Theological Review* 12 (1967–8), 283–94.

Corradini, R. (ed.) *Ego Troubles: Authors and their Identities in the Early Middle Ages* (Vienna, 2010).

Cosman, M. P. *Fabulous Feasts: Medieval Cookery and Ceremony* (New York, 1992).

Cunningham, M. 'Preaching and Community', in *Church and People in Byzantium, 20th Spring Symposium of Byzantine Studies, Manchester 1986*, ed. R. Morris (Birmingham, 1990), 29–47.

'Dramatic Device or Didactic Tool? The Function of Dialogue in Byzantine Preaching', in *Rhetoric in Byzantium: Papers from the 35th Spring Symposium of Byzantine Studies, Exeter College, the University of Oxford, March 2001*, ed. E. Jeffreys (Aldershot, 2003), 101–26.

Dabrowska, M. 'Ought One to Marry? Manuel II Palaiologos' Point of View', *BMGS* 31 no. 2 (2007), 146–56.

Dalby, A. *Tastes of Byzantium* (New York, 2003).

Daley, B. E. *On the Dormition of Mary: Early Patristic Homilies* (Crestwood NY, 1997).

'At the Hour of our Death: Mary's Dormition and Christian Dying in Late Patristic and Early Byzantine Literature', *DOP* 55 (2001), 71–89, 86.

Dagron, G. 'Manuel Chrysoloras: Constantinople ou Rome', *BF* 12 (1987), 281–288.

Emperor and Priest: The Imperial Office in Byzantium (Cambridge, 2003).

De Mély, F. *Exuviae Sacrae Constantinopolitanae*, III (Paris, 1904).

Demetracopoulos, J. A. 'Pope Benedict XVI's use of the Byzantine Emperor Manuel II Palaiologos' Dialogue with a Muslim Muteritzes', *Archiv für Mittelalterliche Philosophie und Kultur* 14 (2008), 264–304.

'Palamas transformed, Palamite Interpretation of the Distinction between God's 'Essence' and 'Energies' in Late Byzantium', in *Greeks, Latins, and Intellectual History 1204–1500*, eds. M. Hinterberger and C. Schabel (Leuven, 2011), 263–372.

'Thomas Aquinas' Impact on Late Byzantine Theology and Philosophy: The Issues of Method or 'Modus Sciendi' and 'Dignitas Hominis', in *Knotenpunkt Byzanz. Wissenformen und Kulturelle Wechselbeziehungen*, eds. A. Speer and P. Steinkrüger (Berlin, 2012), 333–410.

Dendrinos, Ch. Ἡ ἐπιστολὴ τοῦ αὐτοκράτορος Μανουὴλ Β΄ Παλαιολόγου πρὸς τὸν Ἀλέξιο Ἰαγούπ καὶ οἱ ἀντιλήψεις του περὶ τῆς σπουδῆς τῆς θεολογίας καὶ τῶν σχέσεων Ἐκκλησίας καὶ Πολιτείας', *Φιλοσοφίας Ἀνάλεκτα*, vol. 1 (2001), 58–74.

'Co-operation and Friendship among Byzantine Scholars in the Circle of Emperor Manuel II Palaeologus (1391–1425) as reflected in their Autograph Manuscripts', Paper presented at International Colloquium, Unlocking the Potential of Texts: Interdisciplinary Perspectives on Medieval Greek, organized by the Centre for Research in the Arts, Social Sciences and Humanities, University of Cambridge, 18–19 July 2006, Cambridge, United Kingdom, 18/07/06– 19/07/06.

'Manuel II Palaelogus in Paris (1400–1402): Theology, Diplomacy and Politics', in *Greeks, Latins, and Intellectual History 1204–1500*, eds. M. Hinterberger and C. Schabel (Leuven, 2011), 397–422.

'Palaiologan Scholars at Work: Makarios Makres and Joseph Bryennios' Autograph', in *From Manuscripts to Books: Proceedings of the International Workshop on Textual Criticism and Editorial Practice for Byzantine Texts (Vienna 10–11 December 2009)*, eds. A. Giannouli and E. Schiffer (Vienna, 2011), 23–51.

Dennis, G. T. *The Reign of Manuel II Palaeologus in Thessalonica (1382–1387)* (Rome, 1960).

'Four Unknown Letters of Manuel II Palaeologus', *Byzantion 36* (1966), 35–40, reprinted in G. T. Dennis, *Byzantium and the Franks, 1350–1420* (London, 1982), Study VII.

'An Unknown Byzantine Emperor, Andronicus V Palaeologus (1400–1407?)', *JÖB 16* (1967), 175–87, reprinted in G.T. Dennis, *Byzantium and the Franks, 1350–1420* (London, 1982), Study II.

'The Deposition and Restoration of Patriarch Matthew I, 1402-1403', *BF 2* (1967), 100–6, reprinted in G. T. Dennis, *Byzantium and the Franks, 1350–1420* (London, 1982), Study VI.

'The Byzantine-Turkish Treaty of 1403', *OCP 33* (1967), 72–88, re-printed in G. T. Dennis, *Byzantium and the Franks 1350–1420*, (London, 1982), Study XII.

'Two Unknown Documents of Manuel II Palaeologus', *TM 3* (1968), 397–404, reprinted in G. T. Dennis, *Byzantium and the Franks, 1350–1420* (London, 1982), Study VIII.

'Official Documents of Manuel II Palaeologus', *Byzantion 61* (1971), 45–58, reprinted in G. T. Dennis, *Byzantium and the Franks, 1350–1420* (London, 1982), Study IX.

'Rhadenos of Thessalonica, Correspondent of Demetrius Cydones', *Byzantina* 13 (1985), 261–72.

'Death in Byzantium', *DOP* 55 (2001), 1–7.

'Demetrios Kydones and Venice', *in Bisanzio, Venezia e il mondo Franco-Greco (XIIe-XVe s.)*, eds. C. Maltezou, P. Schreiner (Venice, 2002), 495–502.

'John VII Palaiologos: A Holy and Just Man', in *Byzantium, State and Society: In Memory of Nikos Oikonomides*, eds. A. Avramea, A. E. Laiou and E. Chrysos, (Athens, 2003), 205–17.

'The Late Byzantine Metropolitans of Thessalonike', *DOP* 57 (2003), 255–64.

Diehl, C. *Byzantine Empresses*, trans. H. Bell and T. de Kerpely (London, 1963).

Djuric, I. *Le crépuscule de Byzance* (Paris, 1996).

Dölger, F. 'Die Krönung Johannes VIII zum Mitkaiser', *BZ 36* (1936), 318–19.

Doumerc, B. 'Cosmopolitanism on board Venetian Ships (Fourteenth–Fifteenth Centuries)', *Medieval Encounters* 13 (2007), 78–95.

Duby, G. and Ariès, P. (eds.) *A History of Private Life, II, Revelations of the Medieval World*, trans. A. Goldhammer (Cambridge MA, 1988).

Du Cange, C. *Familiae Augustae Byzantinae (Historia Byzantina, Pt. 1)* (Paris, 1680).

Ducellier, A. *Chrétiens d'Orient et Islam au Moyen Age, VIIe–XVe siecle* (Paris, 1966).

'La France et les iles Britanniques vue par un byzantin du XVe siècle: Laonikos Chalkokondylis', in *Economies et sociétés au Moyen âge; mélanges offerts à Edouard Perroy* (Paris, 1973), 439–45.

'L'Islam et les musulmanes vus de Byzance au XIVe siecle', *Byzantina* 12 (1983), 95–134.

Dölger, F. 'Johannes VII, Kaiser der Rhomaer 1390-1408', *BZ* 31 (1931), 21–36.
'Zum Aufstand des Andronikos IV gegen seinen Vater Johannes V im Mai 1373', *REB* 19 (1961), 328–33.
Dvornik, F. 'The Byzantine Church and the Immaculate Conception', in *The Dogma of Immaculate Conception: Its History and Significance*, ed. E. D. O' Conor (Notre Dame, Indiana, 1958), 87–112.
Byzantium and the Roman Primacy, trans. E. A. Quain (New York, 1966).
Early Christian and Byzantine Political Philosophy, Origins and Background, 2 vols (Washington DC, 1966).
Eichner, W. 'Accounts of Islam', *in Doctrine and Debate in the East Christian World*, eds. A. Cameron and R. Hoyland (Farnham, 2011), 109–72.
Estangüi-Gómez, R. *Byzance face aux Ottomans. Exercice du pouvoir contrôle du territoire sous les derniers Paléologues (Milieu XIVe- Milieu Xve siècle)* (Paris, 2014).
'Actes autographes de l'empereur Manuel II Paléologue conservés dans les archives du Mont Athos', in *Peribolos: Mélanges offerts à Mirjana Zivojinovic*, eds. B. Miljkovic and D. Dzeldelzic (Belgrade, 2015), 409–26.
Estopañán, S Cirac. 'Ein Chrysobulles des Kaisers Manuel II Palaiologos (1391–1425) für den Gegenpapst Bennedikt XIII (1394–1417/23) vom 20. Juni 1402', *BZ* 44 (1951), 89–93.
La Unión, Manuel II Paleólogo y sus Recuerdos en España (Barcelona, 1952).
Famigletti, R. C. *Royal Intrigue. Crisis at the Court of Charles VI 1392–1420* (New York, 1986).
Feissel, C. and Spieser, J. M. 'Inventaires en vue d'un recueil des inscriptions historiques de Byzance, II: les inscriptions de Thessalonique. Supplément', *TM* 7 (1979), 303–46.
Fine, Jr, J. V. A. *The Late Medieval Balkans: A Critical Survey from the Late Twelfth Century to the Ottoman Conquest* (Ann Arbor, 1987).
Fleet, K. ed. *The Cambridge History of Turkey: Byzantium to Turkey*, vol. 1 (Cambridge, 2009).
Fleming, R. 'Writing Biography at the Edge of History', *American Historical Review* 114 (2009), 606–14.
Forbes Manz, B. *The Rise and the Rule of Tamerlane* (Cambridge, 1989).
Förstel, C. 'Metochites and his Books between the Chora and the Renaissance', in *The Kariye Camii Reconsidered*, eds. A. Klein, R. Ousterhout and B. Pitarakis (Istanbul, 2011), 241–66.
Foss, C. 'Late Antique and Byzantine Ankara', *DOP* 31 (1977), 27–87.
France, P. and St. Clair, W. (eds.) *Mapping Lives: The Uses of Biography* (New York, 2002).
Frede, M. 'John of Damascus on Human Action, the Will and Human Freedom', in *Byzantine Philosophy and its Ancient Sources*, ed. K. Ierodiakonou (Oxford, 2002), 63–97.
Fryde, E. *The Early Palaeologan Renaissance (1261 – c. 1360)* (Leiden, 2000).
Galatarioutou, C. 'Travel and Perception in Byzantium', *DOP* 47 (1993), 221–41.

Ganchou, Th. 'Autour de Jean VII: luttes dynastiques, interventions étrangeres et résistance orthodoxe a Byzance (1373–1409)', in *Colonisér au Moyen Age*, eds. M. Balard and A. Ducellier (Paris, 1995), 367–85.

'Démetrios Kydones, les freres Chrysoberges et la Crete (1397–1401)', in *Bisanzio, Venezia e il Mondo Franco-Greco (XIIe–XVe s.)*, eds. C. Maltezou, P. Schreiner (Venice, 2002), 435–93.

'Ilario Doria le gambros génois de Manuel II Paléologos: beau-frère ou gendre?', *REB* 66 (2008), 71–94.

'Zampia Palaiologina Doria: épouse du prétendent ottoman Mustafa', in *Impératrices, princesses, aristocrates et saintes souveraines. De l'Orient Chrétien et Musulman au Moyen Age et au début des temps modernes*, ed. E. Malamut and A. Nicolaides (Aix-en-Provence, 2014), 133–69.

'Les chroniques vénitiennes et les unions ottomans des filles de l'empereur byzantine Jean V Palaiologos, Eirènè et Maria (1358 et 1376), in *La transizione bizantino-ottomana nelle cronache veneziane*, eds. S. Kolditz and M. Koller (Rome and Venice, 2018), 163–96.

Garland, L. 'Mazaris' Journey to Hades: Further Reflections and Reappraisal', *DOP* 61 (2007), 183–214.

Gaul, N. 'Eunuchs in the Late Byzantine Empire c. 1250–1400', in *Eunuchs in Antiquity and Beyond*, ed. S. Tougher (Cardiff, 2002), 199–217.

'The Partridge's Purple Stockings: Observations on the Historical, Literary and Manuscript Context of Pseudo-Kodinos' Handbook on Court Ceremonies', in *Theatron: Rhetorische Kultur in Spätantike und Mittelalter*, ed. M. Grünbart (Berlin-New York, 2007), 69–103.

Thomas Magistros und die spätbyzantinische Sophistik. Studien zum Humanismus urbaner Eliten der frühen Palaiologenzeit (Wiesbaden, 2011).

Gerstel, S. 'Civic and Monastic Influences on Church Decoration in Thessalonike: In Loving Memory of Thalia Gouma-Peterson', *DOP* 57 (2003), 225–339.

Gill, J. *The Council of Florence* (Cambridge, 1959).

'John V Palaeologus at the Court of Louis I of Hungary', *BSI* 38 (1977), 31–8.

Byzantium and the Papacy, 1198–1400 (New Brunswick 1979).

'Matrons and Brides of 14th-Century Byzantium', *BF* 10(1985), 39–56.

Gleason, M. W. *Making Men: Sophists and Self-Presentation in Ancient Rome* (Princeton, 1995).

Gosset. L. *Le palais du Louvre* (Paris, 1933).

Gregory, T.E. *Isthmia, V, The Hexamillion and the Fortress* (Princeton, 1993).

Grierson, P. and Bellinger, A. R. *A Catalogue of the Byzantine Coins in the Dumbarton Oaks Collection and in the Whittemore Collection*, vol. 5 (Washington DC, 1999).

Grosdidier de Maton, V. D. and C. Förstel, 'Quelques manuscrits grecs liés à Manuel II Paléologue', in *Proceedings of the 6th International Symposium on Greek Paleography, Drama, Greece, 21–27 September 2003*, eds. B. Atsalos and N. Tsironis, vol 1 (Athens, 2008), 375–86.

Guberti Bassett, S. 'John V Palaiologos and the Golden Gate in Constantinople', in τό Ἑλληνικόν: *Studies in Honor of Speros Vryonis Jr*, vol. 1, eds. J. S. Langdon et al. (New Rochelle and New York, 1993), 117–27.

Guenée, B. 'Documents insérés et documents abrégées dans la Chronique religieux du Saint Denis', *Bibliothèque de l'Ecole des Chartes* 152, 2 (1994), 375–428.

'Le vœu de Charles VI. Essai sur la dévotion des rois de France aux XIIIe et XIVe siècles', *Journal des Savants*, no 1, (1996), 67–135.

'Le portrait de Charles VI dans la *Chronique du religieux de Saint-Denis*', *Journal des Savants*, no 1, (1997), 125–65.

Guran, P. 'Patriarche hésychaste et empereur latinophrone. L'accord de 1380', *RESEE* 39 (2001), 53–62.

Gurevich, A. *The Origins of European Individualism* (Oxford, 1995).

Haldon, J. 'Humour and Everyday Life in Byzantium', in *Humour, History and Politics in Late Antiquity and Early Middle Ages*, ed. G. Halsall (Cambridge, 2002), 42–72.

Halecki, O. *Un empereur de Byzance à Rome* (Warsaw, 1930; reprinted London, 1972).

Harris, J. *Greek Emigres in the West, 1400–1520* (Camberley, 1995).

'A Worthless Prince? Andreas Paleologus in Rome – 1464–1502', *OCP* 81 (1995), 537–54.

'Edward II, Andronicus II and Giles of Argenteim: A Neglected Episode in Anglo-Byzantine Relations,' in *Porphyrogenita: Essays on the History and Literature of Byzantium and the Latin East in Honour of Julian Chrysostomides*, in eds. Ch. Dendrinos et al. (Aldershot, 2003), 77–84.

The End of Byzantium (New Haven and London, 2010).

'Manuel II Palaiologos (1391–1425) and the Lollards', *Greek Orthodox Theological Review* 57 (2012), 213–34.

Hatlie, P. 'Life and Artistry in the Publication of Demetrios Kydones' Letter Collection', *GRBS* 37/1 (Spring 1996), 75–102.

'Images of Motherhood and Self in Byzantine Literature', *DOP* 63 (2009), 41–57.

Hennessy, C. *Images of Children in Byzantium* (Farnham, 2007).

Henry III, P. 'A Mirror for Justinian: the *Ekthesis* of Agapetos', *GRBS* 8 (1967), 381–408.

Herrin, J. 'L'énseignement maternel à Byzance', in *Femmes et pouvoirs des femmes à Byzance et en Occident (VIe–XIe siècles)*, eds. S. Lebecq et al. (Lille, 1999), 91–102.

Hetherington, P. 'The Jewels from the Crown: Symbol and Substance in the Later Byzantine Imperial Regalia', *BZ* 96 (2003), 157–68.

Hilsdale, C. *Byzantine Art and Diplomacy in an Age of Decline* (Cambridge, 2014).

Hinterberger. M. *Autobiographische Traditionen im Byzanz* (Vienna, 1999).

Hladký, V. *The Philosophy of Gemistos Plethon: Platonism in Late Byzantium, Between Hellenism and Orthodoxy* (Farnham, 2014).

Holmes, C. *Basil II and Governance of the Empire (976–1025)* (Oxford, 2006).

'Political Literacy', in *The Byzantine World*, ed. P Stephenson (London, 2012), 135–47.

Houston, M. G. *Medieval Costume in England and France* (London, 1939; reprinted 1996).

Hunger, H. 'Das Testament des Patriarchen Matthaios I (1397–1410)', *BZ* 51 (1958), 288–309.

'On the Imitation (ΜΙΜΗΣΙΣ) of Antiquity', *DOP* 23/24 (1969/70), 15–38.

Schreiben und Lesen in Byzanz (Munich, 1989).

Ierodiakonou, K. (ed.) *Byzantine Philosophy and its Ancient Sources* (Oxford, 2002).

'The Anti-Logical Movement in the Fourteenth Century', in *Byzantine Philosophy and its Ancient Sources*, ed. K. Ierodiakonou (New York, 2002), 219–237.

Ierodiakonou, K. and Byden, B. (eds.) *Many Faces of Byzantine Philosophy* (Athens, 2012).

Imber, C. *The Ottoman Empire, 1300–1650: Structures of Power* (New York, 2002).

İnalcık, H. 'Ottoman Methods of Conquest', *Studia Islamica* 2 (1954), 103–29.

'Bayezid I', in *The Encyclopedia of Islam*, vol. 1, eds. H. A. R. Gibb, J. H. Kramer, E. Levi-Provencal and J. Schact (Leiden, 1986), 1117–19.

'How to Read Ashık-Pashazade's History', in *Studies in Ottoman History in Honour of Professor V. L. Ménage*, eds. C. Heywood and C. Imber (Istanbul, 1994), 117–38.

Irwin, T. H. 'Aristotle on Reason, Desire and Virtue', *The Journal of Philosophy* 72.17 (1975), 567–78.

Ivanović, F. 'Byzantine Philosophy and its Historiography', *BSl* 68 (2010), 369–380.

Jacoby, D. 'Foreigners and the Urban Economy in Thessalonike ca. 1150– ca. 1450', *DOP* 57 (2003), 86–133.

Jones, M. (ed.) *The New Cambridge Medieval History: c. 1300–1415, vol. VI* (Cambridge, 2008).

Jugie, M. 'Le voyage de l'empereur Manuel Paléologue en Occident (1399–1403), *Echos d'Orient* 15 (1912), 322–32.

'Le discours de Démétrius Cydonès sur l'Annonciation et sa doctrine sur l'Immaculée Conception', *Echos d'Orient* 17 (1915), 97–106.

La mort et l'assomption de la Sainte Vierge (Rome, 1944).

Kaegi, W. *Heraclius: Emperor of Byzantium* (Cambridge, 2003).

Kafadar, C. *Between Two Worlds* (Berkeley and Los Angeles, 1995).

Kakulide, E. D. 'Βιβλιοθήκη τῆς Μονῆς Προδρόμου-Πέτρας στὴν Κωνσταντινούπολη', *Ἑλληνικά* 21 (1968), 3–39.

Kaldellis, A. 'Historicism in Byzantine Thought and Literature', *DOP* 61 (2007), 1–24.

'A Byzantine Argument for the Equivalence of all Religions: Michael Attaleiates on Ancient and Modern Romans,' *International Journal of the Classical Tradition* 14 (2007) 1–22.

Hellenism in Byzantium: The Transformations of Greek Identity and the Reception of Classical Tradition (Cambridge, 2007).

'The Study of Women and Children: Methodological Challenges and New Directions', in *The Byzantine World*, ed. P. Stephenson (London, 2010), 61–71.

'Byzantine Philosophy Inside and Out: Orthodoxy and Dissidence in Counterpoint,' in *The Many Faces of Byzantine Philosophy*, eds. K. Ierodiakonou and B. Bydén (Athens, 2012) 129–51.

Ethnography After Antiquity (Philadephia, 2013).

A New Herodotos: Laonikos Chalkokondyles on the Ottoman Empire, the Fall of Byzantium and the Emergence of the West (Washington DC, 2014).

The Byzantine Republic (Cambridge MA, 2015).

Kalogeras, N. *Byzantine Childhood Education and Its Social Role From the Sixth Century Until the End of Iconoclasm* (PhD thesis, The University of Chicago, 2000).

'What do they think about Children? Perceptions of Childhood in Early Byzantine Literature', *BMGS 25* (2001), 2–19.

Kaltsogani, E. 'Zur Entstehung der Rede des Manuel II Palaiologos auf die Heilige Maria von Ägypten (BHG 1044c)', *Parekbolai* 1 (2011), 37–59.

Kantorowicz, E. *Frederick the Second 1194–1250* (New York, 1967).

Kapriev, G. *Philosophie in Byzanz* (Würzburg, 2005).

'Modern Study of Byzantine Philosophy', *Bulletin de Philosophie Médiévale* 48 (2006), 3–13.

Karathanassis, A. 'Philip and Alexander of Macedon in the Literature of the Palaiologan Era', in *Byzantine Macedonia, Identity, Image and History*, eds. J. Burke and R. Scott (Melbourne, 2000), 111–15.

Karlıdökme Mollaoğlu, F. '"Düzmece" olarak anilan Mustafa Çelebi ve Bizans (1415–1416/17)', *Ankara Üniversitesi Dil ve Tarih-Coğrafya Fakülesi Dergisi*, no 49/2 (2009), 173–85.

Karpozilos, A. 'Byzantine Apologetic and Polemic Writings of the Palaeologian Epoch against Islam', *Greek Orthodox Theological Review* 15 (1970), 213–48.

'Realia in Byzantine Epistolography X–XII c.', *BZ 77* (1984), 20–37.

'Realia in Byzantine Epistolography XIII–XV c.', *BZ* 88 (1995), 68–84.

Kastritsis, D. J. *The Sons of Bayezid: Empire Building and Representation in the Ottoman Civil War of 1402–1413* (Leiden and Boston, 2007).

Kazhdan, A. 'The Aristocracy and the Imperial Ideal', in *The Byzantine Aristocracy from IX to XIIIth Centuries*, ed. M. Angold (Oxford, 1982).

'Ships in Storms: On Imagery and Historical Interpretations', in *Studies on Byzantine Literature of the 11th and the 12th Centuries*, eds. A. Kazhdan and S. Franklin (Cambridge, 1984), 264–78.

'Innovation in Byzantium', in *Originality in Byzantine Literature, Art and Music*, ed. A. R. Littlewood (Exeter, 1995), 1–14.

Kennedy, G. *Greek Rhetoric under Christian Emperors* (Princeton, 1983).

Kianka, F. *Demetrius Cydones (c. 1324 – c. 1397): Intellectual Diplomatic Relations between Byzantium and the West in the Fourteenth Century* (PhD dissertation, Fordham University, 1981).

'The Letters of Demetrios Kydones to Empress Helena Kantakouzene Palaiologina', *DOP 46* (1992), 155–64.

'Demetrios Kydones and Italy', *DOP 49* (1995), 99–110.

King, E. J. *The Grand Priory of the Order of the Hospital of St John of Jerusalem in England. A Short History* (London, 1924).

Kiousopoulou, T. 'La notion de ville chez Manuel Chrysoloras: ς Παλαίας και Νέας Ρώμης', *BSl* 59 (1998), 71–9.

Emperor or Manager: Power and Political Ideology in Byzantium before 1453, trans. P. Magdalino (Geneva, 2011).

Khoury, Th. 'L'empereur Manuel II Paléologue (1350–1425), esquisse biographique', *Proche-Orient Chrétien* 15 (1965), 127–44.

Les théologiens Byzantins et l'Islam: texts et auteurs (VIIIe–XIIIe siècles). (Louvain and Paris, 1969).

Klein, H. 'Eastern Objects and Western Desires: Relics and Reliquaries between Byzantium and the West', *DOP* 58 (2004), 283–313.

'Refashioning Byzantium in Venice, 1200–1400', in *San Marco, Byzantium and Myths of Venice*, eds. H. Maguire and R. Nelson (Washington, 2010), 193–226.

Knežević, M. (ed) *The Ways of Byzantine Philosophy* (Alhambra, California, 2015).

Knobler, A. 'The Rise of Timur and Western Diplomatic Response, 1390–1405', *Journal of the Royal Asiatic Society of Great Britain and Ireland* 3, 5 (1995), 314–49.

Krueger, D. *Liturgical Subjects. Christian Ritual, Biblical Narrative and the Formation of the Self in Byzantium* (Philadelphia, 2014).

Koder, J. 'Latinoi – The Image of the Other According to Greek Sources', in *Bisanzio, Venezia e il Mondo Franco-Greco (XIII–XV secolo)*, eds. Chr. A. Maltezou and P. Schreiner, (Venice, 2002), 25–39.

Kohl. G. *Padua under the Carrara, 1318–1405* (Baltimore and London, 1998).

Kolbaba, T. *The Byzantine Lists: Errors of the Latins* (Chicago, 2000).

Kolbaba, T. 'Repercussions of the Second Council of Lyon (1274): Theological Polemic and the Boundaries of Orthodoxy, in *Greeks, Latins, and Intellectual History 1204–1500*, eds. M. Hinterberger and C. Schabel (Leuven, 2011), 43–68.

Kolias, G. T. "Η ανταρσία Ἰωάννου Ζ´ Παλαιολόγου ἐναντίον Ἰωάννου Ε´ Παλαιολόγου (1390)', *Ἑλληνικά* 12 (1952), 34–64.

Konstantinides, K. 'Οἱ ἀπαρχὲς πνευματικῆς ἀκμῆς στὴ Θεσσαλονίκη κατὰ τὸν 14° αἰῶνα', *Δωδώνη* (1992), 133–50.

Kotzabassi, S. (ed) *The Pantokrator Monastery in Constantinople* (Leiden and Berlin, 2013).

Kubiski, J. 'Orientalizing Costume in Early Fifteenth-Century French Manuscript Painting (Cité des Dames Master, Limbourg Brothers, Boucicaut Master, and Bedford Master)', *Gesta* 40 (2001), 161–80.

Kyriakidis, S. *Warfare in Late Byzantium (1204–1453)* (Leiden, 2011).

Kyritses, D. 'The Imperial council in Byzantium and the tradition of Consultative Decision-Making in Byzantium', in *Power and Subverison in Byzantium,*

Papers from the 43rd Spring Symposium of Byzantine Studies, Birmingham, March 2010, eds. D. Angelov and M. Saxby (Farnham, 2013), 57–67.

Laiou, A. E. 'Economic Concerns and Attitudes of the Intellectuals of Thessalonike', *DOP* 57 (2003), 205–23.

Lamberz, E. 'Das Geschenk des Kaisers Manuel II an das Kloster Saint-Denis und der 'Metochitesschreiber' Michael Klostomates', in *Λιθόστροτων: Studien zur byzantinischen Kunst und Geschichte. Festschrift für Marcel Restle*, eds. B. Barkopp and T. Steppan (Stuttgart, 2000), 156–9.

Lampros, Sp. 'Ἐπιστολὴ Μανουὴλ Παλαιολόγου πρὸς τοὺς Σιεναῖους', *Νέος Ἑλληνομνήμων* 6 (1909), 102–4.

Ἰωάννου Ζ' Παλαιολόγου, ἐκχώρησης τῶν ἐπὶ τῆς βυζαντιακῆς αὐτοκρατορίας δικαιωμάτων εἰς τὸν βασίλεαν τῆς Γαλλίας Κάρολον ΣΤ', *Νέος Ἑλληνομνήμων* 10 (1913), 248–57.

Lappa-Zizicas, E. 'Le voyage de Jean Paléologue en Italie', *REB* 34 (1976), 139–42.

Larner, J. *Culture and Society in Italy, 1220–1420* (London, 1971).

Lascaratos, J. and Manduvalos, V. 'Cases of Stroke on the Throne of Byzantium', *Journal of the History of the Neurosciences* 7.1 (1998), 5–10.

Laurent, V. 'Une nouvelle fondation monastique des Chumnos: la Néa Moni de Thessalonique', *REB* 13 (1955), 109–32.

'Les droits de l'empereur en matière ecclésiastique: L'accorde 1380-82', *REB* 14 (1955), 5–20.

'Ecrits spirituels inédits de Macaire Choumos († c. 1382), fondateur de la 'Nea Moni' à Thessalonique', *Ἑλληνικά* 14 (1955), 40–86.

'Les préliminaires du concile de Florence. Les neuf articles du pape Martin V et la réponse inédite du patriarche de Constantinople Joseph II', *REB* 20 (1962), 5–60.

'Le trisépiscopat du Patriarche Matthieu 1er (1397–1410): un grand procès canonique à Byzance au début du XVeme siècle', *REB 30* (1972), 32–111.

Lauxtermann, M. *Byzantine Poetry from Pisides to Geometres* (Vienna, 2003).

'Byzantine Didactic Poetry', in *Doux remede, poésie et poétique à Byzance, actes du IVe colloque international philoloqiue, Paris 23–24-25 Février 2006*, eds. P. Odorico and P. Agapitos (Paris, 2009), 37–46.

Le Goff, J. 'The Whys and Ways of Writing a Biography: The Case of Saint Louis', *Exemplaria* 1 (1989), 207–25.

Saint Louis (Paris, 1999).

Lemerle, P. *Le premier humanisme Byzantine* (Paris, 1971).

Leonte, F. 'Advice and Praise for the Ruler: Making Political Strategies in Manuel II Palaiologos's Dialogue on Marriage', in *Papers from the First and Second Postgraduate Forums in Byzantine Studies: Sailing to Byzantium*, ed. S. Neocleous (Newcastle, 2009), 163–83.

Rhetoric in Purple: The Renewal of Imperial Ideology in the Texts of Emperor Manuel II Palaiologos (PhD thesis, Central European University, 2012).

'A Brief "History of the Morea" as seen through the Eyes of an Emperor-Rhetorician: Manuel II Palaiologos's Funeral Oration for Theodore, Despot of the Morea', in *Viewing the Morea Land and People in the Late Medieval Peloponnese*, ed. S. Gerstel (Washington DC, 2013), 397–417.

Imperial Visions of Byzantium. Manuel II Palaiologos and Rhetoric in Purple (Edinburgh, 2020).

Littlewood, A. R. (ed.) *Originality in Byzantine Literature, Art and Music* (Exeter, 1995).

'Imagery in the *Chronographia* of Michael Psellos', in *Reading Michael Psellos*, eds. C. Barber and D. Jenkins (Leiden, 2006), 13–56.

Loenertz, R. J. 'Manuel Paléologue et Démétrius Cydonès: remarques sur leurs correspondances', *Echos d'Orient* (1937), 271–87; 474–87 (1938), 107–24.

'La première insurrection d'Andronic IV Paléologue (1373)',*Echos d'Orient* 38 (1939), 334–45.

'Un prostagma perdu de Théodore I Paléologue regardant Thessalonique (1380/ 82?), *EEBΣ* 25 (1955), 170–2.

'Manuel Paléologue, épitre à Cabasilas', *Μακεδονικά* 4 (1956), 38–46.

'Une erreur singulière de Laonic Chalcocondyle', *REB 15* (1957), 182–3.

'Notes sur le règne de Manuel II à Thessalonique, 1381-1387', *BZ* 50 (1957), 390–6.

'Jean V à Venise (1370–1371)', *REB 16* (1958), 217–32.

'Le chancelier imperial à Byzance au XIVe et au XIIIe siècle', *OCP* 26 (1960), 275–300.

'Pour l'histoire du Péloponnèse au XIVe siècle', in *Byzantina et Franco-Graeca*, eds. R.J Loenertz and P. Schreiner (Rome, 1970), 227–65.

'L'éxil de Manuel II Paléologue à Lemnos 1387-89', *OCP* 38 (1972), 116–40.

Losin, P. 'Aristotle's Doctrine of the Mean', *History of Philosophical Quarterly* 4.3 (1987), 329–41.

Lowden, J. 'The Luxury Book as Diplomatic Gift', in *Papers from the Twenty-fourth Spring Symposium of Byzantine Studies, Cambridge March 1990*, eds. J. Shepard and S. Franklin (Aldershot, 1992), 249–60.

Lowry, H. *Fifteenth-Century Ottoman Realities: Christian Peasant Life on the Aegean Island of Limnos* (Istanbul, 2002).

The Nature of the Early Ottoman State (New York, 2003).

Louth, A. *St John Damascene. Tradition and Originality in Byzantine Theology* (Oxford, 2004).

Lutrell, A. 'John V's daughters: a Palaiologan Puzzle', *DOP 36* (1986), 103–12.

Macrides, R. J. 'Subversion and Loyalty in the Cult of Saint Demetrios', *BSl* 51 (1990), 189–97.

'The Ritual of Petition', in *Greek Ritual Poetics*, ed. P. Roilos and D. Yatromanolakis (Cambridge MA, 2004), 356–70.

(ed.) *History as Literature in Byzantium. Papers from the 40*[th] *Spring Symposium of Byzantine Studies, University of Birmingham, April 2007* (Aldershot, 2010).

'Emperor and Church in the Last Centuries of Byzantium', *Studies in Church History* 54 (2018), 123–43.

Magdalino, P. 'Hellenism and nationalism in Byzantium', in *Tradition and Transformation in Medieval Byzantium*, ed. P. Magdalino (Aldershot, 1991), Study XIV, 1–29.

The Empire of Manuel I Komnenos 1143–1180 (Cambridge, 1993).

Makris, G. 'Ships' *EHB*, (2002), 91–100.

Maksimović, L. *The Byzantine Provincial Administration under the Palaiologoi* (Amsterdam, 1988).

Malamut, E. 'La monastère Saint-Jean Prodrome de Pétra de Constantinople', in *Le sacré et son inscription dans l'espace à Byzance et en Occident*, ed. M. Kaplan (Paris, 2001), 219–33.

Marciniak, P. 'Byzantine Theatron – A Place of Performance?', in *Theatron, Rhetorische Kultur in Spätantike und Mittelalter*, ed. M. Grünbart (Berlin and New York, 2007), 277–85.

Margolis, N. *An Introduction to Christine de Pizan* (Gainsville, Florida, 2011).

Marinesco, C. 'Manuel II Paléologue et les rois d'Aragon, commentaire sur quatre lettres inéedites en Latin, expédiées par la chancellerie byzantine', *Académie Roumanie, Bulletin de la Section Historique* 11 (1924), 192–206.

'Du nouveau sur les rélations de Manuel Paléologue (1391–1425) avec l'Espagne', *Studi Bizantini e Neoellenici* 7 (1953), 420–36.

'Deux empereurs byzantins en Occident: Manuel II et Jean VIII Paléologue, vus par des artistes parisiens et italiens', *Bulletin de la Société Nationale des Antiquaires de France* (1958), 38–40.

Markopoulos, A. 'Autour des chapitres de Basile Ier', in Εὐψυχία. *Mélanges offerts à Hélène Ahrweiler*, eds. M. Ballard et al., vol 11 (Paris, 1998), 469–79.

Martin, G. 'Rhetorical Exercise or Political Pamphlet? Thomas Magistros' exploitation of Demosthenes' Against Leptines', *GRBS* 46 (2006), 207–26.

Matschke, K. P. *Die Schlact bei Ankara und das Schicksal von Byzanz* (Weimar, 1981).

'Thessalonike und die Zealoten. Bemerkungen zu einem Schlüsselereignis der spätbyzantinischen Stadt undReichsgeschichte', *BSI* 55 (1994), 19–43.

'The Late Byzantine Urban Economy, Thirteenth–Fifteenth Centuries', *EHB*, (2002), 463–95.

'Die Stadt Konstantinopel und die Dynastie der Palaiologen', in K. P. Matschke, *Das spätbyzantinische Konstantinopel, Alte und neue Beiträge zur Stadtgeschichte zwischen 1261 und 1453* (Hamburg, 2008), 8–87.

Matschke, K. P. and Tinnefeld, F. *Die Gesellschaft im späten Byzanz. Gruppen, strukturen, lebensformen* (Cologne, Weimar and Vienna, 2001).

Meiss, M. *French Art in the Time of Jean de Berry. The Limbourgs and Their Contemporaries*, 2 vols (London and New York, 1974).

Melvani, N. 'The Tombs of the Palaiologan emperors', *BMGS* 42, 2 (2018), 237–60.

Mercati, G. *Notizie di Procoro e Demetrio Cidone, Manuele Caleca e Teodoro Meliteniota, ed altri appunti per la storia della teologia e della letterature bizantina del Secolo XIV* (Vatican, 1931).

Mergiali-Sahas, S. *L'enseignement pendant l'epoque des Paléologues* (Athens, 1996).

'Manuel Chrysoloras (ca. 1350–1415), an Ideal Model of a Scholar- Ambassador', *Byzantine Studies* 3 (1998), 1–12.

'A Byzantine Ambassador to the West and his Office during the Fourteenth and Fifteenth Centuries', *BZ 94* (2001), 388–604.

'Byzantine Emperors and Holy Relics. Use and Misuse, of Sanctity and Authority', *JÖB* 51 (2001), 41–60.

'An Ultimate Wealth for Inauspicious Times: Holy Relics in Rescue of Manuel Palaeologos' Reign', *Byzantion 76* (2006), 265–75.

Messis, Ch. 'La memoire de 'Je Souffrant'. Construire et écrire la mémoire personelle dans les récits de voyage', in *L'écriture de la mémoire: la littérarité de l'historiographie, Actes du colloque international sur la littérature Byzantine, Nicosie 6–8 mai 2004*, eds. P Odorico and P. Agapitos (Paris, 2006), 107–46.

'Fiction and/or Novelisation in Byzantine Hagiography', in The *Ashgate Companion to Byzantine Hagiography*, vol. 2, ed. S. Efthymiadis (Farnham, 2014), 313–42.

Mesarovič, S. *Jovan VII Paleolog* (Belgrade, 1996).

Meyendorff, J. 'La procession du Saint-esprit chez les Pères orientaux', *Russie et chrétienté* 3/4 (1950), 158–78.

Introduction a l'étude de Palamas (Paris, 1956).

'Jean-Joasaph Cantacuzène et le projet de concile oecumenique en 1367', in *Akten des XI. Internationalen Byzantinisten-Kongresses, München 1958* (Munich, 1960), 363–9.

'Byzantine Views of Islam', *DOP* 18 (1964), 263–86.

A Study of Gregory Palamas, trans. G. Lawrance (London, 1964).

Byzantine Theology: Historical Trends and Doctrinal Themes (New York, 1974).

Byzantine Hesychasm: Historical, Theological and Social Problems (London, 1974).

'Mount Athos in the 14th Century: Spiritual and Intellectual Legacy', *DOP* 42 (1988), 157–65.

Meyer, W. 'Homiletics', in *The Oxford Handbook of Early Christian Studies*, eds. S. Ashbrook Harvey and D. G. Hunter (Oxford, 2008), 565–79.

Miller, T. J. *Poetic License: Authority and Authorship in Medieval and Renaissance Contexts* (New York and Oxford, 1986).

Miller, T. S. *The History of John Cantacouzenus (Book iv): Text, Translation and Commentary* (PhD thesis, The Catholic University of America, 1975).

Miller, W. 'The Gattilusj of Lesbos (1355–1462)', in W. Miller, *Essays on the Latin Orient* (Amsterdam, 1964), 313–54.

Moffatt, A. 'The Byzantine Child', *Social Research* 53 (1986), 705–23.

Momigliano, A. *The Development of Greek Biography* (Cambridge, 1991).

Mompherratos, A. *Διπλωματικαὶ ἐνέργειαι Μανουὴλ Β᾽ τοῦ Παλαιολόγου ἐν Εὐρώπῃ καὶ Ἀσίᾳ* (Athens, 1913).

Morrison, C. 'The Emperor, the Saint and the City: Coinage and Money in Thessalonike from the Thirteenth to Fifteenth Centuries', *DOP* 57 (2003), 173–203.

Morrison, C and Cheynet, J. C. 'Prices and Wages in the Byzantine World', *EHB* (2002), 815–78.

Mullett, M. 'The Classical Tradition in the Byzantine Letter', in *Byzantium and the Classical Tradition: University of Birmingham Thirteenth Spring*

Symposium of Byzantine Studies 1979, eds. M. Mullett and R. Scott (Birmingham, 1981), 75–93.

'The Madness of Genre', *DOP* 46 (1992), 233–43.

'Originality in the Byzantine letter: The Case of Exile', in *Originality in Byzantine Art, Literature and Music: A Collection of Essays*, ed. A. Littlewood (Oxford, 1995), 39–53.

Theophylact of Ochrid: Reading the Letters of a Byzantine Archbishop (Aldershot, 1997).

'How to Criticise the Laudandus', in *Power and Subversion in Byzantium, Papers from the 43rd Spring Symposium of Byzantine Studies, Birmingham, March 2010*, eds. D. Angelov and M. Saxby (Farbham, 2013), 247–62.

Munitiz, J. 'War and Peace Reflected in some Byzantine Mirrors of Princes', in *Peace and War in Byzantium. Essays in Honour of George T. Dennis*, eds. T. Miller and J. Nesbitt (Washington DC, 1995), 50–61.

Muratore, D. *Una principessa Sabaudo sul trono di Bisanzio* (Chambéey, 1909).

Mureşan, D. I, 'Une histoire de trois empereurs: aspects des relations de Sigismond de Luxembourg avec Manuel II et Jean Paléologue', in *Emperor Sigismund and the Orthodox World*, ed E. Mitsou (Vienna, 2010), 41–100.

Necipoğlu, N. 'Economic Conditions in Constantinople during the Siege of Bayezid I (1394–1402)', in *Constantinople and its Hinterland*, eds. C. Mango and G. Dagron (Aldershot, 1995), 157–67.

'The Aristocracy in Late Byzantine Thessalonike: A Case Study of the City's Archontes (late 14th and early 15th centuries)', *DOP* 57 (2003), 133–51.

Byzantium between the Ottomans and the Latins: Politics and the Society in Late Empire (Cambridge, 2009).

Nelson, R. 'The Italian Appreciation and Appropriation of Illuminated Byzantine Manuscripts 1200–1450', *DOP* 49 (1995), 209–35.

Nicol, D. *The Byzantine Family of Kantakouzenos, ca. 1100–1460* (Washington DC, 1968).

'A Byzantine Emperor in England: Manuel II's visit to London in 1400–1401', *University of Birmingham Historical Journal* 12.2 (1971), 204–25, reprinted in D. Nicol, *Byzantium: its Ecclesiastical History and Relations with the Western World*, (London, 1972), Study x.

'Byzantium and England', *Balkan Studies* 15 (1974), 179–203, reprinted in D. Nicol, *Studies in Late Byzantine History and Prosopography* (London, 1986), Study xvii.

'Kaisersalbung: Unction of Emperors in Late Byzantine Coronation Ritual', *BMGS* 2 (1976), 37–52, reprinted in D. Nicol, *Studies in Late Byzantine History and Prosopography* (London, 1986), Study i.

Church and Society in the Last Centuries of Byzantium (Cambridge, 1979).

'Thessalonica as a Cultural Centre in the 14th Century', Ἡ Θεσσαλονίκη μεταξὺ Ἀνατολῆς καὶ Δύσεως. Πρακτικὰ Συμποσίου Τεσσαρακονταετηρίδος, Ἑταιρείας Μακεδονικῶν Σπουδῶν (1980), 121–131, re-printed in D. Nicol, *Studies in Late Byzantine History and Prosopography* (London, 1986), Study x.

The Immortal Emperor: The Life and Legend of Constantine Palaeologus, The Last Emperor of the Romans (Cambridge, 1992).

Byzantium and Venice: A Study in Diplomatic and Cultural Relations (Cambridge, 1992).

The Last Centuries of Byzantium, 1261–1453 (Cambridge, 1993).

The Byzantine Lady: ten portraits, 1250–1500 (Cambridge, 1994).

The Reluctant Emperor: A Biography of John Cantacuzene, Byzantine Emperor and Monk, c. 1295–1383 (Cambridge, 1996).

Nicol, D. and Bendall, S. 'Anna of Savoy in Thessalonica: The Numismatic Evidence', *Revue Numismatique, 6th Ser, xix* (1977), 87–102.

Nuti, E. 'Manuel Chrysoloras' Περὶ τοῦ Βασιλέως λόγου: Genre, Aims, Content, and Sources', *GRBS* 56 (2016), 164–97.

Obolensky, D. *Six Byzantine Portraits* (Oxford, 1988).

O'Carroll, H. M. *A Theological Encylopedia of the Blessed Virgin Mary* (Eugene, Oregon, 1991).

Odorico, P. and Agapitos, P. A. (eds.) *Pour une nouvelle histoire de la littérature Byzantine : problèmes, méthodes, approches, propositions. Actes du colloque international philologique 25–28 Mai 2000* (Paris, 2002).

Odorico, P. 'Les miroirs des princes à Byzance. Une lecture horizontale', in *L'éducation au gouvernement et à la vie: la tradition des régles de vie de L'antiquité au Moyen Age. Colloque International Pise, 18 et 19 Mars 2005*, ed. P. Odorico (Paris, 2009) 223–46.

Oehler, K. 'Aristotle in Byzantium', *GRBS* 5.2 (1964), 133–46.

Oikonomides, N. 'John VII Palaeologus and the Ivory Pyxis at Dumbarton Oaks', *DOP* 31 (1977), 329–38.

'La chancelliere impériale de Byzance du 13e au 15e siecle', *REB* 43 (1985), 167–95.

'The Contents of the Byzantine House from the Eleventh to the Fifteenth Centuries', *DOP* 44 (1990), 205–14.

'The Holy Icon as an Asset', *DOP* 45 (1991), 35–44.

Origo, I. *The Merchant of Prato. Francesco di Marco Datini, 1335–1410* (London, 1957).

Origone, S. *Giovanna di Savoia: Alias Anna Paleologina, Latina e Bisanzio (c. 1306–1365)* (Milan, 1998).

Orme, N. *Medieval Children* (New Haven, 2001).

Ostrogorsky, G. *History of the Byzantine State* (New Brunswick, 1957).

Page, G. *Being Byzantine: Greek Identity Before the Ottomans* (Cambridge, 2008).

Paidas, K. *Η Θεματική των Βυζαντινών Κατόπτρων Ηγεμονίας ' της Πρώιμης και Μέσης Περιόδου (398–1085)* (Athens, 2005).

«Κάτοπτρα Ηγεμόνος» της Ύστερης Περιόδου (1254–1303): Εκφράσεις του Βυζαντινού Βασιλικού Ιδεώδους (Athens, 2006).

Pall, F. 'Encore une fois sur le voyage diplomatique de Jean V Palaéologue en 1365/66', *RESEE* 9 (1971), 535–40.

Papadakis, A. *Crisis in Byzantium: The Filioque Controversy in the Patriarchate of Gregory II of Cyprus (1283–1289)* (New York, 1983; repr. 1997).

The Christian East and the Rise of the Papacy: The Church 1071–1453 A.D (New York, 1994).

'The Byzantines and the Rise of Papacy: Points for Reflection (1204–1453), in *Greeks, Latins, and Intellectual History 1204–1500*, eds. M. Hinterberger and C. Schabel (Leuven, 2011), 19–42.

Papadapoulou, E. 'Περί της ηλικίας καὶ του γήρατος ἀπό τη γραμματεία του ενδέκατου και δωδέκατου αιώνα', *Byzantina Symmeikta* 17 (2005), 131–98.

Papadopoulos, A. T. *Versuch einer Genealogie der Palaiologen 1259–1453* (Amsterdam, 1962).

Papaioannou, S. 'Letter Writing', in *The Byzantine World*, ed. P. Stephenson (London and New York, 2010), 188–99.

Michael Psellos. Rhetoric and Authorship in Byzantium (Cambridge, 2013).

Parani, M. *Reconstructing the Reality of Images* (Leiden, 2003).

Patasci, G. 'Joseph Bryennios et les discussions sur un council d'union (1414–1431)', *Κληρονομία* 5 (1973), 73–96.

Patlagean, E. 'De la chasse et du souverain', *DOP* 46 (1992), 257–63.

'L'immunité des Thessaloniciens', in *Εὐψυχία. Mélanges Offerts à Hélène Ahrweiler*, 2 vols. (Paris, 1998), 591–601.

Peers, G. 'Manuel II Palaeologos' Ekphrasis on a Tapestry in the Louvre: Word Over Image', *REB 61* (2003), 201–14.

Petanović, L. *Elena. L'ultima imperatrice bizantina* (Milan, 2002).

Philippides, M. *Constantine XI Dragaš Palaeologus (1404–1453): The Last Emperor of Byzantium* (London, 2018).

Philippides-Braat, A. 'La captivité de Palamas chez les Turcs, dossier et commentaire', *TM* 7 (1979), 109–22.

Pitarakis, B. 'Material Culture of Childhood in Byzantium', in *Becoming Byzantine: Children and Childhood in Byzantium*, eds. A. Papaconstantinou and A. M. Talbot, (Washington DC, 2009), 167–252.

Pizzone, A. (ed.) *The Author in Middle Byzantine Literature. Modes, Functions and Identities* (Berlin, 2014).

Podskalsky, G. *Theologie und Philosophie in Byzanz. Der Streit um die theologische Methodik in der spätbyzantinischen Geistesgeschichte (14/15 Jhr. Seine systematischen Grundlagen und seine historische Entwicklung)* (Munich, 1977).

Polemis, I. *Theologica varia inedita saeculi XIV* (Turnhout, 2012).

(ed.) *Theodorus Metochita Carmina* (Turnhout, 2015).

'Manuel II Palaiologos between Gregory Palamas and Thomas Aquinas', in *The Ways of Byzantine Philosophy*, ed. M. Knežević (Alhambra, California, 2015), 353–60.

Porter, R. (ed.) *Re-writing the Self: Histories from the Renaissance to the Present*, (London, 1997).

Prinzing, G. 'Beobachtungen zu integrierten Fürstenspiegeln der Byzantiner', *JÖB* 38 (1988), 1–31.

'Emperor Manuel II and Patriarch Euythmios II on the Jurisdiction of the Church of Ohrid', in *Le Patriarcat oecuménique de Constantinople et Byzance hors frontières (1204–1586)*, eds M. H. Blanchet, M. H. Congourdeau and D. I. Mureşan (Paris, 2014), 243–71.

Pucci, J. *The Full Knowing Reader: Allusion and the Power of the Reader in the Western Literary Tradition* (New Haven, 1998).

Radošević, N. 'The Emperor as the Patron of Learning in Byzantine basilikoi logoi', in *Τὸ Ἑλληνικόν: Studies in Honor of Speros Vryonis Jr*, vol. 1, eds. J. S. Langdon et al. (New Rochelle, New York, 1993), 267–88.

Rautman, M. L. 'Observations on the Byzantine Palaces of Thessaloniki', *Byzantion* 60 (1990), 300–6.

Redon, O., Sabban, F. and Servent, S. (eds.) *The Medieval Kitchen: Recipes from France and Italy*, trans. E. Scheider (Chicago and London, 1998).

Reinert, S. W. 'Manuel II Palaeologus and his Müderris', in *The Twilight of Byzantium*, eds. S. Ćurčić and D. Mouriki (Princeton, 1991), 39–51, reprinted in S. W. Reinert, *Studies on Late Byzantine and Early Ottoman History* (Farnham, 2014), Study IX.

'The Palaiologoi, Yildirim Bayezid and Constantinople: June 1389-March 1391', in *Τὸ Ἑλληνικόν: Studies in Honor of Speros Vryonis Jr.*, ed. J. S. Langdon et al., 2 vols. (New Rochelle, NY, 1993), i, 289–365, reprinted in S. W. Reinert, *Studies on Late Byzantine and Early Ottoman History* (Farnham, 2014), Study IV.

'A Byzantine Source on the Battles of Bileća (?) and Kosova Polje: Kydones' Letters 396 and 398 Reconsidered', in *Studies in Ottoman History in Honour of Professor V. L. Ménage*, eds. C. Heywood and C. Imber (Istanbul, 1994), 249–72, reprinted in S. W. Reinert, *Studies on Late Byzantine and Early Ottoman History* (Farnham, 2014), Study III.

'What the Genoese Cast upon Helena Dragash's Head: Coins, not "Confecti"', *BF* 20 (1994), 235–46, reprinted in S. W. Reinert, *Studies on Late Byzantine and Early Ottoman History* (Farnham, 2014), Study VIII.

'Political Dimensions of Manuel II Palaiologos' 1392 Marriage and Coronation: Some New Evidence', in *Novum Millennium: Studies on Byzantine History and Culture Dedicated to Paul Speck*, eds. C. Sode and S. Takács (Aldershot, 2001), 291–303, reprinted in S. W. Reinert, *Studies on Late Byzantine and Early Ottoman History* (Farnham, 2014), Study VII.

'Coping with Political Catastrophe in 1387: Representations of Nature in Manuel II Palaiologos' Epistolary Discourse to Kabasilas', in S. W. Reinert, *Studies on Late Byzantine and Early Ottoman History* (Farnham, 2014), 1–21, Study V.

Rigo, A., Ermilov, P. and Trizio, M. (eds.) *Byzantine Theology and its Philosophical Background* (Turnhout, 2011).

Robertson, D. W. Jr. *Chaucer's London* (New York, 1968).

Rochette, R. 'Les despotes à Thessalonique', in *Impératrices, princesses, aristocrates et saintes souveraines. De l'Orient Chrétien et Musulman au Moyen Age et au début des temps modernes*, eds. E. Malamut and A. Nicolaides (Aix-en-Provence, 2014), 89–96.

Rollo, A. 'A proposito del Vat gr 2239: Manuele II e Guarino', *Νέα Ῥώμη* 3 (2006), 375–88.

Roux, S. *Paris in the Middle Ages*, trans. J. A. Mc Namara (Philadelphia, 2009).

Runciman, S. 'Manuel II and the see of Moldavia', in Καθηγήτρια: *Essays presented to Joan Hussey for her 80th Birthday*, ed. J. Chrysostomides (Camberley, 1988), 515–20.

Russell, E. *St. Demetrius of Thessalonica: Cult and Devotion in the Middle Ages* (Oxford, 2010).

Literature and Culture in Late Byzantine Thessalonica (London, 2013).

Russell, N. 'Palamism in the circle of Demetrius Cydones', in *Porphyrogenita: Essays on the History and Literature of Byzantium and the Latin East in Honour of Julian Chrysostomides*, eds. Ch. Dendrinos et al. (Aldershot, 2003), 7–25.

'Prochoros Cydones and the Fourteenth-Century understanding of Orthodoxy', in *Byzantine Orthodoxies. Papers from the 36th Spring Symposium of Byzantine Studies, University of Durham, 23–25 March 2002*, eds. A. Louth and A. Casiday (Farnham, 2006), 75–94.

Ryder, J. R. *The Career and Writings of Demetrius Kydones: A Study of Fourteenth-Century Byzantine Politics, Religion and Society* (Leiden, 2010).

Schilbach, E. 'Die Hypothyposis der καθολικοὶ κριταὶ τῶν Ῥωμαίων vom Juni 1398 (?)', *BZ* 61 (1968), 44–70.

Schlosser, F. E, 'Wearing a Precious Web: The Use of Textiles in Diplomacy', *BSl* 63 (2005), 42–52.

Schlumberger, G. *Un empereur de Byzance à Paris et Londres* (Paris, 1916).

Schmitt, O. J. 'Kaiserrede und Zeitgeschichte im späten Byzanz: Ein Panegyrikos Isidors von Kiew aus dem Jahre 1429', *JÖB* 48 (1998), 209–42.

Schreiner, P. 'Hochzeit und Krönung Kaiser Manuels II im Jahre 1392', *BZ* 60 (1967), 70–85.

'Zur Geschichte Philadelphias in 14. Jahrhundert (1293–1390)', *OCP 35* (1969), 375–431.

'Chronologische Untersuchungen zur Familie Kaiser Manuels II', *BZ 63* (1970), 258–99.

'Ein seltsames Stemma. Isidor von Kiev, die Leichenrede Kaiser Manuels auf seinen Bruder Theodoros und eine moderne Ausgabe', in *Lesarten: Festschrift für Athanasios Kambylis zum 70. Geburtstag. Dargebracht von Schülern, Kollegen und Freunden*, eds. I. Vassis et al. (Berlin and New York, 1998), 211–25.

Schrijver, F. 'Daily life at the Blachernai Palace: The Servants of the Imperial Bedchamber (1261–1354), in *The Byzantine Court. Source of Power and Culture. Papers from the Second Sevgi Gönül Symposium, Istanbul 21–23 June 2010*, eds. A. Ödekan, N. Necipoğlu and E. Akyürek (Istanbul, 2013), 83–7.

Searby, D. (ed.) *Never the Twain Shall Meet? Latins and Greeks Learning from Each Other in Byzantium* (Berlin and Leiden, 2018).

Ševčenko, I. 'Nicolas Cabasilas' "Anti-Zealot" Discourse: A Re-interpretation', *DOP* 11 (1957), 79–171.

'The Decline of Byzantium seen through the Eyes of the Intellectuals', *DOP 15* (1961), 167–86.

'A Postscript on Nicolas Cabasilas' "Anti-Zealot" Discourse', *DOP 16* (1962), 403–8.

'Society and Intellectual Life in the 14th Century', in *Actes du XIVe Congrès International des Etudes byzantins, Bucarest 1971*, vol. 1, (Bucharest, 1974), 69–92, re-printed in I. Ševčenko, *Society and Intellectual Life in Byzantium*, (London, 1981), Study 1.

'Agapetos East and West. The Fate of a Byzantine Mirror of Princes', *RESEE* 16 (1978), 1–45.

'Levels of Style in Byzantine Prose', *JÖB* 31/1 (1981), 307–12.

Shahar, S. *Children in the Middle Ages* (London, 1990).

Shawcross, T. 'A New Lykourgos for a New Sparta: George Gemistos Plethon and the Despotate of the Morea', in *Viewing the Morea: Land and People in the Late Medieval Peloponnese*, ed. S. Gerstel (Washington DC, 2013), 419–52.

Smyrlis, K. 'The State, the Land and Private Property: Confiscating Monastic and Church Properties in the Palaiologan Period', in *Church and Society in Late Byzantium*, ed. D. Angelov (Kalamazoo, 2009), 58–87.

Spaak, P. H. 'Deux empereurs byzantins, Manuel II et Jean VIII Paléologue, vus par des artistes occidentaux', *Le Flambeau*, nov–déc. (1957), 758–62.

Spieser, J. M. 'Inventaires en vue d'un recueil des inscriptions historiques de Byzance, I: Les inscriptions de Thessalonique', *TM* 5 (1972), 145–80.

Sphatarakis, I. *The Portrait in Byzantine Illuminated Manuscripts* (Leiden, 1976).

Stringer, C. L. *Humanism and the Church Fathers: Ambrogio Traversari* (New York, 1977).

Sussman, A. *Anglo-Byzantine Relations During the Middle Ages* (PhD thesis, University of Pennsylvania, 1966).

Talbot, A. M. 'Old Age in Byzantium', *BZ* 77 (1984), 267–78.

'Late Byzantine Nuns: By Choice or Necessity?', *BF 9* (1985), 59–102.

'Women's Space in Monasteries', *DOP 52* (1998), 113–27.

Telfer, W. 'Autexousia', *Journal of Theological Studies* 8.1 (1957), 123–9.

Theocharides, G. 'Δύο νέα ἔγγραφα ἀφορῶντα εἰς τὴν Νέαν Μονὴν Θεσσαλονίκης', *Μακεδονίκα* 4 (1957), 315–51.

Thomson, I. 'Manuel Chrysoloras and the early Italian Renaissance', *GRBS* 7 (1966), 63–82.

Thorn-Wickert, L. *Manuel Chrysoloras (ca. 1350–1415): eine Biographie des byzantinischen Intellektuellen vor dem Hintergrund der hellenistischen Studien in der italienischen Renaissance* (Frankfurt, 2006).

Tinnefeld, F. 'Vier Prooimien zu Kaiserurkunden, verfaßt von Demetrios Kydones', *BSl* 44 (1982), 13–30, 178–95.

'Kriterien und Varianten des Stils im Briefcorpus des Demetrios Kydones', *JÖB* 32/2 (1982), 257–64.

'Freundschaft und Παιδεία. Die Korrespondenz des Demetrios Kydones mit Rhadenos (1375–1387/8)', *Byzantion* 55 (1985), 210–44.

Die Gesellschaft im späten Byzanz. Gruppen, Strukturen und Lebensformen (Cologne, Weimar and Vienna 2001).

'Intellectuals in Late Byzantine Thessalonike', *DOP* 57 (2003), 153–72.

Briefe des Demetrios Kydones: Themen und literarische Form (Wiesbaden, 2010).

Todt, K. P. *Kaiser Johannes VI Kantakuzenos und der Islam. Politische Realität und theologische Polemik im palaiologenzeitlichen Byzanz* (Würzburg, 1991).

Torrance, A. 'Precedents for Palamas' Essence-Energies Theology in the Cappadocian Fathers', *Vigilae Christianae* 63 (2009), 47–70.

Repentance in Late Antiquity. Eastern Ascetism and the Framing of the Christian life c. 400–650 CE (Oxford, 2013).

Toth, I. 'Rhetorical Theatron in Late Byzantium: The Example of Palaiologan Imperial Orations', in *Theatron, Rhetorische Kultur in Spätantike und Mittelalter*, ed. M. Grünbart (Berlin and New York, 2007), 429–48.

Tougher, S. *The Reign of Leo IV: Politics and People (886–912)* (Leiden, 1997).

Trapp, E. 'Der Sprachgebrauch Manuels II in den Dialogen mit einem "Perser"', *JÖB* 16 (1967), 189–97.

'Zur Identifizierung der Personen in der Hadesfahrt des Mazaris', *JÖB* 18 (1969), 95–9.

(ed.) *Prosopographisches Lexikon der Palaiologenzeit*, 14 vols. (Vienna, 1976–96).

'Quelques textes peu connus illustrant les relations entre le Christianisme et l'Islam', *BF* 29 (2007), 437–50.

Triantafyllopoulos, Ch. 'The Thomist base of Prochoros Kydones' anti-Palamite Treatise "De essentia et operatione Dei" and the Reaction of the Byzantine Church', in *Knotenpunkt Byzanz. Wissensformen und Kulturelle Wechselbeziehungen*, eds. A. Speer and P. Steinkrüger (Berlin, 2012), 411–30.

Trizio, M. 'Byzantine Philosophy as a Contemporary Historiographical Project', *Recherches de Théologie et Philosophie Médiévales* 74 (2007), 247–94.

Tsirpanlis, C. N. 'Byzantine Parliaments and Representative Assemblies from 1081 to 1351', *Byzantion* 43 (1973), 432–83.

Tuffin, P. and McEvoy, M. 'Steak à la Hun: Food, Drink and Dietary Habits in Ammianus Marcellinus', in *Feast, Fast or Famine: Food and Drink in Byzantium*, eds. W. Mayer and S. Trzcionka (Farnham, 2005), 69–84.

Turner, C. J. G. 'Pages from the Late Byzantine Philosophy of History', *BZ* 57 (1964), 348–57.

Urmson, J. O. 'Aristotle's Doctrine of the Mean', *American Philosophical Quarterly* 10.3 (1973), 223–30.

Van Millingen, A. *Byzantine Constantinople: The Walls of the City and Adjoining Historical Sites* (London, 1899).

Vasiliev, A. A. 'Putešestvie vizantijskago imperatore Manuila Palaeologa po zapadnoi Evrope (1399–1403)', *Žurnal Ministerstva Naradnago Prosveščeniia*, N. S. 39 (1912), 41–78, 260–304.

'Il viaggio di Giovanni V Palaeologo in Italia e l'unione di Roma', *SBN* 3 (1931), 153–92.

Vassilaki, M. 'Praying for the Salvation of the Empire?', in *Images of the Mother of God: Perceptions of the Theotokos of Byzantium*, ed. M. Vassilaki (Aldershot, 2004), 263–74.

Vassilopoulos, D. and Poulakou-Rebelakou, E. 'The Three Last Years of Manuel II Paleologus' Reign between Two Stroke Attacks, Aphasia or Not?', *Historical Neuroscience* 20(2011), 277–83.

Voordecker, E. 'Les 'Entretiens avec un Perse' de l'empereur Manuel II Paléologue (à propos de deux éditions récentes)', *Byzantion* 36, (1966), 311–17.

Vryonis, Sp. 'Isidore Glabas and the devshirme', *Speculum* 31 (July 1956), 433–43.

The Decline of Medieval Hellenism in Asia Minor and the Process of Islamization from the Eleventh through the Fifteenth Century (Berkeley and Los Angeles, 1972).

Warren, W. 'Biography and the Medieval Historian', in *Medieval Historical Writing in the Christian and Islamic World*, ed. D. Morgan (London, 1982), 5–18.

Webb, R. *Ekphrasis, Imagination and Persuasion in Ancient Rhetorical Theory and Practice* (Farnham, 2009).

Weiss, G. *Joannes Kantakuzenos. Aristokrat, Staatsmann, Kaiser und Mönch, in der Gesellschaftsentwicklung von Byzanz im 14. Jahrhundert* (Wiesbaden, 1969).

Weiss, R. 'The Medieval Medallions of Constantine and Heraklios', *Numismatic Chronicle* 7, 3 (1963), 129–44.

Wenger, A. *L'Assomption de la T. S. Vierge dans la tradition Byzantine du VIe au Xe siècle. Etudes et documents* (Paris, 1955).

Wessel, K. 'Manuel II Palaiologos und seine Familie. Zur Miniatur des Cod. Ivoires A 53 des Louvre', in *Beiträge zur Kunst des Mittelalters. Fetschrift für Hans Wenzel*, ed. R. Becksmann (Berlin, 1975), 219–29.

Willard, C. C. *Christine de Pizan: Her Life and Works* (New York, 1984).

Wilson, N. G. 'Libraries of the Byzantine World', *GRBS* 8.1 (1967), 53–80.

'Books and Readers in Byzantium', in *Byzantine Books and Bookmen*, eds. C. Mango and I. Ševčenko (Washington DC, 1975), 29–45.

Scholars of Byzantium (London, 1996).

Wirth, P. 'Die Haltung Kaiser Johannes V. bei den Verhandlungen mit König Ludwig I. von Ungarn zu Buda im Jahre 1366', *BZ* 56 (1963), 271–2.

'Zum Geschichtsbild Kaiser Johannes VII Palaiologos', *Byzantion* 35 (1965/1967), 592–94, 599–600.

'Manuel II Palaiologos und der Johanniterorden', *Byzantina* 6 (1974), 387–89.

Woodhouse, C. M. *George Gemistos Plethon* (Oxford, 1986).

Wylie, J. H. *History of England under Henry the Fourth*, (1399–1404), 4 vols. (London, 1884).

Zachariadou, E. A. 'John VII (alias Andronicus) Palaeologus', *DOP* 91 (1977), 339–42.

'Manuel II Palaeologus on the Strife between Bayezid I and Kadi Burhan al-Din Ahmad', *Bulletin of the School of Oriental and African Studies* 43 (1980), 471–81.

'Süleyman Çelebi in Rumili and Ottoman Chronicles', *Der Islam* 60 (1983), 268–96, reprinted in E.A. Zachariadou, *Studies in Pre-Ottoman Turkey and the Ottomans* (Aldershot, 2007), Study xi.

'Religious Dialogue between the Byzantines and Turks during the Ottoman Expansion', in *Religionsgespräche im Mittellalter*, eds. B. Lewis and F. Niewöhner (Wiesbaden, 1992), 289–304, reprinted in E. A. Zachariadou, *Studies in Pre-Ottoman Turkey and the Ottomans* (Aldershot, 2007), Study 11.

Zakythinos, D. A. *Le despotat grec du Morée. L'histoire politique.* (Athens, 1953; reprinted London, 1975).

Le despotat grec du Morée. Vie et institutions (Athens, 1953; reprinted London, 1975).

'Μανουὴλ Βʹὁ Παλαιολόγος καὶ ὁ καρδινάλιος Ἰσίδορος ἐν Πελοποννήσῳ', in *Mélanges Octave et Melpo Merlier*, III, (=Collection de l'Institut Français d'Athenes, 94), (Athens, 1957), 45–67.

Index

For EU product safety concerns, contact us at Calle de José Abascal, 56–1°,
28003 Madrid, Spain or eugpsr@cambridge.org.

www.ingramcontent.com/pod-product-compliance
Ingram Content Group UK Ltd.
Pitfield, Milton Keynes, MK11 3LW, UK
UKHW020433240426
470322UK00017B/499